Encompassing a wide range of issues in Japanese literature and culture, the twenty-nine original essays in this book focus on how cultural and literary genres and norms have developed in response to historical and cross-cultural influences.

Currents in Japanese Culture deals with various aspects of Japanese culture—Japanese literature from the Heian period to the present (including poetry, drama, fiction, and autobiographical writing), film, visual arts, and social and intellectual history. Contributors to this volume touch on such topics as the art of translating Takuboku, the poetry of Saitō Mokichi's *Shōen*, the influence of nō on Joyce's *Finnegans Wake*, James McNeill Whistler as a metaphor for Japan in a poem by Amy Lowell, a study of Taoist influence on early seventeenth-century Haikai, the transformation of Hayashi Fumiko's fiction, and the nature of literary influence in the poetry of Bashō.

Broad in scope and comprehensive in its presentation of Japanese traditions, *Currents in Japanese Culture* will be of vital interest to students and professors of all aspects of Japanese literature and culture.

Currents in Japanese Culture

Translations and Transformations

Currents in Japanese Culture

Translations and Transformations

AMY VLADECK HEINRICH
EDITOR

Columbia University Press
NEW YORK

Columbia University Press
Publishers Since 1893
New York   Chichester, West Sussex
Copyright © 1997 Columbia University Press. Chapter 21, copyright ©
    1997 Amanda Mayer Stinchecum.

Library of Congress Cataloging-in-Publication Data
Currents in Japanese culture : translations and transformations / Amy
    Vladeck Heinrich, editor.
        p.   cm.
    Includes bibliographical references and index.
    ISBN 0–231–09696–8 (alk. paper)
    1. Japan—Civilization.   2. Japanese literature.   I. Heinrich,
    Amy Vladeck.
    DS821.C86   1997
    952—dc21   96–46271

Printed in the United States of America

c 10 9 8 7 6 5 4 3 2 1
p 10 9 8 7 6 5 4 3 2 1

Contents

Preface   ix

Preface

Donald Keene is an extraordinary teacher. Certainly almost everyone who has read some Japanese literature in English translation or learned about it through English texts—not to mention all the people who have read his work in Japanese—are in some sense Donald Keene's students.[1] It is those of us fortunate enough to have studied directly with him, however, who are privileged to contribute papers to this anthology in his honor. His deep commitment to his students is expressed in his desire that the volume include the work of any student who wanted to contribute.

The contributors are united in sharing deep gratitude to Donald Keene for teaching us; his guidance has enriched our lives. Privately, all of us have felt the respect and support that he believes are due his students and that defined his teaching career. Donald Keene's delight in his students was publicly apparent at the symposium honoring his retirement in 1992.[2]

The title of this collection, *Currents in Japanese Culture*, refers obliquely to Keene's translation, included in his *Anthology of Japanese Literature*, of the opening lines of Kamo no Chōmei's *An Account of My Hut*: "The flow of the river is ceaseless and its water is never the same."[3] Donald Keene's career as a teacher has been invaluable in ensuring the continuing flow of the study of Japanese culture.

The subtitle is drawn from the symposium, and the authors of the chapters took the themes included in the subtitle to heart. Each chapter deals with some aspect of the translation of culture and the transformations that it entails: in the form of stories from genre to genre, or genres from culture to culture, or texts translated from Japanese to English, or the internal transformations that take place in the world of Japanese literature—all the alterations accomplished by time, imagination, and creative action.

The contributors to this book are a diverse group, with far-ranging interests. The chapters cover Japanese literature from the classical Heian period to our own late twentieth century and genres from traditional poetry to modern drama, as well as the ways that Japanese traditions have influenced and been influenced by other cultures and cultural movements. In this way, the topics represent developments of Donald Keene's own work, which has similarly traveled through Japanese literature and culture with a sense of unlimited possibilities. What is clear in all his writing, as well as in his teaching, is the joy he takes in his studies. He communicated that joy to his students and, with it, a sense that the study of Japanese literature and culture is a shared endeavor. He was not only willing and eager to teach us; he assumed we would learn from one another, and he was willing and eager to learn from us as well.

Although the twenty-nine chapters could have been organized in a variety of ways—systematically by genre or chronologically by topic—in the spirit of Japanese poetry, they are instead linked by association. The structure of the whole is something like a *renga*, a poem with many links, each link (or chapter) related to the previous one by image, tone, subject—demonstrating the shared endeavor—but each opening new directions. Donald Keene's vast body of work is the hypothetical *hokku*, or opening verse, the one that is traditionally composed by the master and that can stand alone. It sets the tone and standard for all that follows.

Amy Vladeck Heinrich

NOTES

1. In a review article entitled "The Mission of Literature," Aileen Gatten writes about her first experience reading, under protest, Keene's *Anthology of Japanese Literature*: "Long before I reached the end of the anthology I was hooked on classical literature, and began searching the library and bookstores for more. There is nothing unusual about this story. That is what makes it worth telling: it applies to most of the readers of this article." *Journal of the Association of Teachers of Japanese* 29 (April 1995): 27.

2. The symposium, "Translations and Tranformations," was organized by the Donald Keene Center of Japanese Culture and held at Columbia University on March 2, 1992, in honor of Professor Keene's retirement. Professor Barbara Ruch was the director of the center at the time, and Victoria Lyon-Bestor was the program officer.

3. Keene, *Anthology*, p. 197.

1

Load Allmarshy! Yes we have nō transformations!
So lend your earwicker to a zing-zang meanderthalltale!

◉

Eileen Kato

There is ample evidence that James Joyce, Ireland's most famous exile, was, among other things, a jappyknowledgist. In Roland McHugh's monumental *Annotations to Finnegans Wake*[1] we find a positively astonishing number of words or groups of words marked J for Japanese. The number has risen considerably in the revised edition, and many more such words will no doubt show up in the third edition. Although any undergraduate could pillage a Japanese dictionary and have phun showing off, one must recognize—whether or not one likes James Joyce—that he was up to more than that. A close examination of his Japanese allusions demonstrates that he knew indeed what they meant and that they were painstakingly and unerringly fitted into a preordained and faithfully followed scheme to buttress the central theme of this complex and chaotic-seeming work, which was nevertheless, I believe, conceived along clear and simple lines by Joyce's basically well ordered mind.[2]

So much of the Japanese allusion in *Finnegans Wake* evokes the nō, most especially the play *Kakitsubata*,[3] that I have become convinced this play holds a key, if not the principal key, to that hilariously recondite work.

I first read *FinnegansWake* when I was an undergraduate at University College Galway in the early 1950s. Like so many other Irish undergraduates, I was addicted to punning: *FinnegansWake* was the bible of our rejoycing crowd, and I can say truthfully that we sometimes came up with puns that James Joyce himself might well have envied. I think none of us then, however, had any glimmering of what *Finnegans Wake* might be about. Nonetheless, it seemed all the more mysteriously admirable to us for being virtually incomprehensible!

By that time I was already familiar with the Fenollosa/Pound version of the nō play *Kakitsubata*, and in spite of its imperfections—not then detectable by me—I found it fascinating but read it as a pretty flower-fairy tale and saw no possible connection between it and James Joyce. Then, in the late 1950s, I saw *Kakitsubata* in Tokyo and was indescribably moved. In the mid-1960s when I studied it in the original Japanese in Donald Keene's nō class at Columbia, I finally came to understand what an extraordinary piece of literature this lyric drama was. A few years before that, I had had an unusual encounter with a most unusual Japanese in Kanazawa, and ever since, I have seen *Kakitsubata* through his wise eyes.

In 1982 I reread *Finnegans Wake* in Tokyo and, to my amazement, found myself seeing Joyce's work, too, through the eyes of the man in Kanazawa. Page after page brought *Kakitsubata* to mind! The entire work now seemed to make a lot of sense.

Joyce began writing *Finnegans Wake* in 1922 (although the date 1923 is more often cited). For several years, extracts from it appeared as "Work in Progress," many of which were heavily reworked before the final publication of the book in 1939. Seventeen years of the life of a great genius spent on this one book! Some have doubted Joyce's sanity, but there is no doubting his high seriousness of purpose. There is no doubting, either, his low seriousness of purpose, just as relentlessly followed as the high. W. B. Yeats is pursued on both levels (among many other literary figures but more than any other).

There was in Joyce a frustrated poet who could never quite make the top grade in poetry and occasionally exhibited what seems like a childish tendency to take this out on Yeats, who was not only Ireland's greatest poet but also, I believe, the greatest of his time in the English-language world. The author of "Pomes Penyeach" and "Chamber Music" couldn't hold a candle to Yeats in that field, but Joyce could and did achieve greatness as the antithesis of Yeats.[4] Yet Joyce never quite got out from under the shadow of the older man and remained obsessed with Yeats and his preoccupations. It is easy to demonstrate how mercilessly Joyce spoofed Yeats. His jabs and jibes at Yeats's mannerisms, like the oft-repeated "findrinny" Yeats-speak, his constant playing on "shee" "sidhe" (fairies), his snide digs at Yeats's occult and theosophical interests in association with Madame Blavatsky and so on, or his spoofs on Yeats's "A Vision" throughout *Finnegans Wake* are well known. I find also a sustained spoof of Yeats the aspiring nō playwright that so far has not been noticed. Joyce's preoccupation with nō, however, seems to have gone far beyond mere spoofing.

Let me return to the man in Kanazawa. I forget the year, but it had to have been in the early 1960s. My husband and I went to Kanazawa for a few days' holiday. It had to have been early in June because the famous iris garden in the Kenrokuen (park) was in full bloom. We had hired a car and driver for the day and about midafternoon visited the park. There in all their glory stood the aristocrats of the iris family, *kakitsubata* and *ayame* and some others of their kin, in a patch of wetland crossed by a zigzag plank bridge, just as described in the nō play *Kakitsubata*. My husband, a great nō devotee, began to talk about that play. The driver, who had been discreetly silent since morning, now suddenly and eagerly joined in. He was sixtyish, impeccably groomed, polite as only a Japanese can be, with eyes full of quiet humor. It turned out that he too was an ardent nō fan and frequent visitor to nearby Sado Island (with its long nō tradition dating from Zeami's exile there).[5] He used to be a fisherman and farmer, but an old war wound made it difficult for him to do much physical work any more, so he had moved into Kanazawa where he now worked as a driver. He had an intimate knowledge of not only nō but also all the ancient lore and superstitions of the countryside that underlie so much of nō. He thereupon began to explain *Kakitsubata* for the foreigner.

From the most ancient times, iris have been very special, our driver told us. You see, they are Man and Woman: the leaf is *otoko no are* (the man's you-know-what) and the flower is *onna no are* (the woman's you-know-what). *Kakitsubata* and *ayame* thrive only in marshland, which is the symbol of the womb and fertility. The color of these irises is purple, the color of the deepest passion and also of the highest nobility. The word (and same character) *iro* means both "color" and "amorous passion." Our driver talked about Ariwara no Narihira, the *mukashi-otoko* (man of old) who was one of Japan's most famous *iro-otoko* (man of color, that is, great lover). Narihira was an aristocrat; a poet; an exile; a wanderer; an avatar of the deity Kannon, the bodhisattva of song, music, and dance; and an incarnation of In—Yō no kami (the god of yin—yang). Because of its configuration of leaf and flower, the iris is a symbol of yin—yang. The bridge has a zigzag shape because that is the symbol of forked lightning, of the thunderbolt, which in turn symbolize the sudden planting of love in the human heart by the thunder god, who is also the god of love and marriage. Lightning in Japanese is *inazuma*, written with the characters for rice ear (denoting fertility) and wife. Lightning is also the symbol of all direct communication between heaven and earth, such as poetic inspiration. But lightning also kills; indeed, love and death are always close. A bridge is a symbol of all kinds of joining, from copulation to the reconciliation of opposites, the fusion that occurs when yin meets yang, and even the passage from this world to the next. Mikawa, the river in the play *Kakitsubata*, means "river of life," "beautiful river," "body's river," "sacred river," and "three rivers" (referring to the triple river the soul must cross at death before it can find its place in the next world). The zigzag bridge in the play is called Yatsuhashi, literally "eight bridges." The figure 8 in Sino-Japanese script ∧ is a meaningful character in itself: unlike the Western figure 8, it is an open system, narrow above and broad below, and symbolizes many things, for example, the birth canal, open legs, a river reaching the sea, a delta, and a mountain with an opening on top like a volcano. The number eight need not be taken too precisely, however; it often is used just to denote plurability, as in *yae-zakura* (literally "eight-petaled cherry blossom").

All this information is more helpful than the famous Reizei commentary on the *Tales of Ise* cited by Susan Blakely Klein in a note to her translation of *Kakitsubata*,[6] that is, that the eight bridges represent the eight women Narihira could not abandon and that the three rivers, Mikawa, refer to his three true loves (there were, of course, eight such women and three special loves in the *Tales of Ise*).

In 1982 the whole world was celebrating the centenary of James Joyce's birth, and Tokyo was particularly active. I attended several interesting lectures on Joyce and decided I had to reread *Finnegans Wake* and also several essays by eminent Joyce specialists. They told me, and *Finnegans Wake* confirmed, that the novel was about exile, wandering and return, about life and love, about Man and Woman, about Eros and Thanatos, about the fusion of opposites, with motifs of river and delta and bog (that is, marsh) and mountain. In *Finnegans Wake*, Joyce showed an excessive preoccupation with color, bridges, thunder and lightning, and the rainbow, this last being again color and a mythic bridge, which is personified in the West as Iris. All coincidence? The human adventure is much the same everywhere, and primitive symbols tend to be universal.

James Joyce never saw a nō play or met the man from Kanazawa. What could he have known about *Kakitsubata*? That name does not occur once in *Finnegans Wake* nor does that of Ariwara no Narihira, and its Iris is the rainbow and not a flower. Nor have I found in any one book about nō from Joyce's time or since all the information so eagerly passed on to me by the theater-loving driver. Yet I feel that Joyce had discovered all of it, just as this quasi-maniacal researcher discovered so much else, and that he was also well informed about Chinese and Japanese writing techniques. "The unfacts did we possess them, are too imprecisely few to warrant our certitude."[7]

It is no doubt impossible to pin down just what Joyce did know about the nō, but he certainly knew the Fenollosa/Pound versions published in 1917. These

include a translation of *Kakitsubata*, very imperfect but in places beautiful—
there was a poet on the job—and containing a number of things that could have
interested Joyce. Indeed, of all the plays in this collection, I can see no other so
likely to appeal to Joyce. On his first perusal, it perhaps would have been more
intriguing than informative for him, but a number of things could have been
clarified through discussion—even with Pound, whom he knew well. In 1921,
Arthur Waley's *The Nō Plays of Japan* was published, and Joyce surely was familiar with this book, too. He also would have had access to Noël Péri's French
translations, as Joyce lived in Paris, and Péri's detailed introduction to the art of
the nō to which Waley referred. Joyce also could have questioned Japanese
acquaintances: "checking chinchin chat with nipponippers" (p. 485, l. 36–p.
486, l. 1). Did he ever meet someone like the Kanazawa man? At any rate, Joyce
knew the word for the main actor in nō, the *shite* (pronounced sh'tay) that we
meet on page 142, line 7, and that an Irish reader would no doubt read to
rhyme with "rite," making it the common Irish way of saying "bullshit!"

The story of Yeats's encounter with the nō is well known. The great shock of
delight for the poet playwright was the discovery that the lyric dramatic form
toward which he had been groping for years was not impossible to attain. It
already existed and had been brought to the highest degree of perfection in
Japan, a country and culture that he clear-sightedly admired. On the strength of
this discovery, Yeats launched into "my Noh plays," as with typical modesty he
called his dance dramas. Despite being proudly indebted to the nō, not one of
these dance dramas even comes near to being a true nō play, though some of
them are fine stage works in their own right, and even the poorest of them is
stamped with the genius of a great poet. (Joyce was less charitable toward them
and is not the only one who underestimated them.)

It seems to me that for Joyce, too, the greatest satisfaction he could have
derived from his growing acquaintance with the Japanese language and literature would have been finding confirmation of the feasibility of what he had been
aiming at and experimenting with for years: layered language, not only single
words but whole narratives, pivot words, and associative words, that is, "putting
it as between this yohou and that honmonymh" (p. 490, ll. 12–13) as "if it was
in yappanoise language, ach bad clap" (p. 90, l. 27). Yahoos and houyhnhnms lie
down! By now, such techniques are taken for granted in English writing, but in
Joyce's day they were a sensational innovation. Unfortunately the English language, for all its flexible genius, does not lend itself to this kind of thing as naturally as the Chinese and Japanese languages and their writing systems do.

To understand *Finnegans Wake*, it is essential to have read all that Joyce wrote
before and especially *Ulysses*, but he would hardly have progressed from that to

the *Wake* without some stimulus such as I am assuming he learned from Japan and China. I believe it was his obsession with Yeats that started Joyce on the East Asia trail.

The Fenollosa/Pound translations were first published in the United States in 1917 under the title *"Noh" or Accomplishment, a Study of the Classical Stage of Japan* (Knopf). Yeats was in close association with Ezra Pound while the latter was editing and "finishing" (that is, polishing) the versions translated by the late Ernest Fenollosa with the help of his nō teacher, Umewaka Minoru, and an interpreter. It is no wonder that translations written under such circumstances so long ago should seem woefully imperfect in the light of today's exacting scholarship. However, each of the men involved was remarkable in one way or another and deeply dedicated. Notwithstanding all its sins, the end result has many merits, and Pound's polishing is often brilliant. Indeed, Yeats was so fascinated that he had four of the plays published in advance by his sisters' Cuala Press in 1916 under the title of *Certain Noble Plays of Japan*, and for this he wrote a remarkable introduction which, I believe, did more than anything else to change the condescending attitude shown up to then by Westerners when commenting on the Japanese theater. Péri had already done fine work in French on nō plays but reached too small an audience to have much impact at the time. Pound and Yeats certainly reached Joyce. Yeats's famous introduction throws light on many a spot in *Finnegans Wake*. Even his publishing sisters, nicknamed Lolly and Lily, turn up there frequently, especially Lily, in a variety of avatars. I think that one of the possible readings of "nonobli" (*Finnegans Wake*, p. 64, l. 30) is "noh annobli" and that the pun on Shaw's and Yeats's Nobel Prize also harks back to the *Noble Plays of Japan*. "Will-of-the-Wisp and Barney-the-Bark two mangolds noble to sweeden their bitters" (p. 211, l. 23).

The two great cycles of storytelling in ancient Ireland were the *Red Branch*, or *Cuchulainn Cycle*, and the *Fenian*, or *Finn Mac Cool Cycle*. The ink was hardly dry on his introduction to the *Noble Plays* before Yeats was off and running on "my Noh plays" and soon absorbed in conceiving a Cuchulainn series of nō. Cuchulainn is curiously, or perhaps not so curiously, absent from *Finnegans Wake*. Yeats's antithesis would naturally choose the Finn Cycle, thereby inevitably banishing Cuchulainn.

In *Finnegans Wake*, page 166, line 30, we find a "Margareena . . . velly fond of chee." McHugh gives "tea" and "cheese" for this. The Japanese word for tea is *cha*, but the Japanese way of pronouncing the syllable *tee* is *chee*. This is also—especially if softened in the French way—suggestive of "piss," so well attested in the *Wake* and often vulgarly used in Ireland to denote weak or badly prepared tea. In lines 31 to 34, we find "the important influence excercised on everything by this East Asian import has not been till now fully flavoured." Is Joyce still talking about tea only? I think not. The kind of tea used then in Ireland was not an *East* Asian import. The phrase "fully flavoured" jogs the memory. It was J. M. Synge's phrase for the quality of native genuineness he thought a stage play should have.[8] Even Yeats's most ardent admirers, of whom I am one, find his *Noh Plays*, as Irish plays, sadly far from being "fully flavoured," but none of us could fault *Finnegans Wake* on the same account. *Finnegans Wake*, page 32, line 1, asks, "And shall Nohomiah be our place like?" As well as McHugh's "no place like home," "Bohemia," and "Nehemiah," I think Noh is relevant here and is related to the "problem passion play of the millentury" (p. 32, l. 32) that Joyce is slyly offering us. "I tell you no story. Smile!" (p. 52, l. 2). Might that be Yappanoise? Japanese has no articles.

Finnegans Wake is closer to a vision nō than anything conceived by Yeats, and I am more and more inclined to believe that this was a part of its purpose. "Be secret and exult," Yeats advised a friend "whose work had come to nothing." I imagine Joyce determined that his work would come to something, secretly exulting as he went about upstaging the Japan-inspired Yeats, seriously producing what is no play and yet a nō play "behind the butteler's back" (p. 12, l. 4). Yeats was so proud of the Butler name! Page 52 again is strongly evocative of Yeats and suggests Joyce's intention of "stealing his thunder" (l. 31). On page 303 in a long list of writers, "all the characters in the drame" (Irish dream and French drama: vision nō?) we find line 7, "This is Pshaw. This is Doubbllinnbbayyates." This obviously refers to Shaw and W. B. Yeats, but in the insistent "doubling" of Yeats, is Joyce dropping a hint of what he is doing (at least one of the several things he is doing) in *Finnegans Wake*? We are definitely dealing with a very devious "doblinganger" (p. 490, l. 17).

This story has no beginning and no end. Here is a simple, incontrovertible statement about *Finnegans Wake* that commentators have repeatedly made and that is often accompanied by learned references to Vico.[9] Although there is no doubting Joyce's interest in Vico, this statement also just happens to be a line spoken by the Iris lady in the Fenollosa/Pound *Kakitsubata*.[10] Fenollosa, the actual translator, is not once referred to by his full name in *Finnegans Wake*, but we might be able to detect veiled references to him in, for example, "the charmful water*loose* country" (p. 8, ll. 2–3), which could less charmingly be called a *fen*, a marsh being in any case the setting for *Kakitsubata*. Again, in a hilarious spoof on French cuisine, we find "his Poggadovies alla Fenella" (p. 84, l. 31). Is this mere fennel? Again, at the bottom of page 291, footnote 6, we have "See the freeman's cuticatura by Fennella."

There is considerable wordplay on asthma in *Finnegans Wake*, for example, "the King of the Yeast" and his "caspian asthma" (p. 579, ll. 3–5). Might it not refer to *Adzuma* (Azuma in east Japan)? Pound has Narihira both coming from there (error) on page 123 and heading for it on page 127. "His asama" (p. 130, l. 5) clearly refers to Mount Asama, the volcano mentioned in *Kakitsubata* (pp. 127–28).

Ariwara no Narihira is never mentioned, unless he is the "Arra irrara hirrara man" of page 497, line 4, but even so, the hero of the *Wake* has many of his attributes. First, he was an avatar. Earwicker is "the vilest bogeyer but most attractionable avatar the world has ever had to explain for" (p. 42, ll. 15–16). It must be remembered, however, that Joyce had been interested in avatars since at least 1902, when he visited AE (George Russel) and discussed "the Irish avatar" with him. The *Tales of Ise,* attributed to Narihira, are not mentioned either, unless "Isegrim" (p. 244, l. 21) alludes to Ise and pilgrims as well as to the wolf Isengrim. But Joyce surely knew about that work, at the very least from Waley's half-page comment on *Kakitsubata* in his *Nō Plays of Japan* (p. 262). Waley translates the eighth episode of the *Tales of Ise,* in which Narihira in the iris marsh composes his famous anagram on the iris that expresses his love and longing for wife and home. (Joyce never reached that standard of layering words and meaning!) Waley translates: "When he had done singing, they all wept over their dried rice till it grew soppy." We find in *FinnegansWake,* page 314, line 33, "wiping the rice assatiated with their wetting." McHugh deciphers this as "wiping their eyes" and "the rice associated with their wedding." It is not only in Kanazawa, of course, that rice is used as a fertility symbol, but the rice here is definitely wet with weeping. A few lines later (l. 34) we have "he sicckumed of hominis terrars" from which one can deduce a layer meaning that he was homesick. Is he a doblinganger for Narihira?

What convinced me that Joyce knew a great deal about Narihira is the reference to "Iro's Irismans ruinboon pot" (p. 612, l. 20). It refers, no doubt, to Irish devotees of Eros and to Iris the rainbow, but surely also to the great *iro otoko* of the Iris story *Kakitsubata.* On the same page a few lines down, he is styled a "sager." Pound (p. 122) calls him, oddly, "the old sage Narihira," but *sager* in German also suggests a teller of tales. Narihira was also a nobleman. Joyce's "respectable prominently connected fellow of Iro-European ascendances with welldressed ideas" (p. 37, l. 26) is, I believe, at least in part inspired by Narihira. I would not be surprised to discover sometime that Joyce knew about another famous iro-otoko of Japanese literature, the hero of Saikaku's *Kōshoku ichidai otoko* (*shoku* being the Chinese reading of *iro*).[11] How Joyce, if he could read Japanese, would have envied Saikaku's mastery of the verbal techniques he pursued!

Finnegans Wake is a riot of color. Joyce's interest in colors certainly predates this book. There are lots of colors in *Ulysses,* and they were a part of what he admired in *The Book of Kells*, but in *Finnegans Wake* he is, to use his own word, suffering from "chromitis" (p. 232, l. 2). "Who'll search for *Find me Colours*" (p. 626, l. 17) he challenges us. The italicized phrase contains Finn Mac Cool ("find" being an old variant of "Finn"). *My* is commonly pronounced "me" in Ireland. Are we being urged to investigate what color means to James Joyce? In the *Wake*, it is identified, I believe, with the Japanese *iro*, "color" and "amorous passion." A very fat volume would be needed to say all that could be said about this case of chromitis; I will limit myself to pointing out just a few symptoms of it.

On page 63, lines 12–13, we have "Myriam Huey and Colores Archer under Flaggy Bridge" ("look at my myriad hues" and "rainbow"). There is a Flaggy Bridge in Ireland, identified by the indefatigable McHugh, but I think it relevant to note that *flag* is another name for the iris. On page 7 we find "What if she be in flags and flitters?" Again, *flag* can mean iris flower or the other flag, alias the colors. "Flitters" suggests bats and twilight, the time of the play *Kakitsubata* as well as the fluttering of a flag. At any rate, we have come a long way from rags and tatters. I pick at random "Lokil calour" (p. 51, l. 26), "a funny color" (p. 38, l. 17) "the calour of her brideness" (p. 223, l. 6), "flush-caloured" (p. 205, ll. 8–9); I could go on all day.

There are constantly recurring references to the rainbow and its colors and almost as frequent references to flowers and their hues. Even fruits are used to represent colors. The hero of *Ulysses* was named Bloom. Joyce already showed a great preoccupation with flowers in that book, but in *Finnegans Wake*, they seem to be important mainly for color. On page 494, lines 2–4, is "that skew arch of chrome sweet home. . . . Talk about iridecencies," which seems to play between the iridescence of the rainbow and the iris flower whose botanical family name is Iridaceae. The rainbow is presented in an unbelievable parade of aliases, for example, regenbogen (p. 3), reignbeau (p. 203; a court beau like Narihira?), ruinboon (p. 612), and even Tuwarceathy (p. 490, from its name in Gaelic, *tuar ceatha*), but its personal name is Iris for the Greek goddess. Incidentally, the Gaels of Ireland prided themselves on their Greek origins.

On page 285, lines 26–27, Joyce seems to be taunting Yeats and assuming his inability to understand what is going on here. "For a surview over all the factionables see Iris in the Evenine's World.[6] Binomeans to be comprendered; . . . Inexcessible as thy by god ways" (identified by McHugh as alluding to Yeats's "A Vision," "as inaccessible as God or thou," p. 143). Joyce's footnote 6 then gives the reader an Archimboldo Iris to chew on; "tomatoes, malmalaid with De Quincey's salade can be tastily served with Indiana Blues on the violens." Chromitis, did we say? Oh yes, and a very bad case indeed! To return to the factionables. Is Joyce suggesting that they can be comprehended by

means of nō? There are funns far more forced than that on every page of
Finnegans Wake!

Japanese sufferering from chromitis are often described it as having dipped
themselves in the Somegawa (river Dye). I diligently looked for this river
among the hundreds of rivers in *Finnegans Wake*. It is not there as such. Did it
perhaps drown in the Somme on page 208, line 19, as "sommething quaint"? Or
is it confluent with the Dee? On page 200, lines 16–17, the rivers Dee and
Doon are evoked in the same breath, recalling the liar who vowed, "I'd lay me
doon an' dee" for Annie Laurie, "dee" being Scots for "die" (dye?). The river Dee
is mentioned several times in the *Wake*, most suggestively on page 226: "In the
Dee dips a dame." Just before this, beginning on line 11 of page 226, is a lovely
passage: "She is fading out like Journee's clothes, so you can't see her now. Still
we know how Day the Dyer works in dims and deeps and dusks and darks. And
among the shades that Eve's now wearing she'll meet a new fiancy, tryst and
trow." One of the shades of that passage is surely purple, and the Dee coming
just after that may well indeed be the Somegawa. The passage is also another but
gentler than usual spoof on Yeats and his poem "He wishes for the Cloths of
Heaven."[12] Incidentally, there was a Dublin dyer whose name was Day! The
"Journee's clothes" intrigue me. Also "journey's"? They remind me of the *tabi-
goromo* or traveling clothes of nō. In his translation of *Kinuta*, Pound has the
maidservant say: "The day is advancing and I, in my travelling clothes, travel
with the day" (p. 89). Joyce knew that, too. Did he know that a full, five-play, nō
program is usually called a *journée* by French commentators? The "fading out"
also suggests the fading away of the vision *shite* in nō.

The most important color in *Kakitsubata* is purple. One does not have to be
Japanese to live a purple passion or to be born to the purple, but I feel that
Joyce's repeated references to it had much to do with his Japanese gleanings. We
even find it in Corcor Andy (p. 504, l. 20), *Corcair* being Gaelic for "purple."
Purpurando (p. 504, l. 17) hints at a possible new interpretation of *purpurandus*,
Vatican parlance for one declared fit to be elevated to the cardinalate. Another
color with which Joyce seems obsessed is indigo. In Japanese, indigo is *ai* and is
a homonym of the word *ai* meaning "love." In the *Wake*, "eye" frequently occurs
next to indigo or variant puns.

The question arises as to why Joyce—if indeed he took inspiration from
Kakitsubata—would not have emphasized Iris the flower rather than Iris the
rainbow. First, I suspect that this man—so proud of his own "kunning"—would
not give his game away too easily. Second, there is no body of stories about the
iris in Ireland, but there are endless rainbow tales, so the impact of a rainbow
Iris would be far greater. The flower associated with bogland in Ireland is the bog

cotton, and it thrives in the *Wake*, too. There are lots of irises in Irish wetlands, but they are the common yellow flag. The rainbow is an ideal vehicle for the color theme. Ireland has no tradition of zigzag bridges, but the rainbow is a mystic bridge between heaven and earth. On page 612, lines 27–28, it is presented as "Balenoarch," evoking the Italian *arcobaleno*, the Celtic fire god Baal, and Noah's ark and rainbow. Robert Boyle points out that *baleno* in Italian means "lightning flash."[13] All that in a back-to-front rainbow!

But Joyce does not by any means abandon Iris the flower. She often appears in conjunction with Lily, as in "Iris Trees and Lily O'Rangan" (p. 30, l. 1). Here we have a stage Iris, the English actress Iris Tree, who doubles as Irish trees and means green. Lily may be Elizabeth Yeats. The lily is white. Lily O'Rangan is the orange lily. It all adds up to the Irish national flag, green, white, and orange: that *flag* again! But Iris and Lily are worth knowing better. If the iris is an erotic symbol, the lily is a chastity/purity symbol.

Joyce lived in France, where he would have been daily reminded of the fleur-de-lys. *Lys* means "lily," but anyone can see and many note that the conventional fleur-de-lys emblem does not look like a lily at all. There is a good reason for that. It was originally the sign of the blue flag, or purple iris. It carried the symbolism the Kanazawa man gave to kakitsubata and ayame, and it was known as the *fleur délice*. It is well attested under that name, even in English poetry up to Elizabethan times. It is said that the famous Queen Blanche de Castille, pious mother of Saint Louis, found it an inappropriate emblem for a Christian realm and so had it changed to a fleur-de-lys to symbolize the white lily associated with the Virgin Mary and almost always included in pictures of the Annunciation. Although the flower and name were changed, the conventional form remains to this day. Instead, it was the rose that took over the erotic symbolism of the banished "aglo iris" (p. 528, l. 23); see *Le Roman de la rose*. Does this have anything to do with "Rosa and Lily Miskinguette" (Mistinguette and Miss can get) on page 33, line ll?

The aristocrats of the iris family are no doubt the purple kakitsubata and ayame. Also mentioned in the Fenollosa/Pound version of the nō play *Kakitsubata*, the ayame is now well known in western Europe as the Japanese iris or Kaempfer's iris (*Iris Kaempferi spontanea*), named for the German Dr. Engelbert Kaempfer (1651–1716) who came to Japan in 1690 as the doctor for the small Dutch colony of traders in Nagasaki. He wrote a valuable account of his years in Japan, including a visit to the court of the shogun (Joyce's "shugon," p. 535, ll. 19–20) in Edo (the old name for Tokyo) (or Yedo: Joyce's "yeddo not need light," p. 535, l. 9). Like other doctors of his time, Kaempfer had to know medicinal herbs and be something of a botanist. He discovered and classified several

Japanese plants, later introduced to Europe, including rhododendrons, East Asian willows, and ayame. We meet him in a Dutch and double-Dutch context on page 383 as Mr. Deaubelow Downbelow Kaempersally (sally for willow?).

There was another Dr. Kaempfer in Joyce's life, however. Two hundred years after Engelbert Kaempfer's death, in 1917 in Locarno, Joyce met a young German woman, Dr. Gertrude Kaempfer, and fell in love with her. The only positive result seems to have been Joyce's giving her name to the girl Gerty in the Nausicaa chapter of *Ulysses*[14] and perhaps the stirring of an interest in her namesake. I have not checked a possible family relationship.

Joyce specialists, including Joyce himself, do not fail to point out the recurring Eros–Thanatos theme in *Finnegans Wake*. There are a few allusions to it that have not yet been discussed. We find on page 293, line 22, "aiaiaiai." This is a common French expletive expressing grief or frustration, but it is something else, too. Joyce certainly knew that *ai* means "love" in Japanese, and he learned enough of the language that we may assume he knew how to count to ten in it. He therefore would surely have found out that the number four is unlucky, being a homonym of *shi*, death, which is why Japanese hospitals avoid having a room number 4. And in *ai* quadrupled, we have Eros–Thanatos. Again in "Ay,ay.Aye,aye,baas" (p. 608, l. 15), we have the same kind of neat trick and, for good measure, the Gaelic word for death at the end, *bás*. Here we have not only Eros–Thanatos but also a Joycean reconciliation of opposites. *Pace* Kipling! Far East and Far West meet in love and death. Joyce can toss off this kind of thing effortlessly, thanks to his "Lipponease longuewedge wambles" (p. 339, l. 1).

Finnegans Wake mentions bridges over and over again, but there are none in zigzag form symbolizing a thunderbolt or lightning. There are, however, innumerable references to these phenomena. Samuel Beckett cites Vico "in the beginning was the thunder."[15] It rolls already over the first page of *Finnegans Wake* in a babel of languages, including the yappanoise *kaminari*. But it never really stops rolling right through the book, and the lightning flashes on page after page. In fact, to cite in full all the instances of crashing and flashing, I would need far more than the number of pages allowed for this chapter. Many of the thunder and lightning references are in the form of wordplay on Crom Cruach, the thunder god of ancient Ireland. In *Finnegans Wake*, the god Crom is often combined with Oliver Cromwell, the most hated "planter" in Irish history. It is not easy to see why. Does the fact that some of Yeats's antecedents were Cromwellian settlers have any bearing on this? Be that as it may, the number of Crom Cruach references is impressive. Among the most ancient Celtic symbols known in Ireland is the zigzag line. This is surely the sign of Crom Cruach, whose very name in Gaelic evokes a crooked angular line, forked lightning. Love and death! Joyce certainly had a *coup-de-foudre* zigzag in mind for the "zing-zang" (p. 20, l. 22) I use in my title. He doubles it with yin–yang, or male and female. And he seems to be throwing in singsong for good measure. A hint at poetic inspiration?

Yin–yang was never far from Joyce's mind in the *Wake*. My favorite reference to it comes in the form of a pun on chiaroskuro, page 612, line 18, "shiroskuro," that is, Japanese *shiro*, "white," and *kuro*, "black," joined by *s*. In Gaelic the copulative *is* (sibilant), often shortened to *s*, can replace *agus*, for "and." The old Celtic emblem for yin–yang was a circle divided into equal areas of black and white meeting not in a straight line but in an S form, suggesting fluidity and overlapping fusion. This same symbol is found all over East Asia. The "sheeroskuro" on page 317, line 33, seems also to be saying "sheer obscurity" and "although obscure, can be seen through."

The "shiroskuro" of page 612, line 18, is immediately followed by the intoxicating "blackinwhitepaddynger," referring to two well-known brands of Scotch and Irish whiskey. Irish whiskey is spelled with an *e* for the *uisce* or *uisge* (water) of its Gaelic name, *uisge beatha*, meaning water of life, which brings us to Joyce's "translated water, whereamid . . . violet vesper vailed" (p. 606, ll. 3–4). Mikawa of the nō play could in fact be translated into Gaelic as *uisge beatha*, but Joyce can do better than that. He has—consciously I believe—translated it into Anna Livia Plurabelle, which contains everything that Mikawa with its rich homonymic resonance says in Japanese and then a bit more.

Anna deserves a book of explication all for herself. In Gaelic she is Abha na Life—in English the river Liffey—but the two-syllable Gaelic "Life" can be read as the one-syllable English word *life*. Here I leave her with a question. Why does Joyce so often juxtapose her with Joachim? There was a biblical Anna whose husband was called Joachim. For "Joakimono" on page 114, McHugh offers Joachim de Flora and kimono, and also Joachim Creek. Then, for "her joki's nose" he tells us helpfully that *joki* is Finnish for "river," but there may be more to it. If Joyce had read Waley and Péri, as I am assuming he had, he would know that *mono* in Japanese is often used to mean nō play, as in *kamimono* (god play) or *sanbanme-mono* (third-category play). Is Joyce also telling us that he is giving "muddle crass" us a *jokimono* (river play) and a *jokey mono* (comic play)? In *Finnegans Wake* we have both of these in a special way, and they are "samuraised twimbs" (p. 354, l. 23). Makoto! (p. 233, l. 35). Really!

I do not claim for a moment that nō or *Kakitsubata* can explain everything in *Finnegans Wake*. As the illustrious author is at pains to point out that "there are sordidly tales within tales" (p. 522, l. 5) and, just as certainly, "no one end is known" (p. 48, l. 24). The most striking contrast between nō and *Finnegans Wake* is the latter's "superexuberabundancy." Joyce's themes and aims and ideas were manifestly plurabelle, but he had them all under control.

Finnegans Wake is a verbal masterpiece of Celtic interlacing, but like the illuminations—as the interlaced designs of the old Irish and other insular manuscripts were called—it is precision work of the most exacting kind. Joyce's admiration for *The Book of Kells* is well known. He clearly refers to it in the *Wake* and especially to the superb Tunc illumination (p. 122, l. 23). The Tunc illumination is often cited as the key to the form of *Finnegans Wake*, an idea I find plausible. Each illumination is an intricate interweaving of a multiplicity of strands, all distinct and every one a necessary part of the overall design that it enhances. The river-of-life theme is, to me, the most important strand in the *Wake* that I can identify, and it also provides the unifying image so important in a nō play and so admired in that context by Fenollosa, Pound, and Yeats. *Finnegans Wake* is, above all, as is *Kakitsubata*, a celebration of life and love and a glorification of erotic love.

Surely Joyce is not only linking Aesop's fable of the fox and the grapes to the Mookse and the Gripes when he says, "As none of you knows Javanese I will give you my easyfree translation of the old fabulist's parable" (p. 152, l. 12). Has he not been doing the same thing for another fabulous tale? I believe that that is what we have here, and it is a delight and a marvel to see how the river and the lowlands of Mikawa and the wanderings of Narihira are translated into vibrant Joyce and how Iris who attained Buddhist illumination in *Kakitsubata* goes on to achieve Celtic illumination in a new avatar in *Finnegans Wake*.

And now, chapjappy cheerycherrily Seyoh narar my fiends! Banzaine! Chin, chin! Chin, chin!

Aman!

Omen!

NOTES

1. Roland McHugh, *Annotations to Finnegans Wake*, rev. ed. (Baltimore: Johns Hopkins University Press, 1991). Also useful is McHugh's *The Finnegans Wake Experience* (Berkeley and Los Angeles: University of California Press, 1981).

2. I lack the space to give any adequate idea of the already vast and steadily growing Joyce bibliography, but the following are essential reading for anyone with an interest in the subject under discussion: James Joyce, *Finnegans Wake* (London: Faber & Faber, 1939; New York: Viking Press, 1939 [reedited in 1975]); and *Ulysses* (New York: Random House, 1961).

Richard Ellmann, *James Joyce*, rev. ed. (New York: Oxford University Press, 1982).

A number of Joyce puns not identified by page and line of *Finnegans Wake* are scattered throughout these pages. I am responsible only for 'jappyknowledgist' (p. 1, l. 2), and even there the "jappy" is Joyce. The final salutation is all Joyce. Donald Keene's *odeshi* do not need any further elucidation.

3. For the text of *Kakitsubata* in a translation available to Joyce, see Ezra Pound and Ernest Fenollosa, trans., *The Classic Noh Theatre of Japan* (New York, 1917; New Directions paperback, 1959), pp. 120–30. For accurate later versions, see Chifumi Shimazaki, trans., *The Noh*, vol. 3: *Woman Noh 2* (Tokyo: Hinoki shoten, 1977), pp. 73–103. The translation is parallel to the romanized original text. Also see the translation by Susan Blakely Klein in Karen Brazell, ed., *Twelve Plays of the Noh and Kyōgen Theaters* (Ithaca, NY: Cornell University East Asia Papers, no. 50, 1988), pp. 64–79. For the source, consult Helen Craig McCullough, trans., *Tales of Ise: Lyrical Episodes from Tenth Century Japanese* (Stanford, CA: Stanford University Press, 1968). For nō in general, I believe Joyce would have consulted Waley and Péri as well as Pound. See Arthur Waley's *The Nō Plays of Japan* (London: Allen & Unwin, 1921; reprinted New York: Grove Press, 1957); and Noël Péri, trans., *Le Nō* (Tokyo: Maison franco-japonaise, 1944). Much of the content of this Péri collection appeared in learned journals in Paris in the second decade of this century.

4. See Frank O'Connor, *The Backward Look* (London: Macmillan, 1967), pp. 194–211.

5. See Susan Matisoff, "Kintōsho: Zeami's Song of Exile," *Monumenta Nipponica* 32 (Winter 1977): 441–58.

6. Klein, *Kakitsubata*, p. 68, n. 4.

7. James Joyce, *Finnegans Wake* (London: Faber & Faber, 1975), pp. 57, ll. 16–17. Subsequent quotations are from this edition. My 1982 reading was enhanced by having heard and read Donald Keene on the subject of decorative language and artistic puns.

8. In a preface to his most famous work, *The Playboy of the Western World,* Synge vouches for the authenticity of the high-flown language he puts in the mouths of the Irish peasantry and argues for the necessity of language natural to the characters. "In a good play every speech should be as fully flavoured as a nut or apple—" J. M. Synge, *Plays, Poems, and Prose* (London: Dent, 1941), p. 108.

9. Giambattista Vico (1668–1744), Neapolitan philosopher-historian whose cyclic theory of the history of cultures had many points in common with ancient Celtic and Asian beliefs.

10. Pound and Fenollosa, *Classic Noh Theatre*, p. 126, penultimate line.

11. Ihara Saikaku's *Kōshoku ichidai otoko* (literally a "color-loving man"), first published in 1682. Donald Keene renders this title *The Life of an Amorous Man*.

12. W. B. Yeats, *Collected Poems* (London: Macmillan, 1950), p. 81: "He wishes for the cloths of Heaven."

13. Robert Boyle and E. L. Epstein, eds., *A Starchamber Quiry: A James Joyce Centennial Volume 1882–1982* (New York: Methuen, 1982), p. 116.

14. See Ellmann, *James Joyce*, p. 418.

15. Samuel Beckett et al., *James Joyce/Finnegans Wake: A Symposium: Our Exagmination Round His Factification for Incamination of Work in Progress* (Paris: Shakespeare and Company, 1929; New York: New Directions paperback, 1972), p. 5.

2

The Nō Play Motomezuka *as a Poem Narrative:*
A Study of Transtextuality, Wordplay, *and Sexual Overtones*

◎

ETSUKO TERASAKI

In the medieval period, it was the general practice for nō texts to borrow from earlier literary material—legends, folk tales, poems, and prose—found in various anthologies and literary canons. The first act of *Motomezuka* (The Sought-After Grave) is characterized by a rich infusion of earlier poetry,[1] and the narrative, forming a sequential thread, was created from this transtextual practice.[2]

Nō scholars have pondered the question of why Unai, the maiden in the play *Motomezuka*, must be punished so severely in the Buddhist inferno. According to some commentators' readings of the old legend of "the contention for the bride" (*tsuma-arasoi*), the maiden Unai's indecision alone leads her to commit suicide, but they maintain that the maiden is naive and innocent of any guilt. The reason for the maiden's tortures is not revealed.[3]

Many answers to this question are possible. One Japanese critic noted that the maiden's fall into the inferno means no more than the continuation of a "sacrificial rite" by a communal body to maintain order and harmony and to ensure its survival. Since her indecision defies the communal law, she is condemned to punishment for her transgression.[4] When considering this view, it should be remembered that this critic's thesis is based on a social–anthropological analysis of the legend, which he extends to the nō play.

I believe that the answer to this question must be sought in the text of the play itself and that it can be found in the two opposing signifying structures appearing in the text. One uses the "literalistic" trope based on the phenomenal or quotidian world of nature, which is metonymical. The other explores reflective consciousness based on imagination, which is metaphorical. "Metaphor," according to Paul de Man, is "on the side of inwardness, imagination, contemplative withdrawal, and all that belongs to the realm of pure, self-delighting creative reverie." Metonymy is a "literalistic trope that works on the basis of external or real-world relationships." Whereas metaphor creates a world of unified thought and has a totalizing tendency, metonymy is often perceived as fragmented and heterogeneous.[5]

As applied to the nō play, these signifying structures are seen as the material of rhetorical operation in which the domain of mind conflicts with the world of natural objects. The narrative's persistent practice of incorporating a different "content" drawn from a prior poetic context (pre-text) takes us into the world of irony and ambiguity. A network of new relations is introduced, and the narrative turns into a literary construct based on quotations or allusions from the "ghost" texts, in the process transforming the meaning of the text. Furthermore, this "imagining" (consciousness) must rely on the images of everyday natural objects for its expression. This kind of insertion from another system creates incompatibility because the substitute "reality" brings with it specularity and distortion. In this way, transtextual wordplay produces heterogeneous and dissimilar reading effects, because the otherness of the appropriated text constantly introduces both relatedness and conflict. In addition, various figures of speech function dually as methods of concealment and of revelation.

The first act of *Motomezuka* is a good example of this type of rhetorical mode. The text shows that the narrative moves toward rhetorical negativity, in which disfiguration takes place. Disfiguration is defined as "the repetitive erasure by which language performs the erasure of its own position."[6] By examining the individual as well as the sequential function and the reading effects of the poetic signs, we find that the play of significations reveals the text's own desire.

A number of oppositions are created by the text's practice of transtextuality and its rhetorical mode. These oppositions are the romantic and idealized past (the inner world of imagination) versus the grim and hostile present (the external world of natural objects)—that is, the elegant mode of life in the capital over the harsh surroundings of the rural area—the aesthetic in the life of the aristocracy versus the pragmatic necessity of the socially marginal working people, and the fundamental ideological difference between Buddhism and Shintoism.[7] Social relations and cultural and political elements are inscribed in their rhetorical manifestations.

The Plot

Motomezuka is a two-act play, with the first act divided into two scenes and an interlude between the acts. The first act takes place on an early spring morning in Ikuta in Settsu Province near Kyoto. The second act takes place at the sought-after grave (*motomezuka*), a historical site.

ACT I, SCENE I

An itinerant priest and his companion are on their way to the capital. They arrive in the village of Ikuta, where they meet a group of maidens gathering fresh herbs in the marsh. When the companion priest asks the unfriendly maidens where the sought-after grave is, they do not answer. Soon all the maidens except one leave. Perplexed, the priest asks her why she alone remains in the field, and she tells him that she will lead them to the grave.

SCENE 2

At the site of the grave, she recounts its history: Long ago, there was a maiden called Unai whom two young men wanted to marry. They sent her passionate letters and gifts at the same time and on the same day, but she could not decide which man to choose. They competed for her hand in various contests, but each time they proved to be equal in skill and strength. Unable to decide which man to choose and lamenting her predicament, the maiden recited a poem and then drowned herself in the Ikuta River. The two suitors, in despair, stabbed each other. Three graves were dug and marked in their memory.

After pleading with the priest to help her restless soul attain enlightenment, the maiden disappears into the grave.

INTERLUDE

A villager happens to walk by and confirms the story the priest and his companion have heard. He also tells them that since the maiden died while she was being courted, the grave, formally known as Otomezuka (Maiden grave), is now called Motomezuka (Sought-after grave). He adds that a tragedy occurred because one man, a native of the province, was buried with a sword, and the other, from another province, without one. The priest then tells the villager about the mysterious maiden he encountered. The villager convinces the priest that this maiden must be the incarnation of Unai and suggests that the priest and his companion offer a prayer on her behalf.

ACT 2

While the two priests recite a sutra, the spirit of the maiden appears and tells them how she longs for the human world and how much she appreciates their prayers. She has barely finished speaking when she is attacked by creatures from hell. Her two suitors have become fiery demons, and a pair of mandarin ducks have been transformed into ferocious iron birds with steel beaks and claws that pick at her brain. She cannot run forward because an ocean blocks her way, and she cannot run back because flames stand in her path. The maiden's body is charred as she is forced to embrace a burning pillar. When the flames disappear, she confesses her sins and describes the burning inferno, the Eighth Great Hell, where she must endure unspeakable pain and suffering. As she is telling them about her tribulations, darkness suddenly falls, and she disappears into the grass by the grave.

The Two Opposing Tendencies: Shinto and Buddhism

The two-act structure of the play *Motomezuka* divides the text into two opposing ideological tendencies, native Shintoism (first act) and Buddhism (second act). The Shinto religion is concerned with human life (birth, marriage, renewal, and so forth) and nature worship. It is celebratory, creative, and generally optimistic, whereas Buddhism's primary concern is with death and life after death. It considers the living world as a place of suffering and impermanence and thus is basically pessimistic.

The first act of *Motomezuka* deals with the living world and the activities of the herb-gathering maidens in which the spirit of Shinto prevails, whereas the second act depicts the Buddhist inferno scenes in which the maiden suffers incredible pain and agony after death.

The subtle interactions of these two opposing tendencies also are contained in smaller units. Even in the first act, the celebration of the spring (Shinto), Buddhist pessimism constantly undermines the prevailing optimistic spirit.

The Young Herbs, the *wakana*, and Sexual Overtones in Act 1

In act 1 of *Motomezuka*, the chain of signifiers in the narrative disseminates the meaning of the poetic discourse. The theme is the celebration of youth, that is, social relations or images of sexual implications. The relationship between the "human"—as opposed to the nonhuman world or perhaps "nature"—is portrayed in a setting in which concerns for the pragmatics of life and the beauty of nature conflict with each other. The overall mood conveys a fundamental pessimism, yet optimism—attributable to the basic Shinto way of life—also is evident. It is embodied in the abundant natural images, such as the young herbs, *wakana*; in images of topography, Ikuta (literally "living field"), the Ikuta River, and the Ikuta sea; in the celebration of the coming of the new year, the anticipation of spring, of renewal of life; and, most important, in images of sexuality.

When the itinerant priests arrive at the village of Ikuta, they find a group of maidens gathering fresh herbs to make the "seven-herbs" soup to celebrate the new year, a major Shinto celebration which, according to the lunar calendar, coincides with spring. Wakana is an important key word generating complex variants in the narrative. For example, the image of sexuality is always encoded in the words *wakana tsumu*. The word *wakana* literally means a young herb but figuratively stands for a young woman. Consequently, the phrase "plucking the fresh herbs" means to seduce or to deflower a woman. *Wakana* thus playfully evokes images of sexuality in ways that must have delighted the medieval audience.

The initial model of the young herb image as a natural object can be seen in the following passage, in which the maidens are chanting to one another.

MAIDEN AND COMPANION: While we gather our young herbs,
the morning wind
in the little marsh of Ikuta
is still cold, as we felt it
under our fluttering sleeves.

This passage already contains a seed of contradiction. The opposition between nature and human sensibility—the chilly wind against the maidens' sleeves—becomes the theme of hardship and discomfort that is developed in the first act. The details are revealed as the narration continues:

MAIDEN: "Deep in the mountains, snow
still remains on the pine branches.

MAIDEN AND COMPANION: But in the capital, this must be
                         the season for gathering
                         young herbs in the little marsh."[8]
                         How envious we are,
                         just thinking about
                         the pleasantness of it all.
         COMPANION: This place is so far out
                         in the country.
MAIDEN AND COMPANION: For us rustics,
                         life is inevitably difficult
                         here in Ikuta-by-the-sea.
                         Till the water source and
                         our bodies are exhausted,
                         we must pursue
                         our miserable livelihood.
                         We must go out
                         in the cold meadows
                         where it is not yet spring.

As a variation on the first dialogue, the chilly "morning wind" is replaced by even colder snow on the pine branches. In addition, a radical displacement is seen in the location shifting from the little marsh of Ikuta—a rural area—to the vicinity of the capital. Here we find a play of significations—the alliteration, *miya*, in "between the mountainside," *miyama*, and the "capital," *miyako*. In medieval Japan, the word *capital* often evoked the life of the aristocracy, and here the maiden's active flight of imagination—her consciousness—takes her to pastoral activities in the distant capital. The climate in the capital area is known to be moderate, not as harsh as that of the mountains. Gathering herbs in the capital is thus considered a pleasurable pastime for the nobility. But ambivalence becomes apparent in this passage when the maidens refer to their struggle for livelihood. Their perception of the harsh phenomenal world is reflected in the language: "how envious we are," "us rustics," "life is difficult," "our bodies are exhausted," and "our miserable livelihood." The erasure of pleasure by hardship—a negative movement—now becomes evident.

A complex verbal play is introduced here with *amasagaru* (far away or distant from heaven), which is the *makurakotoba* (pillow word, a standard epithet) for *hinabito* (the rustics), in contrast to nobility. *Uki* (wretched, unhappy) and *inochi* (life, livelihood) also are pivoted on Ikuta, the toponym or place-name. The *iku* in Ikuta produces a homonym, *iku* (a modified form of *iki*), "to live." In turn, this *iku* acts as the preface (*jo*) for the subsequent wordplay between *mi o* (our bodies) and the homonym *mio* (water source). In the next line, *uki* is repeated twice, with the latter occurrence pivoting *haru* (clear, as in the weather), its *engo* (related word), with its homonym *haru* (spring, as in the season). Because *haru* is followed by a negative, it means "cloudy," thereby implying that it is not yet spring.[9]

What may be surprising is that this comparison between the capital and the mountainside, which matches the actual landscape, is a direct quotation from the poem "Deep in the Mountains" from the *Kokinshū* (compiled in 905). By using this literary pre-text, "culture" is substituted for "nature." Although the context here differs from that of classical literature, the topical relationship is still close because the quoted poem belongs to the same category of nature, "early spring." In the maiden's imagination, the harsh "reality" of life in the country is replaced by a scene that takes place in the capital. The opposition between action and reflection is apparent, illustrated by the differing dimensions of country life and life in the capital.

This signifying movement focused on the wakana is developed with variants that introduce complexity and multiplicity.

MAIDEN AND COMPANION:　"These must be the footprints
of other villagers who
come to gather the young herbs;
The field turned into
many melted patches."
Even though there is
hardly a path,
we shall find our way:
". . . threading our way
we shall gather the young herbs
in the little marsh today.
For if we wait for the snow to melt,
the herbs will be too old."
The storm rages in the forest,
and in the shadows of trees
the little marsh lies frozen.
The snow remaining on it
makes us even more cold.
Although it is too cold
to be spring, let us gather herbs for
the seven-herb soup of Ikuta.[10]

The first insertion, "These must be the footprints," was adapted from a poem by Fujiwara no Tamesada (1293–1360) in the *Fūgashū* (Spring). The second insertion, "threading our way," is an allusion to the second stanza of a poem by Emperor Kōgon (1313–1364) in the *Shin senzaishū*, which also appears under the heading Spring. A different sort of social relationship and a different time constraint are now added to the pressing situation of harvesting the scarce herbs. Utterances such as "footprints of other villagers" and "there are many patches" indicate the presence of competitors, and "the herbs will be too old" demonstrates the urgency. This "pressing situation" seems applicable to the working context of the play. The scene of searching for the young herbs (or maidens) and the competition with other pickers can be interpreted as a seduction. The context and the associations evoked by the pre-texts thus create a difference by means of a play on words. The pre-texts are not eliminated, however, because like ghosts, their aura still hovers over the new usage. Therefore, on one hand, these passages still evoke the perception of pragmatic reality, calling attention to the suffering in this life, which is the basic tenet of Mahayana Buddhism. On the other hand, the wordplay points to a figurative meaning of seduction, which is the Shinto element.

In the next passage, the herb image is developed further through a metonymic structure by use of the toponym Ikuta. Ikuta is a well-known historical site of the medieval period where the traveling priests in the play decide they must stop for a visit. Curious about the graves of the maiden Unai and her two suitors, a priest asks the herb-gathering women, but their reply is evasive.

COMPANION MAID   *(unconcernedly):*
                      We have heard the name but where it might be,
                      we really do not know.
MAIDEN: You, sir, traveler,
                      Why do you ask about something so trifling? You are
                          wasting our time
                      when we need to gather the fresh herbs.
MAIDEN AND COMPANION: You yourself are on a hurried journey.
                      Why do you pause here?
CHORUS: Well, you know the old poem, . . .
                      "What halts a traveler
                      on his path
                      are the fresh herbs
                      in the little marsh of Ikuta."

Pointless, though,
for you to be asking us why!

Every word in the poem that describes this encounter seems to be innocuous. The maidens' reply (by the chorus) is in fact a direct quotation from a poem by Minamoto no Moroyori in the *Horikawa hyakushu* (compiled in 1106). This poem is clearly double edged, with both literal and figurative meanings. The young herbs are metonyms of the young maidens picking herbs who cause the traveler to pause on his trip. That is, the poem implies that by stopping to talk to the maidens, the pilgrims are needlessly delaying reaching their destination, and for their part, the maidens counter that their work is being interrupted. Figuratively, this is a scene of seduction, in which the maidens' distraction or temptation could be a serious obstacle to the travelers' religious pilgrimage.[11]

The image of *michi* (path) also has a traditional double meaning: literally, it can be a road or journey, and figuratively, it can stand for a Buddhist religious practice. When this idea is combined with the word *samatage* (impediment, obstacle, or interruption), the poem becomes a Buddhist signifier, conveying its doctrinal intent that those in religious pursuits must not be distracted by sexual matters. The play on words in this scene thus unfolds from its likeness to everyday reality to a figurative usage. The doubled-edged words in these poems are "undecidable" because they can have either literal or figurative meanings. As polysemes, they no longer have a unitary meaning.

In this way, a different system of relationship derived from classical literature is constantly infused into the play, and because of this, the transtextual wordplay creates an oscillation between practical action and imagination.

The greatest displacement of the everyday world is perhaps the maiden's allusion to a part of the well-known *Kokinshū* poem 21, composed by Emperor Kōkō (r. 884–887).

For our lord, we shall go out
in the spring marsh to gather
the young herbs while
snow alights continually
on our sleeves.

The narrative voice and the time and space of the countryside are now completely dislocated, since the poem refers to a pastoral scene in which the elegant Heian court ladies in the capital are out in the marsh gathering herbs as a leisurely pursuit. The pre-text evokes the brilliant visual image of the white snow alighting on the scarlet robes of the court ladies in the green pastures. The phrase "for our lord" shifts the context and the meaning of harvesting the herbs, indicating that this activity is an aristocratic pastime. The pre-text splits the subject itself by activating another ghostly presence of the subject from the distant past, creating differences and fissures between the two texts. By differing in this way, the narrative alternates between the maiden's perception of discomfort in the present moments—the image of everyday struggle—and the pleasure produced by her imagination—the fiction of the past.

What brings us back to the beginning of the play is the change in the last line of the poem, "our sleeves are cold" (referring to a pragmatic and mundane situation), which replaces the "while snow alights continually on our sleeves" of the pre-text. The sleeves are of different kinds—one set belongs to the working woman (metonymic), and the other sets are those of the elegant court ladies (metaphoric)—producing a momentary discontinuity.

The immediate world is represented as visual and tactile images of natural objects such as snowflakes, thin ice, and blue-green drops, which we perceive as cold and sharp. The snow image continues throughout the poem by means of its omnipresent "chilliness." But there is more—such as the sexual overtones in the language "pluck the herbs from under the snow" or the hymenal "thin ice" or "wade through the water to gather the watercress" (connoting the lower half of a woman's body) or "dripping" water.

> CHORUS: Let us gather the herbs
>   from under the snow.
>   Let us gather them
>   snowflakes and all.
>   The thin ice remains
>   on the edge of the swamp,
>   but I shall wade through the water
>   to pluck the watercress,
>   dripping with blue-green drops;

Through its associative links, the narrative finally turns into a nonliteral periphrasis. Near the end of the passage, the duality of the key word is transformed into a literary signifier of sexuality. The narrative is made up of a string of literary fragments based on the classical canons. Perhaps this passage illustrates most abundantly the text's figurative structure and its relationship to the pre-texts. Although reflective of the maiden's consciousness, a metonymical

description of the natural objects prevails in the wordplay. It is extremely elliptical, and the allusive structure sometimes makes the decoding difficult.

CHORUS:	Beware of the spring meadow, . . .	1
MAIDEN:	"In the spring meadow,	
	the person who came to gather violets"	
	not only collected the herbs of	
	the pale purple Murasaki	5
	but also the fickle name as well.	
CHORUS:	Oh, yes, speaking of purple,	
	—the color of relationship—	
	the rapeseed stalks of Sano,	
	where it is said	10
	the "lovers' bridge" was dismantled	
	and so was their love,	
	are putting on youthful growth.	
MAIDEN:	Their green color, too,	
	is as famous as	15
	the Shepherd's Purse of Ch'ang-an,	
	the Chinese hot-herbs.	
	At dawn, the white-root herbs	
	mixed in the snow are	
	hardly discernible to pluck.	20

The spring meadow in the first and the second lines and "to gather violets" in
the third line refer to a poem by Yamabe no Akahito (fl. 724–737) found in the
Man'yōshū (Collection of Ten Thousand Leaves, compiled in the late Nara or
early Heian period). It reads:

To the spring meadow,
I have come to gather
some violets; so delighted
by the field,
I spent a night there.

With the spring meadow and the violets as the main referents in Akahito's
poem, when we read the nō passage, this ghost text begins to echo in our minds.
This kind of retroactive association is important to the reading of nō texts and
produces depth and complexity. For example, an extended metonymy is often

created, based on a transtextual wordplay and also by the overdetermination of the poetic structure.

The herb image of wakana is now displaced and becomes a violet, a purple-flowered plant. "Beware of the spring meadow" in the first line and "the spring meadow" repeated in the second line suggest a seduction scene by means of the interplay of words in Akahito's poem, such as "I have come to gather," and "only collected" found in the nō text. A scene of seduction is thus created and affirmed by the echoing lines in the pre-text, the metonyms "to gather some violets," "so delighted by the field," and "spend a night." The allusion in this passage thus has a dual significance, concealing and revealing at the same time. The violets are then quickly linked to *The Tale of Genji*, and the narrative takes a further turn. The "pale purple Murasaki" in the fifth line is unmistakably a metonym of the heroine, the young Lady Murasaki (*murasaki* means purple), in the *Tale*.

At this point, the theme of sexuality has far-reaching and multiple echoing effects and is elliptically linked to the hero, Prince Genji, whose numerous sexual exploits are so well known as to be a kind of cliché. In addition, the passage hints in the sixth line that Genji has become an object of gossip, earning the "fickle name," *na o tsumu*, a skillful pun. As we have seen, the phrase "plucking the herbs" connotes deflowering, which is abundantly evident in *The Tale of Genji*. Name, *na* in Japanese, is a homonym of the *na* in *wakana*, young herbs, and is a deliberate paronomasia (play on words) here. In this way the key word is concealed in its sexual implications.[12]

The analogical structure using transtextual wordplay in regard to the theme of sexuality turns even more elliptical at this point. In the seventh line, "purple" is further linked to the "color of relationship" found in the eighth line. This "relationship" joins the toponyms Sano and Funahashi (boat bridge), where the "lovers' bridge" is located (lines 9, 10, 11, and 12). Thus the signifying chain is associated with the two names frequently cited in the classic texts. An image such as the "rapeseed stalk" has sexual overtones, and "the lovers' bridge was dismantled" calls attention to the threat of lovers being separated; of these two images, the "lovers' bridge" becomes a negative signifier. The allusion to the plight of lovers, derived from an anonymous poem in the "Songs of the East" section of the *Man'yōshū*, echoes the lovers' direct and passionate voice in the pre-text.

> In the province of Kamitsuke,
> the Boat Bridge at Sano Ferry
> is taken apart. Our parents
> are shunning us. Would we be
> torn apart? Never![13]

In the nō text, the Boat Bridge (Funahashi), a well-known toponym in poetry, is deliberately replaced with the "lovers' bridge" in order to emphasize the text's desire. On the other hand, in the ninth line, the herb theme is retained in the allusion to Sano, as a reference to its famous product, the rapeseed stalk, evoking a sexual image. This inflection of the herb image is further displaced to conceal the sexuality theme.

The text also takes an unexpected turn to things Chinese, an exotic foreign country, referring to the "Shepherd's Purse of Ch'ang-an" (line 16) and the "Chinese hot mustard greens" (line 17). Because Ch'ang-an was the capital of T'ang China, T'ang, or Kara (an old Japanese reading for China), is homonymous within *karai* (hot), a play on words that establishes an extended double meaning. The rapeseed (a native product) is compared to the Shepherd's Purse of China (foreign). The use of a verse in Chinese from the *Wakan rōeishū*, alluding to the Shepherd's Purse of Ch'ang-an, by Minamoto no Shitagō (911–983), further deflects and erases the theme of sexuality by means of these ingenious transtextual punnings.[14]

At this juncture, the string of allusions to classic texts completely undermines the literal imagery. The metonymic figures of sexuality (associative links) surface and then disappear. The herb imagery used here no longer refers to the literal object per se but now functions as a dual sign to facilitate the wordplay in order to produce readings of multiple dimensions.

In the approaching dusk, the herb-gathering maidens leave the field and then "vanish" before the priests' eyes, effecting a further erasure. The first act thus comes to an end. This act is a celebration of life, with abundant sexual overtones, and portrays a struggle in the opposition between the poetically charged imaginary landscape and the phenomenal world, which leads to disfiguration.

Death, Delusion, and Confession in Act 2

Transtextual poetic wordplay is used only once in the second act, when the priests stand before the graves and recite their prayers. The graves signify the deaths long ago of the maiden and her suitors, buried side by side. The priests' presence and prayers for the lost souls make this a sacred site for the meeting between the dead and the living. The gloomy setting of the graveyard is evoked as the priests allude to a poem by the *Man'yōshū* poet Hitomaro:

We shall spend the night
by this *grave* and pray for

the lost soul who, rising from
the shadows of the grass around
the mound, showed herself but for
an instant, "narrow as is the space
between a stag's horns."

Hitomaro's text is

Even *narrow as is the space*
between the horns of a stag,
crossing the summer field,
do not forget for *an instant*
my love for you. (emphasis mine)[15]

This passage instantly reverses the text's orientation from sweet longing for love and life, positive and optimistic, to something gloomy and deadly, negative and pessimistic. The key phrase for the wordplay between the two texts is "the space between the horns of a stag" (*ojika no tsuno no tsuka no ma* or *kusa*). Two entirely different sets of logic govern the meaning of the two texts. In Hitomaro's poem, the words *tsuka no ma* mean literally the shortest possible duration with the imperative "do not forget me." The words insist on the urgent abundance of passionate love. Moreover, the expression the "stag's horns" (*tsuno*—an alliteration with *tsuka*) metonymically connotes male sexuality, and the summer field implies a mating season. We are reminded of the legend of the two suitors in their pursuit of the maiden.

In the play, the allusion to the pre-text is made negative and is destructive. It subverts the original meaning by underscoring sexual transgression in Buddhist terms. The double-edged word *tsuka,* "grave," becomes "undecidable" because it signifies both passionate sexuality (Hitomaro's text), and *tsuka no ma,* a moment in which the ghost—a lost soul—appears from the grave (the nō play), signifying human delusion and death. Because this key word, *tsuka,* links the two texts simultaneously here, the result is an eerie sort of fissure between the two meanings. The figure of sexuality in Hitomaro's poem is disfigured and debased in the play, and we sense that it has become something deadly, ghostly, and gloomy. Because our reading of Hitomaro's poem is lyrical and passionate, its effect in the nō text is all the more uncanny. In the play, the word *tsuka* becomes indeterminate, something that is incompatible with the connotation of *tsuka no ma* of the pre-text.

The wordplay here rests on the deceptive transfer from homophony to antinomy, a contradiction between two differing logics working simultaneously. The word *grave* remains true and literal to its function, the word placed in the right place. It is capable of being at once the wrong word (*catachresis*) and the right word. Here the grave is structured to read as it is meant to read, as a reference to its own mode. However, used as a pun, it signifies another transtextual referent lurking in the background and letting the reader experience through retroactive association another realm of logic. In this way, the "real" of the grave site is reversed and made literary. The effect of this type of transtextual word-play remains powerful in nō texts. Hitomaro's poem is inserted in this text as the sexuality code challenging at the same time another code—delusion and death—signified by the grave symbol.

Outcome

Act 1 of *Motomezuka* presents scenes in which the Buddhist priest hears from the "lost soul"—*prosopopoeia*—her nostalgia for life replete with youthfulness and sexuality. By using a profuse transtextual wordplay—allusions from classical canons—the text unfolds a world that is fragmented and heterogeneous. Since the language appropriated from the pre-texts can be taken either literally or figuratively, no unitary meaning can be ascribed to it, thereby creating undecidability. A play of significations displays two incompatible rhetorical manifestations. One is the operation of external or mundane occurrences and the description of natural objects, a metonymical structure based on the maiden's perception of the phenomenal world. The other is the mode of consciousness—reflections on the aristocratic past—which takes the form of the maiden's flight of imagination, the metaphorical structure. These opposing modes, in which mind takes priority over the natural world, progress step by step toward disfiguration; the figures of pleasure are erased by those of the hardship, causing the dislocation of the topos and finally bringing about the erasure of the figures of sexuality by the powerful figure of the grave.

The world constructed in this play is a world of socially marginal people whose ordinary everyday activities such as gathering herbs are dramatized. The language in the play is symptomatic of the emergence of the voice of the common people insisting on being heard. Their world is in conflict with their toil in the field and their yearning for the aristocratic culture of the past: Buddhist suffering, on one hand, and Shinto optimism, on the other. In this way, the social, political, and ideological meanings in the play are inscribed in the play of signifiers.

Human activities, presenting playful notions of seduction and sexuality, are skillfully woven into the wakana theme. As mentioned, the theme of sexuality is basically celebratory of life, at least not considered a "sin" in Shinto belief. In the first act, the examples are selected from the older texts and are organized so as to create images of sexuality, and in no way does the text repress these suggestions. However, at the end of the first act, the text's progression from the descriptive pastoral scenes to the various motifs of sexuality becomes clear as a preparation for the hideous tortures to which the maiden is subjected in the inferno.

In the second act, the theme of death, delusion, and confession completely displaces the sexuality reference. The most powerful warring signification, leading to disfiguration, is seen in the passage alluding to Hitomaro's poem. Here the text's internal differentiation is clearly seen.

In my critical reading, one of the answers to these opposing movements lies in the text's conflicting desire—to sanction and even celebrate sexuality and at the same time to satisfy the demand of the institutional ethical teaching of Buddhism as the cultural force of the period. Buddhism brands sexuality as one of the most serious ways in which humans are led astray, and it is considered a great obstacle on the path to salvation. The inferno scene describes the maiden being tortured and the agonies of fires—metonyms of her desire and delusion. The Buddhist goal is to send her on her way to enlightenment after she reexperiences her "transgression" by way of "confession" (*keka*). The medieval audience must have been well entertained by the plural meanings—the juxtaposition of nature, sexuality, and desire—evoked by the artistic play of signification through poetic allusions to the classic pre-texts. But at the same time they must have been terrified by the dramatization of the doctrinal lesson—the fearful consequences that sexuality can have.

As I observed at the beginning of this chapter, traditional nō scholars claim that because of "the way the legend was written, the cruel punishment in the inferno hardly seems justifiable." However, when we examine the signifying structure of the old legend of the "contention for a bride," then the sexual complicity between the two suitors and the maiden becomes a powerful theme. The "Otomezuka" (The Maiden's Grave) episode in *The Tale of Yamato*, which predated the nō play, picks up this unmistakable motif and richly thematizes it in several poems composed by the ladies-in-waiting at the imperial court. As we have seen, the nō play, too, does not fail to weave the theme of sexuality in the narrative, using wordplay and various tropes.

Why is this facet of the nō play not recognized or discussed by most critics? One Japanese critic points out the "extremely passionate nature of the encounter" between the maiden and her suitors, asserting that the "sexuality, which is extravagant and expendable," has no capacity for continuation and so must eventually be destroyed by the absolute rule of the communal body, whose main interest lies in ensuring its own continuity and survival. He reasons that the maiden's fall into the inferno is therefore the result of her defying this communal law.[16] Perhaps the kind of communal law to which he refers in his argument, which is basically anthropological, is inscribed in the cultural code of the period when *The Tales of Yamato* were conceived. I maintain that it seems as though two centuries later, the emphasis shifted, as we have seen in *Motomezuka*, toward the individual subject accepting his or her karmic consequence and away from the communal law that usually decided a person's fate. Consequently, this critic's argument cannot be extended to the nō play.

Finally, it has become increasingly clear that Unai's punishment is purely a medieval Buddhist construct. Nothing in the legend indicates what happens to the maiden after she is buried. The herb-gathering and inferno scenes in the play have been added to the legendary core; that is, the legend of *Motomezuka* was rewritten to suit the cultural predilections and religious beliefs of the period.

ACKNOWLEDGMENTS

My deep appreciation goes to Alton Heinz and David Gooding for their helpful suggestions. This article was written with a grant from the National Endowment for the Humanities, for which I am very grateful.

NOTES

1. Traditional Japanese scholarship identifies in *Motomezuka* twelve poetic allusions, fourteen pivot words, six related words, two verses in Chinese, and one preface appropriated from the Japanese classic tradition, all in the short space of two or three pages. The narrative structure of the nō text is unique. In creating dialogues and narrative thread—a plot—for its dramatic purpose, it uses for the most part repetitions of 5–7–5 or 7–7 syllable lines, which are normally reserved for poems, producing a lengthy rhythmic prose-style progression. This "poem narrative" structure results in a crisp, spare style replete with ellipses, imageries, and allusions. The dialogues are spoken by both the characters and the chorus, although the chorus often speaks for the main character.

2. The theory of intertextuality, generally credited to Mikhail Bakhtin, Roland Barthes, and Julia Kristeva, is defined as "a relation between two or more TEXTS which has an effect upon the way in which the *intertext* (that is, the text within which other texts reside or echo their PRESENCE) is read." The term "*transtextuality* is reserved for more overt relations between specific texts, or between two particular texts." See Jeremy Hawthorn, *A Glossary of Contemporary Literary Theory* (London: Arnold, 1992), p. 126. I use *transtextuality* in this essay.

3. *Motomezuka*, in Omote Akira and Yokomichi Mario, eds., *Yōkyokushū I*, in *Nihon koten bungaku taikei* (hereafter abbreviated *NKBT*), vol. 40 (Tokyo: Iwanami shoten, 1960), pp. 66–74. I used the annotations from this work throughout this chapter.

4. Torii Akio, *Chinkon no chūsei* (Tokyo: Pelikansha, 1989), pp. 21–55.

5. Christopher Norris, *Paul de Man: Deconstruction and the Critique of Aesthetic Ideology* (New York: Routledge, 1988), p. 49. This is one of Paul de Man's theoretical arguments.

6. Paul de Man, *The Rhetoric of Romanticism* (New York: Columbia University Press, 1984), p. 119.

7. In this text, I cannot detect the *honji-suijaku* theory, which preaches incarnations of buddhas and bodhisattvas as Shinto gods and asserts that the two religions are generally integrated. I find this opposing tendency prevalent in many nō plays, however.

8. An adaptation of an anonymous poem, "Spring," in the *Kokinshū*, poem 19: "Deep in the mountain,/ snow still remains/ on the pine branches,/ but in the capital,/ this must be the season/ for gathering young fresh herbs in the meadow" (*NKBT*, vol. 40, p. 67, n. 12). All the translations are my own.

9. See *NKBT*, p. 67, n. 14, 15 and 16, and p. 68, n. 1.

10. *Na* in *nanakusa*, the seven-herb soup, is alliterative with the negative *nai* following spring—hence "unlike spring"—and is a preface for *iku*, "many," in the following Ikuta. See *NKBT*, vol. 40, p. 68, n. 7.

11. This type of encounter between a Buddhist priest and a beautiful woman must have been a rather popular theme in this period, as such encounters are found frequently in medieval literature. See my paper on this topic, "Is the Courtesan of Eguchi a Buddhist Metaphorical Woman? A Feminist Reading of a Nō Play in the Japanese Medieval Theater," *Women's Studies, an Interdisciplinary Journal* 21 (1992): 431–56.

12. This type of poetic device comes under the heading "Names of things," which was a traditional poetic game. Considerable skill was required of the players.

13. "Rapeseed"—literally the "flower stalks of Sano." See poem 3406 in the *Man'yōshū*, vol. 3, *NKBT*, vol. 6, p. 421. The Boat Bridge poem is also from the *Man'yōshū*, poem 3420, p. 424. *Sakuragae*, a verb form using the eastern dialect ending *gae* (a rhetorical question) in the last line, expresses the direct emotional tone of the common people of this period. I translated it by using a homonym *saku* (a root form), meaning "to shun," on the fourth line and *saki*, meaning "to tear apart," on the fifth line.

14. *Chōbō* section, *NKBT*, vol. 73, p. 210. It is based on a composition in Chinese (poem 626) by Minamoto no Shitagō: "Looking at the distant trees of Chang-an city, they look like millions of the blue stems of the Shepherd's Purse." There also are several colors (purple, green, and white: the white-root herbs in the eighteenth line and the snow in the nineteenth line) which bring a kind of exotic and visual variation on a literary level to the theme of the wakana.

15. This poem is no. 1373 in *Love*, vol. 5 of the *Shinkokinshū*, *NKBT*, vol. 28, p. 285.

16. Torii, *Chinkon no chūsei*, 50.

3

Subversive Transformations: Atsumori and Tadanori at Suma

◉

KAREN W. BRAZELL

Literature, theater, and the arts are constantly rewriting history, redrawing cultural geography, redefining heros, and transforming and subverting earlier texts to create new systems of meaning and value. These newly espoused values may bolster or undermine the legitimacy and power of the ruling class. This process of transformation was particularly evident during the time of Ashikaga Yoshimitsu (1358–1408), who became shogun when he was only ten years old and remained in control of the government until his death. To further his dreams of a military monarchy, he clothed himself in aristocratic as well as bureaucratic and military precedent.[1] This meant donning court ranks and offices; in 1394 he accepted the highest court position, that of *dajōdaijin* or chancellor, and shortly thereafter retired to rule from behind the scenes as cloistered emperors had done before him.

Assuming the mantle of aristocratic legitimacy also meant patronizing the arts, and Yoshimitsu did this with great success. In addition to supporting *waka*, the traditional poetry of the court, he also promoted the more contemporary arts of *renga* (linked verse) and nō, then known as *sarugaku*. Among the many artists he supported was the actor and playwright Zeami (1363–1433), whose plays helped create and express the emerging values of the time. Thanks largely to Zeami, nō became a part of high culture, a new "aristocratic" art, integrating earlier texts and techniques with contemporary subject matter and ideas. His plays—especially those featuring the ghosts of warriors—also contributed directly to the legitimization of the ruling class, by helping create and propagate the figure of the military aristocrat, the warrior as both cultural and military hero, excelling in aesthetic creativity and sensibility (*bun*) as well as military skills and virtues (*bu*).

In this chapter I explore a small segment of this process, how Zeami appropriated the poetic toponym (*utamakura*) Suma, making it the setting for his versions of the deaths of Atsumori and Tadanori and thereby conferring on these warriors the status of cultural heroes. Or, to put it the other way around, how Zeami transformed the Suma of the classical waka tradition by adding warriors to its population of lovers and exiled aristocrats. Later visitors to Suma, such as the poet Bashō (1644–1694), encountered the ghosts of warriors along with those of Yukihira and the shining Prince Genji.[2] To explain this process, I briefly trace the development of the Suma toponym in the poetic tradition from the *Manyōshū* (compiled ca. 750) to the mid-fourteenth century and then examine its appropriation in the *kusemai* called *Saikoku kudari* (Traveling to Western Provinces) and in Zeami's nō plays *Atsumori* and *Tadanori*.[3]

By the time of the *Manyōshū*, the geographical Suma, a spot on the Inland Sea in present-day Kobe, was already associated in poetic practice with a set of images and ideas centering on the seafolk (*ama*) of the area, their work-worn garments (*kinu* or *koromo*), and their livelihood—boiling brine to obtain salt (*shioyaki*). These images became metaphors for love, often through the use of wordplay. In the two following examples, the threads in the rough weave of the clothes the seafolk wear are as widely spaced (*matō*) as the meetings of lovers, and both the clothes and lovers may be *nare* (well worn or intimate):

> Suma seafolks   boil brine in garments   of wisteria fiber weave
> as sparse as our meetings   and still uncomfortable

> Manyōshū, *book 3, poem 413, by Ōami no Hitonushi*

> *Suma no ama no / shioyaki kinu no / fujigoromo / matō ni shi areba / imada kinarezu*

> Were I as intimate with you   as the Suma seafolk are
> with the well-worn garments   they don for boiling brine,
> would I forget to think of you   even for a single day?

> Manyōshū, *book 6, poem 947, by Yamanobe no Akahito*

*Suma no ama no/shioyaki kinu no/narenaba ka/hitohi mo kimi o/
wasurete omowamu*

These poems combine the local color of a distant place with courtly love as
practiced in the capital. An anonymous poem in the first imperial anthology, the
Kokinshū (compiled ca. 905), expanded the images associated with Suma by
using smoke to evoke unfaithful love:[4]

The smoke from salt fires   of Suma seafolk   assailed by the winds
has drifted off   in an unexpected direction

Kokinshū, book 14 (Love), poem 708

Suma no ama no/shioyaku keburi/kaze o itami/omowanu kata ni/tanabikinikeri

A poem attributed to Ki no Tsurayuki (ca. 866–945) hides Suma in the word
korizuma, "not learning from experience" or "unchastened."[5] As often occurs in
the waka tradition, a headnote describes the poetic persona:

*When I was secretly calling on the daughter of a certain man, he heard us
and scolded me fiercely. Returning home, I sent her this:*

The wind assailed it so   the yielding smoke   rose up and left,
yet still unchastened   is my love for Suma Bay.

Gosenshū, book 12 (Love), poem 865

kaze o itami/kuyuru keburi no/tachiide mo/nao korizuma no/ura zo koishiki

The Suma landscape is invaded by the poet Ariwara no Yukihira (ca. 816–893)
who, according to the headnote of the following poem, "lived in enforced retirement at Suma in Tsu Province during the reign of the Emperor Tamura" (aka
Montoku, r. 850–858).

Should perchance   someone ask after me,
reply that I grieve   here at Suma Bay   as brine drips from seaweed

Kokinshū, book 12 (Miscellaneous), poem 962

wakurawa ni / tou hito araba / suma no ura ni / moshio taretsutsu / wabu to kotae yo

A second Yukihira poem, which earned a place in an imperial anthology only much later, describes another aspect of Suma:

The traveler's   sleeves are   quickly cooled;
blowing through the barrier,   a seabreeze from Suma

Shokukokinshū, book 10, poem 868

Tabibito wa / sode suzushiku / narinikeri / seki fuku koyuru / Suma no urakaze

Suma, once only a remote spot whose romanticized features were used as metaphors for courtly love, now had become a place of exile for courtiers forced to live outside the capital.

By the early eleventh century, however, Suma was still not a particularly popular toponym in poetic practice. *Nōin utamakura*, a mid-eleventh-century primer for poets, does not include Suma among the thirty-five places it lists in Settsu Province, and the second and third imperial anthologies (*Gosenshū*, 951, and *Shūishū*, 1006) together contain only four poems about Suma, although they include twenty-six and twenty-one poems referring to neighboring Naniwa and Sumiyoshi, respectively.[6]

Without the influence of *The Tale of Genji*, the Suma toponym may have languished; instead, however, new life was breathed into it by this narrative. The hero of the tale, the shining Genji, retreats to Suma before he can be exiled to some less attractive place, and his departure and stay there are described in a pivotal chapter of the work entitled simply "Suma." The text compares Genji with several well-known exiles, including Ariwara no Yukihira.[7] In a farewell poem written just before his departure, Genji himself ruefully offers a less elegant comparison:

When will I again   see the blossoms   of the spring capital,
forgotten by the times   I'll live as a mountain rustic

(NKBT, vol. 15, p. 27; Seidensticker, Tale of Genji, p. 228)

Itsu ka mata / haru no miyako no / hana o min / toki ushinaeru / yamagatsu ni shite

The *yamagatsu* label sticks; the text identifies Genji at Suma with the mountain rustic on two other occasions. This usage clearly expands the *Nōin utamakura* definition of *yamagatsu* as someone who is unknown (*hito ni shirarenu*), does not know deep thoughts (*mono omoi o shiranu*), is mean in appearance (*ayashiki hito*), and lives in a mountain village (*yamazato ni sumu*).[8]

The fact that "Suma" contains forty-eight poems, more than any other chapter,[9] reinforces Suma as a poetic toponym, a place in poetry, and a place for poetry. The thirty-one poems written after Genji's arrival at the seacoast include love poems he exchanged with women left behind. These poems often picture the women and / or Genji as seafolk (*ama*). In the following example, the recipient, Fujitsubo, is an ama of another sort as well, as she had become a nun (also pronounced *ama*).

How is it with the   Matsushima ama   in her thatched hut?
For the man of Suma Bay   the days are full of dripping brine.

(NKBT, vol. 15, p. 31; Seidensticker, Tale of Genji, p. 231)

Matsushima no / ama no tomaya mo / ika narame / Suma no urabito / moshio taruru koro

Murasaki, Genji's cherished consort, sends this poem:

Man of the shore   dipping brine,   compare your sleeves
with the night robes   of one across the waves

(NKBT, vol. 15, p. 34; Seidensticker, Tale of Genji, p. 233)

urabito no / shio kumu sode ni / kurabe mi yo / nami ji hedatsuru / yoru no koromo o

When the exiles at Suma composed poems for themselves or one another, they used somewhat different imagery to express their lonely isolation. This poem, which Genji wrote to console himself, is typical:

Flocks of plovers   choral voices calling   beneath dawn's moon
comfort one who lies alone   awake upon his bed

(NKBT, vol. 15, p. 46; Seidensticker, Tale of Genji, p. 241)

tomo chidori / morokoe ni naku / akatsuki wa / hitori nezame no / toko mo tanomoshi

As *The Tale of Genji* gradually became an acceptable, and then a necessary, source of allusions for poets, images from these and other poems were added to the lexicon of the Suma toponym. The following poem by Minamoto no Kanemasa (1074–1128), included in the fifth imperial anthology, the *Kinyōshū* (1127), and in the *Hyakunin isshu* (ca. 1235) of Fujiwara no Teika (1162–1241), evokes the sadness of travel by drawing on Genji's poem:

By the calling voices   of plovers crossing   to Awaji Isle
how many nights   is he kept awake   the border guard at Suma.

Kinyōshū, book 4 (Winter), poem 270

Awaji jima / kayou chidori no / nakugoe ni / iku yo nezamenu / suma no sekimori

Both Teika and his father Fujiwara no Shunzei (1114–1204) admired *The Tale of Genji* and claimed that knowledge of this work was essential to composing waka.[10] Their advice was taken seriously, and *Genji* joined the *Kokinshū* and the *Tales of Ise* as the focus of medieval literary scholarship and practice.

Nijō Yoshimoto (1320–1388), a high-ranking courtier, a leading poet, an intimate of Yoshimitsu, and a supporter of the young Zeami, also encouraged renga poets to turn to *Genji*. "Conventional associations (*yoriai*) from *Genji* are the best," he claimed, and he participated in the compilation of two *Genji* handbooks written for renga adherents.[11] The *Hikaru Genji yoriai no koto* includes summaries of each chapter of the tale, and both it and the similarly titled *Hikaru Genji ichibu renga yoriai* (1365) contain lists of *Genji* words, phrases, and occasionally entire poems, to be used in composing renga. The longest list consists of seventy-seven words and phrases from the Suma chapter.[12] The images used in waka usually came from *Genji* poems; however, the renga *yoriai* are drawn largely from prose passages such as the following (the words in boldface are *yoriai*):

One night Genji awoke, and **rising from his pillow** listened to the **winds from all directions**. It seemed that the **waves were right here**. Unawares he wept until his **pillow was almost afloat**.

(NKBT, vol. 15, p. 38; Seidensticker, Tale of Genji, pp. 235—36)

The smoke near at hand would be, he supposed, that of seafolk boiling brine. In fact, in the **hills to the rear**, the **stuff called brushwood** was smoldering.

(NKBT, vol. 15, p. 44; Seidensticker, Tale of Genji, p. 240).

Words commonly used in the waka tradition, such as smoke, seafolk, and boiling brine, are not included in the renga lists, possibly because they were already known to all renga poets. Many of the selected phrases had already been used by earlier writers, so the contribution of these lists was to organize the references and authorize their use in renga.

In the late thirteenth century, when renga was still in its infancy, a song genre called sōga (or sōka) was created in Kamakura. Sōga can be viewed as an early attempt at appropriating materials from classical culture to express medieval concerns and to help legitimize the power of the military rulers by proving that they too had "culture." The 173 extant songs in this genre are contained in anthologies compiled between 1270 and 1322, mostly through the efforts of a man known by the priestly name Myōkū (born about 1245). References to sōga in the Tsurezuregusa (Essays in Idleness, ca. 1330) of Yoshida Kenkō and in Sarugaku dangi (Zeami's reflections on sarugaku, 1430) attest to the genre's continuing popularity.[13] The songs, which often take the form of lists, draw extensively on earlier works in both Japanese and Chinese. One of the works most often alluded to is The Tale of Genji, and "Suma" is among the most popular chapters: seventy-nine of the 173 sōga contain 191 allusions to Genji (only the Kokinshū has as many references), and fourteen of these seventy-nine allusions are to the "Suma" chapter.[14] For example, a poem entitled Genji shimyō ryōeiga (The Double Glory of Genji's Murasaki and Akashi), quotes phrases from Murasaki's letter to Genji at Suma, and a poetic catalog, Matsutake (Pines and Bamboo), mentions the bamboo fence and pine pillars of Genji's Suma dwelling.

Another sōga, Nadokoro koi (Love at Famous Places), contains this variation on Yukihira's poem:

If perchance,   someone should inquire,
at Suma Bay   excessive sad sobs   do not wet my sleeves
    seafolk sleeping afloat   don't have wet sleeves

wakurawa ni / tou hito araba / suma no ura no / amari ukine ni / sode wa nureji

In *Shukuya no chū* (Constant Loyalty), *Genji* characters are appropriated as models of medieval virtues:

> Koremitsu and Yoshikiyo served the shining Genji . . .
> on the Suma and Akashi seashores,
> troubled sleep in travellers' beds,
> following the rocky shore to that coast,
> passing years in seafolks' dwellings—
> a makeshift life of suffering surrounded by seaweed,
> yet not a trace of rebellion in their hearts:
> superior, sensitive exemplars from among retainers of old.[15]

Thus by the mid-fourteenth century, Suma as poetic toponym was accepted in waka, renga, and sōga practice. Its landscape was peopled with lowly seafolk engaged in humble tasks, imaginary border guards awakened by crying plovers, travelers passing by the wind-swept barrier, and exiled aristocrats living in lonely isolation. Several nō plays are set in this "classical" Suma: *Matsukaze* features two young women (ama) who claim to love Yukihira, and *Suma Genji* features the shining Genji, presenting him first as a mountain rustic (yamagatsu) and then as his young, former self revealed as a divine figure come to save humankind.[16]

Although Suma, the poetic toponym, was still populated with figures from the Heian period, many other events had occurred at the geographical place, especially during the civil war of the twelfth century when the western provinces along the Inland Sea where Suma is located were the stronghold of the Taira clan. Suma lies between Fukuhara, where Taira Kiyomori moved the capital briefly in 1180, and Ichinotani, where the Taira clan lost a major battle to the Minamoto in 1184. These events are not reflected in early medieval poetry, and although the sōga genre does contain many travel songs, none depicts journeys to the western provinces. This is hardly surprising, as sōga were created by and for the Kamakura military elite, whose lands and power lay to the east.

Neither do sōga draw on material from *Heike monogatari* (The Tale of the Heike), the major narrative about the Taira–Minamoto battles. On the other hand, *The Tale of the Heike* ignores Suma as a poetic toponym. The Kakuichi-bon, the most poetic of the numerous versions of the tale, mentions Suma only five times.[17] In the autumn of 1180, when the capital had been transferred to Fukuhara and courtiers wanted to go moon viewing, some of them went "along the coast from Suma to Akashi to seek out traces of Genji of old." In Kenreimon'in's recapitulation of the history of the Taira family in terms of the six realms, in "The Initiates' Chapter," she describes their sufferings "along the coast from Suma to Akashi, places once known to me only by name." The three other references are to Suma as a spot where the troops lodged or passed through during the battle of Ichinotani.

The Suma toponym was eventually transformed by the insertion of Heike warriors into the poetic landscape. The first known piece to attempt this is the kusemai entitled *Saikoku kudari* (Traveling to Western Provinces). Zeami's treatise *Go-on* preserves the text of this kusemai and indicates that the words are by Tamarin and the music by Kannami. Material provided in *Sarugaku dangi* dates the piece rather precisely to between 1376 and 1381.[18] Tamarin, also known as Rin'a, was probably a waka and renga poet, a student—along with Nijō Yoshimoto—of the renga poet Gusai (also read as Kyūsei; d. ca. 1376) and an acquaintance of Kannami. Takemoto Mikio suggests that for a poet to incorporate *Heike* material into his writing was a radical innovation:[19] such usage was not permitted in waka or renga, and it did not occur in sōga.

Saikoku kudari describes the Taira clan's exodus from the capital in 1183. Taking the event from the *Heike monogatari*, the kusemai transforms it by drawing heavily on poetic traditions. After the Taira reached Fukuhara, they put out to sea headed for Dazaifu in Kyushu.[20] Tamarin has them pass by Suma—the Suma of the poetic tradition, described with phrases drawn from *Genji monogatari* (in boldface):

> When we arrived at **the Suma seacoast**
> **winds from all directions** fiercely
> sounded, **blowing through the barrier,**
> and evening **smoke** from **hilltops behind,**
> from smoldering **stuff called brushwood,**
> an unfamiliar, poignant sight.

Then, after alluding to the Gosechi dancer's visit to Genji at Suma and mentioning Akashi, the *Saikoku kudari* continues with an idea that reappears in the nō play *Tadanori*:

> We changed from ships to carriages,
> intending to linger a while, and yet
> the seacoast from Suma to Akashi
> was the road Genji had traversed;

> how would it be for Heike forces, we worried
> and soon pushed off from these shores.

The shining Genji, the fictional aristocrat, is identified with the Genji, the Minamoto warrior clan. This rightly worries the Heike (the Taira clan), for according to the kusemai, their days of glory do come to an end soon after they pass Suma.[21]

The pathos of the fall of the Taira, lamented in general terms in *Saikoku kudari*, is elaborated further in Zeami's nō play *Atsumori*, which also presents the life and death of an individual warrior.[22] Like the earlier kusemai, the nō play places the Taira in the poetic landscape of Suma. This is immediately suggested in the *waki*'s (supporting actor's) travel song (*michiyuki*). He goes not merely to the geographical Suma but also to the Suma where "waves roll in right here" (*nami wa kokomoto ni*). This phrase is a renga yoriai from the "Suma" chapter of *Genji*.[23] The *kuse* scene (major narrative scene) in act 2 uses numerous phrases from the poetic tradition to describe the Taira at Suma:

> That <u>famous autumn</u>, leaves lured by **winds from all directions**, scattered here and there in leaf-like boats bobbing on the waves, we sleep, not even in our dreams returning home, caged birds longing for cloudy realms, **ranks of homing geese** broken, scattered, uncertain skies, aimless travel gowns tied and layered sunsets, moonrises, months, a year journeys by, returns to spring here at Ichinotani secluded <u>for a while</u> <u>here on the Suma seacoast</u> we live. **From the hilltops behind** winds roar down to coastal fields keenly cold our **boats** draw up; no day or night without the cries of **plovers**, our <u>sleeves too dampened</u> by the waves that drench our <u>rocky</u> **pillows**; in **seaside shacks** we huddle together befriended only by Suma folk, bent like wind-bent pines on the strands of <u>evening smoke</u> arising from fires—**brushwood, it's called**, this stuff piled up to sleep upon. Our worries too pile up in **rustic** Suma, in **a place like this** we live out our lives becoming simple Suma folk—such is the fate of our clan, how <u>miserable</u>!

Nine of the phrases in boldface have been identified as identical or similar to Yoshimoto's lists of yoriai from *Genji*. "Smoke" and "a place like this" are not in these lists, but they do appear in the "Suma" chapter of *Genji*.[24] What is not generally recognized, however, is that all the underlined words appear in *Saikoku kudari*, whose strategy of appropriating the Suma toponym for the warrior class is expanded in *Atsumori* and *Tadanori*.[25]

The Heike did not in fact end their days at Suma; their final defeat was at Dannoura some miles farther down the coast and some months later. Atsumori, however, did die near Suma Bay at the battle of Ichinotani, and the nō play identifies Atsumori with the Suma exile Yukihira. The following lines from the end of the *shite*'s (main actor's) entrance scene include an expanded version of one of Yukihira's poems:

> If anyone should ask,
> my reply would speak of lonely grief
> here on Suma's seacoast
> where brine drips from seaweed.
> Should anyone learn who I am,
> then I too would have a friend.

The enactment of this passage provides the basic structure of the play; that is, the action of the poem becomes the action of the play.[26] The speaker (a grass cutter who is the embodiment of Atsumori's ghost) is living at Suma Bay; someone (the waki portraying Atsumori's slayer Kumagai) comes to ask after him, and Atsumori's ghost (in its "true" form in act 2) replies, describing how the Heike passed desolate days on the Suma seacoast. Moreover, once the visitor (his former enemy) learns Atsumori's identity, he becomes a "friend in Buddha's law" (*nori no tomo*), whose prayers promise their mutual salvation. By ascribing Yukihira's poem to Atsumori and enacting it on stage, the play not only serves as a requiem for the souls of the warriors, but it also elevates the social status of the warrior class by identifying them with the noble exiles of the Suma toponym.

One other characteristic of Atsumori, common to the *Heike monogatari* and the nō, is his love for the flute. His return to camp to retrieve his precious flute caused him to miss the fleeing ships and led directly to his death. The instrument is also associated with the "Suma" chapter of *Genji* because Tō no Chūjō presented Genji with a fine flute there.[27] In act 1, the waki hears and admires the flute playing of the grass cutter, just as Kumagai had heard and admired Atsumori's flute playing from the opposing camp the night before their deadly encounter. In the nō, that evening is presented through an elegant, medium-tempo dance (*chūnomai*), an unusual choice for warrior plays in general but appropriate to this play's depiction of Atsumori as a cultured man. It is especially suitable because the dance is performed to strains of flute music. Immediately after this graceful dance, the play turns to an enactment of the brave Atsumori's death in battle.

Tadanori focuses even more sharply on the double role of the warrior in the late fourteenth century. This play, which Zeami himself considered an excellent (*jōka*) work, both produces and expresses the medieval ideal of the warrior—

the man who combines the literary and martial arts and who has the sensitive soul of the poet and the brave heart of the warrior. The depiction of Tadanori as a cultured warrior did not begin with the nō, however.[28] There are two *Heike* sections used in the play: Tadanori's return from the mass retreat of the Heike from Kyoto to present some poems to Shunzei, and his death at the hands of the Genji warrior Rokuyata. Both changed substantially in the course of the complex development that led to the Kakuichi-bon version of *Heike monogatari*.[29] The section depicting Tadanori's death probably began as a tale about the heroic exploits of Rokuyata, but gradually more attention was given to the brave, yet poetic, Tadanori. The Kakuichi-bon and other late texts include the "traveling 'til dark" poem (discussed later), which they attribute to Tadanori, and end the section with the declaration: "How sad! He was a great general equally proficient in military pursuits and in the way of poetry" (*NKBT*, vol. 33, p. 217; McCullough, *Tale of the Heike*, p. 314).

The influence of *Saikoku kudari* is evident in *Tadanori*. For example, the travel song of the waki, the poet Shunzei's retainer who has taken religious vows, includes the following phrases, which also appear in the kusemai:

> We make our way toward the Southern Palace, past Yamazaki, separated from the Capital by hills, Sekido in name only remains . . . the river Akuta, bamboo grass at Ina . . . the moon shining brightly in Koya Pond . . . through leaves of reeds.

In act 2, Tadanori turns back to go to Shunzei's house from "Rangiku Kitsune River." Commentators generally point out that although there is a Kitsune River, it is not the place-name used in any of the numerous versions of the *Heike*, and they refer to a couplet by Po Chü-i: "Owls hoot from the branches of pines and laurels; foxes (*kitsune*) hide among orchids and chrysanthemums (*rangiku*)."[30] What they overlook, however, is that Po's couplet occurs in *Saikoku kudari* to describe the deserted former Taira capital of Fukuhara.[31] In *Tadanori* the phrase introduces a section that borrows both its basic idea and its images from the kusemai passage partially quoted earlier (the words in boldface repeat or echo kusemai phrases):

> Once more **with bow and arrow** adrift **on waves in Western Seas; for a while** we took refuge at **Suma Bay**, but the **dwelling place** of Genji was not good for the **Heike**, though we knew it not, alas!

In describing Suma, *Tadanori* uses a string of words from traditional poetic diction, only some of which appear in *Saikoku kudari*: *uki* (float/sad), *korizuma* (unchastened/cutting, gathering/Suma), *shioki* (driftwood), *nare koromo* (well-worn gown), *ura* (bay/lining), and *ama* (seafolk). The nō text then declares, "Well now, this place called Suma Bay has earned a reputation for being lonesome," and commences to list a number of items that prove it so. The first is Yukihira's "Should anyone inquire" poem, and then as though to back this up with direct observations, the text continues: "Indeed, the fishing seafolk in their small boats, smoke from fires boiling brine, and wind through the pines, can any one of these be considered other than sad?" Needless to say, these "real" images also come from the poetic tradition.

The mountain rustic (*yamagatsu*) embodiment of the ghost in act 1 evokes the shining Genji as well as another figure. When the shite explains that he breaks off blossoms and adds them to his load of firewood, the listener trained in the poetic tradition might recall the metaphor presented in the preface to the *Kokinshū* describing the poetry of one of the six sages of poetry (*kasen*): "Otomo no Kuronushi's form (*sama*) is poor. It might be compared to a mountain man with firewood on his back resting in the shade of blossoms."[32] The effect of the allusion is to emphasize Tadanori as a poet.

In addition to being a mountain rustic, the shite is also one of the seafolk (*ama*); hence his task is twofold, drawing water and carrying firewood. The waki questions this dual identity:

WAKI: If you are one of those seafolk, you ought to live on the shore;
         if you work in the mountains, you should be called a man of
         the mountains.
SHITE: Would you have me draw salt water and not boil it down?

This double responsibility foreshadows the dual functions of the ideal warrior: making war and creating culture. Likewise, the blossoms stuck into the firewood the shite carries prefigure the poem paper (*tanzaku*) attached to an arrow, the hand prop used in act 2.

Although the nō depicts Tadanori's valiant death in act 2, it is primarily a play about poets and poetry. The poetic heart (*hana no kokoro*) is embodied in the blossoming tree, which stands at the center of the work. This image also appears in the "Suma" chapter of *Genji*:

At Suma the year changed, and as the long days passed slowly, the young cherry tree planted [the year before] began to bloom in the fine, balmy weather arousing memories in Genji and causing him to weep.

(*NKBT, vol. 15, p. 48; Seidensticker, Tale of Genji, p. 243*).

In *Tadanori*, after a single cherry tree in the shelter of Suma's hills is identified as the marker of Tadanori's remains, its nature is elaborated:

> Indeed Suma Bay is quite **unlike other places** for what most blossoms fear are mountain **storms** rushing down from the peaks with a loathsome roar; but for the **young cherry tree** of **Suma**, separated only **slightly from the sea**, the mountain cherry blossoms too are scattered by passing sea breezes (the words in boldface are from *Genji*).

The *Tadanori* cherry is not only *Genji*'s young cherry tree; it is also a mountain cherry, and for a listener with any knowledge of Tadanori's poetry, the mountain cherry suggests his most famous poem, the one contained in the anthology the *Senzaishū* without Tadanori's name:

> Waves ripple in at   Shiga, the old capital   lies in ruins
> unchanged from the past, Mount Nagara's   mountain cherries bloom
>
> *sasanami ya / shiga no miyako wa / arenishi o / mukashi nagara no / yamazakura kana*

Although this poem is never directly referred to in *Tadanori*, its presence is strongly felt. The fact that the poem was anonymously included in an imperial anthology so haunted Tadanori's ghost that (in the nō play) it returns to earth and requests that his name be attached to his poem. In addition, the subject of this poem, the enduring nature of the cherries, is a theme of the play. The nō audience might also be aware that this poem is alluded to in *Shiga*, a play about the *Kokinshū* poet Ōtomo no Kuronushi, and is quoted in two other plays about Tadanori, *Shunzei Tadanori* and *Shiga Tadanori*.[33]

Tadanori's tree is most closely associated with another poem:

> Traveling 'til dark,   should the shelter of a tree   become my lodging, would its
> blossoms be   my host tonight.
>
> *Yukikurete / ko no shita kage o / yado to seba / hana ya koyoi no / aruji naramashi*

The poem, which appears in the *Heike monogatari*, is immediately recognized, by the waki, as Tadanori's. The enactment of this poem structures the play: someone, a courtier turned priest, travels until dark and spends the night under a tree whose blossoms (the shite, Tadanori) serve as his host, that is, entertain him with the story of Tadanori's life. In the course of the play, Tadanori is equated with the blossoming tree; the poet is identified with his poem.

The poem is repeated several times in the play, each repetition making a new identification. The first recitation identifies the blossoms as the waki's host; the waki then repeats the poem, recognizing Tadanori as the poet. Near the end of the play, immediately after Tadanori's death, the second repetition informs Rokuyata that the man he has killed is Tadanori. The last lines of the play contain a variation of the poem:

> You entered into the shelter of these blossoms, and I detained you til dark could fall that I might tell this tale.
> Now, there is no doubt—gale winds from all directions—blossoms to the roots return, please pray for my remains. When for travel lodgings you take the shelter of a tree, blossoms will be the host.

One night's temporary lodging has become a promise of recurrent shelter, with the speaker as the host, but the speaker is no longer a traveler anticipating a lonely night in the open; rather, he is the blossoming tree itself, the medieval warrior providing shelter and entertainment, protection and culture to a traveling priest from the capital. The cherry tree planted by the shining Genji has become the symbol of the warrior.

By the late fourteenth century, the Heian social and cultural orders had been gradually subverted by the rise to power and prominence of the warrior class, and artists under the patronage of these new rulers deftly appropriated classical materials and techniques, including the poetic toponym Suma, and used them to transform the image of the warriors themselves. The warriors of the Kamakura period established the bakufu to control much of the territory of Japan, but it was left to the Ashikaga, who returned to the aristocratic center (Kyoto), to incorporate the aristocratic cultural legacy into the warrior-centered medieval way. Even as the historical warriors invaded Kyoto and put on the mantle of aristocratic rule, so too did literary warriors, such as the Atsumori and Tadanori of nō, infiltrate the poetic toponym of Suma, slipping into the garments of its prior inhabitants and clothing themselves in the aura of the classical landscape.

Zeami and the other artists of the period may have helped legitimize warrior rule, but they also looked after their own interests. At the same time that *Atsumori* and *Tadanori* express the new warrior ideal, they also furnish the new age with its music and poetry. The plays overtly emphasize the value of music, dance, poetry, and telling tales; they advocate the arts of the theater. Even as the lowly grass cutter or mountain rustic proves to the higher-class traveler that humble folk can play the flute and sing, that they are sensitive to the beauty of the blossoms (*hana*), so the performers (also members of the lower class) present their own worth to their audiences. *Tadanori* proposes blossoms as a symbol for the warrior class, but Zeami also uses the word in another sense. *Hana* is his technical term for successful theatrical effects and artistic skill. Thus at the end of *Tadanori* while the "cherry blossoms" are promising to shelter and entertain the traveler, the performers are guaranteeing that each time a person comes to the theater, the blossoming of the actors' art will provide entertainment. Zeami, cognizant of past poetic traditions, attuned to the social and political realities of his time, and ardently advocating his chosen way, manages to combine these concerns in the handsome and powerful stage figures of Atsumori and Tadanori.

NOTES

1. Yoshimitsu's aspirations appear to have included making his son the emperor. See Imatani Akira and Yamamura Kōzo, "Not for Lack of Will or Wile: Yoshimitsu's Failure to Supplant the Imperial Lineage," *Journal of Japanese Studies* 18 (1992): 45–78.

2. See Haruo Shirane's chapter in this volume, "Matsuo Bashō's *Oku no hosomichi* and the Anxiety of Influence."

3. *Kusemai* is a medieval song and dance form that was incorporated into nō by Zeami's father, Kannami (or Kan'ami, 1333–1384). The nō plays *Atsumori* and *Tadanori* have been translated numerous times. See Chifumi Shimazaki, *Battle Noh*, vol. 2 of *The Noh* (Tokyo: Hinoki shoten, 1987); Kenneth Yasuda, *Masterworks of the Nō Theater* (Bloomington: Indiana University Press, 1989); and Royall Tyler, *Japanese Nō Dramas* (Harmondsworth: Penguin Books, 1992). The Japanese texts are in Yokomichi Mario and Omote Akira, *Yōkyokushū*, vol. 1, in *Nihon koten bungaku taikei* (hereafter *NKBT*), vol. 40 (Tokyo: Iwanami shoten, 1960), pp. 233–48.

4. Another Suma love poem, *Kokinshū* poem 758, reworks the images already mentioned. I am not arguing that the poems quoted here were necessarily the first to associate a particular image with Suma; rather, they are simply well-known, early examples of such usage.

5. Another possible meaning, "to cut (*kori*) and gather" (*tsumu*), is activated in other poems relating to Suma.

6. Two variants of *Nōin utamakura* are published in Sasaki Nobutsuna, ed., *Nihon kagaku taikei*, vol. 1 (Tokyo: Kasama shobō, 1963), pp. 69–107. Katagiri Yōichi's *Heian waka utamakura chimei sakuin* (Kyoto: Daigakudō shoten, 1972) lists 224 poems using Suma, thirty-one of them appearing in the first eight imperial anthologies. See also Jacqueline Piegot, *Michiyuki-bun: Poétique de l'intinéraire dans la littérature du Japon ancien* (Paris: Éditions G. P. Maisonneuve et Larose, 1982), pp. 78–81.

7. References to Yukihira's poems appear in Edward G. Seidensticker's translation of "Suma" on pp. 231 and 235 and at the beginning of the "Yomogiu" chapter on p. 290 of *The Tale of Genji*

(New York: Knopf, 1976). In the Japanese text edited by Yamagishi Tokuhei, *NKBT*, vol. 15 (Tokyo: Iwanami shoten, 1959), the relevant pages are 30, 38, and 137.

8. *NKBT*, vol. 15, pp. 45, 49; and Seidensticker, *Tale of Genji*, pp. 240, 244; *Nōin utamakura*, pp. 71, 80.

9. Haruo Shirane, *The Bridge of Dreams: A Poetics of "The Tale of Genji"* (Stanford, CA: Stanford University Press, 1987), p. 230, n. 2.

10. Ibid., pp. xvii, 225.

11. The quotation is from *Kyūshū mondō* (1376) printed in Okami Masao, *Yoshimoto renga ronshū*, vol. 2, in *Koten bunko*, vol. 78 (Tokyo: Kotenbunko, 1954), p. 191. The passage is quoted in Janet Goff, *Noh Drama and the Tale of Genji: The Art of Allusion in Fifteen Classical Plays* (Princeton, NJ: Princeton University Press, 1991), p. 21. Both handbooks are published in Okami, *Yoshimoto renga*, vol. 3.

12. The next most popular chapters are "Kiritsubo," with thirty-five phrases and four poems, and "Akashi," with thirty-two phrases.

13. See Donald Keene, trans., *Essays in Idleness* (New York: Columbia University Press, 1967), p. 160 (translated as "popular songs"); and J. Thomas Rimer and Yamazaki Masakazu, *On the Art of the Nō Drama: The Major Treatises of Zeami* (Princeton, NJ: Princeton University Press, 1984), p. 205.

14. Tonomura Natsuko, *Sōka no sōzō to tenkai* (Tokyo: Meiji shoin, 1988), p. 75.

15. For a complete text, see Takano Tatsuyuki, *Nihon kayō shūsei*, vol. 5 (Tokyo: Tokyo dō shuppan, 1960), pp. 83–84. Tonomura, *Sōka no sōzō to tenkai*, discusses these poems on pp. 393 and 68.

16. Royall Tyler, "The Nō Play *Matsukaze* as a Transformation of *Genji monogatari*," *Journal of Japanese Studies* 20 (Summer 1994): 377–422, discusses the use of Suma in some detail. For *Suma Genji* see Goff, *Noh and Genji*, pp. 150–65.

17. The references may be found in Takaki Ichinosuke et al., eds., *Heike monogatari*, 2 vols., in *NKBT*, vols. 32 and 33 (Tokyo: Iwanami shoten, 1960), vol. 1, p. 338, vol. 2, pp. 185, 218, 226, 436; and in Helen Craig McCullough, trans., *The Tale of the Heike* (Stanford, CA: Stanford University Press, 1988), pp. 170, 295, 315, 320, 435.

18. Omote Akira and Katō Shūichi, *Zeami Zenchiku* (Tokyo: Iwanami shoten, 1974), pp. 228–29, 277. The latter is translated in Rimer and Yamazaki, *On the Art of the Nō Drama*, p. 198.

19. Takemoto Mikio, "Rin'a kō—Nanbokuchō-ki kusemai sakusha no yokogao," *Geinōshi kenkyū* 53 (April 1976): 1–14.

20. According to Tomikura Tokujirō, little is known about their actual journey or even the date of their arrival at Dazaifu. See *Heike monogatari zenchūshaku*, vol. 2 (Tokyo: Kadokawa shoten, 1967), p. 468. The text for *Saikoku kudari* is in Omote Akira and Katō Shūichi, *Zeami Zenchiku*, in *Nihon shisō taikei*, vol. 24 (Tokyo: Iwanami shoten, 1974), pp. 228–29.

21. In "*Saikoku kudari* oboegaki," *Nōgaku taimuzu* 332 (November 1979): 7, Matsuoka Shinpei points out that the *Saikoku kudari* depicts the fall of the Heike only metaphorically, through images of the moon setting and its light sinking into the sea.

22. In act 1 of this play, the secondary actor (*waki*), playing the monk Renshō who was formerly the warrior Kumagae, travels to Ichinotani to pray for the soul of Atsumori whom he killed there. He meets a grass cutter (played by the *shite* or main actor) and his companions (*tsure*), who inform him that lowly folk also can make music. After his companions leave, the grass cutter hints that he is the ghost of Atsumori. In act 2, Atsumori appears in his "historical" form, narrates the sad fate

of the Heike at Suma, reenacts his death at the hands of Kumagae, recognizes that Kumagae-turned-Renshō is his friend in Buddhist law, and requests prayers for his soul.

23. The michiyuki also uses several of the place-names that occur in *Saikoku kudari*.

24. Wada Eiko "*Atsumori* no kuse to *Genji* yoriai," *Nō: kenkyū to hyōron*, July 1976, 14. She also points out that "wind-bent pines" was associated with the Suma toponym.

25. I have not seen any edition or translation of either *Atsumori* or *Tadanori* that notes the influence of this kusemai. Takemoto ("Rin'a," 1978) describes influence on nō, but not on either *Atsumori* or *Tadanori*. Goff discusses its use in the waki travel song in *Tadanori* (*Noh and Genji*, p. 65). After writing this chapter, I learned that she has translated *Saikoku kudari* and discussed its relationship to sōga and some nō plays, including *Tadanori*, in Thomas B. Hare, Robert Borgan, and Aharalyn Orbaugh, eds., *The Distant Isle: Studies and Translations of Japanese Literature in Honor of Robert H. Brower* (Ann Arbor, MI: Center for Japanese Studies, 1996). I am indebted to her for showing me her manuscript and for making helpful comments on a draft of this chapter.

26. I describe this process in more detail in "*Atsumori*: The Ghost of a Warrior on Stage," *Par Rapport* 5 and 6 (1982–83): 13–23.

27. Hence "flute" is a renga yoriai. Also, the *Saikoku kudari* phrase "the melody helps them [courtesans] pass through this sad and fleeting world" (*ukiyo o wataru hitofushi*) is applied in the nō to the "grass cutter's flute and woodmen's songs."

28. In the play, a monk (a waki) who had once served the poet Shunzei is traveling to Suma, where he encounters an old woodsman (the shite), who, after describing his life in the mountains and on the sea, hints that he is the ghost of Tadanori. In act 2, Tadanori returns in his "true" form and requests that the monk encourage Shunzei's son to attach Tadanori's name to his poem in the imperial anthology that Shunzei had edited. His name had been omitted because Tadanori had fought on the losing side of the wars and was hence labeled an "enemy" of the throne. Tadanori's ghost then enacts his death in battle at the hands of the Genji warrior Rokuyata.

29. Kitagawa Tadahiko, "Tadanorizō o keisei," *Kokugakuin zasshi*, September 1975, pp. 44–56; and Yamashita Hiroaki, "Zeami to *Heike monogatari*: *Tadanori* o megutte," in *Nagoya daigaku bungakubu, sanjūshūnen kinen ronshū* (Nagoya: Nagoya daigaku, 1978), pp. 640–629 (sic).

30. Kami Hiromi, "Sakuhin kenkyū *Tadanori*," *Kanze*, March 1976, p. 5, and Itō Masayoshi, *Yōkyoku shū*, vol. 2 (Tokyo: Shinchōsha, 1986), p. 304, are two examples.

31. It is also mentioned in *Sarugaku dangi* as a particularly interesting passage of *Saikoku kudari*. See Omote and Katō, *Zeami Zenchiku*, p. 277. Goff, *Tadanori*, also points out these similarities.

32. This metaphor is embodied in the nō play *Shiga*, in which Kuronushi (the shite) is described in act 1 as "a mountain rustic, on whose heavy load of firewood is attached a branch of blossoms, resting in the shade of some blossoms."

33. *Shiga Tadanori* is no longer in the active repertory. The text is printed in Haga Yaichi and Sasaki Nobutsuna, eds., *Kōchū Yōkyoku sōsho*, vol. 2 (Tokyo: Hakubunkan, 1914, reprinted in 1987, Tokyo: Rinsen shoten), pp. 108–11.

4

Warriors as Courtiers: The Taira in Heike monogatari

◉

PAUL VARLEY

Japan's entry into the medieval age (1185–1573) in the late twelfth century was accompanied by an epochal transition in leadership of the country, when the emperor and the ministers who served him at his court in Kyoto relinquished national rule to provincial warrior chieftains. But this transition did not occur immediately, nor was it ever carried to completion in medieval times. Through much of the Kamakura period (1185–1333), for example, government continued to be divided between the court and the new warrior regime (bakufu) that was founded by Minamoto no Yoritomo in Kamakura. And even during the Muromachi period (1336–1573), when the court's political fortunes sank to their nadir, the emperor and his ministers still held high authority and the potential to exercise at least some political power.

In addition to thus retaining a measure of rulership, however slight, throughout the medieval age, the court (comprising imperial and courtier families) influenced and in various ways shaped and even culturally transformed the character of the warrior elite that increasingly dominated the age. Court influence was especially intense during the times when warrior rulers resided in Kyoto. These rulers included the Rokuhara magistrates (*tandai*), who were in Kyoto from 1221 until the overthrow of the Kamakura bakufu in 1333; the Ashikaga shoguns of the Muromachi period; and the daimyos or regional barons who served the Ashikaga and, from at least the late fourteenth century, also lived more or less permanently in Kyoto and visited their domains only infrequently.[1]

The Ise Taira

The forerunners of the medieval warrior rulers who resided in Kyoto were the Ise branch of the Taira (or Heike) family. Victors in the Heiji Conflict in 1159–1160, the Taira under their leader Kiyomori rose to power in Kyoto during the two decades or so from the Heiji Conflict until the Genpei (Minamoto–Taira) War of 1180–1185. Unlike their medieval successors, the Taira did not establish new institutions of warrior rule; rather, they entered court government and in large part emulated the political practices of the Fujiwara regents, even marrying into the imperial family and becoming maternal relatives of the emperor.

The great war tale *Heike monogatari* (The Tale of the Heike) tells us that the Ise Taira were—to coin a word—"aristocratized"[2] during their decades of prominence in Kyoto. Not only did they engage in court government; they actively participated in court society and embraced courtier culture and ways. The *Heike*, although based on history, is—as is well known—a highly embellished work of literature, having been molded and developed over a period of at least two centuries, especially by tale singers who chanted its stories while accompanying themselves with lutes (*biwa*).[3] Hence the *Heike*'s account of how the Ise Taira were aristocratized during their years in Kyoto cannot be accepted uncritically as history. But it is history of a kind, since Japanese through the centuries—even until very recent times—have believed it to be a generally accurate record of the past.[4] The image of the Ise Taira as "courtiers" or courtly warriors was particularly powerful during the medieval age, making their story, primarily as it is given in the *Heike*, the starting point for any study of how the court, court life, and court culture recurrently affected the warrior elite as it evolved during medieval times.

The Taira, along with that other famous warrior family, the Minamoto (or Genji), were descended from the imperial family. Historians have traditionally recounted how surplus princes, excluded from the imperial family in a process of "dynastic shedding" and given the surnames of Taira or Minamoto, went out from the capital during the early Heian period (794–1185) to occupy offices in the provincial governments and, after completing their terms of office, settled down to become leaders in the emerging warrior society of the provinces. In fact, many of these men also continued to maintain residences in Kyoto and, in some cases, to spend more time there than in the provinces. An example is the Minamoto chieftain Yoshiie, victorious commander in the Later Three Years War (1083–1087) in northern Honshu in the late eleventh century, who spent most of his life after the war (he died in 1106) living in Kyoto.

Many provincial warrior chieftains also established patron–client (*shujū*) relations with leading courtiers or members of the imperial family that were very much like the lord–vassal ties of warriors and their followers. The Ise Taira from the time of Kiyomori's grandfather, Masamori, in the late eleventh century, for example, became clients of the senior retired emperors (*in*) who, from about the same time, increasingly surpassed the Fujiwara regents as wielders of power at court.

Not only did provincial warrior chieftains establish private patron–client relationships with courtiers and members of the imperial family, they also avidly sought court titles and posts in both the central and provincial governments. Thus, by the time the Ise Taira rose to national prominence in the second half of the twelfth century, the provincial warrior chieftains as a class had become, both privately and publicly, deeply involved in court life and court affairs; they had, in short, become substantially aristocratized. This does not mean that they were accepted as equals by court society. On the contrary, as the case of the Ise Taira in *Heike monogatari* clearly illustrates, warrior chieftains in Kyoto continued to be despised by courtiers as essentially barbarians, even though—as in the cases of the Taira and Minamoto—they may have been descended from royalty.

Taira no Tadamori

In its famous introduction, *Heike monogatari* announces the theme of and sets the tone for the story that is to be told. It will be a somber story, heavily colored by pessimistic Buddhist views of the impermanence of all things and, especially, the decline of the world during what was believed to be the age of *mappō*, or the "end of the Buddhist Law." The Ise Taira family, under the leadership of Kiyomori, has risen to a dizzying height of grandeur and is headed for a fall, a fall that will be particularly great, and perhaps also very swift, both because of the height to which they have risen and the wickedness of Kiyomori as a ruler.

But before embarking on the story of the Ise Taira under Kiyomori, the *Heike* relates an incident in the life and career of Tadamori, Kiyomori's father, who greatly advanced the family fortunes while in the service of the senior retired emperor Toba during the middle decades of the twelfth century. Toba, we are told, wishes to bestow special reward on Tadamori for building a

Buddhist temple that he, Toba, has personally promised to have erected. The reward is appointment to a provincial governorship and permission to "attend," that is, to participate in courtier affairs, at the imperial palace (Seiryōden).[5] This permission is extraordinary, if not unprecedented, both because it is granted to a warrior and because Tadamori holds only the senior fourth rank, lower grade, and attendance has by tradition been restricted to courtiers of the third rank and higher.

It is difficult, if not impossible, for us living in the present age to appreciate fully the pervasive importance of social status to a class such as the courtiers of ancient Japan. This status, believed to be granted by the gods and based almost exclusively on birth, was figuratively the air that the courtiers breathed. Violations of status were regarded as ethical transgressions of the most serious kind. We can imagine that the courtiers responded in a spirit of truly righteous indignation when Tadamori, in 1132, was granted the right of attendance at the palace. In the *Heike* account, the courtiers' indignation gives rise to a plot to assassinate Tadamori when he first appears at the palace, which is on the occasion of a banquet in the twelfth month.

Although brief, the account of this assassination plot and how Tadamori foiled it (told in "The Night Attack at the Palace") is critical to an understanding of the *Heike* as a whole. We usually think of the *Heike* as the story of the rise and fall of the Ise Taira, but in a larger sense it is a record, admittedly much romanticized, of how and why warriors supplanted courtiers as the ruling elite of Japan in the late twelfth century. Seen in this light, the confrontation between Tadamori and the courtiers in "The Night Attack" becomes a parable for this momentous historical transition in ruling elites.

Informed in advance of the plot, Tadamori, upon his arrival at the palace, ostentatiously displays a large dagger he has brought with him in what is evidently a breach of proper court conduct. Startled by the display of this weapon, the courtiers are truly alarmed when they observe that one of Tadamori's retainers, armed with a sword, is seated in a garden outside the hall where the banquet is being held. When questioned, the retainer states that he has come because he has heard that there is to be an attempt to kill his lord that night.[6]

Obliged to abandon their plot, the courtiers seek some satisfaction by singing, while Tadamori dances as part of the evening's entertainment, a satirical verse that contains a phrase with several plays on words that can be taken to mean either "the Ise Heishi (or Heike; Tadamori) is squint-eyed" or "the bottle from Ise is a roughly made article" (or "is a vinegar bottle"). One meaning mocks Tadamori as physically flawed, and the other characterizes him as a countrified boor from the wilds of Ise.[7]

After the banquet, the courtiers submit their complaints about Tadamori to retired emperor Toba, claiming that he has violated court regulations, which stipulate that one may not, without special imperial authorization, enter the palace with a weapon or in the company of an escort. But Tadamori proves he has not broken the regulations because his dagger is a sham weapon, made of wood, and the retainer came not as an escort but of his own accord. Far from punishing Tadamori, Toba praises him for his resourcefulness in dealing with a difficult situation.[8]

This story of Tadamori and the courtiers is like a parable because it can be taken to signify, although in exaggerated form, the qualities that distinguished courtiers from warriors (represented by Tadamori) in this age and made inevitable the victory of the latter as the future rulers. Whereas Tadamori is determined, realistic, and resourceful, the courtiers are arrogant and aloof, unbending in their commitment to status and class privileges and to the rules that for centuries have tightly governed conduct at court. As Nagazumi Yasuaki points out, the *Heike* subtly enforces the courtiers' rigid commitment to privileges and rules by having them employ elaborate, Chinese-style language when they lodge their complaints about Tadamori with Toba.[9]

Although it may be interpreting too much from a few words voiced in anger, we can regard the courtiers' description of Tadamori as a "vinegar jar from Ise" as an indication of their unwillingness to recognize him as anything other than a barbarian. Yet we have observed that provincial warrior chieftains of this age frequently visited and resided in Kyoto, served at court, and participated in court life and culture. As heir to his father's (Masamori's) preferment in the service of the senior retired emperor, Tadamori had probably spent most of his life in Kyoto. Even the *Heike* alludes to Tadamori's courtliness when, in mentioning an affair he had with a court lady "of refinement," it describes him as a man of "elegance."[10]

Taira no Kiyomori

As he is portrayed in the *Heike*, Kiyomori is an archvillain who rivals all those heinous characters of Chinese and Japanese history who "did not obey the rule of their lords or former sovereigns, led dissolute lives, ignored admonitions, were not aware of the world's disorders, and were blind to the suffering of the people."[11] Through the first half of the *Heike*, until his death in book 6, Kiyomori as archvillain looms over the story, representing a primary (although not the sole) reason that the Ise Taira are headed for decline and destruction.

The organization of book 1 of the *Heike* conveys the sense that the rise of the Ise Taira under Kiyomori occurred very rapidly. If Tadamori faced formidable social and status barriers at court, his son Kiyomori, in the *Heike* account at least, seems scarcely troubled by them. With little commentary, the *Heike* relates Kiyomori's almost meteorlike ascent of the twin ladders of court rank and office to become chancellor *(daijō daijin)* with junior first rank. As he thus rises to the summits of court society and status, Kiyomori carries his entire family in his train, as we quickly learn from a listing of the preferments in office and rank given to other Ise Taira men and from the marriages arranged between Ise Taira women and members of the highest courtier families, including the Fujiwara regent family and even the imperial family (Kiyomori later becomes the grandfather of an emperor, Antoku).[12] So grand do the Ise Taira become that in the words of one of them, "all who do not belong to this family cannot be considered human beings."[13]

Although Kiyomori is now, in regard to office and rank, the preeminent courtier of the land, the *Heike* tells us almost nothing else about how aristocratized or courtly he may have become. Aristocratization does not mean simply the attainment of office and rank at court but also the acquisition of those special qualities of attitude, bearing, and taste that distinguish courtiers from others. As portrayed in the *Heike*, Kiyomori is essentially a political leader, and not a very courtly one at that. Despite his occupancy of the office of chancellor, in times of crisis, for example, he usually responds not as we would expect a courtier of such exalted position to respond but rather like a warrior chief, by resorting to arms. In this, he differs most markedly from his oldest son and heir apparent, Shigemori.

Taira no Shigemori

In earlier war tales—*Hōgen monogatari* (The Tale of Hōgen) and *Heiji monogatari* (The Tale of Heiji)—Shigemori is the leading battlefield commander of the Ise Taira. In the *Heike*, however, he is almost entirely divested of his military attributes, becoming not only a "courtier" but one who exemplifies the highest ideals of the courtier as minister. We must here distinguish between two personae of the courtier: the courtier as minister and the courtier as romantic or lover. Shigemori's courtliness is completely in the ministerial realm; the *Heike* says nothing about his possessing a romantic side. He is married to a court woman, but we are told almost nothing about her or their marriage. Yet others among the Ise Taira, as we will see, display their courtliness primarily as romantics, reciting *waka* poems, playing musical instruments, having affairs with elegant court ladies.

As many commentators have observed, Shigemori the courtly minister functions in the *Heike* as a medium to defend the traditional rights of the imperial family and the courtier class in the face of the relentless assault on them by Shigemori's own family, led by his father Kiyomori.[14] Shigemori defends these rights primarily in two sustained admonitions he delivers to his father in 1177, at the time of discovery of the Shishigatani plot to overthrow the Ise Taira. Kiyomori reacts to the revelation of the plot by summarily executing some of the conspirators and preparing to take military action against others, including the senior retired emperor Goshirakawa.

Shigemori delivers his second, longer admonition after rushing to Kiyomori's residence to forestall a plan to march on and seize Goshirakawa. In contrast to Kiyomori and the other Taira and family retainers assembled at the residence, who have donned their armor, Shigemori is attired—as he is always attired in the *Heike*—in courtly robes.[15] Kiyomori, invariably flustered when confronted by this son who is universally admired for his unswerving adherence to the highest Confucian and Buddhist precepts, tries to hide his armor by hastily pulling a monk's robe over it. He then sits in silence as Shigemori speaks.

In the admonition, Shigemori talks of fate and karmic retribution, touching on themes that permeate the *Heike*. But the central point of his argument is the theory of imperial absolutism.[16] After chiding his father for violating the law that a chancellor must never wear helmet and armor, he calls on Kiyomori to adhere to the supreme obligation of men to obey their sovereign.[17] Although in fact the sovereign is the emperor, Shigemori here refers to senior retired emperor Goshirakawa who, as Uwayokote Masataka notes, is a political schemer capable of straining the faith and commitment of any subject.[18] Shigemori acknowledges that Goshirakawa's thinking can be "unpredictable" but nevertheless asserts that it is the subject's duty to serve him and the court with unstinting loyalty.

Shigemori's courtliness is unique among Ise Taira in the *Heike*. No other member of the family assumes, in any significant way, the qualities of the courtier as minister. Rather, the aristocratization of other Ise Taira, apart from the receipt of court ranks and offices, lies largely in their acquisition of what I have called the romantic attributes of the courtier. But little is said about the Ise Taira as courtly romantics until the *Heike*'s second half, when the Genpei War has begun and the family is launched on the road to what we know will be defeat and doom.

Courtly Warriors in the Genpei War

The Genpei War began in 1180 when an imperial prince, Mochihito, disgruntled because he had been bypassed through Kiyomori's interference in the succession to the emperorship, dispatched an edict to Minamoto chieftains in the provinces calling on them to rise up and overthrow the Ise Taira. Among the first to accept this call to arms against the Ise Taira were Minamoto no Yoritomo in the Kantō and his cousin Yoshinaka in Shinano Province.

In the Genpei War, as it is narrated in the second half of the *Heike*, there is little doubt about the eventual outcome of the warfare between the Minamoto and the Ise Taira. The Minamoto, especially those from the eastern provinces of the Kantō, are famous as fierce fighting men—they are the cream of the horse-riding warrior class that had evolved in the provinces since early times. The Ise Taira, on the other hand, represent what the *Heike* categorizes as "western" warriors, who lack both the martial prowess and physical and mental toughness to stand up to their eastern adversaries.[19] Although some Taira chieftains, such as Noritsune and Tadanori, are in fact impressive fighters, most are no match for their Minamoto counterparts.

The Taira problems in the *Heike*'s version of the Genpei War begin with weak leadership. In 1179 Shigemori dies, convinced that the fortunes of the Ise Taira are nearing their end, and then in 1181 Kiyomori dies, angry and unrepentant to the last, less than a half year after the war's start. Although dictatorial and erratic, Kiyomori was at least a decisive leader. His successor as the head of the Ise Taira, his second son Munemori, is not only indecisive; he is quite devoid of martial spirit. When, for example, Minamoto no Yoshinaka leads his army to the gates of Kyoto in 1183, Munemori decides to take the child emperor Antoku (his nephew and Kiyomori's grandson) and flee the capital, rejecting the advice of other Taira chieftains who wish to remain and defend against Yoshinaka. Munemori gives as his reason for abandoning the capital his unwillingness to expose members of the imperial family, including the emperor and his mother, Kenreimon'in (Munemori's sister), to the distress of battling with Yoshinaka.[20]

Munemori's fainthearted—one is tempted to say courtierlike—behavior in the face of the Yoshinaka threat sets the tone of the chapters in book 7 of the *Heike* that describe the sad departure of the Ise Taira from Kyoto and, indeed, of the work's entire second half. Until this point, the reader has generally despised the Ise Taira because of the evilness of Kiyomori and the hubris of the family as a whole; from here on, however, the reader is increasingly led to sympathize with them.

One reason for this newly felt sympathy is the disparity in fighting ability between the Ise Taira and their Minamoto adversaries: the reader pities the Taira as manifest underdogs. But another and, I believe, stronger reason for the elicitation of the reader's sympathy is the series of revelations about the romantic courtliness of Taira leaders. It can even be suggested that the Ise Taira become surrogates for the courtier class and that their destruction in the Genpei War symbolizes the historical displacement of this class as a ruling elite by rough warriors from the provinces.

The Ise Taira flight from Kyoto in 1183, at least as described in the *Heike*, is less tragic than pathetic. Some of the Taira are tough and are ready to fight. But the family in general is bewildered and in disarray. Munemori sets the tone by weeping when he informs his sister Kenreimon'in that they must leave the capital.[21] The Minamoto also cry in the *Heike*, for example, Yoshitsune when his intimate follower, Satō no Tsuginobu, is killed defending him at the battle of Yashima early in 1185.[22] But the Minamoto shed only "manly" tears—tears for fallen comrades or for the anguish of war itself. Munemori, on the other hand, cries like a courtier—drenching the sleeve of his robe—from a sense of frustration and impotence. Other Taira weep in similar courtly fashion, for example, Shigehira when parting from a mistress he is allowed to see briefly after he is captured by the Minamoto following the battle of Ichinotani.[23]

In preparing for flight, the Taira decide to take their women with them (they also take Emperor Antoku, but that is for an important political reason: to give legitimacy to their cause). With the women in tow, the Taira are far from a typical army. Women seldom accompany armies in the war tales, and the presence of the Taira women during the flight from the capital contributes as much as anything to the sense of courtly poignancy surrounding what we know will be the family's inevitable fate in the Genpei War.

Although they occasionally rally and win battles, after Kyoto the Taira are essentially pathetic fugitives, afflicted at every turn by homesickness and depression resulting from grief over their plight and ceaseless longing for the capital and the life of luxury and glory they once knew. The Taira men would surely have been homesick and depressed without their women, but the presence of the women intensifies these feelings and, I believe, enhances the impression that the *Heike* conveys of the Ise Taira as surrogate victims for the courtiers who are losing out as a ruling elite in the transition to the medieval age.

After leaving Kyoto, the Taira visit Fukuhara, their former base on the Inland Sea to which Kiyomori had once moved the imperial capital.[24] Assailed by memories of Fukuhara's transient grandeur and made wretched by its present desolate and deteriorated state, the Taira spend only one night there, "their tears

mixing with dew on the grassy pillows of their travellers' beds."[25] The description of the Taira departure from Fukuhara the following day is one of the sad-
dest and most courtierlike passages in the *Heike*:

> As dawn broke, the Taira set fire to the Fukuhara palace and, with the emperor,
> they all boarded the boats. Departing the capital had been more painful, but still
> their feelings of regret were great indeed. Smoke at eveningtime from seaweed
> burned by fisherfolk, the cries of deer on mountain peaks at dawn, waves lapping
> the shore, moonbeams bathing their tear-drenched sleeves, crickets chirping in
> the grasses—no sight met their eyes nor sounds reached their ears that failed to
> evoke sadness or pierce their hearts. Yesterday they were tens of thousands of
> horsemen with their bits aligned at Ōsaka Barrier; today, as they loosened their
> mooring lines on waves in the western sea, they numbered a mere seven thou-
> sand. The sky was cloudy and the sea calm as dusk approached. Lonely islands
> were shrouded in evening mists; the moon floated on the sea. Cleaving the waves
> to the distant horizon and drawn ever onward by the tides, the boats seemed to
> row up through the clouds in the sky. Days had passed, and they were already sep-
> arated far from the mountains and rivers of the capital, which lay behind the
> clouds. They seemed to have gone as far as they could go. All had come to an end,
> except their endless tears.[26]

As Ishimoda Shō has observed, the *Heike* differs from the earlier war tales in
containing passages such as this one, written in a tone of classical lyricism and
presenting visual images like scenes from *Yamato-e* (Japanese-style pictures).[27]
Drawing on the *aware* aesthetic of courtly taste, the scenes in this passage are suf-
fused with a sadness deriving from the haunting sights and sounds depicted and
the uncontrollable grief of the Taira and also from the many metaphors related
to water—sea, waves, tears, floating, tides, mists. These images heighten our
awareness that the once supremely proud family of Kiyomori, now greatly
reduced in strength, has literally lost its political and social moorings ("with the
loosening of their mooring lines") and is drifting toward an unknown, but
inevitably dark, fate.

    There is irony in the water metaphors inasmuch as the Ise Taira first gained
fame as a sea power in the Inland Sea. The once great "kings of the water" are
now its victims, carried along by its changing tides and shifting currents. There
is irony also in the fact that the Taira are fleeing to the west, for they were not
just a sea power but a "western" sea power as well. In the *Heike*, the war between
the Ise Taira and the Minamoto is presented geographically as a conflict between
the Minamoto of the east (land power) and the Taira of the west (sea power).

The ultimate irony of this pairing is revealed, of course, in the final defeat of the Taira by the Minamoto in the sea battle of Dannoura in the west in the third month of 1185. But another irony deriving from the association of the Taira with the sea and the west appears in the *Heike* in the description of the family's flight from Kyoto and Fukuhara. Although by heading westward to Kyushu, the Taira hope to gather support from former adherents in that region, the *Heike*, as in the passage just quoted, portrays the west as remote and lonely, distant from the high civilization of the capital. The Taira, who have become aristocratized, now see their western heritage differently: compared with the "civilized" capital, the west is "uncivilized." Sharing the sentiments of courtiers through the ages, they are agonized by their forced departure from the capital and can conceive of happiness only in terms of returning to Kyoto.

Tadanori and Tsunemasa

The *Heike*'s description of the Taira flight from Kyoto emphasizes their courtliness also by highlighting the departure of two members of the family who exemplify acquisition of the courtly arts: Tadanori the poet and Tsunemasa the musician.

Tadanori was a younger brother of Kiyomori and one of the leading field commanders of the Ise Taira. More than any other member of his family as they are portrayed in the *Heike*, he combines the qualities of warrior and romantic courtier. In one of his early appearances in the *Heike*, Tadanori serves as the second in command of an ill-fated expeditionary force sent by Kiyomori to the Kantō against Minamoto no Yoritomo, shortly after Yoritomo rises in rebellion in 1180. We are told that for many years, Tadanori had been conducting an affair with the daughter of a princess and that the daughter, distressed that he must now leave on a military expedition, sends him a poem along with the gift of a robe. In responding to the daughter, Tadanori composes a poem that is described as containing lines of "great refinement":

Wakareji o	Why lament
nani ka nagekan	Our parting,
koete yuki	When the barrier I cross
seki mo mukashi no	Leads to the sites
ato to omoeba	Of bygone days?[28]

Among the warriors in the *Heike*, only the Taira recite poetry. Even in the affairs they occasionally have with courtly women, the Minamoto are poetically silent.[29] The inclusion in the *Heike* of thirty or so poems by Taira—most of them in the work's second half, which describes the Genpei War—is one of the more important indices of how courtly the Taira have become during their years of ascendancy in Kyoto.

We know that Tadanori was, in historical fact, a poet of some distinction.[30] The *Heike* develops Tadanori's courtier poet side to make his flight from Kyoto with his Taira kinsmen and his subsequent death at the battle of Ichinotani one of the more poignant of the many tales of how the Taira perish, one after another, in the various battles of the Genpei War. As the Taira prepare to leave Kyoto, Tadanori visits Fujiwara no Shunzei, one of the leading court poets of the day, with whom he has studied poetry for many years. He implores Shunzei to read a scroll of poems he has written, in the hope that one or more may be included in a future anthology of imperially authorized poetry.[31]

Tadanori is killed attempting to escape when the Minamoto, in the second month of 1184, rout the Taira from the fortress they have established at Ichinotani on the shore of the Inland Sea. The enemy knows Tadanori to be a high-ranking Taira commander because his teeth are blackened in the courtly fashion. He is able to make a precise identification when he finds a poem, written and signed by Tadanori, in Tadanori's armor. There are none among friend or foe, we are told, who do not shed tears upon hearing of Tadanori's death: "How sad! [everyone said]. He was a person who excelled in both the martial arts and the way of poetry. He is a general who will be sorely missed."[32]

When Shunzei compiles the anthology *Senzaishū* in 1187, he in fact includes one of Tadanori's poems. But because the Ise Taira, having by then been defeated and destroyed in the Genpei War, are regarded as enemies of the court, Shunzei is obliged to label the poem "anonymous":

Sazanami ya	Though the old Shiga capital
Shiga no miyako wa	Lies in ruins,
are ni shi o	The mountain cherries
mukashinagara no	Ripple like waves
yamazakura kana	As of yore.[33]

Tsunemasa was a nephew of Kiyomori, who as a youth had served at Ninnaji (temple) in Kyoto and who, because of his extraordinary musical talent, had been entrusted by the temple's abbot with the famous lute Seizan, which centuries earlier had been brought to the Japanese court from China. The bestowal of Seizan, an instrument once prized by emperors, upon a young Taira was an extraordinary tribute to the skill of a warrior in one of the courtly arts. Although it is possible that Tsunemasa was given Seizan to curry favor with the powerful Taira family, the *Heike* avers that he fully deserved it—presumably above potential courtier recipients—on grounds of his musicality alone.[34]

As the Taira prepare to abandon Kyoto, Tsunemasa hurries to Ninnaji to return Seizan to the abbot. Weeping, Tsunemasa says that he cannot bring himself to take such a treasured instrument into "the dust of the hinterland."[35] What he means, metaphorically, is that he must leave behind "civilization" (or culture, represented by Seizan) because he is heading into the "uncivilized" (and hence uncultured) western provinces. He expresses the hope that if the fortune of the Taira should through some miracle change and he is able to return to the capital/civilization, he might be given Seizan to play once again. After exchanging poems of parting with the abbot, he leaves Ninnaji. Tsunemasa's performance in this touching scene—his relinquishment of the lute, his weeping, his dread of venturing into the "hinterland," his exchange of poems with the abbot—is thoroughly courtly.

The theme of the Taira warrior as musician reappears in the famous story of Tsunemasa's younger brother Atsumori. The setting is again the Minamoto rout of the Taira at Ichinotani. Atsumori, who is only sixteen or seventeen, is attempting to escape to the Taira ships moored offshore and fights with the fearsome Minamoto adherent Kumagai no Naozane. Wrestling Atsumori to the ground and tearing off his helmet to behead him, Naozane is amazed to see the face—with blackened teeth—of a beautiful youth. To Naozane, Atsumori is like a courtier. He also reminds Naozane, who wishes to spare him, of his own son. But Naozane is forced to kill Atsumori when he sees a band of Minamoto approaching and knows they will show the youthful Taira no mercy. Later, Naozane discovers a flute in a pouch at Atsumori's waist and realizes that it had been Atsumori playing the flute in the Taira fortress that morning. Observing that none among the Minamoto would think of bringing a flute to a battle, Naozane proclaims: "These lofty people [the Taira] are truly men of refinement!"[36]

The End of the Ise Taira

The Taira journey to Kyushu in the distant west avails them little, for they are driven also from that region, which had once been an important family base, by a renegade former vassal. Adrift again, they make their way to Yashima off Shikoku Island, where Munemori and the other Taira, all of whom hold high court ranks, must "spend their days in the rush-thatched huts of fishermen and their nights in mean hovels."[37] The Taira are, however, able to win some battles against forces sent from Kyoto by Yoshinaka, who is under increasing threat from his cousin and rival for Minamoto leadership, Yoritomo of Kamakura.

In the first month of 1184, Yoshinaka is destroyed by an army under the half brothers Minamoto no Yoshitsune and Noriyori, dispatched from Kamakura by Yoritomo (another half brother). With Kyoto secured, the quick-acting Yoshitsune attacks the fortress that the Taira have meanwhile established at Ichinotani on the Honshu littoral of the Inland Sea, near Fukuhara. The Taira loss at Ichinotani is devastating; the *Heike* lists among the family dead ten of its most prominent members, including all three of those discussed in the last section—Tadanori, Tsunemasa, and Atsumori. [38]

Only one Taira commander, Kiyomori's son Shigehira, is captured at Ichinotani. Shigehira, as we find him in the *Heike*, rivals his uncle Tadanori as a possessor of outstanding qualities as both warrior and romantic courtier. Much of the *Heike*'s book 10 is devoted to Shigehira in captivity (he is held for about a year and a half before being executed after the Genpei War), during which time he is taken to see Yoritomo in Kamakura. In an earlier meeting with a mistress (mentioned earlier) and while on the trip to Kamakura, Shigehira shows himself to be a person of great courtly sensitivity, composing waka poetry, engaging in a brief affair with a girl at an inn, and charming people with his lute playing and chanting at Kamakura. Yoritomo pronounces him to be "the most cultivated of men." [39]

There is no need, for the purpose of this chapter, to describe the final year of the Genpei War; it is enough to note that the Ise Taira are badly defeated again at the battle of Yashima in the second month of 1185 and are driven westward once more in their boats. A month later they are decimated in the naval battle at Dannoura. Most of the remaining Taira leaders are killed or drown themselves, along with the child emperor Antoku, at Dannoura. The few Taira who are captured, including Munemori, are subsequently executed, and other Taira who did not participate in the Dannoura fighting, including children, are hunted down and killed. The *Heike* is brought to a conclusion with the final pronouncement, after the execution of Shigemori's grandson (and Kiyomori's great-grandson) Rokudai, that "thus the progeny of the Heike [Taira] came finally to an end." [40]

Conclusion

As I noted at the beginning of this chapter, the Kakuichi version of the *Heike monogatari* that I used was completed in 1371 and was the product of nearly two centuries of textual development and embellishment, especially by itinerant tale singers. The picture of the Ise Taira as aristocratized or courtly warriors in the Kakuichi *Heike* is therefore historically inaccurate (although the Taira certainly became aristocratized to some extent during their years of ascendancy in Kyoto), and it does not even necessarily represent the tastes and attitudes of the late twelfth century, the time of the *Heike*'s story. Rather, at least some, if not a great deal, of what we find in the Kakuichi *Heike* reflects the tastes and attitudes of the early Muromachi period. We know, for example, that in the early Muromachi period, the Ashikaga and other members of the warrior elite, most of them maintaining their principal residences in Kyoto, were commencing a historical process in which they themselves became aristocratized and that they enjoyed being informed about courtier-warriors of the past, especially the Ise Taira of the Genpei age. Zeami, one of the creators of the nō theater, who began his career in the theater about the time of the completion of the Kakuichi *Heike*, catered to this desire of the Muromachi warrior elite to learn about the Ise Taira as courtier-warriors by creating the warrior category of nō plays and by basing all his warrior plays on the Kakuichi *Heike*.[41]

The transformation of the Ise Taira into courtly warriors in the Kakuichi *Heike* is achieved by various means. Among these are the constant use, and thus highlighting, of Taira-held court ranks and titles (the Minamoto in the *Heike*, with few exceptions, have no such ranks and titles); the recording of poems composed by Taira; the description of Taira, especially from the time of their forced departure from Kyoto in 1183, weeping when moved by such unmanly or un-warrior-like feelings as longing for a loved one, homesickness (for Kyoto), and the bewilderment and frustration caused by the disruptions of the Genpei War; and the narration of the love affairs the Taira have with court ladies. Among the most prominent Taira lovers, as they are identified in the *Heike*, are Tadamori, Tadanori, Michimori, and Shigehira.[42] Although the Minamoto also occasionally engage in affairs with court ladies in the *Heike* (for example, Yoshinaka and Yoshitsune), we are told nothing about their styles of courtship.

When speaking of the intrusion of Muromachi tastes into the war tales that recount the Taira–Minamoto stories of the Genpei age, Helen McCullough has commented on "the idealization of the fleeing Taira as elegant and bewildered aristocrats."[43] This comment appears, in fact, in a discussion of how Minamoto no Yoshitsune, who remains manly and warriorlike throughout the *Heike*, is aristocratized in *Gikeiki* (Chronicle of Yoshitsune), a Muromachi-period work whose primary focus is on the flight of Yoshitsune and a small band of supporters to the northern provinces after the Genpei War to avoid the wrath of Yoritomo, who is determined to destroy—and finally succeeds in destroying—

Yoshitsune. One should be cautious about drawing analogies between *Heike monogatari* and *Gikeiki*, since they are very different kinds of works. Nevertheless, in both we see the "flight" used prominently as a narrative device for the purpose of transforming warriors into courtly warriors.

Still another important means by which the *Heike* transforms the Taira into courtly warriors is through the use of classical court language, such as the language in the description quoted earlier of the Taira flight from Fukuhara and in the stories of their affairs with court ladies. The classical language we find in this and other sections of the *Heike* is one of the reasons it, alone among the war tales, is admired as a literary masterpiece.

Many other examples of Ise Taira aristocratization or courtliness in the *Heike* could be cited. But I hope what I have presented conveys a general sense of the extraordinarily rich tradition, in both history (insofar as people regard the *Heike* as history) and literature, of this family as courtly warriors, especially romantic courtly warriors, as they are portrayed in the *Heike*'s second half when they flee from Kyoto, are hunted down, and are annihilated in the Genpei War and its aftermath.

NOTES

1. Records of the fourteenth century, especially the war tale *Taiheiki*, suggest that many daimyos had already voluntarily taken up residence in Kyoto before they were required to do so by the third Ashikaga shogun Yoshimitsu. The first third of *Taiheiki* can be found in English translation in Helen Craig McCullough, trans., *Taiheiki: A Chronicle of Medieval Japan* (New York: Columbia University Press, 1959).

2. The Japanese term for aristocratization is *kizoku-ka*. See the reference to this in Yasuda Motohisa, *Heike no gunzō* (Tokyo: Hanawa shobō, 1967), p. 18.

3. See Kenneth Dean Butler, "The Textual Evolution of the *Heike Monogatari*," *Harvard Journal of Asiatic Studies* 26 (1965–66): 5–51. See also the summary of the *Heike*'s textual evolution in Paul Varley, *Warriors of Japan, as Portrayed in the War Tales* (Honolulu: University of Hawaii Press, 1994), pp. 82–85.

4. Yasuda, *Heike no gunzō*, pp. 14, 77. Yasuda cites two important Tokugawa-period histories, the Mito school's *Dai Nihon shi* and Rai San'yō's *Nihon gaishi*, that use the *Heike* as a primary source.

5. Takagi Ichinosuke et al., eds., *Heike monogatari*, vol. 1, in *Nihon koten bungaku taikei*, vols. 32–33 (Tokyo: Iwanami shoten, 1959), p. 84. This is the 1371 Kakuichi text of the *Heike*, which is the work's *rufubon*, or the most widely disseminated of the hundred or more surviving versions of the *Heike*. My chapter is based solely on the Kakuichi *Heike*, and the translations are mine. For a full English translation, see Helen Craig McCullough, *The Tale of the Heike* (Stanford, CA: Stanford University Press, 1988). The reference to Tadamori's receipt of a provincial governorship and permission to attend at the imperial palace appears on p. 24 of the McCullough translation.

6. Takagi et al., *Heike monogatari*, vol. 1, p. 85; McCullough, *Tale of the Heike*, p. 24.

7. Ibid.

8. Takagi et al., *Heike monogatari*, vol. 1, pp. 87–88; McCullough, *Tale of the Heike*, pp. 25–26.

9. Nagazumi Yasuaki, *Heike monogatari o yomu* (Tokyo: Iwanami shoten, 1980), pp. 19–20.

10. Takagi et al., *Heike monogatari*, vol. 1, p. 89; McCullough, *Tale of the Heike*, p. 27.

11. Takagi et al., *Heike monogatari*, vol. 1, p. 83; McCullough, *Tale of the Heike*, p. 23.

12. Takagi et al., *Heike monogatari*, vol. 1, pp. 92–94; McCullough, *Tale of the Heike*, pp. 27–30.

13. Takagi et al., *Heike monogatari*, vol. 1, pp. 90–91; McCullough, *Tale of the Heike*, p. 28.

14. For example, Tomikura Tokujirō, *Heike monogatari* (Tokyo: NHK, 1972), p. 56.

15. Takagi et al., *Heike monogatari*, vol. 1, p. 171; McCullough, *Tale of the Heike*, p. 74. There is one occasion in the *Heike* when Shigemori presumably wears armor: in book 1, where he is said to assume responsibility for defending several gates of the imperial palace against warrior monks. Takagi et al., *Heike monogatari*, vol. 1, p. 135; McCullough, *Tale of the Heike*, p. 53.

16. See the discussion of this in Uwayokote Masataka, *Heike monogatari no kyokō to shinjitsu* (Tokyo: Hanawa shobō, 1985), vol. 1, pp. 81–88.

17. Takagi et al., *Heike monogatari*, vol. 1, p. 172; McCullough, *Tale of the Heike*, p. 75.

18. Uwayokote suggests that the *Heike*'s author(s) used Shigemori to criticize Kiyomori because Goshirakawa was too embroiled himself in court politics to be a credible critic. *Heike monogatari no kyokō to shinjitsu*, vol. 1, pp. 85–86.

19. See the analysis of the differences between "eastern" and "western" warriors by Saitō no Sanemori, an eastern warrior allied with the Taira. Takagi et al., *Heike monogatari*, vol. 1, pp. 372–73; McCullough, *Tale of the Heike*, pp. 188–90. See also the discussion of this subject in Varley, *Warriors of Japan*, pp. 91–92.

20. Takagi et al., *Heike monogatari*, vol. 2, p. 94; McCullough, *Tale of the Heike*, p. 242.

21. Ibid.

22. Takagi et al., *Heike monogatari*, vol. 2, pp. 314–16; McCullough, *Tale of the Heike*, pp. 365–66.

23. Takagi et al., *Heike monogatari*, vol. 2, p. 247; McCullough, *Tale of the Heike*, p. 330.

24. Kiyomori moved the capital to Fukuhara in the sixth month of 1180 and returned it to Kyoto five months later.

25. Takagi et al., *Heike monogatari*, vol. 2, p. 115; McCullough, *Tale of the Heike*, p. 254.

26. Takagi et al., *Heike monogatari*, vol. 2, p. 116; McCullough, *Tale of the Heike*, pp. 254–55. Tomikura Tokujirō notes that this passage of the Taira flight from Fukuhara has, because of its lyricism, been one of the favorites of the *Heike* tale singers. See his *Heike monogatari* (Tokyo: Kadokawa shoten, 1975), p. 235.

27. Ishimoda Shō, *Heike monogatari* (Tokyo: Iwanami shoten, 1957), pp. 167–68.

28. Takagi et al., *Heike monogatari*, vol. 1, pp. 367–68; McCullough, *Tale of the Heike*, pp. 185–86. The *Heike* goes on to say that the "sites" Tadanori refers to must be the places where Taira no Sadamori was victorious when he led an expedition eastward in the ninth century to subdue the rebel Masakado.

29. There are two exceptions to this statement. Kajiwara no Kagetaka recites a poem before charging into battle at Ichinotani in book 9, and Minamoto no Yorimasa, identified in the *Heike* as an ardent poet, is the author of several poems in book 4. But the case of Yorimasa is unusual, since he was the only prominent Minamoto to side with the Taira in the Heiji Conflict of 1159–60 and, as a result, the only one to remain in the capital thereafter. Despite his Minamoto surname,

Yorimasa is really like a Taira in the *Heike*, that is, one who was aristocratized in the years leading to the Genpei War.

30. Sixteen of Tadanori's poems are in imperially sponsored anthologies. Kajiwara Masaaki, *Heike monogatari* (Tokyo: Shōgakkan, 1982), p. 230.

31. Takagi et al., *Heike monogatari*, vol. 2, pp. 102–4; McCullough, *Tale of the Heike*, pp. 246–47.

32. Takagi et al., *Heike monogatari*, vol. 2, pp. 215–17; McCullough, *Tale of the Heike*, pp. 313–14.

33. Takagi et al., *Heike monogatari*, vol. 2, p. 104; McCullough, *Tale of the Heike*, p. 247. Shiga, in Ōmi Province, had once in ancient times been the imperial capital.

34. Takagi et al., *Heike monogatari*, vol. 2, pp. 107–8; McCullough, *Tale of the Heike*, pp. 249–50.

35. Takagi et al., *Heike monogatari*, vol. 2, p. 106; McCullough, *Tale of the Heike*, p. 248. I have taken the word *hinterland* from the McCullough translation.

36. Takagi et al., *Heike monogatari*, vol. 2, pp. 219–22; McCullough, *Tale of the Heike*, pp. 315–17.

37. Takagi et al., *Heike monogatari*, vol. 2, p. 135; McCullough, *Tale of the Heike*, p. 266.

38. Takagi et al., *Heike monogatari*, vol. 2, p. 226; McCullough, *Tale of the Heike*, p. 320.

39. Takagi et al., *Heike monogatari*, vol. 2, p. 226; McCullough, *Tale of the Heike*, pp. 340–41.

40. Takagi et al., *Heike monogatari*, vol. 2, p. 422; McCullough, *Tale of the Heike*, p. 425. Helen McCullough provides a freer, more dramatic translation of this passage: "Thus did the sons of the Heike vanish forever from the face of the earth."

41. See the discussion of this in Thomas Blenman Hare, *Zeami's Style* (Stanford, CA: Stanford University Press, 1986), p. 185.

42. Michimori's courtship of and marriage to the court lady Kozaishō and her suicide by drowning when she learns of his death in the battle of Ichinotani are recounted in "Kozaishō's Suicide," the last chapter of book 9. Tadamori, Tadanori, and Shigehira as lovers have been discussed.

43. Helen McCullough, trans., *Yoshitsune* (Stanford, CA: Stanford University Press, 1966), p. 54.

5

The Placatory Nature of The Tale of the Heike:
Additional Documents and Thoughts

◉

HERBERT PLUTSCHOW

In my book *Chaos and Cosmos: Ritual in Classical Japanese Literature*, I discuss a number of texts suggesting that the *Heike monogatari* (The Tale of the Heike) was recited in part to placate the spirits of its heroes. These texts range from legends such as "Earless Hōichi" and "Earless Danichi" to war tales (*gunki-mono*), historical works, and diaries. I introduce the pioneering research of Tsukudo Reikan and others who interpret *The Tale of the Heike* as placatory literature. Furthermore, I support my hypothesis with a discussion of the fear of vengeful spirits in Japanese religion and refer to the traditional role of blind performers in placating them.[1]

Based on a combination of these factors, I conclude that the account in *Tsurezuregusa* (Essays in Idleness) of the role of Priest Jien (1155–1225) in producing *The Tale of the Heike* needs serious reconsideration:

> During the reign of the Emperor Go-toba, a former official from Shinano named Yukinaga enjoyed a reputation for learning. . . . The priest Jichin [Jien], who made a practice of hiring men with artistic talent even as menials and treating them kindly employed this lay priest of Shinano.
>
> Yukinaga wrote the *Heike monogatari* and taught a blind man named Shōbutsu to recite it. . . . *Biwa* entertainers today imitate what was Shōbutsu's natural voice.[2]

Although Jien fails to mention *The Tale of the Heike* in his own writings, he is well-known through his *Gukanshō* (a moral history of Japan based on imperial and Buddhist law written around 1219) as the most vehement proponent of the need to protect the nation by placating evil spirits. Moreover, as a prominent member of the most powerful (*sekkanke*) branch of the Fujiwara aristocracy and high priest of the Enryakuji (since 1192), a temple that owes its existence to warding off evil, Jien is likely to have played a role in the inception of the *Heike*.

Additional texts further support this theory. The following are excerpts from Jien's *Hatsugan-bun* (Petition) to build the temple Daisenpōin:

> Thus from the Hōgen era [1156–1159] until now when the nation is in turmoil, vengeful spirits fill the heavens. The spirits of fallen warriors are all over. However, no amnesty has yet been proclaimed to save the nation from their evil. Furthermore, no deliberations have yet taken place about national renewal. . . . Appeasing these evil spirits helps the state. In so doing, we must rely solely on the power of the Buddhist dharma. . . . Among these evil spirits stand out the sacred soul of ex-Emperor Sutoku [1119–1164] and the vengeful ghost of Chisokuin [Kujō Yoshitsune, 1169–1208]. . . . Therefore vengeful spirits and the spirits of fallen warriors fill the nation. By performing *ekō*, we must have them abandon their evil ways, return to normal and help them overcome their pains by providing them with *raku*. By practicing the Buddhist dharma and the laws of good government and by the Buddhas and deities invisible to them, we must turn misfortune into fortune and bring about happiness and peace. This is not only my own wish, but is has always been the desire of the Buddhas and deities to benefit mankind. [3]

Jien expresses the same thoughts in his *Gogan-bun* (Petition for Special Services at Daisenpōin):

> Since the disturbances started in the Hōgen [1156–1159] and Genryaku [1184–1185] eras, warriors were constantly on the move, causing anxiety among the people. . . . Evil ministers and rebellious warriors disturbed the nation and caused war, and many died away from home and turned into evil demons. It is like the southern barbarians aspiring to high office and eastern barbarians who lost their way on the path toward prosperity. We must protect the country by escaping from the pains of these evil times and turning these evils around. [4]

Through these petitions, Jien reiterates the need to placate by means of *ekō* and *raku* the many malevolent spirits of those who died away from home. *Raku* means to guide someone back to a normal, desirable mental and physical state. *Ekō* means that someone uses power or merit accumulated through discipline to benefit someone else and to guide that someone toward enlightenment. Both terms can be applied to the recitation of the *Heike*. Jien fails to mention the Heike by name in these petitions and concentrates instead on the spirits of ex-Emperor Sutoku and Chisokuin. He does, however, mention the Heike (also Taira) in his *Gukanshō*: "The Heishi all disappeared without leaving a trace. . . . there are numerous vengeful spirits of the Heike who, from the invisible world, act out [their vengeance] according to the laws of cause and effect."[5]

Unfortunately, little is known about the early stages in the development of the *Heike*. According to the *Tōdōyōshū*, the first *Heike* text was written under Jōichi, who lived about half a century after Jien.[6] We must therefore resort to other evidence to support the view that the *Tale* was recited to placate the Heike.

One such piece of evidence comes from a close examination of the passages about the drowning of the child emperor Antoku at the battle of Dannoura in 1185. Before throwing herself into the ocean with the emperor in her arms, the wet nurse Nii-dono (Lady Second Rank) consoles him, saying: "There is also a capital at the bottom of the sea," implying the existence of a paradise at the bottom of the ocean. In addition, according to the Enkei text version of the *Heike*, Nii-dono composed a death poem expressing the same sentiments:

Ima soshiru	Now you will know
Mimosusogawa no	There is also a capital
Nagare ni wa	At the bottom
Nami no shita ne mo	Of Mimosuso River.
Miyako ari to wa[7]	

The Mimosuso River stands for the Ise shrine (Naikū), where the ancestral deity of the imperial family is enshrined. By mentioning this, Nii-dono suggests that Antoku will control the gentle flow of the river and live in peace at the home of his ancestors. According to the Kakuichi text, in the "Rokudō no Sata" section, Kenreimon'in, Antoku's mother and the daughter of the Taira chieftain Kiyomori, dreams that Nii-dono told Antoku: "There will be for you a palace by far more splendid than the one in Kyoto, where the late emperor and all the nobles of the Heike will offer you a banquet." Having never heard about such a palace, Antoku asked: "Where is this?" Nii-dono replied: "The dragon's palace."[8] The Enkei copy reports similarly: "Thus all those who sank into the sea will no doubt become one with the dragon."[9] The Kakuichi version even suggests that Antoku was the dragon who "came down from heaven and turned into a fish at the bottom of the sea."[10]

When Emperor Antoku drowned at Dannoura, the imperial sword, one of the three symbols of imperial power, sank with him to the bottom of the sea. According to the *Gukanshō*, only the sword's empty box was picked up by a warrior.[11] This sword, according to the Enkei text, was never found, despite special prayers ordered to be held at temples and shrines, because it "was taken by the dragon and placed in his palace."[12] The Enkei text in fact suggests that the sword was taken back by its original owner, the dragon killed by the deity Susanoo. The *Genpei seisui ki* recounts the story of two divers who, when searching for the lost sword, met the dragon and saw the sword at his palace.[13]

All *Heike* texts attribute the great earthquake of 1185 to the vengeful spirits of the Heike, but by implication it also is ascribed to the dragon, which is seen as the main cause of earthquakes, floods, landslides, and other natural calamities. Jien's *Gukanshō* confirms this: "This is an extraordinary event that was caused by the earth-shaking dragon deity and people claimed that the dragon had become Taira Shokoku [Kiyomori] and that it was he who shook the earth."[14] In his chapter entitled "Why Emperor Antoku Was Drowned," Jien elaborates:

> This emperor [Antoku] became emperor because Kiyomori offered prayers at Itsukushima shrine. It was the blessing of this deity of Itsukushima in Aki Province. This Itsukushima deity is the dragon's daughter, they say. A person knowledgeable in these matters said that the deity responded to the deep respects Kiyomori had paid and turned into this emperor who, in the end, returned to the sea. I think this is true.[15]

Perhaps Kiyomori selected the Itsukushima shrine on Miyajima (island) as his ancestral shrine because the shrine was believed to be the abode of the dragon's third daughter. The Enkei text agrees with Jien's *Gukanshō* interpretation that the dragon sought revenge for having been killed by Susanoo by introducing the Taira into the imperial line.[16] Before that, only Fujiwara—and not Taira— women were eligible to produce emperors. The *Heike*'s section on the loss of the imperial sword also agrees with Jien's interpretation:

> An expert made a divination and revealed: "The great snake that Susanoo-no-mikoto slew at the upper course of Hino River in Izumo Province has deeply resented the loss of the sacred sword and, according to its eight heads and eight tails, retook it after the eightieth human reign from an eight-year old emperor and returned to the bottom of the sea."[17]

In his *Gukanshō*, Jien affirms that thanks to Kiyomori's fervent prayers, the dragon became Antoku. That is, Antoku and the dragon are one and the same. The *Heike* also makes this association quite clear. It describes Antoku just before his death as an exceedingly handsome boy wearing a *binzura* hairstyle.[18] Indeed, Ubukata Takashige and others believe that Antoku's hairstyle, usually worn by deities and buddhas, suggests an unearthly being.[19]

The dragon not only appears in texts such as *The Tale of the Heike* but also was related in many ways to their blind reciters. According to the *Mōsō yurai*, blind reciters were summoned by Empress Genmei (661–721), when the court was disturbed by unusual events.[20] In order to ward off the evil, the blind recited the *Chijin-kyō* (literally, Earth deity's sutra) accompanied on the biwa.[21] It reports that during the rites, a snake appeared and fell on the white sand of the Shishinden palace but was chased off. The *Chijin mōsō engi*, which deals with the *Chijin-kyō* in particular, mentions a large snake seeking "revenge against the court."[22] The text explains the origin of the snake not in terms of the dragon but as the snake that prevented Priest Saichō (767–822) from building the Enryakuji (temple). Such stories may be mythical rather than historical in nature, but they well represent the ideology of the blind reciters and of the court that regarded the placation of opposed forces as one of its most important functions.

By reciting the *Chijin-kyō*, the blind priests were engaging in a placatory effort of national proportions. Yanagita Kunio points out that blind priests were often summoned to perform rites in villages suffering from droughts or floods.[23] The popular legends that resulted reveal the belief that all blind people were related to the dragon, that they controlled the dragon and therefore had the power to appease it when it caused calamities. The *Chijin-kyō* refers to the dragon king and the deities who served the dragon, such as the snake and water deities. According to this text, the five directions (east, west, north, south, and center) are controlled by the dragons. One of them has controlled the wind and waves of Japan ever since it was pacified. The Heike thus must be placated because they were related to this dragon.

Finally, we can gain insight into the purpose of reciting *The Tale of the Heike* by considering where and when it was recited. The Tōdō group gathered every year on March 24, the anniversary of Emperor Antoku's death, on the bank of the Kamo River at about the level of the Shijō Street to recite the *Tale*.[24] Before beginning their recitation, the group built a pagoda with pebbles and stones, a custom still observed today in the construction of stone pagodas (five-storied pagodas, *sotoba* and other forms of stupas, *jizō* [guardian deities], and simple earth mounds) in dry riverbeds, crossroads, slopes, and passes. The erection of such pagodas probably goes back to the *nenbutsu* priests who placated evil spirits at such places. The locations of these pagodas are unmistakably liminal, to use the term that Victor Turner labeled much ritual activity. These places were believed to separate the world of the living from the world of the dead.

Pagodas built at such places served as *yorishiro*, that is, places in which priests invoked the spirits to descend so that the ritual could be performed in their presence. As such, stone pagodas are mentioned in many documents, including the *Honchō seiki* (a history covering the years 935 to 1153) and the *Meikō orai* (text of the late Heian period describing the daily ceremonies of nobles and commoners).[25] According to the *Nihongiryaku* (a history from the first emperor until 1036, of unknown authorship and date), stone pagodas were ordered to be built at all crossroads in the vicinity of Kyoto during the epidemic of 994.[26] From such sources, we learn that pagodas were built at crossroads, gates, and other important locations in order to prevent the evil spirits that cause natural calamities from entering the capital and disrupting the conduct of state affairs.

A good example of such a liminal place is Shinomiya-gawara (dry bed of the Shinomiya River) in Yamashina in northeast Kyoto. Believed to be inhabited by the Shuku or Shiku deities (potentially evil water deities), this was a place where one could link the world of the living with the world of the dead in order to placate evil spirits who seek revenge on the capital from the northeastern *kimon*, or the gate of hell. It was not far from the Seki myōjin (shrine) on Mount Ausaka (or Osaka, between Kyoto and Ōtsu), dedicated to the blind Semimaru, who was worshiped as a tutelary deity of biwa players and also as a deity that protected the access to Kyoto at the Ausaka pass. Semimaru was the fourth prince of Emperor Daigo (885–930) and is thought to have lived near the site of today's shrine.[27] Since he was the fourth prince, the area was also known as Shinomiya (Fourth Prince) and was the place where the Tōdō group performed their rites. Saneyasu, who is worshiped by the Tōdō reciters as their artistic and tutelary deity, also happened to be a fourth prince (of Emperor Ninmyō, 810–850).[28] The two fourth princes were therefore amalgamated in the tradition of the *Heike*'s reciters.

Through folk etymology, which played an important role in Japanese religion, these two fourth princes also were associated with the Ten Deities, called Shiku, of Mount Hiei's Sannō deity. In its Japanese reading, Shiku can also be read Shinomiya, hence the association. In the Shinomiya area, we also find a jizō and the temple *Jūzenji gongen*. Jūzenji refers to ten priests (*naigubu*) selected by Emperor Kōnin in 772 to hold prayers at the imperial palace and included Saichō (797) and Ennin (848). They were believed to be reincarnations of the jizō. The jizō were worshiped as deities that saved souls who erred in the unenlightened Rokudō realm, of which Shinomiya was believed to be one of the crossroads.[29]

There the blind *Heike* reciters built a stone pagoda on a biwa-shaped rock. The pagoda served as a symbol of the prince who was called on to assist the reciters in their art. At the same time, it served as *yorishiro* for the evil ghosts of the Heike that had to be appeased there to prevent their intruding into the capital and wreaking havoc. These spirits are the *mono* that the *monogatari* addressed.

There is still another dimension to the *Heike* recited at such places as Shinomiya-gawara and Shijō-kawara. These were liminal places where the blind reciters were able to identify with their heroes, where they could lend their bodies to these vengeful spirits. As is amply demonstrated in the nō theater, spirits are more effectively placated when the identities of the ghost and his storyteller blur and the reciter speaks as if it were the ghost himself telling his own story. For example, in the nō play *Sotoba Komachi*, nenbutsu prayers are offered at a stone pagoda in an effort to appease the spirits of Ono no Komachi and her unfortunate lover Shii no Shōshō. Not only do they end up exchanging their identities, and therefore their sins and pains, but they also assume the role of the nenbutsu performers as well. These are the ending lines of the play, sung by all:

> By building a pagoda out of sand
> We make a Buddha and offer flowers;
> We are entering the way of enlightenment,
> We are entering the way of enlightenment. [30]

Such shifts and mergers of various identities frequently encountered in the nō theater were no doubt placatory devices available to exorcists and placators, including the blind reciters of *The Tale of the Heike*.

From the Edo period on, Tōdō group reciters also performed their rites at Shijō-kawara, as we have seen. Shijō-kawara was also a liminal place, used for the execution of criminals, for worship of the dead such as *segaki-e* (Buddhist offerings of food to the hungry ghosts feared to cause calamities), and also as a place of purification and divination.

Socially, Shijō-kawara was a place frequented by itinerant nenbutsu priests, outcasts, artists, and low-class performers. The performance of so many different rites at the same place points to the ambivalence we observe in much Japanese art and religion. Placation also means purification, a place polluted with evil spirits that is also a place of renewal. As is clear in the myths of Izanagi's pollution resulting from his visit to the world of the dead and his subsequent purification in a nearby river, purification and world-renewing rituals are often held at the most polluted sites. This fact is consonant with Japanese religion, which places its emphasis not so much on the simple expulsion of evil but, rather, on its conversion to good. The example of Sugawara no Michizane (845–903) is a case in point. Worshiped as Tenjin, a deity of learning and agricultural fertility, Tenjin is a converted devil who, in revenge for having been unjustly exiled, inflicted calamities on the emperor and his rivals.

At Shijō-kawara, the blind reciters performed a ritual called *kyō-nagashi* or *nagare gonchō*, consisting of floating downriver portions of the Lotus sutra that they had copied themselves.[31] On March 24, they did so expressly for the appeasement of Emperor Antoku's soul. Yet there is also another dimension to this rite. Shijō-kawara is in the vicinity of the Yasaka shrine dedicated to Gozu Tennō, who was a deity of epidemics, that is, a deity who could both cause epidemics and prevent them. Gozu was believed to be a manifestation of none other than the deity Susanoo whom we have already encountered. Maybe Gozu was associated with Susanoo—a bull-headed demon of hell—because Susanoo was exiled by the heavenly deities to Izumo, an area associated with the netherworld in ancient Japanese cosmology. At Shijō-kawara, therefore, *Heike* reciters worshiped the spirits of Emperor Antoku and the Heike and also that of Susanoo, in an effort to combine the worship of these original antagonists into one ritual.[32]

Given such multidimensional values and different, that is, malevolent and benevolent, identities, Susanoo was perhaps a kind of scapegoat on whom one could heap all the evil ravaging of a community. But he was also a deity who could purify and appease evil spirits. Susanoo therefore fulfilled many of the same functions as the jizō and other such scapegoat deities one finds all over Japan. As a prominent heroine of *The Tale of the Heike*, Empress Kenreimon'in was also a kind of scapegoat who, according to the "Rokudō no Sata" section of the *Heike*, assumed all the sins committed by the Heike. The *Heike*'s reciters, too, are scapegoats as they heap on themselves the sins of the very heroes whose stories they recite. Their highly dramatic and lyrical recitations help erase the separation between reciters and their heroes.

In conclusion, a thorough study of where, when, and by whom *The Tale of the Heike* was recited is likely to reveal dimensions that hitherto have remained hidden from us. The result of such study would help us show that the heroes and the reciters of the *Heike* were related to one another and to the heterogeneous religious rituals and deities in a multidimensional, grandiose scheme through which the nation sought to rid itself of its past violence and the bad conscience it was causing. By trying to associate Antoku's death with mythical traditions concerning the creation of Japan, the *Heike*'s reciters seem to have abided by a historical determinism from which Japan seeks delivery. In the light of these facts, it is evident that the *Tale* was recited for placatory, and not exclusively artistic, purposes.

NOTES

1. Herbert Plutschow, *Chaos and Cosmos: Ritual in Early and Medieval Japanese Literature* (Leiden: Brill, 1990), pp. 220–28.

2. Donald Keene, trans., *Essays in Idleness: The Tsurezuregusa of Kenkō* (New York: Columbia University Press, 1967), p. 186 and n. 1, 3, 4, and 7. Jien was the son of the *kanpaku* (chief adviser) Fujiwara no Tadamichi. At the age of eleven, Jien entered the Enryakuji (temple) and was ordained two years later. In 1192 he became the head priest of Enryakuji. He is known as the author of the *Gukanshō* and as one of Japan's most prolific poets.

3. Added to the end of the *Daisenpōin jōjō keisei no koto*, reprinted in *Dainihon shiryō*, vol. 5, part 1 (Tokyo: Tōkyō daigaku shuppan-kai, 1981), p. 529. See also *Jien, jinbutsu sōsho*, vol. 15 (Tokyo: Yoshikawa kōbunkan, 1963), pp. 126–27. Kujō (Fujiwara) Yoshitsune was assassinated the night before he expected the emperor's visit.

4. *Dainihon shiryō*, vol. 4, part 10 (1910), pp. 259 ff. See also Fukuda Akira, "Kataribon no seiritsu," *Nihon bungaku*, June 1990, p. 58.

5. *Nihon koten bungaku taikei*, vol. 86 (Tokyo: Iwanami shoten, 1967), pp. 304–5 (hereafter abbreviated *NKBT*). See also Delmer Brown and Ichirō Ishida, trans., *The Future and the Past: A Translation and Study of the* Gukanshō, *an Interpretive History of Japan Written in 1219* (Berkeley and Los Angeles: University of California Press, 1979), p. 182.

6. The *Tōdōyōshū* is a collection of documents pertaining to the Tōdō-za group of blind *Heike* reciters, of unknown date and authorship, and containing information about the origin of the Tōdō group; legends about the founder, Prince Saneyasu; the ritual calendar; protective deities and buddhas; the origin of the various *Heike* texts; and the establishment by Kakuichi of a bureau of blind priestly reciters. It also includes instructions (and punishments) for the reciters. The *Tōdōyōshū* tried to establish the art of reciting the *Heike* as a sacred art related to emperors and the Tendai school of Buddhism. The earliest extant copy is dated 1741, copied from a 1684–1688 manuscript. It is printed in *Nihon shomin shiryō shūsei*, vol. 17 (Tokyo: Sanichi shobō, 1972), p. 231.

7. Yoshizawa Yoshinori, ed., *(Ōei shosha Enkei-bon-) Heike monogatari* (Tokyo: Hakuteisha, 1971), p. 881. The Enkei text is a 1310 version of the Kakuichi manuscript of the *Heike monogatari* related to the Kajūji family in Kyoto.

8. *Heike monogatari*, part 3, *NKBT*, vol. 33 (Tokyo: Iwanami shoten, 1960), p. 439. Kakuichi (d. 1371) established the Kakuichi *Heike* text and helped form the Tōdō-za group. He is said to have recited the *Heike* as a prayer for Kō no Moronau's health. The Kakuichi text, issuing from an earlier Yashiro text version, was the main recitative text of the Tōdō-za.

9. "Hōō Ōhara e gokō naru koto," in Yoshizawa, *Heike monogatari*, pp. 989–90.

10. *NKBT*, vol. 33, p. 337.

11. *NKBT*, vol. 86, p. 246.

12. Yoshizawa, *Heike monogatari*, pp. 889–93.

13. *(Kōtei-) Genpei seisuiki* (Tokyo: Hakubunkan, 1911), pp. 1158–61.

14. *NKBT*, vol. 86, p. 268.

15. Ibid., p. 265.

16. Yoshizawa, *Heike monogatari*, p. 893.

17. *NKBT*, vol. 33, pp. 348–49.

18. Ibid., pp. 336–37.

19. *Heike monogatari no kisō to kōzō— Mizu no kami to monogatari* (Tokyo: Kindai bungeisha, 1984), pp. 22–23.

20. Printed in *Nihon shomin seikatsu shiryō shūsei*, vol. 17, p. 247. The *Mōsō yurai* explains the origins of the blind priestly reciters, their cults and exploits. According to this text, the ancestor of the reciters is not Prince Saneyasu but a person recorded as Yukyōreishi. The oldest text, in the possession of Iwata Koyata, is dated 1301.

21. The *Chijin-kyō* is printed with its various versions in *Nihon shomin seikatsu shiryō shūsei*, vol. 17, pp. 119–29.

22. *Nihon shomin seikatsu shiryō shūsei*, vol. 17, pp. 225–27. The *Chijin Mōsō engi* is a religious text related to the Myōonji in Chikuzen Province and used by the Chikuzen and Hizen groups of reciters.

23. *(Teihon-)Yanagita Kunio shū*, vol. 8 (Tokyo: Chikuma shobō, 1962), pp. 309–11.

24. *Nihon shomin seikatsu shiryō shūsei*, vol. 17, p. 230.

25. See in particular *Honchō seiki, (shintei zōho-) kokushi taikei*, vol. 9 (Tokyo: Yoshikawa kōbunkan, 1933), p. 12.

26. *(Shintei zōho-) kokushi taikei*, vol. 11, pp. 177–79.

27. See Susan Matisoff, *Legend of Semimaru: Blind Musician of Japan* (New York: Columbia University Press, 1978), pp. 38 ff.

28. *Tōdō yōshū*, in *Nihon shomin seikatsu shiryō shūsei*, vol. 17, p. 229. Prince Saneyasu (831–872) entered the priesthood in 859. He was the younger brother of Emperor Kōkō.

29. For further discussion, see Hyōdō Hiromi, *Katarimono josetsu: Heike-gatari no hassei to hyō gen* (Tokyo: Yūseidō, 1985), pp. 119 ff.

30. *Yōkyoku taikan*, vol. 3 (Tokyo: Meiji shoin, 1931), p. 1730. The pagoda (*sotoba*) is referred to earlier in the play as a prayer allowing one to leave the Three Evil Paths.

31. Hiromi, *Katarimono josetsu*, pp. 122 ff.

32. For more discussion, see Fukuda Akira, "Shukujin-gatari no keifu," *Ritsumeikan bungaku*, nos. 472, 473, and 474 (October, November, and December 1984): 22 ff; and Neil McMullin, "On Placating the Gods and Pacifying the Populace: The Case of the Gion *Goryō* Cult," *History of Religions* 27 (February 1988): 270–93.

6

*The Power of Fudō Myōō: Ichikawa Danjūrō and His Soga Gorō
Character in the Kabuki Play* Tsuwamono kongen Soga

◉

LAURENCE KOMINZ

By the late Edo period, Soga Gorō had become a religious icon in Edo. He was
one of the most frequently depicted characters on large *ema* donated to temples
and shrines, and he was featured on woodblock prints that were thought to have
religious power. The shogun Minamoto Yoritomo had ordered the Soga brothers enshrined as Shinto gods shortly after they were killed in 1193, but the
emergence of Soga Gorō as an urban cult hero and religious symbol in the 1700s
was the direct result of frequent portrayals on the kabuki stage by actors of the
Ichikawa Danjūrō line.

The transformation of Soga Gorō from a local, rural deity and hero of historical tales into a religious icon widely recognized throughout Edo began in
1697 with the performance of *Tsuwamono kongen Soga* (The Genesis of the Soga
Warrior), a smash-hit kabuki play coauthored by[1] and starring the first Ichikawa
Danjūrō (1660–1704). In this play Danjūrō both borrowed from and satirized
esoteric Buddhist ritual to invest Soga Gorō with the power of Fudō Myōō, the
deity he himself revered above all others at this stage of his life. Fudō Myōō is
an incarnation of the cosmic Buddha, fanged and fierce of aspect. A direct
Gorō–Fudō relationship is nowhere present in any version of the narrative tale
of the Soga vendetta, but Danjūrō's new Soga Gorō, given power and strength

by Fudō, became the enduring incarnation of the character in Edo for the remainder of the Tokugawa period.

We are fortunate that a text for *Tsuwamono kongen Soga* is still extant—it is the second oldest surviving play text by Danjūrō I. It is in the form of an *e-iri kyogen bon*, an illustrated book, more like the novelization of a screenplay than an actual theater script. In the case of the *Tsuwamono kongen Soga* e-iri kyogen bon, however, many of the actors' most important lines are recorded as dialogue, not converted into narrative as is typical of the genre. *Tsuwamono kongen Soga* reads like a play in a way that many e-iri kyogen bon texts do not. The e-iri kyogen bon text and accompanying pictures help us envision what took place on stage in 1697 that so moved and excited Danjūrō's audiences.

In many ways *Tsuwamono kongen Soga* marks new beginnings in the development of Edo kabuki. Whereas medieval Japanese drama and early kabuki and *jōruri* had often depicted deities on stage, their portrayal had remained within the contexts of received religious tradition and ritual, repeating the stories told by priests and borrowing from books of mythology and religious lore. Danjūrō exercised a new freedom with his deities, taking them out of the temple and away from their traditional settings, and bringing them into the lives of his heroes.[2] In doing this he followed his own religious inclinations, for he imagined the deities as ever present. When he felt the need for divine assistance, he often went up on the roof of the kabuki theater or of his own home and addressed his prayers to the open sky.[3]

The man who created *Tsuwamono kongen Soga*, the first Ichikawa Danjūrō, left enough autobiographical evidence to give us a picture of his personality. His own diary shows him as ambitious, hard working, short tempered, sometimes philosophical, and often arrogant. He recorded his prayers and religious vows and was a devout believer in and supplicant to various Buddhist and Shinto deities. On the eighth day of the third month of 1690, for example, Danjūrō made the following pledges:

- to dedicate himself to supporting his parents and caring for his wife and children.
- to give up drinking alcohol as long as his parents remained alive.
- to give up extramarital sex, with both men and women, for three years.
- to strive for three years to combat all forms of immorality by means of ritual activities performed at home, including regular morning ablutions, special religious devotions three days each month, and special rites to the deities of the sun, moon, and stars on the twenty-eighth of every month.

- for three years to make regular pilgrimages to the Hall of the Two Saints at Kan'eiji in Ueno and to conduct services on sacred days to Aizen Myōō.
- for three years to serve Fudō Myōō by performing special rites and offering a wooden sword on the twenty-eighth day of each month, and making yearly pilgrimages to Narita Shinshōji, either in person or by means of a designated representative.[4]

In return for these acts of devotion and abstinence, Danjūrō asked the various deities to protect his family and to make the name Danjūrō known throughout the land.[5]

From 1690 to 1692 he was true to these vows, and his career was crowned with success. He wrote:

> Look at myself. Among all the arts, there is not one I have mastered, not one I am better at than anyone else. I am not naturally skilled in martial arts, nor am I exceedingly clever. It is Sanbōkōjin, Ganzan Daishi, Dainichi, Aizen Myōō, Fudō Myōō, and Nitten who shine on me, and because the deities protect me, I am called "unrivaled in Japan," "the finest actor," "the founder of a new temple of kabuki in the modern age." My name is revered, but this is not the work of a mere mortal.[6]

The three years designated in Danjūrō's vows came to an end. He began experiencing difficulties in his career—poorly received plays and poor reviews in the *hyōbanki* (actor rating books). In late 1693 no theater in Edo would employ him. At this time, by his own confession, he was involved in romantic liaisons with at least three actors. Looking back on this period of his life, he observed:

> As they say, truly the room of religion is as wide as the ocean, but if your heart leads you astray, there is nowhere to go. If my behavior continued to surge about like waves, it was likely I would come to grief later on. If your heart strays, even just a little, it is a simple thing for huge mountains to crumble away instantly. If you let your will weaken, all can turn to dust. And in fact, after I relaxed my attitude, all sorts of problems arose.[7]

So once again, in 1693, Danjūrō drew up a long list of vows, pledging abstinence from immoral conduct and service to many deities. This time he requested the deities to grant him specific rewards in return for his devotion: that he become the master of a fine house and be able to pass his name on to his oldest son, Kuzō; that he be ranked among the top actors of all time in the hyōbanki; that he be acclaimed a major actor during his upcoming season in Kyoto, though he recognized this would be difficult for an actor of martial leads in Kansai; that he one day become one of the great *zamoto* (kabuki producers) of all time; and that he be considered unique in the kabuki world.[8]

The following hyōbanki entry shows that as early as age twenty-eight (1688), critics recognized Danjūrō as a cut above the average Edo kabuki actor:

> This guy called Ichikawa is the number one sexy lover boy unparalleled in three thousand worlds. He looks great when he comes swaggering on stage. His lines move all under Heaven. It is unlikely that there will ever again be a performer in Japan or abroad who will go as far as he will. Whether he does realistic roles, villains, or anything else, he always does it well. He excels most remarkably in learning, and his fame as a playwright is widespread. He is the founder of flamboyant acting in this age, and there is no actor his equal in Edo. The radiance of his glory shines down from Heaven, and he is likely to become the model for actors down through the ages.[9]

It was a prophetic description. The hyōbanki entry praises Danjūrō's learning and skill as a playwright, and his surviving plays testify to the breadth of his education, but nowhere in his autobiographical writing do we find evidence that he revered knowledge for its own sake. Rather, for Danjūrō, knowledge, like morality, religious devotion, and artistic training, served a utilitarian purpose. When properly exercised, all these skills and virtues ensured success on the stage, which in turn meant the acquisition of wealth and stature. Stature gave one the ability to control one's career and achieve even greater personal success, and wealth gave one the ability to discharge filial and parental obligations. Danjūrō's writings make it clear that for him, religious worship, filial piety, moral conduct in his off-stage life, and work on the stage were part of a holistic concept of life and fate.

Given his religious devotion, it is not surprising that Danjūrō turned to the iconography and ritual of esoteric Buddhism to provide inspiration and physical models for his *aragoto* (wild acting style) art. Gunji Masakatsu, Hattori Yukio, Suwa Haruo, and others have examined in detail Danjūrō's incorporation into kabuki of the costumes, poses, and *chikara suji* (power sinews) of fierce guardian deity statues, the choreography of *yamabushi aramai* (the wild dances of mountain ascetics), the loud, droning chants of priests, and other aspects of esoteric iconography and ritual.[10] Over the course of his career, Danjūrō enacted numerous esoteric deities on stage, Fudō more often than any other. Unfortunately, he never wrote about what portraying deities meant to him, but he had this to say about his acting: "I don't know about other actors, but for me, when I go on stage, I don't feel my body to be my own. It transfers itself to the character and is consumed by the performance."[11] This would suggest that when Danjūrō played deities, he felt in some way fused with the divine spirit. Records of audience response to his plays indicate that many spectators felt this to be the case; they threw coins and other offerings onto the stage (some days totaling up to ten *kanmon*) and directed their own personal prayers to Fudō. Descriptions of the *Tsuwamono kongen Soga* production are the first record of this kind of response to a deity presented on the kabuki stage.

For Danjūrō, art, family life, professional life, and religious life were fused in the process of actualizing *Tsuwamono kongen Soga*, from conception, to casting, to performance, to postperformance ritual. The play portrayed the power and virtue of a deity, but it also had a religious context in the actor's personal life. Danjūrō considered the play an offering of thanks to Fudō for granting him a son, Kuzō, born in 1688 and destined to become Danjūrō II. Called "Fudō's gift" by his father, Kuzō made his stage debut in *Tsuwamono kongen Soga* as Fudō, appearing first in the guise of a *yamabushi* priest. Celebrating Fudō on stage was also a form of divine insurance to Danjūrō, making it likely that Fudō would protect the young Kuzō during his first crucial performance.[12] Danjūrō's expressions of thanks to Fudō on the occasion of the play extended to the material wealth he gave to Fudō's temple in Narita: when the play closed, Danjūrō led a pilgrimage of worshipers to his patron temple, the Shinshōji in Narita City, some forty-five miles northeast of Edo. There he gave generous gifts in thanks for his theatrical success.[13]

Even more than his depiction of the story of Soga Gorō and Fudō in the play, Danjūrō the man stood as living testimony to the power and efficacy of Fudō. For the audience, *Tsuwamono kongen Soga* was as much about Danjūrō and his family as it was about the story presented on stage. By 1697 Danjūrō's wealth, his personality, and his religious beliefs were public knowledge. He was a man who had made vows to several deities (Fudō included), who had lived up to those vows, and who had been rewarded for this with great wealth. For many years he had prayed to Fudō for a son, and finally this wish had been granted. Theatergoers, in fact most Edo townsmen, were as pragmatic in their religion as Danjūrō himself was. It was an age of *hayarigami*,[14] the rapid rise and fall of popular cults and worshipers' frequent changing of preferred deities. Edo townsmen worshiped many deities, but they remained with the gods that delivered the goods. They saw that Fudō had come through for one famous and wealthy man, and this was important evidence about Fudō's reliability. Both the plot of the play and Danjūrō's life story attested to the efficacy of Fudō worship:

a powerful twofold advocacy by a famous contemporary man and by a historical hero in a fictional story.

Religious conviction and gratitude to Fudō inspired Danjūrō's concept for the play, but it required intellectual knowledge to create it. Danjūrō relied primarily on *kojōruri* (pre-Chikamatsu puppet play) texts and on two medieval sources,[15] the *rufubon* (vulgate, or popular) version of *Soga monogatari* (Tale of the Soga Brothers) and Miyamasu's nō play, *Chōbuku Soga*. From the kojōruri texts and the *Soga monogatari*, Danjūrō took the basic plot of the Soga story. *Chōbuku Soga* is the first work of literature in which Gorō relies on Fudō worship, and in Danjūrō's play, Fudō appears at exactly the same point in the story as in the nō play—right after the *taimen*, Gorō's first meeting with Kudō Suketsune.[16]

By 1697 Danjūrō had mastered the crafts of acting in and writing for aragoto kabuki. He knew that traditional sources needed considerable reworking in order to become hits on the kabuki stage. We have discovered from his writings that Danjūrō was striving not just to survive in the competitive world of Genroku kabuki but also to become the most popular and highest-paid actor in Edo. In order to do so, he wrote, he needed to be in one or two major hit plays each year.[17]

One basic change in the traditional Soga story that Danjūrō made for *Tsuwamono kongen Soga* was to transform the entirely verbal conflict of the traditional taimen scene into a physical encounter on the kabuki stage. In the rufubon, and in nō and kojōruri plays, Gorō wishes to attack Kudō at Hakone temple, but he is too intimidated by Kudō and, in the end, too prudent to convert his desire into action. Furthermore, in the traditional story, Gorō is still a temple acolyte during his first encounter with Kudō. For priests, personal vendettas and acts of violence are sins, not heroic deeds. Danjūrō clears up Gorō's moral ambiguity in the taimen scene by having him leave priestly life and take his adult, samurai name before he meets Kudō, at a point much earlier than in any previous version of the Soga story. In *Tsuwamono kongen Soga*, Gorō is thus completely free to act against his enemy when the taimen scene occurs, and he does in fact attack Kudō twice. Both times, the mature, powerful Kudō pins the young Gorō to the floor. Gorō's superhuman strength at the end of the act is all the more striking for the pathetic "bird wing" blows he strikes against Kudō during the taimen scene.

In *Tsuwamono kongen Soga*, Danjūrō reversed the child and adult roles as he found them in *Chōbuku Soga*. In the nō play, a child actor (*kokata*) plays Gorō (who is still known by his childhood name of Hakoō) and the *shite* (main actor) plays Kudō Suketsune in the first part of the play and Fudō in the second part. Fudō, as played by the shite, is ferocious and powerful. Fudō appears out of the flame of the *goma* altar, and after a wild dance, he takes out his straight sword and strikes off the head of an effigy of Kudō Suketsune, thus promising Gorō eventual success in his vendetta. The ceremony consoles young Gorō, who is bitterly disappointed that he was unable to challenge Kudō during their recent meeting. Fudō's assistance to Gorō in the nō play is symbolic and moral, but in *Tsuwamono kongen Soga* it is eminently practical. Fudō transforms Gorō into a physically powerful warrior in a way that the audience can witness before its very eyes, and then Fudō prevents Gorō from getting hurt or wasting his strength by fighting a man who is in fact his ally.

The ritual and symbolic action of Fudō in the nō and his direct assistance to Gorō in the kabuki play present an interesting contrast between medieval and urban Edo worshipers' expectations of the same deity. In the kabuki play, Fudō's supernatural powers were demonstrated in his magical disappearance, presumably in the choreography of his dance (of course, there is no way to be sure), in the ease with which he controls two violent and powerful men, and, most of all, in Gorō's transformation.

In act 2 the audience must have particularly enjoyed watching Gorō perform his comically exaggerated "wild training" exercises and witnessing his physical transformation through a series of quick changes in costume and makeup done when Danjūrō ran off stage. Asahina, the other leading strongman of the Kamakura period, appears much earlier in the kabuki play than he does in previous versions of the Soga story. The reason is simple—Gorō's newly earned physical strength is best demonstrated on stage by a fight with the man Gorō defeats later on in traditional versions of the story, in the *kusazuribiki* tug-of-war.

The structure of this fight scene is a gradation of increasingly impressive acts of physical prowess, and it showcased the acting styles used for different heroic character types. The scene begins with four samurai who struggle with but cannot control a wild horse. Next, Asahina, a comic hero, appears. He picks up the horse and throws it in the sacred river. Finally Gorō enters and challenges Asahina to fight. Their fight is stopped by Fudō (see illustration 6.2 accompanying the text).

Although it is clear that Danjūrō fashioned act 2 to highlight his own talents, if the audience's response to child actors in current kabuki is any indication, then it is easy to imagine that nine-year-old Kuzō stole the scene when he was on stage. In fact, performance records show that the audience loved the scene when Kuzō, as Fudō, emerged from a rock cave, and they also loved the verbal interchanges and glaring contests (*nirami ai*) between father and son.[18] Kuzō's father gave the boy plenty of opportunity to demonstrate his talent and charm: a *michiyuki* dance, an ad-libbed dialogue with the Soga family retainer Dōsaburō, and a Fudō dance at the climax of the act. Even though Kuzō was given few lines of text in the e-iri kyogen bon, this does not mean that his was a bit part. Illustrations in e-iri kyogen bon depict the most important and popular scenes and characters, so the fact Kuzō is featured twice in illustrations accompanying the text (see illustrations 6.1 and 6.2) is strong evidence of his importance to the scene.

Tsuwamono kongen Soga was one of the biggest hits of Danjūrō's career. Important scenes and images from the play were repeated over and over again on the kabuki stage. Parody and imitation are, of course, strong indicators of influence and popularity, and in 1703 the Edo *wagoto* (gentle acting style) star Nakamura Shichisaburō took the lead role in *Keisei Asama Soga*, a play that included several parodic scenes inspired by *Tsuwamono kongen Soga*. In one scene from *Keisei Asama Soga*, for example, in a plot to sidetrack the Soga brothers' vendetta, a villain impersonates Fudō and "appears" with instructions to Gorō that he should not attack Kudō Suketsune. This scene from *Keisei Asama Soga* stands as evidence that just a few years after *Tsuwamono kongen Soga*, the association of Soga Gorō and Fudō had taken root in Edo kabuki.

Tsuwamono kongen Soga was not just a play about Soga Gorō and Fudō. It was a public statement of faith in and gratitude to a deity, by a man of wealth and fame. In its presentation of Kuzō, the play was a celebration of the Ichikawa family's bright future.[19] When audience members watched Kuzō perform, they were conscious of multiple layers of meaning in what went on stage. They enjoyed seeing the activities of a yamabushi and of Fudō as characters in a play, and many of them regarded the on-stage Fudō as invested with divine power. Audience members also watched and evaluated a new child performer. They must have compared Kuzō with his father and with other young actors, wondering if this boy would become Edo's next big star. Kuzō's ad-libbed lines more likely than not contained an admixture of lines in character with expressions of gratitude to his father, his teachers, and his audience.[20]

One of the attributes of kabuki that has kept it alive, and has kept audiences coming in large numbers, is the close connection its audiences feel to its stars. This connection is weaker today than it was in the Edo period, but it is still achieved to some degree through the relative ease of access to dressing rooms,[21] through a few activities, such as *nihon buyo* (classical dance), that are shared by actors and certain members of the audience, and through public, on-stage celebrations of family ties—name-taking rituals (*shumei*) and direct addresses to the audience (*kōjō*) during which actors express gratitude to the audience in the same respectful terms they use when addressing teachers and family elders.

With *Tsuwamono kongen Soga*, Danjūrō I took a major step in the creation of a very loyal group of fans and patrons, people who would continue to support his descendants. He did this by inviting audience members to share in his family happiness and family religion, by in effect extending his family group, the most basic in-group in Japanese society, to include audience members and professional associates.

Danjūrō I was murdered on the nineteenth day of the second month of 1704 by fellow *tachiyaku* (lead role) actor Ikushima Hanroku at the Ichimura theater. Hanroku was apprehended the same day and died some months later during interrogation. He was pronounced guilty posthumously, but the details of the crime and his motives remain a mystery. Numerous contradictory accounts survive from around the time of the murder. One description of the crime says that Hanroku hid in the folds of the stage curtain and stabbed Danjūrō with a metal stage sword when Danjūrō came off stage. For the previous scene, Danjūrō had been armed only with a wooden sword.[22] The juiciest contemporary explanation of Hanroku's motive runs as follows: Hanroku's son Zenjirō was taking acting lessons from Danjūrō at the time, and Danjūrō criticized Hanroku for excessive debauchery with young actors in front of Zenjirō and the other young actors. This public criticism so angered Hanroku that he murdered Danjūrō.[23]

No matter the motive for the crime, when Danjūrō died in 1704, it was as if thousands of Edoites had lost a family elder. The last hyōbanki to evaluate Danjūrō was *Daijin mitsu sakazuki*, probably by Ejima Kiseki, and the author concludes as follows: "For a long time I have known that all men must take this road, but for this to happen now. . . . The deities we rely on should be impervious to harm. From now on, whenever I pray to the Narita Fudō, it will be him that I see."[24] In the same hyōbanki, the characters for Ikushima Hanroku were cut from the woodblock, leaving as a last statement only his mediocre rating, eighteenth out of twenty-two Edo tachiyaku.[25] It is significant that the author of this hyōbanki recognizes the close connection between Danjūrō and Fudō and suggests that he is a believer in Fudō himself.

Kuzō became Danjūrō II a half year after his father's death, and he and each of his successors portrayed Fudō on the kabuki stage. Their activities on and off stage brought increasing prosperity to Shinshōji in Narita. When Danjūrō II bought a summer villa in Meguro, he located it near several temples on a Fudō pilgrimage route, and he became a patron of another Fudō temple, Myōōin, in Meguro.[26] Danjūrō II had made his debut as Fudō, but the role he played more often than any other during his fifty-seven-year career was that of Soga Gorō. The version of Soga Gorō that he created for the play *Ya no ne* became the most frequently depicted in ema and ukiyo-e prints. In creating this version of Gorō, Danjūrō II borrowed many attributes of Fudō imagery, and *Ya no ne* Gorō eventually took his place among Edo's religious icons.[27] Varied sources show that by the turn of the nineteenth century, numerous fans and professional associates of Danjūrō V and Danjūrō VII had become worshipers of Fudō[28] and that Fudō worship had become one of Edo's most popular cults.

The current Danjūrō XII is reviving this tradition. He is a devout believer in Fudō and an active supporter of Shinshōji. He has organized four kabuki plays to coincide with and support major memorial celebrations at Shinshōji.[29] Before his shumei ceremony in 1986, he performed one week of ritual austerities in Narita and led two chartered Skyliner train loads of fans from Tokyo to worship at the temple. At the Kabuki-za in August 1992, with the support of Shinshōji, he produced and starred in a revival of Danjūrō I's last Fudō play, *Naritasan funjin Fudō*. The play commemorated the 850th anniversary of the death of the Shingon saint Daigyō Daishi and was marked by the practice of two ritual customs that began with *Tsuwamono kongen Soga*—throwing coins on stage during the Fudō scene as an act of worship and Danjūrō's leading fans and worshipers on pilgrimage to Narita. In May 1993, Danjūrō played Soga Gorō in *Uiro uri* (The Medicine Peddlar) at Tokyo's Kabuki-za, in a performance that commemorated the 800th anniversary of Gorō's death. The stage was decorated with amulets from the Shinshō temple in Narita, reaffirming the connection between Soga Gorō and Fudō.

A translation follows of the most dramatic and popular section of the play *Tsuwamono kongen Soga*: Gorō's encounter with his blood enemy; his transformation, through Fudō's power, into a superhuman strong man; and the appearance of Fudō himself.

Tsuwamono kongen Soga *(The Genesis of the Soga Warrior): Translation of part of act 2*[30]

Ichikawa Danjūrō and Nakamura Akashi Seizaburō

Characters:

Hōjō Tokimasa

The Hakone temple abbot

Soga Gorō Tokimune

Kudō Suketsune

Ōmi and Yawata (Kudō's retainers)

Dōsaburō (a Soga family retainer)

Tsūrikibō, a yamabushi (Fudō in disguise)

Asahina

Monks

Four warriors

Summary of the action of act 2 preceding the translated portion: Act 2 opens with the Soga retainers Ōnio and Dōsaburō disguised as blind men in order to approach Kudō Suketsune surreptitiously. When they confront Kudō, he denies all responsibility for the death of the Soga brothers' father. Hōjō Tokimasa visits Hakone temple and secretly performs a genbuku (coming of age) ceremony for the boy Hakoō, who is given the adult name Soga Gorō Tokimune. The ceremony changes the child's status from temple acolyte to adult samurai. The abbot, thinking that Hakoō has disappeared, calls for a general search. Tokimasa tells the abbot what he has done and calls for Gorō, who appears dressed in fine samurai clothes.

TOKIMASA: Look at him, doesn't he look like a fine man? His new name is Gorō Tokimune.[31]

ABBOT: So, you've changed your name from Hakoō to Gorō, have you? I'm upset. Why did you keep your plans secret from me? You and I were so very close. Now who will be my closest companion? Well, what is done is done. Now you must work hard to excel at the martial arts.

TOKIMASA: Gorō has done this because he has a lofty goal—to kill his blood enemy.

ABBOT: Yes, I know about it.

GORŌ: I am grateful for your understanding.

NARRATOR: As Gorō is joyfully expressing his thanks to the abbot for his support, the announcement is made that Kudō Suketsune has arrived at the temple. When Gorō hears the news that his blood enemy has arrived, he begins to shake.

TOKIMASA: Why are you shaking?

GORŌ: I'm so happy that I'll have the chance to attack my blood enemy, I'm shaking all over.

ABBOT: Someone tie up Suketsune and bring him in here!

NARRATOR: The abbot begins to strip for action and a great commotion begins, but Hōjō Tokimasa calms everyone down. Soon Suketsune enters.

TOKIMASA: Is it true that you have come to Hakone as the shogun's envoy? I too have come on pilgrimage to Hakone temple.

SUKETSUNE: My dear abbot, you should be pleased. Because of my frequent petitions to the shogun, he has decreed that your construction projects are to proceed as scheduled. You should be pleased.

NARRATOR: Outside the room, Gorō grips the lattice door, quivering in agitation.

SUKETSUNE: What's that?

ABBOT: That? It's the mice. That's how out of control they've gotten.

SUKETSUNE: Is that right? I think I'll have a look for myself.

NARRATOR: At this moment Gorō enters, bringing tea for the guests. He glares at
              Suketsune as he serves him tea, then withdraws to his seat.

SUKETSUNE: I have heard that Kawazu Saburō's second son, Hakoō, is studying at
              this temple. Is Hakoō here?

ABBOT: Indeed he is. This is Hakoō.

SUKETSUNE: So, you're Hakoō. I am Kudō Saemon Suketsune. If you have any
              request of me, please let me know.

GORŌ: Thank you very much.

TOKIMASA: I had the pleasure of putting his first samurai cap on him in his com-
              ing-of-age ceremony. His name is now Gorō Tokimune.

SUKETSUNE: Is that right? I am a little put out that you didn't consult with me at
              all on the matter. But that's all right. After all, today is my first meet-
              ing with him.

NARRATOR: Suketsune gives Gorō a short sword to commemorate his coming of
              age. Gorō receives the dagger, thanking Suketsune politely. Then he
              draws it and tries to stab Suketsune. Suketsune seizes Gorō's hand
              and holds it tight.

SUKETSUNE: What's the matter with you? I don't understand. You are very
              upset . . . do you have something against me?

TOKIMASA
AND ABBOT: Please let the child go.

NARRATOR: Kudō acquiesces.

SUKETSUNE: That's one detestable kid. He gives me a stomachache. Let's get out
              of here.

ŌMI AND
YAWATA: By all means, yes, let's leave.

ABBOT: Wait, let me give you a shoulder rub to relax you.

GORŌ: Wait, let me twist your arm off at the shoulder!

NARRATOR: Gorō hits Suketsune on the shoulder. *(Gorō hits Suketsune with a flurry
              of light blows.)*

ABBOT: He said he'd hit Suketsune on the shoulder hard, but look at him try-
              ing to do it.

TOKIMASA: Arms just like a bird's wings. None are as intimate as parent and child
              birds. Look under the eaves. There a swallow has built its nest and is
              raising its children. It reminds me of the story of the hawk and the
              dove. Long ago, during the reign of Empress Kōken, in the northern
              land of Dewa, there was a certain samurai commander who had a
              superb hawk.[32] The hawk gave birth to five fledglings. The empress
              heard about it and ordered that a fine fledgling be given to her. The
              mother hawk grieved for the loss of her child, and so she flew off,

heading for the capital. She landed on the Akoya pine[33] to rest her
wings, but an evil eagle spied her there, attacked her, and ate her up.
The news of her death reached the capital and the fledgling went to
Hachiman shrine to pray for revenge. In response to its prayers, a
dove appeared and joined it, flying with it to the north country.[34]
Once, the fledgling spotted the eagle resting in a treetop. The fledgling wanted to attack, but because the sacred dove wasn't with it at
the time, it held back.

NARRATOR: Gorō had seen before his eyes a chance to fulfill his deepest desire,
and that is why he attacked Suketsune. But he understood that
Tokimasa was telling him not to attack without the aid of his brother,
Jūrō. How frustrated he must feel. He runs over to Suketsune and
grabs him. Suketsune pins the boy to the floor.

SUKETSUNE: You're an impertinent lout. Do you think a stripling like you has a
chance against me? Lord Hōjō is a bad man, and I especially detest his
story about the hawk and the dove. I know he told you not to attack
me unless Jūrō is with you, but that story will just get you in a lot
of trouble.

NARRATOR: With a final word of warning . . .

SUKETSUNE: Don't forget what I've told you!

NARRATOR: Suketsune leaves for Kamakura. Gorō is so angry he tries to run out
after Suketsune, but the abbot and Tokimasa hold him back. Gorō is
so upset and frustrated that he collapses in tears and falls asleep in the
middle of his prayers to the Buddha.[35] Presently Tokimasa and the
abbot wake Gorō.

TOKIMASA
AND ABBOT: We understand how you feel. You should join us in some saké and try
to calm down.

NARRATOR: When they look at Gorō, they see that his face has mysteriously
changed color. Gorō grabs the abbot and begins to slap him on
the face.

TOKIMASA: That's just the way you hit Suketsune. Gorō; there's something strange
about you. Your face is turning red. Do you have any idea why?

GORŌ: I was so upset that in my heart of hearts I prayed to Fudō. I asked him
to grant me bravery and strength, to make me a demon or a god so I
can avenge my father. At first I thought my face was changing color
because of the smoke from the holy fire, but if it's really turning red,
it means my prayers are being answered. This is wonderful!

NARRATOR: Gorō runs out of the temple and down a mountain path. The abbot
and Dōsaburō shout:

ABBOT AND

DŌSABURŌ: Did you hear him? Did you see how red his face was?

NARRATOR: Now they see Gorō coming back, and what an incredible sight he is. A ferocious warrior, charging up the steps.

(Danjūrō accompanies the following narration with an aragoto dance.) (For this scene, see illustration 6.1.)

NARRATOR: His wild training is frightening to behold. The first seven days he rips apart seven new hoes. The second seven days he uproots large bamboo. *(There is a danced interlude featuring the abbot doing a comic routine and Gorō ripping up bamboo by the roots.)* The third seven days he smashes stupas. The abbot and Dōsaburō are terrified and call everyone to take refuge inside the temple. Presently the priest Tsūrikibō enters. *(Ichikawa Kuzō, Danjūrō's son, enters and does a michiyuki dance.)*

YAMABUSHI: I come begging alms.

NARRATOR: Dōsaburō ventures out to greet him.

DŌSABURŌ: Where do you come from, little priest?

(The yamabushi and Dōsaburō engage in an ad-libbed comic dialogue.)

NARRATOR: Gorō spies them.

GORŌ: You look like a clever priest. How would you like me to grab you and kill you?

NARRATOR: As he speaks these words, the yamabushi suddenly disappears.

DŌSABURŌ: That was witchcraft! We've got to do something! We've got to stop the evil spirit!

NARRATOR: He rushes off to the Sagami River to perform daylight lustration rituals. *(At the river, four warriors do a dance depicting a fight over a horse.)* Asahina enters, leading a horse named Black Fan K'uai[36] to the river, where it stops to drink. *(There is jōruri accompaniment from this point to the end of the act.)* Gorō now enters.

GORŌ: You upstart lout! How dare you pollute the lustration site! I'll take you on and give you a big surprise.

NARRATOR: Gorō splashes into the river, panicking Black Fan K'uai.

ASAHINA: Who are you? You look like a kid. Where do you come from?

GORŌ: I come from the land of Brahma!

ASAHINA: You look like a tough kid. Okay, let's fight!

Illustration 6.1.   On the right Soga Gorō (Ichikawa Danjūrō) uproots living bamboo, the second task of his three-part "wild ritual training" (aragyō). Smashing hoes was the first task, and fragments can be seen in the lower right corner of the picture, along with a stupa that is to be broken as Gorō's last task. On the left, the little yamabushi Tsūrikibō (played by Danjūrō's son, Kuzō) appears before Dōsaburō (Ichikawa Dannojō) and the Hakone abbot (Saikoku Heisuke). The family crest in the pattern of three concentric squares indicates members of the Ichikawa family or close disciples of Danjūrō. The illustration has been attributed to Torii Kiyonobu and Torii Kiyomasu. (Published by Kaifuya in 1697.) (COURTESY OF TŌKYŌ GEIJITSU DAIGAKU.)

NARRATOR: They fight furiously, back and forth. Then suddenly the little yama-bushi reappears.

YAMABUSHI: Both of you! Stop fighting and listen to me! In answer to Gorō's prayers to Fudō, from now until the time he meets his blood enemy, Gorō shall be granted strength greater than the breakers on the shore. But Soga and Miura are from the same family and must not fight. I am, in fact, Fudō Myōō. Behold my true appearance! *(Ichikawa Kuzō does a Fudō dance.) (For this scene, see illustration 6.2.)*

NARRATOR: Both men express profuse thanks. They bow in worship to this mani-festation of Fudō that has appeared before them in real life. Stouthearted and full of joy, each returns to his home; Gorō to Soga, and Asahina to Kamakura.

(End of act 2)

Illustration 6.2.   The little yamabushi reappears in his true form, as the deity Fudō (played by Danjūrō's son, Kuzō), to break up the fight between the two strongest men in Japan, Kobayashi no Asahina (Nakamura Denkurō) and Soga Gorō (Ichikawa Danjūrō). The illustration has been attributed to Torii Kiyonobu and Torii Kiyomasu. (Published by Kaifuya in 1697.) (Courtesy of Tōkyō Geijitsu Daigaku.)

NOTES

1. In Ihara Toshirō, *Kabuki nenpyō*, vol. 1 (Tokyo: Iwanami shoten, 1956), p. 205. Ichikawa Danjūrō is listed as the coauthor of the play. The other author cited is Akashi Seizaburō. In his "Ganmon," in an entry from Genroku 8 (1695), Danjūrō mentions that Akashi Seizaburō is a playwright for the Nakamura-za. See Ichikawa Danjūrō I, "Ganso Danjūrō no zangeroku," in Ihara Seiseien, ed., *Danjūrō no shibai* (Tokyo: Waseda daigaku shuppanbu, 1934), p. 135. *Tsuwamono kongen Soga* was a Nakamura-za production in 1697. In his study of Ichikawa Danjūrō as a playwright, Suwa Haruo states that Danjūrō is the primary playwright in plays in which he is cited as a coauthor. Suwa Haruo, *Genroku kabuki no kenkyū* (Tokyo: Kasama shoin, 1967), p. 113.

2. In this, Danjūrō was the leader of a general trend that Gunji Masakatsu identified in Genroku-period kabuki plays about gods and buddhas. See Gunji Masakatsu, *Kabuki no hassō* (Tokyo: Nishizawa shoten, 1978), pp. 182–84.

3. Danjūrō I, "Ganso Danjūrō no zangeroku," pp. 129, 134.

4. Ibid., pp. 113–14.

5. Ibid., p. 114.

6. Ibid., p. 117.

7. Ibid., p. 126.

8. Ibid., p. 129.

9. "Yarō Yakusha Fūryū Kagami," in Kabuki hyōbanki kenkyūkai, eds., *Kabuki hyōbanki shūsei*, vol. 1 (Tokyo: Iwanami shoten, 1972), pp. 277–78.

10. Four of the numerous works dealing with the religious origins of *aragoto* acting are Gunji Masakatsu, *Kabuki yōshiki to denju* (Tokyo: Gakugei shorin, 1969); Hattori Yukio, "Danjūrō no aragoto to shōmin shinkō," in Hattori Yukio, *Ichikawa Danjūrō* (Tokyo: Shochiku, 1984); Hattori Yukio, *Edo kabuki ron* (Tokyo: Hosei daigaku shuppankyoku, 1980); Misumi Haruo, "Minzokugaku yori mita aragoto no bijutsu," *Kabuki*, January 1971.

11. Danjūrō I, "Ganso Danjūrō no zangeroku," p. 147.

12. Ihara Toshirō, *Kabuki nenpyō*, p. 207.

13. Ibid., p. 206. After the play closed, Danjūrō gave to Shinshōji a holy mirror, a curtain, and five hundred *mon* in cash. The records are not clear about what became of the money and gifts offered by spectators to Fudō during the run.

14. See Miyata Noboru, *Kinsei no hayarigami: Nihonjin no kōdō to shisō*, vol. 17 (Tokyo: Hyōronsha, 1975), for a study of the *hayarigami* phenomenon.

15. It is hard to know how much Danjūrō took from recently published kabuki and jōruri texts about the Soga brothers or from Soga kabuki and jōruri plays he had seen or heard about. In *Genroku kabuki no kenkyū*, Suwa Haruo argues convincingly that Danjūrō learned much about the craft of play writing while he was in Kyoto in 1693–94. He may have read the earliest Kansai Soga kabuki text (*Wakoku fūryū kyōdai kagami*), but there is no evidence he saw that play performed in Osaka in 1694. He would certainly have known about it because it starred Sakata Tōjūrō, and we know that Danjūrō was very interested in Tōjūrō's career. No texts for Soga kabuki plays predate 1694, but that does not mean that Danjūrō could not have read texts that have since been lost. Chikamatsu wrote only two Soga puppet plays before *Tsuwamono kongen Soga*, but neither of them deals with the main plot of the Soga vendetta. If Danjūrō knew anything about Chikamatsu's 1696 kabuki play, *Soga tayū Zome*, it could well have influenced him in terms of the author's freedom in changing the central story of the vendetta. None of Danjūrō's scenes or lines is borrowed from that play, however.

16. For an English translation of the play, see Laurence Bresler, "Chōbuku Soga: A Noh Play by Miyamasu," *Monumenta Nipponica* 29 (1974):69–81.

17. Danjūrō I, "Ganso Danjūrō no zangeroku," p. 134.

18. Ihara Toshirō, *Kabuki nenpyō*, pp. 205–7.

19. At the close of his diary, in 1696, Danjūrō wrote that he was blessed with a healthy family (both parents were alive and well, and he had a wife and four children) and a successful career. He realized how fleeting this happiness might be, because he described in detail the accidental death of a friend's daughter and two fires that devastated Edo, noting the suffering he saw around him. For his thankfulness for his and his family's well-being at the close of his diary, see Danjūrō I, "Ganso Danjūrō no zangeroku," p. 150.

20. I am guessing at this, based on common practice today for ad-libbed lines.

21. Nakamura Matazō, *Kabuki Back Stage, on Stage*, trans. Mark Oshima (Tokyo: Kodansha, 1990), p. 81.

22. Ihara Seiseien, *Danjūrō no shibai*, p. 6. The original account is from a 1705 record entitled *Hōei Tadanobu monogatari*.

23. Ihara Seiseien, *Danjūrō no shibai*, p. 6. The original account is in *Musashino zokudan*.

24. Kabuki hyōbanki kenkyūkai, ed., *Kabuki hyōbanki shūsei* (Tokyo: Iwanami shoten, 1973), vol. 3, p. 576.

25. The author of *Daijin mitsu sakazuki* also erased Danjūrō's name because Danjūrō had a new, posthumous Buddhist name by the time the book was published. The hyōbanki retained its description of Danjūrō's acting skill, the passage mourning his loss, and a high rating: *jō-jō-kichi*. In *Daijin mitsu sakazuki*, the wagoto actor Nakamura Shichisaburō also received a rating of jō-jō-kichi and was rated just above Danjūrō as the best tachiyaku actor in Edo. Kabuki hyōbanki kenkyūkai, ed., *Kabuki hyōbanki shūsei*, vol. 3, pp. 575–77. The other 1704 hyōbanki, *Yakusha mai ōgi*, also gave Danjūrō a rating of jō-jō-kichi but placed him at the top of the list of tachiyaku actors, just above Nakamura Shichisaburō. Suwa, *Genroku kabuki no kenkyū*, p. 403.

26. Ichikawa Danjūrō II, "Nisei Danjūrō no nikki," in Ihara Seiseien, ed., *Danjūrō no shibai* (Tokyo: Waseda daigaku shuppanbu, 1934), pp. 166–73.

27. In the play *Ya no ne*, Gorō does a pillar-entwining mie (pose), a very rare and dramatic mie thought to derive from the dragon that coils around Fudō's sword. Ueharu Teru, "Minzoku geinō to kabuki jūhachiban," in Gunji Masakazu, ed., *Kabuki jūhachiban Nihon no koten zusetsu*, vol. 20 (Tokyo: Shūeisha, 1979), p. 123. The most important attribute deriving from Fudō that appears in ukiyo-e representations of *Ya no ne* Gorō is that he sits facing straight ahead, glaring at the viewer. By the early eighteenth century, pictures with this pose were thought to possess the power to ward off evil spirits. Hattori Yukio, *Edo kabuki ron* (Tokyo: Hōsei daigaku shuppan kyoku, 1980), pp. 293, 294.

28. The large ema donated to Shinshōji and other Kantō Shugendō temples are one important source of information about who in Edo worshiped Fudō at the end of the eighteenth and beginning of the nineteenth centuries. The ema often depict scenes from kabuki and so tell a lot about the connections between Fudō worshipers and kabuki.

29. Mizuochi Kiyoshi, "Junisei Danjūrō jishu kōen," *Naritasan funjin Fudō*, performance program (Tokyo: Honzan Naritasan Shinshōji & Shochiku, 1992), pp. 26–27.

30. The text used for this translation is Ichikawa Danjūrō and Nakamura Akashi Seizaburō, "Tsuwamono kongen Soga," in Hattori Yukio, ed., *Kotobuki kongen Soga, Kokuritsu gekijō jōen shiryō shū* (Tokyo: Kokuritsu gekijō, 1970), pp. 86–90.

31. In the play, Gorō is sometimes called Sukegorō. For consistency's sake, I use the name Gorō throughout the translation.

32. Empress Kōken reigned from A.D. 749 to 758. At that time Dewa comprised what is now Yamagata and Akita Prefectures.

33. Akoya is the archaic name for Chitoseyama in Yamagata City. It was famous for an ancient pine that grew on its slope.

34. Hachiman is the patron god of war, and the dove is his messenger.

35. The thread of the story seems to break here. We are told that Gorō falls asleep during his prayers before we are told that he began his prayers. This sort of oversight sometimes occurs in e-iri kyogen bon. The Buddha referred to here must be Fudō, who is an incarnation of Dainichi Nyorai, the central Buddha of the esoteric pantheon.

36. "Black Fan K'uai" in Japanese is "Hankai kuro." Fan K'uai was a general who fought for the first Han emperor.

7

Transformation of a Heroine: Yokobue in Literature and History

◉

BARBARA RUCH

If Donald Keene had only one message in all his courses, his speeches, and his books, it was that the joys of Japanese literature are a very personal matter, a matter of personal experience and personal judgment. For my presentation at the symposium in honor of his retirement and in my contribution to this volume, I wanted to think of something in my work on Japanese literature that was both academic and at the same time a matter of personal experience, judgment, and joy that I could share.

In looking back over my own years in the field, I decided to detach myself from my present research and to take another look at the first piece of work that I had ever shown to Donald Keene, to see if it would give me any ideas.

My first substantive translation of classical Japanese was done years ago for my master's degree at the University of Pennsylvania. When I entered the doctoral program at Columbia, it was natural that I should have to show it to Professor Keene. It must have been "satisfactory," since he accepted me as his student in that same field, medieval popular literature. After the fact, I can now see, as he must have seen then, all the errors of a beginning student. But that aside, when I looked at my translation again after more than three decades, a lot of memories came flooding back concerning the amazing set of personal circumstances that had led me to select the literary piece in question, the Muro-machi-period work *Yokobue no sōshi* (The Story of Yokobue).

More than thirty years ago, an astonishing and mysterious series of events happened that I remember as if they happened yesterday.

For my master's thesis I had to present a translation and analysis, about one hundred pages in length, of a substantive work of premodern literature. I personally wanted to work on medieval fiction. Who would dare to work on Arthur Waley's *Genji*, without a *Genji* specialist at one's side? And I had made up my mind that I definitely did not want to do Edo-period literature. All the first generation of American scholars had chosen that. Donald Keene and Donald Shively worked on Chikamatsu. William Theodore de Bary and Howard Hibbett worked on Saikaku. I had nothing against their fine translations and scholarship (nor indeed against Chikamatsu's or Saikaku's beautiful use of the Japanese language). I simply found the works wholly uncongenial. It may be literature that men like to read. But most of the women depicted seemed to me preposterous, and if on rare occasions they seemed like real and human women, they were nonetheless treated so badly that I preferred not to depress myself by getting involved with such stories.

Nonetheless, if it was to be medieval fiction—then how to choose?—since indeed, there were more than five hundred such works to choose from. At that time there were virtually no annotated texts, and reading through the tales themselves was very difficult for me. Books on the subject were few, and there was not, of course, a single book in a Western language on the subject.

It is only fair to say that Donald Keene had translated and published two-thirds of one of these medieval stories, called "Sannin hōshi" (The Three Priests), though he never went back to the genre again.[1] But this, too, surely, is a work depressing to a woman reader. It is the story of a serial killer who murders and robs his victims and justifies his crime as the only way he can support a wife and children. His 308th victim turns out to have very long and lovely hair, and learning of this, the wife decides to go out to where her husband left the corpse and cut off this hair and bring it home, since her own is growing thin with age and she thinks she could make a hairpiece with it. The serial killer is struck dumb with horror at his wife's act, and lamenting that he had ever slept with a woman of such base character, he abandons her and his children and becomes a priest.

The second priest, with whom the killer-priest is now conversing on Mount Kōya, had been a husband deeply in love with his young wife, who, it turns out, was the woman with the beautiful hair, the last victim to be murdered by this very same killer-turned-priest. How does this all end? The killer-priest says, "I'm sorry, don't hate me," and the husband-priest replies, "How can I hate a fellow priest," and there on the top of Mount Kōya, in the sacred precincts from which all women are rigorously excluded, they have this male-bonding thing and feel good about it all.

This was not my kind of story. And yet in his introduction Donald Keene suggested that this story was "the finest of the *otogi zōshi* [late medieval companion stories] genre." I was depressed, to say the least. I also was at a loss as to how I could evaluate such a gigantic body of Muromachi-period literature and choose one work I felt was not only important and appropriate but one that I liked as well.

Then a series of events occurred that were truly mysterious.

In the library one day I found a small dark blue book with *Otogi zōshi* written in gold on its spine. It was a beautiful small book from the *Yūhōdō bunko* series, containing almost forty Muromachi-period works.[2] It rested comfortably in the palm of my hand, and somehow it reminded me of the small "Book of Hours" prayer books that were so beloved throughout Europe during the Middle Ages.

I took it into a quiet corner of the library that morning and sat looking through it. The book, though printed in 1926, was in pristine condition. It had never been taken out. As Japanese books so often do, it had a ribbon bookmark bound into it, and without thinking I opened the book to that spot. It fell open exactly in the middle of the book, and before my eyes appeared "The Story of Yokobue," which I started to read.

Although a fictionalized work, the story was based on actual events that took place sometime between 1179 and 1181, a true-life tragedy about a historical woman, Yokobue, who must have been born around 1164. Yokobue's talents and training in musical instruments, *imayō* song, *rōei*, and *waka*, has led her—still very young, apparently about fourteen years old—into a modest official post in service to the young Empress Tokuko, daughter of Taira no Kiyomori, who is later known, after the death of her husband Emperor Takakura in 1181, as the retired Empress Kenreimon'in. A young samurai named Takiguchi Tokiyori is in service to Tokuko's brother, Taira no Kiyomori's son Shigemori. Takiguchi catches sight of Yokobue at the empress's residence when on an errand for Shigemori and, at the tender age of about sixteen, falls in love with her. His father, who hopes for a strong political marriage for his only son, forbids the relationship, but over a period of about three years their involvement deepens, and the father disowns his son. This insoluble conflict between love for Yokobue and filial respect for his father, in which to betray either would in his view be a sin, leads Takiguchi, by then about eighteen or nineteen years old, to abandon secular life and become a monk. He tells neither Yokobue nor his father of his plan.[3]

Yokobue then makes an extraordinary search for him by foot into the western hills of Kyoto where rumor places his monastery, and she finds him in a tiny temple residence called Ōjōin, in the Hōrinji complex near the Ōi River.[4] Yokobue at least wants to understand his decision. She knocks on the gate and begs him to hear what she has to say, but he refuses to see her, fearing that he will be overcome by his love for her and lose his religious resolve.

Historically, all we know about the outcome of this affair is that Takiguchi decides that his retreat is too close to the capital and moves to a temple on Mount Kōya where he will be far from secular pressures. As for Yokobue's fate, three or four versions of her end were recorded; more about that later.

Without knowing why, I felt drawn to the story and decided I wanted to study this particular work of historical fiction. But this lovely little blue book, too, had almost no annotations, and so my grasp of the story and its historical and literary significance were still hopelessly superficial.

Then the second amazing event.

It could not have been more than a day or two later when the librarian came over to me and said, "This newly published book has just arrived from Japan, and I think you may be interested in using it." She placed in my hands the beautiful, newly published, persimmon-colored *Otogi zōshi* volume of the *Nihon koten bungaku taikei* (series) published by Iwanami shoten and meticulously edited with many headnotes.[5] This was the series that was to become the "bible" of postwar studies of Japanese literature. I looked through it with great pleasure. Inserted in the book was the usual little brochure-like supplement, the *geppō*, and I began to look through it as well. My eyes were drawn to a small black-and-white illustration in a short article about a late-Muromachi-period, hand-painted *Nara ehon* version of Yokobue's story. The label under this small illustration said that it was the scene depicting the moment before she threw herself into the waters of the Ōi River and killed herself (one of the versions of her tale).

It was a very sad, lonely scene showing a young woman seated at the edge of a high riverbank, her hands in prayer, seated very still. She had hung her outer silken robe on the branch of a tree where it billowed in the wind. The picture, extremely simple though it was and produced in a minuscule black-and-white illustration, was quite wonderful. Yokobue herself was the quiet, seated center of the scene. Deeply quiet. Deeply sad.

As I was looking at this picture, an incredibly strange thing began to occur in my memory. The name Yokobue, indeed the woman herself, seemed somehow to be familiar to me, though I could not imagine why. I felt as if I knew something about this woman already but could not retrieve what it could be from deep in my memory. Then suddenly, like an electric shock, I remembered something that had happened to me long ago.

It happened one day in the early 1950s. I had been in Japan only a short time, having just recently arrived to work for the American Friends Service Committee. I could not yet speak Japanese at all except for one or two words. On a visit to the Kansai area, some friends took me to visit famous places in Nara, and one of the places I was taken to see was Hokkeji. Hokkeji is a beautiful convent founded in the eighth century by Empress Kōmyō. My hosts had wanted especially to show me Hokkeji's main object of worship, the famous Jūichimen Kannon. But at that time, I still knew very little about Buddhism, somehow all temples looked alike, and my eyes had not yet been opened to the meaning of the statues of the buddhas and bodhisattvas, so I do not remember much about the visit.

As we were leaving, however, we stopped in a side building, and there my eye was caught by a small papier-mâché statue, only about twelve inches high, of a young bareheaded nun seated in prayer. I was immediately entranced by the figure. Somehow it moved me deeply, and I asked about her. My hosts were not experts on the subject, but they did their best to explain that something had forced the man she loved to become a monk, and so she had become a nun. This small statue that indeed dates back to the late twelfth century had been made out of the love letters that this woman had received from him so that she would always be seated, forever praying for his salvation even after her death. I did not understand the story fully, but my hosts gave me a small Japanese brochure that I could not read, in which I saw there was a photo of the tiny nun's statue, so I was very happy to have it. The little statue was so small and sad looking. At the same time it gave me such a feeling of intimacy, and the story moved me so much, that for some reason when I went home, I cut out the picture of the little nun from the brochure that I could not read, and I carried the picture in my wallet, together with a photo of my mother, father, and younger brother, for many years thereafter. I do not understand, myself, quite why I did that. But somehow I felt close to her.

And so, years later, sitting in the university library that day with the bright new persimmon-colored book before me and its geppō in my hand, lightning went through my brain. I reached down into my handbag and took out my wallet. The picture of the little papier-mâché nun was faded and partly stuck to the plastic of the wallet window, but I opened the window and took out the picture for the first time in years. I had long ago folded back the edges so that it would fit into the window, and now I delicately unfolded the fragile, crumbling edges of the paper. To my utter astonishment, there, at the bottom of the picture, were the Chinese characters Yokobue. Now I could read her name; now I knew who she was. I was stunned.

Somehow I did not know whether I had chosen her, or she had chosen me.

Illustration 7.1. Statue of Yokobue as a nun, in papier-maché, 34 cm high. Late twelfth century. (COURTESY OF HOKKEJI CONVENT, NARA.)

The Literary Transformation of a Woman's Life

Without a doubt, it was Yokobue and her story that made me want to go deeper into the medieval world and so brought me to Columbia to study with the young Donald Keene. Now at his retirement, his festschrift has brought me back to Yokobue again. Over the years, I admit, I had encountered Yokobue's name in passing, in genres and eras other than my own specialties, but by then I had always been focused on other matters and had no time to follow the new trails or divert my attention from the tasks at hand.

Now, motivated to go back, to discover what became of her, I uncovered in a short space of time almost thirty different Japanese literary works in which Yokobue is the central heroine, ranging in time from the thirteenth through the nineteenth century, in at least ten different literary genres.

I have always been interested in Japanese literary works less as objects of beauty or as autonomous aesthetic entities in and of themselves than as tools for the cultural historian: cultural vessels, the content of which takes on the shapes and reflects the beliefs and penchants—the worldview—of both the creators of these works and the consumers who transformed them into the best-sellers of their culture. What I wanted most to find out now was what subsequently happened to this woman in the Japanese imagination, a young woman whose real life story so moved the Japanese over the centuries that apparently they could never let her go. If her story changed with the centuries, and it did, how and why did it do so? A shift in the received wisdom of a story or in the perception of a heroine does not occur in a vacuum.

Yokobue, more than any other historical woman (even more than Kenrei-mon'in or Tomoe or Shizuka or Tokiwa Gozen) moved the Japanese deeply. Her origins, her life, and her predicament fit some deep cultural preference, and they pulled her back into their literature, drama, and song again and again. Writers of each new era depict her and her dilemma in differing ways—like Helen of Troy who appears in Homer and then Virgil, Euripides, Marlowe, and Goethe and like Cleopatra in Shakespeare and Dryden and Shaw. As the centuries passed and the storyteller changed, Yokobue was appropriated and used in a manner compatible with the era and the needs of the time, a barometer of the morality and aesthetics of the age, a marvelous reflecting glass giving off new light to illuminate the shifting temper of the time.

Yokobue's story is recorded in almost every literary form. We trace her through numerous versions of *Heike monogatari* and differing texts of *Genpei seisuiki*. She emerges as the central figure and in the title role in many works. There are two separate *heikyoku* (performance compositions for *biwa* and narrative voice based on passages from the *Heike monogatari*) entitled *Yokobue*, even one that was published in modern times with the voice and biwa music in Western-style score! Two medieval nō plays of unknown authorship are called *Yokobue*. Three Muromachi-period short stories tell her story: *Takiguchi engi*, a two-scroll *emaki* owned by the Seiryūji (temple), which originally was in Nara ehon book format; a one-scroll emaki version also remade from a Nara ehon, now owned by Hiroshima University; and a manuscript book in the Keiō University Library. In the same genre, there are four early-Edo-period illustrated editions (see, for example, illustration 7.4), including the well-known *Otogi bunko* (Companion library) version (see illustration 7.2), and two Edo manuscript copies.[6]

In the puppet and Kabuki theater, there is the 1674 *kojōruri* text, *Yokobue Takiguchi koi no dōshin*, used by the Osaka chanter Itō Dewa no jō, the conclusion to which has been lost, and the 1676 *TakiguchiYokobue momiji no yūran*, narrated by the Kyoto chanter Yamamoto Tosa no jō Kakudayū. In the 1690 printed book *Jinrin kinmō zui*, an unknown artist has captured Kakudayū's portrait as he sits in performance hidden from the audience chanting an unidentifiable play.

By great good fortune the artist Furuyama Moroshige, in a late 1680s book, *Yakusha ezukushi*, depicted Ise no Taijō's puppet theater in a performance of the scene of Yokobue arriving at the Ōjōin gate (see illustration 7.3). Yokobue appeared frequently on the kabuki stage between 1661 and 1681, and the artist Hishikawa Moronobu portrayed the actor Tamagawa Sen no jō, also in the moving scene at the brushwood gate, in a 1678 book, *Kokon yakusha monogatari*, which commemorates outstanding Edo actors (see illustration 7.5).[7] Chikamatsu Monzaemon's play about Yokobue and Takiguchi, entitled *Kaoyo uta karuta*, was written in 1714 when Chikamatsu was already sixty-one years old. His *michiyuki* for Yokobue (in a kind of verbal tour, a use of words to embrace beloved places) is so close to that of Kakudayū's authorized version of 1676 that until quite recently scholars were under the misimpression that Kakudayū's Yokobue was a work of Chikamatsu's youth and that *Karuta* was his later rewriting of his own earlier work.[8]

The decade from 1887 to 1898 showed another revival of creative interest in Yokobue and produced two more *nagauta* (long narrative songs) about Yokobue, one choosing suicide and the other, nunhood. In 1891, the first modern print edition of the seventeenth-century woodblock *Otogi bunko* set of stories, including the *Yokobue no sōshi* that began this chapter, was published, and thus for the first time a broad general public was able to read Yokobue's story rather than see or hear it in a vocally performed medium. The last major work

Illustration 7.2.   *Yokobue no sōshi* from the *Otogi bunko* set of printed books published by Shibukawa Seiemon of Osaka, ca. 1700. (COURTESY OF THE NATIONAL DIET LIBRARY, TOKYO.)

to deal with Yokobue and Takiguchi is the Meiji-period novel by Takayama Chogyū, *Takiguchi nyūdō*.

The vocalized literary tradition in which Yokobue's life history had emerged and was kept alive (heikyoku, yōkyoku, kojōruri, nagauta, and so forth) preserved, as all oral literature does, those aspects that society most values and is determined to transmit to future generations—those qualities in Yokobue that made her story important to preserve: her skills in music, song, dance, and poetry; her courage on the journey to Saga; the faithfulness of both Takiguchi and Yokobue to each other, each in their own ways; and the determination of each to aid in the salvation of the other even if forever separated by events and the dictates of social pressures. Over time, audiences instinctively experienced Yokobue and Takiguchi's tragedy as something more than a private matter, as deeper in meaning than a single historical event in the lives of two people. The purity and the wholeheartedness of youthful emotion of the Takiguchi and Yokobue story has that universality found worldwide in the stories-become-legend of Tristan and Isolde, Troilus and Cresseda, and Romeo and Juliet.

The concerns of each era also emerge in the retelling of Yokobue's story. *Genpei seisuki* emphasizes a girl who is low born and whose talents and skills were nur-

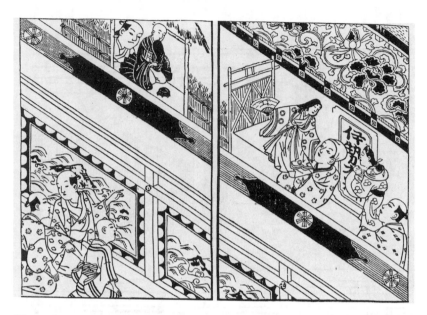

Illustration 7.3.   Yokobue, followed by Karumo and her baby, at the gate of Takiguchi's hermitage in Saga, as performed in the theater of Ise no Taijō. *Yakusha ezukushi,* three-volume printed book, ca. 1688. Illustration by Furuyama Moroshige (Hishikawa studio). (Courtesy of Rinsen shoten, Kyoto.)

tured as the daughter of the proprietor of a wealthy house of pleasure in Kanzaki where she was born and raised. So great were her beauty and gifts that Taira no Kiyomori himself picks this young *yūjo* (entertainer) to serve his daughter, the Empress Tokuko, and she is named for a kind of flute (a *yokobue,* a lateral flute) by Kiyomori's son, Shigemori, because of her musical skill. In the fifteenth-century *Takiguchi engi,* Yokobue is all the more of heroine quality and a worthy counterpart of the "sage" Takiguchi because she is a *mōshigo* (child born as the result of prayer), a gift to her parents from the deity of Kurama. In the absorption and retelling of a *Kojiki* legend, it is related that as a miraculous mōshigo, Yokobue was named for the flute left long ago as a keepsake by the Great Snake of Mizoro Pond and later treasured by the great founder of Mount Kōya, the monk Kōbō Daishi.

Another Muromachi manuscript, the *Keio-bon,* prefers to give Yokobue literary value in her readers' eyes by comparing the Yokobue and Takiguchi love tragedy to that of Onna Sannomiya and Kashiwagi in *The Tale of Genji,* and to the love between Kyōgoku no Miyasudokoro and the priest of Shiga, while at the same time emphasizing less the pathos and tragedy of events than the moral necessity that such great passions should be overcome.

At the end of the seventeenth century, the Osaka publisher Shibukawa Seiemon published twenty-three medieval stories, including *Yokobue no sōshi*, in his *Otogi bunko*, with the intent of marketing it as a trousseau item. His Yokobue is neither a beautiful pleasure quarters entertainer (hardly an appropriate model for young brides) nor merely a beautiful attendant to the empress, as most narratives had described her, but a lady (*nyōbo*) in service to Kenreimon'in. For the first time, Takiguchi is described as *yasashii*, a gentle, thoughtful, as well as handsome man, qualities that no one had thought to tell us about before but that apparently constituted the type of man desirable in the eyes of the Edo woman reader, especially if Yokobue's love tragedy (which here ends in suicide) was to be believable from a woman's point of view.

One might think that the suicide element was not particularly felicitous in a trousseau book. But this is not an Anna Karenina story. The emphasis is on the faithfulness of two lovers who had known and loved no other and who considered themselves man and wife. When social pressures separated them, they remained true to their love, she hoping, and in a way dying, for his salvation, and he devoting himself to hers after her death.

Over the years, as the oral history of Yokobue and Takiguchi settled into the written texts of vocal narrative and performance, as it did in nō, heikyoku, and nagauta texts, and the story became more literature than history, the emphasis shifted from transmitting data about an extraordinary event to becoming a play on themes and Yokobue a value-laden symbol. Two moments in the tragic story become the focus of poetic devotion. In all genres, these two moments in time became the literary highlights of both performance and reading texts. The first was Yokobue's michiyuki: hearing the rumor that Takiguchi has become a monk, distraught, she slips out of the palace and travels on foot into the western hills of Saga searching for the unknown monastery now said to be sheltering him. With lavish affection for the well-known places that she passes and with seasonal references to map Yokobue's heartbroken journey, the creators of the michiyuki passage in virtually every genre heightened it in shimmering wordplay and deeply moving meter, thereby setting the stage for the second and most beloved climactic passage: Yokobue's arrival at the brushwood gate of the tiny cloister where Takiguchi now resides and from which she is sent away. Her long search ends when near the bridge at Arashiyama, at the Hōrinji (temple), she lies prostrate in prayer before the statue of Kokūzō, and the deity appears to her in a dream in the guise of a monk and tells her at last where Takiguchi is. She crosses the bridge at once, heads north and, just as instructed, finds the small cloister. She hears Takiguchi's voice reciting sutras, knocks on the gate, and a companion monk emerges only to deny that the person she seeks is there. This passage is

marked by an exchange of what can only be described as religious love poems—
poems that only lovers would exchange but that rejoice in each other's having
found that path to salvation. In some versions, the exchange of poems takes
place immediately, the lovers separated by cloistered walls, able to hear each
other's voices only through the brushwood gate. In other texts Takiguchi sends
a poem from his final monastic retreat on Mount Kōya to Yokobue, who is by
then a nun, and she then sends a like poem in reply. Thus, true to the Japanese
literary tradition throughout the ages, Yokobue's story took on the very literary
forms most cherished by the Japanese: the michiyuki and the poem exchange
(by means of words, two people embrace).

What does it mean that of all the dozens of versions of this love tragedy only
two, the Seiryūji emaki entitled *Takiguchi engi* and the Meiji novel *Takiguchi
nyōdō*, are in effect "Takiguchi's Story," whereas all other titles over the ages bear
either both their names or hers alone? True, in many ways Yokobue's story is a
kind of *hosshindan*, the story of how Takiguchi reached a religious enlightenment
and thus became a monk. It tells the story behind the startling news of young
Takiguchi's tonsure related by Yoshida no Tsunefusa in his diary in 1181 right
after it happened and before people learned the details. But clearly once the facts
came out, it became the story of a couple and then more and more *her* story.

There is no reason, either, to accept Yokobue's dramatic suicide that is
recounted in many versions. For a male audience, a woman's suicide may be a
more interesting end; it certainly has more drama and touches on violence. It
may even seem somehow erotic. Also, for a male reader, the woman's death
makes a more complete severance. The anxiety is gone, leaving the man free to
pursue his religious faith without distraction, hindrance, or attachment. Such
versions depict the man as the seeker and the woman as both the prize and
impediment. But for a female audience, why would the death of Yokobue be
more satisfying than nunhood? One can only admire anew the brilliant perceptiveness and awareness of her varied readers that Murasaki Shikibu displays in
The Tale of Genji when she makes Ukifune into a woman who is simultaneously
both a suicide and a nun, depending on which character has heard which report
of what happened to her.

There is no doubt that I was prejudiced by my long-ago encounter at
Hokkeji, but on other grounds those early *Heike* accounts of Yokobue's taking
the tonsure seem truest to life: deep grief at the unexpected external pressure
that suddenly interrupted her relationship with Takiguchi and destroyed their
union; her attempt at nunhood (because Takiguchi had fled into monkhood); her
wish that his religious enlightenment could be the source of hers as well. But
Yokobue's grief slowly drained her heart until it became clear that even the rit-

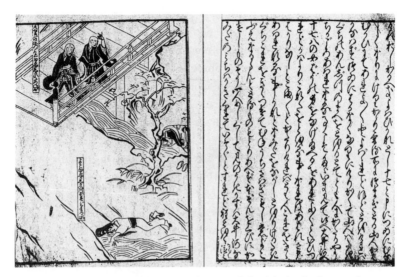

Illustration 7.4. Takiguchi and fellow priest discover Yokobue's body after her suicide in the Ōi River. *Yokobue Takiguchi no sōshi,* printed book published by Yamada Ichirōbei, 1658. (COURTESY OF THE NATIONAL DIET LIBRARY, TOKYO.)

uals and serenity of nunhood could not hold firm the meaning of her existence. Her loneliness for Takiguchi finally took her away in death, which was for her an erasing of all memory.

The fourteen versions of *Heike* that mention Yokobue fall roughly into three groups: those that do not mention her death, those that say she became a nun at Hokkeji in Nara and later died there, and those that say she drowned herself, sometimes having first become a nun at any of several Kyoto temples. Just as the great *Heike* story was composed by various hands from various vantage points—some recorded as national history, some as individual family records, some as religious lessons—so Yokobue was viewed and used for various purposes.

But "suicide because of lost love" must surely be a later fictional attachment to Yokobue's true life story. It would contradict the long history of set patterns for female suicide in Japanese history and literature. There are almost no such cases of suicide over lost love in the classical literature. Since the earliest Japanese accounts, women have drowned themselves, never out of frustrated love, but rather, out of having been pressed to the limits of their endurance by rival men. Crushed between the attentions of two men and unable to hurt either by saying no, they flee into death. From women such as Tekona and Sakurako and Unai otome in the *Man'yōshū* to the same Unai in *Yamato mono-*

gatari and the nō play *Motomezuka*, and even in the case of Ukifune, who tried but failed, they committed suicide not because of lost love but because they were loved and fought over by two men. They escape into suicide, sacrificing themselves in order to resolve the unresolvable conflict of men.

Even in the later otogi zōshi version itself, which ends with Yokobue's suicide, remnants of the older story line, closer perhaps to the actual events, can be found. Yokobue seeks Takiguchi at his cloister in Saga not to reestablish their love affair but because she, too, wishes to become a nun so that they might live in close communion in a cloister and help each other gain enlightenment. She articulates what must be for some women the picture of an ideal life:

> I am not asking you to care for me as you did in the past. I came this far in search of you thinking that I, too, like you, would change my garb for religious robes and live together with you in the same cloister. There I would give water to the flowers that you pick for the altar, and we would be reborn on the same lotus leaf in Amida's paradise.

This is reminiscent of the beautiful, peaceful, and happy scene in the "Nun's Scroll" of the *Shigisan engi*, in which the older sister, Amagimi, a nun, seeks and finds her younger brother, the monk Myōren, in his cloister on Mount Shigi, and they then live together following the Buddhist path in that little mountain retreat until the day they die.

There can be no doubt that the gender of the author and/or the anticipated audience plays an important role in the depiction of character, and it clearly has influenced the evolution of Yokobue's image in different eras. The evidence leads us to assume that the authors of *Heike* and *Genpei seisuki*, as well as the nō texts, were male but that their audiences were of both genders. In these works Yokobue is treated with great sensitivity and respect. The authors of otogi zōshi are unknown, and diary notations lead us to believe they too had both male and female readers. But Shibukawa's *Otogi bunko* was intended for a female audience, and as we have seen, numerous subtle aspects of the Yokobue narrative in this genre make it appealing to women.[9]

The kojōruri theater of the early Edo period, however, is another story. The paying guests then anticipated in the pleasure quarters' theaters were primarily male, and the adoption of the Yokobue and Takiguchi story into the kojōruri repertory reflects that. And with Chikamatsu's adaptations, we find a decidedly male view of Yokobue, and there even emerge additional comic touches more to a male than a female taste. At first, when Takiguchi arranges a liaison with Yokobue, he carries off the wrong lady-in-waiting by mistake, and Yokobue goes off with the wrong man, though of course, they all find out just in time. In a greatly elaborated tale, Yokobue's friend Karumo is caught in a love triangle and has troubles of her own. Pregnant by the man she loves, she is kidnapped by her lover's rival, who threatens to kill her unless she reveals the name of the child's father. In an intricate plot complicated by lovers separated and thought to be dead, and even tonsures, the play nonetheless ends happily after a sword fight between Takiguchi and company and some villainous men, whereupon Kagekiyo (!) intervenes and makes peace.

Following Yokobue throughout the ages has brought me at last to Takayama Chogyū's novel *Takiguchi nyūdō*, written in 1894. Having been initiated into the mysteries of Meiji novels by Professor Ryūsaku Tsunoda (too much like oil paintings on velvet for my taste, I thought), I certainly never anticipated that I would voluntarily read another. But this was the final stop. I guess I have to forgive Chogyū his excesses and what he did to Yokobue, since he wrote it when he was only a college freshman. It did, nonetheless, win second prize in a contest run by the *Yomiuri* newspaper for the "best new historical novel or play." The contest was judged by such Meiji greats as Tsubouchi Shōyō, Ozaki Kōyō, and Kōda Rohan, and although they considered Chogyū's the best entry, they refused to award a first prize.[10] When I learned that, I felt a little better. Nonetheless, *Takiguchi nyūdō* became a blockbuster best-seller. Despite all the weaknesses of story and character, without a doubt the beauty of Chogyū's language—its pace and meter reminiscent of the poetry of Akashi no Kakuichi's *Heike* itself—contributed to both the critics' and readers' positive response.

Chogyū was true to the temper of his time (and of course to his own college-age interests). His novel is a curious amalgam of male-centric neo-bushi-ism mixed with a romanticism reminiscent of Goethe's *Sorrows of Werther*—whose love tragedy, I think not coincidentally, had just been attracting Japanese attention and had even been compared in an 1891 newspaper review with Japan's own Takiguchi/Yokobue love tragedy.[11] For Chogyū, however, the story belongs to Takiguchi, as his title *Takiguchi nyūdō* makes clear. Throughout the novel, Yokobue floats in the background, much like a later-to-come Sōseki heroine, chiefly functioning as a source of pain in the friendship between two men. Yokobue is reduced to a pure and idealized love object desired by Takiguchi and his friend, another Taira foot soldier, Shigekage, whom Chogyū has made into Takiguchi's rival over Yokobue. In the best tradition of Meiji misogyny, Yokobue is the cause for the disintegration of a noble warrior. Both men catch a glimpse of her from afar and fall in love with her on sight. She is inundated by love letters from two men she has never seen, loves neither, has one of those dreadful maids whom Shigekage has persuaded to press his suit over that of Takiguchi, and who also

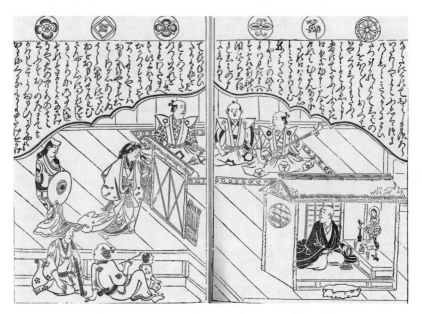

Illustration 7.5.   Yokobue, Karumo and child, and Takiguchi on the Kabuki stage with
the words spoken by Tamagawa Sen no jō. *Kokon yakusha monogatari,* printed book, 1678;
reprinted 1915. Illustration by Hishikawa Moronobu. (Courtesy of the Asia Library,
University of Michigan.)

warns her mistress that a woman "has only ten years to bloom in beauty and then
is spent," so she better hurry and give in. Shigekage further betrays his friend by
telling Takiguchi's father that love is destroying the warrior spirit of his son, a fictional elaboration of the cause for the falling out between father and son.
Unaware of these betrayals and with only silence from Yokobue, Takiguchi—out
of both filial piety and loyalty to Shigekage, not wanting to court and win a girl
that his friend also loves—enters a monastery and becomes a priest.

Yokobue is blamed by the palace women as well as by her maid for having driven, by her indifference, a noble warrior to the cloister, and she assumes the
burden of this guilt. Appalled when she hears of this unknown samurai's obsession with her, his emotional disintegration, and his tonsure, she takes responsibility for it all by going to Saga to seek his pardon and, when he refuses to see
her, by then becoming a nun and then getting wholly out of the way by dying.
The novel continues at length, free of women, and in the end Takiguchi commits
suicide himself (a new touch). But this is a *junshi* suicide out of loyalty to fellow
Taira warriors who have just died, including, it is important to note, his loyalty
to his old rival for Yokobue, who earlier had confessed his jealous duplicities and

had received the monk's absolution. (Somehow we are back to the bonding of men on Mount Kōya!)

Whereas Western tradition has made women like Helen of Troy into scapegoats for men's troubles and held them responsible as the cause of catastrophe, Yokobue may be a sacrificial victim but never a scapegoat—not until Chogyū's novel. In otogi zōshi versions, for instance, she is warned by an attendant not to make a man suffer by failing to reply to his love letters. But the dialectic does not blame her for the end of Takiguchi's military career and his tonsure. Chogyū's novel, in contrast, is steeped in a Neo-Confucian ethos not merely of male-to-male loyalty but of a view of women as members of a separate world that makes dealing with them a lapse, a weakness. The correlation between the intensity of patriarchy and the degree of separation between the private and public spheres in human societies was demonstrated by the historian J. Kelly.[12] *Takiguchi nyūdō* adds Japanese evidence in support of this correlation.

After coming this far, one has lost touch with the real Yokobue. She has become a tale with no longer any but the loosest grounding in fact or history. Although each Yokobue, transformed in each new era, had real meaning to her respective audiences, I go back to where this all started, to the Yokobue who was most real to me—and who, I maintain, is the Yokobue closest to history. I go back to that Kamakura-period statue of a young girl encountered when I too was still young. I remember her impossible situation. I remember the courage of her journey to Saga. And I remember the strength and the fragility and yet the serenity of that small statue she had made of herself as a nun that still to this day sits in prayer at Hokkeji. Although Yokobue died centuries ago, in many ways she has become a part of me. She helps give me both courage and serenity (when they so often escape me), the very qualities indispensable to the life of scholarship. As Donald Keene always made clear, the joys of Japanese literature are a very personal matter.

NOTES

1. Donald Keene, "The Three Priests," in Donald Keene, ed., *Anthology of Japanese Literature* (New York: Grove Press, 1955), pp. 322–31.

2. Edited by Fujii Shiei, 1926.

3. Yoshida no Tsunefusa remarks in his diary (*Kikki*, 11/20/1181) that he heard about Takiguchi Fujiwara no Tokiyori having taken the tonsure at Hōrinji (temple) in Saga at the young age of eighteen and that people were still at a loss to explain the reason. Kannotō Akira, "*Yokobue no sōshi no seiritsu made—Muromachi jidai monogatari ron no tame ni . . .*" *Nihon bungaku* 26 (February 1977): 72.

4. Apparently there was at that time a small building known as Ōjōin in the compound of Hōrinji. This should be distinguished from the Ōjōin founded later, sometime after 1219, by Nenbutsubō (1156–1251) and destroyed by fire in 1222. Sanbōji, also known as Takiguchidera (Takiguchi temple), likewise in Saga and now housing late-Kamakura-period statues of Takiguchi and Yokobue, also postdates the events surrounding Takiguchi's tonsure, despite the tradition claiming it as the site of his retreat.

5. Edited by Ichiko Teiji, 1958.

6. For the evolution of the early- Edo-period *Otogi bunko*, see Barbara Ruch, "The Origins of *The Companion Library*: An Anthology of Medieval Japanese Stories," *Journal of Asian Sudies* 30 (May 1971): 593–610.

7. Shinoda Jun'ichi, *Ningyō jōruri butaishi* (Tokyo: Yagi shoten, 1991), discusses these two illustrations, 7.3 and 7.5, on pp. 110 and 139.

8. See the clarification of this confusion in Sakaguchi Hiroyuki, "*Takiguchi Yokobue momiji no yūran* to sono shūhen—Chikamatsu zongisaku shiron," *Jinbun kenkyū* 30 (1978): 20–42.

9. See also Susan Matisoff's "Deciphering the Code of Love: *Yamato kotoba* in Literature and Life," chapter 8 in this volume.

10. Takayama Chogyū, *Takiguchi nyūdō* (Tokyo: Iwanami shoten, 1990 (51st reprint since 1938), pp. 109 ff., in Sasabuchi Yuichi's postscript.

11. Ibid., p. 115. See in particular the article "Werther's Love Tragedy," in *Yamagata nippō* newspaper, July 9, 1891.

12. Joan Kelly, "The Social Relation of the Sexes: Methodological Implications of Women's History," in her *Women, History and Theory: The Essays of Joan Kelly* (Chicago: University of Chicago Press, 1984), p. 14.

8

Deciphering the Code of Love: Yamato kotoba *in Literature and Life*

◉

SUSAN MATISOFF

In the late-Muromachi-period short story *Minazuru*, there is a scene in which several women are gathered together, struggling to read something written in Japanese and having a very hard time figuring out the meaning. The women sit side by side, staring at the text, but "they still can't read it. If they know the first character, they don't know the next one. And even if they know a certain character, they can't get the sense of its reading."[1] The description certainly reminded me of my own personal experience.[2] The exasperatingly puzzling text is a letter, written by a suitor who is courting their mistress Minazuru. Laughing over the incompetence of the man who would write such an incomprehensible letter, they are about to rip it to shreds without delivering it to Minazuru. However, Minazuru's nurse Rensei[3] intercedes and delivers the letter. Rensei cannot read it herself, but Minazuru proves able to fathom its contents. The suitor is none other than the great hero Yoshitsune, certainly no cultural incompetent, and Minazuru's ability to read the letter sets her apart from her nurse and serving women. The scene of the arrival of the letter is preceded by one in which Minazuru has already assured herself of Yoshitsune's suitability by noting his qualities as a musician and testing his knowledge of classical poetry from *Genji*, *Sagoromo*, *Koitsukushi*, *Kokin*, *Man'yō*, *Ise monogatari*, and the eight imperial anthologies.[4]

Several other late-Muromachi or early-Edo-period *otogi zōshi* (works of popular fiction) contain similar instances in which a cultured, educated woman can decipher a letter meant for her, even though its meaning remains opaque to her servants. The very popular *Yokobue no zōshi*, an elaboration on the "Yokobue" chapter of *Heike monogatari*, includes such a scene, even though the *Heike* version and its early variants make no mention of a letter.[5]

In this case, the young courtier Takiguchi Tokiyori is so taken with Yokobue's charms that he has fallen ill with "lovesickness." With the collusion of Yokobue's nurse, he sends a letter to his beloved. The nurse pretends she has found the letter by chance; in any case, she cannot read it. She says to Yokobue, "Although you are still young, because you have read *Genji*, *Sagoromo*, *Kokin*, *Man'yō*, and *Ise monogatari*, you should be able to explain these words to me. Please figure it out and read it for me." Yokobue takes up the letter, not realizing it is meant for her, and succeeds in reading it. When she has finished, the nurse reveals who it is from.

Sekkyō-bushi, "sermon-ballads," were a style of puppet performance derived from narratives first developed by itinerant street performers. They enjoyed a period of intense popularity in the seventeenth century, and many were published in printed form for the enjoyment of readers. In style and degree of reading difficulty, sekkyō-bushi texts are for the most part similar to otogi zōshi. That is to say, both genres were relatively easy for contemporary audiences to read.

Two sekkyō-bushi, *Oguri* and *Shintokumaru*, include examples of puzzling courtship letters.[6] The letters are quite similar, and the circumstances surrounding them are identical. In both cases the letter is written by a man attempting to court a woman with whom he has fallen in love at first sight. His intermediary is a peddler. The woman for whom the letter is intended can read it, but her attendants cannot.

The peddler who helps Oguri says he feels hesitant about serving as a go-between for people of such high status and so asks Oguri to write a letter. The paper and brush are lovingly described. The peddler delivers the letter to the residence of Oguri's beloved, Terute. The letter's phrasing causes Terute's attendants much laughter, as they find the letter muddled and disconnected and think its author may have been out of his mind. But when Terute sees the letter, she praises the calligraphy, the ink, and the scent of the paper. And she is able to read it, telling her women, "I'll give you the *kun* reading of this letter."

In *Shintokumaru*, Otohime receives a similar letter from her unknown suitor Shintokumaru; its phrasing baffles her attendants. She too offers a "kun reading" of the letter and asks her attendants, "Shall I read it as *yamato kotoba* or for its meaning?" Literally translated, *yamato kotoba* simply means "Japanese words," just as a "kun reading" means reading a character with its native Japanese pronunciation rather than its Sino-Japanese pronunciation. In the case of these letters, however, yamato kotoba means something more specific. It refers to a kind of code, something requiring decipherment. It would appear from the comments made by their servants that the intended recipients of these letters are able to understand them not simply because they "know the characters" but also because of their knowledge of a small canon of classic texts, the sources of poetic allusions. In addition, the "kun reading" means a rephrasing in straightforward prose.

The details of this sort of code and the complex origins of the term yamato kotoba are the subject of this chapter. But certain conclusions may follow from the letters' contexts alone. As these four examples suggest, letters using yamato kotoba appear in late medieval fiction in plots involving groups of people, some who can read well and some who cannot. They seem to be a product of their time—a time when literacy was spreading rapidly. Such letters are found in some of the earliest literary texts to circulate in printed form, and they were appreciated by an audience that must have included many who were, in effect, first-generation readers. The nature of literacy itself is called into question by the challenges of deciphering yamato kotoba letters. These letters might seem to reflect an ever growing range of readers who recognized the need for training in the literary classics, as they seem to valorize the technical ability to read, that is, to understand the writing system, and to endorse a version of "cultural literacy."[7]

The yamato kotoba letter in *Yokobue no zōshi* is quite short. As Yokobue reads the letter, the reader of *Yokobue* sees, as if through her eyes, five lines referred to as *uta*, though not in the standard form of a "poem":[8]

mi wa ukigumo no gotoku nari	My body is like a floating cloud
ume no tachie no uguisu wa	A bush warbler in the upper branches of a plum tree
kishi utsu nami no fuzei shite	Appearing like waves breaking on the shore
nonaka no shimizu	A meadow spring
tani no mumoregi	A tree buried in a valley

These lines are followed by two standard waka that are not discussed or explicated in the text. Next, Yokobue turns to explaining the puzzling lines. That done, the nurse reveals that the letter is actually intended for Yokobue, not something picked up by chance, and that she is acting as an intermediary for the sender, Tokiyori.

Yokobue's explication of the yamato kotoba lines is not a perfect match. This is presumably a textual problem, perhaps indicating a copying error somewhere along the lines of transmission of the text. Nothing is made of the unmatched lines, however, and clearly the reader is meant to find no flaw in Yokobue's knowledge or intelligence. To avoid confusion, I skip Yokobue's explanation for a completely different first line and turn directly to the four lines where the explanation fits. Each puzzling line is repeated, followed by its decipherment.

"My body is like a floating cloud," means "Because of you who are beyond the heavens, my heart wanders in vain longing."

"A bush warbler in the upper branches of a plum tree," means "just raising my voice and crying."

"Appearing like waves breaking on the shore," means "to break one's heart."

"A meadow spring," means "to live alone, visited by none."

Yokobue then explicates a line that does not match the last line of the letter. To avoid confusion, I skip it here. It is clear from the context that Yokobue's ability to decipher the letter shows her intelligence and education—and her charm. Because her knowledge of the classics has been mentioned, the reader might reasonably assume that she understands the lines because she catches certain poetic allusions, but there are no poems cited as sources for the lines.

In the case of *Minazuru*, Yoshitsune deliberately writes in a manner he knows Minazuru's ladies will be unable to understand. His calligraphy is elegantly "scattered," like "plumes of grasses or falling maple leaves." Again, the reader first encounters the content of the letter as seen through its recipient's eyes.

Katsuragi ya	Katsuragi
Mine no shirakumo	White clouds on the peaks
Kasuga no wakamurasaki	Young lavender at Kasuga
Tokiwa no mori	Tokiwa woods
Iwade no yama	Mount Iwade
Noki no shinobu	Haresfoot ferns by the eaves
Tsukubayama	Mount Tsukuba

"Yes, Rensei, it's reasonable that you couldn't read it," Minazuru said.

"Now, about the first words: where it is written 'white clouds on the peaks,' that is in the sense of

yoso ni nomi	Is it only from a distance
mite ya yami nan	That I shall be able to gaze

katsuragi ya	At the white clouds on the peaks
takama no yama no	Of Katsuragi and Mount Takama?
mine no shirakumo?[9]	

"Where it is written 'young lavender,' that is, in the sense of

kasugano no	Just as the young purple
wakamurasaki no	Of Kasuga plain
surigoromo	Dyes a robe in a tangled pattern,
shinobu no midare	The wild disorder of my yearning heart
kagiri shirarezu	Knows no limits.[10]

"Where it is written 'Tokiwa woods,' that is, in the sense of

omou to mo	My longing
kou to mo shiraji	and my love for you
Yamashiro no	Perhaps will be unknown,
Tokiwa no mori no	If Tokiwa woods in Yamashiro
Iro ni ideneba.[11]	Does not show its colors.

"Where it is written 'Mount Iwade,' that is, in the sense of

omoedomo	Although I long for you
iwade no yama ni	I've passed the years
toshi o hete	At Mount Iwade, without speaking.
kuchi ya hatenan	Shall I rot into old age,
tani no mumoregi?	Like a tree buried in a valley?"[12]

As with *Yokobue no zōshi*, the text is flawed. At this point, two more lines are explained by allusions to poems. The first poem matches the final line of the letter, "Mount Tsukuba," but there is no match here for "haresfoot fern by the eaves"; instead, the final poem matches a line meaning "to lie down weeping," which is not in Minazuru's first reading of the letter.

Still, despite the slightly imperfect match, the explication of this letter is obviously different from the "reading" in *Yokobue*. The reader of *Yokobue* may infer that Yokobue's knowledge of poetry gives her the ability to decipher the images in her letter, but the reader of *Minazuru* is shown the full poems that are the sources of allusion and, thereby, of meaning. The meaning is not actually spelled out, but the first five lines would work out something like this:

Katsuragi	I want to draw close to you
White clouds on the peaks	
Young lavender at Kasuga	My heart yearns without limit
Tokiwa woods	Perhaps my longing is unknown to you
Mount Iwade	Shall I rot into old age?

This pattern, citing relatively familiar poems but not spelling out the prose explanations of the allusions, ends abruptly with the sixth poem. The letter continues for five more lines, however, now in the same pattern as *Yokobue*. Minazuru says this "about the next words":

"Where it is written 'pale-tinted autumn leaves' (*usumomiji*), it has the sense of 'do not think my feelings shallow.'"

(The same term appears in the yamato kotoba letter in *Shintokumaru* but is explained differently.)

"Where it is written 'a meadow spring' (*nonaka no shimizu*), it means 'to clarify one's feelings in solitude.'"

(This term is also found in *Oguri*, *Shintokumaru*, and *Jōruri jūnidan zōshi* with varying, though related, "readings." We have already seen it in *Yokobue*, given the meaning "to live alone, visited by none.")[13]

"Where it is written 'a boat rowed in the offing' (*oki kogu fune*), it means 'to burn with longing.'"

(This yamato kotoba is read with the identical meaning in *Jōruri jūnidan zōshi*. In *Oguri*, its meaning is "I burn with passion for you, hurry to me." And in *Shintokumaru*, the reading is "with your heart floating and unsettled, hurry to me.")

"Where it is written 'sweet-flag' (*ayamegusa*), it has the sense of 'I want to meet you sometime.'"
      "Where it is written 'a damaged boat' (*katawarebune*), it has the sense of 'having no one to rely on.'"

For the reader of *Minazuru*, the six phrases in the letter that are matched to complete poems might even have served as a sort of primer of poetic allusions. The elegant letters (*ensho*) that appear in early-seventeenth-century *kana zōshi* (notably *Uraminosuke* and *Usuyuki monogatari*) are known to have been used as practical guides for writing love letters.[14] However, the letters in kana zōshi, though thick with snippets of old poems to the point of stultification, are not in yamato kotoba riddle form. The typical yamato kotoba letter takes the the form of the latter half of the Minazuru letter, with prose explications rather than the citation of poems.

In *Oguri* and *Shintokumaru*, the letters are not given a first reading without explication; rather, each yamato kotoba phrase is immediately deciphered by the recipient as she reads the letter out loud. The letters in the two texts are similar; the *Oguri* letter, with transcription and translation combined, is as follows. For simplicity's sake I have put it in the form of a chart, omitting phrases such as "where it is written" or "is read as."

Oguri yamato kotoba letter

A round log bridge over a narrow valley stream (*hosotanigawa no marokibashi*)
Read this letter without stopping; go right through to the end and give me an answer.
Haresfoot ferns by the eaves (*noki no shinobu*)
As dusk falls along the road, I wait impatiently for you.
A meadow spring (*nonaka no shimizu*)
Tell no one of this, but settle your mind alone, in secret.
A boat rowed in the offing (*oki kogu fune*)
I burn with passion for you; hurry to me.[15]
Waves striking the banks (*kishi utsu nami*)
May you be giving in and longing for me?
Smoke from salt kilns (*shioya no kemuri*)
If the wind blows off the bay, yield to me for one night.
A sash that is too short (*shakunai obi*)[16]
Someday our love will be fulfilled, and we will be bound together.
Hail on ground-bamboo (*nezasa ni arare*)
If I touch you, yield to me.
Double stalks of plume grass (*futamoto susuki*)
Someday our love will reach fruition, and we will be tangled together.
Three sacred mountains (*mitsu no oyama*)
If I ask, grant my entreaty.
A wingless bird and stringless bow (*hane nai tori ni tsuru nai yumi*)
Now since I first fell in love with you, though I would go I cannot; though I would stay, I cannot.

Four of the twelve yamato kotoba in *Shintokumaru* are not in any of the texts discussed so far. They are as follows:

> The high peak of Fuji (<u>*Fuji no takane*</u>)
>> As I gaze at the moon in the sky
> Deer standing on a mountaintop (<u>*mine ni tatsu shika*</u>)
>> I am not a stag in autumn, but I long for a mate.
> Reeds on the beach at Ise: a salt maker's hut (<u>*Ise no hamaogi, shioya*</u>)
>> If a strong wind blows, yield to me for one night.[17]
> Water oats in a pond (<u>*ike no makomo*</u>)
>> If I draw you to me, yield to me.

There are a few other otogi zōshi or sekkyō-bushi texts with some slight traces of yamato kotoba,[18] but only one more that extensively uses this riddling technique. This is *Jōruri jūnidan zōshi*, the extremely popular story of yet another of Yoshitsune's romances. Some kind of account of the love of Yoshitsune and Lady Jōruri was already popular as early as 1485, and the story was transmitted through performances with musical accompaniment. Eventually the label *jōruri* became the common designation for a distinct style of recitation in performances utilizing puppets.[19] The version of this tale cited here is a modern annotated printed edition based on a movable-type printed book published sometime during the Keichō period (1596–1615).[20] Probably because performances of this tale remained popular for a long time, a bewildering variety of transcriptions and written versions have been identified, in all some thirty-five manuscripts and twenty-four variant printed texts.[21]

In *Jōruri jūnidan zōshi*, Yoshitune turns to yamato kotoba at a point when the Lady Jōruri has grown cool in her treatment of him, having previously welcomed his attentions. It is worth noting, however, that in this case the yamato kotoba are not written in a letter but are spoken directly to the lady, who immediately deciphers them. Although the yamato kotoba are identical or similar in form and content to those in other tales, here they are presented as a kind of *oral* wordplay:

"After hearing what she had said, Yoshitsune used for her the metaphors (*nazorae*) of yamato kotoba, and what he said was fascinating."[22] Of course, she cannot help but respond. She gives her reasons: "I wasn't going to answer, but those who don't respond to poems they've been sent will be reborn for ages on end as tongueless snakes. . . . and those who don't answer letters they've been sent will be reborn blind, so I'll just answer this."

This comment would seem to imply a written answer, but the lady in fact is responding orally. As in other otogi zōshi, the reader first reads the string of yamato kotoba and then sees each repeated and explained. This text is consistent in that each of the lady's explanations properly matches the phrase spoken by Yoshitsune, but there is great variation among the yamato kotoba sections of the many texts of this tale. Most versions contain fifteen to eighteen yamato kotoba, and the longest is a list of twenty-one. Comparing six variant texts, Kazayoshi Fujikake found a total of forty-six puzzle phrases, of which only three are common to all six texts. One, the "meadow spring," should by now be familiar to the readers of this chapter. However, at least in the particular version being discussed here, the decoding of this phrase is different from what we have already seen. Here "meadow spring" is taken to mean "to make one's way through something" (*kakiwake mairu*).[23]

Yoshitsune frames his string of yamato kotoba by declaring, "If I liken my love to various things." Each yamato kotoba is followed by a phrase such as "and it also can be compared with . . ." (. . . *ni mo tatoetari*). Each decoding is followed by "is that in the sense of . . . ?" (. . . *no kokoro ka*) or "is that to say?" (*to ōse ka*) or the like. I have omitted these tags to conserve space and focus more clearly on the yamato kotoba and their explications. The following is the full exchange:

Jōruri jūnidan zōshi yamato kotoba exchange

Mount Asama in Shinano (<u>*Shinano naru asama no take*</u>)
    Passions burst into flame.
Water in a round well (<u>*tsutsui no mizu*</u>)
    No way to find my heart's ease.
A meadow spring (<u>*nonaka no shimizu*</u>)
    To make one's way through something.
An untethered horse (<u>*tsunaganu koma*</u>)
    I am without a wife.
A stringless bow (<u>*tsuru naki yumi*</u>)
    I want to draw you to me, yet I cannot.[24]
Hail on ground-bamboo (<u>*nezasa no ue no arare*</u>)
    If I draw you to me, yield to me.
Arrowroot spreading underground (<u>*shita hau kuzu*</u>)
    Though once intact, my heart is broken in thousands of pieces.[25]
A bamboo flute (<u>*fuetake*</u>)
    Pledge your love for me, even for one night.
A clump of plume grass (<u>*hitomura susuki*</u>)
    Yield when I draw you to me.

A narrow valley stream (*hosotanigawa*)
 Yield all at once and join with me.
A carpenter's marking line (*utsu suminawa*)
 Decide resolutely.
A river with two forks (*futamatagawa*)
 To meet up together.
The slope at Kiyomizu (*Kiyomizuzaka*)
 Many eyes are watching.
A beautifully patterned sash (*keshō no obi*)
 Let us be bound together.
A boat rowed in the offing (*oki kogu fune*)
 To burn with longing.
The sacred mountain at Nachi (*Nachi no oyama*)
 If I ask, grant my entreaty.
Buried fire (*uzumibi*)
 To burn in secret, giving off smoke.
Deep crimson (*koki kurenai*)
 To show one's passion.

With thirty-six different examples (seven occurring in more than one text), it is possible to make some generalizations about the yamato kotoba in otogi zōshi and sekkyō-bushi.[26] Setting aside the first half of the letter in *Minazuru*, certain patterns emerge. First, and not surprising, the vocabulary of these yamato kotoba is entirely of native Japanese origin. There are few place-names in these examples, virtually none of the codified *utamakura*, or "poem pillows"—conventionalized references to famous places—found in waka. Nor are these the same as *makura kotoba*, the conventional poetic "pillow words" of great antiquity. There are two main nexuses of meaning through which yamato kotoba are deciphered, either by conceptual meaning or through homophony (*kakekotoba*), as explained in notes 17 and 25.

Despite the standard list of classics sometimes invoked to describe the heroines' abilities as readers, the yamato kotoba usually do not seem to be allusions to famous poems. Given their contexts, the yamato kotoba passages in these works reflect a general understanding that waka were used in elegant courtship. But again, with the exception of *Minazuru*, there is little to indicate that the anonymous authors of these tales actually knew very much traditional poetry. As discussed in note 13, the phrase *nonaka no shimizu* appears in *Kokinshū*, *KT* no. 887. But the phrase is interpreted differently in various yamato kotoba contexts, and none of the interpretations appears to mirror the *Kokinshū* poem.

Hosotanigawa no marokibashi is a different case. These are the second and third lines in a pair of poems in *Heike monogatari*. In the first poem, the following line is *fumikaesarete*, used in the double sense of "repeatedly trodden" and "returning (spurning) a letter." In the response poem, the following line is *fumikaeshite*, meaning both "repeatedly trodden" and "returning (responding to) a letter."[27] The first yamato kotoba in *Oguri* is deciphered to mean, in part, "give me an answer (to my letter)." Clearly this is an allusion to the poem exchange, and the source is apt, a courtship exchange in *Heike monogatari*. Still, since *Heike monogatari* was transmitted through performed recitations as well as reading texts, knowledge of these poems might have been gained entirely aurally. Knowing the *Heike* tale of Michimori's courtship of Kozaishō would not necessarily mean having broad familiarity with classical poetry.

The correspondence in the kana zōshi *Uraminosuke* and *Usuyuki monogatari* seems to have had a particular appeal to women seeking epistolary models. But the yamato kotoba "letters" in otogi zōshi and sekkyō-bushi would not make useful models, as they are not actually answered. Whether in the guise of letters or as speech, they are presented by men and deciphered by women. In otogi zōshi and sekkyō-bushi, yamato kotoba were brainteasers rather than practical guides to exchanging fancy correspondence.

In his compelling dictionary of varieties of Japanese wordplay,[28] Suzuki Tōzō includes two separate sections entitled "Yamato kotoba." I shall discuss the first type of yamato kotoba later. The second type of yamato kotoba itself actually includes two kinds—"those used as love riddles and found in 'classics' [*koten*] from the Muromachi period onward and those found in the poetry dictionary *Yamato kotoba*, and other dictionaries, particularly those terms having the character of riddles."[29] Nearly two-thirds of the examples in this article are included in Suzuki's list. (His list does not include citations from *Minazuru* or the sekkyō-bushi texts.) Suzuki notes six of the examples we have seen—*uzumibi, oki kogu fune, katawarebune, nonaka no shimizu, fuetake,* and *marokibashi* —as appearing in the dictionary *Yamato kotoba*. This is also the source of most of his 230-odd examples (ten or so are from *Usuyuki monogatari* and a few from the otogi zōshi called *Ko otoko*).

The first dictionary with the title *Yamato kotoba* was printed, using movable type, sometime between the Genna and Kan'ei periods (1615–1644). A block-printed edition from 1663 is the earliest dated dictionary with this same title.[30] Through the ensuing years, as many as twenty-five different dictionaries of yamato kotoba were in circulation, some of them revisions or unrevised reprintings of earlier editions under new titles.[31] It is evident that such books were very popular. They generally were lists of elegant language—that is, native Japanese poetic terminology—most often images found in the twenty-one imperial anthologies, with the meanings explained and the source poems sometimes cited. The books were most commonly organized by readings, though a few were ordered by conceptual categories. They were not general kana dictionaries but, rather, selective glossaries of what one would need in order to read and write poetry and, by extension, to use these skills in order to write superior letters. The vogue for acquiring such knowledge coincided with the growing popularity of linked verse (*renga* and *haikai*), and the dictionaries were considered particularly useful in the education of women.[32]

Although some of the puzzle-type yamato kotoba we have seen in otogi zōshi and sekkyō-bushi do appear in some yamato kotoba dictionaries, a few examples from a typical yamato kotoba dictionary show that they incorporate a range of basic poetic vocabulary, not just opaque metaphors:

> *Akitsushima*—a name for Japan/*hinomoto*—also a name for our country/*moro-koshi*—means China/*azumaji*—means the road to the east/. . . *mubatama* means night/*nubatama*—means dream/*kuzu no ura kaze*—means resentment [not explained in the dictionary; apparently it was considered evident that the reason is homophony between *ura* in the expression that literally means "wind blowing under arrowroot leaves" and the *ura* of *urami*, "resentment" or "grudge"].[33]

There is some overlap between yamato kotoba dictionaries and the yamato kotoba of otogi zōshi and sekkyō-bushi, but many of these latter examples seem subtly different from the dictionaries' elegant expressions. We also need to consider Suzuki's other selection of yamato kotoba, listed as type I, with the prefatory note "Used until recent years in remote mountain areas of Kii and Yamato; a collection of love riddles."[34] Most of Suzuki's type I "love-riddle" yamato kotoba were originally collected by or for the ethnologist and folklorist Minakata Kumagusu and were published in the journal *Shūko* in 1922.[35] Inhabitants of a small community in Hidaka County of Wakayama Prefecture reported using these yamato kotoba in courtship notes and as verbal messages passed along to one another. Minakata mentioned the yamato kotoba section of *Jōruri jūnidan zōshi* as indicating a long tradition of using the term in the sense of "love riddles." Although there are no exact duplicates, he found the otogi zōshi yamato kotoba and the village variety essentially similar. Minakata speculated that the practice had previously been more widespread, and he found some people in neighboring villages who said that the use of yamato kotoba had persisted in their villages until about forty years earlier, that is, around the beginning of the Meiji era.

In 1980 the otogi zōshi scholar Ōshima Tatehiko accompanied a team of folklore researchers investigating customs in remote mountain villages along the
upper reaches of the Hidaka River, in the same general area as the community
where Minakata first encountered yamato kotoba. Yamato kotoba were by then
no longer used in this area, but Ōshima collected more than seventy-five examples that elderly people could still remember having heard.[36] Most of the people who could recall such expressions were born in the 1890s or the first decade
of the twentieth century. They noted that they had not themselves used such
expressions when courting one another but had heard them from their elders.
The active use of yamato kotoba in actual courtship seems to have remained
popular in this area throughout the 1920s, then to have declined suddenly. The
aging practitioners sustained their memories of yamato kotoba by transforming
the riddles and their explications into a social drinking game. By now, even these
final memories of local yamato kotoba are probably gone.

Ōshima collected forty-five examples of yamato kotoba, generally in the
form of . . . *to omoimasu*, "I think of you as . . ."; he was told this was the form in
which they were used, both orally and in letters. Here are a few examples:

Kawa mukai no satsuki (Azalea on the far side of a river) = "Pretty, but out of
reach." This is similar to an example collected by Minakata in 1922, *kawa mukai
no senryōbako* (a box containing a thousand *ryō* on the far side of a river) = "desirable but unreachable." *Okuyama no kobushi no hana* (Wild magnolia on a remote
mountain) = "Pretty when seen from a distance, but up close, nothing special."

All three examples can be unraveled conceptually, but as with the examples
in otogi zōshi, others depend on puns:

Senaka no teppō (A gun on one's back). The "answer," *ōte hanashitai*, is a pun
meaning both "I want to carry and shoot it" and "I want to meet and talk with you."

Shii no ki ni kama hatchō (eight sickles on an oak tree). This is deciphered as
yakamashii (noisy, boisterous) via wordplay on *ya* (eight), *kama* (sickle), and *shii*
(oak). (This is more like a rebus than the traditional kakekotoba of the kind found
in waka.)

Mikuni ichi no Nachi no taki (Nachi waterfall, the finest in three provinces).
This is a pun on the phrase *mizu ni horeta*, meaning both "entranced by the water"
and "to fall in love without seeing (someone)."

Ōshima notes that conceptual, or metaphorical, examples, like the first
three here, were less common than the more humorous type based on puns. He
also observes that these regional yamato kotoba derive from the local spoken
language rather than from poetic, "elegant language" (*gago*).

Minakata sees the otogi zōshi and local yamato kotoba as essentially similar, whereas Ōshima emphasizes their differences. Certainly, the examples

collected in the twentieth century utilize an unlimited vocabulary, including words in Sino-Japanese *on-yomi* (for example, *teppō* meaning "gun"), along with kun readings. My own feeling after reading all these types of "correspondence" is that the yamato kotoba of otogi zōshi and sekkyō-bushi are closer in spirit to the local yamato kotoba than to the elegant, poetic yamato kotoba of kana zōshi and most of the entries in the seventeenth-century yamato kotoba dictionaries.

The early-Edo-period texts containing the most elaborate yamato kotoba passages—the sekkyō-bushi texts of *Oguri* and *Shintokumaru* and the otogi zōshi texts of *Jōruri jūnidan zōshi*—derive from earlier performance traditions. Their most ancient forms were presumably "oral compositions."

According to Ōshima, the same people in the Kii peninsula who were adept at constructing yamato kotoba also used a completely nonverbal form of communication called "letters" (of a sort). *Kusabumi*, "grass (or plant) letters," were either letters, in the usual sense of the word, tied to certain grasses or other objects, or just the objects themselves. An example is a young woman bundling together *susuki* and *yomena* (plume grass and wild chrysanthemum) and sending it to her chosen young man, who would have understood <u>susuki</u> and <u>yomena</u> as *anata ga* <u>suki</u> *dakara*, <u>yome</u> *ni shite hoshii*: "I like you and I wish to be your bride."

In the early years of Meiji, an investigator of folk customs reported being shown a kusabumi in the Yunomine area of the Kii peninsula. He was told that it, too, was a courtship custom. One example involved binding together the leaves of plants called *omoiha*, *nezumochi*, and *matsu no ha* (pine needles) together with *koishi* (small stones). The reading for this is *omoeba koishi, nezu ni matsu*: "I long for you lovingly; I wait without sleeping."[37]

In the otogi zōshi *Minazuru* and *Ko otoko*, lovers send their courtship letters "bound in Yamato style." In the latter case the letter is bound together with a sprig of pine needles. For some contemporary readers the lovers' nonverbal communication—"I wait, I pine for you"—might have been transparent. Perhaps this, too, is evidence of the influence of local culture (though the cultural area may have been much wider than the last remnants in the mountains of Kii) and of "oral" (or even silent) language on the development of sekkyō-bushi and otogi zōshi.

Although they were used in notes as well as in speech, the traditional rural yamato kotoba were based on oral techniques, not literary allusions. Perhaps they were originally used verbally and came to be used in courtship notes only as literacy spread to the hinterlands. As mentioned earlier, the range of meanings of the term *yamato kotoba* (some of which are not germane and so not discussed in this chapter) is quite complex. In the case of the rural tradition, one evidently deeply rooted in the Kii–Yamato region, "yamato" kotoba may simply have meant a riddling tradition well known to local (that is, Yamato) people.

The origins and authorship of otogi zōshi and sekkyō-bushi also are obscure. The large numbers of textual variants and the lack of clear dating make it impossible to trace with certainty the evolution of any particular narrative. In many cases, such as *Jōruri jūnidan zōshi, Oguri* and *Shintokumaru*, an originally oral narrative presumably underwent a long development before first acquiring a written form. Perhaps the oral art of courtship riddling, the Kii–Yamato type of yamato kotoba, came first, and examples of this sort of riddling made their way into early oral narratives.

In the first half of the seventeenth century, just as otogi zōshi and sekkyō-bushi were becoming popular as reading texts, yamato kotoba—in their alternative sense of elegant, poetic vocabulary—became prized knowledge for newly literate groups bent on the composition of poetry and refined correspondence. With the exception of the first part of the letter in *Minazuru*, the yamato kotoba of otogi zōshi and sekkyō-bushi are not the typical yamato kotoba of the dictionaries. Rather, the yamato kotoba of otogi zōshi and sekkyō-bushi are essentially similar to Suzuki's type I local riddles, given a superficially literary guise. They are represented as the amorous correspondence of elevated women whose superior knowledge of classical literature accounts for their ability to read and "translate" the letters they receive.

The text of *Jōruri jūnidan zōshi* just discussed might reflect a transitional stage, with the riddles presented orally yet referred to almost as if they were a letter and, like a letter, requiring immediate response. The texts I have considered clearly place great value on both technical and cultural literacy, on both the ability to read and the ability to recognize and decipher classical allusions. But ironically, the phrases deciphered in the "letters" in these texts seem to have originated mainly in an essentially oral, preliterate art. Among the texts discussed, only *Minazuru* actually shows considerable authorial familiarity with classical source poems. In *Minazuru* we can see the convergence of two streams of yamato kotoba. Before long, the literary stream submerged the rural, so to speak, leading to the poetic, allusion-filled letters of kana zōshi. The yamato kotoba "letters" of otogi zōshi and sekkyō-bushi stem from a particularly interesting temporal juncture. In these texts, respect for literacy and literary skill is apparent, yet through them we can still glimpse the vitality of yamato kotoba as a spontaneous, oral, courtship ritual.

NOTES

1. *Minazuru,* in Yokoyama Shigeru and Matsumoto Ryūshin, eds., *Muromachi jidai monogatari taisei,* 15 vols. (Tokyo: Kadokawa shoten, 1985), vol. 13, pp. 13–23. (The letter is on pp. 16–17.) The manuscript transcribed in this volume is a *Nara ehon,* an inexpensively produced illustrated manuscript from the Kan'ei period (1624–1644). The editors give evidence to suggest that the story may have been in circulation as early as 1537, and they mention a 1585 diary reference to a Kōwakamai ballad drama performance of a text with the same title.

2. No doubt, choosing topics for articles in honor of Donald Keene has been easy for all of us contributors, as there surely is no subject in the field of Japanese literature unrelated to Professor Keene's writings. I have chosen this topic because the scene in question reminded me of the final moments of preparation for his seminars (puzzling over texts side by side with several other women graduate students) and of the pleasure I took in those classes as knots of incomprehension came untied and meanings became clear. The article is offered in gratitude to a wonderful teacher.

3. She is called Reisen when her name first appears in the text. It soon metathesizes to Rensei.

4. I am not sure just what *Koitsukushi* refers to. There is a certain redundancy here because *Kokinshū* is one of the eight imperial anthologies.

5. Ichiko Teiji, ed., *Otogi zōshi,* in *Nihon koten bungaku taikei,* vol. 38 (Tokyo: Iwanami shoten, 1958), pp. 346–60. (The letter is on pp. 348–49.) This is the Otogi bunko version of the story, published around 1700 by Shibukawa Seiemon. It seems closely based on a movable-type edition from the Genna period (1615–1624). See Barbara Ruch's chapter, "Transformation of a Heroine: Yokobue in Literature and History," in this volume.

6. Both texts can be found in Muroki Yatarō, ed., *Sekkyō shū* (Tokyo: Shinchōsha, 1977). *Oguri* is on pp. 209–98, and the letter is on pp. 222–24. Muroki's *Oguri* is based primarily on a scroll dating from sometime during the Kan'ei through Meireki periods (1624–1658). Muroki also used several other texts for comparison and supplementation, which are listed on pp. 420–21. *Shintokumaru* is on pp. 153–207, and the letter is on pp. 172–74. The primary basis for Muroki's edition is a printed book entitled *Sekkyō Shintokumaru,* published in Shōhō 5 (1648).

7. This is E. D. Hirsch's term for a common core of knowledge necessary for full participation in an educated society. Whatever one thinks of Hirsch's arguments, the concept seems eminently transferable here. See E. D. Hirsch Jr., *Cultural Literacy: What Every American Needs to Know* (Boston: Houghton Mifflin, 1987).

8. In this and following examples, I underline the phrases that may be understood to be the *yamato kotoba,* leaving various ancillary grammatical particles and phrases unmarked.

9. This is the first love poem in the *Shinkokinshū,* in *Kokka taikei,* rev. ed. (hereafter abbreviated *KT*), no. 990 (Tokyo: Kadokawa shoten, 1983–92). It appears in a variant form in *Taiheiki,* in *Toshiyori zuinō, Mumyōsho,* and elsewhere and must have been very widely known.

10. This love poem is *Shinkokinshū, KT,* no. 994. It is also found in *Ise monogatari* and various private collections.

11. *Zoku Gosen, KT,* no. 665.

12. This is the first love poem in the *Senzaishū, KT,* no. 651.

13. Although *Minazuru* cites no poem as the source for this phrase (nor do any of the other texts in which it appears), a possible basis for the allusion is *Kokinshū, KT,* no. 887: *inishie no / no-*

naka no shimizu/nurukeredo/moto no kokoro o/shiru hito zo kumu (The meadow spring/of long ago/may now be tepid,/yet those who knew it as it was/still scoop its waters). This is the suggestion of Noda Hisao in his annotation of the same phrase when it is used in the kana zōshi *Uraminosuke*. See Noda Hisao, *Kana zōshi shū, jō* (Tokyo: Asahi shinbunsha, 1960), p. 137.

14. These works are discussed in Donald Keene, *World Within Walls* (New York: Holt, Rinehart and Winston, 1976), pp. 149–52.

15. Explained by the similar sounds of *kogu*, "to row," and *kogaru*, "to burn," coupled with the conception of a boat approaching a harbor. Muroki, *Sekkyō shū*, p. 224, n. 1.

16. Some other *Oguri* texts have the form *shakunaga obi*, "a long sash," rather than *shakunai obi*, which is, at best, an odd waying of saying "a sash without length." With *shakunaga*, the riddle makes more sense. See Yokoyama Shigeru, ed., *Sekkyō shōhonshū* (Tokyo: Kadokawa shoten, 1968), vol. 2, pp. 58, 84.

17. Muroki, *Sekkyōshū*, p. 173, n. 10, cites a poem from *Zoku kokinshū* that he suggests as a possible allusive source. In note 11, Muroki explains the "reading" as "if a strong wind blows . . ."—*karakaze fukaba*—as follows: *Karakaze* "empty wind," means a strong wind without rain or snow; here it is introduced through homophony with *kara*, "bitter," which comes from the association with salt/salt maker's hut.

18. These would include the sekkyō-bushi *Aigo no waka* that contains a short passage in a letter using yamato kotoba, the otogi zōshi *Monogusa Tarō* in which the hero puzzles out a series of place-names presented to him in riddle form by the woman he is courting, and the otogi zōshi *Ko otoko* that includes a flowery letter somewhat resembling yamato kotoba. That letter is only perfunctorily deciphered.

19. For details, see Charles Dunn, *The Early Japanese Puppet Drama* (London: Luzac, 1966); and Donald Keene, *Bunraku* (Tokyo: Kodansha International, 1965), pp. 30–32.

20. In Matsumoto Ryūshin, ed., *Otogi zōshi shū* (Tokyo: Shinchōsha, 1980), pp. 9–74. The yamato kotoba passage is on pp. 50–51.

21. Fujikake Kazuyoshi, *Muromachi ki monogatari no kinseiteki tenkai* (Osaka: Izumi shoin, 1987), pp. 122–36. Fujikake devotes his entire third chapter to yamato kotoba in the *Jōruri* tale. He compares six versions and suggests that the oldest are two that do not use the term *yamato kotoba*, although he is not able to date precisely the first use of the term.

22. Matsumoto, *Otogi zōshi shū*, p. 49.

23. Matsumoto's note suggests that the connection here would be the similarity to separating grasses to find the pure water bubbling below.

24. The decipherment in *Oguri* (line 11) makes fuller sense of this.

25. "Once intact" (*moto wa hitotsu*) is a homophone for "one root," the single root from which arrowroot tends to spread rampantly.

26. Here, in *gojūon* order, are all the examples previously mentioned. Those in boldface occur more than once: **asama no take**/*ayamegusa*/*ike no makomo*/*Ise no hamaogi, shioya*/*ukigumo*/*uzumibi*/**usumomiji**/*utsu suminawa*/*ume no tachie no uguisu*/**oki kogu fune**/*katawarebune*/**kishi utsu nami**/*Kiyomizuzaka*/*keshō no obi*/*koki kurenai*/**shakunai obi**/*shioya no kemuri*/*shita hau kuzu*/*tani no mumoregi*/*tsutsui no mizu*/*tsunaganu koma*/**tsuru na(k)i yumi**/*Nachi no oyama*/**nezasa ni arare**/**noki no shinobu**/**nonaka no shimizu**/*hane nai* (or *hana nuke*) *tori*/*hitomura susuki*/*fuetake*/*Fuji no takane*/*futamatagawa*/*futamoto susuki*/**hosotanigawa**/*marokibashi*/**mitsu no oyama**/*mine ni tatsu shika*.

27. In Takagi Ichinosuke et al., eds., *Heike monogatari, ge* (Tokyo: Iwanami shoten, 1960), pp. 234–35. Translated in Helen Craig McCullough, *The Tale of the Heike* (Stanford, CA: Stanford University Press, 1988), pp. 323–24.

28. Suzuki Tōzō, ed., *Kotoba asobi jiten*, rev. ed. (Tokyo: Tōkyōdō, 1981).

29. Ibid., p. 521.

30. "Yamato kotoba," in *Nihon koten bungaku daijiten*, 6 vols. (Tokyo: Iwanami shoten, 1983–1985), vol. 6, p. 83.

31. My main source of information on yamato kotoba dictionaries is Mashimo Saburō, *Fujin go no kenkyū* (Tokyo: Tōkyōdō, 1969), pp. 204–17.

32. For example, *Onna chōhōki*, an influential guide to women's deportment published in 1692, includes a section on yamato kotoba.

33. Fujikake, *Muromachi ki*, p. 132, gives the list. Mashimo, *Fujin go*, pp. 206–7, lists twenty-three examples (out of a total of 770) from *Zōhō yamato kotoba*, Empō 9 (1681), emphasizing that their sources were mainly waka.

34. Suzuki, *Kotoba asobi*, p. 515.

35. The original article, from March 1922, and an additional note on the subject from the November issue of the same year, are included in *Minakata Kumagusu zenshū*, 12 vols. (Tokyo: Heibonsha, 1971–1975), vol. 3, pp. 385–90.

36. Ōshima Tatehiko, "'Yamato kotoba' no denshō," *Gengo* 6 (June 1981): 54–59.

37. There is a similar example in vol. 3 of *Seishuishō*, a collection of comic anecdotes by Anrakuan Sakuden, written in 1623. An elderly couple are living apart but longing for each other. The old man sends the woman *ubara* (= *ibara*, brambles) with *koishi* (little stones). The woman adds *konuka* (rice bran) and sends the bundle back. She has understood his message as *ubara koishi* (I long for you, old woman), and her response is explained as meaning *ubara koishikuba konuka* (If you're longing for this old woman, won't you come here?). Quoted in Ōshima Tatehiko, "Otogi zōshi to kotoba asobi," *Kokubungaku* 22 (December 1977): 46–51.

9

Yosano Akiko in Heaven and Earth

◉

JANINE BEICHMAN

Even one who does not believe in a world beyond draws
phantoms that cannot exist in this one.

The Firebird, 1919[1]

Yosano Akiko (1878–1942) is always counted among the giants of modern
Japanese poetry. Strangely enough, however, popular opinion is that she wrote
nothing of real literary importance after her twenties. Even though she published prolifically for nearly forty-five years, almost up until her death at the
age of sixty-four, her reputation today rests almost entirely on two works,
both written before she was twenty-five: *Midaregami* (Tangled Hair, 1901), her
first collection of *tanka* and one of the classics of modern Japanese poetry; and
"Kimi shinitamau koto nakare" (Beloved,You Must Not Die, 1904), a modern-
style poem of only forty lines. In part, this assessment reflects the fact that
youthful love—the predominant subject of Akiko's early poetry—always has
more popular appeal than anything to do with life past thirty. As Donald
Keene wrote,

> Though her later poetry was technically and artistically superior, flaming youth
> rather than the ripeness of age was what the public asked of Akiko, and they found
> it in *Tangled Hair.* LikeThéophile Gautier, always remembered in terms of the red
> vest he wore to the opening of *Hernani,* even when he was an old man, Akiko cap-
> tured so vividly the headstrong emotions of a sensual girl that readers never per-
> mitted her to grow up.[2]

An equally important factor was the attacks of the Araragi school of tanka poets,[3] especially Itō Sachio (1864–1913) and Saitō Mokichi (1882–1953). These had a damaging effect on Akiko's reputation, an effect only now beginning to be undone by the reevaluations of Akiko and other female writers that women's studies has inspired.[4] Mokichi's priceless comment, made to a friend after Akiko's funeral in 1942—"She was a genius, to be sure. . . . But what's a woman, in the end?"—suggests the sexism that tainted his (and his teacher Sachio's) view of Akiko. There were genuine artistic differences as well, and they are usually summed up by the terms *realism* (for Araragi) and *romanticism* (for Akiko and the Myōjō poets). The simplicity of the scheme conceals as much as it reveals, but if realism can be defined in the context of the modern Japanese tanka as fidelity to the everyday, then Akiko and many of the Myōjō poets were united by a longing for the sublime. Akiko's distinctive quality, as both a poet and a human being, was that in her this longing was grounded in a firm sense of reality. Travel back and forth between the real world and imagined ones was a basic dynamic of her personality as well as her poetry.

In the rest of this chapter, I trace early appearances of this dynamic in Akiko's childhood and adolescence and suggest how they relate to the poetry she wrote later. My approach combines biography with literary analysis and gives equal weight to the child's inner life and the adult's poetry.

Childhood

Ōtori[5] Shō, later to become Yosano Akiko, was not a wanted child. Sent to live with a maternal aunt when just a month old, she returned home a short time before she reached the age of two,[6] but her mother, preoccupied with her household duties and the family store as well as trying to please a demanding mother-in-law, left Akiko's care to servants. Her father, who had not wanted a girl from the beginning, showed little interest in her. In "Osanaki hi" (Childhood Days, 1909), one of the article-length memoirs that Akiko, like many other Meiji-period writers and artists, was commissioned to write, she remembered:

> When I stood before the mirror in my older brother's hand-me-down red flannel shirt, fumbling with a collar button that I could not fasten no matter how hard I tried, or when I lit my own lamp at night to fetch hot water from the kitchen, then went to bed, alone in the dark, I wondered if the couple I called my parents were my real mother and father.

Father was always abrupt, but Mother was terrifying. Once when I . . . spilled my bowl of rice, Father rushed over saying, "Pick it up before she sees!" and hurriedly helped me clean up the mess. My younger brother was still nursing from Mother's breast when he was seven. I used to wish I were him.[7]

Bitter as these memories were, the spiritual isolation in which Shō grew up was not extreme enough to stunt her. It had, in fact, the virtue of leaving room for the flowering of imagination and an intense inner life that served her well as a poet in adulthood.

The Ōtori home and store were near Yokokōji, a neighborhood of doll makers, and the Aguchi shrine, familiarly called Big Temple. Shō often visited both, taken by a maid she called Bei. In Yokokōji, she saw "the first thing I hated." It was the Empress Jingū doll, one of the dolls made for the Doll Festival in May and thus found in every store. Clad in red-threaded armor and a warrior's headband, the doll, her face all sweet femininity, knelt on one knee, leaning forward as if to join combat at a moment's notice. It was, thought Akiko later, that strange combination of femininity and fierce aggression that had inspired her fear and loathing.

When Shō was three, the Empress Jingū doll and the shrine came together in a dream. Akiko related it later, in "Childhood Days":

I heard people talking about an exposition in Nara. I think my father had taken my older brother and sisters. I tried again and again to sketch an image in my head, but try as I might, I could not imagine what it could be. Then one night in a dream I saw open-air stalls flanking the stone path that led to Big Temple, with Empress Jingū dolls displayed in them. "This," I was told, "is an exposition."

After that dream, I thought that expositions must be horrible things, and at the same time, I realized, with frustration, that certain things in this world were beyond my powers of imagining.[8]

"I was told" (*oshierarete*), Akiko said, but not by whom. The information doubtless came from an adult, but the words, their source unspecified, suggest the nonhuman voice of religious revelation or artistic inspiration. It is as if the child stood before the door to the outside world, the will to explore so great that even as she slept it went right on working, until she transcended her own physical boundaries, flying in her dream from Sakai to an imaginary Nara. As the modern American poet Anne Sexton once said, "Sometimes the soul takes pictures of things it wishes for but has never seen."[9]

The lineaments of the adult are so clear here that I do not know whether to call the dreamer Shō, as she was then, or Akiko, the name she took later. Both shared that same instinctive movement from the world of reality to the world of dreams and the equally instinctive movement back, so that the absoluteness of vision coexisted with the practical sense of one's own limited powers. Three decades later, speaking through the heroine of her autobiographical novel *Akarumi e* (To the Light, 1913), Akiko wrote an extended defense of her poetry, which concluded,

> I dream of the life a genius leads and write as if it were my own. . . . I may be an ordinary person but I am not only that: I am an ordinary person who dreams of genius. When I write of myself without lying, this double life of necessity becomes the poem.[10]

Ōtori Shō, the three-year-old child, frustrated by the gulf between her own limited reality and the great world outside, already understood the conflicting claims of reality and imagination. Yosano Akiko, the poet, used that contradiction to her own advantage, nourished by its fertility.

Adolescence

"From the age of seven or eight," Akiko wrote when she was in her thirties, "I felt I was a creature from another world."[11] This sense of alienation from her surroundings made it impossible for her to share with anyone the terrifying fantasies of her own death that began, as she wrote in the autobiographical essay "Aru asa" (One Morning, 1911), when she was ten. Instead, she sought escape in activity, reading omnivorously in the classical literature (especially *The Tale of Genji*) that later influenced her poetry so deeply.[12] Then at about fifteen,[13] as if the extravagance of those imaginary worlds had emboldened her, Akiko created her own solution to the fear of death, in the vision of a world beyond so beautiful that death seemed almost desirable:

> I came to believe in a vague way that somewhere in the universe there existed a world, call it Paradise, call it Heaven, at any rate a world happier than the real one, pure and beautiful, and difficult to know with the human mind. I saw it often in my dreams. I wanted so much to die in my sleep and be reborn into this beautiful world that I even spread flowers to sleep on. Before I slept, I prayed to a god who was not Buddha or the Christian god but an unknown god of my own.[14]

Like the vision of the exposition at age three, this one, too, had its practical side. Just in case the world she had imagined turned out not to exist, the young Akiko hedged her bets by reading secretly in pharmaceutical texts, seeking a formula that would make her into a fossil to survive eternally. For all the intensity of her inner life, though, she continued to lead an outwardly normal existence. From the age of twelve, she kept the accounts in the family store (her family owned the Surugaya, a well-known confectionary) and spent many hours wrapping the *yōkan* that was its principal product. She did well in school and got along well with family, friends, and the store employees.[15] As Akiko later put it, "I was living in a separate fantasy world, but for the sake of my pride tried to behave impeccably in this one."[16]

All along she was reading and, probably from the age of seventeen, writing. Sometime after she published her first poem in 1895,[17] the young Akiko had a sudden realization:

> After my elder sister married, I worked in the store, keeping the accounts, and in the intervals I used to wrap the yōkan. In those days we used bamboo bark in quantity; the folding, wrapping, inserting, tamping down, and pressing meant that my fingers were constantly at work. I used to make up poems as I worked looking down. . . . But eventually I realized they were all mediocre. "It must be because I'm stuck in a woman's body," I thought, and decided to write as if I were a man.[18]

The same powerful imagination that had scaled the wall between her own circumscribed reality and the world beyond at the age of three now tore down, with the same innocent daring, the boundary between male and female. *Tangled Hair*, that classic of erotic poetry, began with a young woman's decision to undo gender; it was the poetic equivalent of cross-dressing. From the male model, Akiko took a strength, an insistence, an aggressiveness that she could never have permitted herself as a woman. But the emotions that she was expressing were romantic ones, and it was a woman that was voicing them. The voice that evolved from this union of male and female sometimes seems suprahuman, as though echoing from great distances. Akiko herself later wrote that in this early poetry, "without realizing it, my imagination had come to transcend the sexes."[19]

By the time Akiko entered her twenties, the attractions of the fantasy world had yielded to those of poetry. In August 1900, already an important contributor to *Myōjō*, the leading poetry journal of that time, she met and fell in love with its editor, Yosano Tekkan,[20] who as the founder of the New Poetry Society was a leader in the effort to reform Japanese poetry. The next year, after a dramatic courtship and flight from home, she married Tekkan and embarked in earnest on her poetic career. In one of her simpler formulations of this sea change, Akiko wrote: "After I turned twenty, my life as a poet opened before me, and the fear of death gave way to a heady pursuit of the joy of being alive."[21]

The Poet: Immortal Voices

From early on, Akiko's poetry had the same strong sense of connection to unseen worlds that had colored her life from early childhood. Her first tanka collection, *Tangled Hair*, opens with this poem:

> A star that once
> within night's velvet
> whispered all the words of love
> is now a mortal in the world below—
> Look on this swirling hair![22]

> *yo no chō ni / sasamekitsukishi / hoshi no ima wo / gekai no hito no / bin no hotsure yo*

Once there was a star in heaven who spent whole nights into the dawn in perfect loving bliss. But now, reborn as a mortal woman on earth, she is sleepless with frustrated passion, expressed in her unkempt hair. A strange figure, this woman, this star—passionately female and unquestionably human, but at the same time transcendent and incorporeal, her body represented only by her hair. Vivid and obscure at the same time, she and similar figures who might be her sisters or cousins populated many of the poems in *Tangled Hair*.

With this poem about the descent from heavenly perfection to human desperation, Akiko placed herself, whether intentionally or not, in the line of heaven-sent women that runs through classical Japanese literature, from the moon maiden Kaguyahime to the angel of the nō play *Hagoromo*. The more immediate provenance, though, was undoubtedly the image of *hoshi no ko*, or "child of the stars," that appeared in several poems by members of the New Poetry Society from 1900 onward.[23] Even before that, there was Akiko's own long-standing sense of difference: In the background of this poem, like a shadow, floats the image of the child of "seven or eight" who already felt she was "a creature from another world."

Akiko's husband, Tekkan, was one of the most reliable interpreters of her poems. It seemed obvious to him that the speaker of the first of the following two poems was an incarnation of the goddess of love.[24] The second is, in my view, best read in the same way.

> Pressing my breasts
> I softly kick aside

the curtain of mystery
> How deep the crimson
> of the flower here[25]

chibusa osae/shimpi no tobari/soto kerinu/koko naru hana no/kurenai zo koki

"Let men pay for their
many sins!"—so came the words
when I was made
> with my face so fair
> and this long flow of black hair[26]

tsumi ooki/otoko korase to/hada kiyoku/kurokami nagaku/tsukurareshi ware

If the star recalled Kaguyahime or the angel of *Hagoromo*, these incarnations of the goddess of love bring to mind Venus. But too strong an identification with any existing mythical figure is misleading; all were creatures of Akiko's own private, unformulated mythology, creations of the same irrepressible imagination that in her teens had invented her own paradise and its reigning god, borrowing elements of Buddhism and Christianity and yet parting from both.

A slightly later variation on these powerful speakers appeared in Akiko's second collection, *Saōgi* (The Little Fan, 1904):

Farewell my love,
to youth farewell
Sleep on stones
> and grieve
>> for the light of spring[27]

kimi saraba/saraba hatachi wo/ishi ni nete/haru no hikari wo/kanashimitamae

The speaker is addressing a young friend who has chosen a life of renunciation, probably the priesthood. "Sleep on stones" is a metaphor for austerities. "The light of spring" is youth, love, sexuality. The speaker is human and mortal, for she has a youth to bid farewell to. But the sweeping, imperious tone comes from somewhere beyond. She may be on earth, but something that transcends the human is speaking through her.

Prisoner of Love to Birthing Woman

In 1902, Akiko's first child, Hikaru, was born. By 1904, when her second, Shigeru, arrived, she felt trapped. She later recollected: "Unable to do anything because of the children, I felt that I was falling apart and resolved to establish myself as a poet."[28] As the poet in her real life moved deeper into the female space of marriage and childbirth, the love goddesses of the early poetry receded. The poet's imaginary selves reflected the changing facts of her own life. In a tenderly ironic poem in *The Little Fan*, the speaker compared herself as a poet with a decaying minor deity, and herself as a lover with a penned-up lamb waiting for slaughter, perhaps, or sacrifice:

> A feather shed
>   by a love-aged god
> here hymns
>   o little lamb
>   your jail joys[29]

koi ni oishi / kami no nukeba no / mi wa koko ni / kohitsuji kimi ga / ori no sachi yomu

As the star of the *Tangled Hair* poem was reduced to a lock of human hair, so here the poet herself, once a god of love, is now no more than its molted feather. The lamb is herself as a captive lover bound, literally, in matrimony. That is, the poet is describing her own poems ironically, as songs of praise for her own imprisonment. The "country of spring, kingdom of love" (*haru no kuni, koi no mikuni*)[30] that once seemed to promise boundless freedom has become its own prison. And yet that prison, once lost, is missed.

The first tanka of *Yume no hana* (Dream Flowers, 1906) moved in a logical progression from disillusion to fear and then to a sense of emptiness:

> In terror the heart
> awakes from love—
>   And where shall it look?
>   Is there no jail
>   to take my eyes?[31]

osoroshiki / koizame gokoro / nani wo miru / waga me toraemu / hitoya wa naki ya

Then, in the poems of middle age, a new and weary voice, absorbed by the sorrow of aging and the downside of a long relationship, emerged. In contrast to the oracular tone of much of Akiko's early poetry, this was closer to a sad whisper to the self, as in the 1909 *Saohime*:

. . . don't know
which goes first,
heart or body,
but
it's sad . . .[32]

kokoro mazu / otoroenikemu / katachi mazu / otoroenikemu / shiranedo kanashi

Or this from the 1911 *Shundeishū* (Spring Thaw):[33]

. . . alone
is better
    nothing sadder
    than two
    depressed together[34]

ichinin wa / nao yoshi mono wo / omoeru ga / futari aru yori / kanashiki wa nashi

For this speaker, it was not heaven that had been a golden age but, rather, those first early years of love on earth:

. . . can't forget
those three years of my life
when it seemed as if
    gods and buddhas
    had touched the earth . . .[35]

kami hotoke / arawareshi goto / omowareshi / waga yo no mitose / wasurekanetsumo

Hi no tori (The Firebird, 1919), published when Akiko was forty-one, contains poems that bespeak an even bleaker inner landscape:

Even at the bottom of my heart
there's nothing
left for you beyond these words
The nothing
hurts[36]

mizukara no / kokoro no soko mo / kimi ni iu / kono kotoba yori / naki ga itamashi

Side by side with this tired, sad voice was another one, just as earthly but without the weariness, full, instead, of passion and fire. Audible as early as 1906, this voice surfaced again in some of Akiko's modern-style poems about middle age, which she wrote at almost the same time as the bleakest of the preceding tanka, and reached its finest expression in the birth poems of 1911 and afterward.

This intense, almost surrealistic tanka was from the 1906 *Maihime* (The Dancing Girl, 1906):

Peony in my hair
becomes a flame
the sea burns
    Mad with love
    earth's child dreams[37]

kazashitaru / botan hi to nari / umi moenu / omoimidaruru / hito no ko no yume

The speaker here, unequivocally human, a "child of earth,"[38] was the paired opposite of the star woman with which *Tangled Hair* opened. The affirmative identification with planet earth had displaced a sense of heavenly origins. The famous and much-translated modern-style poem *Yama no ugoku hi kitaru* (The Day the Mountains Move Has Come), which Akiko contributed in 1908 to the debut issue of *Seitō*, Japan's first literary feminist magazine, continued the same identification.

Other poems imagined a different kind of fire, as brightly colored as the earlier one, but silent and unmoving. Passion remained but had become interiorized. The modern-style poem "Sanjū onna no kokoro" (The Heart of a Thirtyish Woman, 1915), written when Akiko was thirty-seven, compared the heart of a woman in her thirties to the blazing evening sun:

The heart of a thirtyish woman
is a shadowless, smokeless,

soundless ball of fire, a crimson sun
set against the evening sky,
unmoving . . .
burning, burning, burning . . .[39]

The voice of the earthly speaker was strongest and most powerful in Akiko's poems about birth. As Akiko in her twenties had broken the taboo on speaking about physical love, so now in her thirties she broke the taboo on speaking about the act of birth. She developed her own image of birth as a journey to death and back, with the birth giver compared with a warrior. She challenged the traditional attitude that the woman should bear her pain in silence. She expressed with searing honesty the anger and fear that the birthing woman could feel, as well as her joy.

Akiko's earliest poems about birth were first published in several different magazines and newspapers in 1911. The following year they appeared, with additions, in *Seigaiha* (Blue Waves on the Sea, 1912), as a twenty-seven-poem tanka sequence describing the birth of Akiko's second set of twins, her sixth and seventh children.[40] Then came the modern-style poems *Ubuya no yoake* (Dawn in the Birthing Room, 1914), written on the birth of her ninth child, Hélène, and *Dai'ichi no jintsū* (The First Labor Pain, 1915).[41]

"Dawn in the Birthing Room," which uses the baby's real name, is as much an autobiographical document as it is a poem. The speaker lies on the bed, exhausted after giving birth. But as the dawn sun colors the white walls, she revives and ends by stretching out her hands to the sun, deriving inspiration from its endurance.

Through the window glass comes dawn,
like a pale cocoon . . .
Then something crawls silently
across the maternity room wall,
trailing a faint thread of coral light.
Or so I thought . . . but no,
it is the early winter sun,
a fragile butterfly, emerging.

Here lies a woman
eight times escaped to return from death—
she is myself, a pale woman,
with my daughter Hélène,
like a wild camellia's firm bud,

in her fifth day of life,
and a vase of roses
and the pale peach-color butterfly sun,
shy as first love.
Such a silent, pristine dawn!
Noble sun, how I missed you.
I lie down now
like a soldier wounded in battle,
exhausted.
But my newfound joy
is like the belief of sun worship.
Accept my outstretched hands,
O sun, empress of the dawn!
You know both night and winter,
and for millions of years
with the heroic power of your heavenly flames
have endured infinitudes of deaths
and always returned to life.
I will follow you.
I have returned alive only eight times,
a mere eight times come through
the screams, the blood, death's darkness.[42]

Perhaps it was the spirit behind these poems that Akiko was thinking of when she said that in her poetry after 1911, "I returned to the female."[43]

Portraits of the Artist

In a note at the end of *The Firebird*, Tekkan explained that the firebird was the phoenix, the beautiful multicolored bird of Egyptian legend that "immolates itself in the sun's holy flames and then at once is reborn from its own ashes . . ., a symbol of immortality."[44] From *Tangled Hair* onward, many of the titles of Akiko's more than twenty tanka collections seem like figurative eponyms. *The Firebird* was no exception. One of its poems seemed to record the psychic death of one self and the birth of another:

And then one morning,
  surprised,

I found myself
　　at the brink of wisdom,
　　　　having forgotten love[45]

to aru asa / koi wo wasurete / kenjin no / kiwa ni narinu to / odorokinu ware

Another poem moved into a new realm altogether, that of the artist, which it depicted as a figure who, like the phoenix, transcended life and death:

Half-horse
　half-woman
　　on me red rains of coral
　　　　　　　　fall
　　blue showers of lapis lazuli[46]

mizukara wa / hanjin hanba / furu mono wa / sango no ame to / hekiruri no ame

A centaur-like creature gallops about the heavens, bathed in a rainbow of jewels, perhaps showers of iridescent shooting stars. The figure evokes the *tenba*, or heavenly horse of Chinese legend, as well as heroic Pegasus and the centaurs of Greek myth. There is also a hint of our final glimpse of the angel in the nō play *Hagoromo*, who showers the earth with jewels as she ascends to the sky. Yet none of these images fits. Unlike the tenba and Pegasus, this creature is half human. Unlike the coarse male centaur, the creature's human half, in this autobiographical poem, is female. And of course, she is no angel either. We are again in the realm of Akiko's private mythology, as seen in her early visions of paradise. The reader is challenged to complete the image to which the words point. But this one can say without doubt: as the phrase *tenba sora wo yuku*—meaning that one's thoughts are as free and unrestricted as the heavenly horse that gallops around the heavens—implies, this poem is not about the realm of love but about that of art, the liminal Eden of the imagination where the poet roams. It is a metaphoric portrait of the artist.[47]

It would be false to imply that the artist as speaker emerged only after the disappearance of the lover. In fact, Akiko always wrote in several voices, and those poems depicting the liminal world of the artistic imagination began much earlier. In the 1911 "Waga uta" (My Poems), a modern-style poem, the speaker explained why she wrote the short tanka.

Because my songs are brief,
People think I hoarded words.
I have spared nothing in my songs.
There is nothing I can add.
Unlike a fish, my soul swims without gills.
I sing on one breath.[48]

The premise is that the poet's soul must dive into the metaphoric sea of imagination in order to create—but, being without gills, can stay there only briefly,
hence can create only short poems. The poet is a sort of mermaid, a cross
between a human and an animal, like the "half-horse half-woman" of the tanka
from *The Firebird*. (The ease with which Akiko crosses these interspecies boundaries is reminiscent of the ease with which she crossed gender boundaries to
create the oracular voice of her early poems.)

The same metaphor of the sea as the poet's imagination was at the base of the
allegorical poem "Kanashikereba" (I Was Sad, 1928):

I was sad so I said
"I'll row a boat"
I rowed the boat but still was lonely
Then I said "I'll wait for moonrise"
    For a long time
    the sea lay still, like a closed book
    with no voice for me
    and then
a round moon
danced out upon
the waves and I said
    "I want a long pole,
    to hook that coral fish!"[49]

Here the poet, longing for a poem, tests the waters of her own mind, which is a
sea, but it is "like a closed book" without words. Finally, after waiting, an idea for
a poem, an inspiration, appears on that unroiled sea, bright and beautiful. Its
image is the moon, which in turn is compared to a coral fish. To "hook" the fish,
take it up, and return to land is to write the poem. The poet is a fisherwoman,
an *ama* in a boat, and inspiration is an imaginary moon on the waters of the mind.

Only four years earlier, in the collection *Ryūsei no michi* (The Meteor's Path,
1924), Akiko had published a poem that forms a diptych with the tanka "half-

horse half-woman" and, like it, benefits from being read with accompanying matter, in this case Akiko's own preface to the collection, in which she wrote:

> I am delighted that there is a publishing house kind enough to take on the poems of an amateur who stands outside the main currents of the world of tanka and that there are still a small number of friends who read me.
>
> I escaped death in the Great Earthquake last year and recovered from illness this spring, but I have always had a presentiment that my life will be short and feel that I will not be writing for many more years. *The Meteor's Path*, a fleeting memento of one small personality, will doubtless be swallowed up in the darkness of eternity.[50]

This is the first poem of *The Meteor's Path*:

Half its way
across the sky
is light,
the other half is dark:
the meteor's path[51]

misora yori / nakaba wa tsuzuku / akaki michi / nakaba wa kuraki / ryūsei no michi

This can be taken as a realistic description of the path of a meteor. But when read against the preface, the meteor is clearly meant as an emblem of Akiko herself, both the woman moving from life and light to death and darkness and the artist, falling from heaven, first brilliantly bright with the early celebrity of *Tangled Hair* and the glorious early days of *Myōjō* and then lost in darkness, just as *Myōjō* waned while *Araragi* waxed.

In contrast to the portrait from *The Firebird*, which leaves behind the vagaries of literary history and Akiko's own career for the transcendent realm of art, the preface and first poem of *The Meteor's Path* are vitally connected to both. The sense of evanescence and mortality are as strong here as the affirmation of eternity is in *The Firebird*. And yet the covert message is almost as powerful as anything in *The Firebird*: that she might not be visible to others but was still a denizen of the skies, their vast mystery the only metaphor that could express her cosmic sense of self. In spite of its bleakness, the meteor poem suggests the vaster view that sustained Akiko. It almost seems to be speaking to us now, telling us to shine our light into the darkness of "the other half."

Epilogue

The poet and novelist Satō Haruo (1892–1964) was not the most reliable of biographers, but his vision of Akiko's ghost provides an irresistibly fitting last image of her traveling back to this world after her death, as easily and matter-of-factly as in life she traveled between the real and the imaginary, weaving her seamless web between worlds.

In 1948, six years after Akiko's death, Haruo had a long-awaited reunion with the poet and translator Horiguchi Daigaku (1892–1981) at the home of Daigaku's wife, deep in the Niigata countryside. Haruo and Daigaku had been close friends ever since Akiko and Tekkan had introduced them more than thirty-five years ago, and much of their talk was devoted to fond reminiscences of Akiko, who had been very kind to both.

The night before Haruo and his wife were to leave, Haruo, having drunk a bit too much, woke in the middle of the night to relieve himself. As he emerged from the toilet, a familiar voice addressed him in a friendly tone, asking, "Did you eat something that disagreed with you?"

There was Akiko, "standing in the corner of the corridor, her head inclined forward. She shone dimly, like a phosphorescent body." Then, in the delicate voice he knew so well, she recited this tanka twice:

I came to enjoy myself in this mortal world
It's better than Paradise, for memories fill it

She added:

Everyone travels from the Western Paradise to the other ones, but hardly anyone comes back to this world. I guess I'm just as odd as I always was. I was with you all the way from Akakura in that bus and then that horribly crowded train. I wondered what the two of you would talk about after such a long time apart. I felt sure you'd talk about us. I wanted so much to hear what you would say. There are so few people left these days who remember us. Thank you so much for having me today.[52]

How like Akiko, who in reality traveled all over Japan in her later years and whose poems so often involved cosmic travel, to make the journey back to this world after her death. And how like her, too, to come back out of nostalgia, affection, and curiosity rather than any of the usual murderous or tortured impulses that traditionally afflict Japanese ghosts. The phrase, "she shone dimly, like a phosphorescent body," is especially striking. It is as though Akiko had stepped out of one of her own poems, half human and half divine.

ACKNOWLEDGMENTS

I would like to thank Carroll Aikins Beichman, Andrew C. A. Jampoler, and Susan Matisoff for their helpful comments. Parts of this chapter have appeared in different form in the *Japan Quarterly*, *Journal of the Association of Teachers of Japanese*, and *The Japan Times*.

NOTES

1. *nochi no yo wo/nashi to suru mi mo/kono yo nite/mata ariezaru/maboroshi wo kaku. Hi no tori* in *Teihon Yosano Akiko zenshū* (hereafter abbreviated *TYAZ*), vol. 4 (Tokyo: Kōdansha, 1982), p. 3.

2. Donald Keene, *Dawn to the West: Japan Literature in the Modern Era, Poetry, Drama, Criticism* (New York: Holt, Rinehart and Winston, 1984), pp. 24–25.

3. The Araragi school traced its origins back to Masaoka Shiki (1867–1902), whose haiku activities were responsible for the resurgence of the haiku as a serious art form in the Meiji period and who later applied himself to the tanka as well. Sachio studied tanka with Shiki, and Mokichi studied with Sachio, but both were more doctrinaire and disputatious than Shiki. See Janine Beichman, *Masaoka Shiki* (New York: Kodansha International, 1986); and Amy Vladeck Heinrich, *Fragments of Rainbows: The Life and Poetry of Saitō Mokichi, 1882–1953* (New York: Columbia University Press, 1983).

4. The late Yoshida Seiichi, the preeminent critic of modern romanticism in Japanese poetry, used typically sexist arguments to support his contention that nothing Akiko wrote after her early thirties had significance as literature. See Janine Beichman, "Bungaku ni okeru seisabetsu: Yosano Akiko no hyōka wo megutte," *Kashin* 1 (August 1987): 29–35. The quotation from Mokichi in the next paragraph is from p. 30.

Contemporary critics engaged in reevaluating Akiko's later poetry include Baba Akiko, Michiura Motoko, Ōoka Makoto, and others. Their path has been made easier by the work of such members of the previous generation as the tanka critics Kimata Osamu and Shinma Shin'ichi.

It must be mentioned that Araragi's views of Akiko, influential as they were in creating the popular conception of her work, were not accepted by some of the leading literary figures of the Meiji and Taishō periods, including Mori Ōgai and Arishima Takeo. Their admiration was echoed by certain members of the next generation, such as the great scholar of Chinese literature Yoshikawa Kojirō, who in Kyoto in the 1950s asked Donald Keene if he were going to include Akiko's work in his anthology of Japanese literature.

5. Akiko herself read her surname as Ōtori, not Hō. See *TYAZ*, vol. 1 (Tokyo: Kōdansha, 1979), p. 36, poem 53, which necessitates that reading in order to scan it.

6. All ages given are in the modern *man* style. When my source is in traditional *kazoedoshi* style, I have converted it.

7. *Fujin kurabu* 2 (October 1909): 29.

8. "Childhood Days," pp. 26–27. Akiko gives her age here as five. However, she is using kazoe-doshi and, because she was born on December 7, was a *toshiyowa* child. This and the comparison with childhood reminiscences she wrote in the Taishō period, when she consistently used *man* to count ages, make it clear that by modern count she was three.

9. Diane Wood Middlebrook, *Anne Sexton: A Biography* (Boston: Houghton Mifflin, 1991), p. 358.

10. *TYAZ*, vol. 11 (Tokyo: Kōdansha, 1980), pp. 110–11.

11. "Watakushi no teisōkan," in *TYAZ*, vol. 14 (Tokyo: Kōdansha, 1980), p. 374.

12. *Waseda bungaku*, July 1911, p. 239.

13. It could also have been sixteen or seventeen. "One Morning" does not make the exact age clear.

14. "One Morning," pp. 241–42.

15. Ibid., p. 240.

16. "My Conception of Chastity," p. 378.

17. *TYAZ*, vol. 1, p. 299, has the poem.

18. Quoted in Shimamoto Hisae, *Meiji no joseitachi* (Tokyo: Misuzu shobō, 1966), p. 372.

19. *Gendai tanka zenshū Yosano Hiroshi shū Yosano Akiko shū* (Tokyo: Kaizōsha, 1929), vol. 5, pp. 410–11.

20. Tekkan's real name was Hiroshi, also read Kan, and he reverted to it after 1905.

21. "One Morning," p. 242.

22. *TYAZ*, vol. 1, p. 3. I follow the interpretation of Yosano Tekkan in his *Tekkan kawa*, as quoted in Satake Kazuhiko, *Zenshaku midaregami kenkyū* (Tokyo: Yūhōdō, 1969), p. 3. He took *ima wo* as an ellipsis for *ima wo koi no egataki ni yasete* and *hotsure yo* as another ellipsis, for the imperative *hotsure wo mitamae*. Assuming the grammatical subject of *yasete* to be *gekai no hito*, this means that *gekai no hito* belongs, syntactically, to both the previous *hoshi no ima wo* and the following *bin no hotsure yo*. In other words, it proves to be an example of zeugma, which, as Robert H. Brower pointed out, is a kind of *kakekotoba* (pivot word). See Robert H. Brower, "Masaoka Shiki and Tanka Reform," in Donald H. Shively, ed., *Tradition and Modernization in Japanese Culture* (Princeton, NJ: Princeton University Press, 1971).

23. Satake, *Zenshaku*, p. 2.

24. Quoted in ibid., p. 80.

25. *TYAZ*, vol. 1, p. 12.

26. Ibid., p. 59.

27. Ibid., p. 68.

28. "Bundan shōka nenpu 9," *Shinchō*, September 1916, p. 92.

29. *TYAZ*, vol. 1, p. 68. This poem is one of the most obscure in a collection so difficult that Kimata Osamu, in disgust, gave up teaching it. See Itsumi Kumi, *Yosano Akiko daini kashū Saōgi zenshaku* (Tokyo: Yagi shoten, 1988), p. 269. Itsumi (pp. 10–11) offers an interpretation, the only published one I have found, but my own interpretation is different. Unfortunately, I do not have room here to explain why.

30. *TYAZ*, vol. 1, p. 5.

31. Ibid., p. 197.

32. *TYAZ*, vol. 2 (Tokyo: Kōdansha, 1979), p. 16.

33. The translation of the collection's title is from Jay Rubin, *Injurious to Public Morals,Writers and the Meiji State* (Seattle: University of Washington Press, 1984), p. 213.

34. *TYAZ*, vol. 2, p. 79.

35. Ibid., p. 85.

36. *TYAZ*, vol. 4, p. 69.

37. *TYAZ*, vol. 1, p. 152.

38. The phrase *hito no ko* exists in opposition to the earlier *hoshi no ko*, "child of the stars," which Akiko would have had at the back of her mind when she wrote this poem. Therefore, I consider "earth's child," as the antithesis of "star's child" (or "child of the stars"), truer to the actual meaning of the phrase *hito no ko* than a more literal rendering, such as "child of man" or "human child," would be.

39. *Sanjū onna no kokoro wa / kage mo,keburi mo, / oto mo nai hi no katamari, / yūyake no sora ni / ichirin maaka na taiyō, / tada jitto tesshite moete iru.* *TYAZ*, vol. 9 (Tokyo: Kōdansha, 1980), pp. 284–85. Later published in *Maigoromo* (The Dancing Cloak, 1916).

40. *TYAZ*, vol. 2, pp. 193–97. All told, Akiko gave birth to thirteen children, of whom eleven survived to adulthood. The oldest, Dr.Yosano Hikaru (1902–1992), studied public health at Johns Hopkins University in the 1930s and made important contributions to the development of the postwar medical system in Japan. The youngest, Mori Fujiko (b. 1919), is still active and sometimes lectures informally about both her parents, to whose memory she is devoted.

41. *TYAZ*, vol. 9, pp. 251–53. For translations and commentary on the tanka sequence and "The First Labor Pain," see Janine Beichman, "Yosano Akiko: Return to the Female," *Japan Quarterly* 37 (April–June 1990): 220–26.

42. *TYAZ*, vol. 9, pp. 93–95. *Garasu no soto no akebono wa / aojiroki mayu no kokochi . . . / Ima hito-suji honoka ni / otosenu edasango no hikari wo hikite, / waga ubuya no kabe wo hau mono ari. / To mireba, ureshi, / hatsufuyu no kayowanaru / hi no chō no izuru nari. / Koko ni aru wa, / yatabi shi yori nogarete kaereru onna—/ aozameshi onna ware to, / umarete itsukame naru / waga yabutsubaki no kataki tsubomi nasu musume Erennu to / ichibin no bara to, / sate hatsukoi no gotoku hanikameru / usumomoiro no hi no chō to . . . / Shizuka ni sugasugashiki akebono kana. / Tōtoku natsukashiki hi yo, ware wa ima, / tatakai ni kizu tsukitaru mono no gotoku / tsukarete hikuku yokotawarinu. / Saredo, waga atarashiki kangeki wa / hainichi kyōto no shin no gotoshi, / waga sashinoburu morode wo ukeyo, / Hi yo, akebono no jōō yo. / Hi yo, kimi ni mo yoru to fuyu no nayami ari, / senmannen no mukashi yori ikuoku tabi, / shi no ku ni taete wakagaeru / amatsu honō no chikara no ōōshiki kana. / Ware wa nao kimi ni shitagawan, / waga ikite kaereru wa wazuka ni yatabi nomi / wazuka ni yatabi zekkyō to, chi to, / shi no yami to wo koeshi nomi.*

43. Yosano Akiko, "Kōki," *Yosano Akiko shū Yosano Hiroshi shū*, in *Gendai tanka zenshū*, vol. 5 (Tokyo: Kaizōsha, 1929), pp. 410–11.

44. Quoted in Shinma Shinichi, *Yosano Akiko* (Tokyo: Ōfūsha, 1986), p. 81.

45. *TYAZ*, vol. 4, p. 56.

46. Ibid., p. 5.

47. The interpretation of this poem as a portrait of the artist is in Hirano Banri, *Akiko kanshō* (Tokyo: Sanseidō, 1949, repr. 1979), p. 375. Shinma, *Yosano Akiko*, p. 206, also has a useful discussion.

48. *Waga uta no mijikakereba, / kotoba wo habuku to hito omoeri. / Waga uta ni habukubeki mono nashi, / mata nani wo tsuketasan. / Waga kokoro wa sakana naraneba era wo motazu / tada hitoiki ni koso*

utaunare. *TYAZ*, vol. 9, p. 294. The translation is by Shio Sakanishi, in Donald Keene, ed., *Modern Japanese Literature: An Anthology* (Rutland, VT: Tuttle, 1974), p. 202.

49. *Taegataku kanashikereba/ware wa iinu [Fune ni noran.]/Noritsuredo nao sabishisa ni/mata iinu [Tsuki no de wo matan.]/Umi wa tojitaru shomotsu no gotoku/yobikakuru koto naku,/shibaraku shite, maruki tsuki/nami ni odoritsureba iinu,/[Nagaki sao no hoshi,/kano sango no uo wo tsuru.] TYAZ*, vol. 9, pp. 39–40.

50. *TYAZ*, vol. 4, pp. 247.

51. Ibid., pp. 249.

52. Seki Yōko, *Nihon no uguisu: Horiguchi Daigaku kikigaki* (Tokyo: Kadokawa shoten, 1980), pp. 25–26, 33. I wish to thank Takeo Yamamoto for bringing this book to my attention. Akiko's "us," by the way, is not the royal "us," but "my husband and me." The poem, which is not in *TYAZ*, is *ware hitori/edo ni asobinu/nakanaka ni/jodō ni masaru/omoide no tame*. Daigaku assumed it was Haruo's creation.

Ghosts who recited their own poems were not unknown in classical Japanese literature. One example is *Shinkokinshū*, poem 814 (*furusato ni/yuku hito mogana/tsugeyaramu/shiranu yamaji ni/hitori madou to*), an English version of which is in Ōoka Makoto, *A Poet's Anthology*, trans. Janine Beichman (Santa Fe, NM: Katydid Books, 1994), p. 107. This version is slightly revised:

O for someone to
go to my old home and tell
them all how on these
wild mountain paths I wander
astray, alone and lost!

10

Moments of Respite: Poems from Saitō Mokichi's Shōen

◉

A M Y   V L A D E C K   H E I N R I C H

In the late 1920s, Saitō Mokichi—already a famous poet for his early collections *Shakkō* and *Aratama*—wrote about the demands of his profession as a neuropsychiatrist:

> In my calling
> there is not a single
> moment of respite:
> I think about insanity
> both waking and sleeping[1]

> *(Tomoshibi)*

> *nariwai wa / itoma sae nashi / monogurui no / koto o zo omou / nete mo samete mo*

The final line, *nete mo samete mo*, translated as "both waking and sleeping," is all-inclusive: all human activities are encompassed in these two actions.

About twenty years later, having retired from the practice of medicine, Mokichi wrote another poem with a similarly constructed last line:

To see the charcoal
flourish into flame—
brightly, brightly!—
a sudden tranquillity,
yesterday, today . . .

(Shirokiyama)

akaaka to / okoreru sumi o / miru toki zo / hayamo yasuragu / kinō mo kyō mo

The final line, *kinō mo kyō mo*, translated as "yesterday, today . . . ," includes, beyond the two points in time, unlimited stretches of experience both before and after. As worry filled all possibilities of being for the poet in the earlier *tanka*, tranquillity is a possibility at all times later on, and in the end it is discovered in sights and in sounds as well:

Is this what
quietude is like?
on a winter night
the sounds of the air
which surrounds me

(Shirokiyama)[2]

shizukesa wa / kaku no gotoki ka / fuyu no yo no / ware o megureru / kūki no oto su

The possibility, and the experience in various forms, of tranquillity permeates the collections of poems Mokichi wrote in retirement. Since the poet is Mokichi, however, it is a complex tranquillity he finds, hard won and, consequently, deeply cherished. It follows great losses, which underlie the peace, and the poet is seeking healing as well as expressing gratitude[3] for the moments of respite.

These two cold, bright moments of peace are poems from the collection *Shirokiyama* (White Mountains), widely considered one of the peaks of Mokichi's long and illustrious poetic career. It was published in August 1949 and includes poetry written in 1946 and 1947. Before Mokichi could climb those snowy peaks, however, he had to spend some time wandering in closer quarters.

The collection *Shōen* (The Small Garden), published in April 1949 and containing poems written from 1943 through 1945, documents this wandering.

I discovered one of the poems from *Shōen* while wandering myself, through
television channels one day in a Tokyo hotel. The following poem was being discussed on the NHK education channel:

No words are left
  to tear at my heart—
  the flames frolic
  in the hearth
  evening in winter

kuyashimamu / koto mo taetari / ro no naka ni / hono'o no asobu / fuyu no yūgure

It is arresting and deeply moving. There is the sadness of loss in the opening
lines, a sense of the weariness of survival. But there is also a peculiar kind of
fierce peace in the final images, a peace hard won and almost painfully precious.
It seems to hold a key to the achievement of Mokichi's later poems. I began to
read more of *Shōen.*

In his afterword (*goki*) to that collection, Mokichi wrote that he created the
volume by selecting the "peaceful ones"—*heiwa no mono*—from his poems written in 1943 and 1944 and adding to them most of the poems he had written
when he had been evacuated from Tokyo and returned to Kanakame, the village
of his birth and childhood in Yamagata Prefecture. "At first," he explained, "I
intended to make a volume only of the poems from my stay in Kanakame, but
the number of poems was somewhat insufficient, so I decided to add poems
from during the war."[4]

Certainly the war was a major source of the sense of loss with which Mokichi
had to come to terms in order to find tranquillity. He lost to the fires of war not
only his home and hospital in Tokyo but to some degree also the medical career
that had so engrossed him. Clearly, he had also lost some sense of self-respect as
a result of the role he had played as a popular and public advocate of the war
effort. His choosing to suppress the poems he wrote in that role—as he eliminated all but the "peaceful ones" for *Shōen*—makes the loss apparent.

Mokichi went on, in the afterword, to mention that the composition of the
poems corresponded on the whole "to the period when I was sixty-two, sixty-
three, and sixty-four years of age." He *felt* old, not because he was old chronologically, but because the life he had made for himself seemed to be over:

The color of copper
it has turned,
my bald head—
to become like this
have I lived on.

akagane no / iro ni naritaru / hageatama / kaku no gotoku ni / ikinokorikeri

Unnoticed,
how I have aged!
in the dark night
even my buttocks
freeze, these days—[5]

hito shirezu / oitaru kanaya / yo o komete / waga isarai mo / hiyuru kono goro

In 1943 and 1944, he had spent a great deal of time outside Tokyo, first in Hakone and then in Yamagata, where he stayed with his younger sister and her husband. They had room in their home, Mokichi remembered, because all three sons were away at war. His role in their lives was, he felt, a burden, since his social functions were no longer of great value. "At first I intended to help with the farming, but when I actually tried, I could not weed the fields adequately. So I watched the children, swept the garden, at most gave some slight help." Mokichi had been adopted in his youth by a distant relative, who had trained him as his successor in the new field of neuropsychiatry and had arranged for him to marry, more or less unhappily, his daughter. When he returned to his childhood home, Mokichi did not have the skills to function productively in a farming village. "Since I left to go to Tokyo in Meiji 29, at age fifteen, it was after a fifty-year absence that I returned to live in this village a second time."[6]

It was the combination of these two situations—leisure and his childhood landscape—that provided him with the opportunity to wander in search of tranquillity:

Because I had nothing very important to do, I often went out walking. I walked to the mountains and was silent; I walked to the riverbank and was silent; I went to the Kannon temple in the neighboring village and watched the carp swim. Then I'd walk to Kaminoyama and go into the hills behind it and sit until the sun

went down. Now the outdoors was all rough; it was not gentle like a park. Still,
I walked nearly everywhere: the hills of Kanakame, the temple in the neighboring village, the shrine precincts, Fudō in the gorge. And I knew that it was a
return to the experiences of my youth.[7]

Indeed, images and ideas from earlier experiences recur in Mokichi's poems.
Mokichi had returned to Kanakame during those fifty years to visit, if not to
live, most notably in 1913, when he was called to his mother's deathbed. The
poem sequence he wrote about that period, *Shinitamau haha* (My Mother Is
Dying), was one of the foundations of his fine reputation as a poet.[8]
    This visit seems to have been on his mind as well when he returned during
the war:

> When day after day
> I taste the steamed barley
> she comes to mind—
> my mother who nurtured me,
> my mother in Michinoku

> *mugi no ii / higoto ni kumeba / Michinoku ni / wa o hagukumishi / haha shiomooyu*

The combination of leisure time and childhood memories made the landscape of his early years particularly precious. In the preceding poem, the verb
hagukumu, translated as "to nurture," is associated with a familiar food—a "comfort food" in today's vocabulary—and with his mother. Later, the landscape
itself, as in the following poem about Mount Zaō, is described in terms of the
same verb *hagukumu*, "to tend, to rear, to foster—to nurture."

> Soaring skyward
> that my soul may receive
> nurturance—
> Mount Zaō in morning enshrouded
> in snow blown gray as smoke

> *tamashii o / hagukumemasu to / sobietatsu / Zaō no yama no / asa yukigemuri*

In fact, Mount Zaō, which looms so large in the poems of *Shōen* and especially
Shirokiyama, also appears in "My Mother Is Dying," in the last section, in which

the poet describes walking through the mountains of his familiar landscape after his mother's death and funeral:

> There are patches of snow
> on Zaō mountain;
> as evening came
> in brilliance
> I walked the steep paths.

> *Zaōsan ni / hadara yuki kamo / kagayaku to / yū sarikureba / sowa yukinikeri*

But Mokichi selected a slighter, less awe-inspiring facet of the consoling nature of his birthplace as the title for the volume: the phrase "the small garden" is from a poem in the series *Kanakame Evacuation Songs*:

> Columbine blossoms
> in the small garden
> anemone blossoms
> in the high fields
> their fragrances mingling

> *shōen no / odamaki no hana / no no ue no / okinagusa no hana / tomo ni nioite*

The scent of the columbine blossoms, *odamaki no hana*, mingles with that of the anemones, or *okinagusa*, literally "old man's grass," much as his present consciousness mingles with visions and memories of his youthful self.

Ueda Miyoshi points out that the images of columbine and anemone that resonate in this poem also were used in "My Mother Is Dying."[9] One such poem, mentioning columbine blossoms, is from the second part of that long sequence, in which the poet watches and describes the process of his mother's dying set against the images of spring surrounding them:

> Bowing before the sunlight
> coming out of the mountains,
> the columbines
> are blossoming
> abundantly.

yama izuru/taiyōkō o/ogamitaru/odamaki no hana/sakitsuzukitari

The other occurs in the third section, which follows the funeral procession to the crematorium:

By the country road
where anemones flower
red throated,
the light streams forth
and we walk on.

okinagusa/kuchi akaku saku/no no michi ni/hikari nagarete/warera yukitsu mo

There is a change in Mokichi's use of the images, however. In "My Mother Is Dying," the abundant natural beauty is poignant, indeed, almost an affront when it is juxtaposed against the pain of bereavement. The beauty is apparent in the columbines "blossoming abundantly" and in the anemones that "flower red throated," but those seeing them walk on. The poet's attention, though drawn to their beauty, is in fact focused elsewhere—first on his dying mother and then on the funeral rites. In *Shōen*, those flowers are central. Mokichi's leisure permitted a fuller focus, a greater absorption in the natural world: he had returned to center himself in the landscape.

Even more important, Mokichi's sense of returning allowed the "motherland" of his youth, filled with images of nature, to replace the "fatherland" of the war years, filled with images of battles. Ueda describes this as a transformation of the passion Mokichi had poured into the war poems—the "shouting" as he calls it— a transformation facilitated by the silence of his wanderings around Kanakame. Leaving Tokyo had meant leaving the dramatic physical manifestations of war. The quietness of the country, where the war was experienced through what was missing (sons, food), stood in dramatic contrast to the noise and frenetic activity of the city, where the war was experienced through air raids and firebombing. Quietness permitted meditation. Eventually, images of nature, central to both the tanka tradition and Mokichi's earlier work, pointed in a new direction.[10]

This direction took Mokichi walking through the landscape:

Earnestly yearning
to find peace at heart

for even a day
I'd cross over them,
the high hills, myself

hitohi naru / kokoro yasuragi o / koinegai / mama no takaoka / koeyuku ware wa

But it was not an easy change.

There are times
when my loneliness
becomes unbearable.
I set fire to pinecones
on the flatness of the earth—

taegataki / made ni sabishiku / naru koto ari / matsukasa o taku / tsuchi no taira ni

The clear distinction between the emotion and the activity in this poem is emphasized by the grammatical structure. The first three lines are encapsulated by the final phrase, *koto ari*, "it happens" or "there are times." The loneliness is coherent and complete. By contrast, the activity of the closing two lines is directionless and random. This random quality is heightened by the grammatical reversal of the last two lines, so the activity does not quite stop; rather, it trails off. The poem separates into two parts, as the poet is isolated even from the fire he sets.

Fire and light become increasingly important as points of focus:

The grief itself
when I reflect on it
I think of as
a spark of light like
the firefly that evening . . .

kanashisa mo / kaerimi sureba / aru yoi no / hotaru no gotoki / hikari to zo omou

This poem separates neither structurally nor imagistically. Instead, it is one sentence, moving smoothly from beginning to end—from grief (*kanashisa*), the first word of the poem, to thought (*omou*), the last word, in a final form. The poet is connected to the world of nature again, albeit tenuously, and he is also reconnecting to his own past, in *aru yoi*, "that certain evening."

Fire, finally, becomes the source of cleansing and rebirth:

> From the midst of
> utter destruction, even I
> will become a
> phoenix, and fly forth—
> although so small

kaijin no / naka yori wa mo / fuenikisu to / narite shitobamu / chiisakeredomo

There is nothing striking about the image of a phoenix rising from ashes except in the scale of the reborn self: *chiisakeredomo*, "although so small." Unlike the triumphant soaring of the mythical phoenix, Mokichi's rebirth is as a being not yet complete, with much to learn. Many of the poems that follow have a sense of wonder, even bewilderment, at the poet's silent wandering; he is not yet of the world.

> Hearing the sound
> of the scythe reaping rice—
> can it be heard
> so lucidly?
> since early morning

ine o karu / kama oto kikeba / sayakeku mo / kikoyuru mono ka / asa madaki yori

He has brought his old self with him, the survivor of the "utter destruction," the one who "lived on." This double layering of experience in the best poems in *Shōen* accounts for their sense of depth.[11] In them, Mokichi returns to the "everyday poems" that had long been a source of his poetic strength, poems in which the world is seen—or heard—anew. In this poem, the scything sound, a mere whisper, also emphasizes Mokichi's distance from the everyday life around him, the world through which he wanders. Yet amazement at the world heard anew through the filter of his own silence offers a new sense of possibility:

> It seems all things
> achieve serenity—
> in the mountain gorge

rays of autumn sunlight shine
on streambed sand

mono nabete / shizuka naramu to / yamakai no / kawara no suna ni / aki no yo no sasu

If all things can become serene, perhaps so can the world; perhaps so can the poet. In a sense, when Mokichi left Tokyo, as Kajiki Gō points out, the war ended for him. His return to Kanakame was a liberation from his public role as a citizen, and it allowed him to return to his role as a private individual. The effort that had gone into what Kajiki calls the "howl" of Mokichi's public war poetry was eventually diverted into his private nature poems.[12]

Mokichi's diaries for 1944 chronicle this deepening silence, in two ways. On the one hand, they contain notations concerning requests for commemorative poems from newspapers—the *Asahi shinbun, Tokyo shinbun, Mainichi shinbun*—which he increasingly found himself unable to write. "I couldn't" (*dekinakatta*) and "I declined" (*kotowatta*) dot the pages.[13] On the other hand, his diaries contain similar notations of activities he referred to in the afterword to *Shōen*:

8/19   I came to the shade of the reeds at the edge of the field near the dry
            riverbed and was silent, meditated. Then some poetic urge arose to a
            small degree. In the afternoon, too, I sat meditating in the shade of
            the cherry trees.

8/21   . . . and then I went to the Kannon temple, meditated.

8/23   . . . after that, on the way back, I drank some ice water, worshiped
            the deity of the Fukuda shrine, meditated.

9/16   . . . afterward, in silence, did nothing, didn't read. I was just vacant.

9/17   Heavy rain; silently watched it.[14]

As a private individual, Mokichi gave himself over to the natural world surrounding his old home. It not only gave him a glimpse of serenity, it also could share the burden of his grief, as in the following poem marking Japan's surrender:

O grieve! when you soar
through the sky
of this realm—
wild geese heading south
on a rain-soaked night

kono kuni no / sora o tobu toki / kanashimeyo / minami e mukau / amayo karigane

There is some ambiguity about the term *kono kuni*, "this realm": it is both Japan as a whole and the poet's home prefecture of Yamagata. But clearly, the wild geese heading south are flying toward the regions made desolate by the war, and grief is spreading through the natural private world as the public world collapses. In the following poem, the single persimmon leaf, "the color of ancient steel," also points south: *nanbantetsuiro* is literally "the color of southern barbarian steel," from ancient rifles. But it is a personal advance for the poet to pick up the leaf. The fissure that so many commentators describe between the public poet exalting the war and his silence in the combination of exile and homecoming could heal only when the past and present were reintegrated. The very act of going out and bringing back the martial-colored leaf marks this progress:

I went out and
brought back with me
back to the tatami
a single persimmon leaf
the color of ancient steel

ide yukite / tatami no ue ni / mote kitaru / nanbantetsu iro no / kaki no ha hitotsu

As there is ambiguity in the referent for "realm" in the earlier poem, there also is ambiguity in the source of the silence in the following:

O look at me
in my own silence!
so on the massed clusters
of the deep black grapes
the rain pours down

chinmoku no / ware o miyo to zo / hyakufusa no / kuroki budō ni / ame furisosogu

The silence is both that of the poet, drawn to the beauty of the sight, and that of the grapes themselves, submitting to the rhythms of the cycles of nature and attracting the poet's gaze. In this light, the poem on NHK—which Satō Satarō interprets as a description of the family sitting around the fire eating dinner and talking about their sons at war, when gradually the conversation dies down[15]—is instead a description of an internal silence, achieved during

Mokichi's wandering. The flames frolicking in the hearth then become a source of potential tranquillity.

> No words are left
> to tear at my heart—
> the flames frolic
> in the hearth
> evening in winter.

> *kuyashimamu / koto mo taetari / ro no naka ni / hono'o no asobu / fuyu no yūgure*

The structure and sounds of the poem support this interpretation. The first two lines are a complete sentence: "nothing is left / to tear at my heart." The next two lines are again a complete sentence, literally "in the hearth the flames play." The ending, though a sentence fragment, does not trail off. The final line is a context for both situations, "evening in winter" (*fuyu no yūgure*), in which they can coexist. Even more, each makes the other possible. Because he is left empty and more or less at peace, the poet can enter the mood of the frolicking flames; because he can penetrate the spirit of the frolicking flames, he can find peace. The drawn-out *o* sounds of the phrase, *ro no naka ni hono'o no asobu*, accentuate the peacefulness.

This reading is supported by the following poems:

> O, when the winter
> storms blow in and blanket
> the mountains!
> the voices I hear
> fade far away

> *kogarashi no / yama o ōite / fuku toki zo / ware ni kikoyuru / koe tōzakaru*

In this poem too, the intensity of the poet's focus on the natural world erases to a degree the encroachment of the human world, which is so much harder to comprehend. But the natural world helps in that process:

> The mountains
> turning white
> as I watched

as though alive
winter deepened.

yamayama wa / shiroku naritsutsu / manakai ni / ikeru ga gotoku / fuyu fukamikeri

Even the mountains age, as though they were animate; even the landscape "lives on" (*ikinokori*). The natural world and the everyday experience of it that the silence has enabled help the poet integrate the past and the present.

I can't forget the bell
reverberating through
this village,
that the end of the war
was drawing near.

tatakai no / shūmatsu chikaku / kono mura ni / narihibikitaru / kane o wasurezu

The possibility of tranquillity learned in the moments of respite that Mokichi found in Kanakame was realized during his stay in Ōishida and most clearly expressed in *Shirokiyama*. It did not last forever: the poems in his last collection, *Tsukikage*, reflect the shock of returning to an altered Tokyo and adapting to a culturally changed world, real problems with aging, and family worries, which together created a different kind of poem:

Night after night
I feel in my breast
that I cannot breath

as though I have come
to the limits of this world.

yo na yo na ni / mune no atari ga / ikigurushi / kono yo no hate ni / wa ga koshi gotoku

Wondering if
years remained to me
or if I had no years left
I climbed to the second floor
to sleep in broad daylight.

zannen wa / aru ka naki ka no / gotoku ni te / nikai ni nobori / mahiruma mo inu

But while wandering in the small garden, Mokichi achieved a kind of peace—a kind in which resignation is an achievement rather than a failure, coming to terms with the world rather than giving up on it. It is this sense of reconciliation—an acceptance that has the feel of an embrace—that provides the tranquillity in Mokichi's later poems. Walking through the natural setting of his old home allies him with the natural world and gives him a precious if brief freedom, expressed in both the images and the relaxed and irregular form of the following tanka:

Yet again
snow piling up—
    tracks of a horse-drawn sled
      tracks of an ox-drawn sled
        tracks of high rubber galoshes

atarashiku / yuki furitsumite / umazori no ato / ushizori no ato / gomu nagagutsu no ato

NOTES

1. For other poems concerning Mokichi's medical profession, see Amy Vladeck Heinrich, *Fragments of Rainbows: The Life and Poetry of Saitō Mokichi, 1882–1953* (New York: Columbia University Press, 1983), pp. 133–44.

2. All the poems translated in this essay can be found in *Saitō Mokichi zenshū* (hereafter abbreviated *SMZ*), vols. 1–3 (Tokyo: Iwanami shoten, 1973–1975). See also Heinrich, *Fragments*, pp. 70, 145.

3. Satō Satarō, "*Shōen sho*," in *Saitō Mokichi kenkyū*, vol. 36 of *Kindai sakka kenkyū sōsho* (Tokyo: Nihon tosho sentaa, 1984), p. 65.

4. "Goki" to *Shōen*, in *SMZ*, vol. 3, p. 541.

5. Heinrich, *Fragments*, pp. 142–43.

6. "Goki," *SMZ*, vol. 3, p. 542.

7. Ibid., p. 543.

8. For a translation of the whole sequence, see Heinrich, *Fragments*, pp. 158–66; and for an analysis, see Amy Vladeck Heinrich, " 'My Mother Is Dying': Saitō Mokichi's '*Shinitamau haha*,' " *Monumenta Nipponica* 33 (Winter 1978): 407–39.

9. Ueda Miyoji, *Mokichi bannen* (Tokyo: Yayoi shobo, 1988), pp. 58–59.

10. Ibid., pp. 59–60.

11. Satō, "*Shōen to Shirokiyama*," in *Saito Mokichi kenkyū*, p. 83.

12. Kajiki Gō, *Zōho Saitō Mokichi* (Tokyo: Kinzan shuppan, 1977), pp. 214–16.

13. *SMZ*, vol. 31, pp. 595–729. Cited in Nakamura Minoru, *Saitō Mokichi shiden* (Tokyo: Asahi shinbunsha, 1983), pp. 285–86.

14. *SMZ*, vol. 31, pp. 595–719. Cited by Ueda, *Mokichi bannen*, pp. 62–63.

15. Satō Satarō, *Mokichi shūka*, vol. 2 (Tokyo: Iwanami shoten, 1978), pp. 105–6.

11

Matsuo Bashō's Oku no hosomichi *and the Anxiety of Influence*

◉

HARUO SHIRANE

Shelley once said that poets of all ages contributed to one Great Poem perpetually in progress. He meant of course that poems arise not so much in response to the present time but, rather, in response to other poems. More recently, advocates of intertextuality have argued that a literary text is comprehensible only in terms of the other texts that it takes up, prolongs, cites, refutes, or transforms. Harold Bloom, one of the leading intertextual critics, has compressed this notion of intertextuality into a relationship between a text and a particular precursor text, between a poet and his or her major predecessor—a relationship that results in what Bloom calls the "anxiety of influence": "Poetic influence—when it involves two strong, authentic poets—always proceeds by a misreading of the prior poet, an act of creative correction that is actually and necessarily a misinterpretation."[1] In Bloom's view, all major English Romantic poets are engaged in a struggle with strong precursors in an effort to carve out imaginative space for themselves. Taking a Freudian or "family" approach to the problem, he argues that strong poets, striving for immortality and fearful of falling in the shadow of their literary masters, are constantly engaged in an Oedipal struggle to overcome and "slay" the poetic father. This kind of Freudian approach would seem antithetical to a culture that emphasizes filial piety and to such communally oriented literature as *haikai*. But the anxiety of influence provides a useful tool, as both a model and an antimodel, for understanding the highly intertextual nature of Japanese poetry and avoids the tendency, which predominates in classical studies and commentaries, to see the pre-text solely as either a source of influence or the basis for allusive variation.

On the surface, the relationship between Matsuo Bashō (1644–1694) and Saigyō (1118–1190), the late Heian *waka* poet whom Bashō admired and whose path he followed on the famous journey commemorated in *Oku no hosomichi* (Narrow Road to the Far North), seems to be the opposite of Bloom's antagonistic struggle. In Japan's medieval period, travelers often embarked on journeys as a way of paying their respects to the spirits of the dead. Poetic travel diaries were often written on important anniversaries—usually the first, third, fifth, thirteenth, or thirty-third—of the death of a teacher, lord, or parent. Similarly, *Oku no hosomichi* can be seen as an offering or tribute to Saigyō on the five-hundredth anniversary of his death. Saigyō died in 1190, and Bashō started on his journey through Michinoku, or the Far North, in 1689. Bashō was drawn to both Saigyō's lifestyle—as a recluse, a monk, and a poet traveler, who visited the Far North twice—and Saigyō's poetry, particularly the medieval aesthetics of *sabi*, which Bashō incorporated into his haikai. As the ultimate host of Bashō's journey, Saigyō becomes the object of various poems of gratitude, tribute, or remembrance. The vast majority of the *hokku* that Bashō composed were greetings, or *aisatsu*, to Bashō's hosts on the road, to the spirit of the land, to nature, and to Shinto and Buddhist deities. A number are salutations to spiritual teachers or to the spirits of the dead, such as those of Saigyō and Sōgi, whose traces Bashō wanted to explore.

In European travel literature, the author tends to travel to unfamiliar places. The interest of the narrative usually lies in the traveler's encounter with the Other, the unknown, the unexpected, the unusual. By contrast, in Japanese poetic travel diaries, particularly medieval *kikōbun*, the traveler gravitates toward the familiar, especially *utamakura* (poetic places), which represent nodes in the poetic tradition and links to poetic ancestors. (Indeed, for Heian aristocrats, utamakura were a way of traveling without traveling. Utamakura existed primarily as places in the poetic imagination, particularly in the Far North, which was rarely visited by the aristocracy but which had been the subject of poetry from as early as the *Man'yōshū*, particularly in the Sakimori-uta and Azuma-uta poems.) By visiting the utamakura, the poet was able to come in contact with the "heart" of the ancient poets. Travel represented a movement across time toward one's poetic roots or a return to one's poetic ancestors.

Although *Oku no hosomichi* can be interpreted as a tribute to the dead, to the spirits of ancient poets, particularly Saigyō, Bashō also carved out his own poetic space, sometimes at the expense of his poetic father. More specifically, Bashō remapped much of the poetic landscape of the Far North, recasting or replacing the utamakura rooted in the Heian classical tradition—particularly those found in the *Sandaishū* (*Kokinshū, Gosenshū, Shuishū*), the first three imperial waka anthologies—with utamakura closely associated with the *Tale of the Heike* and the *Gikeiki*. Bashō accomplished what might be called, to use a modern suffix, the Yoshitsune-ization of the Far North, altering the poetic landscape from the images of exile, salt burning, fishermen, thatched huts, autumn winds, frustrated love, longing for home, and such found in Heian classical views of the Far North, to a dreamlike landscape of medieval warriors, particularly fallen heroes such as Yoshitsune and Sanemori, and of medieval monks and hermits. He accomplished this, at least in part, through the use of nō drama, which enabled him to pay tribute to his poetic fathers and also to create new poetic space.

In *Zōdanshū* (1692), Kikaku, one of Bashō's leading disciples, comments that "*utai* is the *Genji* of haikai," that is, the texts of the nō drama were as vital to the composition of haikai as *The Tale of Genji* was to the writing of classical poetry. By the end of the seventeenth century, nō theater had become popular among *chōnin* (townspeople) in the form of the *utai*, the singing of nō librettos, and nō texts became important subtexts for Tokugawa haikai, particularly Danrin school haikai, which frequently cited and parodied nō texts. During the journey of 1687–88 (Jōkyō 4–5), which is commemorated in *Oi no kobumi* (Letters in a Satchel), Bashō began taking a different approach to nō drama, casting himself playfully in the role of the actors, particularly the *waki*, the wandering priest in a "dream play" (*mugennō*), who travels to a historic site, encounters an ancient spirit, listens to the story narrated or reenacted by that spirit, and then quietly offers prayers for the spirit's salvation.

One of the earliest examples occurs at the end of *Oi no kobumi*, commemorating a journey Bashō took in 1687–88 to visit Suma, a well-known utamakura associated with fisherfolk (*ama*), salt burning (*shioyaki*), seaweed (*mirume*), brine, firewood (*tsumugi*), smoke *keburi*), boats, a lonely coast, exile, autumn winds, and the sound of the waves—all of which provide the *hon'i*, or poetic essence, of Suma as an utamakura. Bashō, however, found none of these classical associations at Suma, particularly since he came in summer, the wrong season. Instead, he had a vision of another past, the battleground of Ichinotani and the defeat of the Heike at Suma, and the narrative assumes the atmosphere of a warrior nō play, specifically *Atsumori*, in which the waki priest (the former Minamoto warrior Kumagai no Naozane, now the priest Rensei) comes to Ichinotani, on the Bay of Suma, to pray for the spirit of his former enemy (the young Taira warrior

Atsumori) and encounters a young reaper who is playing a flute and who turns out to be Atsumori's spirit or ghost. In the second part of the nō play, the *shite* (main actor; here, Atsumori's ghost) and the waki recount the night before Atsumori's death when Kumagai was moved by the sound of Atsumori's flute, which Kumagai later found on the body of the slain warrior. The scene in *Oi no kobumi* climaxes with the following poem (composed in 1688):

> *Sumadera ya*   at Suma Temple—
> *fukanu fue kiku*   the sound of an unblown flute
> *koshita yami*   in the darkness beneath the trees

Standing in the dark shade beneath the thick leaves of a summer tree (*koshita yami*)—which suggests the name of Atsumori's flute Aoba (Green leaf) or Saeda (Small branch)—Bashō hears Atsumori's flute as if in a dream or faintly in the distance. In this series of poems on Suma, Bashō replaces the Heian associations of exile and loneliness with his own nō-esque vision of medieval warriors.

A similar battle scene appears at a climactic moment in *Oku no hosomichi*: Bashō's visit to Hiraizumi, where Yoshitsune and his loyal retainers (Benkei and Kanefusa) met their end.

The glory of three generations of Fujiwara vanished in the space of a dream; the remains of their Great Gate stood two miles in the distance. Hidehira's head-quarters had turned into rice paddies and wild fields. Only Kinkeizan, Golden Fowl Hill, remained as it was. First, we climbed Takadachi, Castle-on-the-Heights, from where we could see the Kitakami, a broad river that flowed from the south. Koromogawa, Robe River, rounded Izumi castle and, at a point beneath Castle-on-the-Heights, it dropped into the main river. The ancient ruins of Yasuhira and others, lying behind Koromo no seki, Robe Barrier, appeared to close off the southern entrance and to guard against the Ainu barbarians. With his chosen loyal retainers, Yoshitsune fortified himself in the castle, but his glory turned in a moment to grass. "Countries may be destroyed, but mountains and rivers remain. When spring comes to the castle, the grass turns green." With these lines from Tu Fu's poem in my head, I lay down my bamboo hat, letting the time and tears flow.

> *natsugusa ya*   summer grasses—
> *tsuwamonodomo ga*   the dreams of brave warriors,
> *yume no ato*   the traces

Bashō

> unohana ni   in the white hydrangea
> Kanefusa miyuru   Kanefusa appears—
> shiraga kana   a white head of hair

Sora

In Bashō's day, Hiraizumi was known for two prominent utamakura: Koromo no seki (Robe Barrier) and Koromogawa (Robe River), both of which were associated in the classical tradition with "robe" (*koromo*) imagery, "sewing" (*tatsu*), and the vicissitudes of love.[2] One of the earliest examples is an anonymous poem in the *Gosenshū* (compiled in 951) in which Robe Barrier becomes a symbolic guard against an overly aggressive man.

> tadachi tomo   I wish you would not
> tanomazaranamu   count on me so quickly—
> mi ni chikaki   Something called
> Koromo no Seki mo   Robe Barrier lies
> ari to iu nari   next to my body.

Misc. II, poem 1160

Another utamakura at Hiraizumi, albeit a minor one, was Tabashine Mountain, which was famous for its cherry blossoms, especially as a result of this poem by Saigyō:

I went to Hiraizumi in the Far North, where there is a mountain called Tabashine. It was covered with cherry trees as far as the eye could see, as if there were almost no other kind of tree. Seeing the flowers in bloom, I wrote:

> kiki mo sezu   I never heard
> Tabashineyama no   that cherry trees
> sakurabana   as beautiful as these
> Yoshino no hoka ni   on Tabashine Mountain
> kakarubeshi to wa   bloomed outside of Yoshino

Sankashū, poem 1442

Bashō was obviously aware, as all poets of the time were, of the significance of Robe Barrier, Robe River, and Tabashine Mountain as utamakura, and yet in *Oku no hosomichi* he deliberately ignores their poetic associations and does not even mention Tabashine Mountain, engaging in what Harold Bloom calls "creative correction."

The word *dream* in Bashō's hokku not only refers to the warriors' dreams of glory in battle—specifically those of the three generations of Fujiwara who valiantly conquered the Ezo barbarians and those of Yoshitsune's brave retainers (Benkei, Kanefusa) who fought bravely for their master—but also implies that those dreams of glory are like dreams, being ephemeral and impermanent. The dream can also be interpreted as the dream of the waki priest in a warrior nō play who visits the site of a former battlefield, encounters the spirits of the dead, and watches the shite reenact his most tragic moments on the battlefield.

In this context, *natsugusa* (summer grasses), which was associated in the classical tradition with love and the "binding together of blades," is transformed into the grass pillow of the traveling waki priest who at the end of the nō play wakes up from a vivid dream of the dead. The summer grasses become a polysemous image of impermanence and renewal, of life and death. The Tu Fu poem alluded to in the prose suggests that although civilization and its creations may come and go, the grass remains and is renewed each year. Natsugusa becomes the grass of the past, on which warriors spilled their blood, as well as the grass of memory, given life by the waki priest and renewed by each visitor (and reader) who comes and remembers. The dreams of the soldiers have faded, but the memory, the traces of the dream (*yume no ato*), remain. Sora's poem, which was probably written by Bashō himself, continues the dreamlike scene. According to *Gikeiki*, Kanefusa, one of Yoshitsune's most loyal retainers, helped Yoshitsune's wife and children commit suicide; saw Yoshitsune to his end; set fire to the fort at Takadachi; felled Nagasaki Tarō, an enemy captain; grabbed Nagasaki's younger brother under his arm; and then leapt into the flames.[3] In the hokku, the poet sees—much like a waki priest in a nō "dream" play—the swirling white hair (*shiraga*) of Kanefusa, famous for his loyalty and ferocity, in the white flowers of the *unohana* (deutzia, translated here as hydrangea).

At the end of the *shuramono*, or warrior play, the waki priest often offers a prayer to console the spirit of the dead warrior. In a similar fashion, Bashō's poems can be interpreted as prayers to the spirits of the dead. Indeed, both the Suma scene in *Oi no kobumi* and the Hiraizumi scene in *Oku no hosomichi* closely follow the conventions of a classic Chinese prose genre, *ko senjō o tomurau bun* (mourning for the spirits of the dead on an ancient battlefield), in which the narrator stands on a height, looks down on a former battlefield, imagines the terrible carnage, and laments the fate of the dead soldiers. (This is in fact the title of this section, which later appears in *Fūzoku monzen*, a *haibun* anthology edited by Kyoriku, one of Bashō's disciples.) This Chinese genre has its roots in such early poetry as *Kuo-shang* (The Kingdom's Young Dead)—one of the nine songs in the *Ch'u-tz'u* (Songs of the Ch'u)—which was a ritualistic song intended to honor and pacify the souls of young warriors who gave up their lives for their kingdom.

Another offering to the spirit of the dead was made when Bashō visited Kaga Province (near Kanazawa), where he discovered a temple that preserved the helmet and robe of Sanemori, the famous Heike warrior described in *The Tale of the Heike* (book 7). Not wanting others to realize his advanced age, Sanemori dyed his white hair black and fought valiantly before being slain by the followers of Kiso no Yoshinaka.

> We visited Tada shrine where Sanemori's helmet and a piece of his brocade robe were stored. They say that long ago, when Sanemori belonged to the Minamoto clan, Lord Yoshitomo offered him the helmet. Indeed, it was not the gear of a common soldier. A chrysanthemum and vine design inlaid with gold extended from the visor to the ear flaps, and a two-horn front piece was attached to the dragon head. Kiso Yoshinaka offered the helmet and a prayer sheet to this shrine after Sanemori died in battle, and Higuchi Jirō acted as his messenger—such details in the shrine history made the past appear before my very eyes.

muzan ya na	"How pitiful!"
kabuto no shita no	beneath the warrior's helmet
kirigirisu	cries of a cricket

The first line in Basho's hokku, "How pitiful!" (*muzan ya na*), is taken from *Sanemori*, a warrior nō play by Zeami, in which a wandering priest (*yugyō shōnin*) encounters the ghost of Sanemori (the shite) who narrates the story of his death in battle. In a passage narrated by the ghost, Higuchi Jirō, one of Yoshinaka's retainers, is summoned to identify the washed, white-haired head of the slain warrior and exclaims, "Oh, how pitiful!/It's Saitō Bettō!" In *Oku no hosomichi*, the traveler, presumably reminded by Sanemori's helmet of the washed head of the slain warrior, utters the words of Higuchi Jirō, "How pitiful!" and then, awakening from these thoughts of the distant past, hears a cricket (*kirigirisu*) under the helmet. The following poem by Saigyō in the *Shinkokinshū* (Autumn, poem 472) exemplifies the classical associations (especially lonely cries) of the kirigirisu, a seasonal word for autumn.

kirigirisu	As the autumn nights
yosamu ni aki no	grow cold,

naru mama ni	the cricket
yowaru ka koe no	seems to weaken, the voice
tōzakari yuku	fading into the distance.

The voice of the kirigirisu in the frosty autumn night embodies the pathos and loneliness of fading life. In Bashō's poem, these associations, particularly the pathos of old age, resonate with the drama of *Sanemori*. Some commentators, such as Yamamoto Kenkichi, believe that the spirit of Sanemori appears in the form of the cricket and that the cries are those of his anguished soul, which Bashō, like the wandering priest in the nō play, pacifies with a poetic prayer.

Bashō also uses Chinese poetry to transform the classical landscape of the Far North. A good example is the famous scene at Kisagata, a passage written in a highly Chinese style.

> The next morning, when the skies cleared and the morning sun came out brightly, we took a boat to Kisagata. Our first stop was Nōin Island, where we visited the place where Nōin had secluded himself for three years. We docked our boat on the far shore and visited the old cherry tree, on which Saigyō had written the poem about "rowing over the cherry blossoms." . . .
>
> We sat down in the front room of this temple and raised the blinds, taking in the entire landscape at one glance. . . . The face of the bay resembles Matsushima, but it is different. If Matsushima is like a person laughing, Kisagata is like a resentful person. A feeling of sorrow was added to that of loneliness. The land was as if in a state of anguish.

Kisagata ya	Kisagata Bay—
ame ni Seishi ga	Hsi Shih asleep in the rain,
nebunohana	flowers of the silk tree

In the classical tradition, Kisagata was associated with fisherfolk (*ama*), the moon, thatched huts (*tomaya*), and the loneliness of exile and travel. Nōin (d. 1050) made Kisagata famous with the following travel poem in the *Goshūishū* (519).

> On the way to Dewa Province, Nōin composed this poem at a place called Kisagata:

yo no naka wa	I have spent my life
kakutemo hekeri	this way,
Kisagata no	making the grass hut

ama no tomaya o	of the fishermen
waga yado toshite	at Kisagata my lodging.

Bashō also thought of the following poem, which he attributed to Saigyō (the poem does not appear in *Sankashū*):

Kisagata no	The cherry blossoms
sakura wa nami ni	at Kisagata are buried
uzumorete	in waves:
hana no ue kogu	a fisherman's boat rowing
ama no tsuribune	over the flowers

Bashō mentioned the fisherfolks' thatched huts and visited Nōin Island and an old cherry tree associated with Saigyō, thereby paying respect to his two poetic fathers, but in the end he radically transformed the utamakura by comparing it to Hsi Shih (J. Seishi), the legendary Chinese beauty who was used during the Chou dynasty to seduce an enemy emperor and cause his defeat and who was thought to have a constant frown, her eyes half closed, as a result of her tragic fate. Bashō juxtaposed the image of this brooding Chinese beauty with the delicate *nebunohana* (literally "sleeping flower"), flowers of the silk tree, an elegant flower with hairlike petal leaves that close up at night as if to go to sleep. Once again Bashō presents a double vision, but this time it takes the form of a *mitate*, of "seeing" a Chinese landscape in a Japanese landscape.

The utamakura was not only a poetic topos and a source of poetic inspiration, it was also a palimpsestic text, a place to be revisited, reremembered, reread, reinterpreted, and rewritten. The poet visiting a famous utamakura hoped not just to learn from his poetic fathers and explore the existing traces; he also had—if he had any hope of achieving poetic immortality—to leave a trace, a lasting mark, usually in the form of a poem or a poetic travel diary, to be read by future visitors. In the Bloom-ian model of intertextuality, an utamakura becomes a point of struggle between major poets across time in which earlier traces are often willfully distorted or erased.

Sometimes the new poet is drowned out by the voices of the past and left with no poetry. In *Oi no kobumi*, when Bashō visited Yoshino, one of the most famous utamakura in Japan, he wrote:

We stayed for three days at Yoshino, while the cherry trees were in full bloom, and saw Yoshino both at dawn and at dusk. The beauty of the early morning moon sent my heart racing, filling me with emotion. I was swept away by thoughts of

that famous poem on Yoshino by Fujiwara Yoshitsune and was left directionless at
Saigyō's signpost, by his poem on Yoshino, and I recalled the poem that Teishitsu
had tossed off—"What a scene! What a scene!" I had nothing to say, could not
even compose a single poem, and ended up shutting my mouth—all to my great
regret. I had come charged with enthusiasm, but now it had all died.[4]

In *Oku no hosomichi* Bashō has a similar experience at Shirakawa Barrier, an utamakura dominated by the traces of Nōin, Saigyō, and Sōgi, Bashō's great precursors. In the *michiyuki* (poetic travel) passages, in which the narration floats from
one poetic association to another, the poet is often little more than a transmitter
of literary tradition or a conduit for his or her poetic father. But when Bashō
becomes what Bloom calls the "strong" poet—at such passages as Hiraizumi and
Kisagata—he ignores or erases the traces of his poetic fathers, carving out his
own poetic space, even as he traces the paths of his poetic mentors.

Bashō not only remapped much of this classical landscape—replacing the
Heian images of the Far North with medieval and Chinese images—he also created new poetic places, what may be called *haimakura*.

When we had crossed Nezu no Seki, Mouse Barrier, we hurried our steps toward
the soil of Echigo and came to Ichiburi, in Etchū Province. During this period of
nine days, I suffered in the extreme heat, fell ill, and did not record anything.

fumizuki ya	The seventh month—
muika mo tsune no	the sixth day doesn't resemble
yo ni wa nizu	a usual night.
araumi ya	A wild sea!
Sado ni yokotau	the Milky Way laid sideways
Amanogawa	to Sado Isle.

One of the difficulties of new poetic places—and the reason that poets avoided
them—is that like new seasonal words, they usually came with few, if any,
poetic associations. By drawing on Sado Island's historical associations, however,
Bashō was able to view the landscape through the eyes of the past, as he does at
utamakura and ancient battlefields. Sado, an island across the water from
Izumozaki (Izumo Point), is known for its long history of political exiles:
Emperor Juntoku, Nichiren, Mongaku, Zeami, the mother of Zushiō, and others. As a consequence, Sado Island, surrounded here by "wild seas" (*araumi*) and
standing under the vast Amanogawa (literally "river of heaven"), or Milky Way,
comes to embody the feeling of loneliness, both of the exiles at Sado and of the

traveler himself. The poem has a grand, majestic, slow-moving rhythm, especially the drawn-out *o* sounds in the middle line (*Sado ni yokotau*), which suggests the vastness and scale of the landscape.

Bashō arrived at Izumo Point on the fourth day of the seventh month, but
when he wrote *Oku no hosomichi* many years later, he added a hokku about the
sixth day of the seventh month, thereby associating the "wild seas" poem with
Tanabata (seventh day of the seventh month), when the legendary constella-
tions, the Herdsboy and Weaver Girl, cross over the Milky Way for their annual
meeting. In this larger context, the island surrounded by "wild seas" embodies
loneliness as well as the longing of the exiles (and implicitly that of the poet) for
their distant loved ones. The Milky Way becomes like a boat or a bridge reaching out across the dark waters to the waiting exiles at Sado, reaching out to the
lonely soul of the poet.

By Bashō's time, the seasonal words (*kigo*) in haikai formed a vast pyramid,
capped by the most familiar seasonal topics of the classical tradition—the
cherry blossoms (*hana*), the cuckoo (*hototogisu*), the moon, and the snow—representing spring, summer, autumn, and winter, respectively. Spreading out
from this narrow peak were the other less prominent topics from the classical
tradition, such as the warbler (*uguisu*) and the frog (*kawazu*), and then, further
down, those added by the *renga* tradition such as *kiri* (paulownia). Occupying
the bottom and largest area were the seasonal words that had been added by
haikai poets and that by the mid-seventeenth century numbered in the thousands. Under the entry for midspring in Matsue Shigeyori's *Kefukigusa* (1638),
for example, we find such nonclassical items as dandelion (*tanpopo*), garlic (*nin-
niku*), and Japanese horseradish (*wasabi*). A similar, albeit less defined, pyramid
existed for utamakura, with famous Heian utamakura (established in the
Sandaishū) such as Suma, Yoshino, Matsushima, Shirakawa Barrier, and Sue no
Matsuyama occupying the top, the minor or lesser utamakura such as Kisagata
and Koromogawa standing in the middle, and haimakura such as Sado Island sit-
uated at the bottom. The *Ruiji meisho waka shū*, a handbook of utamakura that
Bashō undoubtedly used, lists fifty-nine different waka from Matsushima and
ninety-four for Shinobu no Sato. The same collection contains only six poems
on Robe River (Koromogawa), ten on Robe Barrier (Koromo no seki), two on
Kisagata, and none on Sado.

The Edo-period haikai handbooks vastly widened the field for seasonal topics, but the actual number of different seasonal topics used in haikai collections
was still surprisingly small—at most, two hundred or three hundred—and most
hokku were on familiar topics (warbler, plum blossom, mist, cherry blossoms)
from the classical tradition. In *Kyoraishō*, Bashō is quoted as saying, "If one can

find even a single new seasonal word, it will be a present for future generations."
But there is only one new kigo that Bashō contributed to the pyramid for certain: *take uuru hi* (bamboo-planting day), on the thirteenth of the fifth month.

Bashō himself wrote very few hokku with new kigo, and then only in his last
years. Instead, he devoted himself almost entirely to seeking new poetic associations (*hon'i*) in traditional topics. Bashō similarly composed relatively few
poems on haimakura such as Sado Island. Instead, like other haikai poets, he usually based his poems on classical utamakura, attempting to find "newness" in the
"old," to work against the tradition rather than outside it.

With its circle of associations, classical kigo, like classical utamakura, provided a special pipeline to the reader, greatly increasing the complexity and
capacity of the seventeen-syllable hokku. By contrast, new kigo, like haimakura,
had very few associations and usually none that were poetic, consequently making it extremely difficult to create a complex poem in seventeen syllables and to
parody or work against classical associations and conventions. In the famous frog
poem, for example,

furu ike ya	an ancient pond—
kawazu tobikomu	a frog leaps in
mizu no oto	the sound of water

Bashō works against the hon'i of *kawazu* (frog), a classical seasonal word associated with singing, longing for a lover, the bright yellow *yamabuki* (kerria), crys-
talline mountain streams. In place of the plaintive voice of the frog singing in the
rapids or calling out for its lover, Bashō gives us the humorous plop of the frog
jumping into the water. And instead of the elegant image of a frog in a fresh
mountain stream beneath the bright yellow yamabuki, the hokku presents a
stagnant pond. Haikai poets likewise worked against the classical associations of
utamakura, but in contrast to classical kigo, utamakura also were invested with
the spirits of ancient poets who could inspire as well as haunt the poet, both give
him poetic life and squelch his voice. Bashō frequently sought to "creatively cor-
rect"—as he does at Hiraizumi/Koromogawa—or to find less untrammeled
territory—as he does at Sado Island. As Bloom notes, "The precursors flood us,
and our imaginations can die by drowning in them, but no imaginative life is
possible if such inundation is wholly evaded."[5]

Bashō in fact was most successful with minor utamakura such as Kisagata and
Hiraizumi/Koromogawa and with haimakura, which represented new ground,
than with the major utamakura (at the top of the pyramid) such as Matsushima,
Sue no Matsuyama, and Shirakawa Barrier, where he left no poems or denied

ever writing any. In contrast to medieval poetic travel diaries, such as Sōgi's *Shirakawa kikō* (Journey to Shirakawa) or the Edo haikai master Sōin's *Matsushima ikkenki* (A Visit to Matsushima, 1662–1663), which are named after major uta-makura, Bashō took his title from an obscure road called *Oku no hosomichi* (near present-day Sendai), which makes only a cameo appearance in the text.

In short, Bashō's seemingly paradoxical relationship to Saigyō, to ancient poets, and to poetic toponyms reflected a larger, creative tension in his litera-ture: on the one hand, a movement back to the past, an integration of haikai into the larger poetic tradition, and a yearning for the poetic father who could pro-vide spiritual strength and inspiration and who could, like the ghosts of dead warriors, initiate a poetic dialogue; and, on the other hand, an equally strong, haikai-esque impulse to work against the tradition, to twist and parody the clas-sical conventions and associations, to break off from the "family," to seek new poetic ground and diction. As Basho's poetic ideal of *fueki ryūkō* (the unchanging and the ever changing) suggests, one was not possible without the other.

NOTES

1. Harold Bloom, *The Anxiety of Influence* (New York: Oxford University Press, 1973), p. 30.

2. Saigyō wrote on Robe River, playing on the homophones *kitaru* (to wear, to come) and *shimu* (to penetrate, to dye):

When I arrived at Hiraizumi on the twelfth of the tenth month, snow was falling, and there was a fierce storm. I had been anxious to see Robe River, and when I arrived at the bank of the river, the walls of the castle on Robe River seemed unusual. The edge of the river was frozen, and it was particularly cold.

toriwakite	Particularly cold,
kokoro mo shimite	it dyes even my heart,
sae zo wataru	Robe River
Koromogawa mi ni	that I came to see,
kitaru kyō shimo	to wear today.

Sankashū, poem 1131

3. See the eighth volume of *Gikeiki*. Helen Craig McCullough, trans., *Yoshitsune* (Stanford, CA: Stanford University Press, 1971), pp. 292–94.

4. Bashō in fact composed a poem here but apparently was not satisfied with it.

5. Bloom, *Anxiety of Influence*, p. 154.

12

Adaptation and Transformation: A Study of Taoist Influence on Early Seventeenth-Century Haikai

PEIPEI QIU

Haikai (comic linked verse) evolved from *renga* (linked verse) during the sixteenth and seventeenth centuries. From renga to *haikai no renga* and then to the shortest poetic form of haikai, *haikai hokku* (*haiku*), Japanese poetry experienced drastic changes in both form and nature: full-length poetry became an extremely condensed, seventeen-syllable genre; an aristocratic parlor art turned into a popular poem that had internalized irony as its core. In the process, conflicts between old rules and new ideas inevitably arose, and haikai poets constantly searched for proper poetic concepts and methods to sustain the legitimacy of this embryonic poetic form. The three major schools whose names are always associated with the rise of haikai—the Teimon, the Danrin, and the Shōmon schools—shared an interest in Taoist teaching, especially the *Chuang-tzu*.[1] Although each school had its own goals, they all sought poetic inspiration from the Taoist classics. In order to understand haikai, we first must examine its literary significance.

This chapter focuses on, first, the inner factors of haikai that occasioned the poets' encounter with the Taoist thinkers and, second, how Taoist concepts were transformed and retransformed during their adaptation for haikai. The significance of the Taoist influence on the development of haikai demonstrates that cultural influence and literary adaptation can never be mechanical. Rather, it is through dynamic transformations and metamorphoses that a diverse world literature evolves.

The Teimon School and the *Chuang-tzu*

The word *haikai* comes from the Chinese word *fei-hsieh*, meaning "facetiousness" or "humor." In T'ang-dynasty (618–907) China, the term was used to designate a witty poetic style. The first Japanese imperial poetry anthology, the *Kokin wakashū* (905), also used the same two characters to refer to witty and humorous *waka*. But haikai-style poems did not gain much literary importance in Japan until haikai no renga developed in the later medieval age.

When renga first emerged in medieval Japan, it referred to a kind of entertaining poetic game in which the participants competed with one another by adding their own witty lines of verse to the preceding ones, forming linked verses of alternating three- and two-line units. The *ushin renga* (serious renga)[2] masters' orthodox theories generally denied the original entertainment purpose of linked verse and, instead, turned it into an elegant art form that could be extended to as many as a thousand links.

The first collection of renga, *Tsukubashū* (Collection of Tsukuba, 1356), contained a separate haikai section for comic (as opposed to elegant) renga. Another important renga collection compiled when the verse form had matured, the *Shinsen Tsukubashū* (Newly Selected Collection of Tsukuba, 1495), contained no haikai no renga at all, and thereafter, haikai no renga were not included in anthologies of renga.

This exclusion of haikai from the more elegant renga had a lasting effect on its development. Although haikai has the same form as renga, it was considered to be a deviant, even inferior, poetic form because of its comic (sometimes vulgar) intent. Consequently, the haikai masters were forced to look for different poetic ideas and theories to uphold the identity and legitimacy of their chosen verse form. The haikai poets' encounter with the *Chuang-tzu* in the seventeenth century was a result of this search.

The first haikai no renga bespoke a liberal spirit and boldness of expression. In the first half of the sixteenth century, Yamazaki Sōkan (?–1553), Arakida Moritake (1473–1549), and other poets disregarded the rigid rules governing renga and instead made haikai no renga a lighthearted and unconstrained poetic form. One verse by Sōkan that is often cited to illustrate such characteristics is as follows:

saohime no	The goddess Sao
haru tachinagara	Now that spring has come, pisses
shito wo shite	While still standing.[3]

Such poems had no lasting literary value because their principal appeal was their boldness and facetiousness, and so they were soon dropped from the main repertoire of Japanese poetry. Despite this seeming setback, the cultural proclivities of the samurai and townsmen at the beginning of the seventeenth century were fertile ground for the comic verse. In addition, praise by Matsunaga Teitoku (1571–1653) for haikai no renga as a proper art form for the new era made haikai a major genre of Japanese poetry.

Teitoku's Teimon school flourished in the early seventeenth century, when Japan was at peace under the rule of the Tokugawa shogunate. Throughout his life, Teitoku played a double role as both a historical and a literary figure,[4] taking great pride in the secret traditions of learning in which he had been trained since his youth and also giving public lectures on traditional literature, which earlier had been taught only privately in the noble families. This double role gave rise to the contradiction of Teitoku's being a conservative leader of his haikai school and, at the same time, a reformer of haikai no renga.

Although Teitoku made great efforts to establish haikai as a legitimate literary form, his method was to constrict it by means of codes, the same fate that had befallen waka and renga. Teikoku's critical writings were centered on technical regulations, and the principal distinction he made between haikai and elegant renga was the use of *haigon* (vernacular words and Chinese words that were not permitted in waka and the elegant renga). Accordingly, Teitoku was often accused of destroying haikai's free-flowing style. Nonetheless, his efforts to tame the verse by means of formal regulation and his emphasis on haigon helped satisfy the demand for a popular yet artistic comic verse form, and in this way, Teikoku saved haikai from degenerating even further.

As a codifier of haikai, Teitoku wrote little about the connection between haikai and Taoist thought. But we do know that he was familiar with the *Chuang-tzu* and was perhaps greatly impressed by it. Teitoku often used the literary name Shōyūken, which undoubtedly came from the "Hsiao-yao-you" (Shōyōyū in Japanese, "Free and Easy Wandering") chapter of the *Chuang-tzu*. Other evidence shows that the Teimon poets began to think of the *Chuang-tzu* in conjunction with haikai theory even before the Danrin poets enthusiastically advocated haikai as a kind of Chuang-tzu-style *gūgen*.[5] In 1671, the Teimon school poet Yamaoka Genrin (1631–1672) published *Takaragura* (The Treasure

House), a collection of prose and poetry which, according to his son, imitated the *Chuang-tzu*.[6]

Takaragura consists of seventy-two short prose essays on household implements. These pieces contain frequent allusions to Lao-tzu and Chuang-tzu, and each concludes with a hokku that contains either *tsuki* (the moon) or *hana* (cherry blossoms) as its central image. The structure of the work is like that of a parable. Because the moon and cherry blossoms in Japanese poetry are traditionally symbols and synonyms for beauty and poetic elegance, by deliberately associating ordinary household implements with these traditional symbols of beauty, Genrin demonstrated his concept of haikai through a Taoistic vision:

Leave everything to the limitless power of *zōka*, then

> *ame tsuchi ya*   Heaven and earth
> *kore tsuki hana no*   became a treasure house
> *takaragura*   of *tsuki* and *hana*.[7]

Zōka (*tzao-hua* in Chinese), a term cited from the sixth chapter of the *Chuang-tzu*, encompasses several key notions of Taoist thought. First, zōka refers to Nature's working, the actual reflection of the Tao.[8] Second, it suggests that the existence of all things and beings is the direct result of Nature's working and, therefore, that each thing and being embodies the Tao. Finally, following Nature's working means at the same time following the Tao. By "leaving everything to the limitless power of zōka," Genrin means that total adherence to Nature is both the prerequisite and the ultimate goal of haikai composition. To Genrin, haikai is more a fablelike device to reveal the truth than just a literary form, as is made clear in the afterword to *Takaragura* by Genrin's son Genjo:

> Recently, [my father] wrote essays on such things as writing brushes and ink and clogs and sandals. He entitled the collection *The Treasure House*. Although it is mainly an imitation of gūgen and *shigen*, the work is intended to harmonize all things with the Heavenly Equality and, by so doing, to redress man's mind.[9]

Gūgen, *shigen*, and the phrase "harmonize all things with the Heavenly Equality" come from the twenty-seventh chapter of the *Chuang-tzu*. Yü-yen (*gūgen* in Japanese) describes the characteristics of Chuang-tzu's writing style as "imputed words (*gūgen*) make up nine tenths of it; repeated words (*jūgen*) make up seven tenths of it; goblet words (*shigen*) come forth day after day, harmonizing things in the Heavenly Equality."[10] According to Chuang-tzu's own explanation of a similar expression, "harmonizing things in the Heavenly Equality" refers to a state completely free of any conceptual restrictions and harmonious with nature:

> What do I mean by harmonizing [things] with the Heavenly Equality? Right is not right; so is not so. If right were really right, it would differ so clearly from not right that there would be no need for argument. If so were really so, it would differ so clearly from not so that there would be no need for argument. Waiting for one shifting voice (to pass judgment on) another is the same as waiting for none of them. Harmonize them all with the Heavenly Equality, leave them to their endless changes, and so live out your years. Forget the years; forget distinctions. Leap into the boundless and make it your home.[11]

Compared with other Teimon poets, Genrin displays a much deeper understanding of the *Chuang-tzu*. He catches the important point that although Chuang-tzu's gūgen is a literary device to convey truth, it does not transmit religious teaching or moral lessons but, rather, explicates a unique way of thinking, a way that Chuang-tzu characterized as harmonizing with nature. But by imitating the *Chuang-tzu*, Genrin intended to "redress man's mind." Thus his perspective of the gūgen-style is still based on a pragmatic concept.

This pragmatic concept of Chuang-tzu's gūgen is expressed more clearly in the writing of Teitoku's disciple Kitamura Kigin (1624–1705). When asked how one should judge the merits of Teitoku's verses on the theme of love, which contain obvious erotic elements, Kigin answered:

> A verse composed by a person whose heart is occupied entirely by sexual desire and a verse by a person who understands that the essence of haikai is to teach rightful moral principles have different souls. They are not the same kind of poem, even though they may resemble one another. . . . As seen in the fifty-four chapters of the *Genji monogatari*, Murasaki Shikibu's original purpose was to make the book a vehicle to convey the five cardinal articles of morality[12] and to encourage the pursuit of salvation. Yet on the surface, it looks like merely an amorous tale. Chuang-tzu's gūgen talks about the principles by means of pure fabrications, but if anyone takes his gūgen as an ordinary lie, we should say that he did not understand the *Chuang-tzu* very well. The whole idea of Lin Hsi-i's[13] annotation [of the *Chuang-tzu*] is nothing else but what I have just said.[14]

Three points in this passage should be explained. First, Kigin is defending Teitoku's poetry on the basis of a didactic theory. The idea that "the essence of haikai is to teach rightful moral principles" is typical of the concept of the

Teimon school, which used the pragmatic literary tradition to legitimatize haikai. Second, Kigin is trying to strengthen his argument by referring to Japanese critical history, especially those medieval commentators who justified the *Genji monogatari* as a gūgen conveying moral lessons.[15] Third, Kigin is reading the *Chuang-tzu* through Lin Hsi-i's *Chuang-tzu chüan-chai k'ou-i* and is applying a didactic interpretation to the *Chuang-tzu* as well as to Lin's annotations.

Kigin was one of the major spokesmen of the Teimon school after Teitoku's death. His comments reflected the general critical view of the Teimon poets and became the foundation of their lengthy dispute with the Danrin school in the 1670s.

The Danrin School and Chuang-tzu's Gūgen

The rise of the Danrin school is described by Japanese literary historians as a reaction to the formalism of the Teimon poetry. After flourishing for some forty years, the tepid humor of the Teimon haikai had lost its appeal. At the beginning of the 1670s, those haikai poets desiring a new style looked to Nishiyama Sōin as their leader. These poets, mainly in the commercial cities of Edo (present-day Tokyo) and Osaka, formed the Danrin school.[16]

The Danrin school sought its authority from the *Chuang-tzu*. In 1674, Nishiyama Sōin (1605–1682) published the hundred-verse *Kabashira* (Mosquito Pillar). The lighthearted cynicism of the work was fiercely criticized by the Teimon poets as harmful to morals and religious belief, and this formed the basis of the two schools' long period of quarrel. In answer to the Teimon school's accusations, Sōin issued his famous statement on the correspondence between haikai and Chuang-tzu's gūgen:

> The art of haikai places falsehood ahead of truth. It is the gūgen of waka, the kyō-gen (comic or mad verse) of renga. It is said to have been the teaching of the poets of the past that one should use renga as a base and also forget renga. I have been wandering on the way of haikai for many years. I heard that someone in China observed: "When one turns fifty, one will recognize the mistakes one has made in the past forty-nine years."[17] How could I, at the age of seventy, not realize my own faults that others have seen? I chose the "wrong way" for various reasons. . . . Whether in the old style, the current style, or the in-between style, a good poet is a good poet, and a bad one is a bad one; there is no such thing as distinguishing which style is the correct one. The best thing is to amuse oneself by writing what one likes; it is a joke within a fantasy.[18]

By "the wrong way," Sōin is referring to the boldness and free spirit represented by Moritake's tradition. Sōin's "reasons" for choosing "the wrong way," though he did not spell them out here, came from the *Chuang-tzu*, as he explained elsewhere: "Haikai, a form of miscellany style, is the gūgen of renga. How can we not learn from Chuang Chou's writings and revere Moritake's tradition?"[19]

Sōin's statement that haika "is the gūgen of waka, the kyōgen of renga" was soon adopted by his disciples, with the result that their elaborations became the theoretical basis of the Danrin haikai, giving rise to that school's characteristic style. In *Haikai mōgyū* (An Introduction to Haikai, 1675), an important discussion of the Danrin school's theory, Sōin's disciple Okanishi Ichū (1639–1711) offers various examples of gūgen from the *Chuang-tzu* and concludes:

> Thus, mixing the concepts of big and small, breaking the common sense of longevity and ephemeral, making falsehood [*kyo*] truth [*jitsu*] and truth falsehood, taking right [*ze*] as wrong [*hi*] and wrong as right—these are not only Chuang-tzu-style gūgen but, indeed, also the very nature of haikai. Therefore, the essence of the art is to exaggerate freely and to create the most outrageous lies.[20]

Here, by mixing right and wrong, Ichū favors the humorous twist of meaning rather than the idea of transcending the worldly boundaries of right and wrong. In addition, "falsehood" and "truth" are used to describe literary fabrication rather than to refer to the mental states required by the *Chuang-tzu* to comprehend the Tao.

Frivolous as it was, the Danrin school's advocacy of haikai as a kind of Chuang-tzu-style gūgen had a positive effect. The Danrin poets ignored Teikoku's rules, believing that "if wedded to old conventions and limited by codes, the style of a verse would become rigid and ossified, thereby losing the essence of the gūgen."[21] Although the Teimon school considered the presence of haigon to be the only feature distinguishing haikai from renga, haigon was less important to the Danrin poets. To them, what constituted a haikai was the spirit of gūgen in its content.[22] These differences from the Teimon school greatly widened the haikai poets' imagination and brought the comic verse a step forward to maturity.

The Nature of Haikai and the *Chuang-tzu*

Previous studies found two major causes for the Teimon and the Danrin poets' interest in the *Chuang-tzu*: the influence of the Genji scholars' critical view and the popularity of Lin Hsi-i's *Chuang-tzu chüan-chai k'ou-i* in Japan at that time.

But the fact that the *Chuang-tzu* inspired so many major haikai poets cannot be explained by these external influences alone. Rather, an important issue has been neglected: the internal factors relating haikai to the Taoist text.

Imoto Nōichi defined the two fundamental characteristics of comic verse as its "extremely short form" and "comic nature."[23] The second characteristic is found consistently throughout haikai's development, from the basic renga, to the lighthearted renga (*mushin renga*), to the haikai no renga, and, finally, to the haikai hokku (haiku). The first characteristic (its extremely short form), however, did not become apparent until the seventeenth century, when the segmentation of haikai no renga became a regular practice and the hokku became an independent poetic form. It was not accidental that the haikai poets were drawn to the *Chuang-tzu* at the same time that haikai was establishing its final form. It was from the *Chuang-tzu* that the extremely condensed comic poetry derived the theoretical basis for strengthening its identity.

As I stated earlier, haikai was always differentiated from other poetry because conventional renga theory named poetry as a way to support the government and educate the people, and the comic poem was thought to lack the qualities that could achieve this goal. In order to gain recognition for haikai, the haikai masters tried to defend comic verse by either referring to its didactic tradition represented in the "Great Preface" to the *Classic of Poetry*[24] or seeking a new theoretical basis from sources that did not belong to the orthodox tradition but were comparably authoritative. These sources were Taoist teachings, especially the *Chuang-tzu*.

The Teimon school, becoming prominent after a long bleak period of haikai no renga, attempted first to regulate haikai, which still depended on theories regarding the traditional waka and renga. Kigin's writings on haikai theory, for instance, often begin with discussions of the didactic theory advocated by the "Great Preface," drawing heavily on pieces by waka and renga scholars. The following statement is a recurrent theme of Kigin's writings: "Humorous poems, though not moral doctrines, convey the truth; haikai, though not an instrument of government, teaches a wonderful lesson."[25]

Although the Teimon poets tried hard to prove the virtue of haikai in accordance with the pragmatic critical tradition, the contradictions between the comic nature of the new poetry and the didactic goal set by the old tradition were not easy to resolve. The Teimon masters constantly had to deal with such problems as using moral values to justify erotic or frivolous verses.

The Danrin school, established later, faced different issues. These poets did not need to worry about the legitimacy of haikai; instead, they tried to transcend old traditions and to create their own theory of haikai. In referring to

Chuang-tzu's gūgen, the Danrin poets touted haikai for its humor and publicly threw off the didactic yoke. For the Danrin poets, Chuang-tzu's careless laughter, his deliberate reversal of concepts, and his fantastic fables provided an authoritative defense for haikai: humor and wit had their own value.

During this time, the development of haikai's other basic feature, its brevity, also heightened the haikai poets' interest in the *Chuang-tzu*. Although even some traditional renga consisted of solely an opening verse, this was not common until the revival of haikai in the early seventeenth century. Beginning with the Teimon school, composing hokku became a very popular activity. Three of Kigin's commentaries on the opening verses in hokku contests have been preserved, showing that in the 1670s, the Teimon school was already sponsoring competitions.

This tendency toward the independence of an individual verse was also evident in the fragmentation of the linked verses. Each verse had to be independent, a significant feature of haikai no renga after Teitoku's time. Indeed, for the Teimon school's haikai, the independent verse was a requirement, as was the use of haigon.[26] The independence of the individual verse led to the condensation of haikai in both form and content. Accordingly, haikai became the representation of a self-contained poetic world by means of seventeen or even fourteen syllables. This format requires the verse to be both emblematic and evocative, in order to enlarge its poetic capacity. Here again, the haikai poets found a connection between the nature of haikai and the characteristics of the *Chuang-tzu*, which is an exceptionally rich source of emblematic depictions and evocative associations.

The awareness of this connection explains Genrin's reason for imitating Chuang-tzu's gūgen in his *Takaragura*: he must have believed that Chuang-tzu's artistic thinking and expression—seeing and embodying beauty and truth in the simplest and most ordinary things—provided a key to "the treasure house" of haikai's highly condensed art form. When Sōin stated that "the art of haikai places falsehood ahead of the truth. It is the gūgen of waka," he probably was also conscious of the importance to haikai of the use of parable. However, by considering the use of parable as the essence of haikai,[27] the Danrin poets pushed their advocacy of Chuang-tzu's gūgen beyond reasonable limits.

Neither the Teimon nor the Danrin poets really understood the profundity of Chuang-tzu's gūgen and the subtle forces operating in Chuang-tzu's literary style, as both schools interpreted Chuang-tzu's text at face value. But the literary significance of his work cannot be fully grasped without also recognizing its literary influences—the conceptualization of Taoist assumptions in Chinese poetics and the embodiment of Taoist tastes in Chinese poetic practice.

Nonetheless, the schools' promotion of the *Chuang-tzu* inspired the younger generation of haikai poets to discover the poetic possibilities suggested by the Taoist classics and to explore their depth of irony. Along with an increasing number of Chinese poetic anthologies and handbooks published from the late 1670s onward, haikai poets' interest in the *Chuang-tzu* moved toward a deeper understanding of Taoist traits in the Chinese poetic tradition, which in turn led to radical changes in both the style and the critical concepts of the comic verse.

The Emergence of the Bashō Style

The Danrin school's assertion that haikai consists of "wild exaggerations" and "the baldest of lies"[28] grew quiet in the late 1670s, and a new trend emerged in the 1680s: Poets who were tired of the frivolous wordplay of the earlier haikai decided that the form should be essentially natural and truthful. This new idea was reflected especially in the works of Ikenishi Gonsui (1650–1722), Shiinomoto Saimaro (1656–1738), Uejima Onitsura (1661–1738), and Matsuo Bashō. They all shared a tendency toward naturalness and profundity, with the most gifted poet of the group, Bashō, epitomizing the characteristics of the new haikai style.

From the end of the 1670s to 1680s, the "Chinese style" prevailed in haikai circles. The force behind this development was a determination to elevate haikai to an art comparable to the best of Chinese poems. It was during this period that Matsuo Bashō founded his haikai school, known as Shōmon. Poets of the Shōmon school sought inspiration from the Chinese poetic tradition and the Taoist classics. The preface to *Inaka no kuawase* (The Rustics' Hokku Contest), published by Bashō's disciples in 1680, clearly illustrates how deeply the Chinese influence colored the school's critical interest:

> Master Tō taught us the "haikai doctrines of the endlessness" in his Kukusai [Flitting and Fluttering Study]. He starts his lecture from the elegant taste of Tung-p'o,[29] the unworldliness of Tu Fu,[30] and the sentiments of Shan-ku.[31] The haikai style he advocates is profound and tranquil. Master Tō said: "Imagine the spring mists over the north bank of the Wei River when you are standing under the cherry blossoms on the Nerima hills; behold the clouds over the east bank of the Yangtze River when you are looking at the moon above the Kasai shore." Inspired by the master's words, Rasha[32] composed fifty verses in the Chinese style and divided them into left and right sides, called "the countryman" and "the boor," respectively. Since the verses are coarse and the expressions robust, the

contest was named the "Rustics' Hokku Contest." It was judged by Master Tō. His comments captured the quintessence of Chuang Chou's [Chuang-tzu's] thoughts; it could make the eloquent Lin Hsi-i speechless.[33]

This short paragraph contains many allusions to Chinese poetry and the *Chuang-tzu*. First, "Master Tō" refers to Master Bashō, who was then writing under the literary name Tōsei. By naming himself Tōsei, "Peach Green," Bashō was comparing himself with Li Po (701–762), the great Chinese poet whose name is written with characters meaning "Plum White." In the preface to *Inaka no kuawase*, Bashō's teaching is referred to as "haikai doctrines of endlessness" (*haikai mujinkyō*), which is reminiscent of the "true doctrines of Nan-hua" (*Nan-hua chen-ching*)—the expression used to refer to the *Chuang-tzu* since T'ang times. The name of Bashō's residence, "Flitting and Fluttering Study," is also from the *Chuang-tzu*: the butterfly in the famous *gūgen* about Chuang Chou's dream is described as "flitting and fluttering." Bashō also used the term as one of his pseudonyms. The literary names for Bashō, his teachings, and his residence are revealing, as they reflect how much Bashō considered in this period the *Chuang-tzu* and Chinese poetry to be major sources for his haikai. The preface indicates that Bashō asked his disciples to associate their own world, the "Nerima hills" and the "Kasai shore," with those of the greatest Chinese poets, Tu Fu and Li Po: "the north bank of the Wei" where Tu Fu had once lived, and "the east bank of the Yangtze River," which refers to Hui-chi, where Li Po spent time composing poetry. According to the preface, Bashō not only required his disciples to return for inspiration to the great Chinese poets but also "captured the quintessence of Chuang-tzu's thought" in his critical norms. His comments on the following verse from *Inaka no kuawase* show what he meant:

tobi ni notte	Riding on a kite
haru wo okuru ni	to see off the parting spring—
shirakumo ya[34]	the white clouds.

Bashō judged this verse to be superior, for the first phrase implicitly alludes to the *Chuang-tzu*, and the whole poem portrays a realm reminiscent of the free and easy wandering celebrated by the Taoist classic. Bashō wrote: "Riding on a kite to wander freely in the boundless infinity—the joy expressed in the verse on the right side is indeed endless."[35] Bashō's wording here shows a striking resemblance to the *Chuang-tzu* as well as to Lin Hsi-i's explanation of the term *hsiao-yao-you* (free and easy wandering). Lin observed: " '*You*' means to have the spirit of heavenly wandering. '*Hsiao-yao*' means unrestrained and free. '*Hsiao-*

yao-you' denotes nothing else but what is called 'joy' in *The Classic of Poetry* and *The Analects*."[36] Lin concluded that expressing inner joyousness without mentioning the word *joy* "is the quintessence of composing a poem."[37] From this, we can see that Bashō not only imitated Lin's wording but also followed his criteria.

In fact, in his annotations Lin Hsi-i closely associated Taoist notions with Chinese poetry and poetics; throughout his interpretation of the *Chuang-tzu*, he refers to the great literary figures and paradigms in Chinese poetic history. He also ascribed the achievements of the great Chinese poets to the reading of the *Chuang-tzu* and asserted that the *Chuang-tzu* was the most important work for literati and poets.[38] This is indeed an important feature to keep in mind when examining the *Chuang-tzu chüan-chai k'ou-i*'s influence on Bashō. His integration of Taoist philosophy and the Chinese poetic tradition indicates the poetic possibilities that the haikai poets sought.

It was through this increasing awareness of the connections between Taoist philosophy and the principles of Chinese poetry that the Shōmon poets distinguished themselves from their predecessors in borrowing from the *Chuang-tzu*. Although in its early stage, the gūgen style was still an important part of the Shōmon poets' interest in the *Chuang-tzu*, creating witty jokes was no longer their main purpose. Instead, they emphasized the thematic profundity, the ultimate truth evoked through allusions. The Shōmon poets explored fictitious and exaggerated expressions to dramatize the ironic nature of worldly phenomena, as the *Chuang-tzu* had originally sought to do, whereas the Danrin poets tried merely to achieve surprising or entertaining effects.

The poetic themes in *Tokiwaya no kuawase* (Hokku Contest of the Everlasting, 1680) are similar. Bashō considered the following verse to be extremely well written:

daidai wo	The tangerine and the kumquat
mikan to kinkan no	laughed at the daidai, saying,
waratte iwaku	"You're big in name only."[39]

The sounds *daidai* in Japanese represent a fruit, and they also suggest "big"; so the good-tasting tangerine (*mikan*) and kumquat (*kinkan*), which are small, ridicule the daidai fruit, which is big but tastes bitter. This poem reworked two important themes of Chuang-tzu's gūgen. One is the limitation of humans' cognizance and understanding. Critics have pointed out that the image of the tangerine and kumquat laughing at the daidai is derived from Chuang-tzu's depiction of the cicada and the little dove laughing at P'eng.[40] In the *Chuang-tzu*, P'eng is a bird that can fly as high as ninety thousand *li* when beginning a six-month flight. The cicada and the little dove laugh at this because they do not believe any bird can fly so far. Through the ignorance of the cicada and the little dove, Chuang-tzu humorously reveals the pitiable limitations of humans' cognizance and existence. The preceding verse imitated Chuang-tzu's gūgen, but instead of depicting a lesser creature's ignorant laughing at a greater creature, the verse satirizes the laughter of the privileged members of the citrus family. The tangerine and kumquat laugh at the daidai because they consider themselves superior to the daidai, which, in their eyes, is a useless fruit. By twisting the relative positions of those who are laughing and the one who is laughed at, the poem introduces another recurrent theme of the *Chuang-tzu*: the absurdity of conventional values.

In the *Chuang-tzu*, many gūgen stories make fun of established values and worldly concerns. For instance, one story describes how Chuang-tzu and Hui-tzu[41] argue over the use of an exceptionally huge gourd. The gūgen relates that Hui-tzu grew a huge gourd that could hold five *piculs*. Because the gourd was so big, Hui-tzu found it unsuitable to be used as either a water container or a dipper, so he smashed it to pieces. Ridiculing Hui-tzu's thinking, Chuang-tzu asks: "Why didn't you think of making it into a great tub so you could go floating around the rivers and lakes, instead of worrying because it was too big and unwieldy to dip into things!"[42] The main point of this gūgen is that established values and human-imposed standards have brought nothing but meaningless limitations to the people and restrictions to the world. Only by violating those conventions can one reach the ideal realm free of worries and harmonious with nature. In the *Chuang-tzu*, this realm is called the "Not-Even-Anything Village" or the "Field of Broad-and-Boundless,"[43] which Lin Hsi-i defines as "the joyful realm within the ultimate Way, the Way of Nature's working."[44]

As the referee, Bashō admires the skillful construction of the poem's double conception, noting that "the tangerine and kumquat laugh at daidai—the verse constructed one conception within another, embodied truth within fabrication. It is a masterpiece that stands out from the other verses. In this hokku, one can see the heart of Chuang Chou. It is indeed the best poem, worthy of pondering."[45] Apparently, Bashō liked the poem not only for its ingenuity in imitating the gūgen-style of the *Chuang-tzu* but, more important, also for its thematic depth, the embodiment of "the heart of Chuang Chou."

The thematic tendency of *Inaka no kuawase* and *Tokiwaya no kuawase* demonstrated the Bashō school's departure from the Danrin school's preferences. Although in the Bashō school's heavy use of Chuang-tzu's gūgen we can still see the traces of Danrin influence, to Bashō and his fellow poets, the essence of haikai was no longer "to make wild exaggerations and create the baldest of lies."[46] Rather, the new school discovered in the *Chuang-tzu* a deeper dimension of humor—an internalized irony based on spiritual freedom and philosophical depths. The preference for the rustic, the joy of free wandering, and the unrestrained laughter at worldly values presented in the two hokku contests exemplified the poetic traits that Bashō later summarized as *fūkyō* (poetic eccentricity) and *fūryū* (elegant unconventionality), both derived from Chinese words. The terms brought together many elements reflecting a Taoist trend in the Chinese poetic tradition. Several salient features of these terms—honoring the unworldly and the austere, preferring the solitary and the simple, and valuing the rustic and the natural—left a mark on Bashō's poetry. From the early period of Bashō's poetic career, *fūkyō* and *fūryū* comprised a significant part of his poetic theory and also changed his way of life. The same year as *Inaka no kuawase* and *Tokiwaya no kuawase* were published, Bashō moved from the city of Edo to Fukagawa, a rustic area on the eastern bank of the Sumida River. Regarding this move, Bashō wrote:

> After nine years living in poverty in the city, I moved my dwelling to the neighborhood of Fukagawa. Someone once said: "Since antiquity, Ch'ang-an has been a place to win fame and fortune, but it is a hard place for those who are empty-handed and penniless to live in." Is it because I myself am poor that I can appreciate the wisdom of the speaker?

shiba no to ni	To my brushwood hut
cha wo konoha kaku	it sweeps leaves for my tea
arashi ka na	the stormy wind.[47]

The lines cited in this passage are from Po Chü-i's (772–846) poem "Seeing off Hermit Chang on His Return to Sung-yang." Bashō compared Ch'ang-an, the ancient and populous capital of China, with the place in the city where he formerly lived and linked his renunciation of worldly concerns to the Chinese poem. In this way, Bashō associated himself with the long poetic tradition of rejoicing in a solitary and austere life. The whistling cold wind is humorously depicted as sending withered leaves to the speaker to use for tea in place of real tea leaves. The contrast between the hard conditions and the humor—one highlights the other—creates an aura of spiritual joyousness, defined by Lin Hsi-i as the quintessence of poetry.

Bashō's move to Fukagawa was an epochal event in his poetic career. The integration of his poetic ideals into his way of life marked the poet's awareness and pursuit of the poetic truth, *fuga no makoto*.[48] Furthermore, the joy he found in his solitary, rustic life revealed his determination to set off on his long journey to "follow Nature's working [zōka] and return to the Natural [zōka]."[49] It was not by chance that in the same period, Bashō wrote the famous hokku still recognized as a landmark in the formation of the Bashō style:

kareeda ni	On the withered branch
karasu no tomaritaru ya	a crow has alighted,
aki no kure	nightfall in autumn.[50]

This is a realistic sketch of late autumn. The poem's natural, simple images clearly point in a new direction. They differ not only from the witty wordplay and exaggeration of the Danrin haikai but also from the conceptual representations of the philosophical truth in *Inaka no kuawase* and *Tokiwaya no kuawase*. The aesthetics of this hokku can be found in Shiinomoto Saimaro's preface to *Azuma no nikki* (Diary of the east), the collection of haikai in which the poem was published.

Azuma no nikki was compiled by Ikenishi Gonsui in 1681. The collection contains sixteen opening verses (hokku) by Bashō, who at that time was still writing under the name Tōsei. Criticizing the endless exchange of attacks between the Teimon and the Danrin schools at that time, Shiinomoto Saimaro pointed out that those who wasted time arguing over stylistic supremacy did not understand the beauty of naturalness and spontaneity and never "saw that true ingeniousness exists beyond artifice." Saimaro ended his preface with citations from the *Chuang-tzu*: "As for judging the old and the new styles, we should wait for the True Man and leave everything to the Way of Heaven."[51]

A term from the *Chuang-tzu*, the "True Man" essentially refers to the Taoist sage who is aloof from worldly concerns and preoccupies himself with the Way of Heaven. According to the *Chuang-tzu*, only through the judgment of the True Man can one know what the way of Heaven is and thereupon acquire true knowledge, the Tao. The *Chuang-tzu* also calls the True Man the "Great and Venerable Teacher."[52] Regarding the relationship among the concepts of the True Man, Heaven, and the Tao, Lin Hsi-i explains: "The Great and Venerable Teacher is the Tao. It is also said that the sage follows Heaven; Heaven follows the Tao; the Tao follows the Natural."[53] Thus in Taoist teaching, the True Man, Heaven, and the Tao are integrated into one under the principle of the Natural.

Saimaro thus was not just criticizing the meaningless bickering between the Teimon and the Danrin schools but was also declaring a critical position based on the Taoist aesthetic preference for the Natural. He was calling for a poetic "aspiration," the pursuit of a new poetic principle, and it was in this sense that Saimaro asserted that "true ingeniousness exists beyond artifice."[54]

From the false to the truthful, haikai completed an important step toward its maturity, and Taoist influence played a significant role in this transition. The Taoist principle of the Natural provided the haikai reformers with suitable theoretical weapons to combat the mannerism of the earlier haikai, and the impact of Chinese poetry further enhanced the impulse for change. Rising in this current, Bashō and his followers did not limit themselves to a mechanical adherence to certain Taoist concepts. Instead, they discovered the poetic possibilities suggested by Taoist assumptions in a much larger context—the poetic tradition that evolved during the long history of China. During the next decade, after being adapted and regenerated through the truly ingenious works of Bashō, these poetic possibilities became an inseparable part of the unique tradition of haikai.

ACKNOWLEDGMENTS

This article grew out of my dissertation research, which was conducted under the guidance of Professor Donald Keene. I would like to take this opportunity to express my deepest gratitude to him for his help and encouragement at every stage of my studies.

Research for this article was supported by the Institute of Oriental Studies of the University of Tokyo, where I was a visiting researcher in 1991, and a Japan Foundation Dissertation Research Fellowship. I owe a great debt to Professors Konishi Jin'ichi, Ogata Tsutomu, Fukunaga Mitsuji, Hirota Jirō, Morikawa Akira, and Hachiya Kunio for their counsel during my research in Japan. This study is also immensely indebted to the stimulation of previous studies by Japanese scholars, particularly Yamamoto Heiichirō, "Haikai to Sōji ga gūgen," in *Kokugo to kokubungaku* 14 (1937) I, pp. 60—87 and II, pp.167—92; Ebara Taizō, "Bashō to Ro So," in *Ebara Taizō chosakushū,* XI, Tokyo: Chūō Kōronsha, 1987, pp. 72—79; Kon Eizō, "Danrin haikai oboegaki—Gūgensetsu no genryū to bungakushiteki jittai," in *Kokugo kokubun kenkyū,* 7 (1953), pp.1—27; Nonomura Katsuhide, "Danrin haikai no gūgenron wo megutte," in *Kokugo to kokubungaku,* vol. 33 (1956), pp. 36—44, and his "Bashō to Sōji to Sōgaku," in *Renga haikai kenkyū* 15 (1957), pp. 33—39; Konishi Jin'ichi, "Bashō to gūgensetsu," *Nihon Gakushiin kiyō,* 18, no. 2 and 3 (1960); and Hirota Jirō, *Bashō no geijutsu— Sono tenkai to haikei,* Tokyo: Yūseidō, 1968.

NOTES

1. Scholars disagree about the authorship of the extant text of the *Chuang-tzu* and the identity of the author Chuang-tzu. It is generally agreed, however, that the seven "inner chapters" constitute the heart of the *Chuang-tzu* and that the remaining chapters may have been written by different writers at different times. For convenience, I have used "the *Chuang-tzu*" to refer to the

thirty-three chapters of the existing text, and the name of the philosopher, "Chuang-tzu," to the Taoist thinker or thinkers who created the work.

2. Translation from Donald Keene, *World Within Walls* (New York: Grove Press, 1978), p. 12.

3. Ebara Taizō, ed., *Kōhon Inutsukubashū* (Tokyo: Ōuchi insatsujo, 1938), p. 1. Translation from Keene, *World Within Walls*, p. 16.

4. See Keene, *World Within Walls*, ch. 2.

5. *Gūgen* (*yü-yen* in Chinese) is a term appearing in the twenty-seventh chapter of the *Chuang-tzu*. Its original meaning, according to Burton Watson, is "words put into the mouth of historical or fictional persons to make them more compelling." *Chuang-tzu* scholars also use the term to refer to the general writing style of the *Chuang-tzu*. In modern Japanese and Chinese, *gūgen* is often translated as "apologue" or "fable," but these translations are not suitable here. In his translation of the *Chuang-tzu*, Watson translated the term as "imputed words." Since the term refers to many important issues in the connections between haikai and the *Chuang-tzu* and since its complex connotations cannot be properly expressed by any existing English word, I have used *gūgen* throughout the text.

6. Yamaoka Genjo's "Postscript to *Takaragura*," in Odaka Toshio et al., eds., *Teimon haikaishū II*, in *Koten haibungaku taikei* (hereafter abbreviated *KHT*) (Tokyo: Shūeisha, 1971), vol. 2, p. 82.

7. Yamaoka Genrin, *Takaragura*, in *KHT*, vol. 2, p. 23.

8. *Zōka* has often been translated into English as "nature," but the concept of nature in the Western sense did not exist in Bashō's time. As seen in my discussion, zōka in both the original Taoist texts and in the writings of haikai poets essentially means "the working of the Tao," which includes the Tao's manifestations in nature—the external world and its phenomena—but is not limited to it. For convenience, I have capitalized "Nature" here as a synonym for the Tao's reference to the natural, as opposed to the artificial, and I have translated zōka as "Nature's working."

9. Yamaoka, *Takaragura*, in *KHT*, p. 82.

10. Translation by Burton Watson, *The Complete Works of Chuang Tzu* (New York: Columbia University Press, 1968), 303. As Watson explains, *shigen*, or "goblet words," refer to words that are like a goblet that tips when full and rights itself when empty—that is, expressions that adapt to and follow along with the fluctuating nature of the world and thus achieve a state of harmony.

11. Lin Hsi-i, *Chuang-tzu chüan-chai k'ou-i* (hereafter abbreviated *CCK*), 1629 edition printed in Kyoto, in Nagasawa Kikuya, ed., *Wakokubon shoshi taisei* (Tokyo: Kyūko shoin, 1976), vol. 11, p. 436. The translation is from Watson, *Chuang Tzu*, pp. 48–49, but here the arrangement of the sentences follows Lin Hsi-i's text. From the context of the second chapter, "Discussion of Making All Things Equal," the word *t'ien-ni* is appropriately translated as "Heavenly Equality," but elsewhere it can also be translated as "the principle of Nature" or "the Tao."

12. *Gorin*, the Confucian principles of the five human relations—father and son, master and servant, husband and wife, brothers, and friends.

13. Lin Hsi-i was a scholar and official of Sung China. The dates of his birth and death are not known. According to the *Sung Yüan hsüeh-an* (an anthology and critical account of the Neo-Confucianists of the Sung and Yüan dynasties), he became a successful candidate in the imperial examination during the Tuan-p'ing era (1234–1227). Lin's annotations of the works of Lao-tzu and Chuang-tzu were widely read in Japan during Bashō's time..

14. "Haikai yōi fūtei," in Ogata Tsutomu, ed., *Kigin hairon shū, Koten bunko* vol. 151, pp. 208–9.

15. See Kon Eizō, "Danrin haikai oboegaki—Gūgensetsu no genryū to bungakushiteki jittai," *Kokugo kokubun kenkyū* 7 (1953): 7.

16. A Buddhist term literally translated as "forest of sermons" that later acquired the meaning of an academy. But this name, supposedly given in jest, by no means indicates any pedantic tendency of the school. See Keene, *World Within Walls*, p. 49.

17. A quotation from the *Huai Nan-tzu*, a twenty-one-volume Taoist text. It is attributed to Liu An, Prince Huai Nan of the Former Han dynasty (206 B.C.–A.D. 24). The "Yaun-tao hsun" chapter states: "When he turned fifty, Chü Po-yü recognized the mistakes he had made in the past forty-nine years."

18. Kihara Sōen, ed., *Orandamaru nibansen* (Tokyo: Koten bunko, 1960), pp. 439–40. Part of the translation is from Keene, *World Within Walls*, p. 49.

19. Nishiyama Sōin, "Sōjizō san," quoted in Hirota Jirō, *Bashō no geijutsu—Sono tenkai to haikei* (Tokyo: Yūseidō, 1968), p. 217.

20. *KHT*, vol. 4, p. 83.

21. Ibid., p. 92.

22. Ibid., p. 93.

23. "Haiku no honshitsu," in Meiji Shoin, *Haiku kōza* (hereafter abbreviated *HK*), vol. 5, p. 18.

24. *The Classic of Poetry* is the oldest Chinese poetic anthology, traditionally said to have been compiled by Confucius. The "Great Preface" was the most influential statement of the Confucian view of the nature and function of poetry in traditional China. Although the actual author and date of the "Great Preface" are not clear, scholars believe that the work probably came out before the first century A.D.

25. *Haikai umoregi* (Haikai: The Bogwood, compiled in 1655 and published in 1673), in Ogata Tsutomu, ed., *Kigin haironshū, koten bunko* (Tokyo: Koten bunko, 1960), vol. 151, pp. 33–34.

26. Ogata Tsutomu, "Teimon Danrin haikai," in *HK*, vol. 5, p. 34.

27. See Okanishi Ichū, *Haikai mōgyū*, in Iida Masakazu, Esaki Hironao, and Inui Hiroyuki, eds., *Danrin haikaishū*, vol. 2 (Tokyo: Shūeisha, 1972), p. 83.

28. Ibid.

29. Su Shih (1037–1101), a famous Chinese poet of the Sung dynasty.

30. Tu Fu (712–770), one of the most outstanding Chinese poets of the High T'ang period.

31. Huang T'ing-chien (1045–1105), a famous Chinese poet of the Northern Sung.

32. Takarai Kikaku (1661–1707). Kikaku was one of Bashō's principal disciples. At that time, he used the literary name Rasha.

33. Hattori Ransetsu (1654–1707), "Preface to *Inaka no kuawase*," in Imoto Nōichi et al., eds., *Kōhon Bashō zenshū* (hereafter abbreviated *KBZ*) (Tokyo: Kadokawa shoten, 1966), vol. 7, p. 357.

34. Takarai Kikaku, *Inaka no kuawase*, in *KBZ*, vol. 7, p. 362.

35. Ibid., p. 363.

36. Lin, *CCK*, p. 412.

37. Ibid.

38. Ibid., p. 410.

39. Sugiyama Sanpū (1647–1732), *Tokiwaya no kuawase*, in *KBZ*, vol. 7, p. 389.

40. See Ōuchi Hatsuo's annotation of *Tokiwaya no kuawase*, in *KBZ*, vol. 7, p. 389.

41. Hui Shih, a logician philosopher of late Chou times. In the *Chuang-tzu*, Hui-tzu is described as "weak in inner virtue, strong in his concern for external things." Translation from Watson, *Chuang Tzu*, p. 377.

42. Lin, *CCK*, pp. 417–18. Translation from Watson, *Chuang Tzu*, p. 35.

43. Lin, *CCK*, p. 418. Translations from Watson, *Chuang Tzu*, pp. 35.

44. Ibid.

45. Ōuchi, *Tokiwaya no kuawase*, in *KBZ*, vol. 7, p. 389.

46. Okanishi, *Haikai mōgyū*, p. 83.

47. *Zoku Fukagawashū*, in *KBZ*, vol. 1, p. 64.

48. Hattori Dohō (1657–1730), *Sanzōshi*, in *KBZ*, vol. 7, p. 174.

49. *Zōka ni shitagai, zōka ni kaere.* Bashō, *Oi no kobumi*, in *KBZ*, vol. 6, p. 75. As I noted earlier, zōka is an extremely important concept in the *Chuang-tzu*. Bashō's understanding of it and his commitment to "follow zōka and return to zōka" led him to emphasize naturalness in the later stages of his development. For an in-depth study of the Taoist principle of the Natural and Bashō's critical thought, see Peipei Qiu, "Poetics of the Natural: A Study of the Taoist Influence on Bashō" (Ph.D. diss., Columbia University, 1994).

50. Ikenishi Gonsui, comp., *Azuma no nikki*, in *KBZ*, vol. 1, p. 63. Translation from Keene, *World Within Walls*, p. 57.

51. Ikenishi, *Azuma no nikki*, in *KHT*, vol. 3, p. 572.

52. Lin, *CCK*, p. 466. Translation from Watson, *Chuang Tzu*, p. 77.

53. Ibid.

54. Ibid.

13

The Sea Girl and the Shepherdess

◉

R O Y A L L   T Y L E R

A comparison between the literatures of love in medieval France (eleventh to thirteenth centuries, Old French and Provençal) and Heian Japan (including material from thirteenth-century tale collections), is fairly obvious, since both are well known to give love a place of honor. Still, it is not inevitable, since love is prominent in many other literatures as well. I make this comparison not only because these are two literatures that I care about but because Donald Keene, too, studied French literature before Japanese and retains a similar fondness for it.

I argue that in matters of love both literatures cover common ground, and then I contrast the two on the issue of tact and crudeness. This contrast brings in the "sea girl" (*ama*) and the shepherdess of the title. Weightier questions, such as why a troubadour should have thought all worth and valor sprang from love, whereas Genji (to say nothing of Tō-no-Chūjō) would have found the same idea bizarre, lie beyond my range.

It seems to me that there must always have been sincere lovers everywhere, even if fewer than the songs and romances claim, and that despite varying habits of thought and expression, their feelings are bound to share a great deal. So it is difficult for me to accept, for example, Georges Duby's conception of a "pre-history of love,"[1] after which the relations between men and women take on (in twelfth-century France) a distinctive pattern governed by feudal social relations

and the church's strictures.[2] For the same reason, I find it hard to believe
Nakanishi Susumu, who rejected any connection between courtly love and love
as known to the Japanese in classical times. Nakanishi wrote that *koi*, the single
word that seems closest to "love" in classical Japanese, designates not the English
"love" but, rather, "longing for" or "missing" someone whose absence is painful;
and he urged his readers to rediscover the native quality of such feelings.[3] To
me, for better or worse, his position is unintelligible.[4]

To highlight what lovers may share despite a thousand differences, I start by
juxtaposing two love scenes, one from *Flamenca* and one from *Genji monogatari*.[5]
Flamenca is a wonderfully fresh and witty verse tale of which some 8,100 lines
survive (the only extant manuscript is incomplete). The language is Provençal,
and the work was probably written between 1240 and 1250. A calendrical clue
provided by the text suggests that the main action took place in 1234.

Near the end of what remains of *Flamenca*, a great baron has invited knights
from far and wide, including the king of France, to a tournament. Presiding over
the tournament is a lady, as was then proper: the baron's wife, Flamenca. Since
every knight entering the tournament is bound by courtesy to render homage
to Flamenca, when the hero arrives, Flamenca's husband takes him right away
to greet her. The hero's name is Guilhem (William). Guilhem has never before
laid eyes on Flamenca—as far as the husband knows. Nevertheless, the husband
does not object to the two meeting:

> *A Guillem dis: "Segner, presen*   He said to Guilhem: "Lord, I am obliged
> *Dei far de vos, per covinen*   by custom to present you
> *A vostra domna, s'a vos plas,*   to your lady, if you please,
> *Per so-us prec ques a lui vengas."*   and so beg that you should come to her."[6]

At the time, Flamenca is sitting with the king of France. Guilhem immediately
salutes the king, informing him that he has "come to see my lady" (*ma domna sui
vengutz vezer*), and since this reference to his host's wife is a gesture of courtesy,
no one takes it as meaning anything personal. Flamenca acknowledges his courtesy quite simply:

> *"Seigner," fai s'il, "vostra merce,*   "My lord," said she, "I thank you;
> *Sezes doncas dejosta me."*   Do then sit down beside me."[7]

She has invited to sit beside her, in the presence of all, a knight who calls her *ma
domna* and whom she has never met before. Public civility could hardly go further—but it does. For then the king gallantly yields to Guilhem his own seat

beside Flamenca and takes his leave, assuring Flamenca that she will be pleased with so splendid a gentleman's company. He says:

Quar ieu sai ben qu'en petit d'ora,	For I know that in no time,
Quant vos aures parlat ab lui,	Once you have talked with him,
Aures oblidat qu'ieu sai fui,	You will forget I was ever here,
Tant vos aura cortes solas.	Such pleasant company he will be.[8]

Far from being hidden, Flamenca is, in effect, being invited to engage in some polite gallantry. Little does the king, still less her husband, know that although she and Guilhem have not seen each other for months, she is Guilhem's *ma domna* in earnest. Until only recently, her husband was a demon of jealousy who kept Flamenca locked up in a tower, and during her incarceration Guilhem courted and won her by the most devotedly ingenious of means. Now, unwittingly, Flamenca's husband is about to give her and Guilhem an honorable reason to retire to a nearby room, where even if they cannot yet do all they would like (that will have to wait until nighttime), at least

De moutas res bon solas tenon;	They had comfort from each other in many ways;
Lur ueilz e lur bocas revenon	their eyes, their mouths knew joy again,
D'aitan com podon, e lur nas.	all they were able, and their noses too.[9]

Never have there been truer or naughtier lovers.

The mention of "their noses" may sound strange. It certainly surprised the text's editor, who suggested emending *lur nas* (their noses) to *lur mas* (their hands). The idea is reasonable, especially since the play of hands under capes and coats is a recurring motif in troubadour poetry. But fond lovers do sometimes playfully rub noses together, and assuming that these two did, then their scene contrasts even more amusingly with one from the "Suetsumuhana" chapter of *Genji monogatari*.

In the world of *Genji monogatari*, a scene like this one from *Flamenca* is unimaginable. The noblest ladies were not seen in public, no matter how restricted that "public" might be. Instead, theirs was a world of curtains and blinds. Even when playing music with gentlemen, they remained invisible, and they conversed with most callers only *monogoshi ni*, "through something" (usually a blind). If the gentleman came through the blind, he and the lady were still either in darkness or in deep shadows broken only by the firefly glow of a distant lamp trimmed low for the night. A lady's looks did count in the end, but it could be a long time before even a lover got a proper view of her figure and face. In France, a high-born woman might be visible to all, and a man unworthy even to speak to her could fall in love on merely seeing her. However, a suitor in Japan might not see his lady until it was too late.[10] *Lur mas* should therefore have been particularly important, and indeed they were, but *lur nas* mattered too. Now and again, in *Genji*, it is only touch or smell that gives one partner a clue to the other's identity.[11]

Suetsumuhana is a princess on whom Genji has projected romantic fantasies worthy of any lonely teenager. Eventually, thanks to some clever maneuvering, he hears her (invisibly) play the *kin* (a seven-stringed Chinese *koto*) for a few minutes. Since her playing is acceptable, he assumes that she is, too, and proceeds with the courtship. Alas, the more involved he gets, the more he realizes that something is wrong. The poor lady is a bit odd. By this time, however, good manners require him to continue, since he has, in effect, already married her. After a miserable night with her (not his first), he at last finds out what she really looks like:

> Since dawn had apparently come at last, Genji himself raised the shutters and looked out over the snow-covered garden. No footprint broke the vast, empty and chillingly lonely expanse. . . .
>
> It was not yet quite light, and by the glimmer of the snow he looked so wonderfully young and handsome that the sight of him brought grins to the faces of the aged gentlewomen. "Do go out to him, my lady," said one encouragingly; "You simply must! It makes such a difference to be nice!" So the lady, who despite her shyness could never say no when told what to do, tidied herself up more or less and slipped out toward him. Genji gazed out into the garden, pretending not to look at her, but he gave her many sidelong glances. What was she like? How glad he would be (ah, foolish hope!) if their intimacy had brought out in her any attraction at all!
>
> Her seated height, first of all, was unusual; she was obviously very long in the back. I knew it! thought Genji, despairing. Next came the real disaster, her nose. He spotted it instantly. She resembled the mount of the bodhisattva Fugen. Long and lofty that nose was, slightly drooping toward the end and with, at the tip, a blush of red: a real horror. In color, she was whiter than snow—even slightly bluish—and her forehead was remarkably broad, although below it her face seemed to go on and on for an extraordinarily long way. . . . Why on earth, he wondered, had he insisted on finding out what all of her looked like? And yet she made at the same time so outlandish a sight that he could not keep his eyes off her.[12]

The situation of young Guilhem and that of young Genji could hardly be more different. Yet both of them are behaving as men do everywhere: they are seeking what in Provençal is called *solas* (comfort, solace) from a lady. Despite the different settings, different fortunes, and different assumptions about the ways of love, they share a great deal.

For example, lovers in France and Japan, as elsewhere, may "burn" with desire. Enz Archimbautz (Sir Archambaut), who marries Flamenca near the start of her tale, burns for her from their first meeting:

> *. . . Mais, poiz quez ac Flamenca vista,*　. . . but no sooner did he see Flamenca,
> *Lo cor el cors l'a enflamat.*　than she set the heart within him
> burning.[13]

Likewise, Komachi's heart burns in one of her famous poems:

> *hito ni awan*　This night of no moon
> *tsuki no naki yo wa*　there is no way to meet him.
> *omohi okite*　I rise in longing—
> *mune hashiri hi ni*　My breast pounds, a leaping flame,
> *kokoro yakeori*　my heart is consumed in fire.[14]

The idea that one can die of love was as familiar in Japan as in France, and both the Japanese poet and the troubadour believed, or claimed to believe, that dreams could unite them with their beloved. For example, Komachi wrote:

> *omoitsutsu*　Thinking about him
> *nurebaya hito no*　I slept, only to have him
> *mietsuran*　appear before me—
> *yume to shiriseba*　Had I known it was a dream,
> *samezaramashi wo*　I should never have wakened.[15]

Komachi's dream was so vivid, she claimed, that she had no idea it was not real; in fact, dream meetings became so popular a motif in poetry that "dream" could simply mean a night of love. The late-twelfth-century troubadour Arnaut de Maruelh (de Mareuil) said in Provençal nearly the same thing as Komachi did. He sang of sighing with longing as he drifted off to sleep, to dream of her:

> *Adoncs s'en vai mos esperitz*　Then my spirit journeys forth
> *Tot dreitamen, domna, vas vos*　straight, my lady, toward you
> *De cui vezer es cobeitos . . .*　whom I so dearly long to see . . .
> *Ab que dures aissi mos soms*　Might this dream of mine last long,

No volri' esser reis ni coms.   I would be neither count nor king,

Mai volria jauzens dormir   but would rather sleep in joy

Que velhan deziran languir.   than, waking, languish in desire.[16]

Of course, Arnaut de Maruelh was a man, and Komachi a woman. Moreover, his song wears a fancier dress than hers and almost swaggers, since the poet claims in it that he goes to his lady whenever he sleeps, night or day. But both poets agree on the possibility of meeting in a dream, and they also agree that the man goes to the woman. In *Flamenca*, Guilhem has similar dreams. After imagining all he would do if he could fondle and kiss Flamenca "and do with her all I wish," he accuses himself of raving from an excess of desire,

Mais per Amor o ai vesat   Though Love herself has led me on,

Que-m fai tenir midon soven   who lets me often, while I sleep,

Tot a ma guisa en dormen.   hold my lady as I will.[17]

Once lovers do meet in the flesh, however, they must part again. Sei Shōnagon put down in her *Makura no sōshi* definite ideas about how a lover, once his visit is over, should take his leave, and surely no one anywhere could find strange what she wrote: "A good lover," she declared, "will behave as elegantly at dawn as at any other time."

> He drags himself out of bed with a look of dismay on his face. The lady urges him on: "Come, my friend, it's getting light. You don't want anyone to find you here." He gives a deep sigh, as if to say that the night has not been nearly long enough and that it is agony to leave. . . .
>
> Presently he raises the lattice, and the two lovers stand together by the side door while he tells her how he dreads the coming day, which will keep them apart; then he slips away. The lady watches him go, and this moment of parting will remain among her most charming memories.[18]

It would surely have pleased Sei Shōnagon to hear her lover, summoned away by the approach of dawn, speak like the knight in this *alba* (a "dawn" song) by Gaucelm Faidit (fl. ca. 1180–1220):

Us cavaliers si jazia   Once a knight so sweetly lying

Ab la re que plus volia;   by the one whom he loved best,

Soven baizan li dizia: said to her with many kisses,

Doussa res, ieu que farai?   O my dear, what shall I do?

Que.l jorns ve e la nueytz vai.	Day comes on, the night is leaving.
Ay!	Ah!
Qu'ieu aug que li gaita cria:	I hear the watchman calling:
Via!	Away!
Sus! qu'ieu vey lo jorn venir	Arise! For I see the day
Apres l'alba.	following the dawn.
. . . .	. . . .
Doussa res, que qu'om vos dia,	O my dear, never believe,
No cre que tals dolors sia	for all men say, there is worse pain
Cum qui part amic d'amia,	than the pain of lovers' parting,
Qu'ieu per me mezeys o sai.	as I know: it is my own.
Aylas! quan pauca nueyt fai!	Alas! How soon the night is gone!
Ay! . . .	Ah! . . .[19]

Shōnagon would have been startled to hear a departing lover actually sing things like that (though he might have put them in a whispered *uta*), but a Provençal lady would have been surprised as well. The *alba* is a conventional genre. A real knight, like a Heian gentleman loath to reach for his trousers, would no doubt have expressed himself in murmured prose.

A particularly famous scene of parting at dawn occurs in the "Yūgao" chapter of *Genji monogatari*. Genji has spent the night with the Rokujō Lady, a beautiful, intelligent, and exacting woman, some years older than himself, whom he actually finds a bit too much. The scene is memorable for its elegant and casually wanton grace:

One very misty morning when, in response to insistent urging, the still sleepy Genji was at last taking his leave, though with many sighs, the gentlewoman Chūjō raised a lattice shutter and moved her mistress's curtain aside, as though to say, "Madam, do see him off!" The lady lifted her head and looked out: there he was, standing before all the colors of the garden as though he did not wish to miss their beauty. No, there was no one like him.

When Genji reached the gallery, Chūjō joined him. With a silk gauze train neatly tied at her waist over an "aster" layering just right for the season, she carried herself with delicious grace. Glancing back, he sat her down by the railing at the corner of the building. Her comely deference toward him, the length of her hair—all seemed to him a miracle. *"I would not be known as one who flits from flower to flower yet in passing fain would pluck this lovely morning glory. What do you suggest?"* he said, taking her hand; but she, with practiced wit, replied, *"Your haste to be off before the morning mists are gone betrays how little your heart cares for your flower,"* so turning his poem to refer to her mistress.

A pretty page boy, handsome in trousers that might have been contrived for the occasion and that were now wet with dew, wandered out among the flowers and brought back Genji a morning glory. One would have liked to paint the scene.[20]

Gaucelm Faidit, too, might have enjoyed this scene. Everything about it, for example, the flirtatious yet benign exchange between Genji and the gentlewoman Chūjō, demonstrates the civilizing influence of courtly ways, letters, and poetry. In *Flamenca*, the heroine praises this influence:

Quar ben conosc que pa ni sal	For well I know that without learning
Negus hom ses letras non val,	no man is worth bread or salt,
E trop ne val meins tot rix hom	nor is he worth much, that rich man
Si non sap letras queacom	who of letters knows nothing at all;
E dona es trop melz aibida	and a lady is far better endowed
S'es de letras un pauc garnida.	if she is somewhat adorned with letters.[21]

It goes without saying that the ladies and gentlemen of the Heian court, at least as we know them from literature, would have agreed. And they also would have subscribed to Flamenca's observation a few lines later:

Que negus repaus non es bos	That leisure has no charm at all
Ad home si letras non sap.	for one quite ignorant of letters.

If the Rokujō Lady had been "quite ignorant of letters," she would not have been enchanted by the sight of Genji "standing before all the colors of the garden as though he did not wish to miss their beauty," nor would he have stood there for her to see. None of this scene, which so beautifully illustrates the charm of leisure, could have been imagined without the writer's knowledge of "letters" or would been plausible without the culture shared by her listeners and readers.

A classic Japanese statement on "letters" of this kind is the famous passage in the preface to the *Kokinshū*: "It is song [that is, poetry] that, without effort, moves Heaven and Earth, touches the unseen spirits and gods, smoothes the relations between men and women, and calms the heart of the fierce warrior." These words suggest that one who can "sing" (that is, who has learning or "letters"), understands the spirit (*kokoro*) of things, and so is a *kokoro aru hito*: a person of "heart." The expression *kokoro aru hito*, "cultivated person," appears often in classical Japanese literature. It seems to mean above all that someone cultivated is capable of responding appropriately to experience and especially to the feelings of others—the typical form of this response being a "song" that "moves Heaven and Earth." It is similar to the responsiveness and sympathy that in *Flamenca* Guilhem discovers through love—the love that Georges Duby, many centuries later, described as a civilizing influence in medieval France.[22] Guilhem observed:

D'amor ha hom cella douzor	It is from love man gains this sweetness
Que-s dol per la dolor d'autrui.	by which he suffers from another's pain.
Anc mais tan pïatos non fui.	Never have I known such pity
Ni-m duelc per las autrui dolors.	nor so felt the pain of others.
E tot aiso m'a fag Amors,	Love it is that has done this to me,
Qu'ieu ai de mi donz pietat	that I should feel pity for my lady,
Quar estai presa mal son grat. . .	who unwillingly is held prisoner. . . [23]

A few lines later, Guilhem sums up his discovery in a particularly striking line:

E de so mal sui eu dolenz,	Her pain it is from which I suffer,
So es amor e chausimenz.	for such is love and love's choice.
D'amor ven merces e comensa.	From love comes forth compassion.

No doubt the idea that "from love comes forth compassion" was foreign to Buddhist Japan, and no doubt Guilhem's discovery of sympathy for others was centered on a fellow human of the opposite sex in a way uncharacteristic of the *Kokinshū* ideal; yet the responsiveness of the heart is what matters in both cases. Someone without *kokoro*, or "heart," is "heartless," even in English.

I now turn to the heartless side of love. Most of the time, Sei Shōnagon probably managed to avoid boorish lovers, but in love, there is worse than boorishness. "Michitsuna's mother" filled her *Kagerō nikki* with the hurt and anger caused by the conduct of her husband, Kaneie. Her voice, too, can be heard in the songs of the troubadours. The comtessa de Dia (fl. ca. 1160), perhaps the best of the *trobairitz* (female *trobador*), had the misfortune to love a man who belittled and neglected her. She wrote:

A chantar m'er de so qu'eu no volria,	Mine it will be to sing of what I would not,
Tant me rancur de lui cui sui amia;	I have such hurt from him whose love I am;
Car eu l'am mais que nuilla ren	For I love him over all things in the world.
que sia:	
Vas lui no.m val merces ni cortezia	Pity and courtesy avail me nothing with him,
Ni ma beltatz ni mos pretz ni	nor my beauty, my good name, nor my
mos sens;	wit;

C'atressi.m sui enganad' e trahia	I am as gulled by him and as betrayed
Com degr' esser, s'eu fos dezavinens.	as I should be were I dull and unsightly.[24]

Although the comtessa de Dia believed she was beautiful, her lover still gave her sorrows she had never thought she would know. Medieval tradition identifies him as Count Raimbaut d'Aurenga (Raimbaut d'Orange), himself a distinguished though not necessarily likable troubadour.

Many a troubadour complained in his songs that his lady would not accept him. For example, when faced with persistent coldness, the sweet but humble Bernart de Ventadorn (Bernard de Ventadour, fl. mid-twelfth century) sighed, "Although I feign joy, I have much sorrow in my heart."[25] Not so Raimbaut d'Orange, who was of a different stamp from Bernart, just as he was of a different standing. In one of his songs on this theme, he tried in vain to repress sheer physical rage. Having started out by protesting that despite his suffering he would ever remain "sweet, loving, loyal, and tender," he soon began offering other lovers very different advice. The very least of his counsel was to win the lady over "with sharp words and ugly songs." He then wrote:

Si voletz domnas gazaignar,	If it is your wish to win the women
Quan crezetz que-us fassan honors	when you think their favors are your due,
Si-us fan avol respos avar,	if they give you disappointing answers,
Vos las pones a menassar:	your proper course is to threaten them.
E si vos fan respos pejors,	and should their answers then wax insolent,
Das lor del punh per mes las nars.	Treat them to a good punch in the nose.[26]

One trembles for the comtessa de Dia.

As far as I know, this is a note not heard in classical Japanese literature. In the gulf between the bitter resolve to be "sweet, loving, loyal, and tender" and the animal urge to "treat them to a good punch in the nose" lies a wide range of troubled moods, the more brutal of which seem not to have received expression in Japan. Physicality itself, however healthy, goes no further than the following sort of poem, by Sone no Yoshitada (fl. late-tenth century):

araiso ni	Thunderous breakers
aranami tachite	crash tonight
aruru yo ni	against a rocky shore:
imo ga nehada wa	so in bed I long, my love,
natsukashiki kana	for your nakedness.[27]

Provençal literature, however, contains many passages like this, for example, a scene in *Flamenca* that involves not one couple but two—two young ladies attached to Flamenca and two young gentlemen attached to Guilhem:

Comjat prenon en totas guisas;	They say good-by in all sorts of ways;
Desotz lur pellissetas grisas	under their little gray tunics
Lasson lur mans et entrebescan,	they join and mingle their hands,
E sai e lai taston e pescan,	feeling and probing here and there,
Baison, abrasson et acollon	kissing, cuddling, and embracing,
E garo-s ben que non s'afollon,	but taking care not to hurt one another;
Quar dousamen e senes gap	for it is gently and in silence
Fai cascus so que faire sap	that they each do what they well know
E so que fin Amors l'ensengna.	and what sweet Love teaches them.[28]

Although there is not quite so much of this sort of thing in Old French, the following lines appear in a song by Guy de Coucy (fl. ca. 1200), who took part in the Third and Fourth Crusades:

Or me lait Diex en tele honeur monter	Now may God so honour me
Que cele u j'ai mon cuer et mon penser	that her to whom my heart and love belong
Tieigne une foiz entre mes bras nuete	I may hold naked in my arms
Ançois qu'aille outremer.	before I cross the sea.[29]

After this, Provençal or French literature may continue on to the "good punch in the nose" of Raimbaut d'Orange or even to the crudeness of William IX of Aquitaine (Guilhem de Peitieus or Guillaume de Poitiers, 1071–1126), a great lord and the first known troubadour. In one of William's songs, the roving singer meets two desirable sisters and tempts them by pretending to be mute, since the mute tell no tales. Once the sisters are persuaded, they get on with the business at hand. For eight days (so he wrote), William remained "in that oven":

Tant les fotei com auziretz:	I fucked them this much, as you shall hear:
Cen et quatre vint et ueit vetz...	One hundred and eighty and eight times...

till every stroke was agony.[30]

This song is not typical, but it nevertheless is in the canon. In *Genji monogatari*, Genji sometimes behaves toward ladies in surprisingly decisive ways, but nothing remotely resembling this sort of thing can be suspected of him. Even the *oni* who repeatedly violated the Somedono empress[31] was a reasonably likable fellow in comparison.

The strikingly civilized character of Japanese writing on love becomes clear when one considers the medieval French song genre known as *pastourelle*. The earliest known *pastourelle* is by the Provençal troubadour Marcabru (fl. early twelfth century). It begins:

L'autrier jost' una sebissa	The other day, beside a hedge,
Trobei pastora mestissa,	I found a pretty shepherdess,
De joi e de sen massissa.	all compounded with wit and grace.
E fon filha de vilana.	She was a lowborn mother's daughter.[32]

In a *pastourelle*, a traveling knight encounters a shepherdess, alone with her flock beside a hedge, as in Marcabru's example, or "where the forest meets the plain," as in a song by the French poet Jehan Bodel (d. 1290):

Entre le bos et la plaine	Where the forest meets the plain
trovai de vile lontaine	and far away from any town,
tose de grant beaute plaine,	a very lovely girl I found
ses bestes gardant.	out minding her flock.[33]

So far, the tale told by a *pastourelle* recalls certain Japanese stories. In Japan, too, a gentleman might travel down to the country (perhaps in exile from the capital) and spot a tempting girl. In Japan, of course, there were no sheep or shepherdesses. Instead, the gentleman almost inevitably ended up by the sea, where there were divers and salt makers collectively known as *ama* (sea people). In the *Man'yōshū*, Ōtomo no Tabito's account of his visit to Matsura, with its accompanying sequence of poems, provides an example. Tabito wrote: "Once I wandered for a while in the district of Matsura. When I visited the abyss of Tamashima, I happened to meet some girls fishing. Their flowery faces and radiant forms were beyond compare."[34] A similar story from *Senjūshō* (mid-thirteenth century) begins as follows: "Of old, there was a gentleman known as Middle Counselor Yukihira. Having misbehaved, Yukihira was sent down to Suma shore, where, with the salt brine dripping from him, he wandered along the beach. Among the divers on Ejima, there was one whom he found singularly attractive."[35]

Even the settings of these escapades—French and Japanese—are similar. Whether it is between land and sea or between forest and open country, the woman inhabits a liminal zone where she seems (to the traveler) to offer herself to the traveler's desire.

At this point, the traveler approaches the girl and strikes up a conversation.

He begins to "talk her up" and, in France, to display the reverse side of the nobly exalted feelings more often associated with courtly love, such as the adoration of a lady whom the poet may approach only in fear and trembling.[36] (Note that the writer of the *pastourelle* and of the courtly love song may be the same man.) This is where the French and the Japanese scenarios part company.

In Provençal, or especially in French and other European languages (the *pastourelle* having become very popular), almost anything could happen. The shepherdess's spirited replies might persuade the knight to leave her alone, but he also might rape her. Or he might be beaten up by the shepherdess's boyfriend and his fellow shepherds.

In addition, *pastourelles* are likely to be jokes. In one, written in a macaronic fusion of French and Latin, the dialogue proceeds as follows:[37]

Dis a la bele:"Icel Seignur qui est redemptor omnium
Vus sauve e gard e doint honur supra coronas virginum!
Vostre humme suy sans nul return, et meum est consilium
Ke nus fasçum le ju de amor: ecce tempus ydoneum."

> To her I said, "Our Lord, who is the Savior of all,
> save, keep, and raise you up above the crowns of all the virgins!
> Your man am I forever more, and it is my desire
> That we should play the game of love: the time for pleasure is at hand."

Ele respunt:"Ne me gabez tuis blandis sermonibus,
Mès vostre dreit chemin tenez, commune stratus ductibus;
Autre respuns de mei ne averez, ni si oppressa viribus.
Mun pucelage me gardez.Veni creator Spiritus.

> She replied: "Don't you give me any of your sweet talk.
> Just keep moving straight ahead—the road's all yours [?].
> That's the only answer you'll get from me, unless you mean to rape me.
> Leave me my virginity. Come, O creator Spirit!

Tute ma vie sans lecherie vixi puella tenera;
Saynt Marie, ke ne sey hunie, me puram pura tollera!
Si cest ribaud par mal me asaut mallem adesse funera,
Kar byen say ke dunc averay eterna Christi munera.:"

> All my life I have lived free of lust, a tender girl;
> Holy Mary, to whom be honor, you who are pure keep me pure!
> If this lout attacks me now, I'd rather be at my own funeral,
> For well I know that I shall have the eternal gifts of Christ!"

So ends this dubious lesson, one actually a little less plainspoken than Marcabru's;

for although in the parent of all *pastourelles* the shepherdess tames the singer, she must first hear the knight remind her that

E seria.us ben doblada	You would look twice as pretty
Si.m vezi' una vegada	if one day I should end up
Sobeira e vos sotrana.	on top and you under me.[38]

This sort of thing gave shepherdesses so doubtful a reputation that one medieval French novel speaks of "shepherdesses and other women of easy virtue."[39] The reputation of ama girls in Japan was exactly the same,[40] although the literature does not explain why. Sea girls do not encounter the trials of the shepherdess, however. Here, for example, is how the story of Yukihira and the diver ends:

Going up to the diver, Yukihira asked, "Where do you live?" She replied:

shiranami no	No home have I of my own,
yosuru nagisa ni	for I,
yo o sugosu	a diver's daughter,
ama no ko nareba	live beside white-breaking waves
yado mo sadamezu	upon the ocean shore.

Then she slipped away. Yukihira, deeply moved, could not refrain from weeping. And what did he do then? One may imagine anything, but so short an exchange and such delicate feelings hardly make a prose *pastourelle*.

Michel Zink described the essential theme of the *pastourelle* as "the pursuit of a single image: that of a woman, a pure object of pleasure, called into being by the wildness and sensuality of nature and wholly foreign to [the poets'] refined sensibility."[41] No doubt Yukihira, too, was aroused by the wild land and seascape of Ejima, peopled by women as strange and as alluring as nymphs; no wonder he found the diver girl so entrancing. But in the *Senjūshō* story, he did not see her as "a pure object of pleasure." The piously Buddhist compiler of *Senjūshō* would have been revolted by what the late-twelfth-century cleric Andreas Capellanus had to say about such women.

Andreas Capellanus was a "chaplain to the royal court," probably that of Champagne.[42] His treatise on love, widely read in both its original Latin and various vernacular versions, is a valuable manual of courtly love. For Andreas, peasant women like shepherdesses deserved no consideration, and his chapter "De amore rusticum" (On the Love of Peasants) surpasses Raimbaut d'Aurenga. The following passage is from a translation into thirteenth-century French verse:[43]

Et, s'ainsi aveint qu'il te preigne	And should you happen to conceive
Talent d'amer fame vilaine,	desire for a woman of low degree,
Se tu pues a bon point venir	then, having found the proper spot,
Tu ne dois mie tenir,	you should not restrain yourself,
Ains dois accomplir ton plaisir	but should take what serves your pleasure
Tantost, sanz querre autre loisir,	there and then, nor ask her leave,
Et a ton pooir t'en efforce.	and go to it all you can.
Se ce n'est ausint com a force,	Without recourse to violence,
Tu i venras a trop grant peine,	you will hardly reach your goal,
Car c'est manière de vilaine	for such is a base wench's way,
Qui s'amour ne vieut otroier,	who obstinately withholds her love,
Tant la sache .I. hom biau proier.	however nicely one may ask.

The line "however nicely one may ask" refers to a request that the girl apparently has no right to refuse. On the contrary, she should be grateful for being asked.

In contrast, the literary Yukihira, a *kokoro aru hito*, treated his diver well. If the *Senjūshō* story about him ends in discreet silence, another gives a similar encounter a happy ending. This one is told in *Shasekishū* (1287), by the priest Mujū Ichien (1226–1312).[44] A courtier had gone down, as governor, to a coastal province where he met on the beach a beautiful young diver girl. A poetic exchange with her left him so impressed by her spirit and wit that he asked her to marry him, and she agreed. He then took her back to the capital, where she gave him many fine children.

Genji did approximately the same thing in "Suma" and subsequent chapters of *Genji monogatari*. Having prudently withdrawn from the capital to Suma, where Yukihira had been in exile before him, Genji met a lady who had been brought up by the sea and who, in both his eyes and her own, might almost have been a diver or a salt maker. Despite her explicit fears that he might take her for a "pure object of pleasure," he married her; she gave him a daughter; and the daughter grew up to become an empress and to make him the grandfather of an emperor.[45] No knight in a *pastourelle* ever marries the shepherdess or even sees her again, no matter how thoroughly she may have tamed him. As Andreas Capellanus wrote, "One should not seek love with ladies with whom it is disgraceful to seek marriage."[46] Shepherdesses, unlike sea girls, do not count.

It would be risky to draw from texts like those discussed here lessons about individual behavior. Human failings do not encourage the faith that on this sort of topic, literature—especially well-mannered literature—reflects what all men actually do. However, young men of good birth really were brought up differently in Heian Japan and in medieval France. Georges Duby described the typical bridegroom as "an adolescent hardly older than [his bride's twelve years] who, since being removed in his seventh year from the care of women, had lived only to ready himself for battle by means of physical training, amid the glorification of manly violence."[47]

The peaceful upbringing of the young Heian noble might well have left unaroused the most brutish desires of most men. At any rate, it seems at least to be true that writing about love in classical Japanese is more reliably civilized than writing about love in Provençal or Old French. Much as I like French literature and miss in classical Japanese its full vigor and range, I also admire Japanese discretion; the relative democracy of love's hope, disappointment, and anguish in the imperial anthologies, for example; and the emphasis on considerate respect that the Japanese failure to write *pastourelle* stories illustrates so well.

NOTES

1. Georges Duby, "Que sait-on de l'amour en France au XIIe siècle?" in Georges Duby, *Mâle moyen-âge* (Paris: Flammarion, 1988), p. 39.

2. Various scholars, including Duby, have also contended that the relationship of suitor to lady in courtly love may represent in part an idealized homosexual bond between the knight and his lord (since the lady is normally the wife of the suitor's lord). This idea was developed by Jean-Charles Huchet in his *L'amour discourtois: La "Fin' Amors" chez les premiers troubadours* (Toulouse: Privat, 1987), in connection with the "first troubadour," Guillaume d'Aquitaine.

3. Nakanishi Susumu, *Nihonjin no ai no rekishi*, Kadokawa sensho no. 29 (Tokyo: Kadokawa shoten, 1978), pp. 7–11.

4. The problem may partly be one of nomenclature. For example, in medieval France, the word *amor* has a more precise meaning, closer to Nakanishi's *koi*, than the general-purpose "love." Duby ("Que sait-on de l'amour," pp. 45–46) defined it strictly as the unfulfilled erotic longing felt by young, unmarried men for inaccessible (forbidden) women.

5. Unless otherwise noted, all the translations in this chapter are my own. For the Provençal, I have been greatly helped by translations into French.

6. René Lavaud and René Nelli, *Les Troubadours: Jaufre, Flamenca, Barlaam et Josaphat* (Brussels: Desclée de Brouwer [Bibliothèque européenne], 1960), pp. 1020–22.

7. Ibid., p. 1022.

8. Ibid., pp. 1022–24.

9. Ibid., p. 1028.

10. In Japan, a high-born noble seems often to have begun courting a lady solely on her reputation without even having seen her. However, Guilhem did the same with Flamenca, and the troubadour Jaufre Rudel made *amor de lonh* (love from afar) famous by falling in trans-Mediterranean love with the countess of Tripoli.

11. For instance, in the passage in the "Yūgao" chapter in which only touch and smell allow Yūgao to guess what sort of man Genji is.

12. Abe Akio, Akiyama Ken, and Imai Gen'e, eds., *Genji monogatari*, 6 vols. (Tokyo: Shōgakkan, 1970–1976), vol. 1, pp. 365–66.

13. Lavaud and Nelli, *Les Troubadours: Jaufre*, p. 653.

14. Donald Keene, ed., *Anthology of Japanese Literature from the Earliest Era to the Mid-Nineteenth Century* (New York: Grove Press, 1955), p. 78.

15. Ibid., p. 78.

16. André Berry, *Florilège des troubadours* (Paris: Firmin-Didot, 1930), pp. 228–30.

17. Lavaud and Nelli, *Les Troubadours: Jaufre*, p. 887.

18. Ivan Morris, trans., *The Pillow Book of Sei Shōnagon* (London: Penguin Books, 1971), pp. 49–50.

19. Berry, *Florilège*, p. 240.

20. Abe et al., *Genji monogatari*, vol. 1, pp. 221–22.

21. Lavaud and Nelli, *Les Troubadours: Jaufre*, p. 892.

22. Duby, "Que sait-on de l'amour," p. 47.

23. Lavaud and Nelli, *Les Troubadours: Jaufre*, pp. 882–84.

24. Berry, *Florilège*, p. 268.

25. Song, "Lo tems vai e ven e vire," in René Nelly and René Lavaud, *Les Troubadours: Le Trésor poétique de l'Occitanie* (Brussels: Desclée de Brouwer, 1966), p. 62.

26. Nelly and Lavaud, *Les Troubadours: Le trésor*, p. 57.

27. *Yoshidada shū*, poem 355, in Hisamatsu Sen'ichi et al., eds., *Heian Kamakura shikashū* (Tokyo: Iwanami shoten, 1964), p. 94. The *Gunsho ruijū* text of this poem has as the last line the stronger *ima zo koishiki* (I want you naked with me NOW!)

28. Lavaud and Nelli, *Les Troubadours: Jaufre*, p. 995.

29. Jean Dufournet, *Anthologie de la poésie française des XIIe et XIIIe siècles* (Paris: Gallimard, 1989), p. 114.

30. Nelly and Lavaud, *Les Troubadours: Le Trésor*, p. 838.

31. *Konjaku monogatari shū*, vol. 20, poem 7; Royall Tyler, *Japanese Tales* (New York: Pantheon, 1987), pp. 78–180.

32. Berry, *Florilège*, p. 100.

33. Quoted by Michel Zink, *La Pastourelle: Poésie et folklore au Moyen Age* (Paris: Bordas, 1972), p. 97.

34. *Man'yōshū* poems 853–71. Nippon gakujutsu shinkōkai, trans., *The Man'yōshū: One Thousand Poems* (New York: Columbia University Press, 1965 [reprint]), pp. 258–59.

35. *Senjūshō*, poem 87 (vol. 9, no. 11), in Nishio Kōichi, ed., *Senjūshō* (Tokyo: Iwanami shoten, 1970), pp. 244–45. Ejima is a picturesque rock, about the size of a large barn, next to the bus and ferry terminal in present Iwaya-shi, at the north end of Awaji. Yabuta Kaichirō, in *Nōgaku fudoki* (Tokyo: Hinoki shoten, 1972), p. 108, insisted for some reason that the diver was a man, but Abe Yasurō described her unequivocally as a girl (*ama otome*). See Abe Yasurō, "Seizoku no tawamure to shite no geinō: *Ama*," in Moriya Takeshi, ed., *Geinō to chinkon* (Tokyo: Shunjūsha, 1988), p. 192. The lovelorn ama girl is a stock motif in poetry.

36. Among the rules of love listed in book 2 of Andreas's treatise, no. 15 states, "Every lover tends to grow pale when his partner looks at him." See P. G. Walsh, ed. and trans., *Andreas Capellanus on Love* (London: Duckworth, 1982), p. 282. Many troubadour poems put the matter more strongly.

37. Zink, *La Pastourelle*, p. 33.

38. Berry, *Florilège*, p. 102.

39. Zink, *La Pastourelle*, p. 59.

40. A document dated 1297 places ama in the same class as *yūjo* and *shirabyōshi* (two kinds of singing girls). See Abe, "Seizoku no tawamure to shite no geinō," p. 192, n. 26.

41. Zink, *La Pastourelle*, p. 97.

42. Walsh, *Andreas Capellanus on Love*, pp. 2–3.

43. The translation is by Drouart la Vache. Less stuffy than Andreas's Latin (Walsh, *Andreas Capellanus on Love*, p. 223), it is equally authentic for my purpose. It was quoted by Zink (*La Pastourelle*, p. 59) from the text as edited by Robert Bossuat: *Li Livres d'amours de Drouart la Vache, texte établi d'après le manuscrit unique de la bilbiothèque de l'Arsenal* (Paris: Champion, 1926), ch. 13, "De l'amour as vilains," lines 4519–34.

44. Watanabe Tsunaya, ed., *Shasekishū* (Tokyo: Iwanami shoten, 1966), pp. 230–31.

45. On the Akashi Lady as an ama, see Royal Tyler, "The Nō Play *Matsukaze* as a Transformation of *Genji monogatari*," *Journal of Japanese Studies* 20 (Summer 1994): 404–5.

46. Rule no. 11 (Walsh, *Andreas Capellanus on Love*, p. 283). Rule no. 29 (p. 285) adds, "The man afflicted by excessive sensuality is usually not in love."

47. Duby, "Que sait-on de l'amour," p. 39.

14

The Fine Folly of the Encyclopedists

◉

Carol Gluck

Chambers's Encyclopædia: A Dictionary of Universal Knowledge for the People. This famous title of 1860 exemplified the encyclopedian creed, lately reaffirmed by the 1993 *Columbia Encyclopedia*'s modest promise "to bring the world between two covers." It is one of the conceits of modern times that "Everything That Everybody Wants to Know" (the subtitle of a 1901 encyclopedia) may be made accessible to anyone who can be persuaded that he wants, or needs, to know it.[1] The long history of the modern encyclopedia pays tribute to the belief in the link between knowledge and progress, for the profit of the people and also of the publisher.

The age-old quest to gather the *omne scibile*—all that is knowable—is here combined with the modern idea that the imagined whole of society requires access to the purported whole of knowledge. The encyclopedia thrives on this pair of odd but beguiling premises, which hold true around much of the contemporary world. Whether or not the knowledge purveyed by the world's encyclopedias is as universal as their editors claim, the urge to compile, publish, and promote these lexica of self- and national learning seems to know no bounds or boundaries. Here, as the encyclopedists would say, is an "epitome" of their story.[2]

Encyclopedias West

Antiquity bequeathed little more than the name to the Western encyclopedic tradition, and that by way of a later misinterpretation. The Greeks made no encyclopedias, though they practiced "the circle of learning" (*enkýklios paideía*), which constituted the general education later called "the seven liberal arts." This curriculum was broad and deep, quite the opposite of the general knowledge we now think of as "encyclopedic" and which the Greeks scorned as superficial and "polymathic." The Roman Pliny, retroactively evoked as the first great encyclopedist, was himself an unwitting one. In his *Natural History*, he cataloged everything in and out of sight, from godhead and the stars through the human race, oddities and freaks, women (in that order), to insects and minerals. Pliny certainly possessed the requisite "taxonomic urge" to classify the "facts" of nature, if without perhaps the missionary sense of encompassing the world.[3]

Early Christian compilers supplied the missionary sense, and more. In his seventh-century *Etymologies*, Isidore of Seville brought together the secular knowledge of antiquity and the teachings of the church as a guide to the new converts in Spain. His twenty books typified two abiding encyclopedic habits. One was the heroic synthesis of disparate traditions, whether sacred and profane in the humanist dictionaries, indigenous and foreign in medieval Islamic works, ancient and modern in the Enlightenment, Latin and vernacular in the Renaissance, or Chinese and Japanese learning and, later, Sino-Japanese and Western learning in the encyclopedias of Japan. The other habit was the attempt to codify an entire tradition for the sake of preserving and transmitting it, lest it be lost, mutilated, or misunderstood. The first famous Islamic compilation minced no words in its title: this was *The Book of the Best Traditions*.[4] Isidore's work also reached the promised land of encyclopedian longevity. "It was popular because it was compendious and succinct in an age which wanted all its learning in tabloid form." That age, it turns out, was the twelfth century.[5]

Other compilers of that century sought to encompass the universe, producing *Summae* and Mirrors of the cosmos, Gardens and Treasuries, of both Words and Things, the dual stuff of which all encyclopedias are made. These medieval compilations perpetuated their cosmic vision within a community of clerics writing largely for other clerics. Their intellectual grasp was encyclopedic, but their social reach remained confined to a European scribal circle, which transmitted its knowledge by laborious copying for the greater glory of God.[6]

Modern encyclopedists preferred the profane. Francis Bacon shifted the ground from the sacred to the scientific in his grand plan of 1620 to organize knowledge into three conspicuously godless categories: Nature, Man, and Man

Acting on Nature. When the word *encyclopedia* was finally used in its modern sense in the seventeenth century, it was as Alsted described his *Scientiarum omnium encyclopædia* (1649): "a methodical summary of human knowledge."[7] The new unity of all things knowable was sought not in cosmology but in the Arts and Sciences, enshrined in capital letters and interconnected in what the French *encyclopédistes* chose to call "the chain of knowledge." The modern encyclopedia depended on print and profit, placed its faith in reason and progress, and practiced patriotism in both language and content. It owed much to the critical spirit of the pathbreaking *Dictionnaire historique et critique* of Pierre Bayle, who in 1697 sought to lay out before the reader both the "reasons for affirming and the reasons for denying." Of his rationalist approach to Catholicism it was said, "he supported Christianity the way a rope supports a hanged man."[8]

The great encyclopedias of the eighteenth century each bore a different national stamp, but all were arranged in the newly touted alphabetical order and were produced by and directed toward the "society of men of letters." In 1728 Ephraim Chambers commended his *Cyclopædia* to the king with the words, "SIR, the ARTS and SCIENCES humbly crave audience of Your Majesty," and concluded with imperial Britannic pride, " 'Tis they, in fine, that make the difference between your Majesty's subjects, and the savages of Canada, or the Cape of Good Hope." His work, he owned, with the usual humility of the encyclopedist, would "contribute more to the propagating of useful knowledge through the body of a people, than half the books extant."[9] With this juxtaposition of "useful knowledge" and "the people," Chambers established himself as a founding patriarch in the realm of the modern encyclopedian tradition.

The luminous French *Encyclopédie* began as a translation of Chambers's *Cyclopædia* but soon departed the commonsensical commonwealth of English letters and embarked upon a radical, progressive, and philosophical attempt, in the words of Diderot, "to change the way people think." Sanctified as it was by reason and grounded not only in the arts and sciences but also in the mechanical arts and crafts (*métiers*), the *Encyclopédie* contributed to the worldview of its successors. But in its radical orientation toward the future and its polemical philosophy, it stood in literally revolutionary terrain that few subsequent encyclopedists found either comfortable or profitable. Most took refuge instead in the haven of objectivity, where the triple cause of modern science, bourgeois conservatism, and expanding readership could simultaneously be served. In 1801 the third edition of the *Encyclopedia Britannica*, already the emblem of weighty British intellectual enterprise, presented itself to the king as a means to counteract the tendency of anarchy and atheism of "that pestiferous work" of Diderot *et cie*.

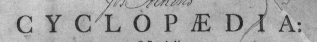

CYCLOPÆDIA:

OR, AN

UNIVERSAL DICTIONARY

OF

ARTS AND SCIENCES;

CONTAINING

AN EXPLICATION OF THE TERMS, AND AN ACCOUNT OF
THE THINGS SIGNIFIED THEREBY,

IN THE

SEVERAL ARTS, BOTH LIBERAL AND MECHANICAL;

AND THE

SEVERAL SCIENCES, HUMAN AND DIVINE:

The Figures, Kinds, Properties, Productions, Preparations, and Uses of Things

NATURAL AND ARTIFICIAL:

The Rife, Progrefs, and State of Things

ECCLESIASTICAL, CIVIL, MILITARY, AND COMMERCIAL:

With the feveral Syftems, Sects, Opinions, &c. among

PHILOSOPHERS,	PHYSICIANS,
DIVINES,	ANTIQUARIES,
MATHEMATICIANS,	CRITICS, &c.

The whole intended as a Courfe of ancient and modern Learning,

Extracted from the beft Authors, Dictionaries, Journals, Memoirs, Tranfactions,
Ephemerides, &c. in feveral Languages.

By E. CHAMBERS, F. R. S.

Floriferis ut apes in faltibus omnia libant,
Omnia nos————————————LUCRET.

THE FIFTH EDITION.

IN TWO VOLUMES.

VOL. I.

LONDON:

Printed for D. MIDWINTER, W. INNYS, C. RIVINGTON, A. WARD, J. and P. KNAPTON, S. BIRT,
D. BROWNE, T. LONGMAN, R. HETT, C. HITCH, T. OSBORNE, J. SHUCKBURGH, A. MILLAR,
J. PEMBERTON, F. GOSLING, M. SENEX, and J. HODGES.

M.DCC.XLI.

Illustration 14.1. Ephraim Chambers, later known as "the great father of the Encyclopaedic enterprize," promised his readers a collection by means of which "a stock of knowledge becomes attainable on easy terms, sufficient for the purposes of most persons, except those who make learning their more immediate profession" (Preface, 1727, to the first edition, 2 vols., 1728). The fifth edition of his *Cyclopaedia* was published in 1741. (COURTESY OF THE GENERAL RESEARCH DIVISION, THE NEW YORK PUBLIC LIBRARY, ASTOR, LENOX, AND TILDEN FOUNDATIONS.)

But the scholarly "Society of Gentlemen in Scotland," who had produced the first *Britannica* in 1771, eventually had less worldwide effect than the German publishers who compiled for the newly identified middle classes. Germany also produced learned encyclopedias like those of France and England, not least Zedler's gigantic *Universal-Lexicon* (1731–1754) in sixty-eight volumes, which at that time was the largest encyclopedia ever printed in Europe. The wave of the future, however, lay less with the society of the learned than with the expanding society of learners. In 1704 Hübner invented the so-called *Conversations-Lexicon* for "curious people" who wanted to understand what they read in the newspapers and to participate in sociable conversation about matters of the day. He forswore any pretense of an "academic *Systema Pansophicum*" or "excathedral erudition" and offered instead the informational key to the "well-informed circles" of the bourgeoisie. A hundred years later, the Leipzig publisher Brockhaus profitably invoked this middle-class readership in the title of his famous encyclopedia, *Conversations-Lexicon für die gebildete Stände*, a conversation-dictionary for the educated classes.[10]

Brockhaus made a long-running family fortune, the *Brockhaus* today still eponymous for German encyclopedias, as *Larousse* is for French. Both were of the type that dominated the "age of the encyclopedia," as the nineteenth century came to be called. Everything knowable was arranged in a way that everyone could know it. The so-called short entries, which were at times short only in comparison to the thick erudition of the *Britannica* or the *Encyclopédie*, appeared in alphabetical order, thus making it possible to "refer" rather than "read" to satisfy the new social need for general knowledge. These "reference books" proposed to supply to the home the benefits formerly conferred only on those who went to school. The Arts and Sciences alone would therefore not suffice; all manner of words and things must be included. When Pierre Larousse combined all manner of (mostly French) words and things in his famous *Grand dictionnaire universel du XIXe siècle*, he redefined universal knowledge as knowledge that was universally accessible. Victor Hugo was not far wrong when he praised Larousse for erecting a monument to the nineteenth century.[11]

As for Brockhaus, his *Conversations-Lexicon* was translated, copied, and pirated around the world—in the United States (patriotically retitled the *Encyclopedia Americana*), in England (as the exceedingly durable *Chambers's Encyclopaedia*), and in France, Italy, Spain, Russia, Japan, and other places. Intended first for the educated classes, but by midcentury having expanded their target to "all classes," the German "popular dictionaries" purveyed the idea that self-education led both to individual success and national progress. For although the French *encyclopédistes* of the eighteenth century had spoken broadly of "the people," they did

Illustration 14.2. In keeping with its scientific bent, the first *Encyclopaedia Britannica*
(1768–71) discoursed in its short entry on "Ark" on the "wood whereof the ark was built," "in
what place Noah built and finished his ark," and "the dimensions of the ark, as given by Moses"
and as "proved geometrically" by modern critics and found to be "longer than St. Paul's church
in London, from East to West," leading to the conclusion that "the ark was abundantly sufficient
for all the animals supposed to be lodged in it." The writer added a practical note: "But it must
be observed, that besides the places requisite for the beasts and birds, and their provisions,
there was room required for Noah to lock up household utensils, the instruments of husbandry,
grains and seeds, to sow the earth with after the deluge." This was surely an addition to knowledge, since, in Genesis at least, the Lord maketh no mention of "household utensils." (Courtesy
of the Rare Books and Manuscripts Division, the New York Public Library, Astor,
Lenox, and Tilden Foundations.)

not sell to them. German publishers like Brockhaus and Meyer advertised
themselves rather extravagantly to "the masses," compressing their own multivolume offerings into inexpensive form, predecessors of what would forever
after be promoted as the "handy" one-volume encyclopedia.[12]

They helped to create a market of middle-class readers susceptible to the
nineteenth-century notion that knowing meant getting ahead, as the American
publishers put it. "What the world wants is the man who knows. This is the age
of universal education. . . . Those who pay court to knowledge by systematic
home study, eventually secure the choice places."[13] Filled with "practical"
knowledge and optimistic about the "opportunities" that awaited "the ambitious
reader," the flood of late-nineteenth- and early-twentieth-century American
titles represented the popular encyclopedian myth in full one-volume flower.

Despite the proliferation of special encyclopedias, the single or multivolume
general encyclopedia still holds to its nineteenth-century tenets, even if it

appears on twentieth-century CD-ROM. The need to need to know, which the encyclopedists worked so hard to help to create, remains well entrenched in our own obsession for what they called knowledge and we worship as information.

Encyclopedias East

Present-day Japan prides itself on its status as an "information society," awash in education, communication, media—and reference books. The Japanese have been one of the modern world's great producers and even greater consumers of encyclopedias. Their proclivity for the genre goes way back and, like so much in East Asian civilization, owes its cultural origins to China.

In China the encyclopedic tradition is long and deep. The earliest encyclopedic dictionary may date from the second century B.C., its cultural status enhanced by retroactive ascription to the time of Confucius. This book, the *Erh-ya*, resembled Pliny's *Natural History* in its catalog of categories, beginning with explanations of Expressions, Concepts, and Words, then Relationships, on to Heaven and Earth, through Birds, Beasts, and Domestic Animals (no freaks or women, at least in the nineteen main headings). By the second century A.D., a more systematic and abiding classification had appeared: the tripartite division of Heaven, Earth, and Man that is fundamental to Chinese cosmology and to Chinese encyclopedias as well.[14]

In the intent to classify all of knowledge, the Chinese "category books" (*lei-shu*) displayed the same taxonomic urge that drove early encyclopedists in the West. But the principle and purpose of the compilations were different. In principle, Chinese encyclopedias were anthologies, collections of quotations, selections, or, sometimes, entire texts. The compilers inserted relatively few of their own words; their contribution lay rather in selection and ordering. They shaped orthodoxy and heterodoxy through their choice, not of which "facts," but of which "texts" they deemed worthy of knowledge.

If Western encyclopedists defined their art, as John Harris did in 1704, as "a dictionary not only of bare words but things," the Chinese defined theirs in terms of "the images of things following principle, and the verification of words following things . . . the *Book of Changes* explained each thing according to its category, thus the making of category books was not out of keeping with the intent of the words of the sages."[15] This linking of words to things to principles and to the Classics affirmed the Chinese practice of learning, which depended on a shared conceptual language of textual precedent, drawn from the past to be consulted and often memorized in the present. Encyclopedias consciously sought to preserve and construct tradition, and in an enterprise sustained over the centuries, the vast imperial anthologies did indeed conserve the record of the thoughts and lives of the cultural and political elite of traditional China. The impelling encyclopedic goal was to foster moral rule. Whether in "mirrors" for the emperor or in collected "treasures" for generations of would-be officials preparing for the examination system, Chinese compilers shared encyclopedic metaphors with medieval European clerics. Yet they labored to serve not the divine unity of revealed truth but the cumulative wisdom of the way of good government.[16]

Later imperial encyclopedias reached both a high standard of scholarship and immense size. Few can refrain from reciting the statistics on the "largest encyclopedia ever written," the fifteenth-century *Yung-le ta tien* (Great handbook of the Yung-le period): 2,169 scholars compiled 22,900 chapters in 11,000 volumes, which if piled atop one another reached a height of 450 feet, or as one British scholar monumentalized it, "nearly 46 feet higher than the top of St. Paul's." Only a fraction of its hand-copied grandeur still survives.[17] But of the other less gargantuan, but still huge, encyclopedias, the eighteenth-century *Ch'in-ting ku-chin t'u-shu chi-ch'eng* (Collection of books and illustrations of ancient and modern times, compiled at imperial command), its ten thousand chapters, which were printed, remain as an invaluable repository of the Confucian world of knowledge up to 1700.

Chinese encyclopedias, of smaller scale, were also produced and preserved outside the capital and by others than the imperially sponsored elite. A great deal of common knowledge, including pharmacopoeia and aids to learning, was caught in the encyclopedic web. In 1607 one imaginative scholar produced an unusual illustrated encyclopedia, the *San-ts'ai t'u-hui* (Collection of illustrations of the three powers), attempting to render all that was knowable of Heaven, Earth, and Man, in annotated visual form. Where the imperial encyclopedias concentrated on historical and philosophical texts, this compiler presented depictions of plants and animals, figures of folklore, and elements of daily life. Indeed, he was later criticized for an excess of illustrative enthusiasm, which, some said, had led him to include too many drawings of plants and utensils and a surplus of mythical creatures more often imagined than observed. Despite, or perhaps because of, this generosity of range, his work gained wide currency.[18] It crossed the seas to Japan, where in 1713 a doctor in Osaka produced a Japanese version, on the premise that one first had to understand heaven, earth, and man before one could treat the sick. Over time it became a compliment of wide learning to be called "a person straight out of the *Sansai zue*." The book remained popular in Japan until the late nineteenth century.[19]

Though deeply indebted in such ways to Chinese antecedents, Japan traversed its own encyclopedian route. The absence of a civil service examination

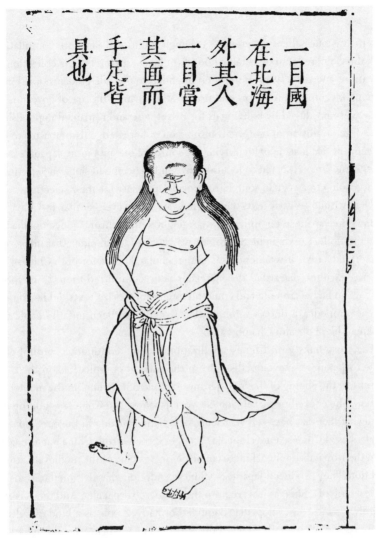

一目國在比海外其人一目當其面而手足皆具也

Illustration 14.3. In "the Land of the One-eyed," which lies "beyond the northern sea, people have one eye in their face and they have hands and feet." This drawing (reproduced from John A. Goodall's *Heaven and Earth*, 1979) is from the section on foreign lands in the Chinese illustrated encyclopedia, the *San-ts'ai t'u-hui* compiled by Wang Ch'i in 1609. The Land of the One-eyed, the Long-haired, and others also appeared on Japanese world maps, just as the One-eyed and the Single-footed continued to be depicted in Western encyclopedias and maps of the same period as the "monstrous creatures" who inhabited the unexplored seas of Asia and the New World. Before drawing any conclusions about the parochiality of such "unscientific" depictions, compare "Noah's Ark floating on the waters of the Deluge" from the *Britannica* (see illustration 14.2).

(COURTESY OF THE NEW YORK PUBLIC LIBRARY, GENERAL RESEARCH DIVISION, ASTOR, LENOX, AND TILDEN FOUNDATIONS.)

system was one salient difference. Although traditional Japanese compilations took the Chinese form of "catalog books" (in Japanese, *ruisho*), the collections of quotations and texts were more often intended to provide guidance in Chinese learning or composing poetry and prose rather than in the art of government. Many were produced by individuals for private use and remained unpublished. Indeed, the tradition of esoteric transmission of knowledge from master to disciple meant that instead of identifying the source of the quotation, Japanese compilers sometimes resorted to locutions like "it has been said since ancient times" or "according to a certain source" to provide authority for their selections.

The attitude toward texts and learning was, however, similar in China and Japan. One Japanese compiler of a late-eighteenth-century encyclopedia had begun to collect texts in his youth but was warned by an elder that unless one memorized a text, it was of no use. So the scholar, known for both Chinese and nativist learning, discarded the materials as he committed them to memory. Only when he became old and could no longer memorize texts did he compile his encyclopedia, a line of thinking that would have been unfathomable to a bookman like Ephraim Chambers.[20]

The close links with Chinese civilization posed a continuous cultural challenge to Japanese encyclopedists, from the earliest compilations in the ninth century to the ebbing of the Sino-Japanese "circle of learning" in the nineteenth century. The encyclopedic relation between Japanese and Chinese erudition was somewhat like that between vernacular and Latin learning in Europe. Japanese scholars used Chinese encyclopedias brought directly from China but also compiled their own using the Chinese language, as was true of the medieval Latinate tradition. They produced Japanese–Chinese encyclopedias designed to translate the learning of China, as it were, into the Japanese vernacular. And they created entirely Japanese encyclopedias compiled of native texts, as a kind of cultural countercanon. Eventually they produced works of a hybrid Sino-Japanese type that amounted to the triumph of the Japanese vernacular but with a rich admixture of Chinese learning in it, just as French and English prevailed in Europe with a large amount of hybridized Latin mixed in. By the eighteenth century, when the sorting out of Japan from China had become a matter of national identity in the modern sense, Japanese works underwent a determined nationalizing similar to the sort that the French *Encyclopédie* did in Germany and Italy, in an age when national encyclopedias were becoming the wordy emblems of national pride.

This Sino-Japanese synthesis was also evident in the household encyclopedias that spread among educated commoner families in the eighteenth and nineteenth centuries. Called *setsuyōshū*, meaning a collection for either economical or occasional use, these books contained a Chinese–Japanese dictionary so the newly educated peasant elite could write letters or keep their diaries using the Chinese characters essential to higher literacy. Increasingly the books added what might be called vernacular material, arranged in *iroha* order, until they became almanacs of useful information regarding etiquette, divination, children's names, rituals, beliefs, and general lore: how to blow one's nose, how to arrange three fish on a platter, how to do the "illness math," which entailed adding the age of the patient to the day and the month he fell ill, multiplying the total by 3 and dividing by 9, leaving a remainder that conveyed whether the illness was critical (time for a funeral), moderate (time for a doctor), or mild (no need to worry).

With felicitous titles such as "treasury," "gold satchel," and "happy sea," these books became prized possessions, their covers forbiddingly labeled to ward off borrowers: "Not to leave the house." In a time of hardship, one family reported that it sold "all our precious old things except our gravestones and setsuyōshū." Yokoyama Toshio, the enterprising scholar who gathered this information, also directed a scientific measurement of the dirt pressed into the pages of the household treasuries. His grime index revealed that the sections most often consulted were not the Sino-Japanese dictionaries but the horoscopes, lists of children's names, and other material of immediate individual and social use.[21] These "gold satchels" were the indigenous Japanese equivalent of the *Brockhaus* or *Larousse*, books for the small but rising rural elite, the proto-*gebildete Stände*, who would later form the middle classes of modern Japan—and buy literally millions of encyclopedias.

But the encyclopedias they bought were of a very different sort. In a sea change wrought by imperialist threat and national determination, the nineteenth century saw China almost entirely replaced by the West in the Japanese "chain of knowledge," and the encyclopedic tradition, too, was transformed. *Rangaku* pioneers of the late 1700s had already mined Dutch translations of European encyclopedias for their rapidly expanding knowledge of the world. In the tradition of good encyclopedists everywhere, they cribbed liberally from Hübner's *Conversations-Lexicon* of 1704, translating its entries on tobacco and adapting its geographical information for Japanese readers. Omitting the name *The New World* from the original Dutch, Watanabe Kazan wrote of America that "no one knew of it until a man called Kirisutopōkusu Koryunbyusu found it in 1492 (kōkoku Meiō gannen)."[22]

In 1811 the shogunate directed its new "office for the translation of barbarian books" to translate the Dutch version of Noël Chomel's *Dictionnaire oeconomique, contenant divers moïens d'augmenter son bien et de conserve sa santé* of

1709. One of the samurai translators described the encyclopedia as "a compendium of necessities for daily household life," which, since the daily household life in question contained such unfamiliar European items as "apple tarts"
and strange Latin names for stomach disorders, made the translation particularly challenging. After Siebold's expulsion in 1829, it became dangerous as
well. But the scholars persevered across three generations and, after nearly
thirty years, completed the *Kōsei shinpen*. When it was done—all neatly
rearranged out of alphabetical order into conventional Sino-Japanese categories
and cleanly copied in forty volumes—the shogunal government to which it was
presented blindly sealed the manuscript against unofficial eyes. It was not found
and published until 1937.[23]

After the unseeing shogunate fell in 1868 and the Meiji government began
its rapid drive toward civilization on the Western model, it led with, among
other things, an encyclopedia. With the country barely unified, the new
Ministry of Education gathered fifty-five men, including scholars of Western
learning from the old regime and apostles of "civilization and enlightenment" in
the new, to translate Chambers's *Information for the People*. The Chambers brothers (no relation to Ephraim), whose nineteenth-century encyclopedias sold
widely in England and the United States, had described their two-volume set
with the usual confidence: "everything is given that is requisite for a *generally
well-informed man* in the less highly educated portions of society. . . . The ruling
object, indeed, has been to afford the means of *self-education*, and to introduce
into the mind, thus liberated and expanded, a craving after still further
advancement."[24] Such a purpose precisely suited the Meiji government's aim to
bootstrap the nation to Western-style civilization through the education and
self-effort of the people.

Fukuzawa Yukichi had already included considerable chunks of Chambers's
Victorian wisdom in his *Seiyō jijō* and other essays. But the volumes of the actual
encyclopedia were rather dry going, consisting of shortish *Britannica*-style treatises on topics from Astronomy and Hydrostatics to Indoor Amusements and
Household Hints: "If the color of your curtains be scarlet, and the color of your
walls or carpet blue, a most inharmonious and unpleasing effect will be produced." Japanese readers, who had neither curtains nor carpets, made what they
would of this helpful hint. The truth was that although several thousand sets
were acquired by the elite, the venture met with no swelling popular success.
But the title, *Hyakka zensho*, evolved into the modern Japanese term for encyclopedia (*hyakka jiten*), literally "a thing dictionary of all sorts of categories."[25]

Where the government failed, commercial publishers succeeded, producing, as in the West, two parallel genres that sold side by side: the multivolume

general encyclopedia and the handy, "by one's elbow" one- or two-volume family encyclopedia. The catholicity of the market was striking. Even the English-language *Encyclopedia Britannica*, which Maruzen promoted as early as 1874, seemed to sell well. Though some Englishmen impugned the Japanese capacity to pay on the installment plan, in 1912 the agent reported that unlike Great Britain, where fewer than half the payments arrived on the promised day, "in Japan less than one per cent of the payments were even one day late, and more than half of them were made the day before they were due, because the Japanese did not like to run the risk of any accidental delay that might make them even one day late." Families of young men at the front in the Russo-Japanese War paid their installments for them, and "the Japanese bought five times as many encyclopedias as were sold in France and Germany combined, fifty times as many as Russia, and more than the people of any other country except India, Australia, and the United States."[26]

These sets obviously sold to the highly educated who could make their way through dense thickets of foreign language, or at least pretend to. They soon developed the predictable *Britannica*-envy that affected those in many nations around the world who coveted an encyclopedia of their national own. Taguchi Ukichi, who produced the first modern encyclopedia about Japan, felt the need for "a Japanese *Britannica*," meaning a Western-style reference book with specially written entries rather than the traditional collection of texts, but with content relating to Japan, not only to the West. Oddly enough, in the late 1880s, Western knowledge was so much the rage that he had trouble finding people to edit it. Describing and classifying elements of Japanese society, he wrote, was like trying "to rebuild a ruined temple."[27]

Cultural conservatives of the period shared his perception. Fearing the loss of Japanese tradition before the onslaught of Western knowledge, Nishimura Shigeki and others retaliated with a traditional encyclopedia, consisting once again of a collection of Japanese texts, but on a scale never before known in Japan. In 1879 they sought government sponsorship, for no commercial publisher could have been expected to buy into the past just as the market was looking to the future. Following the old rule, "precisely cite the classics," the compilers completed one thousand manuscript volumes of the aptly named "Catalog of ancient matters"(*Koji ruien*). The project required thirty-five years and the support not only of the government but of the Grand Shrine at Ise, which conferred both financial donations and the aura of the Sun Goddess on this vast encyclopedic enclosure of Japanese erudition. But even that was not enough to arrest the seismic shift in knowledge. Along with another herculean effort by a private scholar produced in the same period, this collection marked the end of the long Japanese tradition of Chinese-style compilations of texts arranged in conventional categories.[28] Encyclopedias, henceforth, would purvey the informational perquisites of modernity—the facts, figures, and filiations of knowledge deemed necessary for the middle classes of a modern nation-state. And they would do so in Western form, most of them in the Japanese syllabary version of the by then relentlessly standard alphabetical order.

The old form of household encyclopedias (*setsuyōshū*) also gave way to new one-volume works in the manner of the nineteenth-century middle-class handbooks in the West. The last of the old type was published in 1894, with considerably updated contents. Gone was the Chinese–Japanese dictionary and much of the earlier lore, which "civilization" now branded as superstition. In their place was a mélange of material for the modern populace, with the entry explaining *junshi*, the feudal practice of "committing suicide after the death of one's lord," right next to the one defining *ginkō*, the newly conspicuous institution of the modern bank.[29] When the first new-style family encyclopedia appeared in 1906, it modeled itself on a German "*Konversations-Lexikon* for women" and declared itself essential to "each and every household in a civilized nation." From *ai* (love) to Waterloo, the *Brockhaus*-like compendium encompassed the latest knowledge of East and West. Twenty pages were devoted to the preparation of Western cuisine, most of which was unknown to housewives in 1906 but included such later Euro-Japanese standards as the *omuretsu* (omelette) and *karee raisu* (curry rice).[30]

The success of this homely helpmeet spurred the same publisher to offer another "all-new" title just two years later, its editor, Haga Yaichi, having overcome the difficulties of compiling a proper encyclopedia "in our *Britannica*-less, *Larousse*-less, and *Meyer*-less country."[31] By the time Fuzanbō published a multivolume version of its family compendia in 1927, the preface declared encyclopedias "the most useful thing in the world," particularly for middle-class women who cease (the publisher confidently pronounced) "to learn anything new during the course of their daily routine," thereby depleting the proper educational environment of the family. Encyclopedias would educate women and children together, a promotional line that soon became routine.[32]

The large encyclopedia sets traded in the same tender. The first major multivolume Japanese encyclopedia created from scratch had been planned in 1898. With Ōkuma Shigenobu as chairman, the first volume was published in 1908 to much national acclaim, but in 1913 the publisher, Sanseidō, went bankrupt. The complete set of ten volumes finally appeared in 1919, bailed out by patriotic entrepreneurial capital. It had taken twenty-one years for Japan to acquire its "Great Japan Encyclopedia"(*Nihon hyakka daijiten*).[33] From then on

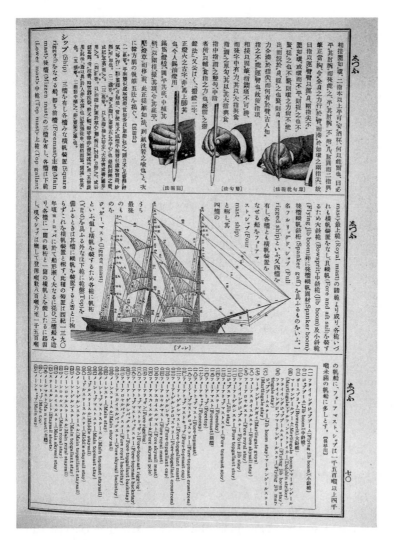

Illustration 14.4. These two entries from volume 5 of the *Nihon hyakka daijiten*—for "*shippitsu*," holding the brush in Japanese calligraphy, and "*shippu*" (ship), both the word and the thing of Western origin—offer on one page a sample of the labors of the modern Japanese encyclopedists. These editors went to great lengths to illustrate the Japanese materials, even hiring actors to perform fighting styles in samurai armor and, in this case, probably drawing from life, since no calligrapher in bygone days would have worn a Western-style jacket. The "*shippu*" posed a different problem, that of translation, which the editors solved in some instances by consulting foreign scholars and diplomats in Tokyo. When it came to such maritime terms as "Martingale guys," however, direct transliteration (as in the word *shippu* from ship) was the only recourse. Modern Japanese soon became accustomed to learning presented in this mixed Euro-Japanese idiom. (Courtesy the Oriental Division of the New York Public Library, Astor, Lenox, and Tilden Foundations.)

the encyclopedias proliferated, making the fortunes of several publishers and selling in large numbers. The emerging urban middle classes carried the encyclopedias in Japan as elsewhere, and after the war, as the economy prospered and the middle classes expanded, the 1960s brought what in Japanese publishing was called the "encyclopedia boom."

Massive sets, some with names like *Grand Napoleon*, competed with one another, each selling in the hundreds of thousands.[34] The *Encyclopedia Britannica* appeared in an all-Japanese edition in 1967, agreeably Japanized and Britannic at the same time, though its door-to-door sales force is said to have brutalized not a few housewives with its pressure pitch on behalf of their children's education. By 1985, when "the great encyclopedia war" between Heibonsha and Shōgakkan commenced, there were already eight million sets of various kinds in 30 percent of Japan's households.[35] For a long time, encyclopedias were an obligatory part of every bride's possessions and sat, "like a piece of drawing-room furniture," occupying space in small Tokyo apartments. Large-format, one-volume encyclopedias, like Kōdansha's *Daijiten DESK*, sought to offer the same this-is-all-ye-middle-class-need-to-know information in more manageable bulk.

As in the West, the encyclopedian creed in Japan has changed little in a century. It still promises the world and personal success in a national binding, and though Japan is a far more reference-ridden society than most, its encyclopedias tell a story that has its versions in many other places.

The Cyclopedic World

The story of the modern encyclopedia may be told at length—the encyclopedic style is itself seductive. But it may also be summarized, or even tabulated, in what encyclopedia publishers peddle as the "concise" form. My own pseudo-*propædia* of encyclopedianism follows, in thematic entries arranged under categories known to neither West nor East.

The Expansion of Knowledge: The *omne scibile*, or what Ephraim Chambers called "the wide field of intelligibles," has expanded: from theology and natural history to Arts and Sciences to practical arts like bookkeeping and phonography (stenography [*sokki*], as the nineteenth century knew it) to sexual preference and rock stars. As a rule, encyclopedists stand open-armed to the universe of information, which has grown in amplitude. We are now obliged and entitled to know an ever-widening world.

At the same time, the "circle of learning" has shrunk, contracted in scope from an interconnected cosmos through a rationalist landscape of human control over nature and society to a collection of loose information that rattles around in a volume that claims to be "all you need to know." As a rule, encyclopedists seek compression. Like Basic English, Theodore Zeldin writes, encyclopedias now bring a form of "Basic Knowledge," which amounts to a reassuring but not inspiriting "Manual of Contemporary Folklore."[36] Not yet reduced to a Book of Lists or a Dictionary of Cultural Literacy, modern encyclopedias have nonetheless flattened the sphere of knowledge.

Voluminous Concision: Encyclopedias have always been fat and, but for time, money, and mortality, would surely have been fatter. As a rule, encyclopedists are greedy, their desire greater than their capacity. That is why the world knows more about "A" and "B" than any other letter: the original *Britannica* devoted 697 pages to the first two letters, leaving 2,000 for the rest.[37] Despite the pretensions to reason of the Scottish gentlemen of letters, this is scarcely a rational apportionment in a universe that does not operate in alphabetical order.

Encyclopedists are obsessed with size. Ersch and Gruber's unfinished German dictionary of arts and sciences broke off after a mere 167 volumes, although it did contain one of the world's longer encyclopedia entries, 3,668 pages on Greece. It is not only the Chinese who boast about vastness: "8,320 pages, 27,000 distinct articles, more than 100 writers," bragged the brothers Chambers, and the great encyclopedia known as the *Espasa* is the pride of Spanish-speaking countries today, not only for its contents but for its size, "the largest in the world."[38] Indeed, twentieth-century publishers have gone to great lengths to thin out the paper—an important consideration in small Japanese apartments—diminish the print, enlarge the page, and yet contain the results "between two strong covers."

At the same time, compilers have constantly called for ever greater brevity and convenience. Horace Greeley wanted a "table-book . . . every general article abridged as much as possible, or, as they say in Vermont, 'boiled down.' "[39] Concentrated knowledge, like maple syrup, was thought to sweeten the learning and make it more accessible. In the war of the concise against the discursive, one-volume encyclopedists inveighed against cost and "cumbrousness" and singled out the "lengthy treatises" of the *Britannica* for particular populist scorn. Like *Beeton's Dictionary of Universal Information* of 1861, the one-volumers promised only "the closest, tersest, and most exact manner." And like Kōdansha's multikilogram "portable," they often aimed not only for the DESK but also for the "living room, the kitchen, the office, the hotel room." But of course their books, too, were fat, stuffed with a surfeit of short entries. There is no such thing as a short encyclopedia.

Figments of Fact: In the modern encyclopedian theology, the ritually intoned credo is Facts, Not Opinions. "Comments, discussions, speculations, criticisms . . . have no fit place in a book of reference, of which the proper object is to give facts of positive knowledge, and not the opinions of men about such facts" (*Johnson's New Universal Cyclopædia*, 1874). Nishimura Shigeki's provision number eight for the compilation of the *Koji ruien* in 1879 sternly decreed: "Citations only, no need to add the views of the compiler." As a rule, encyclopedists are extremely sure of their facts, which they solemnly offer at the high altar of Objectivity.

And how did they define these "tried and true facts"? By the consensus of the day. Theirs was the knowledge commons, where everyone grazed, the beaten path, where all knew the way. They sought to represent the best, or the most important, part of a collectivity of knowledge, sanctified by common use. Alden's *Manifold Cyclopedia* of 1887 proudly announced that it did "not especially attempt originality of treatment, but aim[ed] rather to give the generally accepted views of the most eminent scholars of the world upon all topics discussed." The encyclopedists could be extremely naive about scientific facts, reproducing accuracy and error with equal precision. When it came to social or national facts, they could more easily detect the bias in others than in themselves.

Witness the Chambers brothers' printed disclaimer about the "flagrant abuse" of their encyclopedia in the American edition of Messrs. Lippincott of Philadelphia. The entries so "hateful to the original proprietors" included Free Trade, which the English edition called "the most important and fundamental truth in political economy," altered by the Americans to a doctrine that "had no foothold in the policy of any civilized nation" until the British sophists and propagandists got hold of it. The American edition omitted the English reference to the constitutional sanction of slavery in the United States, adding a defense of the institution "as a social necessity." But the editors found "a much more serious perversion" in the article on Victoria I. Both editions admitted unparalleled material prosperity under the queen's rule. But the English entry continued: "perhaps during no reign has a greater measure of political contentment been enjoyed." The Americans found instead "a growing discontent under her unequal institutions, and a progress toward republicanism." At that point, the Chamberses found themselves quite unable to continue because of a "slanderous imputation concerning His Royal Highness, the Prince of Wales, which we should be ashamed to copy."[40]

Think, too, of the response of the Meiji translators in the hire of the Ministry of Education when they came to this section in the very same Chambers's *Information for the People*:

> As regards civilization . . . the continent of Asia is now, with a few fractional exceptions, in a state of semi-barbarism and stagnant imbecility. . . . China and

Japan, though possessing a literature, laws, and religion—though their people dwell in cities, cultivate the soil with exactitude and care, and exhibit considerable skill in the domestic arts, are little, if anything, in advance of what they were several centuries ago, being destitute of that elasticity and adaptive capacity essential to a progressive civilization.[41]

Of course, bias is usually more subtle than in these examples, but the problem today lies also with the "facts" themselves. Now that we no longer believe in the transparency of truth or the absoluteness of science, on what authority does the principle of encyclopedic selection rest?

The Authoring of Authority: Compilers have nearly always had recourse to the authority of others to gain the imprimatur of value for their work, whether it is to claim truth or objectivity, relevance or universality. As a rule, encyclopedists are cowards. Even when individuals produced the whole work, they called on God or the sages before them as the "source" of their knowledge. The "precise citation" of the classics that informed the traditional East Asian encyclopedias conferred authority on the work. Encyclopedias everywhere are logocentric: if the words are accurate, so then is the thing, or the representation of it. Pierre Bayle, no coward in his anti-Catholic rationalism, perhaps said it best. At the end of a long discourse of disclaimers that amounts to a veritable treasury of authorial alibis and academic apologia, he stated plainly:

Such as will give themselves the trouble to cast their eyes upon the margins of this Dictionary, are desired to remember, that the quotations I have marked with a figure, are those which I have found in the authors, whose passages I relate. I am not answerable for them.[42]

It could scarcely be clearer; errors in the sources, if faithfully transcribed, remain *their* errors: "I am not answerable for them."

When European encyclopedias outgrew the authorship of a one-man compiler-savant—Hübner in 1704 already had a staff of contributors, and Zedler in the 1730s had a staff of editors, one of them with the fitting title of Professor of Worldly Wisdom—the tradition of collective compilation became increasingly common. In Asia, encyclopedias had long been produced by both individuals and collaborative groups, but the authority ultimately rested in the texts, not the author, so the difference perhaps mattered somewhat less. In the *Britannica* and the *Encyclopédie*, which depended on the hands of many contributors, the device of individually signed articles appeared, thus making authorial responsibility clear. But in general this practice remained the exception, and even when articles were signed, subsequent revisions tended to muddy the authorial waters to the point that the undersigned became a ghost of his former self.

The next resort came to be increasingly long lists of "experts," whose names lined the front pages of many nineteenth-century encyclopedias, with degrees and academic positions lumbering suitably behind each one. Some encyclopedias looked as if they had been compiled by an entire metropolitan bureaucracy of specialists, each conferring the weight of his authority on the whole. In many cases, the experts wrote the articles in their specialty themselves. This practice gradually devolved into a group of "consultants," whose expertise was more tenuously connected to the actual words within, which were usually the work of someone else, often long dead, a contributor of three or four revisions before. I think of these groups as an encyclopedic choir invisible, present but not responsible, lending an aura of authority greater than the reach of the editorial eye of its members. In most large contemporary encyclopedias, it is the anonymous horde of checkers, by finger, phone, and fax, who are responsible for "accuracy." In short, both the consultants and the checkers leave no discernible traces. Encyclopedias today are their own authorities.

Paradoxologia I: The word means "the art of explaining paradoxes," and Alsted devoted a section to it in his encyclopedia of 1630. Would that he were here to explain how it is that most modern encyclopedias, which are so vocally consecrated to progress, perform so conservative a role in the perpetuation of knowledge.

Since the eighteenth century in the West, and subsequently in many other parts of the world, encyclopedias have cut themselves from the same mythic cloth of progress in which modern ideology is thoroughly draped. Their compilers rarely failed to present their work as part of *The Growing World; or, Progress of Civilization, and the Wonders of Nature, Science, Literature, and Art*, which was the title of an 1880 American encyclopedia whose frontispiece bore the caption, "From the lowest to the highest type of animal life." The "highest type" was a mustachioed gentleman sitting in a chair reading a book, surrounded by the beasts of land, sea, and air, and one "savage" with a bow and arrows. Whether Social Darwinism, scientific advance, or national progress, the encyclopedias justified their usefulness in progressive terms. To keep up, one needed an encyclopedia.

And the encyclopedias, too, strove to keep up in a constant rat race of revision, each new version explained in terms of the march of progress and the press of contemporary events, "which have never moved as rapidly as in the present age." In the scramble to be "up-to-date," the publisher Brockhaus at one point in 1817–18 found himself in the midst of issuing volumes of three different editions of his encyclopedia at the same time. The "loose-leaf encyclopedias" patented special designs to enable readers to add pages to them as world events tumbled forward. The encyclopedias depended on progress for their profit.

And yet, the information they purveyed was generally the most up-to-date of the out-of-date of a given age. Encyclopedian knowledge was backward learning, gathered in the eddies where the collective wisdom slowed while new knowledge rushed by in the larger stream. In 1727 Ephraim Chambers had written, approvingly, that "the modern is yet wild, and unascertained," but he, too, drew the lexicographic line at newness, likening the lexicographer to the historian who "comes after the affair; and gives a description of what passed." The last Meiji setsuyōshū, published in 1894, also strove to avoid "things likely to change in the future" in favor of "fixed, immutable" portraits from the past and principles of science. Encyclopedias everywhere tended to wait for the reduction to regularity, the sanctification by collective consensus, the anointing by the authority of experts, who themselves were not anointed until seasoned by age. "Each edition," commented one scholar, "is intellectually, if not factually, a generation old the moment it is published."[43] And several have suggested that in both China and Europe, eras of encyclopedic activity coincided with lulls of intellectual creativity, when it was time to codify tradition, not break its mold.

As a rule, encyclopedists are timid. The editorial resistance to contemporary topics and, sometimes, to the inclusion of entries on living people, is partly defensive, for these are anything but "tried and true"—"unascertained," Chambers would say. So encyclopedists brew a mix of the latest "safe" subjects, which they take to mean geographical, scientific, and contemporary historical topics (despite the fact that these entries have a way of dating as fast as the biographies of living people) with the well-ascertained subjects from the past, such as the Battle of Marathon, which seems stable, and the kings of England, whose order of reign never changeth. The initial mix is thus in many respects quite the opposite of up-to-date, and what begins as a conservative grasp grows only more so as successive redactions perpetuate the material—and the errors—from past editions, forever fixed in encyclopedic amber.

Far from presenting universal knowledge, it would seem that modern encyclopedias tend toward serial knowledge of a markedly conservative bent.

Paradoxologia II: The modern encyclopedic world is a relentlessly national one, different from the medieval religious universe in Europe and the sinocentric cultural ecumene in East Asia. For the ideology of progress is profoundly implicated in the development of the modern nation-state, and encyclopedias, since the eighteenth century, have been national in at least three ways. First, they served to construct a national culture by enshrining what is Japanese, Spanish, Polish, Italian, or Turkish in a series of volumes with the national name in the title, written in the national language, and filled, at least partially, with the drama of the national past. (And what will now become of the *Enciklopedija Jugoslavije?*) Second, they helped to create a common national knowledge among the people, who are expected to have at least encyclopedia-level learning about their country, which is inculcated in school but continued thereafter in self-learning through the media and, yes, the encyclopedia. Third, they were vessels of national pride, which is one reason why nations continued to compile them, even if the information was readily available in other forms.

The impressive *Encyclopedia Italiana* of 1929–1936 was the lavish (and often surprisingly evenhanded) product of fascist pomp, with the article on fascism allegedly written by Il Duce himself. Encylopedian patriotism was as often spearheaded by the publishing world as by the state, for there was the promise of money in it. An advertising jingle for the *Konversations-Lexikon* in 1925 made this point in a Burma Shave–like rhyme: "Like a farmer without a blockhouse, Is a German without a *Brockhaus*."[44]

The content of these encyclopedias was national, too, in its treatment of other countries. Panckoucke's *Encyclopédie méthodique*, which he meant to supersede the work of Diderot, appeared in its Spanish translation with the article on Spain intact. It read, "What do we owe Spain? And for two centuries, for four, for ten, what has she done for Europe?" Therewith ended the career of his encyclopedia in Spain.[45] American compilers were forever fretting about the way "the insular mind of the mother-country has never yet fully awakened to the change in the center of civilization which has resulted from the growth of the New World."[46] And several years ago, Japanese editors began to say the same thing about the center of civilization in Asia, which had yet to receive its encyclopedic due. This national stance is not mitigated by the tendency to make international claims for the content of a given encyclopedia. Japanese publishers are particularly fond of titles like "The Great International Encyclopedia," no less so the Americans, with *The World Book* and the like. The *American Remembrancer* of 1795 declared itself "an epitome of universal history, particularly of that part which respects America." The international claim is the obverse of national pride: it insists on the importance of one's own nation in the world.

Yet, at the same time it is a fact of modern national encyclopedias that they are for the most part all copied from one another: the French *Encyclopédie* in Europe; the brothers Chambers and the *Britannica* in North America, the Commonwealth, Japan, and elsewhere; and *Brockhaus* all over the world. A glance at the prefaces of nineteenth-century encyclopedias reveals that the same names appear again and again as the source of "most, but certainly not all" of the entries "in this worthy book." Some editors did not bother to credit the source, since copying and pirating were the lifeblood of compilation. As a rule, encyclopedists are plagiarists. In an entry for Plagiary, Ephraim Chambers had early on exempted dictionary writers "fron the common laws of meum and tuum . . . and if they rob, they do not do it any otherwise, than as the bee does, for the publick service."

What is interesting here, however, is the thought of a substantial mass of international knowledge sitting comfortably in the midst of the determinedly national encyclopedias. That mass can range from 40 to 90 percent of the whole, but even at its least, it is considerable. This international residuum is conspicuous in some cases, especially when the *Brockhaus*-based encyclopedias reveal a penchant for German place-names or artists. In many cases, the twentieth-century encyclopedias seem to have established some harmony between a core held in common and the canon of national knowledge. But the international core does suggest that the diffusion of the myth of progress, the idea of the nation, and middle classes defined in terms of education is no less accidental in the "chain of knowledge" than nationalism and capitalism are in the terrain of history.

Information for the People: The audience for encyclopedias expanded over the centuries: from clergy to laymen, from the learned and leisured to the learners and workers, from the elect to the self-selected, from the aristocracy to the bourgeoisie, from a society of gentlemen to a readership of women and children (and, one presumes, also men), from the middle class to those "in all walks of life." Or so the modern encyclopedists tell us when they announce that "this work brings within the reach of the many, that knowledge which has too long been reserved for the few."[47]

As a rule, encyclopedists are like snake-oil salesmen, peddling commodified knowledge and asserting a "public craving" when they in fact are seeking to create one. For they know what Bayle knew, too: "a work which is bought only by the learned never pays the printer." It paid to attract the widest possible audience and to take advantage of whatever trends of the time promised a new market.

Sometimes the publishers flattered their readers, as when Bradford sought to sell his American version of Abraham Rees's *New Cyclopædia* in Philadelphia in 1820 to "merchants, artists, manufacturers, and private gentlemen . . . possessed of active and well cultivated minds, and still grasping after further improvements in knowledge" but "too busy to explore an entire system of thought" (a slur on the rival *Britannica*).[48] This stress on busyness became an abiding American theme; the country was full of "busy people." The language of class seemed to sit less easily in American commercial society, where encyclopedias were unlikely to be entitled "for the educated classes," as they were in Germany. Instead, the language went the other way around: "In America intelligence and education are not restricted to one favored class, and books for the diffusion of general information should be moderate in size and cost." So argued *Chandler's Encyclopedia: An Epitome of Universal Knowledge* in 1898, seeking to serve "plain people . . . the average farmer or mechanic" rather than "leisurely scholars." Japanese encyclopedias at the turn of the century made the same pitch: "Many works of reference are published for people with leisure, but not for the practical use of ordinary people; this is a general encyclopedia . . . filled with practical knowledge."[49]

A miasma of condescension settles over some of these appeals, particularly in the references to women, so often evoked as the most likely to benefit from learning by virtue of being in the greatest need. The stance was that of the enlightenment mentality wielding knowledge to uplift the ignorant. Later the didactic tone changed to the wooing, cajoling cadences of the modern marketplace, as mothers became the targeted consumers of twentieth-century encyclopedias purchased for the educational sake of their children. But woman, man, or child, the snake oil promised success and status as a result of learning— or even merely of possessing "like a talisman (*omamori*) in the living room"— what the middle classes were supposed to know.[50]

However much the publishers spoke of "Everybody's Book of Reference," the modern encyclopedia was middle-class material both in content and in actual readership, or more accurately, buyership, since we know very little about how much of what was read and by whom. The middle class, of course, is not Everybody, and it is important to recognize that the homogenizing stance of the encyclopedias linked the middle class to the nation and excluded from the inner "circle of learning"—if not by design, then by default—those who did not fit. As a rule, encyclopedists transmit the consensus, and encyclopedias are not sites of debate or social dissent.

This social exclusion did not seem to depend on the *kind* of knowledge being purveyed. Encyclopedias, which had once encompassed knowledge and then stressed education, now conveyed information. No longer need people fear a lifetime "spent in learning what had already been found out," a sentiment of Ephraim Chambers from the eighteenth century. By the twentieth century, popular encyclopedias were promising to ease the "embarrassment of learning" that faced "the ordinary man," by providing "ready access to a comprehensive storehouse of general information." They offered not a bulk of universal knowledge but "a mass of widely diverse facts."[51] The sales pitch remained the same, even as the encyclopedic content changed dramatically.

Encyclopedias thus reflected the turn from universal knowledge to universal education, which meant knowledge for all but no longer all of knowledge. They also moved from general education, in the systematic sense of the liberal arts, to general knowledge, which consisted of dispersed information, often of a highly accessible and popular sort. They had in effect become the reference-book equivalent of a magazine. In a sense, encyclopedic knowledge was more accessible now than it had ever been before.

Accessibility is not, however, the issue. Instead, I think it is the viability of the notion of the modern middle classes that makes the difference. Publishers today in Britain, the United States, and Japan complain that the market for general encyclopedias is the merest shadow of its former self. In 1994 the reference editor of Kōdansha, which published *Grand Napoleon* and *DESK*, told me, sadly but definitively: "The encyclopedia is dead." In this case, death is relative, since Japan still sells reference books in numbers not even dreamt of by publishers elsewhere. Still, there is little doubt that encyclopedic times have changed. That the 1994 winner of the National Spelling Bee in Washington received an encyclopedia for his efforts seemed only to conjoin two anachronisms from an earlier, more innocent America.

Those who argue that the age of the general encyclopedia is now at its end because of the advent of electronic publishing mistake the medium for the message. The encyclopedia is in fact perfectly suited to electronic access, which offers potential intellectual rewards, not least liberation from the tyranny of both thematic and alphabetic order into the spaciousness of keyword retrieval.[52] The real problem is that the Internet is still in many ways as confined to the elite of the world's societies today as medieval clerics once were to the monastic company of one another. Modern encyclopedias, no matter whether they appear in print or in cyberspace, have always depended on an imagined social norm that promises the world but insists on homogeneity, demands self-help and social conformity, and makes bourgeois knowledge the standard for citizenship. The norm also presumes the universality of both the desire and the ability to drink at the fount of encyclopedic wisdom. But the middle classes, once thought to be infinitely expandable, are now contracting even in the advanced societies, not to speak of their irrelevance in much of the developing world. And if society has no way to make good on the promise and presumption of learning one's way to a better life, then the norm that so long supported the encyclopedic enterprise also loses its power to persuade.

The modern encyclopedia exemplified the optimism, objectivism, and nationalism of the past two centuries, not only in the West but around the world. The encyclopedists who compiled them assumed curiosity and comprehensibility. They argued utility and pursued profit; they hailed the people and praised the nation. And they believed unswervingly in the possibility of progress, progress that "everybody" who was willing to abide by the middle-class consensus could conceivably enjoy. If these beliefs now sound quaint, as they surely do in many contexts, then we may indeed be at the end of this particular modern. Yet it is not the folly of the encyclopedists that is at stake, but what it reflects of our own.

NOTES

1. *Ready Reference: The Universal Cyclopaedia Containing Everything That Everybody Wants to Know*, ed., William Ralston Balch, rev. ed. (London: Griffith, Farran, Browne, 1901).

2. This essay is based on a lecture given at the New York Public Library in 1993 and published in *Biblion* (Fall 1994). Because the encyclopedia encompassed knowledge broadly and thrived across cultures, from the first it reminded me, at the height of its achievement, of Donald Keene. The subject pays homage to this master of translations and transformations, who has not only gathered so much of what is knowable but so generously and inspiringly offers it to others.

3. Tom McArthur, *Worlds of Reference: Lexicography, Learning and Language from the Clay Tablet to the Computer* (Cambridge: Cambridge University Press, 1986), pp. 41–44.

4. The *Kitāb 'Uyūn al-Akhbār* of Ibn Qutayba (d. 889) has also been translated as the "quintessence of traditions," traditions referring literally to "historical reports," or profane knowledge, as distinguished from the sacred sayings of the Prophet. Charles Pellat, "Les Encyclopédies dans le monde arabe," *Cahiers d'histoire mondiale* 9, no. 3 (1966): 638–40.

5. Charles Homer Haskins, quoted in Francis J. Witty, "Medieval Encyclopedias," *Journal of Library History* 14 (Summer 1979): 277.

6. Robert Collison, *Encyclopaedias: Their History Throughout the Ages* (New York: Hafner, 1964), pp. 44–80; McArthur, *Worlds of Reference*, pp. 49–56; Alain Rey, *Encyclopédies et dictionnaires* (Paris: Presses Universitaires de France, 1982), pp. 57–69.

7. S. H. Steinberg, "Encyclopedias," *Signature*, new series, no. 12 (1951): 3. According to Collison (*Encyclopaedias*), this version of the title was a later edition of Alsted's famous *Encyclopaedia: Septem tomis distincta* of 1630.

8. Lawrence E. Sullivan, "Circumscribing Knowledge: Encyclopedias in Historical Perspective," *Journal of Religion* 70 (July 1990): 322.

9. Fifth ed., vol. 1 (London, 1741), title page, preface, and p. iii.

10. Brockhaus's first *Conversations-Lexicon* dates from 1808–1811. The first with the title, "for the educated classes," was the second edition, in ten volumes, 1812–1819.

11. Larousse's encyclopedia appeared in seventeen volumes from 1866 to 1890. Hugo's commendation dates from 1864. Anna Arnar, *Encyclopedism from Pliny to Borges* (Chicago: University of Chicago Library, 1990), p. 8.

12. Georg Meyer, "Das Konversations-Lexikon, eine Sonderform der Enzyklopädie: Ein Beitrag zur Geschichte der Bildungsverbreitung in Deutschland" (Ph.D. diss., University of Göttingen, 1965), pp. 9–16.

13. Trumbull White, ed., *The World's Progress in Knowledge, Science, and Industry: A Vast Treasury and Compendium of the Achievements of Man and the Works of Nature* (N.p., 1902).

14. Wolfgang Bauer, "The Encyclopædia in China," *Cahiers d'histoire mondiale* 9, no. 3 (1966): 665–91; Ssu-yü Teng and Knight Biggerstaff, comps., *An Annotated Bibliography of Selected Chinese Reference Works* (Cambridge, MA: Harvard University Press, 1971); Jean-Pierre Diény, "Les Encylopédies chinoises," in Annie Becq, ed., *L'Encylopédisme* (Paris: Éditions Klincksieck, 1991), pp. 195–200.

15. John Harris, *Lexicon Technicum; or An Universal English Dictionary of the Arts and Sciences* (London, 1704); preface to the *Yu-ting Yüan-chien lei-han* of 1701, an imperial encyclopedia completed at about the same time as Harris's (Shanghai: Shang-hai tung-wen shu-chu, 1887).

16. For example, *Huang-lan* (Mirror for the emperor), A.D. 220; the tenth-century *T'ai-ping yü lan* (The emperor's mirror from the era of great peace), compilations for scholar-officials like the thirteenth-century *Yü hai* (Sea of jade), etc.

17. Herbert A. Giles, "Encyclopædia Maxima," *The Nineteenth Century and After*, no. 290 (April 1901): 660.

18. Many of the illustrations in the last great imperial encyclopedia, the *Ch'in-ting ku-chin t'u-shu chi-ch'eng*, were taken from this work. Wang Ch'i, *San-ts'ai t'u-hui* (repr.) (Taiwan: Ch'eng Wen Publishing, 1970). For a small selection of the drawings, see John A. Goodall, *Heaven and Earth: Album Leaves from a Ming Encyclopedia: San-ts'ai t'u-hui, 1610* (Boulder, CO: Shambhala, 1979).

19. Terashima Ryōan, *Wakan sansai zue*, reprinted in *Nihon zuihitsu taisei bekkan* (Tokyo: Yoshikawa kobunkan, 1929); Heibonsha, ed., *Hyakka jiten no rekishi* (Tokyo: Heibonsha, 1964), pp. 35, 46–47; Ōsumi Kazuo, *Jiten no kataru Nihon no rekishi* (Tokyo: Soshiete, 1988), pp. 115–31.

20. Yamaoka Matsuaki, *Ruishū meibutsukō*. See Mitsunaga Yayoshi, *Hyakka jiten no seirigaku* (Tokyo: Takeuchi shoten, 1972), pp. 187–88.

21. Yokoyama Toshio, "Nihonjin hikkei no jisho de atta 'setsuyōshū' kara gendai e no messeji," *Chūō kōron* 99 (February 1984): 280–93; "Nichiyō hyakkagata setsuyōshū no shiyō taiyō no keiryōka bunsekihō ni tsuite," *Jinbun gakuhō*, no. 66 (March 1990): 177–202; "Setsuyōshū and Japanese Civilization," in Sue Henny and Jean-Pierre Lehmann, eds., *Themes and Theories in Modern Japanese History* (London: Athlone Press, 1988), pp. 78–98.

22. Ishiyama Hiroshi, "Daichiri-shi Hyubuneru o megutte," *Ueno toshokan kiyo* 3 (1957), pp. xlvi–lii.

23. Elided from a Confucian classic, the title meant something like "Well-being, new edition." See Ōsumi, *Jiten*, pp. 147–62.

24. Preface to Chambers's *Information for the People*, William and Robert Chambers, eds., New and Improved ed. (4th?), 2 vols. (Philadelphia: Lippincott, 1859). Originally published in Edinburgh in 1833, this work was frequently revised and reprinted in both the United States and Great Britain.

25. Fukukama Tatsuo, *Meiji shoki hyakka zensho no kenkyū* (Tokyo: Kazama shobō, 1968).

26. George Kennan, "Are the Japanese Honest?" *The Outlook*, August 31, 1912, p. 1015.

27. Taguchi Ukichi, *Nihon shakai jii* (Tokyo: Keizai zasshisha, 1891), p. 3.

28. Completed in 1914, the *Koji ruien* was later reprinted in sixty volumes by Koji ruien kankōkai in 1931–1936. See Ōsumi, *Jiten*, pp. 196–210. The private compilation was Mozume Takami's *Kōbunko*, originally completed in twenty volumes in 1916 and reprinted by Meicho fukyūkai in 1976.

29. *Denka hōten Meiji setsuyō taizen* (Tokyo: Hakubunkan, 1894), reprinted by Geiyū sentaa, 1974.

30. *Nihon katei hyakka jii*, Haga Yaichi and Shimada Jirō, eds., 2 vols. (Tokyo: Fuzanbō, 1906).

31. Preface to *Kokumin hyakka jiten* (Tokyo: Fuzanbō, 1908).

32. *Nihon katei daihyakka jii* (Tokyo: Fuzanbō, 1927), "Johen," pp. 1–2.

33. Published in Tokyo between 1908 and 1919, by the Nihon hyakka daijiten kanseikai (Association for the completion of the Great Japan Encyclopedia), which took over after the project had temporarily bankrupted the original publisher, Sanseidō.

34. *Grand Napoleon: Encyclopedia World Now* was the trendy English title of a successful sixteen-volume Japanese encyclopedia published by Kōdansha in 1971.

35. Heibonsha and Shōgakkan, two of the largest and most prolific encyclopedia publishers, energetically competed—sixteen volumes against twenty-five—in an already saturated market. Herbert A. Lottman, "The Great Encyclopedia War and Other Tales of Today's Japan," *Publishers Weekly*, April 5, 1985, p. 21.

36. Theodore Zeldin, "Encyclopedias," *London Review of Books*, October 26, 1989, p. 34.

37. Richard Yeo, "Reading Encyclopedias: Science and the Organization of Knowledge in British Dictionaries of Arts and Sciences, 1730–1850," *ISIS* 82 (1991): 40.

38. Ersch and Gruber, *Allgemeine Encyclopädie der Wissenschaften und Künste* (Leipzig: J. F. Gleditsch, F. A. Brockhaus, 1818–1889); Concluding Notice to the first edition of *Chambers's Encyclopaedia: A Dictionary of Universal Knowledge for the People* (Edinburgh: W. and R. Chambers, 1860). *Enciclopedia universal ilustrada europeo-americana* (the *Espasa*) appeared from 1905 to 1930 in seventy-two volumes and has been expanded by supplemental volumes since then.

39. Preface to *Johnson's New Universal Cyclopædia: A Scientific and Popular Treasure of Useful Knowledge* (New York: A. J. Johnson and Son, 1874). Greeley proposed this book during a drive in Central Park in 1870, and he later took time from his presidential campaign to contribute the entry "Confederate States."

40. *Chambers's Encyclopædia; A Dictionary of Universal Knowledge for the People*, rev. ed. (London: W. and R. Chambers, 1876).

41. Chambers's (1859), vol. 2, p. 276.

42. Preface to the second French edition, *The Dictionary Historical and Critical of Mr. Peter Bayle*, 2nd English ed. (London, 1734), p. 17.

43. Livio Stecchini, "On Encyclopedias in Time and Space," *The American Behavioral Scientist* 6 (September 1962): 5.

44. Arthur Hübscher, *Hundertfünzig Jahre F. A. Brockhaus* (Wiesbaden: F. A. Brockhaus, 1955), p. 238.

45. Clorinda Donato and Robert M. Maniquis, eds., *The Encyclopédie and the Age of Revolution* (Boston: G. K. Hall, 1992), p. 74.

46. *Harper's Book of Facts* (New York: Harper & Brothers, 1895).

47. *Beeton's Dictionary of Universal Information* (London: Ward, Lock & Tyler, 1861).

48. Arner, *Dobson's* Encyclopaedia, p. 177.

49. *Kokumin hyakka zensho* (Osaka: Shōbunkan, 1910).

50. Maeda Ai, "Aete jidai sakugo ni idomu futatsu no hyakka jiten—katsuji banareha (Shōgakkan) vs katsuji chūdokuha (Heibonsha)," *Asahi jaanaru*, December 7, 1984, pp. 65–67.

51. *Funk & Wagnalls Standard Encyclopedia of the World's Knowledge* (New York and London: Funk & Wagnalls, 1912).

52. For example, Microsoft's *Encarta* (Funk & Wagnalls' *New Encyclopedia* 1992); Compton's *Interactive Encyclopedia on CD-ROM*; and the *Britannica*, on line since 1994, at a price.

15

The Metamorphosis of Disguise: Ibsen, Sōseki, and Ōgai

◉

J. THOMAS RIMER

Over the years, both Japanese and foreign scholars have speculated about the significance of the often complex personal relationships among modern Japanese writers. These connections sometimes determined their individual artistic trajectories and, more often than not, helped shape important developments in their personal lives as well. It has therefore always surprised me that the two figures now regarded as the literary masters of the Meiji period (1868–1911), Natsume Sōseki (1867–1916) and Mori Ōgai (1862–1922), could be said to have remained virtually unacquainted. It is true that Ōgai was older by a few years and had gone to Europe a generation earlier than Sōseki did, but nevertheless the respective prominence of both men should surely, in the natural course of events, have put them together. Or so I supposed.

A close reading of the evidence revealed a few traces of contact.[1] Ōgai, answering a newspaper questionnaire in 1910, indicated that he had met Sōseki "once or twice" and that he admired what little of the author's work he had then read. When the younger author died, Ōgai attended his funeral. For his part, Sōseki, who once described Ōgai's writing as possessing a kind of "melancholy, ironic elegance," wrote briefly in 1916, just at the end of his own life, of his admiration for such historical stories of Ōgai as *Sakai jiken* (The Incident at Sakai, 1914) and *Kuriyama Daizen* (1915). Whether Sōseki knew about and had read Ōgai's much-admired translations of European writers, he did not indicate; with Sōseki's strong interest in English literature, however, he may not have been particularly attracted to the works by the German and Scandinavian authors whom Ōgai admired (Goethe, Hofmannsthal, Andersen, and so on).

In a letter written to a friend in 1909, Sōseki mentions that he regretted missing the opportunity to see in the autumn of that year the famous production of Ibsen's *John Gabriel Borkman*, translated by Ōgai, which inaugurated the celebrated activities of Japan's first modern theater company, Osanai Kaoru's Free Theatre. Sōseki goes on to say, however, that "I heard it was very interesting."[2]

Physical proximity and extended personal contact represent one kind of shared knowledge. This opportunity the two men did not have or at least did not take pains to create. Although the two writers spent no significant moments together, they did carry on an important intellectual exchange through what Marcel Proust would have identified as their "real selves," that is, through the medium of their own writings. Here, the evidence is clear, indeed revelatory. Ōgai himself sought to touch the spirit of the younger novelist through an ingenious and touching strategy of literary impersonation.

The implicit friendship between these two men found its expression in two novels. Each in its own way deals with the emotional circumstances surrounding the transmission of ideas from one artist, and so those of his generation, to the next.

In 1908, Sōseki published his novel *Sanshirō*, which describes the life of a young man who leaves the countryside to go to Tokyo in order to study and make his way in the modern world. The narrative (now available in English in an accomplished translation by Jay Rubin), which provides a charming portrait of an appealing and diffident youth, was immediately popular. Despite its relative slightness and laconic style, readers apparently understood the book's more serious overtones, which suggested the urgent need for spiritual independence felt by many young people in the later decades of the Meiji period. Ōgai certainly knew of, and read, the novel.

At this point in his career, despite his time-consuming duties as surgeon general of the Japanese army, Ōgai was busy again writing fiction after a hiatus of many years. In Ōgai's 1909 novel *Vita Sexualis*, the protagonist Kanai remarks that he has examined and admired the new novel by Sōseki. *Sanshirō* thus came to serve Ōgai as a model, foil, and spur, permitting him to create his own version of the interior life of a young man, which he published in serial form from March 1910 to August 1911 as *Seinen* (Youth).[3]

Both novels follow a similar trajectory: a young man comes to Tokyo, where slowly and painfully, he learns of the complexities and ambiguities of adult life.

Intellectually, both protagonists come to know something of the complex, occasionally dispiriting, nature of the political, social, and moral issues facing the country at the end of the Meiji period. Both take their first steps toward emotional development and maturity in seeking to understand women and the nature of their hold on men. In this regard, the narratives parallel each other. In tonality, however, the two works remain somewhat different, to the extent that the casual reader may not think to compare them. This gap in perception suggests something about the two authors' differing artistic attitudes and literary techniques.

Nevertheless, it is clear that *Youth* represents, among other things, Ōgai's homage to Sōseki. *Sanshirō* begins a conversation between the two writers, and *Youth* continues and expands on it. Thus it is in this form of exchange, at least from Ōgai's point of view, that the two writers can "meet" and exchange ideas in print. More striking still, given the nature of both novels, is the fact that it was the eminent Norwegian dramatist Henrik Ibsen (1828–1906) who provided the connecting link for both.

Apparently, Natsume Sōseki himself made no special study of Ibsen, insofar as I have been able to determine. Nevertheless, the great dramatist's name was in the air and also on the page in a variety of Japanese translations. The work of the playwright and the power of his advanced ideas, particularly those concerning the role of women in society, had as powerful an effect among intellectuals in Tokyo as they did in London, Paris, or New York. In *Sanshirō*, Sōseki had already picked up the fashionable lingo: Minako, the lovely and free-spirited girl to whom the protagonist is attracted, is often referred to as an "Ibsen girl," and the playwright's name turns up a number of times during the course of the novel.

At one point, Sōseki even writes that England itself is not sufficiently "Ibsen conscious." Hirota, one of Sanshirō's mentors, discusses the matter in a lightly ironic fashion suggesting as well that from Sōseki's point of view, these European enthusiasms perhaps need not be taken too seriously.

> Look at England. Egoism and altruism have been in perfect balance there for centuries. That's why it doesn't move. That's why it doesn't progress. The English are a pitiful lot—they've got no Ibsen, no Nietzsche. They're all puffed up like that, but look at them from the outside and you can see them hardening, turning into fossils.[4]

In the end, at least in terms of the tonality created by Sōseki for *Sanshirō*, Ibsen seems to be more of a passing fad than a point of philosophical repair.

On the other hand, Ōgai was far more involved with Ibsen, as both an intellectual and a translator. Indeed, it was Ōgai who did more than almost anyone else to make the works of Ibsen available to Japanese readers and theatergoers. He translated parts of Ibsen's poetic *Brand* as early as 1903 and, after Osanai's staging of his *John Gabriel Borkman* translation in 1909, went on to create effective Japanese versions of *Ghosts* in 1911 and *A Doll's House* in 1913.

Both *Youth* and *Sanshirō* share one concern, although as I mentioned earlier, the literary strategies that each author chose to articulate this concern differ greatly. The driving force behind both narratives is the need to explore the question of how new ideas can be transmitted from one generation to the next and how those ideas, linked to the human experience of the younger generation, can be transformed into true experiential knowledge. For Japan at this moment in its history, such matters were crucial, as one means after another was sought to allow the society to transform itself into a modern nation.

Given the period in which Ōgai and Sōseki wrote, the use of the realistic novel was perhaps the inevitable choice as a literary vehicle. Ōgai chose Goethe as his model, and Sōseki sometimes looked to Meredith for literary strategies and techniques. Thus it is perhaps not surprising that Sōseki treats his material in an ironic, sometimes humorous fashion, and Ōgai was intent on revealing the passion with which the young (well, *his* young) attempt to seize on new ideas, particularly those concepts imported from abroad that would necessarily play a role in shaping their own lives. The student discussions in *Youth* may seem too heavily laden with intellectual freight—to a modern reader, perhaps even naive—but they represent a conscientious and often ingenious attempt by the novelist to document how the passions in one mind can find the means to influence another in the realm of ideas. Sōseki's descriptions of that process are more indirect.

At least, they remained indirect in his fiction. But Sōseki was well known as an essayist and speaker as well. A number of his lectures that appeared in print, such as "Watakushi no kōjinshugi" (My Individualism, 1914) or "Gendai Nihon no kaika" (The Civilization of Modern-Day Japan, 1911), represented, and still represent, powerful cultural statements that even now seem, in their artfully rambling way, to sum up the great moral and social issues that Japan faced in the modern period.[5]

It is in this role as lecturer that Ōgai chose to present his vision of Sōseki in *Youth*. Likewise, the transmission of ideas in this relatively direct fashion constitutes Ōgai's chief strategy in his novels. Ideas are poured vigorously from one source after another into the head, and occasionally into the heart, of Jun'ichi, the protagonist.

In an early section of the narrative, Jun'ichi is invited to attend a meeting at a kind of intellectuals' club so that he can hear the speaker of the day, a certain Hirata Fuseki. It is here, too, that Jun'ichi meets Ōmura, an older student who soon becomes his mentor and friend. Together they listen to the lecture. Fuseki is, of course, Ōgai's Sōseki.

Fuseki's demeanor as a speaker seems to match closely other descriptions that have been recorded of Sōseki as a public figure. "Fuseki moved his body toward the table in a listless manner. He waited a certain time for the conversations that continued here and there to die out, and then he slowly opened his mouth to speak. The tonality he chose was that of an ordinary conversation."[6] Ōgai has assigned to his speaker an unusual topic (for him).

> I've learned that all of you would like to have me say something about Ibsen. Actually, I've never thought very deeply about him. My knowledge concerning him is doubtless no greater than your own, I suspect. Still, it takes a lot of effort to listen to something you don't know much about. But it is quite comfortable to sit and hear about something you already know. I think the refreshments have arrived, so please help yourselves and settle back.
>
> You've asked me to speak about Ibsen. Actually, I haven't thought much about him. What I do know is perhaps the same as you know yourselves. It's hard to listen to something you're unfamiliar with.[7]

The rambling now takes focus.

> At first, Ibsen was Norway's Small Ibsen, but after turning to social dramas, he became Europe's Big Ibsen. However, when he was introduced to Japan, he again reverted to the Small Ibsen. No matter what arrives in Japan, it turns into something small. Even Nietzsche became small in our country. And so did Tolstoy. I remember something that Nietzsche once said. At that time, the earth became small, and then everything on earth became even smaller. The last race of human beings will be dancing with superb nimbleness and flexibility. "We've discovered real happiness," this last race will say, their eyes blinking.
>
> The Japanese import all kinds of -isms, and while they toy with these, Japanese eyes are perpetually blinking. Everything and anything is turned into small playthings fingered by the Japanese. So you don't have to be altogether terrified if the "thing" or "ism" in question seems at first quite dreadful.[8]

This passage is striking in several senses. Ōgai has here captured something of Sōseki's ironic manner in the rhetoric he employs, and his use of a shifting scale of size (and thus significance) between Europe and Japan is effectively polemical. Ōgai may also have borrowed this approach directly from Sōseki.[9] In an early scene in *Sanshirō*, Sōseki's protagonist meets on his first train ride to Tokyo an older man (who later befriends him) who tells him, "Remember,

Tokyo is bigger than Kumamoto. And Japan is bigger than Tokyo. And even bigger than Japan, surely, is the inside of your head. Don't ever surrender yourself—not to Japan, not to anything."[10] Nevertheless, Fuseki's remarks about Ibsen were not likely to have come from the mouth of the historical Sōseki. Here Fuseki has metamorphosed back into Ōgai. The references, particularly those to Nietzsche, suggest a familiarity with these texts that belongs to Ōgai, through his extensive reading in German philosophy. If Sōseki knew these works as well, he certainly made no extended references to Nietzsche in this particularly mordant fashion in his own writings.

Here, therefore, the reader is presented with a triple set of masks as complicated as any found in a medieval nō play. Through a sort of double impersonation, Ōgai is able to underscore and validate by European example the ideas he found in *Sanshirō* that so resonated with his own.

Fuseki next discusses what he calls Ibsen's "worldly self," which he locates in *Peer Gynt*, and then goes on to stress that Ibsen possessed other, more important elements in his character:

> Yet Ibsen was not merely that sort of person. In addition, he possessed a social self, and it was this aspect of himself that he really wished to present. It was this side of himself that he exhibited in *Brand*. Why was it that Ibsen wanted to take a rope and pull off the rotten fetters of convention? Having achieved his freedom, he had no intention of throwing himself into the mire. He wanted to cut through the wind with his strong wings; he wanted to fly high and far.[11]

Jun'ichi and the rest of the audience are spellbound as they hear these words. In *Sanshirō*, Sōseki had implicitly urged the young to expand their minds enough to encompass the world. Now a similar message, conveyed through Ibsen and Ōgai, has become both urgent and explicit. In *Youth*, Jun'ichi's encounter with Ibsen, via Fuseki, becomes the driving force pushing him toward his quest for self-understanding.

In his novel, Ōgai seems to have given Sōseki, by way of Fuseki, pride of place in the pantheon of those who might spur on the younger generation; it is he who has the public's ear, he whose work can truly inspire.

In fact, Ōgai has provided a fictional version of an occasion that never took place. Sōseki did give a celebrated public lecture on the role of the artist a year or so before Ōgai wrote *Youth*, and some Japanese scholars of that period assumed that this occasion may have served as the pretext for this striking scene in Ōgai's novel. Perhaps it goes without saying that Sōseki did not speak about Ibsen on that occasion or, insofar as I can determine, on any other similar one. In the end, this speech is really Ōgai's, put into the mouth of Sōseki/Fuseki.

Here Ōgai uses a clever technique of multiple reinforcement, by means of masks behind which Ōgai can project his own voice, thereby reinforcing his deepest concerns.[12] This multiple displacement is a trenchant example of Ōgai's ability to create a literary strategy he deems suitable for his literary and philosophical purposes. During the whole restless period of Ōgai's creative life (until the resolution of his conflicting artistic impulses in his final phase that began several years later when he began to write successful stories in a historical mode), he sought one means after another by which to join his own sense of moral earnestness—such a powerful component in all his works—with persuasive new literary ideas and devices, many adapted from works he so admired by his European contemporaries.

It also is clear that Ōgai had no intention of "deceiving" his readers; much of his fiction in this period was written not to beguile but to inform. He had no wish to prevent his readers from recognizing the literary games and puzzles he was playing; indeed, recognizing these games was, in his eyes, part of the pleasure to be gained from reading his work.

This kind of literary model has been, of course, far more common in continental Europe than it has been in the Anglo-American tradition. A writer like the critic-sometimes-turned-novelist George Steiner comes to mind as a suitable contemporary example. In his 1981 *Portage of San Christobal*, dealing with Hitler, or his 1993 *Proofs and Three Parables*, concerning the collapse of belief in Marxist doctrines in Eastern Europe, the power and tension of ideas—rather than plot or character—inform their pitch, tone, and emotional thrust. In literary texts constructed along these lines, intellectual understanding, rather than emotional response, is the privileged means to grasp the core, the totality of meaning in the work.

Ōgai's commitment to the importance of the life of the mind in the service of both self and nation (his writings swing from one pole to the other during these years) may, it has been sometimes argued, have derived from the moral earnestness of his Tokugawa Confucian heritage. It is certainly true that in *Youth*, Ōgai reveals his belief in the importance of dedication to self-understanding, both intellectual and emotional, to be harnessed in the pursuit of a higher truth. In that regard, even though *Youth* deals with Japan at the end of the first decade of this century, the novel stands—in terms of its philosophical underpinnings and its subterranean moral fervor—as a precursor by three or four years of those magisterial, probing, sometimes visionary works of fiction on larger historical subjects that came to the fore during the last decade of Ōgai's writing career.

Given the urgency and power of Ōgai's moral convictions, it is not surprising that he himself appears so close to the surface of his writing. Though quite capable of creating characters that stand on their own in the works he composed during this period (Otama, for example, in *Gan* [Wild Geese], 1911, or the erratic, disturbing Setsuzō in the brilliant, unfinished *Kaijin* [Ashes], 1912), the kinds of characters Ōgai creates, who in their anguish seek to possess a true moral fire, most resemble the author himself. In some ways, this is not surprising, since Ōgai felt that he was to continue on this quest throughout his life. It was only with the composition of his historical stories, beginning with "OkitsuYagoemon no isho" (The LastWill and Testament of OkitsuYagoemon) in 1912, that the search to represent a character capable of possessing a genuine moral fervor could be displaced from the author's own persona to a historical subject. In the last phase of his work, Ōgai found himself freed from the weight of his own ego. But when removed, the masks in *Youth* still reveal only Ōgai himself.

Many Japanese who admire Ōgai understand this aspect of his moral quest. The eminent Japanese philosopher Watsuji Tetsurō (1889–1960)—himself a disciple of Natsume Sōseki—in remarks written in 1952 on Ōgai's novel, captured a sense of the unusual nature of Ōgai's moral and intellectual energy. For Watsuji, Ōgai's Jun'ichi did not represent the image of any real or typical student but, rather, disclosed the interior world of Ōgai himself, both his powerful intellectual abilities and an inner force of character.

> *Youth* was being serialized in the journal *Subaru* when I was around twenty-one or twenty-two. I read the novel, fully aware that its subject matter dealt with my own generation. Yet there was no erudite youth such as the protagonist known to me among my acquaintances. Looking back, it seems clear to me now that for his novel, Ōgai used such effective materials as his mental state when he returned from Kokura to Tokyo, his study of the French language while living in Kokura, and his new interest in the literary arts of France. Therefore his protagonist, supposedly a man of our own age, possessed all the precocious emotional responses of a literary master well into his forties.

For Watsuji, Jun'ichi and Ōgai are the same; Jun'ichi is a kind of literary holograph created in the mind of the writer himself.

Nevertheless, it must be said that since Ōgai set out to picture a young man, the results did not seem unnatural, even though his protagonist did exhibit such responses. This fact stands as proof that when Ōgai himself was a young man, he possessed the same sorts of precocious responses himself.[13]

Ōgai's desire to convince his readers of the necessity for an intellectually and spiritually committed life was the driving force behind the composition of *Youth*. In trying to achieve his literary purposes, however, Ōgai seemed aware that he needed to move beyond the model of himself in whatever way he could. Through his metamorphosis into the voices of Sōseki and Ibsen—both representing figures that Ōgai deeply admired—he attempted to add confirmation, resonance, and depth to his arguments.

Should such a confluence be dismissed as a sort of "influence study"? To do so, I think, would be to miss much that is striking in Ōgai's literary methods. For what he sets out to do in this passage, as well as in other, later sections of *Youth*, is to show how a set of ideas, mediated through a figure of respect, can ignite the thoughts and emotions of the young. Fuseki must interpret Ibsen for younger Japanese, just as Ōgai had to interpret them both for his readers. These are the techniques required for the passage of ideas from one mind to another and are precisely the technique that Ōgai set out to illustrate in his novel.

As it has sometimes been said, if art is made up of prior artistic examples plus something of the artist's own personal experience, then Ōgai's novel is one example of how this paradigm can be illustrated. In *Youth*, Ōgai set out to portray the intellectual and emotional environment in which ideas can be transmitted. In order to accomplish this, he made free use of his "friends of the spirit," Sōseki and Ibsen, in order to show how this could be done. In hindsight, at least, Ōgai's literary effort would seem to be a gesture of artistic generosity.

NOTES

1. In his meticulously researched article, "Mori Ōgai to Natsume Sōseki," *Kokubungaku kaishaku to kanshō*, November 1992, pp. 41–47, Yamazaki Kazuhide disclosed information concerning several occasions on which the two presumably did meet, mostly at meetings of haiku enthusiasts. Remarkably enough, both writers lived (at different periods) in the same Tokyo house, now reassembled in the outdoor Meijimura museum, near Nagoya. Ōgai lived there from 1890 to 1892, in the period just after his return from Germany; Sōseki lived in the house immediately after his return from London in 1903. Evidently, neither knew of the other writer's period of residence there.

2. The letter, dated November 29, 1909, is reproduced in *Sōseki zenshū* (Tokyo: Iwanami shoten, 1935), vol. 16, p. 762.

3. A recent complete English translation of *Seinen* by Sanford Goldstein and Shoichi Ono can be found in Mori Ōgai, *Youth and Other Stories* (Honolulu: University of Hawaii Press, 1994), pp. 373–517.

4. Natsume Sōseki, *Sanshirō*, trans. Jay Rubin (Seattle: University of Washington Press, 1977), p. 123.

5. Good translations by Jay Rubin of these two lectures can be found in Natsume Sōseki, *Kokoro: A Novel and Selected Essays* (Lanham, MD: Madison Books, 1992).

6. Mori Ōgai, *Seinen, Ōgai zenshū* (Tokyo: Chikuma shobō, 1971), vol. 2, p. 23.

7. Ibid., pp. 23–24.

8. Ibid., p. 24.

9. Sōseki was not, in fact, the only writer and intellectual who, returning from Europe, sensed a diminishment in scale when back in Japan. The poet Takamura Kōtarō (1883–1956), for example, back from Paris in 1909, composed in the following year this mordant commentary:

The Country of Netsuke
Cheekbones protruding, lips thick, eyes triangular, with a
face like a netsuke carved by the master Sangorō
blank, as if stripped of his soul
not knowing himself, fidgety
life-cheap
vainglorious
small & frigid, incredibly smug
monkey-like, fox-like, flying-squirrel-like, mudskipper-like,
    minnow-like, gargoyle-like, chip-from-a-cup-like Japanese

Takamura Kōtarō, in Hiroaki Sato, trans., A Brief History of Imbecility: Poetry and Prose of
Takamura Kōtarō *(Honolulu: University of Hawaii Press, 1993), p. 3.*

10. Rubin, *Sanshirō*, p. 15.

11. *Ōgai zenshū*, p. 24.

12. In other works written during this period, Ōgai explains the use of this technique, notably in his 1909 one-act play *Kamen* (Masks). Here the protagonist, a doctor, explains to his young student the need to achieve an effective exterior "impersonation" in order to find the means to express oneself while managing to carry on through all the vicissitudes of one's life.

13. Watsuji Tetsurō, "Ōgai no omoide," in *Watsuji Tetsurō zenshū* (Tokyo: Iwanami shoten, 1963), vol. 20, p. 460.

16

Different Feelings: The Intellectual Shift Between Meiji and Taishō

◉

STEPHEN DODD

Important generational shifts occurred between the Meiji (1868–1912) and the Taishō (1912–1926) periods, clearly reflected in the literary works of such writers as Shimazaki Tōson (1872–1943), Natsume Sōseki (1867–1916), and Satō Haruo (1892–1964). I am using a rather extended understanding of "Meiji" and "Taishō" for this chapter. In exact chronological terms, 1912 is the year when the periods changed. However, the Russo-Japanese War of 1904–5 was a key point when important shifts began to take place in the way that many writers and others of their generation perceived themselves and their relationship to the rest of society. The seven-year period from the end of the Russo-Japanese War to 1912 corresponds to the last part of Meiji, but it might also be seen as an interesting transitional period during which the first indications appeared of what came to be identified as a distinctive Taishō sensibility. In other words, the characteristics associated with many Taishō youths began to emerge several years before the beginning of the Taishō period proper.

We can detect a hint of this shift in sensibility through the differing responses of Tōson and Satō to rural and urban sites. Both writers originated from the provinces and shared the experience of moving to the capital where they eventually made their literary names. However, whereas Tōson gives the strong impression that he never lost his sense of attachment to his native place, the younger Satō appears far more at ease in a sophisticated, urbane environment.

For Shimazaki Tōson, Tokyo was the place where he enjoyed literary success but also experienced profound personal suffering. Born into a wealthy peasant family in a mountainous area in what is now Nagano Prefecture, when he was eight he was sent to study in the capital. Even though he saw himself as a member of the Yoshimura family that looked after him in Tokyo so that he and the family's son Shigeru "grew up almost as brothers,"[1] he nevertheless keenly felt the separation from his true parents. In Tōson's loosely autobiographical novel, *Sakura no mi no juku suru made* (When the Cherries Blossom, 1919), for example, letters would come from the country home to the young boy, Kishimoto, saying that things were bad at home and that he should study hard in Tokyo:

> Privation and hardship had seemed natural to him. He was never for a day able to forget his profound desire to keep other people in good humor and to find happiness for himself. The willfulness of other youths who sat at their parents' knees and were able to do just as they liked was unknown to him.[2]

The boy can never completely forget the barrier between himself and his adopted family. Deprived of what he sees as an unself-conscious intimacy between parents and their offspring, the boy is forced to seek fulfillment on a more personal level. One of Tōson's main impulses as a writer, too, emerges from a desire to "find happiness for himself" as he tries to overcome his initial dislocation, by reinventing the native place as a textual representation.

The main characters of two of Tōson's important works, *Hakai* (The Broken Commandment, 1906) and *Ie* (The Family, 1910–11), are teachers in the rural district close to Tōson's hometown. And this parallels Tōson's life: he left Tokyo in 1899 to teach for six years at a school in Komoro, Nagano Prefecture. In *The Broken Commandment*, the teacher, named Ushimatsu, is unable to become a full member of the rural community because of his *eta* (outcast) background. Sankichi, the teacher in *The Family*, enjoys country life, but the lack of intellectual stimulation from his city friends is one of the reasons finally drawing him back to Tokyo. In both novels, Tōson depicts an inability to become fully integrated into the rural site, just as he himself was unable to fully "know" the countryside of his youth after many years of living apart in the city, except through the process of his own literary production.

Tōson's early experiences also lend a sense of seriousness to his later literary endeavors. If he wrote his novels partly in order to compensate for a feeling of loss, his work was also involved in the important task of moving away from the older classical language. Classical Japanese was regarded by many writers of the time, particularly the group known as Naturalists, as incapable of articulating the new conditions of modern life, and they preferred to experiment with what they felt were more effective forms of written language closer to colloquial speech. A result of these experiments is Tōson's series of short verbal landscape portraits, *Chikumagawa no suketchi* (Chikuma River Sketches), written during his stay in Komoro but not published until 1912. Tōson's preoccupation with the big literary problems of the day also had serious consequences for the well-being of his own family. When he returned to Tokyo from Komoro in 1905 and devoted himself wholeheartedly to the last stages of writing *The Broken Commandment*, he lost three daughters in a single year, which can be partly attributed to the family's desperate poverty.[3]

Satō Haruo's experience in the capital could not have been more different. The first time he left for Tokyo from his hometown of Shingō, Wakayama Prefecture, was as a boy of fifteen in 1909. The reason was a desire to escape what he felt to be the provincialism of his school, which had suspended him after he delivered a speech on the "controversial" topic of Naturalism. Though only brief, this trip allowed Satō to begin what would become a long-term cordial relationship with a major figure of literary Tokyo at that time, Ikuta Chōkō (1882–1936). Satō returned to the capital the following year to continue his studies, at the First High School and later in the French literature department of Keiō gijuku, then directed by Nagai Kafū.[4]

Satō was not a particularly industrious student, and he left Keiō in 1914 before graduating. His main interest during the early years of this second stay was his own writing and translation of poetry, and he became familiar with other poets such as Yosano Tekkan (1873–1935) and Horiguchi Daigaku (1892–1981). The stories we hear about Satō seem to indicate a highly idiosyncratic writer who did not take life as seriously as Tōson did. He stood out from others during his university days, for instance, by walking around in a red Turkish fez and velvet suit making acerbic comments in the vein of one of his favorite writers, Oscar Wilde.[5] Clearly, Tōson and Satō present two very different images despite their shared provincial origins: the intensely serious writer battling against all odds to finish his work versus the exotic aesthete. But this difference cannot be attributed simply to personal fate or personality. Rather, it points to a major shift in the underlying moods of the Meiji and Taishō periods. To understand this change, we must examine some of the broader transformational trends in society.

By 1912, the Meiji emperor was dead, and figuratively speaking, there was no one to replace him. Rumors that after reading an imperial rescript, the new emperor of the Taishō period would roll it into a "telescope" to peer at his surrounding audience[6] suggest a very different ruler from that of the young Meiji leader of the 1868 Restoration, described in Tōson's *Before the Dawn* as sweeping along the highway from the old imperial center of Kyoto to take up residence in the new capital of Tokyo.[7] Of course, the dynamism of the Meiji emperor was part of the state authorities' careful image-building process that helped establish him as a symbol for a modernizing and increasingly imperialistic nation. Yet there was a certain factual basis for linking the vitality of the person of the emperor himself to the well-being of the state. He actively promoted the ideal of empire by visiting the troops in Hiroshima during the Sino-Japanese War of 1894–95, and even in the 1904–5 Russo-Japanese War the Meiji emperor was perceived as having remained an aloof but concerned presence.[8] In this sense, "Meiji's personality fitted the needs of a heroic age," whereas the Taishō emperor, said to have been mentally debilitated by a bout of meningitis as a youth, "would not affect the office he occupied."[9] Instead, it was the office of the emperor itself that was given precedence during Taishō while the unbecoming personal traits of the emperor were kept hidden as far as possible from the public gaze.

Even though it may be argued that the need to conceal an emperor in order to maintain the dignity of his office represents a diminution of the age compared with Meiji, this resort to illusory techniques in Taishō also highlights it as a time when the disparities between what was and what seemed to be came forcefully to the fore. And it was precisely in these cracks between the surface and the subterranean reality that the seeds of doubt and self-questioning among concerned writers of the day took root. In this sense, Taishō stood for a new and significantly expanded stratum of critical awareness.

In the last stages of the Meiji period, there were several indications that the general intellectual atmosphere might become more oppressive in the future. Katō Shūichi notes that two events of 1910 stand out as indicative of the government's thinking after the Russo-Japanese War: One is Japan's seizure of Korea, which signaled the strength of its imperialist ambitions abroad, and the other is the government's arrest of several left-wing activists and their trial and execution the following year, which showed that subversive elements would not be tolerated at home.[10] Therefore, as the Taishō period was about to dawn, it looked as if curtains were being pulled around political expectations, just as they would cover the deficiencies of the new emperor's mental state. Heroes, imperial or otherwise, were seen as belonging to an earlier age, and the trick now required of government was to maintain and strengthen its own political power through an imperial authority that depended partly on the mere illusion of a strong personal imperial presence. On the other hand, the significance of such events should not be overemphasized and certainly do not add up to some general closing down of hope. Indeed, the Taishō period is best known for its progressive features such as the growth of political party organizations, universal male suffrage, union activity, and other elements frequently referred to under the general term "Taishō democracy."

In any case, such tensions, which have been identified as the conflict of "civilization, self, and society,"[11] were not unknown in the Meiji period, either. The death by suicide in 1894 of the poet and essayist Kitamura Tōkoku (1868–94), whose early disappointment with political action led him to a particularly inward-looking form of Christianity, "marked the end of the career of a man who had done much to develop in his readers an expansive idea of the nature and role of the self."[12] The works of another writer, Natsume Sōseki (1867–1916), prefigured—and, indeed, helped shape—the questions addressed by the following generation of Taishō writers. The problem of balancing the needs of the individual and society, which he took up in his famous 1914 lecture "Watakushi no kojinshugi" (My Individualism), was also brilliantly articulated in novelistic form in works such as *Kokoro*, written in the same year.

In a slightly earlier novel, *Sore kara* (And Then, 1909), Sōseki traces the gradually deteriorating relationship between the principal character, Daisuke, and his erstwhile close university friend, Hiraoka. Whereas Daisuke has come to see himself as a "dandy,"[13] his friend has chosen the path of the business world. Daisuke senses that Hiraoka was probably involved in some shady dealings while working in a Kansai bank, but he cannot be bothered to take it too seriously:

> Daisuke, who lived in twentieth-century Japan, Daisuke, who had barely reached the age of thirty, had already arrived at the province of *nil admirari*. His thinking was hardly so unsophisticated as to be shocked by an encounter with the darker side of man. His senses were hardly so wearied as to take pleasure in sniffing at the hackneyed secrets Hiraoka might harbor. Or from another angle, one might say they were so fatigued that stimuli many times more pleasurable could not have satisfied them.[14]

Daisuke displays a sense of inner exhaustion and detachment from the world entirely removed from the spirit of Meiji characterized by the vigorous call for "national wealth and military strength" (*fukoku kyōhei*). In fact, during the novel, Daisuke is gradually drawn into a form of engagement with the world through his romantic entanglement with Hiraoka's wife, Michiyo. Nevertheless, the closing section—in which having broken his ties with his family for the sake of this married woman, Daisuke dashes off almost mad into the burning summer heat so that his head "began to spin around and around, breathing tongues of fire"[15]—suggests that it is by no means certain that this hypersensitive youth will survive in the "real" world.

Sōseki wrote this novel in 1909, which places it formally in the Meiji period, yet he prefigured the moody introverted kind of youth that would later be associated with Taishō. This indicates that the process of stepping back with a critical gaze, of weighing the gains and losses of the Meiji period—a sure sign that the age was over or at least was coming to an end—had begun even before the Taishō emperor ascended the throne. Harry Harootunian describes how the very fact that "Japan was, by the first decade of the twentieth century, a 'modern' nation" created its own difficulties: "An older model of society, which had achieved its goals, was failing to satisfy new demands, new needs, and to accommodate new social constituencies which the success of earlier policies had now made possible."[16]

There was an important sea change in the general mood just after one of those very "goals"—a military strong enough to be respected by other nations of the world—had been attained: Japan's victory in 1905 in the Russo-Japanese War. The frequently cited slogan of the Meiji period, "establish oneself and make it in the world" (*risshin shusse*), had always contained a useful ambiguity for those who sought advancement, in that personal interest could be placed within the more honorable aim of furthering the greater glory of the state. The postwar period, however, saw the rise of "enterprise fever" (*jitsugyō netsu*),[17] that is, a preoccupation with purely personal financial success—*seikō*, another catchword of the time—without any concern for wider national interests.[18] The feeling was that the time of individual sacrifice was over and people should begin to enjoy the benefits of their earlier efforts.

Among the "social constituency" of intellectuals, meanwhile, a similar reorientation was taking place. Sōseki had already expressed anxiety that the low status of writers in Meiji meant that they were incapable of looking after themselves in the modern world. This was a matter of real concern because only financial freedom would allow for artistic individuality.[19] Perhaps the last great writer to play the role of social critic while also being in "useful" employment in society—the ideal, at least, of the Confucian scholar of the Edo period—was Mori Ōgai, who was the surgeon general of the Japanese army as well as a writer. By contrast, most present-day writers struggled merely to survive, as shown in the case of Tōson.

Earl Kinmonth describes how a new group of youths—the "anguished youth" (*hanmon seinen*) or the "decadent youth" (*tandeki seinen*)—voiced their opposition to their classmates who sought financial success (*seikō seinen*—"success youth").[20] He locates this rejection of worldly ambition less in a vague loss of purpose after the war or a breakdown in the traditional family than in the practical difficulty of finding meaningful and satisfying employment in the workplace, so that many educated youths, turning inward in search of satisfaction, were led to redefine risshin shusse in terms of a "romantic pursuit of self-fulfillment."[21] This student anguish was exacerbated by the increasing difficulty of entering high school from middle school and the corresponding fear of real failure. By 1902, only one in ten were admitted, and this soon decreased to one in twenty.[22]

It was this profound generational shift of attitudes and ambitions, related to changing roles and expectations of writers in society, that set Satō Haruo apart from Shimazaki Tōson. Tōson was writing some of his major works just as the Taishō period was about to begin, but his formative years were firmly located in the Meiji period when he struggled as best he could to reconcile what often seemed the unreconcilable forces of "traditional" Japan and modernity brought in from the West. When *The Family* was published in 1911, Tōson was already thirty-nine years old.

Satō, on the other hand, was only nineteen in the same year and had just begun to search out like-minded young people with literary ambitions in Tokyo, many of whom were less concerned with the "big" questions of tradition and modernity than with ways to validate their inner selves to compensate for a feeling that the great Meiji enterprise no longer met their personal needs. This prevailing atmosphere of intellectual introversion had a lasting influence on Satō's creative responses to the world around him when he came of age as a writer.

Raymond Williams suggests that each generation has a common set of "characteristic approaches and tones in argument" that makes possible its distinctive culture. This "structure of feeling," as Williams calls it, is not something that can be formally learned:

> One generation may train its successor, with reasonable success, in the social character or the general cultural pattern, but the new generation will have its own structure of feeling, which will not appear to have come "from" anywhere. For here, most distinctly, the changing organization is enacted in the organism: the new generation responds in its own ways to the unique world it is inheriting, taking up many continuities, that can be traced, and reproducing many aspects of the organization, which can be separately described, yet feeling its whole life in certain ways differently, and shaping its creative response into a new structure of feeling.[23]

If the generational worlds of Tōson and Satō were experienced "in certain ways differently," Sōseki might be seen as a kind of bridge between the two. In Sōseki's novel *And Then*, Daisuke replies to Hiraoka's accusation that he does not participate as much as he should in society because he is unable to accept the "world-as-it's-given":

> Of course, if Japanese society were in sound spiritual, moral, and physical health—if it were just in all-around good health, then I'd still be talented and promising, don't you see? Because then there would be plenty of incentive to shake me out of my inclination to just loaf. But as things are, it's no good. I'd rather be alone. As for your so-called world-as-it's-given, I'll take it as it is and content myself with having contact with just those things that are most suited to me. To go out and bring other people around to my way of thinking—that's something that can't be done.[24]

Although Daisuke's "loafing" identifies him in Hiraoka's eyes as one of the "decadent youth" who looks on passively while the "real" world goes by, his stated preference that he would "rather" be alone suggests a more determined choice to disassociate himself as far as possible from the perceived shoddiness of modern society. What is more, his own stance is an oblique criticism of Hiraoka, who has become desensitized to the real conditions of life as he aims for monetary "success." For Daisuke, to accept things as they are with anything more than resignation would be a denial of his only reliable source of strength, that is, his self-questioning and inner search.

Sōseki himself made a similar decision to place himself at the margins of society. In 1911, he refused the doctor of letters degree offered to him by the Ministry of Education, much to its amazement.[25] In addition, he would not participate in the Committee on Literature (Bungei iinkai) set up by the government in May of the same year to monitor literary works.[26] While the government was seeking a "spiritual restoration" (*seishinteki ishin*) to rechannel and control what it saw as the negative tendencies of youths after 1905,[27] Sōseki realized that the successful " 'modern' nation" described by Harootunian was now too complex to be directed entirely from the state level. Like Daisuke, he needed to carve out a more personal space for himself.

An echo can be detected here in the way that Ushimatsu, the main character of *Broken Commandment*, was forced to stand apart from the society in which he found himself. The difference is that Sōseki's character, like the author himself, had no desire to be part of a sham and consciously chose to stand outside. Tōson, on the other hand, articulates through Ushimatsu a yearning to relocate his lost rural world, even if in an idealized form, because it still retains the attractive aura of the "real thing." The somewhat ridiculous denouement of *Broken Commandment*—the hero, his eta background exposed, leaves the country for life as a cowboy in Texas!—shows the author's enormous difficulty in trying to integrate the contradictory pieces of his world. In Sōseki's story, Daisuke's realization that changing other people is "something that can't be done" likewise brings no comfort. Though both speak with a deeply sympathetic understanding of their own generation, Sōseki goes further as he gropes for a position of tenuous and somewhat antagonistic individuality on the edges of society and, in the process, feels his way anxiously toward an identification with the concerns of the coming age. In this way, he stands at the point of transition from one "structure of feeling" to another.

But if Sōseki's anxieties and hopes quite literally trace the cutting edge between Meiji and Taishō, Satō is most certainly a man of civilization (*bunmei*) rather than culture (*bunka*)—two other terms frequently used to differentiate the two periods—and he already accepts as natural the conditions of everyday life that were a source of such painful contradiction to Tōson. This is seen most clearly in Satō's easier handling of "Western" influences. Apart from his foreign clothes, his close association with Ikuta Chōkō meant that he had a personal interest in the translations of Western works for which that writer was famous, including his seminal 1911 publication of *Also sprach Zarathustra*, and D'Annunzio's *Il Triumfo della morte* in 1913.[28] Satō himself translated Oscar Wilde, and the opening quotation in Satō's best-known work, *Den'en no yūutsu* (Rural Melancholy, 1919), shows his familiarity with Edgar Allen Poe.[29]

Satō's first short work to gain some attention in the literary world, "Supeinu inu no ie" (The House of the Spanish Dog, 1917), shows how far Western features had become part of his literary creativity. The story describes how the narrator and his dog come upon an isolated and vaguely Western-looking house deep in the woods. Curious, the narrator "tries knocking in the Western manner on the Western-style door." No one is in, but when he peers through the window, he sees a stone basin in the middle of the room from which water gushes onto the stone floor, more reminiscent of an enclosed Spanish courtyard than the inside of a Japanese house. Unable to contain himself, he enters and notices a clock decorated with the moving figures of a Western man and woman, as well as some books written in German on the table. A black Spanish dog is lying in the room, and afraid that it might bite him, the narrator leaves. When he looks back in through the window, he is amazed to see the dog transform itself into a middle-aged man in a black suit.

These Spanish touches and the gloomy atmosphere reminiscent of a German fairy tale, all in a Japanese location, suggest that Satō's perception of his world depended on an eclectic mixture of influences drawn freely from his readings of Western literature, as much as any from "traditional" Japan. Moreover, when it first appeared in a magazine, the fact that Satō described the piece as a "short story for people who like to feel as if they are dreaming"[30] indicates that this patching together of diverse elements had created a sense of unreality in the Japanese psyche, as much as it represents the shift among Taishō writers to depict the imaginative impulses of the mind. In any case, although the story's mysterious quality hints that this is a world in which the writer does not feel entirely comfortable—the narrator is forced out of the dreamlike house by the threat of being bitten—the Western elements are the familiar features he most readily draws on to give literary shape to that unease.

Something else that differentiates Satō from Tōson is his rejection of the earlier writer's seriousness. Tōson's identification with a new, leaner literary style—what his friend Tayama Katai described as "naked description" (*rokotsu naru byōsha*)[31]—was partly a response to the challenge by the critic Tsubouchi Shōyō (1859–1935) in his highly influential 1885 essay *Shōsetsu shinzui* (Essence of the Novel), to reject the "frivolous" late-Edo *gesaku* writings for works with a more serious intent, in keeping with the tone of Meiji.[32] Tōson's writings, as I have already described them, frequently dealt with the tragic reality of physical upheavals, especially in relation to his hometown. Satō, on the other hand, identified far more closely with the urbane writings linked to the Edo period and their emphasis on aesthetics and a well-crafted literary style.

A personal influence on Satō's literary development while he was still at Keiō was Nagai Kafū in the French department. Having only recently returned from France, Kafū was in the process of turning away from what he felt to be the ugliness of modern Japanese life and beginning to seek out the pleasurable aspects (as he saw them) of the fading Edo ambience. In his story, "Reishō" (Derision, 1909–10), for instance, the narrator Yoshino takes a walk among some old temple grave stones and notices that they are engraved with memorial haiku poems:

> He realized how much the men of Edo had sought solace from the monotony of their actual lives through art. Leaving aside the question of the actual worth of the arts in that period, which were given the collective name of "refinement" [*fūryū*], they were afforded such a high position in the lives of Edo men that they were called "accomplishments appropriate to men of that status" [*mi no tashinami*] and were even considered a type of method toward character cultivation.[33]

Satō reveals a similar interest in the significance of "refinement" in people's daily lives in his article on the same subject, "Fūryū ron" (Concerning Refinement, 1924).[34] *Fūryū*, he believed, was an aesthetic sense almost impossible to express exactly in words, but its mystery was intuitively understood by all sensitive Japanese.[35] At a time when everyday Japanese reality was a bewildering mishmash of imported and native influences, Satō highlighted a shared source of pleasure inherited from "the lives of Edo men" as one of the few common experiences still available to people of his own time.

Satō's interest in the easygoing mood of the Edo dilettante, the *tsū*, together with the light wit that he found congenial in the works of Oscar Wilde, are partly a reaction against the austere instincts of writers identified with the Naturalist movement, like Tōson, for whom the very "frivolous" nature of Edo writings rendered them useless. But there is, perhaps, more than simply personal preference in Satō's self-identification with this particularly city-based aesthetic culture, despite his own provincial origins. Although he was "newly arrived" to Tokyo as Tōson had once been, Satō's own hometown of Shingō was located fairly close to the mountainous area of Yoshino south of Nara, the site of Emperor Go-Daigo's (1288–1339) exile during the struggle for imperial legitimacy in the fourteenth-century period of the Southern and Northern Courts (*nanboku chō*). This somewhat tenuous historical link to the imperial family, even if to the branch that was ultimately defeated (although recognized by the modern state as the legitimate line), gave the following generations inhabiting the area a sense that they were not simply run-of-the-mill provincials. In addition, his "aristocratic" background meant that Satō could identify more readily with the conservative literary elements of Tokyo than could his often more "rustic" Naturalist counterparts.

Satō's concern with the "less serious" aspects of life also led to a less dramatic break with his father's generation than that shown by Tōson. His own interest with fūryū is undoubtedly related to the emergence of dandyism in late Meiji, already depicted by Sōseki in his characterization of Daisuke, to signal a rejection of society's ills as well as social conformism imposed by the government.[36] The internal "cultivation" (*kyōyō*) linked by Kafū to Edo-period fūryū and apparent in Satō's inward-looking "House of the Spanish Dog" was, moreover, vigorously taken up and pursued in Taishō by a number of writers and represents a turning away from the former Meiji generation's interest in broader issues. But Satō's self-questioning does not add up to a social critique of the same hard-hitting intensity displayed by Naturalists calling for the destruction of all artifice in literature. In *Rural Melancholy*, for instance, Satō presents a narrator who resembles the sensation-weary Daisuke as he muses wistfully that "there is nothing new under the sun."[37] He considers the difficulty of overcoming his feeling of ennui:

The only way to live anew in this old, old world was to bring about a total transformation of his own state of mind. He realized this, but how, by what method, could he make something fresh of himself in his present condition? What did his father, in his angry letter, mean by the expression "great courage and a valiant heart" [*taiyū mōshin*]? Where could he draw it from, and how could he plant it in his own heart? How was it possible to stir up his heart? He had no idea how this could be accomplished.[38]

Like the term "national wealth and military strength" (*fukoku kyōhei*), the expression used by the father is another imposing four-character Chinese phrase, and with its clearly articulated aims, it places him firmly in the Meiji period. The narrator does not react violently to such advice, however; indeed, he is trying his best to find a way out of his own impasse. It is just that he does not understand any more what his father's words really mean.

But if Satō seemed no longer to understand the rules of society compared with those of the Naturalists who sought to change them, Isoda Kōichi points out that Satō's very inability to comprehend reflects an equally profound, if less strident, transformation of consciousness. He detects this change specifically in Satō's attitude toward the death of General Nogi, a loyal servant of the Meiji emperor who followed his master into death in 1912 by means of ritual disembowelment (*seppuku*) to compensate for having lost the imperial banner during the 1877 Satsuma Rebellion:

> While sympathizing with the drama of idealism observable in Nogi, such sympathy [by Satō] seems not to have been so much for the content of those ideals. Rather, it was directed to the loftiness that produced self-sacrifice to an ideal or to the tragic element brought about by the purification of passion. This different quality of feeling compared with Sōseki and Ōgai is nothing less than a transformation of sensibility separating the literatures of Taishō and Meiji.[39]

By late Meiji, such an act appeared as both the last flicker of a more heroic samurai age and an anachronism in modern Japan. The problem for even those of a slightly older generation to come to terms with these two elements is a major theme of Sōseki's *Kokoro*, in which the troubled Sensei, himself a man of Meiji, could not "fully understand why General Nogi killed himself."[40] But for Satō, who himself found it impossible to "stir up his heart," Nogi's enormous determination to wait thirty-five years in order to display his loyalty brings Satō's admiration, even if the "content of those ideals," like the content of his own father's Chinese phrases, is beyond his comprehension.

This "transformation of sensibility" relates to Williams's shift in "structure of feeling" discussed earlier. Isoda goes further, however, by specifying the nature of Satō's new sensibility as the product of an "emotional revolution" (*kanjō kakumei*) that is given form in his story *Rural Melancholy*. Isoda notes that the usual Japanese translation of the English term "industrial revolution"—an extremely important aspect of modernizing Japan at the time—is usually *sangyō kakumei*, with *sangyō* describing the idea of industrial production. He suggests the use of another Japanese word, *kinben*, to highlight the less frequently noticed English element of industriousness or earnestness. And the Japanese critic goes on to outline a shift in eighteenth-century Europe from the negative connotations of heavy "melancholy," one of the four bodily fluids in the medieval period, to its emergence as a positive element, as a sign of heightened sensitivity in opposition to the earnest (kinben) utilitarianism of industrialization.

In the same way, Satō's use of melancholy in *Rural Melancholy* may be seen as part of a process whereby the value of the emotional life takes precedence over the utilitarianism of modern Japan. Far from being a sign of passive indifference to the times, then, Satō's writing gives shape to a powerful new sensibility to confront the failings of his father's generation, as well as what is for him the excessive earnestness of the Naturalists. In this sense, Satō represents a new and extremely important phase in the modernization of Japanese literary and intellectual life.[41]

Between Meiji and Taishō, there is a shift among writers like Satō from the larger structure of external events to the inner space of doubt and self-questioning, a process that, as we have seen, started earlier, at least from the time of the Russo-Japanese War. Although I have used Tōson and Satō as representatives of their respective ages, it would be foolish to claim that all people of that generation shared exactly the same feelings or, indeed, to claim that either of the writers can be reduced to the rather simplistic oppositional binarism that I have suggested. Such an approach is nevertheless a valuable starting point from which to examine the more subtle complex of changes that undoubtedly arose as distinguishing markers between one generation and the next.

NOTES

1. Shimazaki Tōson, *Chikuma River Sketches*, trans. William E. Naff (Honolulu: University of Hawaii Press, 1991), p. 3.

2. Shimazaki Tōson, *Tōson zenshū* (Tokyo: Chikuma shobō, 1966–71), vol. 5, p. 492.

3. Shimazaki Tōson, *The Family*, trans. Cecilia Segawa Seigle (Tokyo: Tokyo University Press, 1976), p. xi.

4. Donald Keene, *Dawn to theWest: Japanese Literature of the Modern Era (Fiction)* (NewYork: Holt, Rinehart and Winston, 1984), pp. 631–33.

5. Ibid., p. 636.

6. Yanagida Izumi et al., eds., *Zadankai Taishō bungakushi* (Tokyo: Iwanami shoten, 1965), p. 10.

7. Tōson, *Tōson zenshū*, vol. 12, p. 112.

8. Carol Gluck, *Japan's Modern Myths* (Princeton, NJ: Princeton University Press, 1985), p. 88.

9. H. D. Harootunian, "A Sense of Ending and the Problem of Taishō," in Bernard S. Silberman and H. D. Harootunian, eds., *Japan in Crisis: Essays in Taishō Democracy* (Princeton, NJ: Princeton University Press, 1974), p. 7.

10. Katō Shūichi, *A History of Japanese Literature: The Modern Years*, vol. 3, trans. Don Sanderson (NewYork: Kodansha International, 1990), p. 191.

11. Thomas J. Rimer, ed., *Culture and Identity: Japanese Intellectuals During the Interwar Years* (Princeton, NJ: Princeton University Press, 1990), p. 3.

12. Ibid., p. 3.

13. Natsume Sōseki, *And Then*, trans. Norma Moore Field (Baton Rouge: Louisiana State University Press, 1978), p. 3.

14. Ibid., pp. 18–19.

15. Ibid., p. 257.

16. Harootunian, "A Sense of Ending," p. 4.

17. Earl H. Kinmonth, *The Self-Made Man in Meiji Japanese Thought: From Samurai to Salary Man* (Berkeley and Los Angeles: University of California Press, 1981), p. 161.

18. Ibid., p. 158.

19. Minami Hiroshi, *Taishō bunka* (Tokyo: Keisō shobō, 1965), p. 42.

20. Kinmonth, *Self-Made Man*, p. 206.

21. Ibid., p. 212.

22. Ibid., p. 216.

23. Raymond Williams, *The Long Revolution* (New York: Columbia University Press, 1961), p. 49.

24. Sōseki, *And Then*, p. 73.

25. Keene, *Dawn to the West*, p. 332.

26. Senuma Shigeki, *Taishō bungakushi* (Tokyo: Kōdansha, 1985), p. 19.

27. Minami, *Taishō bunka*, p. 48.

28. Other works he translated include *Salambō* (1913), *Das Kapital* (1920), and *The Odyssey* (1922). Keene, *Dawn to the West*, p. 632.

29. Satō Haruo, *Den'en no yūutsu* (Tokyo: Shinchōsha, 1919), p. 2.

30. Keene, *Dawn to the West*, p. 634.

31. Tayama Katai, *Rokotsu naru byōsha*, in vol. 9 of *Gendai Nihon bungaku zenshū* (Tokyo: Chikuma shobō, 1956), pp. 391–93.

32. Keene, *Dawn to the West*, p. 101.

33. Nagai Kafū, *Kafū zenshū* (Tokyo: Iwanami shoten, 1971–74), vol. 4, pp. 310–11.

34. Satō Haruo, *Jisen Satō Haruo zenshū* (Tokyo: Kawade shobō, 1956–58), vol. 9, pp. 85–122.

35. Ibid., p. 90.

36. Harootunian, "A Sense of Ending," p. 20.

37. Satō, *Den'en no yūutsu,* p. 59.

38. Ibid., p. 60.

39. Isoda Kōichi, *Rokumeikan no keifu* (Tokyo: Bungei shunjū, 1984), p. 179.

40. Natsume Sōseki, *Kokoro*, trans. Edwin McClellan (Tokyo: Tuttle, 1978), p. 246.

41. Isoda Kōichi, "Aru kanjō kakumei—Satō Haruo 'Tokai no Yūutsu' ni tsuite," in Isoda Kōichi, *Kindai no kanjō kakumei: Sakkaron shū* (Tokyo: Shinchōsha, 1987), pp. 88–97.

17

Tsubouchi Shōyō on Chikamatsu and Drama

◉

MICHAEL C. BROWNSTEIN

Modern studies of the puppet theater began in 1890 with a handful of essays on the plays of Chikamatsu Monzaemon (1653–1725) by the novelist, playwright, and critic Tsubouchi Shōyō (1859–1935). Three of the essays were on *Shinjū ten no Amijima* (The Love Suicides at Amijima), *Onnagoroshi abura jigoku* (The Woman Killer and the Hell of Oil), and *Meido no hikyaku* (The Courier for Hell). The fourth, "Chikamatsu no jōruri, Chikamatsu ga jojishi no tokushitsu" (Chikamatsu's Puppet Plays and the Characteristics of Chikamatsu's Epics), was an overview. All four appeared in print in 1891–92[1] and served as a point of departure for the Chikamatsu kenkyūkai (Chikamatsu study group) that Shōyō formed in 1894.

I confine my remarks in this chapter to the 1890 essays, the circumstances that led Shōyō to write them, and how his literary views reflect what H. D. Harootunian characterized as "the crisis of political consciousness and conscience that marked Japan's passage into modernity."[2]

Shōyō's fondness for the kabuki theater and the popular fiction of the late Edo period in his youth may account for why both fiction and drama figured prominently in his early career. When his interests turned to Western literature after entering Tokyo University in 1878, he translated Shakespeare's *Julius Caesar*, using the rhythms of kabuki-stage language, as well as Scott's *The Bride of*

Lammermoor. In a well-known episode, Shōyō failed an examination on which he was asked to analyze the character Gertrude in *Hamlet*. This prompted him to begin studying Western literary criticism, which resulted in the influential book *Shōsetsu shinzui* (The Essence of the Novel, 1885). There, Shōyō treats drama and fiction as historically rival modes of representation. His argument for the superiority of the novel over the romance and premodern drama, however, derives from comparisons of mid-nineteenth-century English fiction with kabuki performances, on the one hand, and an evolutionary conception of human behavior, on the other. That is, both drama and fiction moved away from the fantastic and the supernatural toward the realistic depiction of "human emotions and social conditions" (*ninjō setai*), but in the "dark ages" of the uncivilized past,

> human nature was not the same as today. In general, whether pleased or angry, happy or sad, when people were highly agitated, the Seven Emotions appeared spontaneously in their behavior and facial expressions and could be seen by anyone. . . . Therefore, since human emotions and social conditions in those days were completely visible on the surface and not difficult to depict, the more common ones were portrayed even in their various romances and offered for the amusement of readers. But there must have been many human emotions and social conditions that less talented writers of that time found difficult to describe vividly. It is the drama of such an age that excels in showing us the full range of human feelings and customs in all their detail.[3]

Although human nature did not change, according to Shōyō, "as human intellect advanced, people endeavored to restrain their feelings to keep them from appearing on the outside," so that there now exists "a dichotomy between external actions and thoughts hidden within." Since drama did not kept pace with these changes, it gradually lost its value as a "mirror of the age." The novel is therefore better suited to modern times because it could describe things that could not be presented on stage; its greater breadth and depth permitted a writer to paint a more comprehensive picture of society and to reveal subtle differences among similar personalities.[4]

Shōyō tried to put his theory of the novel into practice, first with *Tōsei shosei katagi* (The Character of Present-Day Students, 1885). *Imotose kagami* (A Mirror of Marriage) and *Matsu no uchi* (The New Year Season) followed in 1886 and 1888. With the publication of *Saikun* (Wife) in January 1889, however, Shōyō gave up trying to write fiction and turned instead to criticism and the theater. By the end of the year, he had accepted an invitation to write the literary column for the *Yomiuri* newspaper and joined the newly formed Nihon engei kyōkai (Japan performing arts society). In February 1890 Shōyō moved into a new house in Ushigome, where he began meeting with some half-dozen students from Tōkyō senmon gakkō (Tokyo school of special studies, now Waseda University) to help them with their Shakespeare studies. He wanted them to learn how to analyze Shakespeare's plays but felt that until they were knowledgeable enough to do this on their own, they could write practice analyses on something more familiar and suggested they try Chikamatsu's *sewamono* (domestic dramas).[5] The essays that I am discussing here were written for this group, Shōyō's own practice analyses that deepened his appreciation of Chikamatsu and led to further studies.

It is difficult to say with certainty how familiar Shōyō was before this with either the texts of Chikamatsu's plays or the puppet theater. He does not refer to Chikamatsu by name in *The Essence of the Novel*, although some of the plays he cites were kabuki versions of Chikamatsu plays he probably attended. Woodblock editions of the original librettos were undoubtedly scarce at the beginning of the Meiji period. But new, movable-type editions, called "Musashiya books," after their publisher, started appearing in 1881, and more than fifty plays were published in the next ten years.[6] Because of the long decline since its heyday in the mid-eighteenth century, performances of puppet theater were largely confined to Osaka. In the fall of 1885, however, a troupe featuring the chanter Koshijidayū II (1836–1917) appeared for two months at a new puppet theater in Tokyo. Koshijidayū returned from Osaka in March 1890, this time to the Yose variety theater, where for seven months he gave recitals without puppets to enthusiastic audiences.[7] Between the new editions of Chikamatsu's plays and the crowd-pleasing recitals that spring and summer, a "*jōruri* (puppet play) revival" was then very much in the air when Shōyō suggested to his Shakespeare students that they sharpen their analytical skills on Chikamatsu's plays.

Shōyō wanted his students to apply what he called the "new criticism" (*shinshiki hihyō*) of Richard G. Moulton, Edward Dowden, and other Shakespeare scholars he had studied. The introduction to Moulton's *Shakespeare as a Dramatic Artist*, published in 1885, is subtitled "Plea for an Inductive Science of Literary Criticism." Moulton argues against the "judicial criticism" of his day in favor of an Aristotelian "criticism of investigation":

> The one is the enquiry into what ought to be, the other the enquiry into what is. Judicial criticism compares a new production with those already existing in order to determine whether it is inferior to them or surpasses them; criticism of investigation makes the same comparison for the purpose of identifying the new prod-

uct with some type in the past, or differentiating it and registering a new type. Judicial criticism has a mission to watch against variations from received canons; criticism of investigation watches for new forms to increase its stock of species. The criticism of taste analyses literary works for grounds of preference or evidence on which to found judgements; inductive criticism analyses them to get a closer acquaintance with their phenomena.[8]

Moulton's "inductive criticism" was thus primarily concerned with "differences of kind as distinguished from differences of degree" and "distinguishing literary species."[9] This is precisely the approach Shōyō took in "Chikamatsu's Puppet Plays," in which he tried to classify jōruri according to the Western categories of lyric, epic, and drama and to clarify the general characteristics of Chikamatsu's *jidaimono* (period pieces). "Some people," he argued, "regard jōruri as drama (or translate 'drama' as 'jōruri') and consider Chikamatsu's works to be drama, but that is erroneous. Jōruri are properly considered a kind of verse novel, that is, a kind of epic."[10]

Of course, Shōyō recognized the dramatic qualities of jōruri, but the lack of a prologue and an epilogue and the presence of a narrator (the *tayū*) who comments on the action in addition to reciting all the dialogue were formal aspects that kept Shōyō from considering jōruri as true drama in the classical Western sense. Rather, he grouped Chikamatsu's period plays with *Beowulf* and the *Iliad* as stories about the past told in verse. This view may have been reinforced by Koshijidayū's solo recitals that year, if indeed Shōyō attended them.

On the other hand, Shōyō emphasized that one must consider jōruri as something to be seen and heard, not just as texts to be read, because Chikamatsu's "constant objective" was to appeal to the eyes and ears of his audiences. In this respect, Shōyō stressed that Chikamatsu's use of the vernacular and the various conventions of the puppet theater were designed to appeal to ignorant and illiterate commoners. He praised Chikamatsu as a master of the *wakan gazoku setchū*, a "mixed" style that combined classical language in the narrative with colloquial dialogue, and noted that "one can find in his works almost every figure of speech found in Western rhetorical manuals."[11]

"Chikamatsu's Puppet Plays" was probably the first essay in which Shōyō compared the Genroku-period playwright with Shakespeare, whose plays were superior, he felt, in part because he mistakenly believed that Shakespeare wrote only for the nobility, whereas Chikamatsu's audience came from the lower classes. Furthermore, their basic goals were different: Shakespeare, according to Shōyō, wanted to bring history alive, but jōruri for Chikamatsu was an art solely intended for aesthetic enjoyment, without regard for historical accuracy.

Dowden's *Shakespeare: A Critical Study of His Mind and Art* is an attempt to trace the growth of Shakespeare's "intellect and character, from youth to full maturity"[12] through an analysis of the characters in his plays. Shōyō's essays on *Amijima* and *Woman Killer*, however, show that he was less interested in reaching the mind of Chikamatsu through his characters than in analyzing them to show how their fates reveal "the law of cause and effect." In *The Essence of the Novel*, Shōyō had been rather vague on the relationship between personality and fate, stating that "success or failure are not necessarily a consequence of a person's nature."[13] Moreover, he advised,

> When creating a character and depicting his emotions, a writer first supposes that the character already has desires. He must plainly show his hidden depths, describing in great detail what the character feels when stimulated by such and such an incident, how such feelings influence his many other emotions, and how the nature of his occupation and prior education affect his emotional processes, to say nothing of his disposition.[14]

Needless to say, this excerpt offers a rather passive view of human nature, of characters reacting to circumstances rather than shaping them. Shōyō's essays on *Amijima* and *Woman Killer* offer a different perspective in that he emphasizes how the main characters change during the course of the plays, and by citing passages of dialogue, he tries to demonstrate their growing awareness of how their fate ultimately results not from impersonal forces but from flaws in their own emotional makeup.

In *Amijima*, for example, Shōyō speculates that when Jihei the paper store owner first met the prostitute Koharu, it was "love at first sight" (he uses the English expression), a purely physical attraction that became an irrational obsession. Koharu's feeling for Jihei, on the other hand, was not a blind passion but a discriminating, "rational" love based on her many experiences with men in the pleasure quarters and mixed with a certain pride based on her "strong sense of self" and "self-respect." This is seen in the way she rebukes Jihei's rival Tahei for spreading rumors about Jihei and in her promise to Jihei's wife Osan not to let Jihei kill himself.

Jihei awakens from his obsession with Koharu in stages marked by his blaming others before he finally acknowledges that all his troubles stem from his own heart. The first episode occurs in act 1, when he overhears Koharu's conversation with his brother and believes she has betrayed him. His blind love immediately turns to an equally blind hatred, and he curses her. The second such episode occurs in act 2, when Jihei begrudges his rival Tahei's freedom to ransom Koharu, only to learn from his wife Osan that Koharu did not deceive him and may kill herself. Although Osan urges him to redeem Koharu, he realizes what this would do to Osan and confesses: "Even if the punishment for my crimes against my parents, against Heaven, against the gods and the Buddhas fails to strike me, the punishment for my crimes against my wife alone will be sufficient to destroy all hope for my future life. Forgive me, I beg you."[15] At this point, Shōyō argues, Jihei is torn between *giri* (obligations) or "public feelings" (*kōjō*) and *ninjō* (emotions) or "private feelings" (*shijō*), that is, his love for Koharu combined with his obligation to save her, on the one hand, and, on the other, his love for his children and his sense of obligation toward his wife not to let her sacrifice herself.

In act 3, according to Shōyō, Jihei attains a kind of enlightenment. Waiting in the shadows for Koharu outside the Yamato house, he sees his brother Magoemon, accompanied by Jihei's son Kantarō and the servant Sangorō, and "cries out in his heart": "He cannot leave me to my death, though I am the worst of sinners! I remain to the last a burden to him! I'm unworthy of such kindness!" Later, as Jihei and Koharu make their way to Amijima, he comforts Koharu, declaring: "Our bodies are made of earth, water, fire, and wind, and when we die, they revert to emptiness. But our souls will not decay, no matter how often they are reborn. And here's a guarantee that our souls will be married and never part!" He then cuts off the top knot of his hair and declares: "I have fled the burning house of the three worlds of delusion; I am a priest, unencumbered by wife, children, or worldly possessions. Now that I no longer have a wife named Osan, you owe her no obligations either."

Shōyō points to this moment especially as evidence that Jihei and Koharu have changed places. Still clinging to her obligation to Osan, Koharu "confuses pride with duty." She has become "a fool" wandering on the edge of madness, her spirit unable to accept death even as her body is about to perish. Jihei, on the other hand, has gone "from lust to love, and from love to enlightenment," from being the passive victim of his own volatile emotions unaware of his obligations to one who acts decisively. Conscious of his sins, Jihei knows that "he must reap what he has sown."[16]

The essay on *Woman Killer* is the longest of the group. It centers on detailed character analyses of the wayward son Yohei and his stepfather Tokubei. Yohei's selfish and ultimately criminal behavior, Shōyō asserts, are the result of Tokubei's inability to rise above his former status as a clerk in the family business and carry out his responsibilities as a father. Yohei himself admits as much in act 2,[17] but Shōyō comments:

He is concerned with his obligations toward an individual person [his former master] and forgets his obligations to society. He devotes himself to his role as a servant and forgets his role as someone's parent. Though he knows that he must repay the kindness of his master, he errs in the way he should repay it.[18]

If Tokubei's flaw is a strong but misplaced sense of giri, Yohei's is an utter lack of it. Like Jihei in *Amijima*, Yohei also changes in the course of the play and attains a kind of enlightenment. In the end, Shōyō contends, Yohei realizes that there are other people in the world besides himself, that "selfish desires are unavoidable, that at the same time giri and ninjō are necessary, that there is right and wrong, and that retribution for one's deeds is inevitable." In his own summary at the end of the essay, Shōyō concludes that the play is about the conflict between "infinite personal desires and the finite word of society (the floating world of giri-ninjō)," between "society and a selfish person who does not know society."[19]

The impact of Shōyō's simultaneous reading of Chikamatsu and Shakespeare can be seen in the essays he wrote immediately afterward. In "Azusa miko" (The Catalpa-Bow Shaman), published in May 1891, he began referring to Chikamatsu as the "Shakespeare of Japan."[20] In "*Makubesu hōshaku no sogen*" (Preface to a Commentary on *Macbeth*), published the following October, Shōyō stated that the difference between Chikamatsu and Shakespeare was "one of degree, not kind" and that the two were comparable because their works "resembled nature" and not because the events depicted or the characters portrayed in their plays were "realistic."

Moreover, like nature, their plays were open to all kinds of interpretations, no one of which could ever exhaust their full meaning. In the same essay, Shōyō defined two kinds of literary criticism: one was a commentary on the language of the text—the meaning of words, grammar, and figures of speech—and the other Shōyō characterized using the English word *interpretation*, namely, an explication of the author's intent or the "ideals" found in the whole.[21] The latter kind of criticism describes Shōyō's approach in his essays on Chikamatsu's plays, but he apparently lacked the confidence to attempt the same with *Macbeth*. As he notes, effective "interpretation" depends on the critic's erudition and perceptiveness: "When done by someone of modest learning, there is the danger that he might mistake a cat for a tiger and lead ignorant readers into misunderstanding."[22] Shōyō was doubtless aware of the other uncertainties of "interpretation" that Moulton pointed out in connection with "Central Ideas":

The criticism that addresses itself to the function of interpreting literature was early attracted to the discovery of Central Ideas in plays and poems. For one thing, critics were found not to agree in their results: and, when different suggestions were put forward, each as a complete explanation of the same work, the suspicion naturally would arise that the interpreters had put into the plays the ideas which they professed to bring out of them. Moreover, a hasty use of terms led to the confusion between a "central idea" and a mere lesson, or reflection, derivable (with fifty others) from the course of a story, in the way in which an accomplished preacher will draw the whole gospel out of half a clause.[23]

Despite the confusion surrounding the notion, Moulton does argue for the "existence of some harmony binding together all varieties of detail into a unity" that can be formulated in words as a Central Idea. This idea "must be based, not upon the authority of the expounder, nor even on the beauty of the idea itself, but entirely upon the degree in which it associates itself with the details of which the play is made up."[24] One can detect here Moulton's influence on Shōyō's concept of *botsurisō* or "submerged ideals," a term that he first used in "The Catalpa-Bow Shaman" and again in "Preface to a Commentary on *Macbeth*" and that sparked his famous debate with Mori Ōgai, the so-called *botsurisō ronsō*, or "debate over hidden ideals."

Shōyō did not use the terms "central idea" or "submerged ideals" in his discussions of Chikamatsu's plays, but he clearly tried to connect their details in terms of a single conflict between giri and ninjō. His view of this conflict as the heart of Chikamatsu's plays has since become a critical commonplace, but it may have been suggested by Dowden's comment that "it is evident, not from one play, but from many, that the struggle between 'blood' and 'judgment' was a great affair of Shakespeare's life."[25] However appropriate and useful the giri–ninjō interpretation might seem, the possibility that he had, in Moulton's words, "put into the plays" the ideas that he had "professed to bring out of them" raises the issue of the historicity of interpretation. Shōyō himself was aware of the problem: through Moulton and other studies of Shakespeare, he learned that Shakespeare's reputation and the interpretations of his plays were shaped by centuries of scholarship and suggested that if Chikamatsu's works had been subject to the same process, his reputation would be far greater than it was then.[26] With this in mind, I now turn to the issues that may have influenced Shōyō's thinking and the impact of his study of Shakespeare and Chikamatsu on his views of contemporary fiction.

In his essay "Between Politics and Culture," H. D. Harootunian writes that "as early as the 1890's Japanese intellectuals began to record a sense of futility over the apparent separation of private and public, the destruction of politics as a means of mediation, and the meanings such an event might hold for a modernizing society." Their response was

a defense of the inner life as a means of arresting what they conceived to be the progressive shrinkage of the realm of private activity. The defense centered on the effort to dramatize the importance of the private realm as a necessary counterbalance to the world of public requirements. It dissolved into an acceptance of public requirements as a condition of the existence of the private realm and defining its content.[27]

I would add that this defense was a response not only to "the apparent separation of private and public" and "the destruction of politics as a means of mediation" but also to the failure of fiction to meet that challenge. Much of the literary criticism of that time—from Tokutomi Sohō's lament over the trivialization of the *seiji shōsetsu*, or "political novel," in July 1887, through the debate between Kitamura Tōkoku and Yamaji Aizan in the spring of 1893—testified to the fact that literature created under such circumstances seemed in danger of becoming irrelevant to both the public and the private. More specifically, this potential irrelevance was blamed on the "Saikaku revival" led by Ozaki Kōyō (1867–1903) and his Kenyūsha ("Friends of the inkwell") circle of young writers. In *The Essence of the Novel*, Shōyō had tried to show the way to modern Japanese fiction by pointing to the novels of George Eliot and other nineteenth-century British writers, but Ozaki Kōyō and Kōda Rohan (1867–1947) had discovered in the Genroku-period novelist Ihara Saikaku (1642–1693) a more congenial model of realism.[28] Shōyō himself was disappointed in this development. His interest in Shakespeare, his "discovery" of Chikamatsu, and the valorization of Chikamatsu as the "Shakespeare of Japan" can thus be seen as an effort to find an alternative model to Saikaku for modern Japanese fiction.

Moulton's argument against the "judicial criticism" of taste also coincided precisely with Shōyō's dissatisfaction with contemporary Japanese criticism, which seemed more concerned with evaluating fiction than with analyzing it. In "Shōsetsu sampa" (Three Schools of Fiction), published in December 1890, Shōyō analyzes four stories that appeared as he was writing his essays on Chikamatsu's plays for his Shakespeare study group.[29] Using Moulton's inductive criticism, Shōyō defines three categories of fiction, corresponding roughly to the epic, the lyric, and the drama, and he places the stories he reviews into the first two. Stories in the first category are "objective" and plot centered, and those in the second are "subjective" and character centered. The weakness of these stories and, by implication, current Japanese fiction in general, is the lack of character development or, if there were some depth to the characters, the absence of a causal relationship between the characters and the events that transpire. By contrast, Shōyō uses the English word *drama* to characterize the third school.

Although he is discussing fiction, Shōyō cites Shakespeare's plays as ideal examples in which character and plot are closely bound together, in which the main character's inner convictions and emotional conflicts are the primary "cause" (*in*) of a chain of events leading to the final "result" (*ga*). And although Shōyō cites only Shakespeare, behind the examples of *Macbeth, Hamlet, Julius Caesar,* and *Othello* that he gives in the essay lie Chikamatsu's *Amijima* and *Woman Killer.* As he wrote elsewhere: "Chikamatsu . . . took great care in depicting the clash between giri and ninjō; thus he always hid giri behind ninjō, put ninjō in the shadow of giri, and thereby wove characters and events together with the (invisible) thread of inevitable cause-and-effect."[30]

By using the term *drama* in this way, Shōyō was not advocating that Japanese writers should abandon fiction for the theater but, rather, was trying to identify the technical shortcomings of contemporary stories. It is also clear that Shōyō saw drama not in the narrow sense of plays but as a mode of narrative representation that integrated plot and character, the "objective" epic and the "subjective" lyric in a dynamic synthesis.[31]

The separation between public and private, individual and state, and the disappearance of politics as a means to mediate between them, was thus marked in literary circles by the decline of political fiction and the Saikaku revival. In Shōyō's literary criticism, this separation appears first in *The Essence of the Novel,* as a disassociation between inner thoughts and outward behavior that Shōyō believed characterized modern people. In Shōyō's reading of Chikamatsu's plays, it appears as a conflict within the protagonists between giri and ninjō: looking back at Chikamatsu's domestic dramas in this light, Shōyō sees characters who invited their own tragic ends because the depth and intensity of their "private" feelings blinded them to their sense of their "public" obligations and threatened to destroy the social fabric. In "Three Schools of Fiction," the gap between public and private appears as a difference between the plot-centered versus the character-centered narratives that Shōyō thought typified contemporary stories. In arguing for a narrative mode exemplified by both Shakespeare's and Chikamatsu's plays, Shōyō, too, sought to defend the importance of the inner life by redefining the essence of the novel as "drama."

NOTES

1. The essays are collected in Tsubouchi Shōyō, *Shōyō senshū*, vol. 8 (Tokyo: Shunyōdō, 1926).

2. H. D. Harootunian, "Between Politics and Culture: Authority and the Ambiguities of Intellectual Choice in Imperial Japan," in Bernard S. Silberman and H. D. Harootunian, eds., *Japan in Crisis: Essays on Taisho Democracy* (Princeton, NJ: Princeton University Press, 1974), p. 112.

3. Tsubouchi Shōyō, *Shōsetsu shinzui,* in *Tsubouchi Shōyō shū,* vol. 3 of *Nihon kindai bungaku taikei* (Tokyo: Kadokawa shoten, 1974), p. 61.

4. Ibid., pp. 61–69.

5. Shuzui Kenji, Kondō Takayoshi, and Otoba Hiroshi, eds., *Chikamatsu*, in vol. 10 of *Kokugo kokubungakushi taikei* (Tokyo: Sanseidō, 1964), pp. 24–27.

6. *Chikamatsu*, pp. 19–20.

7. Toyotaka Komiya, ed., and Donald Keene, trans. and adapter, *Japanese Music and Drama in the Meiji Era*, vol. 3 of *Japanese Culture in the Meiji Era* (Tokyo: Toyo bunko, 1956), pp. 22, 154.

8. Richard G. Moulton, *Shakespeare as a Dramatic Artist: A Popular Illustration of the Principles of Scientific Criticism*, 3rd ed. (Oxford: Clarendon Press, 1893), p. 2.

9. Ibid., pp. 29, 32.

10. Tsubouchi Shōyō, "Chikamatsu no jōruri," in *Shōyō senshū*, vol. 8, p. 666.

11. Ibid., p. 665.

12. Edward Dowden, *Shakespeare: A Critical Study of His Mind and Art*, 3rd ed. (New York: Harper Bros., 1902), p. xiii.

13. *Tsubouchi Shōyō shū*, p. 72.

14. Ibid., p. 74.

15. Shōyō, "*Ten no Amijima*," in *Shōyō senshū*, vol. 8, p. 684. This and other translations of dialogue from the play are from Donald Keene's translation of *The Love Suicides at Amijima*, in his *Major Plays of Chikamatsu* (New York: Columbia University Press, 1961), pp. 387–425.

16. Shōyō, "*Ten no Amijima*," pp. 687–90.

17. See Donald Keene, "The Woman-Killer and the Hell of Oil," in his *Major Plays*, p. 442.

18. Shōyō, "*Onnagoroshi abura jigoku*," in *Shōyō senshū*, vol. 8, pp. 697–98.

19. Ibid., p. 724.

20. Tsubouchi Shōyō, *Shōyō senshū*, vol. 7 (Tokyo: Shunyōdō, 1927), pp. 172–75.

21. Shōyō, "*Makubesu hyōshaku no shogen*," in *Tsubouchi Shōyō shū*, pp. 180–87.

22. Ibid., p. 182.

23. Moulton, *Shakespeare as a Dramatic Artist*, p. 264.

24. Ibid.

25. Dowden, *Shakespeare*, p. xiii.

26. "Preface to a Commentary on *Macbeth*," p. 185.

27. Harootunian, "Between Politics and Culture," p. 112.

28. For an overview of the critical issues in 1889–90, see Togawa Shinsuke, "Bungaku gokusui ronsō no ichi," in Miyoshi Yukio and Takemori Tenyū, eds., *Kindai bungaku*, vol. 2 (Tokyo: Yūhikaku sōsho, 1978), pp. 76–84. On the Saikaku revival, see Richard Lane, "Saikaku and the Modern Japanese Novel," in Edmund Skrzypczak, ed., *Japan's Modern Century* (Tokyo: Sophia University Press, 1968), pp. 115–32; and P. F. Kornicki, "The Survival of Tokugawa Fiction in the Meiji Period," *Harvard Journal of Asiatic Studies* 41 (1981): 461–82.

29. *Tsubouchi Shōyō shū*, pp. 168–78. The essay was originally published under the ungainly title "Shinsaku jūniban no uchi kihatsu yonban gōhyō," (A Combined Review of Four Works Already Published Among Twelve New Works), but Shōyō shortened it to "Three Schools of Fiction" when he included it in an anthology of his writings published in 1893.

30. *Chikamatsu*, p. 32.

31. I am indebted to Togawa Shinsuke's detailed discussion of Shōyō's concept of drama in his " 'Noberu' kara 'dorama' e—*Shōsetsu Shinzui* to '*Shōsetsu Sampa*.' " See Togawa, *'Dorama' 'Takai' Meiji nijūnendai no bungaku jōkyō* (Tokyo: Chikuma shobō, 1987), pp. 46–70.

18

Tanizaki Jun'ichirō's "The Present and Future of the Moving Pictures"

◉

JOANNE R. BERNARDI

Tanizaki Jun'ichirō's involvement with the *jun'eiga undō* (pure film movement) between 1917 and 1921 has long been obscured by his literary accomplishments. When his work on film is acknowledged, it is often interpreted as his only recourse during a severe literary slump or an experiment in achieving something that could not be done in literature. It is true that Tanizaki's novels, stories, and plays have provided material for more than fifty films but that his own involvement in film production was regrettably brief. The film scripts that Tanizaki completed between 1920 and 1921 at the innovative, newly established Yokohama studio of the Taishō katsudō shashin kabushiki kaisha (the Taishō Moving Picture Company, later Taishō katsuei, or Taikatsu) represent only a meager output in comparison with his vast literary output. Furthermore, the extent to which they helped stimulate interest in the unique requirements of writing for the screen and the role of the professional scriptwriter tends to be overlooked in favor of concurrent developments at the rival Shōchiku kinema gōmeigaisha (Shōchiku Cinema Company).

Both studios were established early in 1920 for the purpose of making *jun'eigageki* (pure films), that is, artistic films made without the theatrically derived conventions that were standard practice in the industry at the time. The small portion of the audience promoting "pure film" production welcomed the

Taikatsu films made by Tanizaki and his colleague, the Hollywood-trained actor and director Thomas Kurihara, but the studio was underfinanced from the outset and soon abandoned such experimental projects in favor of more commercial fare. Shōchiku, a branch of a powerful and well-established theatrical company, quickly outdistanced and absorbed its smaller rival, surviving to become the foremost producer of contemporary drama films today.

Shōchiku had already commissioned Osanai Kaoru, a leading figure in the movement to modernize Japanese theater, to head its new school for film actors when the Taikatsu studio engaged Tanizaki as a "literary consultant" in April 1920. In view of their contract requesting Tanizaki's presence at the studio once a month, the Taikatsu executives were apparently most interested in using his name and literary reputation to endorse the studio. It is well known, however, that Tanizaki promptly rented a room in Yokohama not far from the studio and began writing stories for Kurihara, although he was under no formal obligation to do so.

Kurihara rewrote Tanizaki's first attempt at an original scenario for the studio's first "pure film," *Amachua kurabu* (Amateur Club), into an American-style continuity script with numbered interior and exterior scenes, locations, camera angles, inserts, and expository and dialogue titles. When the film was completed in November 1920, Tanizaki informed the readers of *Chūō kōron* of his decision to stop working on the novel *Kōjin*, which the journal was serializing at the time. He stated that he had come to the realization that his participation in film required more time and effort than he had expected. He added that he firmly believed such work was more than a passing fancy and that he considered film to be just as important as literature. He even commented that someday he might make a film adaptation of *Kōjin* itself.[1] One month later Tanizaki wrote that unless he learned to write a film script by himself in the future, his involvement in film would "have been meaningless." He added: "I confess that I put my pen to paper with a happiness that I have not felt recently. . . . I cannot help but be grateful for becoming involved in the moving pictures, which I have loved for a long time."[2]

After admittedly apprenticing himself to Kurihara, Tanizaki wrote three scripts at Taikatsu, gradually working toward the continuity-style format he perfected with *Jasei no in* (The Lust of the White Serpent, 1921). All three scripts were published in magazines that were not considered trade publications, an unusual practice at a time when scripts were just beginning to be recognized as an important part of the production process, and very few members of the industry (including the writers themselves) considered them important enough to preserve after they had fulfilled their function.[3]

Osanai Kaoru's formal association with film dates back to 1912 when he began providing commentary at special screenings of imported film adaptations of literary works, but Tanizaki was clearly more committed to the guiding principles of the pure film movement. An avid fan of films from both Europe and the United States, he had written about the new medium as art and the need to distinguish between stage and screen drama as early as 1917, when discussion of "reform," "modernization," and the need to realize the unique artistic potential of Japanese film had reached a peak among the supporters of "pure film."

In his seminal essay, "Katsudō shashin no genzai to shōrai" (The Present and Future of Moving Pictures), Tanizaki focused on the most urgent concerns of the modernization movement. He addressed in particular the need to abolish conventions or practices inherited from or associated with the indigenous theater: the use of *oyama* (female impersonators) instead of actresses; stylized acting characterized by exaggerated gestures and intonations; the *kagezerifu* (lines in the dark) of the *benshi* lecturers that precluded the use of intertitles; and the predominance of interior stage shots.[4] He discussed the importance of introducing innovative camera technique and more realistic stories to replace plots predominantly drawn from theatrical repertories, and he emphasized the need to replace irresponsible managers who pandered to the demands of the popular and powerful benshi with managers who recognized the medium's artistic qualities. In addition, Tanizaki elaborated on those attributes of the new medium that continued to fascinate him long after his active involvement in film production had prematurely ended: its superiority (in his opinion) to all other art forms; its ability to depict both realistic images and illusions; and the as yet largely untapped potential of classical Japanese literature as source material for film drama. With this essay, his first and most comprehensive consideration of the medium, Tanizaki not only contributed to the recognition of the cultural significance of moving pictures and their indisputable artistic value, but he also helped define the requirements for the modern Japanese film of the following decade.

The pure film movement laid the foundation for the modern contemporary film of the 1920s, but it did not emerge in response to popular demand. When Tanizaki's "The Present and Future of the Moving Pictures" appeared in the pages of the literary journal *Shinshōsetsu* in September 1917, the benshi were still the major attraction at the box office, and they dominated the industry backstage as well. Theaters specializing in the domestic product offered a mixed bill of *rensageki* (chain dramas), the combination stage and screen productions that reached the peak of their popularity between 1916 and 1917, *shinpageki* (shinpa films), the prototype for the modern contemporary drama film that derived from the *shinpa* (literally, "new school") theater, and *kyūgeki* (period drama films), especially those starring the industry's most popular public icon, Onoe Matsunosuke.

American films ranked at the top of foreign imports, and Universal's idyllic Bluebird romances, Charlie Chaplin comedies, and serial pictures were immensely popular. It was possible for the more serious fan to keep up with developments abroad by reading about them in the growing number of domestic and imported trade publications, and Japanese audiences were already familiar with many influential European films, such as the Italian historical epics *Quo Vadis?* and *Cabiria*.[5] But much of the groundbreaking work of Hollywood's masters—D. W. Griffith's *Intolerance*, for example—had yet to reach Japan, and discussion of the artistic potential of the new medium was limited to a small but significant part of the domestic audience that was familiar with films and trade publications imported from Europe and the United States. This primarily young, educated elite promoted the serious study of Western films and Western-language film literature, advocating a reformation of the Japanese industry that would acknowledge the technological and artistic advances occurring in the West.

Never formally organized or well defined, the pure film movement's survival throughout the 1910s depended almost entirely on the contributions to domestic trade publications, literary journals, and general readership magazines by these intellectuals who believed the introduction of Western technique was the most effective way to counteract the influence of the indigenous theater. This was particularly true from 1914—when, following the example of the pioneer trade journal *Kinema Record*, subsequent publications took up the discussion concerning the artistic possibilities of the moving pictures and the difference between stage and screen drama—to 1917, when production of the first "pure films" began.[6]

During this period, the theater handbills, studio-sponsored house organs, and privately owned fan magazines that were increasingly prominent after the early 1910s became an important forum for discussing the possibilities for change. The "oppressive popularity" of the benshi, the "anachronistic" female impersonators, and the incompatibility of stage actors with the screen were the most common targets for complaints, but the need to improve the narrative content of the domestic film received special attention. Anonymous writers, members of the film community, journalists, aspiring critics, and a handful of well-known members of the literary world made numerous suggestions in the trade press for a solution to this problem, including the adaptation of classical Japanese literature and traditional legends for the screen, a more realistic depiction of contemporary Japan, and the use of Japanese film as a vehicle to affirm national identity and to promote Japanese culture abroad.

In addition to affirming Tanizaki's support for the modernization movement and his belief in film's value as art, "The Present and Future of Moving Pictures" introduced the readers of magazines like *Shinshōsetsu* to the issues then under debate in the pages of popular trade publications. Although other prominent literary figures (notably the respected novelist and poet Kōda Rohan and the playwright and critic Tsubouchi Shikō) frequently contributed to the trade press on behalf of the modernization movement, Tanizaki brought additional exposure and prestige to the "pure film" debate through his contributions to literary and general readership magazines. By the end of the decade, he had become one of the pure film movement's most eloquent and influential adherents. The film historian Tanaka Jun'ichirō, a teenager at the time and one of the many young advocates of "pure film" production, recalls that the news of Tanizaki's appointment at Taikatsu made him and his friends feel as if they "had gained a million allies."[7]

In the opening paragraphs of "The Present and Future of the Moving Pictures," Tanizaki made clear his desire to participate actively in the production of a new and modern Japanese film.[8] Frank in admitting both his enthusiasm for the medium and his disapproval of certain aspects of the domestic industry, he argued, first, for recognition of the moving pictures as art:

> I have never made a special effort to attempt a thorough study of the moving pictures, nor do I have a great deal of knowledge about them. But I have been their ardent fan for some time now, and I have even thought that given the chance, I would like to try my hand at writing a Photoplay. To this end I have read two or three foreign reference books, and I have visited the Nikkatsu studio. As a result, although I am a layman, I have much to say in general concerning the future of the motion pictures and, in particular, my displeasure and dissatisfaction with the managers of the entertainment industry in Japan.
>
> If I were asked whether there was a chance for the moving pictures to develop in the future as a true art—as an art that could be ranked with the theater and painting, for example—I would answer most emphatically that there is. I also believe that just as the theater and painting will never perish, the moving pictures, too, will last forever. Frankly, I far prefer the moving pictures to the plays of any theater troupe or any theater in Tokyo today, and in some of them I detect an artistic quality not easily achieved in kabuki or shinpa plays. Perhaps this is a slight exaggeration, but I actually think that however short or mindless it might be, any film, providing it has been made in the West, is much more interesting than the Japanese plays of today. (p. 13)[9]

Tanizaki's enthusiasm, which he acknowledged was a result of watching imported films and reading imported Western-language trade publications, reveals his affinity with the majority of intellectuals contributing to the contemporary domestic trade press. He later recalled that particularly between 1915 and 1919 he regularly patronized theaters specializing in imported films,[10] and it is apparent that his interest in imported film publications was equally genuine. Even after he left Taikatsu, he described seeking reprieve from writing in both the "tranquil domain" of Chinese poetry and "that kingdom of cinema, the world of Hollywood" that he explored through the pages of *Motion Picture Magazine, Shadow Land*, and *Photo Play Magazine*.[11]

Tanizaki's unconditional admiration for Western films and disdain for the domestic product were in accord with contemporary intellectual tastes, although for Tanizaki such sentiments were probably influenced by his infatuation with Western culture at the time.[12] It is evident that at this point at least, his preferences precluded a positive appreciation of traditional Japanese drama. Much of the humor in his plot for *Amateur Club*, in fact, centers on a playful parody of two well-known kabuki plays.[13] Accordingly, Tanizaki's argument for recognizing the artistic qualities of film, developed through a comparison of stage and screen drama, began with the conjecture that soon such established forms of entertainment in Japan might have to yield their favored position to the insurgent import from the West:

> Even if we assume that we cannot discriminate among the arts, those forms of art that suit the times will continue to develop while those that go against the times will naturally cease to improve. Although the content of nō and kyōgen drama is not inferior to that of kabuki drama, nō and kyōgen are not as popular as kabuki for this reason. This is the age of Democracy, and the sphere of the arts catering to aristocratic tastes will gradually be pared down. In this respect, the moving pictures, which are even more plebeian than the theater, are an art more suited to the times, with great potential for improvement. Or rather, just as the theater outdistanced nō and kyōgen, there may come a time when the moving pictures become a respectable, high-class art and in turn outdistance the theater. (pp. 13–14)

The contrast between the stage and screen was a particular concern for Tanizaki, and he continued praising the newer medium at the expense of theater even after his involvement in film had ended. After his first experience directing a stage production, in 1922, he admitted that he found directing films more engaging (he had directed portions of *Hinamatsuri no yoru* [The Night of the Doll Festival] at Taikatsu the previous year).[14] Two years later, he commented that movies were more interesting than plays and that he was even happier when he heard that his play *Honmoku yawa* (Honmoku Nights) was to be made into a film than when the play itself had opened on stage.[15]

In "The Present and Future of Moving Pictures," Tanizaki gave three reasons that he felt moving pictures were superior to stage drama. First, whereas each stage performance could be seen only once by a single audience, a moving picture could be shown repeatedly to different audiences in various locations; also, thanks to the durability of celluloid, a moving picture could continue to entertain audiences for many years to come. Second, as a photographic medium, moving pictures were better suited to the portrayal of both realistic and fantastic (*mugen*) subject matter, proving they were a more versatile form of art than stage drama. Third, the moving pictures allowed the writer more freedom: liberated from the physical constraints of the stage, the writer could manipulate the order and location of scenes as well as the composition of the subject matter projected on the screen.

Tanizaki opened his argument for the artistic merits of film by pointing out the durability of celluloid, revealing his fascination—perhaps influenced by his familiarity with imported trade journals and "how to" books—with even the most basic technical attributes of the medium. Keeping in mind his concern with the future potential of moving pictures, he commented that this was one technical attribute that surely would be developed even further with time. Although in this essay Tanizaki was concerned primarily with how moving pictures surpassed the limitations of stage drama, he also pointed out ways in which the moving pictures compared favorably with other forms of art, such as literature and painting. Equating the difference between stage and screen drama with the difference between a handwritten and a printed manuscript, he noted that screen drama was also more directly accessible to a larger audience than painting, which could be circulated only through the relatively indirect method of reproduction, or literature, which needed to be translated before it could be appreciated by foreign readers. He added that the moving pictures, because of their durability and universality, provided special benefits for both audiences and actors. For audiences, the moving pictures brought the art of actors far and wide to their doorstep; for actors, the moving pictures made the entire world their audience, immortalizing their art for future generations, "just like the poems of Goethe . . . or the works of Michelangelo" (p. 14).

In suggesting that screen drama could accommodate a wider range of subject matter than stage drama, Tanizaki introduced the one attribute of the new medium that intrigued him the most: its ability to portray both realistic and imaginary (in particular, surreal or supernatural) images in an equally convincing manner. He pursued variations on this theme in a number of works. He explored the manner in which film could be used to contest the often thin line between the perception of on- and off-screen reality in the story "Jinmenso" (The Growth with a Human Face, 1918).[16] After the Japanese release of *The Cabinet of Dr. Caligari* in 1921, he addressed the relationship between the worlds of reality and illusion as they are portrayed on film.[17] In the novel *Nikkai* (Flesh, 1923), Tanizaki compared the "entire universe–all the phenomena of the world around us" to a film and wondered if perhaps "we are all nothing but shadows that disappear quickly and without a trace while our reality lives on in the film of the universe."[18]

In "The Present and Future of Moving Pictures," Tanizaki attributed film's affinity for subject matter that stirs the human powers of perception to the fact that screen drama is "less artificial" than stage drama. He again referred to shifting trends in the popularity of established, traditional forms of drama in order to illustrate how this quality made the moving pictures better suited to the times and therefore, in his opinion, the more desirable type of entertainment:

> The nō and kyōgen plays, admired today as symbolic productions, seemed realistic to the people of the Ashikaga period. Could it be that just as the nō and kyōgen plays were followed by the more realistic kabuki theater, the moving pictures, which are even more realistic, will dominate the world in the future? I have a feeling this will indeed happen.
>
> The fact that photoplays are more real in all respects proves at the same time that they are appropriate for stories that are much more realistic than stage plays and stories that are much more fantastical than stage plays. Although there is no need to explain why photoplays suit realistic stories, I think works that cannot possibly be adapted to the stage—for example, Dante's *Divine Comedy*, *The Journey to the West*, and some of Poe's short stories, or works like Izumi Kyōka's *Kōya hijiri* [The Saint of Kōya] and *Fūryūsen* [The Elegant Gang's Railroad] (although both of these were already staged as shinpa plays, they were a disgrace to the originals)—definitely would make interesting pictures. Poe's stories in particular—"The Black Cat," "William Wilson," or "The Mask of the Red Death," for example—would be even more effective as photoplays. (p. 15)[19]

The examples of literature that Tanizaki considered particularly suitable for screen adaptation are worth noting. Izumi Kyōka's work, often about romantically tragic heroines of the pleasure quarters, or ghosts, spirits, demons, and other inhabitants of the supernatural world, was to become a favorite source for Japanese filmmakers. Several stories and novels, such as the supernatural "Uta andon" (A Song Under Lanterns), and *Nihonbashi* (the name of a geisha district in Tokyo) and *Onna keizu* (A Woman's Pedigree), have been adapted many times over the years. There have been no fewer than five adaptations of *Taki no Shiraito* (the heroine's name as a performer), a shinpa play derived from the story "Giketsu kyōketsu" (Noble Blood, Heroic Blood).[20]

Thomas Kurihara was also an avid reader of both Izumi Kyōka and Poe (Tanizaki later wrote that when visiting the bedridden Kurihara, he noticed a collection of Poe's stories by his bedside), and Kurihara's and Tanizaki's mutual fondness for Kyōka's work no doubt resulted in their collaboration, after *Amateur Club*, on an adaptation of the writer's *Katsushika sunago* (The Sands of Katsushika).[21]

Tanizaki's emphasis in his essay on the differences between writing for the screen and writing for the stage reflects the influence of the pure film movement's preoccupation with redefining the nature and function of the script. Preproduction scripts were standard in Japan by the midteens (the precedent for a scenario or story department as an independent unit in the Japanese studio system dates back to 1909), but most of these commercial scripts were *serifugeki*, "line plays" written in the style of benshi narration with no indication of camerawork or shooting locations and often little or no dialogue or division of the action into numbered shots or scenes.[22] According to Kinugasa Teinosuke, who entered Nikkatsu's contemporary drama studio in Mukōjima, Tokyo, in 1917 (presumably around the time that Tanizaki visited the studio), scripts for the Nikkatsu shinpa films were then routinely written in four or five days, just enough time to rewrite a three-act shinpa play into a script with about twenty scenes.[23]

"Pure film" advocates criticized the resident studio writers (referred to by one reformist, Mori Iwao, as "hacks," "literary dropouts," or "playwrights past their prime")[24] and challenged the popular assumption that writing for the screen did not require special skills and training. Such criticism escalated after the publication of Kaeriyama Norimasa's *Katsudō shashingeki no sōsaku to satsuei hō* (The Production and Photography of Moving Picture Drama) in July 1917— just two months before the publication of "The Present and Future of the Moving Pictures." Kaeriyama dedicated an entire chapter of his book, the first technical handbook on filmmaking to be published in Japan, to expounding on the need to understand the function of a detailed and well-written film script, which he considered "the foundation of a film" and "very different from the script for stage drama."[25]

In accordance with the progressive opinion that an understanding of the nature and function of the script was crucial to the reformation of the Japanese film, Tanizaki focused on those technical attributes of the moving pictures that offered special challenges to writers like himself. He maintained that the photographic nature of the medium not only offered writers a wider range of material to choose from but also allowed them greater control over their material, two prospects he found appealing. Tanizaki's confidence in perceiving moving pictures as a writer's medium is more understandable when we remember that during the 1910s, the director's role in the production process was still generally unrecognized in Japan. At any rate, Tanizaki did not seem very concerned—as were many of his American counterparts then being courted by Hollywood—that writing for the screen might compromise the writer's art:

> The third merit [of moving pictures] is that the manner of handling scenes is free and unrestricted as well as rich in diversity. How convenient this must be for the scriptwriter, too. He is unencumbered by bothersome conventions, unlike the process involved in constructing a story for a stage play. Moreover, rather than having to build [a set] on a stage with a limited amount of floor space, he can use any manner of magnificent background or grand-scale building in any way he wishes, and he can even shorten an incident that occurs over a long period of time in a distant land into a short drama of one or two hours. This is yet another reason that the possibilities for source material are so numerous. (pp. 15–16)

Elaborating on the technical advantages of the moving pictures, Tanizaki drew a parallel with painting, pointing out that film provided the option of composing each shot individually, an advantage that could not be achieved on stage. He observed that the new medium also made it possible to control the distance between the performers and the camera—in effect, the distance between the performers and the audience. As a result, each member of a film audience had a better chance of fully appreciating the movements and expressions of the performers on screen. In this respect, Tanizaki paid particular attention to the close-up shot (one year later it became a prominent feature of "The Growth with a Human Face"), noting that "cutting out a part of a scene and enlarging it—in other words, showing a detail—greatly increases the effect of the drama and adds variety." He was quick to add that although the close-up shot enhanced the dramatic impact of a moving picture, it also encouraged greater respect for realistic detail. He explained that for this reason it was customary in the West, for example, for a beautiful actress to play the part of a beautiful woman and for older performers to play older parts. Because an actor's or actress's face appears larger than life in a close-up, screen actors cannot deceive the audience with the garish make-up used on stage. Thus, Tanizaki concluded, screen actors had more opportunities to explore the full potential of their acting ability, and so their performances were less artificial (p. 16).

Tanizaki's lengthy discussion of the merits of the close-up shot led him to a consideration of color and sound for moving pictures. Like many of his contemporaries both in Japan and abroad, he contended that such additions were both unnecessary and undesirable, as they would only weaken the unique visual intensity of moving pictures. He also believed that the absence of such techniques enhanced the medium's affinity with the "spirit" of painting, sculpture, and music—more proof of the superior artistic quality of the moving pictures in comparison with stage drama:

> The human face—even an ugly face—is such that if you stare at it intently, it seems to conceal a mysterious, solemn, and eternal beauty. When I look at a "close-up" of a face in a moving picture, this feeling is especially strong. Every individual part of the face or body of a person who ordinarily would escape notice possesses an indescribable energy, and I can feel its compelling force all the more keenly. Perhaps this is not only because film is a magnification of the real object but also because it lacks the sound and color of the real object. Perhaps the lack of color or sound in moving pictures is an asset rather than a limitation. Just as painting has no sound and poems have no shape, the moving pictures, too, because of their limitations, manifest the purification— Crystallization—of nature that is necessary to art. I believe this aspect of the moving pictures will enable them to develop into a more advanced form of art than the theater. (pp. 16–17)[26]

After discussing the merits of moving pictures, Tanizaki launched into a critique of what he observed to be the domestic industry's major deficiencies. He began by pointing an accusing finger at the businessmen in control, siding with the "pure film" advocates who criticized the industry management for exploiting the medium for the sake of instant profit. Stressing the need to replace present management policies with ones that both complemented the special properties of film and allowed for the introduction of new techniques, Tanizaki wrote:

> Everyone is already fully aware of most of the advantages of the moving pictures that I have described above, and it is not necessary for me to explain them once more. I am reiterating these well-known points only because I particularly want the moving picture management to read them. To say the least, [I am writing this] because I believe they do not sufficiently acknowledge these merits—or, even if they do acknowledge them, they do not put them to good use. (p. 17)

Tanizaki was particularly critical of the staging in period films in which the actors assembled on a stage and delivered their lines from stationary positions. He argued that because the managers, "stage directors," and actors involved in such productions perceived everything in terms of the theatrical stage, they failed to do justice to the medium at hand (pp. 17–18).

But his main concern was that greater attention in general be given to achieving more realism. He deplored the Japanese custom of having men play female roles, pointing out the absurdity of this "ridiculous" practice, compared with the zealous pursuit of authenticity in the West. There, he wrote, actors occasionally were given real liquor before drunk scenes and, in some cases, were told the plot only one scene at a time so that their emotions would appear more genuine.

In contrast, Japanese screen actors, particularly the oyama, appeared on screen in the same costumes and makeup that they wore on stage, "apparently with the impression that they can thus delude the audience." He lamented the custom of using layers of white paint to simulate a woman's fair complexion and of drawing thick black lines for wrinkles in order to appear aged. "Women should play female parts and elderly actors should play elderly roles," he wrote, warning that "as long as the moving pictures remain imitations of the theater, they will never be able to surpass it. . . . Actors in moving pictures today have not realized that they have their own characteristics and purpose, and it is not surprising that these actors are scorned by their colleagues" (p. 18).

Tanizaki concluded, however, that the actors themselves were not solely responsible for their shortcomings. In fact, he believed their acting gradually would improve as they became more aware of the special requirements of their art. Once again, he put the burden of blame on managers, who chose to produce scripts that were tailored more to the needs of the benshi than to those of the performers (pp. 18–19). Above all, he urged filmmakers to improve the content of their work by "returning to nature." There was no need for huge spectacles involving "train crashes" and "exploding railway bridges." Simple stories expressing "Japanese customs and human sentiment" would suffice. The simpler and more natural the content was, the better, for it would be unreasonable "to begin immediately with literary pictures of high quality" (p. 19).

Tanizaki noted that several popular foreign pictures with negligible plots (he specifically mentions Francis Ford's *The Broken Coin*, 1915) were immensely successful in Japan, thanks to the skillful use of location shooting and the firsthand glimpses they provided of local life—both qualities that literature could not offer. For this reason, he surmised, Japanese novels such as *Ono ga tsumi* (One's Own Sin) and *Konjiki yasha* (The Demon Gold), which were not, in his opinion, very interesting as literature, would make good moving pictures "if they were made in the manner of a Western picture and included ample shots of Japanese landscapes and native customs" (p. 19).[27]

The emphasis in the contemporary trade press on making films that could be considered uniquely Japanese—films that, as one writer put it, expressed a "pure Japanese spirit" (*yamato damashii*)[28]—was, after the midteens, increasingly associated with the desire to create a foreign market for Japanese films. Accordingly, Tanizaki concluded that once the technique of adaptation was perfected, Japan's rich wealth of literary classics could be used to make pictures that would fascinate foreign audiences as much as foreign pictures enthralled the Japanese:

> Going one step further, however, if great managers, great directors, and great actors were to emerge in Japan and if they used the famous and time-honored novels of our country as material for moving pictures, what magnificent films they could make! Just thinking about it makes me take heart. For example, if they filmed *Heike monogatari* [The Tale of the Heike] using the actual settings of Kyoto, Ichinotani, and Dannoura and dressing the actors in the armor and costumes of that time, they could make a film on a par with even *Quo Vadis?* or *Antony and Cleopatra*. Something like the Heian-period *Taketori monogatari* [The Tale of the Bamboo Princess] would be first-rate material for a fairy drama using trick effects.
>
> If we made many films of this kind, we could check the importation of foreign-made films and even export large quantities of films from Japan. Moving pictures that depict the history and human compassion of the Far East would surely capture the fancy of Westerners. (pp. 19–20)

Tanizaki also pointed out the benefits such a production policy would offer screen performers, again emphasizing the medium's advantage over all other arts in crossing international borders:

> It is difficult for Japanese artists in the fields of music, literature, and theater to be recognized by the West, but moving picture actors do not face such obstacles. If the name of a Japanese actor were to resound far and wide throughout the world, just like Charles Chaplin, wouldn't it be wonderful for him as a Japanese? Those who seek fame would do well to become moving picture actors. (p. 20)

Tanizaki saved his criticism of the benshi for the end. Although his earlier comments suggested that he blamed the powerful benshi, together with profit-hungry managers, for the industry's weaknesses, his closing observations were surprisingly pragmatic. Rather than call for the immediate and total abolition of the benshi, as did many other intellectual observers at the time, he simply recommended that their narrative skills be used in moderation. He even went so far as to praise Somei Saburō, the resident benshi of the Asakusa teikokukan (a theater specializing in American serials and the popular Universal Bluebird films) as perhaps the only intelligent man in the entire industry (pp. 20–21). It is clear, however, that Tanizaki was emphatically against the benshi's tampering with plots or interlarding their performances with what he perceived as irrelevant, distracting, and often misleading comments. Apart from using the benshi to translate foreign-language intertitles (subtitles in Japanese were experimented with in the 1920s but became standard only with the introduction of sound), he regarded the narrators as dispensable accessories, little more than substitutes for more sophisticated background music, the more preferable accompaniment:

> Finally, I would like to comment on the pros and cons of the benshi. I would favor completely abolishing benshi commentary if we had suitable musical accompaniment for films in Japan, but under the present conditions I wish the benshi would at least limit their comments as much as possible. Their presence should be limited to situations in which Western music cannot be used, and they need only narrate the plot in a simple and brief manner without ruining the effect of the film.
>
> In the case of Western films, it is enough to translate the English phrases into Japanese and to play Western background music in the shadows off stage. The quiet, delicate timbre of the piano could be used for a wide range of Japanese pictures and perhaps might be appropriate even for a historical film. If benshi commentary is absolutely necessary, I would prefer the benshi do no more than deliver the commentary following the phrases that appear in the film as faithfully and skillfully as possible. Breaking up the entire plot right from the start or bantering the lines of dialogue back and forth between each other should be absolutely forbidden. (p. 20)

In "The Present and Future of the Moving Pictures," Tanizaki revealed an impressive amount of awareness and foresight in his appraisal of the potential of the new medium and the immediate problems facing the emergent modernization movement. Tanizaki's apparent knowledge of issues being discussed in the domestic trade press was undoubtedly of great value to Kurihara when he returned, after a prolonged sojourn abroad, to seek financing for the production of new, exportable Japanese films. The two men already had in common a familiarity with and appreciation of foreign films, but Tanizaki provided an important link between Kurihara and the domestic "pure film" debate. It is therefore not surprising that many of the issues raised in "The Present and Future of the Moving Pictures" were to be addressed in Taikatsu's prospectus published two years later.

It is uncertain to what extent Tanizaki himself recognized the significance of his role in the modernization movement, but to the supporters of "pure film," it was one of great consequence. Together with Kurihara, Tanizaki created new genres for the Japanese film with *Amateur Club*, a caricature of the Keystone slapstick comedies that were popular in Japan at the time, *The Night of the Doll Festival*, a children's story, and *The Lust of the White Serpent*, the first "pure film" adaptation of classical Japanese literature.[29] Tanizaki and Kurihara also set a precedent for the director–writer collaboration at a time when the identification of these two disciplines was limited to viewers of the intellectual elite and nascent film critics. In addition to his achievements at Taikatsu as a scriptwriter, Tanizaki's many articles on film and his countless references to the medium (most common between 1915 and 1925 but continuing into the 1950s) attest to more than a casual interest. It is apparent that his legacy amounts to a great deal more than the prestige that went with his name.

NOTES

1. "Kōjin no genkō ni tsuite," *Tanizaki Jun'ichirō zenshū* (hereafter abbreviated *TJZ*) (Tokyo: Chūō kōronsha, 1966–1970, vol. 23), p. 54. Tanizaki had failed to complete the novel *Nageki no mon* (Gate of Sorrow) in 1918 and was evidently experiencing uncertainty in his writing. His personal life also was unstable. There were rumors that he was involved with his wife's younger sister, the future Taikatsu actress Hayama Michiko (her married name is Wajima Sei), and his lack of regard for his wife led to a highly publicized confrontation with his best friend, the novelist and poet Satō Haruo. See Donald Keene, *Dawn to the West: Japanese Literature in the Modern Era*, vol. 1 (New York: Holt, Rinehart and Winston, 1984), pp. 746–47. The *kōjin* was a mythical creature originating in China. It resembled a merman and was believed to live in southern seas, where it wove cloth on a loom and wept tears that were pearls.

2. "Sono yorokobi o kansha sezaru o enai," *TJZ*, vol. 22, pp. 96–97.

3. *Tsuki no kagayaki* (The Radiance of the Moon), generally considered Tanizaki's first scenario, was serialized in *Gendai* in 1921. The first thirty-eight scenes of *Hinamatsuri no yoru* (The Night of the Doll Festival, 1921) appeared in *Shinengei* in 1923, and the magazine published a longer version the following year. *The Lust of the White Serpent*, his final script, appeared in *Suzu no oto* in April 1922, with a preface by Tanizaki describing his role as scriptwriter in the production of the film. Tanizaki is often credited with having written the lost script for *Katsushika sunago* (The Sands of Katsushika, 1920), a three-reel film based on Izumi Kyōka's novel of the same title, but Tanizaki himself attributed the work to Kurihara, claiming that he wrote only a hasty first draft after having read the original work. See "Kurihara Tomasu kun no koto," *TJZ*, vol. 22, p. 194. Both the

script and the film are believed lost. Tanizaki's original scenario for *Amateur Club*, originally enti-tled *Hishochi no sawagi* (Commotion at a Summer Resort), has not survived either. The continu-ity-style script Kurihara completed based on Tanizaki's scenario was serialized under Tanizaki's name in the trade publication *Katsudō zasshi* 7 (June–October 1921): 6–10. It is difficult to determine the extent of Tanizaki's contribution to this version of *Amateur Club*, although it seems likely that Kurihara's revisions, rendering Tanizaki's original scenario into a version closer to a continuity-style shooting script, were primarily technical.

4. The benshi lecturer was a standard presence narrating, explaining, or otherwise verbally embellishing silent films throughout Japan's relatively long silent period. The relationship between the benshi and the modernization movement was complicated: the performers had indi-vidual styles of delivery, and the institution itself underwent vast transformations during the 1910s and early 1920s. Group performances gave way to the presence of a single benshi, and the more subdued, thoughtful style of commentary by popular narrators like Tokugawa Musei (one of several benshi sympathetic to the modernization movement) gradually replaced the histrionic *kowairo* (emotional changes in the pitch of the voice, or "voice coloring") of earlier performers. Anecdotal evidence suggests that all the "pure films" ultimately had benshi accompaniment, but by a benshi specializing in narrating imported films. Nevertheless, "pure film" advocates unani-mously protested the fact that the benshi often enjoyed more authority in the production process than did the director or scriptwriter. It should be noted that the benshi never disappeared com-pletely and that it is still possible to enjoy performances in Japan, primarily at special screenings, libraries, and civic centers. Videotapes and televised broadcasts of both Japanese and imported silent films are common as well.

5. *Quo Vadis?* (Enrico Guazzoni, 1912) was released in Japan in October 1913 and *Cabiria* (Giovanni Pastrone, 1914) in May 1916.

6. Kaeriyama Norimasa (who was primarily responsible, as both a writer and filmmaker, for formulating the goals of the pure film movement) and his colleagues, a group of young foreign film enthusiasts who called themselves the *katsusha kōyūkai* (Friends of Moving Pictures) published *Kinema Record* (originally *Film Record*) in 1913. Kaeriyama also completed the first "pure films," *Sei no kagayaki* (The Glow of Life) and *Miyama no otome* (The Maid in the Mountains) in 1918. Their release was delayed until September 1919, when they opened simultaneously.

7. Tanaka Jun'ichirō, *Katsudō shashin ga yatte kita* (Tokyo: Chūō kōronsha, 1985), pp. 177–78.

8. All "Katsudō shashin no genzai to shōrai" citations in the text are from *TJZ*, vol. 20, pp. 11–21.

9. The word *Photoplay* appears in English. "Nikkatsu" refers to the major film company at the time, the Nihon katsudō shashin kabushiki kaisha (Japan Cinematography Company), established in 1912.

10. See Tanizaki, "Tokyo o omou," *TJZ*, vol. 21, p. 9.

11. Tanizaki, "Shina shumi to iu koto," *TJZ*, vol. 22, pp. 122–23.

12. Tanizaki had always exhibited a strong interest in foreign cultures, and around the time he entered the film industry, his fascination with the West had become extreme. This obsession with Western culture played an important role in his becoming involved in the motion pictures. His work at Taikatsu marked the climax of his infatuation with the West, but it also presaged its end. The shift from West to East is evident in the shift from the Hollywood-inspired slapstick style of *Amateur Club* to the more traditional subject matter of *The Lust of the White Serpent*. It was while he

was working on location in the western region of Kansai during the filming of *The Lust of the White Serpent* that Tanizaki became interested in that region of Japan and consequently in the traditional aesthetic atmosphere that still permeated the area. See "Tōkyō o omou," p. 23. He moved to Kansai to wait out the reconstruction of Tokyo after the earthquake of 1923 and, a few years later, decided to remain there permanently.

13. In the script, the Kamakura Amateur Club stages a performance of the *yukashita* (under the floor) scene of *Sendaihagi* (the full name of the play is *Meiboku sendaihagi*), a play based on the rivalry between different factions of the powerful Date clan of Sendai, in northern Japan, and the tenth act of *Taikōki*, drawn from the events surrounding the assassination of Oda Nobunaga by one of his generals, Akechi Mitsuhide, in June 1583.

14. "Keikoba to butai no aida," *TJZ*, vol. 22, p. 147.

15. "Eigaka sareta *Honmoku yawa*," *TJZ*, vol. 22, p. 168. This article begins with an explanation of how Tanizaki had obtained special permission from the editor to write what was probably the first article on film to appear in the magazine *Engeki shinchō*.

16. "Jinmenso," *TJZ*, vol. 5, pp. 281–305. Tanizaki later wrote that he had been told that this story had an inherent cinematic quality and remarked that he would like to make it into a film. Plans to adapt the story at Taikatsu were never realized. It was finally made into a film, *Oiran*, in 1982 by the director Takechi Tetsuji.

17. "*Karigari hakase* o miru," *TJZ*, vol. 22, pp. 107–12.

18. *Nikkai*, *TJZ*, vol. 9, pp. 40–41.

19. There is an abridged translation of *Journey to the West* by Arthur Waley entitled *Monkey*, and a full translation by Anthony Yu in four volumes, entitled *Journey to the West*. A screen version directed by Yoshino Jirō was released in Japan in 1917. For a description of the trick photography used in this film, see Shibata Masaru (Omori Masaru), "Jun'eigageki to kouta eiga," in Iwamoto Kenji and Saiki Tomonori, eds., *Kikigaki: Kinema no seishun* (Tokyo: Libroport, 1988), pp. 9–10. Tanizaki was probably not familiar with the Italian director Giuseppe De Liguoro's 1909 screen adaptation of Dante's *Inferno*, which was not released in Japan.

20. See Chiba Nobuo, *Eiga to Tanizaki* (Tokyo: Seiabō, 1989), pp. 102–5, for a list of screen adaptations from 1910 to 1983 of Izumi Kyōka's works. More recently, the actor Bandō Tamasaburō directed a short (fifty-minute) film for commercial release based on one of Kyōka's most popular stories, *Gekashitsu* (The Operating Room). It opened in Japan in February 1992.

21. Tanizaki, "Kurihara Tomasu kun no koto," pp. 194–95. Kyōka's novel, serialized in *Shinshōsetsu* in 1890, is set in the mid-1800s in an area known from ancient times as Katsushika. Katsushika was formerly a county that straddled part of Tokyo and what are now the prefectures of Chiba and Saitaima. Kyōka had trouble naming the piece once it was written and only thought of the title, which can also be read as a woman's name, as he was delivering the manuscript to the publisher.

22. The literal meaning of the word *serifugeki* is "line play" or "dialogue play," although in the latter definition the word *monologue* would be more appropriate. "Pure film" advocates used this word to refer to the commercial script in a derogatory manner. The Japanese screenplay has been referred to as *kyakuhon* (script) and *shinario* (scenario, a loan word from the West and a later addition) since the silent period. After the midteens, *katsudōgeki kyakuhon* (moving picture script) and *eigageki kyakuhon* (film script) were used interchangeably, together with *shinario*. The benshi narration script was commonly referred to as the *benshi daihon*. For excerpts of scripts written

between 1915 and 1919, see Tanaka Jun'ichirō, "Onoe Matsunosuke-geki *Bingo Saburō*, Mukōjima shinpageki *Chichi no namida*, Yamazaki Naganosuke rensageki *Utashigure*, Sawamura Shirogorō-geki *Josō ninjutsu*," in *Horidasareta meisakusen*, suppl. to *Nihon eiga shinario koten zenshū* (Tokyo: Kinema junpō, 1966), pp. 25–31.

23. Kinugasa Teinosuke, *Waga eiga no seishun* (Tokyo: Chūō kōronsha, 1977), pp. 16–17.

24. Mori Iwao and Tomonari Yōzō, *Katsudō shashin taikan*, in Okabe Ryū, ed., *Nihon eigashi sōkō*, suppl. vols. 1–4 (Tokyo: Film Library Council, 1976–78), vol. 2, p. 62. This is a reprint of an unpublished manuscript that Mori wrote in 1919–20.

25. Kaeriyama Norimasa, *Katsudō shashingeki no sōsaku to satsuei hō*, 2nd ed. (Tokyo: Seikosha, 1921), p. 41.

26. The word *Crystallization* appears in English.

27. *Ono ga tsumi* (One's Own Sin, 1899–1900), a best-selling melodramatic novel by Kikuchi Yūhō, was the source for the shinpa play of the same name. The first screen version was made in 1908; it proved to be popular and subsequently was made into a film several times in the early years of the industry, most notably by Tanaka Eizō in 1919. Tanizaki, who admitted his preference for imported films, apparently did not know that a screen version already existed. The stage version of *Konjiki yasha* (The Demon Gold, 1905)—Ozaki Kōyō's last, unfinished novel—was also a staple of the shinpa repertory; Tanaka Eizō directed a screen version of the play in 1918.

28. Mukai Shunkō, "Katsudō shashingeki no shin keikō: Kigeki no zensei jidai kuru," *Katsudō gahō* 1 (March 1917): 3, in Makino Mamoru, ed., *Nihon eiga shoki shiryō shūsei*, 9 vols. (Tokyo: Sanichi shobō, 1990–91), vol. 6, p. 596 (facsimile edition). "Yamato damashii," a phrase dating back to the Heian period (794–1185), has been used in various ways to refer to cultural or spiritual qualities regarded as unique to the Japanese people.

29. The film historian Iijima Tadashi makes this point in his history *Nihon eigashi* (Tokyo: Hakushuisha, 1955), vol. 1, p. 33.

19

Komachi: Medieval Legend as Modern Theater

◉

MARY-JEAN COWELL

Komachi began with my desire to share something of the poet's life and work with a Western audience, one larger than readers of Japanese poetry and nō plays. Many elements in the legends about Komachi seemed likely to have broad appeal: the exoticism and romance of a beautiful woman with many lovers, living in a rarefied court atmosphere of long ago; the tale of a vengeful soul taking possession of another's body; and the timeless emotions associated with frustrated love, remorse over past deeds, and aging and its consequences. From a contemporary perspective, Komachi's persona also has a feminist subtext. As a recognized artist, a great beauty, and an aristocrat, she had more control over her destiny than did most women of her time and culture.

I do not recall any intention of creating a "modern nō." I was and continue to be interested in theater that communicates through interactive elements of dance, text, music, and visual design. At the same time, the piece was certainly influenced by my experience of nō as text and especially as theater. The identification of Komachi with a kimono, not with one particular actor, may have been inspired by the nō *Aoi no ue*,[1] in which Aoi is represented by a kimono that remains folded on the stage throughout the performance. In *Komachi*, each of the actors wears a specific kimono when assuming the character of the poet. In writing the text, I occasionally followed the nō practice of quoting and adapting from appropriate poems and other sources. This technique is particularly evident in scenes 3 and 5.

The content and imagery associated with Komachi were drawn largely from three nō in the current repertory: *Sekidera Komachi, Kayoi Komachi*, and *Sotoba Komachi*.[2] I retranslated some of the poems but could not resist using Arthur Waley's translations of two ancient anonymous waka and Donald Keene's translation of one of Komachi's poems; these are identified in the notes. The five-part structure of *Komachi* evolved spontaneously, not from any intention of following nō tradition.

In contrast to nō, the styles of individual scenes vary markedly. The basic concept of the work is a small troupe of players and musicians presenting Komachi to the audience through a combination of storytelling and enactment at different levels of abstraction. The contrasting modes of presentation reflect my idea of the most theatrically effective way to convey the material and also the necessity of developing the brief legends. The dialogue in scenes 2 and 4 is, of course, invented. I have taken considerable liberty with the character of Captain Fukakusa, making him much more a blunt man of action than an elegant aristocrat fulfilling a court military appointment.

Since *Komachi* is primarily intended to be experienced as theater, I should comment briefly on the original production. The Holy Roman Repertory Company presented *Komachi* in April 1987. (Some readers may know the HRRC from its public radio broadcasts.) I was extremely fortunate in my collaborators. Hollis Huston, the artistic director and creator of HRRC, directed the work and performed in it, as did Edith Taylor Hunter, an accomplished actor. Jeffrey Noonan, the composer of much HRRC music, created all the music and sound effects, selected instrumentation in consultation with Huston and myself, played the guitar, and directed and rehearsed the two other musicians. I choreographed the stylized movements and the dance and performed as the actor-dancer. During the rehearsals, all involved made invaluable suggestions that produced minor revisions in the text and fostered ideas now reflected in the stage directions. *Komachi* was staged in a "black box" studio theater with the audience seated on three sides. The performance ran about thirty-five minutes. Since the integration of the theatrical elements was both the special pleasure and the difficulty of *Komachi*, I can only hope that the text reproduced here conveys the essential atmosphere of the work.

Komachi

I

The stage is bare, except for kimono stands placed diagonally in the up-left and up-right corners. The Captain's costume is on one of the kimono stands. In the dark, a percussionist enters and begins playing sporadically on a drum. The other musicians enter carrying four lighted lanterns. They place them at the four corners of the playing area, then go to the upstage corner opposite the drum(s) and begin playing on a guitar and flute. A pulse emerges from the overlapping patterns of the two instruments, and the drum reiterates and amplifies the rhythm. In dim stage light, the three players—one man and two women—make a ceremonial entry carrying all the other properties and costumes. The players wear simple costumes with some Japanese elements but no strong sense of character. The movement is basically unison walking with a certain austere style, clear spatial definition, and some simple rhythmic patterning.

The players conclude the entry seated in a triangular formation up center with their props on the floor beside them. The main prop is a beautiful, brightly colored kimono with a stylized "old and tattered" reverse side. The man, the up-center point of the triangle, tosses the folded kimono partially open on the floor just before he says "Komachi." The players all participate in a kind of ritual unfolding of the kimono as the speaking continues. Distribution of the lines is flexible in this scene. They were assigned as indicated in the original production. Some music from the guitar and flute continues until "The legend . . . "

MAN: Komachi . . .
            A woman of great beauty,
WOMAN 1:   an aristocrat, a woman of refinement,
WOMAN 2:   a woman of wit and grit and talent,
MAN: One of her country's finest poets.
            Her full name was Ono no Komachi,
            the daughter of a court official in ninth-century Japan.
WOMAN 1:   We know little about her life.
            The facts are less important than her legend,
            a legend that has grown from her own poems
WOMAN 2:   and the plays and tales her countrymen have written
            about her for more than a thousand years.
WOMAN 1:   The legend does not tell us whether she had measles,
            what she liked for breakfast,
            what she read in her "formative years."
MAN: But it tells us the important things:
            for instance, she had many lovers,

(As the speaking continues, Woman 1 and Man put on the Komachi and Captain costumes over their stage uniforms, assisted by Woman 2.)

WOMAN 2:   too many, perhaps, for her own good.
            The legend also says she enjoyed tormenting her lovers.

MAN   *(in a deliberately pseudophilosophical tone):*
    One of those instances of the abuse of power.
    Despite her beauty and talent, she could be . . . well. . . .

II

In Komachi's private rooms at court. Letters on a low table brought in by one of the players dur-
ing the entry and placed by one of the musicians while Komachi and the Captain put on their
costumes. Sparse music at appropriate moments throughout the scene (some suggested later).
Komachi (Woman 1) is seated on the floor by the table. She quickly reads one or two of the let-
ters and tosses them aside with a contemptuous gesture. Meanwhile, her maid (Woman 2) leads
the Captain to the imaginary door of her room, bows, and retreats. The Captain opens the door,
enters, bows, and kneels, but with dignity. The maid returns and kneels outside the door, listen-
ing. During the scene, she quietly reacts to the dialogue.

KOMACHI *(startled):* What? You again? How did you get in? *(spoken as he*
    enters, bows)

CAPTAIN
FUKAKUSA: Your maid is sympathetic to my interests.

    (He sits in an erect, formal position.)

KOMACHI: With your reputation, Captain, I can imagine why she might be
    cooperative.

CAPTAIN
FUKAKUSA: All right, I've loved other women. But for six months now, I've sought
    every opportunity to see you. And only you. . . . Why do you refuse to
    take me seriously? . . . *(faint music)* I wake in the night with a strange
    feeling . . . that I'll love you even after I die. Such love will endure.

KOMACHI: All men say such things, but what happens is something else. . . . Not
    long ago I wrote a poem on this well-worn theme. Have you heard it?

CAPTAIN
FUKAKUSA *(with exaggerated politeness):* The whole court has heard and admired
    it. *(reciting)*
    "With no visible sign it fades,
    the flower of a man's affection in this world."

KOMACHI: Well? If you're so much in love, why haven't you written me a poetic
    rebuttal? I have poems here from other suitors vowing their con-
    stancy. *(reading from one of the letters)*

"My heart, fadeless as the pines on a wind-swept cliff, bends only to your will." *(She picks up another letter, decides not to read it, and tosses it aside.)* And so on. *(A thought about the first poem occurs to her.)* Actually, "bends only to your will" is not too bad after "wind-swept." But the rest is appallingly trite. *(Her attention returns to the Captain.)* Well, when will I receive your poem?

CAPTAIN
FUKAKUSA: Never! *(He laughs and changes from the formal seated position to a cross-legged one.)* I'm a soldier, not a poet. Your reaction to any poem I could write would be scathing. *(He tries to amuse her.)* From a military point of view, my poem would be a tactical error.

KOMACHI *(dryly)*: Lack of poetic talent didn't stop these gentlemen.

(Faint music as she arranges the letters in a pattern, a teasing display of her options.)

CAPTAIN
FUKAKUSA: But don't you see, Komachi, I didn't send you a poem simply because I knew I couldn't write well enough to please you. *(a questioning look from Komachi)* My feelings have nothing to do with the conventional exchange of poems that goes on day after day, night after night, week after week at this court. *(Music begins to fade out.)* Conventional romances end in conventional boredom and parting. Decorous aristocrats may be able to confine their feelings within the required thirty-one syllables. Not me.

KOMACHI *(teasing, assuming an academic tone)*: There *is* such a thing as concise expression of intense emotion.

CAPTAIN
FUKAKUSA: A fine poet—you, at your best—can do that. Not these run-of-the-mill court lechers. *(indicating the letters)*

KOMACHI *(laughing)*: I see. *(She studies him and takes out a fan.)* Just because you don't send me conventional verses, I'm supposed to believe you don't have a conventional case of lust. . . . All right. . . . If your feelings are so deep, or grand, or whatever, send me a poem of . . . one hundred syllables.

CAPTAIN
FUKAKUSA: Komachi! If you insist on some ritual of courtship, set me a task more suited to my character and my abilities. . . . Let me do something . . . unheard of, to prove that my love is different.

KOMACHI: Something suitable. . . . Well then, something that permits you to display your daring, your persistence, your stubbornness, your arrogance,

CAPTAIN
FUKAKUSA: *My* arrogance?

KOMACHI   *(mocking)*: Oh yes, man-who-loves-as-no-other-can. . . . Something requiring action more than words . . . *(laughs)* I have it!

CAPTAIN
FUKAKUSA: Well?

KOMACHI: For one hundred nights you will come to visit me—or rather, you will come as far as my gate. But you will not see me. I may be at a party, or if at home, I may be . . . otherwise engaged.

CAPTAIN
FUKAKUSA: If you don't bother to see me, how will you know I'm following orders?

KOMACHI: Each night you will cut a mark on the post at my gate. The post where they tie up the horses. And no cutting two marks on the same night because I'll count every morning. And no nights off due to bad weather or pressing engagements or . . . anything.

CAPTAIN
FUKAKUSA   *(laughing)*: What other woman would ask, or even think, of such a plan? You're not serious, are you?

KOMACHI: Absolutely. *(Faint music begins again.)*

CAPTAIN
FUKAKUSA   *(studies Komachi, and then)*: . . . And if I do it?

KOMACHI: . . . Perhaps I could believe . . . that you *are* more than a "run-of-the-mill court lecher." . . . On the hundredth night, you need not go home.

CAPTAIN
FUKAKUSA   *(with an elaborate bow)*: I hear and obey. *(The speech and action are deliberately exaggerated; the emotion, resolute.)*

The Captain leaves, placing his costume on one of the kimono stands. Komachi puts her kimono on the other stand. All three players pick up lanterns and move into position to begin a stylized presentation of the nightly journeys.

III

A cyclic pattern begins on the guitar. During the following lines, the players are constantly in motion, largely walking patterns in an even rhythm. Literal miming should be avoided, although stylized gestures may be possible in places. The movement functions to create a sense of momentum and repetition, leaving the words to evoke the action and setting more specifically. The distribution of lines could be other than indicated but should relate to the choreography of the movement.

WOMAN 2: And so the hundred nights began. . . .

MAN: The Captain went on foot,
stealthily, in the dead of night,

WOMAN 1: for Komachi also said his visits must be secret.

WOMAN 2: No fanfare,

WOMAN 1: no friends to cheer him on,

MAN: a silent solitary trudging back and forth,
night after night,
with no companion but the moon
and thoughts of her.

(Flute melodies accompanied by the guitar from this point on.)

WOMAN 2: No poet himself,
he memorized the words of those more skilled
and spoke them to himself to pass the time.

MAN: "They say there is a still pool even in the middle of the rushing
whirlpool—
Why is there none in the whirlpool of my love?"[3]

WOMAN 2: And so the hundred nights went on. . . .

WOMAN 1: Late summer turned to autumn,
autumn to winter,
and still the Captain journeyed back and forth. . . .

MAN: He strode briskly on moonlit nights,
stumbled and cursed on dark ones,

WOMAN 2: endured bleak autumn rain,

WOMAN 1: brushed snow from his sleeves

WOMAN 2: and hunched his shoulders against raw winter wind,

MAN: thinking always of her
and the day she would trust his love. . . .

WOMAN 1: What was Komachi doing on those nights?

MAN: What did she feel as the marks reached seventy,

WOMAN 1: eighty,

WOMAN 2: ninety. . . .

MAN: The legend does not tell us this.

                It only says that on the night before the last. . . .

                (The players stop moving and the music ends.)

WOMAN 1

AND

WOMAN 2:   the Captain died.

MAN: Perhaps it was then that Komachi wrote this poem:

WOMAN 1:   "The flowers withered, their color faded away,

                while meaninglessly I spent my days in the world,

                and the long rains were falling."[4]

                *(The players arrange the lanterns in front of the kimono stand bearing the
                Captain's costume, kneel, and bow in ritual mourning. Then they replace the
                lanterns at the corners of the playing area.)*

IV

*Man kneeling down right; women, opposite side. One of the musicians has placed the low table,
a scroll, a teapot, and cups for the women. Court lady 2 is seated by the table, reading.*

MAN: After the episode of the hundred nights, the legend tells us little
                about Komachi's middle years. But you might say that the predictable
                happened. Or even that she—heartless bitch—got what was coming
                to her.

COURT
LADY 1   *(scurries along an imaginary corridor up stage, slides open a door, and
                bustles in):* My dear, I have the most delicious news!

COURT
LADY 2   *(gestures to have the door—left rudely open—closed; otherwise, little
                reaction):* Well?

COURT
LADY 1   *(shuts door, deflated):* Actually, you may have heard already.

COURT
LADY 2:   Oh, you mean about Komachi? Or rather, her husband

COURT
LADY 1   *(recovering her excitement):* . . . ran off with the foreign minister's
                daughter!

COURT LADY 2	*(dryly)*: Someone was bound to run off with her. Hasn't everyone been going on about her beauty, her melodious voice, her exquisite taste,
COURT LADY 1:	her voluptuous charm—just the tiresome way they used to rave about Komachi. She's certainly not getting any younger.
COURT LADY 2:	Are you? *(pours tea for Court Lady 1)*
COURT LADY 1:	Well anyway, now Komachi knows what it's like to lose a man to another woman.
COURT LADY 2:	Don't tell me you're still annoyed about. . . .
COURT LADY 1:	Of course not! I never cared enough about him to take it that seriously. . . . *(cautiously)* I suppose you've heard about Yasuhide, too?
COURT LADY 2:	The *poet* Yasuhide?
COURT LADY 1	*(with renewed energy)*: It seems he felt sorry for Komachi and invited her to go off to the provinces with him. He's just been appointed governor of . . . oh, I don't remember.
COURT LADY 2:	Undoubtedly some God-forsaken place with so little to administer that the emperor can risk sending a poet. . . . No, I hadn't heard about Yasuhide.
COURT LADY 1	*(delighted with herself)*: Oh well, dear, I guess I'm just a bit more au courant than you are.
COURT LADY 2:	You haven't told me whether Komachi accepted Yasuhide's invitation.
COURT LADY 1:	Can you really imagine Komachi going off to a place like that? Or with him, for that matter? *I* certainly wouldn't, even if he *is* a famous poet.
COURT LADY 2:	Komachi still has one point in her favor. She's a good poet herself. Many women *(pointed look at Court Lady 1)* would just snivel or mope around, but Komachi will get a poem out of these circumstances. Perhaps a memorable poem that people will quote when she's a withered old hag—maybe even after she's dead.

COURT
LADY 1   *(not to be outdone)*: She's already written it. . . . Well, she's written a
             new poem. *(recites melodramatically)* "Despairing and alone, a water
             weed torn from its roots. . . . " Oh, what *was* the rest of it!

COURT
LADY 2:   "Despairing and alone, a water weed torn from its roots,
             should a stream invite, would I not drift its way?"
             I heard the poem this morning . . . but not the gossip about Yasuhide.

COURT
LADY 1:   Of course, all the people who think they know so much about poetry
             are saying it's wonderful, but I don't especially like it.

COURT
LADY 2:   Why not?

COURT
LADY 1:   It's hardly elegant to compare oneself to a water weed!

COURT
LADY 2:   It's hardly elegant to be deserted.

V

A musician clears the table and other properties as the women move upstage. The Man and Woman 1 help the other woman (the actor-dancer) reverse the Komachi kimono to the old-and-tattered side and put it on. Guitar pulse from scene 3 reappears, later joined by flute motifs and accents on the drum(s). Speaking begins after the dancer starts moving. Again, any literal mime should be avoided. The dancer conveys the emotional essence more than the narrative of the lines. Man and Woman 1 move very little until the possession episode; they are narrating the tale for the audience.

MAN: After this, we lose sight of Komachi for many years.

WOMAN 1:   The legend says she lived to be an old and ugly woman.

MAN: Being a poet, she must have thought of the ancient poem:

WOMAN 1:   "If only, when one heard that Old Age was coming,
             one could bolt the door, answer

WOMAN 2:   'not at home'

WOMAN 1:   and refuse to meet him!"[5]

(Meanwhile, Woman 2 is dancing a highly stylized movement image of the old Komachi.)

MAN:	At ninety-nine, Komachi became a lonely derelict.
WOMAN 1:	She begged on the outskirts of villages and took brief refuge in convents.
WOMAN 2:	How I hate for people to see me now!
MAN:	She hid in the forest, gathering nuts and berries like some animal, sleeping in caves when she was lucky.
WOMAN 1:	Once she wrote:
	"How cold I am, a traveler sleeping on the rocks,
	Would they might lend me their moss robes."
MAN:	Often she longed to die.
WOMAN 2:	Why does my body linger here when my heart left this world so long ago?
MAN:	But her heart still clung to the past.
WOMAN 1:	Memory is both a blessing and a curse.

(Komachi moves youthfully and lyrically during the following lines.)

WOMAN 2:	I remember rooms bright with flowers and candlelight,
WOMAN 1:	gowns of silk and brocade,
MAN:	sleeves waving in the dance.
WOMAN 1:	How beautiful she was. . . .
MAN:	Flirtatious glances, nights of love,
WOMAN 1:	a heedless power held over many hearts. . . .
MAN:	such memories bring joy and strength *(dancer's movement quality begins to change)*
WOMAN 1:	but also bitterness and misery
MAN:	and regret . . . and remorse.

(Man approaches Woman 2. They perform movement together during which the robe passes to the Man, who assumes the role of Komachi possessed by the Captain.)

WOMAN 1:	Sometimes while Komachi was begging, she went mad, possessed by the memory of the Captain. But now she remembered a man she never knew, someone angry, threatening, vengeful. . . .

(Woman 2 disengages herself as the Captain/Komachi begins to move in ways combining menace and irrationality with variations on Komachi's earlier move-

ment. He gestures with a closed fan as if it were a weapon. The two other actors take the roles of village women.)

CAPTAIN/ KOMACHI:	Take me to Komachi!
VILLAGE WOMAN 1 (WOMAN 1):	But you *are* Komachi!
VILLAGE WOMAN 2:	Just take this food, dear, and. . . .

(Komachi threatens them physically, and they retreat a bit, watching.)

CAPTAIN FUKAKUSA:	Fools! I have given you an order. Take me to Komachi before I beat the hell out of you.
VILLAGE WOMAN 1 TO VILLAGE WOMAN 2:	When she's like this, she's got the strength of a woman half her age.
CAPTAIN FUKAKUSA:	God, when I think of the nonsense she demanded, those endless trips on foot, alone. She didn't really care if others saw me. It amused her to make the task as tedious as possible.

(The women try to slip away, but he cuts them off.)

VILLAGE WOMAN 2:	Sir, perhaps she really wasn't sure you loved her and was afraid. . . .
VILLAGE WOMAN 1:	Perhaps she really loved you but was too proud to. . . .
CAPTAIN FUKAKUSA:	Oh no! It gratified her arrogance to humiliate me. . . . Have you found her?
VILLAGE WOMAN 2	*(backing off)*: Perhaps she was sorry later. . . .
CAPTAIN FUKAKUSA:	That bitch? Never! Well, where is she?
VILLAGE WOMAN 1:	Look, sir, there she is. *(points behind him)*
CAPTAIN FUKAKUSA:	Where? I don't see her.

VILLAGE
WOMAN 2　　*(catching on)*: Over there, sir, beyond those trees.

VILLAGE
WOMAN 1:　　She's beckoning to you.

(The women run off in the opposite direction.)

CAPTAIN
FUKAKUSA:　　She'll be sorry now!

(He rushes in the indicated direction, shows confusion and diminishing energy, stumbles and falls to his knees—the possession beginning to subside. The stage lighting begins to fade into a moonlight effect. Komachi comes to her senses.)

This would not be had I not. . . .

(Woman 2 returns, kneels behind the Man, arms around him, cradling him, gently takes from him the fan he has brandished as a weapon. The two begin to rock in slow, trancelike unison, gazing at an imaginary moon.)

KOMACHI
(MAN):　　If I could have a heart as cloudless as the moon tonight. . . .

WOMAN 1:　　The legend says a Buddhist priest exorcised the Captain's spirit.

(She moves around the other two in rhythmic walking with a few hieratic gestures. Woman 2 helps the Man take off the kimono. After the exorcism, the three players have a brief movement ritual that ends with the kimono stretched out on the floor as it was in scene 1. In the last lines, all the players are just that, speaking to one another and to the audience about the larger implications of Komachi's life. They kneel around the kimono.)

MAN:　　Perhaps she suffered enough. . . .
　　　　and found peace at last.

WOMAN 1:　　All that lingers now are the poems, the tales,
　　　　and the lessons of her life.

MAN:　　Even the withered branch of an ancient tree can flower in the spring.

(Woman 2 places a beautiful opened fan beside the Komachi kimono. The lights begin to fade.)

WOMAN 2:   Make of her life what you will,
             but let her poems,
WOMAN 1:   her heart-flowers,
MAN: be her penance, and a welcome legacy.

             (blackout)

NOTES

1. A translation of *Aoi no ue* appears in the second volume of Nippon gakujutsu shinkōkai, eds., *Japanese Noh Drama* (Tokyo: Nippon gakujutsu shinkokai, 1955–1960).

2. Translations of *Kayoi Komachi* and *Sekidera Komachi* are included in Donald Keene, ed., *Twenty Plays of the Nō Theatre* (New York: Columbia University Press, 1970). Volume 3 of *Japanese Noh Drama* includes *Sotoba Komachi*, but the translation in Donald Keene, ed., *Anthology of Japanese Literature* (New York: Grove Press, 1960) may be more readily available.

3. Arthur Waley, *Japanese Poetry: The Uta* (Honolulu: University of Hawaii Press, 1976; first published by Clarendon Press, Oxford, 1919), p. 66.

4. Donald Keene's translation of this poem appears on p. 81 of his *Anthology of Japanese Literature*.

5. Waley, *Japanese Poetry*, p. 69.

20

Plovers: A tarō kaja *Play*

◎

CAROLYN A. MORLEY

Plovers is one of the *tarō kaja* (servant) plays that make up about one-third of the kyōgen repertory. The plays are one-act comic skits about forty minutes in length and are traditionally performed with nō plays at nō theaters. A preference for a common, earthy tone and a comic view of the frailties of humankind distinguishes kyōgen plays from nō. The mischievous yet good-hearted Tarō Kaja is representative of the spirit of kyōgen humor. Even though other roles may make greater physical and psychological demands on the actor's talent—such as the fox in *Tsurigitsune* (Fox Trapping) or the blind man in *Tsukimizato* (Moon-Viewing Blind Man)—the actor will not achieve full recognition until he has mastered the role of Tarō Kaja and made it his own.

In addition to the tarō kaja plays, the kyōgen repertory includes master plays, woman plays, mountain priest plays, Buddhist priest plays, farmer plays, bridegroom plays, blind man plays, and miscellaneous plays. All the characters are drawn from commoner life in the fourteenth through the mid-seventeenth centuries when the plays were still improvised and performed before a wide variety of audiences. By the mid-seventeenth century, the plays were recorded in full for the first time. The actors began to organize themselves into troupes in order to align themselves with the dominant nō troupes that were already receiving the patronage of the Tokugawa government.

Of the three kyōgen schools emerging at that time—the Okura, Izumi, and Sagi—the Okura and Izumi have continued into modern times. The various families of actors belong to one of these two schools. The Nomura family of Tokyo, for example, is a member of the Izumi school, and the Shigeyama family located in Kyoto is part of the Okura school. The Sagi school disappeared during the Meiji Restoration when it lost government support.

Tarō Kaja, the servant, has been referred to as "everyman." His relationship with his master is often one of affectionate indulgence. In one kyōgen play, when his master gambles and loses Tarō Kaja in a throw of dice (*Nawanai*, Rope Twisting), Tarō Kaja grumbles openly about his master's disloyalty, prompting the master to apologize. Tarō subsequently behaves so badly to his new master that he is soon returned home again. By all appearances, the master has the right to dispose of Tarō Kaja as he wishes, but in reality he cannot bring himself to do so. Their relationship holds fast throughout, however strained it may appear at any given moment. In the servant plays, Tarō Kaja is generally the butt of the humor, a good-natured, mischievous sidekick, but in the master plays, he is frequently the foil for an illiterate master or lord or the indulgent straight man to his bungling master. In *Hagi daimyō* (Lord of the Bush Clover), for example, his attempt to coach his boorish lord in the niceties of poetry proves a miserable embarrassment to both. Tarō Kaja's character, as it appears to us in texts from the mid-seventeenth century on, is neither defiant nor abject.

These plays do not suggest the stirrings of revolt in the master–servant relationship but, rather, an admiration for cleverness and cunning, whether on the part of the master or the servant. The master's position reflects the fluidity of society in the fourteenth, fifteenth, and early sixteenth centuries, when a man might acquire landlord status overnight through warfare or reclamation of land. Clearly, the master and his servant are not meant to represent the households of the formidable warlords in this and later periods.[1] The best evidence of kyōgen's stature is the fact that it was designated the official state entertainment along with nō during the Tokugawa period. Presumably, the government dignitaries found kyōgen neither subversive nor offensive.

The term *irony* in reference to the theater indicates an almost conspiratorial understanding between the audience and the actor to which the character is not privy. This shared point of view is also what we experience in kyōgen, because kyōgen roles are clearly defined character types whose depiction is dictated by tradition. The actor's attitude toward the character remains consistent throughout the genre and is what accounts for the universality of the character type communicated to the audience.

Through subtle changes in timing and voice modulation, an actor playing Tarō Kaja is able to project his own persona through tightly controlled and highly ritualized patterns of performance, against a backdrop of stylization associated with the character. Thus, instead of merging with the role, as, for example, Charlie Chaplin and Buster Keaton do in their comedies, the kyōgen actor appears to be silently commenting on the character to the audience.

The focus of interest in *Plovers* is the play(s) within the play. The actor performing Tarō Kaja moves in and out of a variety of roles at the same time as he projects a pleasurable immersion in Tarō's mimetic games that goes beyond simple enjoyment in deceit. The audience's perception of the actor's—and thus the character's—transformations is dependent on the degree of the actor's identification with the role at any given moment in the play. This transformation takes place on a number of intersecting planes, beginning with the actor's primary relationship to his character, Tarō Kaja, and preceding to the character's relationship to the roles that he in turn assumes. In his first role, Tarō is his master's innocent messenger. He goes to a wine merchant to buy a keg of wine. We (the audience) are aware that Tarō is already playing a role. That is, he must coax a keg of wine from the merchant without paying for it. Later, in further attempts to obtain the wine, Tarō takes on other roles, each time becoming more deeply immersed in play. For example, he offers to demonstrate the method of plover trapping, which he claims to have witnessed on the shores of Ise on his way to the Tsushima festival. The merchant is delighted, especially since he can participate by singing an accompaniment. Tarō thus becomes one of the children catching plovers at the same time as he is the plover itself crying "Peep peep peep chirp" as he circles the plover (that is, the wine keg). For the audience, the thrill is wondering whether Tarō will get away with his ruse. The actor becomes part of the scene at the same time as he signals the audience of Tarō's intention to abscond with the keg.

In this case, Tarō's intention remains clear. In other plays, however, the mimetic scene itself so preoccupies the character that his original intention is all but forgotten, and the actor seems to invite the audience to join at least momentarily in the world of play that has so absorbed the character. For example, the husband in *Ishigami* (Stone God), disguised as a statue, willingly risks being found out by his wife in order to take pleasure in mimicking her devotional dance. The mountain priest in *Kagyu* (Snail) indulges himself in play for no other purpose than teasing the young boy who has mistaken him for a snail, and in *Suehirogari* (Umbrella/fan) the master so loses himself in his servant's umbrella song that he completely forgets his grievance.

In the final scene of *Plovers*, Tarō entertains the merchant with a scene of ritual horseback archery. The merchant is told to use his fan to sweep aside imag-

inary crowds while Tarō rides through them on a stick horse. Taking advantage
of the merchant's absorption in the mime, Tarō grabs the saké barrel and makes
a beeline for the bridge. Out of the corner of his eye, the merchant catches sight
of Tarō and demands to know where he is going with the saké keg. "You mean
this? This?" Tarō taunts him and, turning toward the exit, calls out, "This goes
to the master. *Here comes the horse, here comes the horse!*" The excitement of tension and release in the plot is enhanced by the engagement and disengagement
of the actor from the mimetic scene and from the character. The finale, with its
ironic use of the chant from the horseback archery scene, enables the actor to
end the play with a wink at the audience.

Plovers is of special interest here because it was the first kyōgen play to be performed publicly by a foreigner. Donald Keene took the role of Tarō Kaja in a
1955 version of the play by the Shigeyama troupe in Kyoto. The audience was a
notable one, as it included the well-known novelists Tanizaki Jun'ichirō and
Kawabata Yasunari. Donald Keene's sobriquet "the blue-eyed Tarō Kaja" dates
from this performance.

Plovers[2]

Characters:

> Tarō Kaja: short *hakama* and robe, striped jacket
> Master: long hakama and robe, checked jacket, small sword
> Wine Merchant: long hakama and robe, checked jacket, small sword

> *(The Master, Tarō Kaja, and the Wine Merchant enter the stage one after the
> other. The Master announces himself, and the other two seat themselves at the
> rear of the stage.)*

MASTER: I live around here. All of a sudden, I find I'm expecting guests this
          evening, so I'm going to call Tarō and send him out to our saké shop
          for a keg. Hey there! Hey, Tarō! Are you around?

          (He approaches the waki seat.)

TARŌ   *(stands):* Yes, sir!

          (He approaches upstage right.)

MASTER: You're here, then?

TARŌ:	In your presence, sir.
MASTER:	Already? Hard to believe. I suddenly find I'm having guests this evening; go and get me a keg from our saké shop.
TARŌ:	Of course, sir, but who'd give me anything? You're not paid up there.
MASTER:	That'll be taken care of soon enough. Come to think of it, I hear you're buddies with the owner. Go entertain him with a funny story and bring me back a barrel.
TARŌ:	You're right. It's true I get on with him, but that doesn't mean he's ever said (*chuckles*), "Here Tarō, have a drink?"
MASTER:	That's enough! If you'll go now, I'll let you open the keg and take the first drink.
TARŌ:	What? What's that? Did you say that if I go and get it, I can open the keg?
MASTER:	Absolutely.
TARŌ:	At your service!
MASTER:	Come back soon. We're busy here too.
TARŌ:	Yes, sir.
MASTER:	Be off. (*orders*)
TARŌ:	Yes, sir. (*receives the order*)

(*The Master exits.*)

TARŌ	(*faces front at the jōza*): Well! There's no one as spoiled as my master! He still hasn't made good on his bill, and yet he keeps ordering me back for more. Anyway, I've got to go. I better hurry. (*starts out*) The fact is, if I go ahead and he gives me something, great. If not, it's a waste of time. Anyway, I'll entertain him well, then he's bound to let me have a keg. (*circles the stage and stops at the jōza*) I'm already here. I'll just let him know. Excuse me? Are you in?
WINE MERCHANT	(*stands*): What? There's someone calling outside. Who is it? Who's there please? (*comes forward to the waki seat*)
TARŌ:	It's me.
MERCHANT:	Ah! Tarō, my good man! I've been waiting for you.
TARŌ:	Oh? And why's that?
MERCHANT:	What're you planning to do about your bill?
TARŌ:	Ah, yes! Please give us a day or two. We'll settle up shortly.

MERCHANT: No, no! I'm sick of hearing "Just a day or two, just a day or two." Pay up now!

TARŌ: What am I thinking of? Of course you're right. It'll be taken care of right away. Actually, I'm here again for the same thing. We're suddenly expecting guests this evening, so the master sent me to say that we'd be grateful if you'd let us have a barrel of that delicious saké of yours.

MERCHANT: That's ridiculous! He hasn't even paid up, and yet he sends you here with another order?

TARŌ: Yes, sir. I knew you'd say that, and I'm ready to pay.

MERCHANT: What? You've brought the money?

TARŌ: Yes, sir.

MERCHANT: Well then, I don't care who takes the barrel. Wait here and I'll go get it.

TARŌ: Yes, sir.

(The Merchant brings a barrel out from the rear of the stage and places it front center. A white strip of cloth is wrapped around it for transporting.)

MERCHANT: Now then, I bottled this and had it put aside ready to send out, but it's so unusual for you to say you'll pay up front that I'm going to let you have it instead. Quick, take it away.

TARŌ: Then, I don't get to sample it?

MERCHANT: No, that's not necessary.

TARŌ: Well then, I'll just pick it up like this and go.

(He carries the saké barrel to the jōza.)

MERCHANT: Hey, hey! Hold on there!

TARŌ: What?

MERCHANT: Pay first, then you can go.

TARŌ: For what?

MERCHANT: For the saké, of course!

TARŌ: Yes, sir. You mean for the saké.

MERCHANT: That's right.

TARŌ: How could I forget? I'll pay you right now. *(looks about)* Huh? I don't get it. I know I brought it with me. I don't know what could've happened. Oh, excuse me. Did I drop anything over there?

MERCHANT: No. There's nothing here. What's the problem?

TARŌ: I did get the money from my master, but I was in such a hurry that I left it on the corner of the shelf. I'll take this now and pay you later.

(He picks up the barrel to carry it off.)

MERCHANT: Hey there! Hold on! First the money, then the saké!

(He takes back the barrel and replaces it at front stage center.)

TARŌ: Well, I can't make you out at all, sir.

MERCHANT: Why is that?

TARŌ: This isn't the first time we've bought saké from you. You could let me take it this once without paying first.

MERCHANT: That's not unreasonable, but there's something I simply don't understand about you.

TARŌ: What's that?

MERCHANT: When you have the money, you go elsewhere. It's only when you don't that you come to me. It's outrageous!

TARŌ: Prove it!

MERCHANT: Shall I? There's never a day when you don't drink, is there?

TARŌ: True, true, there's never a day when we don't drink.

MERCHANT: That's just it! Think about it. The fact that you haven't come recently is proof enough.

TARŌ: Well, of course I haven't. We don't need saké while we're out. I just got back from accompanying my master to the Tsushima festival in Owari.[3]

MERCHANT: Really! You went to the Tsushima festival!

TARŌ: That's right.

MERCHANT: I've heard that festival is very interesting. What'd you see?

TARŌ: It was fascinating. I know you like my stories, so I brought back a tale or two.

MERCHANT: Why, that's excellent! Luckily, we both happen to be free, so let's hear all about it.

TARŌ: All right then, shall I begin?

MERCHANT: Sure.

TARŌ: First off, on the way to Ise from here, there's a spot on the shore where the children trap plovers. Not part of the festival but very interesting.

MERCHANT: Indeed, it must be.

TARŌ: Since I'm going to describe it anyway, shall I show you how it's done?

MERCHANT: Sure.

TARŌ: Then I'll need a partner.

MERCHANT: Who?

TARŌ: You.

MERCHANT: Me?

TARŌ: Yes, yes, you'll do. You say:

> *Plovers on the shores*
> *their voices crying to one another . . .*
> then I sing,
> *Peep, peep, peep, chirp*
> *Peep, peep, peep-peep . . .* [4]
> and we trap the plover.

MERCHANT: Excellent.

TARŌ: We need a plover over here.

MERCHANT: What can we use for a plover?

TARŌ: This saké keg'll do fine.

MERCHANT: No, no, that's too big for a plover.

TARŌ: Maybe so, but if you just pretend it's a plover, it'll do.

MERCHANT: True. If I just pretend, it'll do. All right. Shall I begin?

TARŌ: Quick! Sing!

MERCHANT: All right.

> *Plovers along the shores*
> *Crying out to one another. . . .*

TARŌ: Wait a minute! The plover would notice and fly off if you stared at it like that. Hide behind your fan and sing as though you were sneaking up on the plover.

MERCHANT: Then how will I know when it gets interesting?

TARŌ: I'll signal when it gets to the interesting part, so whatever you do, don't look.

MERCHANT: I'll wait for your signal, then.

TARŌ: Sing!

MERCHANT: All right. (*opens his fan and hides his face behind it*)

> *Plovers along the shore*
> *Crying out to one another. . . .*

TARŌ   (*opens his fan and dances across the stage*):

Peep, peep, peep, chirp

Peep, peep, peep-peep

Peep, peep, peep, chirp

Peep, peep, peep-peep.

Peep, off he flies!

MASTER: *Plovers along the shore*

Crying out to one another. . . .

TARŌ: *Peep, peep, peep, chirp*

Peep, peep, peep-peep

Peep, peep, peep, chirp

Peep, peep, peep-peep

Peep, peep, peep, chirp

Peep, peep, peep-peep.

(*As he dances, he lifts up the barrel. The Merchant watches him.*)

Hey! Why're you watching?

MERCHANT: It sounded so interesting that I looked.

TARŌ: I said I'd signal when it got interesting. Now don't watch.

MERCHANT: I'll be waiting for your signal, then.

TARŌ: Quick! Sing!

MERCHANT: All right.

Plovers along the shore

Calling out to one another. . . .

TARŌ: *Peep, peep, peep, chirp*

Peep, peep, peep-peep.

Peep, peep, peep, chirp

Peep, peep, peep-peep

Peep, and off it flies.

(*He lifts up the barrel and carries it off to the bridge.*)

MERCHANT   (*seeing him*): Hey! Wait up! Where're you off to with
my keg?

TARŌ: This is the part where they trap the plover.

MERCHANT: That's dumb.

(The Merchant brings the keg back and places it at front center.)

Tell me another story.

TARŌ: Well then, this time I'll show you how they pull the festival floats.

MERCHANT: Splendid!

TARŌ: I need a partner again.

MERCHANT: Will I do?

TARŌ: Sure. Go ahead. It's not particularly hard. You just sing "*Yo, heave, ho!*" and I'll yell "*A-one-and-a-two-and-a-three*" and I'll show how they pull the floats.

MERCHANT: Sounds like fun.

TARŌ: Then I need a float over here.

MERCHANT: What'll we use for a float?

TARŌ: Ask 'n see if there's anything inside that we can use for a float.

MERCHANT: All right. *(turns to his left)* Hey! Is there anything inside we can use for a float? Nothing, huh?

(While he calls, Tarō carries the barrel to upstage right.)

Hold on! Where're you going with the barrel?

TARŌ: I wondered if it would do for the float.

MERCHANT: No, no! It would be too small for a float.

(He returns the barrel.)

TARŌ: It's small but if you just pretend it's a float, it'll do.

MERCHANT: True, if I just pretend, it'll do all right.

TARŌ   *(removing the white cotton rope wrapped around the barrel)*: Luckily, there's just the right kind of rope attached. I'll pull it like this. Get going!

MERCHANT: Then, shall I begin?

TARŌ: That's right. Go!

MERCHANT   *(tapping the rhythm on his palm with his closed fan)*: Yo, heave, ho! Yo, heave, ho!

TARŌ   *(dances about as he pulls on the rope which is stretched out to its full length)*: A-one-and-a-two-and-a-three; a-one-and-a-two-and-a-three.

MERCHANT: Yo-heave-ho; yo-heave-ho!

TARŌ: A-one-and-a-two-and-a three; a-one-and-a-two-and-a-three! And-a-one; and-a-one; and-a-one; and-a-one!

(He pulls the keg toward the bridge.)

MERCHANT: Hey there! Where're you off to with my barrel?

TARŌ: This is where they take off.

MERCHANT: That's stupid.

(He returns the keg to center stage and wraps the white rope around it again.)

Show me something else.

TARŌ: Well! You're certainly demanding!

MERCHANT: I'm not demanding. You're just using any chance you can to run off with the saké keg so we never get to the story, and it's boring. Tell me another.

TARŌ: Just a minute! I'm busy at home too. I'll go and get your money. *(starts to go)*

MERCHANT: Hold on now! Wait up! One more story won't take long. Tell it first and then go.

TARŌ: No matter how many stories I tell, you still won't give me the saké, so I'm going home for the money first. *(starts to leave again)*

MERCHANT: Hey now! Hold on a minute! You really know how to get to a man. If your story's good this time, I might just let you have that saké keg on account.

TARŌ: What'd you say? Did you say that if the story's good this time, you might let me take the keg?

MERCHANT: That's right.

TARŌ: Well, all right then, just a short one. But you don't like stories that need the keg, right?

MERCHANT: I certainly don't.

TARŌ: Well then, how about I show you ritual horseback archery[5] this time? That won't need the keg.

MERCHANT: That sounds good. Shall I be your partner? If you need one again?

TARŌ: Yes, go ahead. Open your fan and call out *"Make way for the horses, make way for the horses!"* and clear the path for the horses. I'll say *"Here come the horses, here come the horses"* and perform all sorts of acrobatics.

MERCHANT: Wonderful!

TARŌ: Isn't there anything around here we can use for a horse?

(The stage hand brings out a bamboo stick.)

Look! What luck! This bamboo staff'll be perfect. I'll use it like this
(*straddles the staff*) for a stick horse, so you can clear the path now.

MERCHANT: Shall I clear the way then?

TARŌ: Go on!

MERCHANT: All right.

(*He opens his fan before him, and striking it against his open left hand, he
moves forward.*)

Make way for the horses, make way for the horses!

TARŌ   (*straddling the bamboo stick and following after the merchant*): *Here come
the horses, here come the horses.*

MERCHANT: *Make way for the horses, make way for the horses!*

TARŌ: *Here come the horses, here come the horses.*

MERCHANT: *Make way for the horses, make way for the horses!*

TARŌ: *Here come the horses, here come the horses.*

(*As he circles the stage, he grabs the keg and makes off with it to the bridge.*)

MERCHANT (*noticing Tarō, calls from upstage left*): Hey! What's going on! Hey!
Hey!

TARŌ   (*glancing back from the bridge*): Yeah?

MERCHANT: Where're you off to with my keg?

TARŌ: You mean this? (*lifting up the keg to show the merchant*) This?

MERCHANT: That's right.

TARŌ: This goes to the master. (*turns toward the curtain*) Here comes the horse,
here comes the horse! (*exits*)

MERCHANT (*clapping his hands together*): By the three holy treasures! I've been
had! Where'd that sneak go? Catch him! Get him! Get him! (*chases
Tarō offstage*)

NOTES

1. Plays like *Imamairi* contrast the master's boast of a large household with the presence of only a single servant.

2. *Chidori.* Found in the texts of all schools of kyōgen. It appears as *Hamachidori* in the *Tensho bon* and as *Tsushima matsuri* in the *Kyōgen ki.* This translation is from the Okura school text found

in Koyama Hiroshi et al., eds., *Kyōgen*, in *Nihon koten bungaku taikei*, vol. 1 (Tokyo: Iwanami shoten, 1972).

3. The Tsushima festival takes place on June 14 and 15. It is famous for the lanterns floated on boats down the Tenno River.

4. The chant is based on the song *Uji no sarashi* found in collections of kyōgen song and dance.

5. Performed at shrine festivals. The archer on horseback aims at targets hung on three boards.

21

Images of Fidelity and Infidelity in Kosode *Design*

◉

AMANDA MAYER STINCHECUM

Most of the motifs decorating *kosode* of the Edo period seem to reflect the world in which the people who wore them actually lived. Images of the flowers, grasses, and trees common to the hills of Yamato and the familiar animals and birds inhabiting them; landscapes of seashore and lakefront, mountains and riverbanks, meandering streams and wooded islands; shrines and temples, mansions and thatched huts, bridges and boats; folding fans and decorated boxes, bamboo screens and saké cups, fulling blocks and mortars, fishnets and buckets appear to have been plucked from the matrix of rural and urban lives. In fact many—perhaps most—of them derive from the richly visual imagery of classical Japanese literature.[1] *Waka* poetry (thirty-one-syllable Japanese poems), as well as poems composed in Chinese to accompany them; the repertoire of the nō theater; and especially two Heian-period narrative tales, *Ise monogatari* and *Genji monogatari*, provided the imagery for many kosode—forerunner of today's kimono—created during the seventeenth through the nineteenth centuries. Because poems from the canon of classical poetry would be recognized from a few characters not only by members of the military and court elite but even by a well-read merchant, designs alluding to waka often included written characters (usually embroidered in gold or colors) worked in with a pictorial image alluding to the same poem.

The existence of a large body of kosode and other textiles, as well as paint-ing, lacquerware, and metalwork—decorated not with written characters, however, but with imagery derived from classical Japanese literature—indicates that the use of written characters in textile decoration is only one expression of the visual qualities of literary images.

Sue no Matsuyama (Pine Mountain of Sue) appears first as an *utamakura* (literally "poem pillow"; loosely defined, a place-name with conventional literary associations) in the first royal anthology of waka, the *Kokin wakashū* (usually abbreviated *Kokinshū*). In fact, it appears twice in the collection, once in a poem by Fujiwara Okikaze (one of the compilers of the anthology, which was completed in the early tenth century), included in the Winter Poems section; and once in an anonymous poem from the "Azuma uta" (Poems from Eastern Japan) section, attributed to the province of Mutsu. It is not possible to determine which was composed first, but the poem by Okikaze is conceptually simpler (and correspondingly less interesting):

1	*Ura chikaku*	Snow falling
	furikuru yuki wa	near the shore
	shiranami no	looks as if the white waves
	Sue no Matsuyama	might cover
	kosu ka to zo miru	Pine Mountain of Sue.

(KKS, *book 6, poem 326)*[2]

The use of the line *Sue no Matsuyama*, with no further geographical qualifier, suggests that a mountain called Matsuyama, in Sue, had already become a recognized place (or place-name) by the time the *Kokinshū* was compiled. The poem expresses poetic confusion, likening the gusts of snow swirling around the mountain to the white cresting of waves, an additional element frequently associated with Sue no Matsuyama and often used as a *kakekotoba* (a pivot word) with the verb *shiranu* ("does not know"). The poem also has an underlying negative resonance, as of something improbable or impossible, reinforced by Lady Tosa's poem (3). The second *Kokinshū* example hints more strongly at dark undercurrents.

2	*Kimi o okite*	If I left you,
	adashi kokoro o	setting
	wa ga motaba	my fickle heart elsewhere,
	Sue no Matsuyama	surely the waves would cover
	nami mo koenamu.	Pine Mountain of Sue.

(*Anonymous,* KKS, *book 20, poem 1093)*

Perhaps precisely because the imagery of this poem is simpler than that of Okikaze's, it sounds emotional depths that echo throughout not only the imperial anthologies but also the most influential work of classical Japanese narrative fiction, *Genji monogatari* (The Tale of Genji).[3] The improbability of the sea's sweeping over the top of a mountain here represents a vow of undying love. Although the overall sense of the poem is a pledge of fidelity, the first line, *Kimi o okite* (setting you aside), and the second, *adashi kokoro o* (fickle heart), first presents a supposition of infidelity and then denies it by positing an unlikely—perhaps even impossible—event as a concomitant or resulting phenomenon. Even this promise contains the seeds of betrayal.

A third early poem, by Lady Tosa, appears in the *Gosen wakashū* (usually abbreviated *Gosenshū*), compiled in 951 of leftovers from the *Kokinshū*.

3	*wa ga sode wa*	Are my sleeves
	na ni tatsu Sue no	the notorious Sue
	Matsuyama ka	no Matsuyama?
	sora yori nami no	Drenched by waves from the heavens,
	koenu hi wa nashi	No day passes when they are not engulfed.[4]

(Gosenshū, book 10, poem 683)

According to Katagiri Yōichi, *na ni tatsu*, which I have translated as "notorious," is linked with the adjective *adashi* (unfaithful, as *adashi kokoro*, "fickle heart," in *kimi o okite*) and thus has a pejorative sense. *Sora yori nami* (waves from the heavens) links the waves (*nami*) and Pine Mountain to the poet's tears (*namida*), reinforcing the rather indirectly stated meaning of "tear-drenched sleeves." The theme of betrayal is therefore implied here both by the negative cast given to Sue no Matsuyama through *na ni tatsu* and by the poet's sorrow, revealed in her tears. The poem carries the image of Sue no Matsuyama beyond the descriptive nature of Okikaze's, beyond the promise of *kimi o okite* to a lament of disappointed love.

But it is in the *Genji monogatari*, written about a century later than the compilation of the *Kokinshū*, that the image becomes most strongly associated with intimations and then thinly veiled accusations of infidelity. This meaning develops progressively in the course of the narrative, as it does in the preceding three examples. Its first occurrence in *Genji*, book 6, "Suetsumuhana," serves as an ornament to the natural setting, adding a layer (albeit shallow) of suggestion to the image of snow cascading from the branches of a pine as Genji leaves the dilapidated residence of the princess with the red nose.

Tachibana no ki no uzumoretaru mizuijin meshite harawase-tamau. Urayamigao ni matsu no ki no onore okikaerite sato koboruru yuki mo na ni tatsu Sue no to miyuru nado o ito fukakarazu to mo nadaraka naru hodo ni aishirawamu hito mo ga na to mitamau.[5]

He calls his retainer and has him brush off the mandarin orange tree that has become buried. With an envious look, a pine tree springs upright, and the sudden cascade of snow looks like the famous one of Sue. Even if it were not a deep love, if only there were someone who would respond suitably, he thinks as he looks at the scene.

Abe Akio and his colleagues observed that the Kawachi-bon text reads *nami kosu Sue no* in place of *na ni tatsu Sue no*, which would reflect the flatly unemotional imagery of Okikaze's poem rather than the more highly charged state depicted in the *Gosenshū* poem. This reading would accord more closely with the circumstances, in which Genji longs for a companion who would share his (sometimes purely literary) responses to things. Indeed, it is difficult to associate the grief that causes the *Gosenshū* poet to soak her sleeves with tears daily with this innocuous scene, or Genji's meeting with the red-nosed princess preceding it. As in Okikaze's poem, the image of Sue no Matsuyama here serves as the vehicle of some slight literary play.

The second time it appears in *Genji*, Sue no Matsuyama does not take the form of the entire utamakura (Sue no Matsuyama) but alludes to it more obliquely. In the "Akashi" chapter, during Genji's exile from the capital, he writes in anguish to Murasaki no Ue about his affair with the Akashi lady. Her reply is couched in a tone of quiet reproach:

"Shinobikanetaru on'yumegatari ni tsukete mo, omoiawaseraruru koto ōkaru o. . . ."[6]
    "Concerning the dreamlike incident you could not keep to yourself, there are many similar instances I could think of. . . ."

4   *"Uranaku mo*   "Ingenuously
        omoikeru ka na   I believed it,
        chigirishi o   the promise you made.
        matsu yori nami wa   Waiting for you, I thought the waves
        koeji mono zo to"   would never rise above the pines."

Oiraka naru mono kara, tadanarazu kasume-tamaeru o, ito aware ni uchi-okigataku mita-maite, nagori hisashū, shinobi no tabine mo shitamawazu.

Although she had written so generously, quite out of the ordinary, only hinting at her feelings, it moved him deeply, making it difficult for him to set down her letter. His own regrets lingered for a long while, and for some time he did not make any secret nocturnal visits to the Akashi lady.

Although the word *yama* (mountain) and the place-name, Sue, do not appear in Murasaki Shikibu's poem, the image of the waves rushing over the pine trees; the use of the words *matsu* (meaning both "pine" and "wait," having something of the sense of the English verb "to pine for"), *nami* (waves), and *koeji* (will not rise); and the inclusion of the syllables *ura* (inlet, shore) in the first word of the poem (*uranaku*), point to the author's familiarity with and skillful allusion to the two *Kokinshū* poems.[7] *Nami* also implies the verb *nashi* (there is not), suggesting there is nothing to do but wait (*matsu yori nashi*), as well as *namida* (tears), implying something like "I have cried so much that the level of my tears rises above the tops of the pines." A full reading of the poem requires the reader also to be cognizant of at least the second of the *Kokinshū* poems. Unless the promise of *kimi o okite* is understood, the meaning of its revocation will be lost. The context leaves no doubt in the literate reader's mind that Murasaki no Ue is delicately informing Genji of the pain his affair is causing her.

The third use of the Sue no Matsuyama image in *Genji* occurs in the "Ukifune" chapter. It, too, is an allusion rather than a use of the full utamakura. When Kaoru returns from Uji, having discovered Ukifune's liaison with Prince Niou, his anger veers back and forth between Niou and Ukifune:

> *Michi sugara nao ito osoroshiku kumanaku owasuru miya nari ya. Ika narikemu tsuide ni saru hito ari to kikitamaikemu. Ikade iiyori-tamaikemu. . . . Yamugoto naku omoisome-hajimeshi hito naraba koso arame nao saru mono nite okitaramu. . . .*
>
> *Kashiko ni wa, ontsukai no rei yori shigeki ni tsukete mo mono omou koto samazama nari. Tada kaku zo notamaeru.*[8]

On his way home, he thinks, "That prince is indeed uncannily persistent! On what occasion could he have heard that she was there? How had he made his approach to her? . . . If he himself had begun by treating her as someone of importance in his life, that would be one thing—but as it was, he had left her the way she was."

At Uji, she broods about his messengers arriving more frequently than usual. His message said only:

5	*"Nami koyuru*	Unaware that the time had come
	koro to mo shirazu	when the waves crested over
	Sue no Matsu	the pines of Sue,

> *matsuramu to nomi*   I thought only
> *omoikeru ka na*   that you would surely wait.

Hito ni warawasetamau na. Please do not make people laugh at me."

Here, too, Murasaki Shikibu has not included the word mountain (*yama*) but has shortened the utamakura to the five-syllable Sue no Matsu. In addition to being a place-name, *sue* means "end," so that *shirazu sue no matsu*, although not parsing grammatically, also suggests the meaning "waiting for an end I did not foresee." But once again, the images of the waves cresting and the pines of Sue, along with *shirazu* (unaware) implying the *shiranami* (white waves) of the Okikaze poem, clearly refer to the *Kokinshū* verses. Kaoru's poem is not especially noteworthy for its literary quality, but in the context of the narrative, the harshness of its sarcasm and the coldness of his comment at the end are startling. Here, as in "Akashi," the image of the impossible, unthinkable event come to pass—the waves cresting over Pine Mountain in Sue—is meant unambiguously as an accusation of infidelity. The "Akashi" passage bears relatively little weight in the narrative of Genji and his great love for Lady Murasaki and his lesser loves for others. But Kaoru's discovery of Ukifune's betrayal and his way of revealing this knowledge to her (which might be said to augur Ukifune's false death in the rushing current of the river) are pivotal to the unfolding of the Uji chapters. The image of Sue no Matsuyama has become a memorable one because of its use here.

It occurs again in the *Goshūi wakashū* (usually abbreviated *Goshūishū*), compiled in 1086, after *Genji monogatari* was written, although the poet, Kiyowara Motosuke (908–990), lived a century earlier, before the composition of *Genji*.

> *Kokoro kawarite-haberikeru onna ni hito ni kawarite*
>   Written to a woman whose feelings had changed, in place of her former lover

> 6   *Chigiriki na*   Although wringing out the sleeves
>   *katami ni sode o*   on which we pledged
>   *shiboritsutsu*   our love, now damp with my tears
>   *Sue no Matsuyama*   I had thought the waves would not flood
>   *nami kosaji to wa*   Pine Mountain of Sue.

> (Goshūishū, Koi IV, *poem 770*)

With its sodden sleeves, Motosuke's poem refers most directly to the *Gosenshū* waka, and indeed, since Motosuke was one of the compilers of the latter, he must have been familiar with the poem. The *nami kosaji to wa* of the last line is echoed by the last line of the Akashi lady's poem (4), *koeji mono zo to*, suggesting that Murasaki Shikibu was acquainted with the earlier poet's work before its appearance in the 1086 anthology. The complaint of *Wa ga sode wa* (3) states the poet's feelings, but the source of his tears is completely absent from the poem. This contrasts with *Kimi o okite*, where the object of the poet's love appears in the very first line. Likewise, Genji's allusion to Sue no Matsuyama in "Suetsumuhana" does not contain an implication of a beloved other (certainly not the pathetic red-nosed princess). It is only with "Akashi" and "Ukifune," in which the narrative context provides the persona of the betraying other (Genji in the first, Ukifune in the second), that the direction of *kimi o okite* is decidedly reversed, stood on its head, as it were. The twist given to the meaning of Sue no Matsuyama—first in the *Gosenshū* and then, more forcefully, in *Genji*—throws a shadow over some of the later uses of the image, but a larger number of others follow Okikaze's simpleminded prototype.

Of twenty-two waka that include the utamakura contained in the imperial anthologies compiled after *Genji monogatari*, thirteen are little more than descriptions of a scene or remarks on the passing year.[9] Eight, however (including Motosuke's, written before *Genji* but put into an anthology afterward), incorporate wave-swept Pine Mountain of Sue as an image of love betrayed.[10] A ninth is ambiguous, referring to overwhelming circumstances that may be due to loss of love or some other calamity.[11]

The relation between literary imagery and the visual arts, particularly painting and the decoration of textiles, lacquerware, and metalwork in Japan, goes back to the beginnings of *Yamato-e* (Japanese-style, as opposed to *Kara-e*, Chinese-style, painting) in the Heian period.[12] Not only did the visual arts reflect imagery derived from poetry and prose narrative, but poetry was often composed to reflect images depicted on painted folding screens. In textile design, however, this close relationship lapsed for many centuries, in part because of the popularity of clothing textiles of woven repeat patterns—which would obscure the detail of any image painted or dyed over them—rather than more painterly pictorial designs. The use of literary images in textile design was revived and elaborated more than five hundred years later, in the Momoyama period.

Multilayered meanings embodied in visual motifs, sometimes utilized as rebuses in the mid and late Edo period, first occur as a striking element in the style that flourished at the end of the sixteenth and the early decades of the seventeenth century (called the Keichō style after the name of the era, 1596–1615).[13] It is also in the late sixteenth century that literary imagery begins to reappear in clothing decoration.[14] Other features of the Keichō style, contrasting with the kosode of the late Muromachi and early Momoyama periods, include the use of figured satin or other supple figured silk; dynamic spatial composition; the division of the background into fields of red, black, and white by means of stitch-resist *shibori*; and the complementary decoration of these areas with small embroidered motifs and stencil-patterned gold leaf.[15] This counterpoint is exploited to create a provocative formal ambiguity. On an early example of this style, the surface of which is crowded with overlapping forms, the context of surrounding shapes allows a single white form to be read as either a cloud obscuring a mountain or a grotesque rock in a Chinese-style garden setting.[16]

It was not until the later years of the seventeenth century and more particularly in the eighteenth, however, that literary themes, as well as the use of written characters taken from classical poetry, became the major source of themes in kosode decoration. Textile designers of this period seem to have taken delight in devising ingenious and intricate ways of exploiting such imagery.

Two seventeenth-century kosode clearly illustrating the Sue no Matsuyama theme raise the question of ironic intention in the textile design of that period. On one of these garments—fragments of a black, figured-satin kosode mounted on a two-fold screen from the Nomura Collection now in the National Museum of Japanese History—the crests of white waves, reserved with capped shibori, rise to snowy mountain peaks, divided from the background by a jagged line suggesting the nested-lozenge motif known as *matsukawabishi* (pine-bark lozenge). Fan papers superimposed on clumsily rendered snow roundels are executed in capped and *kanoko* shibori. Chrysanthemums, cherry blossoms, pine boughs, and flowing water embroidered in red, green, and white silk floss further enrich the surface. Traces of gold leaf, sparingly applied, remain, but the stenciled gold pattern can no longer be distinguished. The designer/artist has employed formal ambiguity—a device frequently seen in kosode of the early seventeenth century—to condense the shapes of mountain and snow-covered peak (with the pine-bark lozenges suggesting pine trees), waves breaking over the mountaintop, and falling snow into one cohesive image that mirrors the Sue no Matsuyama image of Okikaze's poem, one that seems to reflect only an ambiguity of nature: the confusion of snow and whitecaps (see illustration 21.1).

On a somewhat later example of visual ambiguity (in the same collection), a bold black crescent that curves from shoulder to hem appears first to be the stout trunk of a pine tree, its branches hung with clusters of wisteria and other vines.[17] At second glance, however, an inlet of the sea—on the right of the black area, a white island bordered with bamboo and pines from which a solitary crane rises, and on the left, a pine-sheltered white beach fringed with blossom-

Illustration 21.1.   The kosode on the right of this two-kosode screen from the Nomura Collection has a black background with mountain peaks, waves, pine-bark lozenges, and snow roundels. The formal ambiguity that condenses the shapes of mountain and snow-covered peak, waves breaking over the mountaintop, and falling snow into one cohesive image mirrors the Sue no Matsuyama image of Okikaze's poem. (Courtesy of the Japanese Museum of National History, Sakura.)

ing cherry trees—emerges from its lower quarter. As far as we know, however, these ambiguities have no literary content (see Illustration 21.2).

The reading of the mountaintops, wave crests, and pine-bark lozenges dyed into the Nomura kosode as a visual representation of Sue no Matsuyama is supported by the design of another seventeenth-century kosode. On a white ground of figured satin, a sweeping, asymmetric arc of blue and brown form a body of water and a mountainside. Smaller forms, including pine trees, waves, and the characters *yama* (mountain) and *koeru* (overwhelm), are depicted in shibori. Judging from the color combination and the strong, asymmetric composition, this kosode probably dates from the mid-seventeenth century, probably later than that on the Nomura screen described earlier.

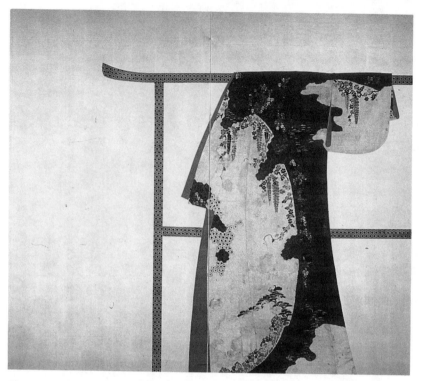

Illustration 21.2.   Another early Edo period kosode from the Nomura Collection uses similar visual ambiguity, merging the stout trunk of a pine tree with a "sandy beach" motif. (Courtesy of the Japanese Museum of National History, Sakura.)

The motifs on the back of the garment, the only part that survives (in the collection of the Tōyama kinenkan, Saitama Prefecture), suggest the imagery of the Sue no Matsuyama poems (2), (3), (4), and (5) but not (1), since the element of snow is missing. Kirihata Ken first identified the imagery of the Toyama kinenkan kosode fragment, associating it with Motosuke's poem.[18] Although not nearly so subtle in its reference or exciting in its execution as the Nomura screen, the more literal Tōyama example indicates that the demimonde of the seventeenth century had not forgotten the imagery so artfully developed in earlier waka.

Some decades after the two kosode were created, two major literary figures of the Genroku era (1688–1704), Matsuo Bashō (1644–1694) and Ihara Saikaku (1642–1693), both mention Sue no Matsuyama in their works. On the eighth day of the fifth month, 1694, Bashō and Sora traveled from Sendai to Shiogama, in present-day Iwate Prefecture, stopping near Sue no Matsuyama. In *Oku no hosomichi*, Bashō elaborates on the pledge:

Sore yori Noda no Tamagawa, Oki no Ishi o tazunu. Sue no Matsuyama wa tera o tsukurite Masshōzan to iu. Matsu no aiai mina haka-hara nite, hane o kawashi eda o tsuranuru chigiri no sue mo, tsui ni wa kaku no gotoki to kanashisa mo masarite, Shiogama no ura ni iriai no kane o kiku.[19]

From there we visited the Tama River in Noda and the Stone of Oki. At Sue no Matsuyama, they built a temple, calling it Masshōzan. Between the pines, the ground was filled with graves, and, my sadness growing as I thought about how lovers' vows of "two birds sharing a pair of wings, two trees with branches intertwined" come to this in the end, I heard the evening bell at the bay of Shiogama.

The pledge (*chigiri*) seems to allude most directly to Motosuke's poem, which contains the word *chigiri*. But its significance in this passage is not disappointment or betrayal (there is no mention here of white waves flooding over the mountaintop), as in Motosuke's poem. Rather, it signifies the promise of fidelity, thus recalling the use of the image in *kimi o okite*, as a vow of undying love.[20] This *chigiri* is reinforced by another allusion, to Po Chü-i's long, romantic poem "Song of Everlasting Sorrow," especially popular in Japan. Near the end of the poem, when the ghost of Yang Kuei-fei appears to the emperor, she reminds him of their vow to remain together for eternity, "in the heavens, as two birds with a single pair of wings; on earth, trees with branches intertwined."[21] Bashō's sadness derives not from any implication of an unfaithful lover but of love's end in death.

In *Kōshoku ichidai otoko*, Saikaku's use of the utamakura serves only to confirm that it was still readily recognized by late-seventeenth-century readers:

Sue no Matsuyama koshi no kagami made, iro no michi wa yameji to. . . .[22]

Saikaku's prose is so entangled here that a direct translation is inevitably awkward, but playing on the meaning of *sue* as "end," the double meaning of *matsu* as both "pine" and "wait," and of *koshi* as "back" and the continuative form of *kosu*, "engulf" or "pass over," the line means something like "Like Pine Mountain of Sue engulfed by the waves, I will wait and not change my way of life but will pursue the path of eros until my back is bent with age." Saikaku employs the utamakura for its verbal enrichment of his description of a famous place, much as Bashō does, rather than playing on any of the preceding poems.

The imagistic quality of both passages (from Bashō and Saikaku) is slight, shedding little light on how the wearer of the Nomura kosode and her social circles might have interpreted the illustration of the wave-swept mountain. Of course, analyses of other allusions to Sue no Matsuyama in the poetry and prose written between the fourteenth and seventeenth centuries might better illuminate the extent to which the seventeenth-century reading public was aware of the layers of meaning carried by the image.

The recognition and appreciation of a literary allusion in the decoration of clothing worn by the increasingly prosperous population of townsmen (and women), which included the merchant class as well as those in the entertainment business, are repeatedly attested to by the large number of surviving kosode, many of which were worn by townswomen. There can be no question of the popularity of images derived from *Genji monogatari* in the decorative arts, particularly in kosode design, of the Edo period. That the seventeenth-century reader was familiar with at least the broad outlines of *Genji* itself is indicated by the existence of series of woodblock illustrations of the whole tale.[23] Historian William Hauser emphasizes that popular culture of the time was heavily influenced by the introduction of movable type in the sixteenth century and the spread of literacy even among merchants and artisans by the late 1600s.[24]

Readers of *Genji monogatari*—in the eleventh, seventeenth, or even twentieth century—would surely recognize the ironic twist introduced in later waka variations of the Pine Mountain theme. The context of Ukifune's betrayal is amplified in the surrounding prose, and the image shifts from a pledge of undying love to a charge of unexpected infidelity and must have been recognized by anyone familiar with *Genji*. The pivotal weight of Kaoru's poem (5) to the events narrated in the last third of *Genji* leaves little doubt that the educated members of the seventeenth-century demimonde would recognize the ironic implication of the kosode's beautifully organized image. That a woman of any social class would choose to wear a stunningly designed and richly decorated kosode illustrating an image so closely connected with the theme of betrayal and infidelity suggests a delicious sense of irony communicated between the wearer and observer (possibly her patron) of such a robe, with its subtly organized image of Pine Mountain of Sue.

ACKNOWLEDGMENTS

I am deeply grateful to Aileen Gatten for her careful reading of and suggestions regarding this manuscript (any errors of interpretation are entirely my own); to Amy Heinrich for her patience and perseverance; and to Donald Keene for his sensitive guidance over many years.

NOTES

1. The art historian Ienaga Saburō observed the following about the relation between literary imagery and the visual arts: "From the very first, Yamato-style painting was connected with literature, and it defies understanding as a genre apart from it." See Ienaga Saburō, *Painting in the Yamato Style*, trans. John M. Shields, *Heibonsha Survey of Japanese Art*, vol. 10 (New York/Tokyo: Weatherhill/Heibonsha, 1973), p. 94. Ienaga's brief account is a good introduction to this important subject, which is beyond the scope of this chapter. For a more comprehensive study, see Ienaga Saburō, *Jōdai Yamato-e zenshi* (Tokyo: Sumimizu shobō, 1966), in which he discusses Sue no Matsuyama as one of the famous spots that were common subjects of *meisho-e*, "pictures of famous places" (p. 181), noting that its image was often associated with cranes and pines (pp. 181, 240). It seems likely that illustrations of Sue no Matsuyama were known in the early Heian period, and one may have been the subject of Okikaze's poem (1). Verbal treatments of Sue no Matsuyama developed without visual imagery after that time; to my knowledge, visual representations of the theme do not occur in the decoration of lacquerware, metalwork, or textiles in the following periods.

For more recent studies of the relation between literature and visual imagery, see Chino Kaori, "Jingoji-zō 'Senzui Byōbu' no kōsei to kaiga-shiteki ichi," *Bijutsushi* 26 (1979): 146–62. See also Murase Mieko, "Sōtatsu-hitsu 'Matsushima zu' byōbu no gadai ni tsuite," *Museum* 312 (March 1977): 12–23.

2. The headnote reads: "Kanpyō no ontoki Kisai no Miya no uta-awase no uta." See Ozawa Masao, ed., *Kokin wakashū*, in *Nihon koten bungaku zenshū*, vol. 7 (Tokyo: Shōgakukan, 1971), p. 162. "A poem from the poetry contest of the empress during the reign of the Kanpyō emperor," probably occurring during Uda's reign (887–897). All translations of Japanese texts are mine unless otherwise noted.

Helen Craig McCullough aptly characterizes Okikaze as "a modestly endowed writer who seldom progressed beyond unimaginative treatments of familiar topics and themes. . . . When he attempts to use reasoning, his favorite technique, in a more innovative manner, the effect can range from the patently contrived to the near-grotesque." See Helen Craig McCullough, *Brocade by Night: "Kokin wakashū" and the Court Style in Japanese Classical Poetry* (Stanford, CA: Stanford University Press, 1985), p. 376. She seems to place his Sue no Matsuyama poem in the former category.

3. McCullough identifies the Azuma uta as a selection of songs "from the repertoire of the Folk Music Office. . . . Folk Music Office Songs from the east [Azuma] were often presented as adjuncts to kagura performances" (*Brocade*, p. 491). Whether or not they were actually folk songs, they were apparently at least intended to appear to be folk songs.

Matsushita Daizaburō and Watanabe Fumio, eds., *Kokka taikan* (Tokyo: Kyōbunsha, 1931), vol. 2, p. 547. This, the great canon of Japanese poetry, a compendium and concordance to the twenty-one imperial anthologies (the last one compiled in 1439) and the earlier collection, the *Man'yōshū*, lists twenty-five occurrence of the phrase Sue no Matsuyama. Okikaze's poem occurs also in the *Shūi wakashū* (compiled around 1011).

4. Katagiri Yōichi, ed., *Gosen wakashū*, in *Shin Nihon koten bungaku taikei*, vol. 6 (Tokyo: Iwanami shoten, 1990), p. 197. Although little is known about the poet Tosa, she appears to have been a woman in court service active during the first quarter of the tenth century (p. 27).

5. Abe Akio, Akiyama Ken, and Imai Ken-e, eds., "Murasaki Shikibu," in *Genji monogatari*, vol. 1 (Tokyo: Shōgakukan, 1972), p. 369, n. 21.

6. Abe et al., *Genji monogatari*, vol. 2 (Tokyo: Shōgakkan, 1972), pp. 249–50. Compare this with Edward Seidensticker, trans., *The Tale of Genji*, vol. 1 (New York: Knopf, 1976), p. 264.

7. Although it does not discuss the Sue no Matsuyama poems, Gunilla Lindberg-Wada's monograph on the relationship between the first imperial anthology and the poetry in *Genji* attests to Murasaki Shikibu's familiarity with the *Kokinshū*. See Gunilla Lindberg-Wada, *Poetic Allusion: Some Aspects of the Role Played by Kokin Wakashū as a Source of Poetic Allusion in* Genji Monogatari, *Japanological Studies* no. 4 (Stockholm: University of Stockholm, Institute of Oriental Languages, Department of Japanese and Korean, 1983).

8. Abe et al., *Genji monogatari*, vol. 6 (Tokyo: Shōgakkan, 1976), pp. 165, 167, 168.

9. *Kinyōshū*, poems 303, 334; *Senzaishū*, poem 219; *Shinkokinshū*, poems 37, 705; *Shinchokusenshū*, poems 749, 1317; *Shinsenzaishū*, poem 18; *Shinyōshū*, poem 159; *Shingoshūishū*, poem 574; *Shinzokukokinshū*, poems 4, 213, 945. The last of these collections was compiled in 1439.

10. *Goshuishū*, poem 770; *Shokugosenshū*, poem 943; *Shokushūishū*, poems 1026, 1027, 1028; *Shingosenshū*, poem 1038; *Shingoshūishū*, poems 1168, 1169.

11. *Shokushūishū*, poem 1104.

12. See note 1.

13. For rebus designs on kosode, see Amanda Mayer Stinchecum, *Kosode: 16th to 19th Century Textiles from the Nomura Collection* (New York: Japan Society/Kodansha International, 1984), color plate 30, pp. 138–39; and Dale Carolyn Gluckman and Sharon Sadako Takeda, *When Art Became Fashion. Kosode in Edo-Period Japan* (Los Angeles: Los Angeles County Museum of Art, 1992), catalog no. 146, pp. 175–76, and fig. 45, pp. 165–66. For a more detailed description and analysis of the Keichō style, see Stinchecum, *Kosode*, pp. 44–48.

14. Kirihata Ken, "Kinsei senshoku ni okeru bungei ishō," in Kyoto National Museum, ed., *Kōgei ni miru koten bungaku ishō* (Kyoto: Shikōsha, 1980), pp. 307–10. The earliest example he cites is a kosode in the Kanebo Collection with embroidered motifs—a courtier's oxcart, a fan, and "moonflower" (*yugao*) vines, flowers, and leaves—identified as an allusion to the "Yugao" chapter of *Genji monogatari*.

15. *Shibori* is a method of resist dyeing—creating a pattern by preventing dye from coloring selected areas of the cloth—that uses pressure to prevent dye penetration. Capped shibori involves stitching the outline and then wrapping the area to be resisted with bamboo sheath and binding it tightly so that no dye will seep through. See Yoshiko Wada, Mary Kellogg Rice, and Jane Barton, *Shibori: The Inventive Art of Japanese Shaped Resist Dyeing* (Tokyo: Kodansha International, 1983), pp. 88 ff.; and Stinchecum, *Kosode*, pp. 31–32.

16. Stinchecum, *Kosode*, color plate 6; see also p. 45. This and the following example are composed of kosode fragments mounted on two-fold screens, which are part of the Nomura Collection, now in the National Museum of History at Sakura.

17. Ibid., color plate 10; see also p. 47.

18. Kirihata, "Kinsei senshoku," p. 310. See also Stinchecum, *Kosode*, pp. 48, 213, n. 11, 12; in the latter I misidentified the character depicted on the Toyama kosode—an abbreviated form of *koeru*—as *shigeru*. The fragment is also reproduced in Gluckman and Takeda, *When Art Became Fashion*, p. 160, fig. 38.

19. Sugiura Shōichirō, Miyamoto Saburō, and Ogino Kiyoshi, eds., *Bashō bunshū*, in *Nihon koten bungaku taikei*, vol. 46 (Tokyo: Iwanami shoten, 1974), p. 81. According to Iino Tetsuji, Sue no Matsuyama is one *chō* (about 119 yards) north of Oki no Ishi, within the precincts of the temple that bears its name, Masshōzan. See *Bashō jiten* (Tokyo: Tōkyōdō, 1989), p. 276.

20. . . . *chigiri no sue* ("end of the vow") plays on the meaning of the place-name Sue, "end," "finish."

21. John A. Turner, trans., *A Golden Treasury of Chinese Poetry: 121 Classical Poems* (Hong Kong: Centre for Translation Projects, Chinese University of Hong Kong, 1976), pp. 180, 181 (Chinese text with English translation).

22. Teruoka Yasutaka and Higashi Akimasa, eds., *Ihara: Saikaku shō*, vol. 1, in *Shinpen Nihon koten bungaku zenshō*, vol. 66 (Tokyo: Shōgakkan, 1996), p. 101.

23. For example, those accompanying the translation by Edward Seidensticker of *Eiri Genji monogatari*, first published in 1650, not long after the creation of the Nomura kosode. See Seidensticker, *Tale of Genji*, vol. 1, p. 2.

24. William Hauser, "A New Society: Japan Under Tokugawa Rule," in Gluckman and Takeda, *When Art Became Fashion*, pp. 56–57.

22

*Genji Meets Masamune: Traditional Aesthetics and
Contemporary Design*

FELICE FISCHER

In his seminal essay "Japanese Aesthetics," published in *Landscapes and Portraits*,[1] Donald Keene focuses on four principles that have defined Japanese taste for nearly a thousand years: suggestion, irregularity, simplicity, and perishability. In looking at contemporary Japanese design, these basic touchstones remain relevant and help define what is "Japanese" about certain products, graphics, furniture, or textiles, despite postwar Western, commercial, and other accretions. The material culture of late-twentieth-century Japan in fact serves as a sort of time capsule of an aesthetic inheritance that was consolidated and fixed in the popular consciousness during the 250 years of isolation in the Edo period (1615–1867). During these centuries, the aesthetic first defined by the Heian aristocracy and then by Zen artists became the aesthetic tradition of all classes of society. Professor Keene's insights allow us to "read" contemporary design. This chapter explores some of the translations and transformations of traditional aesthetics by contemporary Japanese designers.

Suggestion

The brevity of the thirty-one-syllable format of the classical poetic mode, the *waka*, as well as the ambiguity of the Japanese language, contributed to the use of suggestion as a device to expand the possible meanings of the short verse form. Several layers of meaning could be read from a single poem, through the vagueness of singular or plural, masculine or feminine, and the like.[2] Very often, a word or line in a poem alluded to an earlier poem with which the reader would be familiar. This device, *honka-dori*, was used to suggest additional levels of interpretation through its reference to a whole body of existing texts.

Similarly, the use of allusion in contemporary Japanese design gives additional layers of depth, usually to a visual image, through reference to an earlier literary or visual text. For example, the logo created by the well-known graphic designer Matsunaga Shin (b. 1940) for the "Fuku-Masamune" line of saké (illustration 22.1),[3] alludes to the device known as the *Genji-mon* (Genji crests). The Genji-mon were originally devised for the game of incense matching, as a sort of tallying system. These marks in turn were identified by the titles of the fifty-four chapters of *The Tale of Genji*.[4] The Masamune logo does not exactly duplicate any one of the Genji-mon, but the visual allusion is evident. Whereas the saké logo can be interpreted as an appealing "abstract" design on one level, the suggestion of the Genji-mon conveys to the contemporary consumer an additional association of refined connoisseurship. The nuance of the well-bred, literary taste implies that this is saké fit for the nobility.

Another classical allusion, this time to Chinese painting, appears in Kōno Takashi's (b. 1906) 1955 poster for the tea ceremony monthly *Tankō* (*JD*, p. 53, illustration 22.2). The simplicity of the single persimmon in white against a dark green ground echoes the Zen aesthetic underlying the tea ceremony itself. At the same time, the image suggests Mu Ch'i's thirteenth-century ink painting of six persimmons, beloved by tea aficionados.[5] As with honka-dori poetic allusions in the literary tradition, the deeper layers of associations often are properly appreciated only by those in the know. But that is a calculated part of the appeal as well.

Some images have become so pervasive and the allusion so obvious that the challenge for the contemporary designer is to give the hackneyed image a fresh appeal. For example, one of the most successful reinterpretations of Hokusai's famous woodblock print of Mount Fuji "Under the Wave at Kanagawa" (frequently called the "Great Wave" in the West)[6] was rendered by Yamashiro Ryūichi (b. 1920) in a poster for an exhibition of prints at Tokyo's National Museum of Modern Art (*JD*, p. 80). To the image of Mount Fuji and the huge wave rolling in from the left side of the page, Yamashiro added a large diamond shape as a backdrop for the crest of the wave. The diamond shape be meant to suggest the *mimasu* (three saké measures) crest of the Edo-period actors who used the name Ichikawa Danjūrō. Or it may just be an abstract graphic device. The ambiguity of the suggestion itself is part of the traditional aesthetic.

Illustration 22.1. A sake bottle designed by Matsunaga Shin in 1988 alludes to the *Genji-mon* (Genji crests), conveying a sense of refined connoisseurship. (Courtesy of the Philadelphia Museum of Art.)

Visual allusions and puns are common in contemporary graphic design, in which calligraphy and typography come into play as well. Traditionally, calligraphy has been a revered component of Japanese design, on painting scrolls, ceramics, and even textiles. Some of the most beautiful and boldest kimono of the Edo period feature large-scale characters sweeping across their surface.[7] These are echoed in the poster by Hayakawa Yoshio (b. 1917), designed for a kimono exhibition at Kintetsu Department Store (*JD*, p. 51). Hayakawa takes the character *shū* from the sponsor of the exhibition, the Shūsaikai, as the calligraphic focus of the trapezoidal kimono, thus establishing a link with kimono designs of the past.

Calligraphic suggestion also is used in some unexpected corners of contemporary design (*JD*, p. 160, illustration 22.3). The furniture designer Okayama Shinya (b. 1941) produced a series of pieces that suggest written characters. For instance, the stool in the collection of the Philadelphia Museum of Art that he calls "Kaze no ko" (Child of the wind) can be "read" as an abbreviated version of the character *kaze*.

More often, Japanese furniture reflects the architectural tradition. The shape of a rattan stool by Watanabe Riki (b. 1911), for example, suggests the *torii*

Illustration 22.2. The poster design by Kōno Takashi for the magazine *Tankō*, 1955, recalls the famous thirteenth-century ink painting of persimmons by Mu Ch'i. (Courtesy of the Philadelphia Museum of Art.)

Illustration 22.3.   Okayama Shinya's stool, "Kaze no ko," a 1984 design, recalls the shape of the character meaning wind (*kaze*). (COURTESY OF THE PHILADELPHIA MUSEUM OF ART.)

(gateways) of Shinto shrines. The chief designer for Matsushita Electric Company, Mano Zenichi (b. 1916), also hoped to evoke in his 1952 radio design (*JD*, p. 54) the architectural purity of the best-known icon of Japanese architecture, the Katsura rikyū (Katsura detached palace). The left half of the molded plastic housing of the face of the National brand radio DX-350 is reminiscent of the *shitomi* wooden shutters of the buildings, and the pattern on the right half is reminiscent of sliding *shoji* panels. Mano stated that this was a very conscious attempt to impart a sense of tradition and continuity even to designs of objects using the latest technology.[8]

The use of allusion—of ambiguity of form—also has a very playful side. It is the impulse that moved potters in the Edo period to make incense boxes in the shape of fruits or vegetables.[9] The contemporary equivalents can be found in pieces such as Kurokawa Masayuki's serpentine-necked lamps, which are called "Cobra," or in the "Temaki" speakers by Mizobe Tatsuji, whose shape suggest the hand-rolled (*temaki*) seaweed used to wrap sushi.

The examples I have selected focus on a narrower aspect of "suggestion" than Professor Keene did in his essay, and they may seem far removed from the elegant sigh of the poet alluding to the literary past. Yet there is the same sense of belonging to a specific tradition, and most readers understand the allusions without the need of lengthy explanations, showing that an image or a word has retained its power to suggest multiple layers of meaning.

Irregularity

A second aesthetic principle that Donald Keene found to be basic to Japanese culture is irregularity, that is, "a rejection of regularity as well as of perfection" (*LP*, p. 18). This feature is immediately discernible in traditional Japanese architecture, painting, and ceramics, in the preference for the off center, the asymmetrical, the irregularly shaped. Despite the importation and adaptation of many elements of Chinese culture through the centuries, Japanese artists never found the Chinese preference for the balanced symmetry of a building or the perfectly shaped vase to be truly congenial. As Professor Keene points out, the Zen aesthetics of the tea masters did much to reinforce the taste for the tea bowl suggesting the shape of an old shoe. In the end, perfection is not challenging. It leaves no room for the viewer's imagination and "asks our admiration rather than our participation" (*LP*, p. 19).

This traditional artistic principle remains a telling element of contemporary graphic, textile, and product design. The Genji-mon logo on the Masamune saké bottles, for example, is not centered squarely on the label but is placed on the diagonal. Even when the shapes are regular, as in a set of triangular and trapezoidal party trays designed in 1976 by Mori Masahiro (b. 1927), their format is not fixed. That is, they can be rearranged in any number of configurations to avoid the boredom of fixed perfection. The square cabinet with forty-nine drawers by Kuramata Shirō (1934–1991), designed in 1970, contains no two drawers of the same size. Kuramata took his experimentation one step further in a series he called "Furniture in Irregular Forms." The S-shaped cabinet (*JD*, p. 105) with eighteen drawers seems almost in danger of tipping over. The willowy sensuality of the curved profile is reminiscent of the long, lean beauties depicted in Harunobu's Edo-period prints. The shape is found again in a bottle designed by Kaneko Shūya (b. 1937) for the vodka-like *shōchū* alcohol produced by Kikkoman under the name "Komako." Kaneko Shūya designed his bottle as a conscious contrast to the American aesthetics expressed in the Coca-Cola bottle, which, he says, is modeled on Marilyn Monroe.[10] The name "Komako" itself may be a literary allusion to the heroine of Kawabata Yasunari's novel *Yukiguni* (Snow Country).

The large plywood seating units created by Fujie Kazuko (b. 1947) are also lyrical expressions of the beauty of irregular forms. The piece called "Watari-dori" (Migratory bird) is installed at Waseda University in Tokyo.[11] The broad asymmetrical sweep of the lines gives this weighty piece a light, airy quality that does indeed bring to mind a bird in flight. Even as mundane an object as a letter opener yields to the preference for the curve in the 1973 version designed by Watanabe Tokuji (1934–1984).

The love for the imperfect and irregular also finds its expression in the attention paid to objects' surface texture. The tea bowl shaped like an old shoe also should have some firing blemishes and pockmarks on its glazed surface to make it all the more interesting when held in the hand. Likewise, the series of glasses and goblets created by Awashima Masakichi (1914–1979) in the 1950s called "Shizuku," or "Dripping Water," features glass with a rippled surface made by the use of molds (*JD*, p. 61, illustration 22.4). This is a difficult process to achieve in glass and adds a wonderfully tactile level to Awashima's glassware, not unlike that of a Raku tea bowl.

Textile design is another field in which the texture of the materials emphasizes the tactile qualities of irregular surfaces. Arai Junichi (b. 1932) has been one of the great experimenters in creating new effects using modern technology such as heat transfer–printing and computer-driven punch cards to produce complicated weaves. He uses chemical and heat processes to create often unpredictable results in fabrics that pucker, bubble, or shrink.[12] Here, too, it is the preference for the irregular, the interest in the process of change, and the unpredictability of the materials that reflect traditional aesthetic sensibilities.

Simplicity

Simplicity, or "the use of the most economical means to obtain the desired effect" (*LP*, p. 20), is the third aesthetic principle governing much of Japanese literary and artistic creation. It is reflected in the earliest Shinto structures at

Illustration 22.4.   Goblets designed by Awashima Masakichi in 1955 use an irregular, mold-blown surface for the *shizuku* (dripping water) glass. (COURTESY OF THE PHILADELPHIA MUSEUM OF ART.)

the Grand Shrine of Ise, in their austere lines, their unadorned wood and thatch materials. The Zen sensibilities reinforced this tendency to pare everything down to its essence, whether in the spare use of brushwork in monochromatic ink paintings or in the rock and sand gardens of the Zen temples. The preferences of Sen no Rikyū and the tea masters for the astringent atmosphere of the tea hut and the unsophisticated tea bowl were based on the Zen ideals. Simplicity reveals itself in the absence and deliberate avoidance of strong colors, perfumes, or even foods.

Simplicity has remained one of the hallmarks of contemporary Japanese design. It is manifested in the emphasis on clean lines, plain surfaces, and compactness. These are the characteristics that appealed to Western students of Japanese architecture such as Frank Lloyd Wright or Bruno Taut because they seemed to express the ideals of modernism and its reaction to Victorian exuberance.

One of the most ubiquitous and successful examples of the principle of simplicity in postwar Japan is the "Za chair" by Fujimori Kenji (1919–1993) (*JD*, p. 82, illustration 22.5). This L-shaped, legless seat is an ingenious modification of the Western-style chair for floor-level tatami seating. The slight curve of the back lends support as well as elegance to the unpainted wood surface. The look can be changed for the season or the occasion through the choice of cushion (*zabuton*) for the seat. The units can also be easily stacked for compact and efficient storage, thus satisfying another requirement of Japan's typically space-poor interiors.

Illustration 22.5. Fujimuri Kenji's 1961 chair for use on tatami employs new plywood-molding techniques for high-quality chairs that can be mass-produced inexpensively. (Courtesy of the Philadelphia Museum of Art.)

An equally creative and simple solution for Western-style seating in harmony with Japanese interiors was designed as early as 1954 by Yanagi Sōri (b. 1915). His "Butterfly stool" consists of two L-shaped plywood units held together with a brass rod (*JD*, p. 64). The resulting stool echoes the Shinto torii gate in its spare outline, and the love of natural materials is beautifully expressed in the bent plywood, a new technology applied to furniture in postwar Japan. The metal rod can be removed, allowing the L-shaped halves to be stacked for storage.

As in the tea ceremony or in Zen gardens, simplicity of design does not necessarily mean unsophisticated or inexpensive design. Indeed, observers of Japanese culture have often expressed amazement at the great expense and effort taken to produce something very understated or plain. Traditional Negoro lacquerware, for example, is made from layers of red lacquer over black lacquer polished down by age or artifice to reveal the black layer underneath. The result is a very muted, subtle "art concealing art" (*LP*, p. 22).

Isamu Kenmochi (1912–1971), another innovative pioneer in the field of design, conceived of a deceptively simple format for assembling his "Kashiwado" chair from blocks of Japanese cedar. The wood blocks were deliberately "misaligned" to reveal the contrasts of the grains, the only decorative element of the unpainted, unupholstered armchair. The result is a surprisingly comfortable, extremely beautiful piece of furniture embodying the ideal of unobtrusive luxury. Perhaps to underscore his intention of producing an object that was plain and sturdy, Kenmochi named his chair "Kashiwado" after a popular sumo wrestler of the day.

A more recent example of the elegant effects of simplicity on design is the chair called "How high the moon," designed by Kuramata Shirō (*JD*, p. 163). This armchair is made of steel mesh, a medium more likely to be associated with industrial surroundings than home seating. Yet the spare simplicity of the armchair, with its lunar crescent-shaped arms and back, together with the gauzelike transparency of the mesh material give the chair an ethereal, almost spiritual quality, akin to the *yūgen* or "otherworldliness" of the nō theater. As with the aesthetic of suggestion, the taste for simplicity often requires a deeper connoisseurship.

Even on a more down-to-earth level such as ashtrays, the sensitivity to unadorned materials is evident. Yoshitake Mōsuke (1909–1993) designed a series of ashtrays that could be mass-produced by the local foundries in his home prefecture of Yamagata, which were no longer able to survive solely on the manufacture of iron tea kettles for the tea ceremony. Yoshitake retained the time-honored, simple patterns used on the tea kettles and transferred them to his "Arare" (Hailstone) ashtray series.[13] On the tea kettles, the raised hailstones served the function of retaining heat. It might seem that the hailstone pattern was kept as a decorative element. But in fact, on the ashtray perimeters Yoshitake uses the hailstones to prevent the cigarettes from rolling off the edge, an elegantly economic translation of a traditional design element into a contemporary use.

Kenmochi Isamu's design group also designed ashtrays in 1964. The materials used were not traditional, but scrap metal. Press-molded scrap metal sheets were finished in chrome, with a cutout on the rim of the round ashtray to hold a cigarette in place. A molded plastic resin liner insert can be removed for easy cleaning.[14] The ashtrays stack into a compact nest not unlike the lacquer trays for serving sushi.

The Japanese talent for using the most economical means for the desired effect is perhaps best known in the field of electronics and high-tech design. The first pocket-size camera made by Olympus became an instant classic and model for all subsequent production. The innovative use of the plastic housing to protect the lens eliminated the need for extraneous items such as a lens cap or camera case, a simple, practical format combining form and function in a way that ultimately transcends national boundaries. Here too, as Professor Keene comments, "A curious coincidence brings traditional Japanese tastes into congruence with those of the contemporary West" (LP, p. 18).

Perishability

The fourth aesthetic principle that Donald Keene describes in his essay is that of perishability. This aesthetic, too, has been underscored historically in Japan by the Zen Buddhist emphasis on the transience of all things of this world. Without the knowledge that they will be scattered in a few days, the beauty of the cherry blossoms would not be as fully appreciated. As Professor Keene puts it, "The Japanese . . . expressed their preference for varieties of beauty which most conspicuously betrayed their impermanence" (LP, p. 24).

In contemporary Japanese design, there is an entire area of endeavor that is premised on the principle of perishability, and that is package design. What could be more transient and destined for impermanence than a wrapper for candy or a box for soap?

Twenty years ago, an exhibition featuring traditional packaging in Japan traveled throughout the United States. The book published in conjunction with the exhibition had the enticing (sub)title "How to Wrap Five Eggs."[15] Most of the packaging in this exhibition consisted of natural materials, such as straw used to bundle the five eggs, bamboo containers for mushrooms, or cherry tree leaf wrappers for bean paste rice cakes. In this last case, the "wrapping" itself was intended to be consumed along with its contents.

In contemporary design as well, the packaging for traditional foodstuffs is one area in which the care of and sensitivity to the package itself comes to the fore. Wada Kunibō (b. 1900) created for the confectionery firm Arakiya a kind of packaging with a strong traditionalist touch. The materials have changed, as paper and cardboard are used to simulate bamboo and straw, but the strong calligraphy and graphics leave a lasting impression.[16] Indeed, it has been observed by visitors to Japan that the packaging is often more creative and elaborate than the contents. Even as lowly a food item as rice crackers come packaged in whimsical containers modeled on the costumes used for the lion dances in traditional Japan (*JD*, p. 113).

The traditional "packaging" for nonfood items is the *furoshiki*, the all-purpose square of cloth that is still used today, primarily by older, kimono-clad women. The furoshiki expresses the impermanence of things through its infinite changeability of form. As the contents change, the furoshiki changes as well, to accommodate the new, ever changing shape of the objects it enfolds. One contemporary parallel to the furoshiki is wrapping paper, and designers such as Ajioka Shintarō have created patterns for both.

The other contemporary equivalent of the furoshiki is the shopping bag, which is even more perishable than the cloth furoshiki. Nevertheless, many distinguished contemporary graphic artists have created designs for this ephemeral form. In this sense, shopping bags might be more closely related to the ukiyo-e tradition of great printmakers designing theater bills for the late-Edo-period kabuki programs. And so it is that Hokusai's "Great Wave" survives reincarnated on a shopping bag for Yamaya Company, designed in 1985 by Kakutani Shōzō (b. 1928) (*JD*, p. 164, illustration 22.6).

Conclusion

Although the four aesthetic principles of suggestion, irregularity, simplicity, and perishability are not the only ones defining Japanese taste, it is remarkable that they have had such staying power. Largely the result of the accretion of continental Zen ideals onto indigenous preferences for ambiguity, simplicity, or asymmetry, these principles were recorded and analyzed by writers such as Yoshida Kenkō (1283–1350) in his *Tsurezuregusa* (Essays in Idleness). During the ensuing centuries, the rules of taste were embraced by all strata of society, aided in part by the Edo government's policy of isolation from the outside world. Other factors, such as the practice of the transmitting teachings in the arts and literature directly from master to disciple, supported a conservationist atmosphere for aesthetic ideals as well.

In the face of Japan's encounter with Europe and America in the late nineteenth and twentieth centuries, the long-standing aesthetic preferences survived again through the selective acceptance and accommodation of outside influences. As Professor Keene points out, there were many points of intersection

Illustration 22.6.   The shopping bag for Yamaya, designed in 1985 by Kakutani Shōzō, uses a single, thick brush stroke to represent a breaking wave. (Courtesy of the Philadelphia Museum of Art.)

between traditional aesthetics and modernist philosophy and sensibility. Although they grew out of totally different cultural and social environments, both shared a love of the simple line, unadorned materials, and the modular unit.

For contemporary Japanese designers, there has often been a creative tension in the symbiosis of the modern, international outlook with the traditional and regional. To some extent, of course, this is true of designers everywhere. But it seems to me that although Japanese designers may strive to avoid stereotypes of tradition, they do not reject that tradition. Rather, they accept the subdued beauty of Katsura rikyū as well as the monumentality of the Parthenon or

Chartres cathedral. The aesthetic inheritance forms a cultural module, whether conscious or subconscious, that is an inescapable part of growing up Japanese and still remains a vital aspect of Japan's creative experience. As Professor Keene so aptly sums up, "[It] seems safe to say that the aesthetic ideals which have formed Japanese taste over the centuries will find their outlets in media as yet undiscovered and maintain their distinctive existence" (*LP*, p. 25).

NOTES

1. Donald Keene, *Landscapes and Portraits: Appreciations of Japanese Culture* (hereafter abbreviated *LP*) (Tokyo: Kodansha International, 1971), pp. 11–25.

2. Robert H. Brower and Earl Miner, *Japanese Court Poetry* (Stanford, CA: Stanford University Press, 1961), pp. 4–19, 289–92.

3. Kathryn B. Hiesinger and Felice Fischer, *Japanese Design: A Survey Since 1950* (hereafter abbreviated *JD*) (Philadelphia: Philadelphia Museum of Art in association with Abrams, New York, 1994 and 1995), p. 181.

4. Albert J. Koop and Hogitarō Inada, *Japanese Names and How to Read Them* (London: Eastern Press, 1923), p. 119.

5. Asakawa Yasuichi, *Zen Painting* (Tokyo: Kodansha International, 1970), p. 57.

6. Richard Lane, *Images from the Floating World. The Japanese Print* (New York: Putnam, 1978), p. 167 for the Hokusai print and p. 117 for the *mimasu* crest.

7. Amanda Mayer Stinchecum, *Kosode: 16th-19th Century Textiles from the Nomura Collection* (New York: Japan Society and Kodansha International, 1984), pp. 146–47.

8. Mano Zenichi, "2nd Prize Mainichi Industrial Design Award," *Kōgei nyūsu* 22 (February 1954): 28.

9. Christine Guth, *Asobi: Play in the Arts of Japan* (New York: Katonah Museum of Art, 1992), pp. 43–50.

10. Kaneko Shūya, *Package Design* (Tokyo: Kashima, 1989), pp. 145–46.

11. Emilio Ambasz, ed., *The International Yearbook of Design* (New York: Abbeville Press, 1988), p. 98.

12. Asahi Shinbun, ed., *Hand and Technology Textile by Junichi Arai* (Tokyo: Asahi shinbun, 1992).

13. Kōgei Zaidan, ed., *Nihon no indusutoriaru desain: Shōwa ga unda meihin 100* (Tokyo: Maruzen, 1989), p. 61.

14. Ibid., p. 82.

15. Oka Hideyuki, *Tsutsumu: An Introduction to an Exhibition of the Art of the Japanese Package* (New York: Japan Society, 1975).

16. Yao Takeo, ed., *Package Design in Tokyo* (Tokyo: Seibundo shinkosha, 1987), pp. 91–93.

23

Guns as Keys: James McNeill Whistler as a Metaphor for Japan in a Poem by Amy Lowell

◉

MARLEIGH GRAYER RYAN

In June of 1917, the American Imagist poet Amy Lowell (1874–1925) completed a literary piece she named "Guns as Keys: and the Great Gate Swings." It was first published in the August 1917 issue of an aggressive new intellectual magazine, *Seven Arts*, where it attracted considerable critical reaction, as much for its radical style as for its dramatic content. Subsequently the poet included the work as the second of four extended pieces in a volume she named *Can Grande's Castle*, published in September 1918.[1]

The four poems in this volume describe historic military confrontations the poet could not have experienced. "But, living now, in the midst of events greater than these," she tells us in her introduction, "the books have become reality to me in a way that they never could have become before, and the stories I have dug out of dusty volumes seem as actual as my own existence."[2]

"Guns as Keys" deals with the opening of Japan in 1853–54 by Commodore Matthew Perry and his men. The thesis of the poem is that the West—and, in particular, America—gave Japan the materials of war while Japan gave America art. Throughout the work, as a metaphor for Japan's gift to America, Amy Lowell offers the name, work, and painterly atmosphere of James McNeill Whistler (1834–1903), the American artist expatriate in England and France virtually his entire adult life. British, American, and especially French intellectuals and artists of the turn of the century greatly admired Whistler's artistry and ideas and saw him as the model of one who combined the Eastern tradition with his Western heritage. By invoking his name, the poet forcefully conveys her conviction that the West has been culturally enriched by its contact with Japan.

Amy Lowell's poem consciously presents the Perry expedition from two points of view, the American and the Japanese. For the American material, the poet relies heavily on firsthand accounts of the expedition, to which she may have had special access, and on images of it presented by the artists who traveled with the ships.[3] On the whole, her retelling of the events is remarkably true to the materials available to her.

The youngest child of a prominent branch of the New England Lowells, the poet learned about Japan earlier than did most Americans of her generation. Her eldest brother Percival, nineteen years her senior, had been in Korea and Japan for the better part of ten years between 1883 and 1893 and had written a number of major books on Japan and East Asia that had a staggering influence on the West.[4] As a child, Amy had been much affected by the visit of Percival's interpreter, whom he brought home in the fall of 1883. She had received from Percival a steady stream of gifts from Japan, including photograph albums, ink paintings, woodblock prints, and other art objects.[5] Amy Lowell idolized her eldest brother and dedicated her life to emulating his successes; through him the Asia connection was firmly implanted. She frequently spoke of herself as feeling she had lived in Japan, so vivid were her images of the country, although she never traveled there.

Amy Lowell's second published poem, "A Japanese Wood-Carving," which appeared in the February 1911 *Atlantic Monthly*, deals in romantic terms with a carving she had placed above bookcases when she remodeled the library in her family home. This use of Japanese materials presages what we find to be the dominant influence of Japan on Amy Lowell: a projection of herself, as a poet and an observer, into the drama portrayed in an art object from Japan. Even after she had been exposed to the Fenollosa–Pound statements on Japanese aesthetics, which began appearing in 1914, and had tried her hand at the haiku form, she saw Japan predominantly as a drama, visually unfolding before her eyes. It was this drama she attempted to portray in much of her poetry. Japan came to her—as it came to many American and British poets—primarily through its art, and, perhaps because of the limitations of the translations available, only secondarily through its literature. For Amy Lowell, who had cultivated a profound sense of theater even before seriously trying her hand at poetry and who believed that poetry was meant to be appreciated orally, this art was transformed into drama.

The poem on the wood carving appeared with another verbally depicting the scene in a Japanese woodblock print in Amy Lowell's first collection, published in 1912. From then on she repeatedly returned to Japanese themes. Many of these poems were assembled in a volume entitled *Pictures of the Floating World* (1919), which contains 174 poems, the first fifty-nine of which are grouped under the title "Lacquer Prints" and were meant to be modeled on haiku.

In the intervening years, Amy Lowell had briefly been a colleague of the brilliant but mercurial Ezra Pound (1885–1972). She planned to create a literary journal with him when they met in London in 1913, only to find him characteristically fickle in his interest. They had an infamous falling out the following year, but we may be sure she assiduously read the stream of Fenollosa–Pound publications influenced by East Asia that appeared during the following decade. There can be no doubt that Pound's "translations" from Chinese and Japanese affected Amy Lowell deeply, as much because of the rivalry she felt for him as for her early and continuing fascination with Asia.

It was Pound also who drew the analogy between Whistler and the Japanese in heightened terms. Pound was greatly fascinated by Whistler. He emulated the artist's stylized dress and manner, finding in the often outrageous behavior of this earlier expatriate American a model for his own extravagances. More important, he recognized in Whistler a major exponent of abstraction and design as the basic components of a work of art, in contrast to narrative, and attributed this aesthetic position to Whistler's understanding of Japanese art. When Pound was asked in 1912 to submit a poem for the first issue of a new publication, *Poetry*, by its founder, Harriet Monroe, he sent "To Whistler, American." In it he decried his native country's inability to provide a fertile home for art, a thesis that became one of the major themes of Monroe's publication.[6] Monroe sent this and subsequent issues to Amy Lowell, whose support she actively sought.

Amy Lowell's admiration for Whistler, however, long predates any connection with Pound. She had purchased a small seascape directly from Whistler during a visit to London in 1896, "before the paint was dry."[7] In 1899 she obtained possession of the family home in Brookline, Massachusetts, and redesigned its lower floor to create a "baronial" library where she hung the Whistler. It remained there throughout her life.

Thus Amy Lowell brought to bear on "Guns as Keys" a heritage both peculiarly her own and universally American. The Lowell family, so prominent in letters and education, was also deeply involved in New England mercantile life (ironically, Whistler was actually born in the mill town of Lowell, Massachusetts, founded by another branch of the family; Whistler vigorously denied the factory town was his birthplace and is frequently quoted as saying that "no one can be born in Lowell"). The dinner table of her childhood—there were four wildly articulate older brothers and sisters, the closest twelve years her senior, and a host of prominent relatives and friends—was raucous with debates about the Confederate betrayal, American expansionism, and the value of trade. Later as mistress of the family home, she kept it a gathering place for the best minds of Cambridge and Boston. Her second eldest brother, Abbott Lawrence, was president of Harvard University from 1909 to 1933, a condition that colored all of Amy's life in the rarified world of Boston society.

The United States had joined World War I only two months before Amy Lowell wrote "Guns as Keys," marking the dramatic end of its promise to stay out of European affairs. The poet carries into her work the ambivalences that the Lowell heritage created, and the text is studded with commentaries and prophecies regarding the American expedition. War, she notes in her preface, causes the poet to discover "something which has always hitherto struck him as preposterous, that life goes on in spite of war. That war itself is an expression of life, a barbaric expression on one side calling for an heroic expression on the other" (*CGC*, p. ix).

In Part One of "Guns as Keys," the poet juxtaposes passages describing Perry's journey in his paddle wheel steamer, the *Mississippi*, from the Chesapeake Bay to Canton, China, with isolated, free-verse poems offering an encapsulated moment of time in Japan. The journey of the American naval ship is described in a literary form known as *polyphonic prose*, which was essentially Amy Lowell's own invention. She described it as having evolved from French *vers libre* but to be more consciously fugal in style, filled with contrapuntal devices to force the language to reflect the diversity of the events and the thoughts of the author. The poet was drawn to this style by a long-standing fascination with the music of Debussy and Stravinsky, whose work she championed in conservative Boston. Their experiments with nonprogrammatic, abstract composition had inspired her earliest poetic efforts. Consistent with her belief that poetry was meant to be read aloud—and she gained her greatest reputation as a public reader and oral commentator on poetry—she found in polyphonic prose the best possible medium for oral recitation.

By using these two contrasting literary forms—set, free-verse poems when speaking of Japan and polyphonic prose when speaking of America—Lowell was able to demonstrate her highly critical attitude toward the American venture. The frenetic activity associated with the global movement of the American ship is pointedly contrasted with the stasis characterizing the poetry depicting Japan, leaving no doubt in the reader or listener's mind which is the more attractive civilization.

Initially, Lowell presents Japan as a nation of visual beauty, delicacy, and simple if earnest endeavors, with its own tightly prescribed culture—in short, the civilization pictured in the woodblock prints she had owned since childhood and continued to collect throughout her life. She is in effect once again portraying Japanese life as a dramatization of what is depicted in a work of art, acknowledging both its limitations and its excellences.

One of the early poems in "Guns as Keys" set in Japan describes a festival procession in terms that are at once an animation of a woodblock print and immediately identifiable as Whistlerian, filled with the color and forms so characteristic of his work:

The one hundred and sixty streets in the Sanno quarter
Are honey-gold
Honey-gold from the gold-foil screens in the houses,
Honey-gold from the fresh yellow mats;
The lintels are draped with bright colors,
And from caves and poles
Red and white paper lanterns
Glitter and swing.
Through the one hundred and sixty decorated streets of the Sanno quarter,
Trails the procession,
With a bright slowness,
To the music of flutes and drums.
Great white sails of cotton
Belly out along the honey-gold streets.

(CGC, pp. 57–58)

As the work progresses and Perry's ship approaches East Asia, the intensity of the poetic passages dealing with Japan increases, climaxing at the close of Part One with the longest poem in the work, a careful, detailed account of a ritual suicide.

In this first part of "Guns as Keys," Commodore Perry is presented aloof in his cabin, keeping records, writing home, and confident of success; the seamen are less certain of their mission, their vulgar speech and raucous ways punctuating the text as their ship makes its way around the world. The author maintains that the purpose of Perry's mission is trade and that the method is to use the "guns as keys" to achieve that end.

Throughout the American passages, "guns" and the metaphoric "gate" that they will force open appear: "Key-guns, your muzzles shine like basalt above the tumbling waves. Polished basalt cameoed upon malachite" (*CGC*, p. 55). Again, American voices are heard, as the poet adopts a diction she judged characteristic of certain of her countrymen: "These monkey-men have got to trade, Uncle Sam has laid his plans with care, see those black guns sizzling there" (*CGC*, p. 57). And again the Americans speak: "The Gate! The Gate! The far-shining Gate! Pat your guns and thank your stars you have not come too late" (*CGC*, p. 62).

And then as Perry's ship rounds the Cape:

> Down, down, down, to the bottom of the map; but we must up again, high on the other side. America, sailing the seas of a planet to stock the shop counters at home. Commerce-raiding a nation; pulling apart the curtains of a temple and calling it trade. Magnificent mission! Every shop-till in every bye-street will bless you. Force the shut gate with the muzzles of your black cannon. Then wait—wait for fifty years—and see who has conquered.   *(CGC, pp. 63–64)*

At last Perry's ship arrives in Canton:

> The Great Gate looms in a distant mist, and the anchored squadron waits and rests, but its coming is as certain as the equinoxes, and the lightning bolts of its guns are ready to tear off centuries like husks of corn.   *(CGC, p. 71)*

All of Part Two of "Guns as Keys" is in polyphonic prose, reinforcing visually and verbally for the reader the end of Japan as an independent entity. It opens with the arrival of Perry's enhanced fleet of four ships in Edo Bay—"July, 1853, Mid-Century, but just on the turn"—while on land, "arrows rust in arsenals, spears stand useless on their butts in vestibules. Cannons lie unmounted in castle yards, and rats and snakes make nests in them and rear their young in unmolested satisfaction" (*CGC*, p. 75).

The ships drop anchor as crowds watch from the bluffs. "Boats are coming from all directions. Beautiful boats of unpainted wood, broad of beam, with tapering sterns, and clean runs. Swiftly they come, with shouting rowers standing to their oars. The shore glitters with spears and lacquered hats" (*CGC*, p. 77).

But the Japanese seamen are not permitted aboard the American ships, and Perry deliberately insults the most distinguished Japanese vice-governor by refusing to meet him, even though he boards the *Susquehanna*. Lowell visually conveys Perry's arrogance by using initial caps to say of the Commodore: " 'His High Mighty Mysteriousness, Lord of the Forbidden Interior,' remains in his cabin" (*CGC*, p. 78).

With a perfect representation of a Whistler painting, the poetic narrative continues: "Rockets rise from the fort, and their trails of sparks glitter faintly now, and their bombs break in faded colors as the sun goes down" (*CGC*, p. 78). The section ends, bringing together the major images of the work: "Bolt the gate, monkey-men, but it is late to begin turning locks so rusty and worn" (*CGC*, p. 78).

There are conferences and debates and much hesitation on the part of the Japanese, but finally the time is at hand for the formal ceremony at which Perry will present the documents containing the president's message he has brought from Washington. Flags flutter, two American bands play, and the poet speaks for the American seamen:

> Stuff your ears, monkey-soldiers, screw your faces, shudder up and down your spines. Cannon! Cannon! from one of the "black ships." Thirteen thudding explosions, thirteen red dragon tongues, thirteen clouds of smoke like the breath of the mountain gods. Thirteen hammer strokes shaking the Great Gate, and the seams in the metal widen. Open Sesame, shotless guns, and again the grand title: "The Only, High Grand and Mighty, Invisible Mysteriousness, Chief Barbarian" reveals himself, and steps into his barge.   *(CGC, p. 84)*

The text describes the ceremoniousness with which Perry descends to the newly built "Conference House" and has the letters of "rich parchment" from the president transmitted to the Japanese "Princes," as the poet names them. Perry is dismissed by the Japanese officials and in turn promises to return for a reply in the spring. The Japanese are hoping the problem will disappear:

> But ships are frail, and seas are fickle, one can nail fresh plating over the thin gate before Spring. Prince of Idzu—Prince of Iwami—inscrutable statesmen, insensate idiots, trusting blithely to a lock when the key-guns are trained even now upon it.   *(CGC, p. 87)*

The Japanese procrastinate for months while Perry is away, and then in February he returns, his fleet enhanced still more. The poet describes the event in Whistlerian terms:

> Just at the edge of moonlight and sunlight—moon setting; sun rising—they come. Seven war ships heeled over and flashing, dashing through heaped waves, sleeping a moment in hollows, leaping over ridges, sweeping forward in a strain of canvas and a train of red-black smoke.
> "The fire-ships! The fire-ships!"   *(CGC, p. 90)*

In the end, the Japanese relent, and presents are exchanged:

> Who thinks of the Great Gate! Its portals are pushed so far back that the shining edges of them can scarcely be observed. The Commodore has never swerved a moment from his purpose, and the dragon mouths of his guns have conquered without the need of a single powder-horn.   *(CGC, pp. 93–94)*

The author looks to the future, naming the gifts the American expedition brought for the Japanese officials:

> The sands of centuries run fast, one slides, and another, each falling into a smother of dust.
>   A locomotive in pay for a Whistler; telegraph wires buying a revolution; weights and measures and Audubon's birds in exchange for fear. Yellow monkey-men leaping out of Pandora's box, shaking the rocks of the Western coastline. Golden California bartering panic for prints. The dressing-gowns of a continent won at the cost of security. Artists and philosophers lost in the hour-glass sand pouring through an open Gate.   *(CGC, p. 94)*

The text ends with three pages headed "Postlude." The first part consists of a poem about a deserted castle, which concludes:

> Your bowmen are departed,
> Your strong walls are silent,
> Their only echo
> A croaking of frogs.
> Frogs croaking at the moon
> In the ancient moat
> Of an ancient, crumbling Castle.

(CGC, pp. 95–96)

The poem is followed by a polyphonic prose piece headed "1903. Japan." It tells of the suicide at the magnificent Kegon waterfall of a young man who carves his testament on a tree trunk, an event that actually occurred that year and was reported in the press. The poet quotes his testament:

> "How mightily and steadily go Heaven and Earth! How infinite the duration of Past and Present! Try to measure this vastness with five feet. A word explains the Truth of the whole Universe—*unknowable*. To cure my agony I have decided to die. Now,

as I stand on the crest of this rock, no uneasiness is left in me. For the first time I know that extreme pessimism and extreme optimism are one." *(CGC, pp. 96–97)*

Finally "Guns as Keys" ends startlingly with these lines:

1903. America

"Nocturne—Blue and Silver—Battersea Bridge.
Nocturne—Grey and Silver—Chelsea Embankment.
Variations in Violet and Green."
Pictures in a glass-roofed gallery, and all day long the throng of people is so great that one can scarcely see them. Debits—credits? Flux and flow through a wide gateway. Occident-Orient-after fifty years.

(CGC, p. 97)

In these final lines of her poem, Amy Lowell is describing the 1904 Memorial Exhibition of Whistler's works organized by the Copley Society of Boston. In a letter written in 1919, Amy Lowell spoke of the two postludes, the one describing the suicide of the student and the other evoking the Copley Exhibition:

> What I mean to give in both those postludes was the effect that each country had upon the other. In the Japanese section, how difficult it was for the Oriental to assimilate the Occidental habits of thought, how he broke in the effort; in the American part, how, in conquering Japan for our commerce, as we thought, we had ourselves been conquered on the aesthetic plane, and our habits of thought insensibly modified by contact with the Japanese.

Held between February 23 and March 28, 1904, the Whistler Memorial Exhibition attracted an extraordinary number of visitors for its time, 41,111. In the words of one reviewer: "As New York has scored the musical success of the season in 'Parsifal,' so Boston has scored the artistic one in the Whistler Memorial Exhibition."[8] Amy Lowell herself was a contributor to the exhibition, lending her small seascape to the show. She celebrated her thirtieth birthday by going to the exhibition and saved the catalogs in her collection.[9]

Among the major contributors to the exhibition was Charles Lang Freer (1854–1919), a native of Kingston, New York, who was perhaps Whistler's most ardent admirer. The items from his collection shown in Boston, together with others he owned or subsequently acquired, were bequeathed to the nation. He intended them to harmonize with his fine Asian collection, forming a unified whole to be studied and enjoyed by succeeding generations of Americans, housed in the building designed specifically for them, the Freer Gallery of Art, in Washington, D.C. The paintings that Amy Lowell names are in that collection.

She captures Whistler at the moment when his fame in America was at its height, for it was only from 1892 on that his extraordinary talent became recognized fully in his native country. The popular enthusiasm for Whistler followed closely on a surge of interest in Japanese art—primarily woodblock prints, ceramics, metalwork, fabrics and design—which was manifested in a vigorous competition for the purchase of Japanese objects of art and in the production of countless copies and imitations. Throughout the United States, Japanese art influenced home design and decoration, architecture, and gardening, as well as the whole range of pictorial and literary arts. To many Americans of that era, Whistler's painting *was* Japanese; when Amy Lowell identifies him as a direct beneficiary of the relations between the two nations, she is reflecting a commonly held view of his work.

As a young artist in France, Whistler became fascinated with Japanese woodblock prints, and his etchings of the late 1850s already reflect their influence.[10] He was deeply affected by the Japanese decorative and pictorial art he saw at an exhibit in Manchester in 1857 and at the 1862 London International Exhibition.[11] In artistic circles, Whistler enjoyed a considerable reputation as a connoisseur of blue and white Chinese and Japanese porcelain. He also collected Japanese screens, fans, and other objects. His paintings of the 1860s are richly decorated with Japanese items and reflect his knowledge of Japanese prints in their composition and particularly in the placement of figures. The calligraphic use of the brush seen on pottery and in the coloration of nineteenth-century woodblock prints occupied his mind intensely in this period.[12] By the 1870s Whistler's paintings and etchings displayed a profound understanding of Japanese aesthetic principles. In his personal life, he created environments for himself indicating a deep sensitivity to Japanese interior design and was most articulate in espousing, to any who would listen, the superiority of what he perceived as the Chinese and Japanese aesthetic. His own home and studio were famed for their austere decor and the restrained use of oriental objects.

Considering the number of works in the Copley Exhibition—eighty-one oils, sixty-three watercolors and pastels, and 315 etchings, drypoints, and lithographs—one finds special significance in the choices Amy Lowell made. Although the show included many of the paintings of the 1860s most vividly containing emblems of "things Japanese," from kimono to standing screens to woodblock prints, the poet did not cite them. Instead, she turned initially to two of the understated and highly abstract Nocturnes, which by 1904 were recognized as Whistler's finest work. A reviewer wrote:

> On the western wall of Copley Hall hung the final utterances of Whistler's art—the incomparable "Nocturnes." These supreme paintings embodied all the refinement, poetry, feeling, insight, and manual dexterity of the painter's life as an artist. Flawless, marvelous, spiritualized twilight and darkness—it is hard to describe the beauty which seems to be diffused from these splendid canvasses. Their technical simplicity is not the least wonderful thing about them. In these are particularly noticeable a fine poetized glamour—the wistful intangible grace of hidden things—the witcheries and mysteries of night. No other artist has ever expressed the sweet still hush of eventide so exquisitely or so simply. In gazing upon them the observer slowly felt the sober pensive loveliness of dusk and dreams stealing over him. As someone said, "a moment more and one might expect the stars to break through the deep velvety skies, and to see their reflections in the placid waters." It is useless to attempt in words to convey an idea of their memory-haunting loveliness.[13]

"Nocturne: Blue and Silver—Battersea Reach," the first painting Amy Lowell names (she mistook the title; there was no "Battersea Bridge" Nocturne in the exhibit[14]), was painted between 1870 and 1875 and may have been repainted by Whistler in 1892. The view is of Battersea Reach from Chelsea Wharf, near Whistler's home, and is one he painted a number of times. The painting measures 19 5/8 by 30 1/8 inches (see illustration 23.1).[15]

A thick black horizontal line of a barge dominates the right foreground. The line of the barge is cut sharply by a stark, straight, vertical mast, its sail furled. A gaff, almost as long as the mast itself, rises obliquely to the left at its top, forming a strong geometric pattern. Absence of the rigging of the sails contributes to the stark abstract geometric quality of the painting. This pattern is repeated, albeit dimly, through masts standing, seemingly directly in the water, behind the barge to its right. The barges on which these masts stand are not pictured, causing them to appear mysteriously disembodied.

The strong vertical line of the mast in the foreground creates a dramatic asymmetrical division to the painting, across whose upper third lies the horizon, the low buildings of the far shore stretching horizontally across the canvas. This vertical line is echoed on the shore to the left by faint spires, one rising in a line directly above the left edge of the barge, and the masts and spires are reflected faintly in the water of the river. Tiny flecks of light, ranging from pale yellow to bright orange, dot the shoreline.

Illustration 23.1.   James McNeill Whistler, *Nocturne: Blue and Silver—Battersea Reach,*
1870/75, 49.9 by 70.5 cm. (Courtesy of the Freer Gallery of Art, Washington, DC.)

"Nocturne: Grey and Silver—Chelsea Embankment, Winter," the second
painting Amy Lowell names, is thought to be a work of January 1879. Painted
when the Thames was frozen over, it was described by contemporaries as a
"nocturne in snow and silver." The view is from Whistler's studio in Chelsea
looking southwest (see illustration 23.2).[16]

The vertical quality of this painting (it measures 24 5/8 by 18 5/8 inches) is
heightened dramatically by a line of grayish white snow-covered shore on which
three boats, possibly dinghies, are scattered at random as though unexpectedly
frozen in place. The line of snow moves down from the extreme right of the
painting, just above halfway, and widens unevenly to flow beyond the center of
the bottom third of the painting far to the left. The boats appear prominently in
the foreground, flattened against the shore and tilted upward in a manner characteristic of Whistler's Nocturnes. It is a conscious distortion of Western perspective adopted from the Japanese print.

Centered in the upper third of the painting are three river barges, dimly perceived through the darkening shadows of evening, their images faintly reflected
in the ice-covered water. From two rise the same type of vertical mast seen in
"Battersea Reach," with sails tightly furled, gaffs jutting obliquely to the right.

Illustration 23.2. James McNeill Whistler, *Nocturne: Grey and Silver—Chelsea Embankment, Winter*, 1879. (COURTESY OF THE FREER GALLERY OF ART, WASHINGTON, DC.)

Once again, the absence of the lines of rigging transforms the masts and gaffs into geometric patterns. The third barge, barely seen behind the other two, faces the viewer head on.

Beyond the ships lies the shoreline, curving away toward the left, with buildings grouped thickly on the right half of the painting. Faint orange touches mark the windows and reflect in the water below.

Visual information that Whistler acquired from his long association with the Japanese print, Chinese and Japanese calligraphy, and ink painting is eminently clear in these works. In both paintings, the primary figures of the foreground are placed so that they create a strong asymmetrical effect, and in both, the horizon line is well to the top of the painting. The geometric shapes of the boats and their masts, resonating throughout the paintings in shadow and in the shapes of other objects, produce an effect of abstraction.

In "Chelsea Embankment," the composition is divided into horizontal units, with the dramatic forms of the masts and gaffs at the upper reaches of the painting emulating the mountains frequently dominating East Asian ink painting. In both Whistler paintings, the dim coloration produced by the use of gray and black, with only the faintest tinges of blue, link them to East Asian ink painting. Although still identifiable as known places, the Nocturnes gain their power from their universality.

"Variations in Green and Violet," the final Whistler painting that Amy Lowell names in the postlude to "Guns as Keys," is one of a series known as "The Six Projects," believed to have been painted in 1868. It is perhaps the most difficult to read of the six works, which are oil sketches on millboard mounted on wood. It measures 24 3/8 by 18.[17]

The "Six Projects" were widely accepted by the public as "Japanese." In a contemporary review of the 1904 Copley Exhibition, for example, a Boston critic wrote, "Also shown . . . were six of the 'Japanese' paintings, executed in brilliant pigments with a full and liquid brush, superb 'Symphonies' in purple, vermilion, white, blue, green."[18] Another Boston critic noted that in the gallery, there "hung a famous and especially delightful group of . . . decorative studies very Japanese in arrangement and treatment. . . . Their delicacy of color and the illusive grace of their drawing made them of especial note."[19] At least four of the five other "Projects" in this group of paintings have identifiable visual associations with ukiyo-e—primarily in their coloration, the placement of the figures, the line of their bodies, the handling of their parasols, and the prominence of the rear view. Their spatial division is reminiscent of countless Japanese models. But this is decidedly less the case with the "Variations in Green and Violet" named by Amy Lowell, and so we must look beyond the painting for some explanation for her choice of this one of the six.[20]

In "Variations in Green and Violet," two greatly elongated female forms fill virtually the entire space. The figure on the left, swathed in a loose, billowing pale blue robe, her head and face painted in broad undefined curves, is turned toward her companion, her left arm reaching toward her, her right arm drawn up to her face, its hand hidden beneath the wildly swirling lines of the robe. A darkness surrounds her, heightened by rectangular black clouds boldly and sharply drawn and barely showing above her head. Thick black paint underlies her garment at the knees (see illustration 23.3).

To the right, dominating the painting, is a woman in white, her body facing outward, her head and right arm turning toward her companion. Her right arm is raised from the elbow, seemingly pointing outward behind her, and from her hand flows a long, thin purple gauze fabric, blowing backward over her auburn hair. The lines of her robe curve sensuously, their movement defined by an admixture of thick brown paint cutting into the white. This woman's face, a deep pink, is featureless. The sky showing behind her head and to the right, is brighter and clearer than that showing behind her companion. The heads of both women are disproportionately small, particularly that of the woman in blue. It is notable also that the women's feet are not pictured, both qualities characteristic of Japanese painting.

The women stand on a flattened black horizontal surface that dominates the lower quarter of the painting, and a sea green background surrounds the two figures, allowing only a bare minimum of horizontal line across the top of the painting to indicate sky. To the far left of the painting, below the midpoint, white flowers are scattered loosely.

In four of the "Six Projects," the figures stand against the sea. Here too, the strong sea green background and the broad sky showing across the extreme top of the painting, with its ominous clouds to the left and clear horizon to the right, point to a seaside setting. Though less clearly defined than in other of Whistler's seaside paintings, the position of the women's bodies suggest they are leaning against an essentially undefined support, possibly a railing.[21] Wind pulls the flowing purple gauze. It seems possible that Whistler identified the work by the colors of violet and green to focus the viewer's attention on the sea background and the vaporous cloth.

The prevailing coloration of the painting is blue, and the whiteness of both the dominant figure's robe and the flowers is moderated with an admixture of blue, so that the variations within the painting are a matter of degree rather than quality. The brushstrokes delineating the robes vary from thin to thick and are erratic in movement so that they suggest rather than describe the robes.

There is a strong possibility that Amy Lowell's attention was drawn to this particular painting by the comments of Ernest Fenollosa (1853–1908), whose work she knew well through Pound's translations. Fenollosa had identified this *Variation* as one of Whistler's finest achievements, comparable to the works of a great Chinese artist. Although constantly cited in association with the "Six Projects," Fenollosa's published comments have a somewhat curious history. In 1903, when the first of his comments was published, he was attempting to recover his tarnished reputation after a personal scandal that cost him his job as the first curator of Japanese art at the Museum of Fine Arts in Boston. Desperate for money, he persistently wooed Freer, seeking his help in getting engagements as a public lecturer, selling him works of art from his own collection, and acting as Freer's agent and adviser in purchasing Japanese and Chinese art. Freer came to place great confidence in Fenollosa's knowledge, brought him to his home in Detroit to study his Asian collection, and hoped Fenollosa would prepare a catalog of it.

In 1903 Fenollosa contributed an article to an art journal dedicated to Whistler. It was one of many produced by a Salem–Boston art dealer from Japan named Bunkyō Matsuki. Matsuki had been a major source for the Chinese and Japanese art in Freer's collection, and the two men were competing for Freer's respect and favor. Since they both knew of Freer's passionate dedication to Whistler and his art, it is difficult to avoid questioning their effusive enthusiasm for the artist.[22] Fenollosa's article, "The Place in History of Mr. Whistler's Art," describes the artist in these terms:

> The simple truth is that he is the first great master who comes after the union of East and West, the first who creates naturally and without affectation in their mingled terms.
>
> This explains why, in studying any broad range of Whistler's work, whether in water, oil, or the etched line, we continually find such subtle resemblances to all the leading schools of the past. In his grandest figure work, where his broad brush has given us instantaneous sweeps of massy drapery line, we are driven, in spite of the alien material, to trace a parallel to the sculptures of the Parthenon. His broadest color impressions are quite Greek in rhythm. But at the very next moment we are reminded of the broad blunt line of the great Japanese fifteenth-century master, Sesshū. In condensation, in power, to reduce even a mass of foreground figures to a fine—and correct—impressionistic blur of a single tint, he even out-Sesshūs Sesshū. (p. 16)

Illustration 23.3.   James McNeill Whistler, *Variations in Green and Violet*, ca. 1868.
(Courtesy of the Freer Gallery of Art, Washington, DC.)

As a contributor to the Memorial Exhibition, it is likely that Amy Lowell would have been sent a copy of this journal, and Fenollosa's comments might have brought her attention to this particular work in the show.

He wrote about the "Six Projects" again in 1907, in an article entitled "The Collection of Mr. Charles L. Freer," for a periodical called *Pacific Era*, published in Detroit and partially supported by Freer:

> But though Whistler's key to larger range be stolen from the East, it must not be supposed that he falls out of relation to past European achievement. If his work be of universal value, and not freakish, it must have points of contact with all old greatnesses. It is just because he is, first and last, a genuine creator, that his ideas in line, tone and color—drawn up from objective affinities rather than personal whims—are charged with the widest range of analogy. . . . In his grander figure work in oil,—such as the eight [*sic*] supreme "Arrangements," kept by him in his studio till his death, and now, as it were, bequeathed to the American people through Mr. Freer—the long drapery lines rise to such a height of spontaneous splendor that they court comparison with Phidias on the one hand, and with the greatest Chinese painter, Ririomin [Li Lung-mien in Chinese], on the other. (p. 62)

The article is illustrated with a photograph of the "Variations in Green and Violet."[23]

Fenollosa provided the perfect rationale for the inclusion of this painting in "Guns as Keys." The twelfth-century artist he names, Li Lung-mien, was believed to be the painter of a work (with the unfortunate English title "Lohans Laundering") in Freer's collection. It is strikingly rich in thickly etched drapery drawn with masterful strokes.[24] Fenollosa creates a connection between the Chinese artist and the great Athenian sculptor Phidias, to whom the Elgin Marbles are attributed, in order to demonstrate Whistler's role in bringing together the Western and Eastern traditions in a single work of art. To Amy Lowell, such a painting must have seemed an excellent image for the ultimate result of the forceful opening of Japan by the American naval forces.

By naming the Nocturnes and the Variations, whose very titles reflect the poet's own fascination with music, Amy Lowell directs our attention to the most subtle ways in which Japanese art affected James McNeill Whistler. Her choices demonstrate that she had cultivated her own sense of Japanese art and the Japanese aesthetic and was not distracted by the more obvious "Japanese" elements in some of Whistler's more colorful works. It is also clear that she was willing to accept Fenollosa's judgment on the merits of the Variations. She saw that Whistler had absorbed the Japanese model profoundly and had blended it with his sense of the Western tradition to create an original art. To the poet, this total assimilation of Japanese technique and feeling made Whistler the perfect metaphor for the effect on the United States of the opening of Japan.

In the years after writing "Guns as Keys," Amy Lowell embarked on a crusade to bring contemporary American poetry to the American people. On this mission, she traveled countless miles under often arduous conditions, despite nearly continuous physical breakdowns, giving readings in towns and cities across the country. Her interest in Japan (and possibly her rivalry with Pound) led her to provide the introduction to *Diaries of Court Ladies of Old Japan* (1920) and to "translate," with her lifelong friend Florence Wheelock Ayscough, an anthology of "Chinese verse" entitled *Fir Flower Tablets* (1921).

In her last comments on Japan, as in her earliest, Amy Lowell speaks of the woodblock print, and throughout her writing there continues the sharp pictorialization constituting so much of her Imagism. Her affection for East Asia was surely conveyed to her substantial readership, and for many Americans in the first half of this century, Amy Lowell's "Japanese" and "Chinese" poems were their entrée to that mysterious world. Her ability to link the arts—shown so dramatically in "Guns as Keys"—responded to the affection that Americans felt for Japanese objects of art and opened an expanse of understanding and communication often difficult for more academic authors to achieve.

NOTES

1. The title refers to an allusion to Dante's retreat made in a poem describing the artistic recreation of experience through books, in Richard Aldington's poem "At the British Museum." Aldington (1892–1962) was perhaps the most gifted of the seven poets who banded together to produce the three slim volumes, entitled *Some Imagist Poets*, of 1915, 1916, and 1917, which gave the name to this literary movement.

2. Amy Lowell, *Can Grande's Castle* (hereafter abbreviated *CGC*) (New York: Macmillan, 1918), pp. x–xi.

3. It is clear from the text that Amy Lowell was intimately familiar with the Hawks–Perry-authorized *Narrative* (1856) and had studied the images of the expedition made by William Heine and others of the official artists who traveled with Perry. By 1917 a number of other firsthand accounts of the trip, whose publication Perry had originally suppressed, had been published, and the etchings, lithographs, and drawings of Heine and his colleagues had been issued in a variety of editions. Amy Lowell would have had access to virtually all of these. For a review of the literature that would have been available in print to her in 1917, see Frederic Trautman, *With Perry to Japan: A Memoir by William Heine* (Honolulu: University of Hawaii Press, 1990), pp. 215–224.

One of Amy Lowell's biographers, Jean Gould, attributes the poet's detailed knowledge of the expedition to her friendship with the wealthy financier and banker August Belmont (1853–1924), whose mother Caroline was Matthew Perry's daughter. See Jean Gould, *Amy* (New York: Dodd, Mead, 1975), pp. 237–38. The Belmont family was then in possession of unpublished impressions of the expedition to which Amy Lowell may have had access. A number of these have since been published in Roger Pineau, ed., *The Personal Journal of Commodore Matthew C. Perry* (Washington, DC: Smithsonian Institution Press, 1968).

4. Percival Lowell (1855–1916) was sufficiently well regarded in Asia by 1883 to be asked that August to serve as foreign secretary and counselor to the Korean diplomatic mission to the United States. In the course of four trips to Asia, he wrote articles for the *Atlantic Monthly* and published four books on East Asia: *Choson-The Land of Morning Calm* (1886); *The Soul of the Far East* (1888), said to have inspired Lafcadio Hearn, among countless others, to become interested in Japan; *Noto* (1891); and *Occult Japan* (1894). In 1889 Percival Lowell gave a much heralded reading of the poem "Sakura no saku," a work in heroic couplets, for the Phi Beta Kappa Society in Boston (published in the *Boston Post*, June 28, 1889). His poem "Ontake," a work in blank verse, appeared in the journal of the Authors' Club of New York in 1893.

5. Unless otherwise noted, I am indebted for biographical information regarding Amy Lowell to S. Foster Damon's monumental study, *Amy Lowell: A Chronicle, with Extracts from Her Correspondence* (Boston: Houghton Mifflin, 1935). Amy Lowell's contacts with Japan and their effect on her poetry have been carefully reviewed by Sanehide Kodama, *American Poetry and Japanese Culture* (Hamden, CT: Archon Books, 1984), pp. 35–50.

6. It was one of two poems by Pound in this first issue (October 1912) of what became a watershed publication in modern poetry, in good measure owing to Pound's contributions. In the poem he continues a theme he had been expressing earlier—that America was in medieval times, about to embark on the Renaissance—and that he, Pound, was one of those "who bear the brunt of our America / And try to wrench our impulse into art." He described America as a "mass of dolts," but found in such an American artist as Whistler one who could "show us there's a chance at least of winning through." See Humphrey Carpenter, *A Serious Character: The Life of Ezra Pound* (Boston: Houghton Mifflin, 1988), pp. 184–95.

7. In an undated note from Whistler to Amy Lowell's hotel room, confirming the transaction and advising her on having it varnished in six months. Entitled "Blue and Silver: Dieppe," the work has been incorrectly dated in Whistler's *catalog raisonné* as possibly having been done on a trip to Dieppe in August 1898 and sold in that year. See Andrew McLaren Young, Margaret MacDonald, Robin Spencer, and Hamish Mills, *The Paintings of James McNeill Whistler* (hereafter abbreviated *YMSM*) (New Haven, CT: Yale University Press, 1980), no. 499. The painting is now in the New Britain Museum of American Art, Connecticut.

8. *Outlook*, March 5, 1904, p. 541.

9. The exhibition had two separate catalogs, prepared with the utmost simplicity in compliance with Whistler's own tastes. The format directly emulates those he himself designed for his exhibits throughout his lifetime. One listed the oil paintings, watercolors, pastels and drawings, and the other listed etchings, drypoints, and lithographs. Copies can be found in the library of the Freer Gallery of Art and the Glasgow (Scotland) University Library. Amy Lowell willed her vast library with its priceless manuscripts to Harvard. Her papers are housed in the Houghton Library.

10. Katharine A. Lochnan, *The Etchings of James McNeill Whistler* (New Haven, CT: Yale University Press, 1984), pp. 92–95. Lochnan's work is an outstanding study of Whistler as an artist, in addition to being a comprehensive analysis of his etchings.

11. Deanna Marohn Bendix, *Diabolical Designs: Paintings, Interiors, and Exhibitions of James McNeill Whistler* (Washington, DC: Smithsonian Institution Press, 1995), pp. 206–8.

12. Robin Spencer, "Whistler and Japan: Work in Progress," *Japonisme in Art: An International Symposium* (Tokyo: Kodansha International, 1980), pp. 57–81, presents an important analysis of the means by which Whistler absorbed Japanese influences.

13. Maurice Baldwin, "The Whistler Memorial Exhibition," *New England Magazine*, May 1904, pp. 296–97.

14. Her confusion may have been caused by the fact that there was an etching of Whistler's entitled "Battersea Bridge" in the exhibition. Whistler created a number of views of the old Battersea Bridge. He painted a screen in 1872, now at the Hunterian Museum and Art Gallery, University of Glasgow, which he titled "Blue and Silver—Screen with Old Battersea Bridge"(*YMSM*, no. 139). It is often pictured in photographs of his rooms. It was the basis for the painting, also done in 1872, "Nocturne in Blue and Gold: Old Battersea Bridge" (*YMSM*, no. 140) now at the Tate Gallery, London. Both have been frequently compared with Hiroshige's woodblock prints. Neither was in the Copley Exhibition. To the British, the Tate's "Old Battersea Bridge" is perhaps Whistler's most outstanding painting.

The etching entitled "Battersea Bridge" in the exhibition is now known by the title "Old Battersea Bridge" and is numbered in the Kennedy system as 177.

15. *YMSM*, no. 119. It was purchased by Charles Freer in April 1902.

16. *YMSM*, no. 205. This entry cites an 1879 statement that it was " 'fresh from the easel of this artist . . . a nocturne—the Thames by moonlight, with ice coming down the river, an effect seen by Mr. Whistler only the other night.' " However, the Freer Gallery's notes for this work, dated 1977, cite a statement by Susan Hobbs, a former curator of the collection, that it was the earliest of the Nocturnes, having been begun in 1864. Her conclusion is based on information in a letter from Whistler's mother, describing the genesis of the painting.

Charles Freer purchased "Chelsea Embankment" in August 1902. Excellent color plates of both the Nocturnes may be found in David Park Curry, *James McNeill Whistler at the Freer Gallery of Art* (Washington, DC: Smithsonian Institution Press, 1984), plates 25, 30.

17. *YMSM*, no. 83. For a color plate, see Curry, *Whistler*, plate 12. It is known as the "Symphony in Green and Violet." Whistler frequently changed the names of his paintings, and many of his works have had the same name, at least at one time. Adopting musical terms for his titles and associating them with colors fitted his philosophy of his art as abstract rather than narrative. It does, however, lead to massive confusion.

Whistler prized the "Six Projects" and kept five of them with him until shortly before his death. Freer bought the sixth in 1902, from T. R. Way, the son of Whistler's printer and ally, and the others from Whistler in July 1903.

18. In a review of the exhibition in *Studio Talk*, signed A.E.G., undated, p. 361. The review contains a series of photographs of the exhibition, copies of which are in the archives of the Freer Gallery. One is reproduced in Linda Merill, ed., *With Kindest Regards: The Correspondence of Charles Lang Freer and James Mc Neill Whistler, 1890–1903* (Washington, DC: Smithsonian Institution Press, 1995), p. 40.

19. Baldwin, "Whistler Memorial Exhibition," p. 296.

20. Although never completed, the "Six Projects" were conceived as a decorative scheme for the home of Whistler's patron, Frederick R. Leyland. In addition to the clearly Japanese effects, the "Projects" also contain references to the work of contemporary British artists Albert Moore and Edward Burne-Jones, to tiny Greek Tanagra clay figurines, as well as the Elgin Marbles, reinstalled at the British Museum in 1865. Fragments of a frame designed by Whistler for another of the oils in the series indicate that a musical theme may have been meant to accompany the finished series, so that it would have been unified by music rather than narrative content. Whistler saw the "Projects" as an important statement of his evolving "aestheticism." See Richard Dorment, in Richard Dorment and Margaret F. MacDonald, eds., *James McNeill Whistler* (New York: Abrams, 1995), pp. 92–94. Whistler's own high expectation for the series may well have contributed to his inability to complete the project; he took only one of the sketches into full oil paint.

21. Dorment uniquely sees the painting as a "conversation between two figures at what appears to be a garden wall" and reads this as a "confrontation" between two women analogous to several Burne-Jones paintings of the 1860s. See ibid., pp. 92–94.

22. Freer purchased eighty-nine items through Matsuki between 1896 and 1906, a number of which have proved to be treasures. See Yoshiaki Shimizu, "An Individual Taste for Japanese Painting," *Apollo* 118 (August 1983): 144–49. The publication was called *Lotus* and appeared in December 1903 as a "Special Holiday Number in Memoriam" to Whistler. It contained an appreciation of Whistler by Matsuki, a piece announcing the Copley Memorial Exhibition, a short article on ukiyo-e, and another article on the influence of Japanese art on American education. Finally, it included Fenollosa's brief article and items intended to stimulate interest in the Japanese art that Matsuki was selling.

23. The *Pacific Era* article appraised Freer's collection broadly, recognizing the limitations specifically imposed by the collector's personal tastes. Fenollosa's unpublished notes made while viewing the collection with Freer in 1907 are valuable indications of Fenollosa's knowledge of Asian art and of Freer's debts to him. See Thomas Lawton, "Freer and Fenollosa," *Freer: A Legacy of Art* (Washington, DC: Smithsonian Institution Press, 1993), pp. 130–51.

24. Fenollosa sold this painting to Charles Freer in 1902, and it is one of the treasures of the collection. Information later discovered on the scroll reveal it to be a work of 1178 by another Southern Sung painter, Lin T'ing-kuei. One of a large set of paintings believed to have come from China to Japan in the fifteenth century, Fenollosa had received it as a result of his assistance in arranging a show of the set at the Boston Museum of Fine Arts. It had been housed in the Daitokuji. Fenollosa describes the painting and his acquisition of it in a letter to Freer dated October 12, 1902, now in the Freer Gallery of Art archives. The value of the painting is discussed by Thomas Lawton, "China's Artistic Legacy," *Apollo* 118 (August 1983): 127–28.

Freer purchased another painting from this series in Tokyo in 1907, entitled "The Rock Bridge at T'ien-t'ai Mountain." It, too, had been attributed by Japanese scholars to Li Lung-mien, but has been found to be by Chou Chi-ch'ang; it is also dated 1178.

24

Hayashi Fumiko and the Transformation of Her Fiction

◉

JOAN ERICSON

Hayashi Fumiko reached the peak of her popularity and productivity in the immediate postwar era. Her portrayals of struggle and perseverance among the dispossessed and disaffected struck a chord in a broad segment of the reading public. Hayashi's short fiction and serialized works were published in a wide range of venues—major newspapers and mainstream literary journals as well as women's magazines—and her books and collected volumes sold exceptionally well.[1] In the four years before her death in 1951, Hayashi published eleven serialized novels, twenty-two other volumes (principally novels), and more than thirty short stories, among which were considered her most sophisticated and successful works.[2] Her sole literary prize, the Joryū bungaku shō (Women's literary prize) awarded for "Bangiku" (Late Chrysanthemum) in 1949, confirmed her status among the preeminent women writers of the era.[3] In the wake of her premature death at age forty-eight, Hayashi was characterized as "the representative woman writer in our country."[4]

The persistent categorization of her as a "woman writer" (*joryū sakka*) of "women's literature" (*joryū bungaku*), however, ensured that even though she might be especially prominent, her work would also be considered marginal to the canon and would rarely receive sustained critical scrutiny.[5] Even those who closely read and evaluated more than a smattering of her works were hobbled by the received wisdom about "women writers." For example, Fukuda Hirotoshi dismissed Hayashi's early works (including *Hōrōki*) as girlishly sentimental but characterized "Bangiku" as more masculine, or "androgenous" (*chūsei*), and therefore more mature and serious.[6] The irony of Fukuda's presumption—that works by women writers merit critical attention and "women's literary prizes" to the extent that they distance themselves from those characteristics of their gender—underscores the stigma associated with "women's literature." But other critics neglected to observe even this transformation of Hayashi's style and imposed the same fixed "feminine" characterization on wholly dissimilar works. Moreover, the categorization by gender obscured the relation of her work to more salient literary, social, and political trends.

Aesthetic Transformation

By the late Taishō period, notably in Nakamura Murao's 1925 essay in *Shinchō*, a clear distinction had crystallized between *kyakkan shōsetsu* (objective fiction) and autobiography or confessional genres.[7] Kyakkan shōsetsu, also referred to as *honkaku shōsetsu* (authentic fiction), did not directly reflect the author's experiences or views. In contrast, either *shinkyō shōsetsu* (mental attitude fiction), which projected the author's interior states, or *watakushi shōsetsu* (confessional fiction), which revealed largely self-destructive practices, were based on the writer's personal experiences.[8] Tokuda Shūsei, a novelist whom Edward Seidensticker regarded as having a decisive impact on Hayashi's aesthetic development, argued that a writer should begin with autobiography before attempting objective fiction, which he held to be the decidedly superior style.[9] Although this assessment was hotly contested, it appears to be one to which Hayashi adhered.

In the afterword to *Onna no nikki* (A Woman's Diary), first published in 1936, Hayashi described her concerted effort to change her style of writing from the autobiographical *Hōrōki* to the fictional *Onna no nikki* in order, in her words, "to separate myself from the retching [literally "throwing up bloody vomit"] confusion of the autobiographical *Hōrōki*."[10]

"Kaki" (Oyster), published in the September 1935 issue of *Chūō kōron*, was indicative of a decided shift in Hayashi's style. The story, told from a man's point of view, was no longer autobiographical or sentimental but, rather, an unvarnished and straightforward depiction of an inept, possibly retarded man unable to adjust to transitions in his workplace or to resolve tensions in his family life. Due to ill-defined maladies, the protagonist, Morita Shūkichi, a hand sewer of tobacco pouches, is unable to produce the weekly quota or to adapt to machine production. He decides to take his wife from Tokyo back to his family home in Shikoku, which he has not seen in nine years. They plan to stay for a month or two, but when he arrives unexpectedly, his elder sister tells him that he has no right to his ancestral home, having left without ever aiding the remaining family after the parents died. Back in Tokyo, Morita takes up sewing again but is given inferior-quality goods and is forced to work at a lower rate. Neurotic and suspicious, he accuses his wife of infidelity. She thereupon leaves him and their poverty-stricken existence, although within a week she sends him forty yen from her earnings as a live-in waitress. He goes to Chiba to check up on her—certain that she has turned to prostitution—but he cannot substantiate his accusation and so returns to Tokyo alone.[11]

One month after the publication of "Kaki" and a volume of short stories with the same title, Hayashi flouted the publishing industry's conventions by organizing and paying for her own gala celebration in honor of these works.[12] The receipt from the banquet noted that 102 people attended and that the total bill came to 254 yen and fifty sen. Among the literati in attendance were Uno Kōji, Hirotsu Kazuo, Satō Haruo, Hayashi Fusao, Hasegawa Shigure, Yoshiya Nobuko, Kubokawa Ineko, and Tokuda Shūsei. Reportedly in high spirits, Hayashi danced the *dojō sukui* (scooping loaches), much to the derision of some of the literary establishment.[13]

Hayashi had published fictional, as opposed to autobiographical, stories earlier that year—for example, *No mugi no uta* (A Song of Wild Wheat), serialized in *Fujin kōron* from January to March 1935—but with "Kaki," she appears to have wished to call attention to the new approach in her writing.[14] Even at the outset of her career, Hayashi had experimented with a nonautobiographical approach in *Senshun fu* (A Record of a Shallow Spring), serialized in the Tokyo *Asahi shinbun* in January and February 1931. However, when this fictional piece, about an unhappy homeless young woman abandoned by her husband, failed to achieve either critical or popular success, Hayashi returned to writing in an autobiographical voice, with two works both published in *Kaizō* later in 1931: "Fūkin to uo no machi" (A Town of Accordions and Fish) in April and *Seihin no sho* (A Record of Honorable Poverty) serialized beginning in November. Both were well received, but *Senshun fu* was not included in either the Shinchōsha collected works of Hayashi (1953) or the Bunsendō expanded edition (1977).

Contrary to the usual depiction of Hayashi's writing trajectory, her change in style was additive rather than exclusive. In a number of later works, Hayashi returned to the self-referential lyrical approach that characterized *Hōrōki*. Several of these ostensibly autobiographical accounts might best be considered as a revision and elaboration, or a continuation, of the personal odyssey that began with *Hōrōki*.[15] *Hitori no shōgai* (One Person's Life, serialized for one year in *Fujin no tomo* in 1940) begins with a description of recent trips to Kyoto and Beijing. However, the bulk of *Hitori no shōgai* focuses on those few years in the mid-1920s recorded in *Hōrōki*, but organized in a more cohesive prose narrative form. As in *Hōrōki*, thirty free-verse poems play an integral part in the narrative. Hayashi also includes an account of the trip she took to Europe. She had already recounted her 1930 European tour in *Santō ryokō no ki* (Record of a Trip by Third Class, 1933) and further elaborated these incidents in the 1947 publication of *Pari nikki* (Paris Diary). *Hitori no shōgai* was one of a series of confessional diaries—*Yūshū nikki* (Melancholy Diary, 1939), *Nikki* (Diary, 1941), *Nikki II* (Diary, Part II, 1942), and *Den'en nikki* (Rural Diary, 1942)—published in quick succession. Perhaps the most notable of her later autobiographical works was the serialization of *Hōrōki, Part III*, beginning in May 1947. This third version of Hayashi's exploits in the late Taishō period were far more sensational and explicit than the earlier installments.

Hayashi also suggested an autobiographical style by using in the titles such terms as diary (*nikki*), chronicle (*ki*), record (*sho* or *fu*), scribbling (*rakugaki*), and biography (*den*), even though these works were clearly fictional. *Senshun fu* (1931) was the first of such titles; *Sazanami—Aru onna no techō* (Ripples—A Certain Woman's Date Book, 1951) the last.[16]

Miyamoto Yuriko observed that Hayashi would take an idea that could be covered in ten lines of poetry and expand it to fill up a short story.[17] Hayashi conveyed the ability to elaborate on a fragment or single expression or to be inspired by a sentiment or fancy, though this apparent approach to composition was calculated to appear more sophisticated and intellectual.

Hayashi also exhibited a particular penchant for using as the basis for a story an image, often only a title, from a prominent foreign work. This pattern can be seen in many of her titles: *Onna no nikki* (1935), taken from Octave Mirbeau's *Le Journal d'une femme de chambre* (1900) and *Omokage* (Vestiges, 1933), the same as Mori Ōgai's volume of translated European poetry (1889). Hayashi also took her titles from prominent works of Japanese fiction, such as *Ukigumo* (Floating Clouds, 1949), from Futabatei Shimei's work (1887–89), or *Gan* (Wild Geese, 1947), from Mori Ōgai's novel (1911). However, if Hayashi liberally borrowed titles and imagery, her stories were usually wholly unlike their namesake or inspiration. Although this habit of echoing titles may indicate an affectation, her work was not simply imitative. For example, Futabatei's *Ukigumo*, touted as Japan's first modern novel, focuses on the life of Utsumi Bunzō, an ordinary man, who finds his dreams of marriage crushed when he loses his low-level job in the government bureaucracy,[18] whereas Hayashi's *Ukigumo* (Floating Clouds, 1949) describes the malaise and rootlessness of postwar Japanese society, seen through the ill-fated relationship of Yukiko and Tomioka after their repatriation from French Indochina.[19] Hayashi's story has a strong, more fully developed female protagonist who acts as an active agent, and her plot and societal setting are by far the bleaker portrait.

Critical Reception

The critic Nakamura Mitsuo characterized Hayashi's work as quintessentially feminine: "The special characteristic of Hayashi Fumiko as a writer is found . . . in the fact that she remains feminine throughout, and that feminine quality is at times so strong as to be overpowering." He referred to Hayashi as having the ability to work around her "unusually strong female sensibility and female faults," sometimes building on them in her writing.[20] For Nakamura, the "feminine" qualities in her work stemmed from Hayashi's lyrical, poetical, and emotional observations about her personal life that did not share the same sentimental pessimism of the traditional "I-novel." These seemingly playful notes about her life had a direct relation to classical Japanese literary conventions such as the diaries (*nikki*) and poem tales (*uta monogatari*). This linkage to classical Japanese literature drew on a tradition of writing by women.

Nakamura elaborated his assessment of Hayashi through a comparison with Miyamoto Yuriko, both of whom died in 1951:

> Whereas Miyamoto professed fusion with "the people" on an ideological level, in reality she was not able to discard her genteel upbringing. In direct opposition, Hayashi Fumiko was born of common blood and made that the wellspring of her literature. For Miyamoto Yuriko, the masses were the destination to which she mentally aspired; Hayashi Fumiko, conversely, saw the masses as morass through which one was forced to crawl. But at the same time, the common folk also constituted Hayashi's hometown where one did not feel inhibited in one's actions.[21]

Nakamura saw in these two writers a yearning for something that each lacked, notably a station different from that into which they were born. From a good family, Miyamoto longed for the simplicity and authenticity of ordinary people, whereas Hayashi embodied the snobbish social-climbing aspirations of the nouveau riche.[22] Nakamura observed that Hayashi's garish tastes and unsophisticated affectation were themselves of the people.

In 1947, Miyamoto Yuriko criticized Hayashi for having abandoned the natural volatile quality found in *Hōrōki* and for adopting a more refined taste. In her view, Hayashi's later writing contained unnecessary nihilistic and sentimental excesses. Miyamoto indicted both Hayashi and Uno Chiyo as women writers (*fujin sakka*) who embraced the progressive spirit only for personal advancement, not for larger political or aesthetic interests. Miyamoto saw their work as overly individualistic and, at the same time, pandering to issues of gender. Both Hayashi and Uno, she argued, postured as "women writers" and shamelessly promoted their gender in order to secure press coverage and titillate consumers. "The success that they gained as a result served instead to create the boundaries of their literature."[23]

Miyamoto Yuriko's criticism coincided with the condemnation that Hayashi, among many others, faced in the postwar politicized environment for having undergone *tenkō* (apostasy) and for a lack of ideological fealty.[24] Hayashi had first surfaced in the company of anarchist and proletarian writers, but she never exhibited any political commitment to, or even interest in, Marxist ideology. Soon after achieving prominence as a writer, she quickly distanced herself from leftist associations, despite her nine-day detention in the Nakano police station in September 1933 for having purchased a subscription to a Communist Party newspaper.[25] Indeed, her works were often dismissed, as she herself noted, for lacking a political vision.[26]

After the war, however, Hayashi suffered no *crise de conscience* for her active participation in the war effort. Even though she castigated the wartime restrictions and censorship after the fact and bemoaned the lack of outlets for publication (and opportunities for income), she never apologized for—or even rationalized her support for—the war effort. For Hayashi, the dilemmas of the postwar period were personal: whether she would again have the confidence to write and the ability to look at reality straight in the eye.[27]

In 1957, a special issue of the influential journal *Bungei* was devoted to Hayashi. It included the results of a questionnaire of seventy-three prominent writers and intellectuals who were asked, What is your opinion about Hayashi Fumiko's literature? Which of her works do you like the best? What have you learned from Hayashi Fumiko?[28] Most respondents answered briefly, and many chose to answer only selectively and enigmatically. Most commonly, only a favorite work was mentioned, but the answers are nevertheless revealing. Although some respondents were adulatory—Kawabata Chōtarō "read [all] with great pleasure"; Itagaki Naoko, who would be Hayashi's biographer, wrote that her "development from the first work to [the last] was very spectacular"— many expressed an undercurrent of, if not outright, condescension. The critic

Odagiri Hideo noted that "from about the time of *Seishi no sho*, [Hayashi's] self-conscious coquetry was impure; for the most part I stopped reading her works." Yoshida Seiichi, a professor of Japanese literature, also was critical: "I like her work. However, her core (*shin*) is weak, and she is not a first-rate writer." Several thought Hayashi was quintessentially female: the critic Takayama Takeshi wrote that "of Japanese women writers, there are those who have become androgenous (*chūsei*) writers, but the term *joryū sakka* is particularly befitting Hayashi Fumiko." The writer Itō Einosuke thought that "her works [were] full of feminine (*joseiteki*) sensitivity." The disparaging traits associated with femininity were asserted as well. The poet Okamoto Jun described Hayashi's works as "of the people (*minshūteki*) . . . [and] limited in intellect (*chisei*)." And Takayama declared that it "would have been better had she had more of an intellectual contemplative aspect; lacking this, she has left only loveable jewels."

In 1963, in an article published in Japanese, Edward G. Seidensticker defended Hayashi's artistic achievements and criticized those who condemned her work for its lack of social or ideological content.[29] Odagiri Hideo, Ōta Yōko, and others had criticized Hayashi for her lack of intellect and ideology, but Seidensticker found that these charges obscured her artistry:

> Since she is not intellectual to begin with, it may be possible to say that she was not able to rise to the heights of first rate art. But as in the case of Dickens, if one is too obsessed with this aspect, one is liable to overlook important matters. Hayashi Fumiko's vitality when compared with Miyamoto Yuriko is similar to a comparison of Dickens and George Eliot. Furthermore, as far as fiction is concerned, the presence of animation is a more important question than the existence of abstract social or moral ideas.[30]

For Seidensticker, "Hayashi Fumiko at her best had a dramatic imaginative power which was rare for modern Japan, even more so for modern women writers."[31]

Seidensticker accepted the judgment of Nakamura Mitsuo that unlike Miyamoto Yuriko, Hayashi "had all the vices and virtues of a feminine (*onnarashii*) writer."[32] "An all too typical *joryū sakka* in her early career, Hayashi Fumiko abandoned her former feminine fixed outlook with the experience of Japan's defeat. . . . Hayashi wrote some of the best postwar short stories, probably the best by women."[33]

Itagaki Naoko observed that although Hayashi was immensely popular, she was neglected or dismissed by male critics and even by the publishing industry.[34] Other critics agreed that Hayashi's work had yet to receive critical scrutiny. In 1964, Wada Yoshie noted that "although there are commentaries about Hayashi the literary figure (*bungakusha*), there is nothing as yet about Hayashi as a writer (*shōsetsuka*)." However, although he recommended further research on Hayashi, his interest in Hayashi's writing, as opposed to her life, was belied by his proposed approach: "I think that the research lies in *Hōrōki*. To rearrange the three parts in chronological order is the first task."[35] Such an approach can only help relate the entries to incidents in her own life and shows little interest in the works themselves. Muramatsu Sadataka recommended judging Hayashi by her works and not her life or actions, but Muramatsu's article "Hayashi Fumiko's Love Life" nonetheless provides a considerable roster of lovers and spares few details.[36]

Biographies of Hayashi, including those by Itagaki Naoko, Hirabayashi Taiko, and Fukuda Kiyoto, as well as special issues or publications dedicated to Hayashi, such as that in the *Nihon bungaku arubamu* series, also share a relative disregard for an analytic appraisal of her work. Instead, the emphasis has been on organizing a coherent chronology of Hayashi's life, with some discussion of her motivations and influences and comparisons with other writers. Her biographers have tended to accept what she wrote in *Hōrōki, Fūkin to uo no machi* (A Town of Accordions and Fish) and *Seihin no sho* (On Honorable Poverty) as unreconstructed autobiography.[37] Incidents in these literary works are correlated with specific events in her own life and are explained by references to Hayashi's personal experiences. This is in keeping with the prevailing orthodoxy in literary histories, in which confessional fiction is "considered inherently referential . . . its meaning derives from the author's life . . . [and] the work is meaningful insofar as it illuminates the life."[38]

Much of the critical, as well as the popular, interest in Hayashi has derived from a fascination with her as a sort of celebrity. She had a forceful, sometimes outrageous, personality and went some distance to convey to her reading public sensational, if not salacious, intimacies. Tsushima Yūko has described Taishō and Shōwa women writers as needing a passion, vibrancy, or enthusiasm (*jōnetsu*) in order to be successful.[39] Hayashi had that quality, as well as considerable drive, showmanship, and a capacity for self-promotion. Hayashi also could sail close to the winds of scandal, if not simple bad taste. Yet for the most part, she was able to determine what was permissible and popular. Hayashi was somewhat reckless in her personal life, but much of what went into print was cut out of whole cloth. She had a flair for the flamboyant and doggedly sought to preserve her slightly *outré* airs. At the same time, she sought to maintain the image of an understanding wife and attentive mother.

Hayashi's legacy is largely as a "woman writer," the very categorization she sought in her life to escape. Some of her most popular and best-regarded works

(*Hōrōki, Ukigumo*, and *Meshi*) are still in print, in inexpensive paperbacks, published by Shinchōsha and available in the mass-market section of most bookstores. However, books about Hayashi or special editions of her work are shelved in the "women's section." Hayashi is often included in special issues of academic journals focusing on women writers,[40] as well as in collections of women writers' works. In studies devoted to women writers, such as Itagaki Naoko's *Meiji, Taishō, Shōwa no joryū bungaku* (Women's Literature of Meiji, Taisho, and Showa) or Murō Saisei's *Ōgon no hari* (Golden Needles, 1961), discussions of Hayashi's work merit a full chapter. Whereas Hayashi is sometimes included in mainstream literary anthologies—for example, she was the only woman writer represented in the sixteen-volume set of the *Hito to bungaku* series published by Gakushū kenkyūsha in 1980—she is occasionally relegated to a virtual footnote in literary histories.[41] New biographies continue to appear, with assiduously reconstructed details of Hayashi's life that inject a dose of realism into her heretofore romanticized early years, but they do not challenge prevailing interpretations of her work or her place in Japanese literature.[42]

Assessment

Hayashi died of a heart attack on June 28, 1951. She was forty-eight years old. At the time of her death, Hayashi left four serialized works incomplete: *Meshi* for the *Asahi shinbun*, *Shinjubo* (Mother-of-Pearl) for *Shufu no tomo, Sazanami* (Rippling Waves) for *Chūō kōron*, and *Onna kazoku* (A Family of Women) for *Fujin kōron*. She had almost finished the manuscripts of short stories entitled "Raichō" (Snow Grouse) for *Bungei shunjū* and "Kiku obana" (Chrysanthemum Pampas Grass) and "Shin Hōjōki" (A New Hōjōki) for a *Chūō kōron bungei* special collection.[43]

Hayashi's funeral reflected her popular standing: two thousand people attended.[44] The writer and Nobel Prize winner Kawabata Yasunari commented that he would like a funeral similar to Hayashi's, at which after the official literary guests had finished offering incense, the ordinary people lined up for quite a distance outside the house were allowed to file by and pay their respects. Wada Yoshie also described Hayashi's mourners as predominantly women from *shitamachi* (downtown) and apron-clad housewives with shopping baskets. It was this same audience that Hayashi wanted to address: "those who buy their rice by the cup."[45]

Following her death, Hayashi received a range of honors and recognition, both large and small. The literary world paid more attention to her work, as illustrated in the 1957 special issue of *Bungei* and her inclusion in literature anthologies. In 1957, her high school, which had banned her presence in 1931

because of rumored leftist tendencies, erected in front of the school building
a stone monument in Hayashi's honor, with an inscription in Kawabata
Yasunari's hand.[46]

Hayashi left a massive body of work. Itagaki Naoko, her biographer, estimated that only a third of her published writing appeared in the twenty-three
volume *Hayashi Fumiko zenshū* (Collected Works of Hayashi Fumiko), produced
by Shinchōsha from October 1951 to April 1953.[47] In the special issue of *Bungei*,
it was estimated that she had published thirty thousand pages,[48] an average of
roughly thirty pages a week over the twenty years she was actively publishing.

How can we assess her work as a whole? Critics and enthusiasts alike have
tried to characterize her essence. Tamiya Torahiko, writing in 1954, was typical
of Hayashi's supporters in summarizing her work as a reflection of "women's
sorrow and pain." He elaborated that Hayashi had captured "a fragile, pathetic
woman's life . . . caught in a quagmire the moment she tries to make it on her
own, having been thrown out of the social order."[49] Others emphasized her
"feminine sensitivity" (Itō Einosuke) or "overpowering feminine quality"
(Nakamura Mitsuo). But many critics were more hostile: "lacking intellect"
(Takayama Takeshi) or "impure coquetry" (Odagiri Hideo). Itagaki Naoko
argued that male writers and critics tended to ignore her work, imposed pre-
conceived notions, or rushed to premature judgments. In Itagaki's view, they
might read only part of an early work, such as *Hōrōki*, and assess her whole oeu-
vre, unread, as a variation on the same theme.[50] A review of her major publications, taken as a whole, dispels the notion that Hayashi published most often or
was best known for her work in venues that targeted a female readership.

Hayashi published seven longer works in women's journals that were then
picked up by mainstream or parent journals or companies. All except *Hōrōki*
were regarded as fiction. Two short stories and two novels written in the postwar period appeared only in women's journals. Except for *Hōrōki*, the works
published in women's journals were not included in the anthologies published
by Kadokawa, Shūeisha, Shinchōsha, or in the special issue of *Bungei*. That is,
they were not considered among Hayashi's best or her best known. And they
constituted only a small fraction of her major publications: only nine of eighty-
six novels and only two of sixty-two short stories.

Hayashi also serialized seven of her novels in newspapers that were often
considered to cater to a female readership. Newspapers were frequently dis-
paraged, along with women's magazines, as pandering to popular tastes, thus
the lowest common denominator. Muramatsu Sadataka characterized their
readership as housewives who, having seen their husbands off to work, avidly
absorbed the daily installments of family-centered newspaper serials that were

spiced with the dilemmas of marital infidelity.[51] Some newspapers actively promoted their women authors; for example, after the war, the *Mainichi* newspaper sponsored a Joryū bungakusha kai (Literary women's group) and extensively covered their activities and tours.[52] However, even those who distinguished between newspapers and their intended audiences discounted this
venue as a source of serious literature.[53] All of Hayashi's works that appeared in
newspapers, except *Senshun fu*, were also republished in separate volumes, and
all should be considered fiction. A few of these newspaper novels were included
in these single-volume anthologies: Kadokawa included *Uzushio* (Eddying
Current) and *Meshi*, and both the Shinchōsha and *Bungei* collections included
Nakimushi kozō. This might indicate that aside from *Hōrōki*, the novels published
in newspapers were somewhat better known and more highly regarded than
those appearing in women's journals. These serialized newspaper novels constituted only a small percentage of Hayashi's overall body of longer works: seven
of eighty-six.

Most of Hayashi's novels—sixty-two of eighty-six—were initially published
as separate volumes by mainstream presses. Moreover, Hayashi published fifty-
eight short stories in mainstream literary journals. This constituted nearly 94
percent of her published short stories. Although there may be reason to suspect
that the publishers of her separate volumes were targeting a female readership,
there is little evidence to view in the same light her considerable body of short
fiction published in mainstream literary journals.

Women undoubtedly constituted a significant proportion of Hayashi's readership, though the evidence for this conclusion is impressionistic or derives
largely from the presumption that she published principally in venues oriented
toward women's concerns and that such places of publication would determine
the readership. Descriptions of Hayashi's funeral indicated a devoted following
among at least some of the women of *shitamachi* who lined up—some with
babies on their backs—five or six deep, to file past the altar.[54]

Hayashi's simple, accessible style appealed to men as well. The critic Yoshida
Seiichi claimed that it was precisely Hayashi's sweet, lyrical, feminine senti-
mentalism that attracted her male readership.[55] In the *Bungei* survey, the critic
Kubota Masafumi related how he, as a youth, was attracted to her early works
and particularly to her technique of using katakana (one of the Japanese language's syllabaries for difficult kanji [Chinese characters]). He went on to
observe that what he had taken to be a natural, uncalculated style was, in Itō
Sei's opinion, entirely deliberate (*mokuteki ishiki*).[56] The equation of the sex of
the readership with the type of publication should not be automatic. Shibaki
characterized *Chairo no me* as "not necessarily written for women," despite its

publication in a women's supplement to a newspaper.[57] And as we have seen, Hayashi published most of her short fiction in mainstream literary journals and only a fraction of her novels in newspapers or women's journals. Moreover, the evolution of Hayashi's style and her contribution to Japanese letters cannot simply be deduced from where, or how often, she published.

Hayashi continued to publish works that purported to be autobiographical long after she began to write fictional stories and novels. As I noted earlier, many of her ostensibly autobiographical works simply adopted the format of a diary or journal but clearly were fictional. Those explicitly about Hayashi, in effect a continuation of *Hōrōki*, were confessional in form but cannot be taken as an accurate reflection of her life. Written for an audience that was familiar with the incidents and personalities portrayed, these works sought to meet popular expectations about what a woman writer should write. However, when scrutinized, there is enough discrepancy with previous accounts of well-known incidents from her earlier works, in both tenor and detail, that one cannot help but view at least some of her later autobiographies as calculated to conceal the details of her life. Hayashi tended to reinvent herself to fit the times.

Hayashi not only revisited and revised the same incidents or events in successive installments of *Hōrōki* (parts 1, 2, and 3), but she also rewrote or revised the text when new editions were produced. A comparison of subsequent editions of part 1 illustrates the evolution of her style and use of language, and a careful reading reveals indications of Hayashi's aesthetic transformation, even in what is usually assumed to be the same book. Most of the changes were in the opening narratives before the daily entries. The language of these sections in the first 1930 Kaizō edition was more colloquial, spontaneous, and sometimes melodramatic, whereas that of the 1947 Shinchōsha edition was more standard, composed, and grammatically complex.

For example, in the earlier edition, Hayashi wrote, "Shimonoseki was where I breathed my first breath of air"(*watakushi ga hajimete kūki o sutta no wa, sono Shimonoseki de aru*).[58] The 1947 edition reads: "Shimonoseki was where I was born" (*watakushi ga umareta no wa sono Shimonoseki no machi de aru*).[59] In the first version, Hayashi wrote, "I was spunky" (*watakushi wa hatsuratsu toshite ita*)[60] and, later, "At that time I was a very active child" (*sono koro no watakushi wa totemo genki na kodomo datta*).[61] The longer paragraphs of later editions made the text seem less staccato as well. Some passages were altered, some eliminated. The later editions also eliminated subtitles to the diary entries that had originally been published as separate journal installments. This served to rework the text as one seamless whole, instead of random, disjointed pieces. Such emendations might have been a decision by the publishers, but the minor adjustments of the introductory narratives appear so deliberate yet so restrained—similar language in the diary entries remained largely unchanged in all the editions—that presumably only the author would have been so motivated and so selective in revising the text.

The evolution of Hayashi's style has been described by critics as a move from autobiography to fiction. Hayashi herself chronicled her concerted effort as a change from an autobiographical/confessional style to an "objective" (*kyakkanteki*) fiction. I have suggested that incidents in her ostensibly autobiographical works should not be taken at face value. Moreover, even though she tried to establish her literary reputation by placing clearly fictional works in premier mainstream journals, she continued to publish stories that purported and were perceived to be autobiographical.

In somewhat similar fashion, Hayashi attempted to distance herself from the label of "woman writer," even at the outset of her career—for example, in shifting *Hōrōki* to *Kaizō*—and yet continued to embrace opportunities for prominence and publication that such a distinction would present. A larger point is that any assessment of her as a "woman writer" or of her work as autobiographical or fictional fails to identify important continuities and discontinuities between earlier and later works. A review of one of her later short stories, "Suisen" (Narcissus, 1949), illustrates certain key elements in Hayashi's stylistic maturation and helps locate her place in Japanese literary history.

"Suisen" is emblematic of Hayashi's postwar fiction that demonstrates a growing sophistication in use of language and tightness of narrative. "Suisen" portrays the irreconcilable differences and bitter recriminations between a mother and son. Motherhood is characterized as a nightmare from which the protagonist is desperately attempting to awake. The unrelenting petty insults and bickering between two such selfish, vain, and irresponsible characters sets a bleak tone and conveys an especially dark, pessimistic assessment of human relations.

"Saku, I can't tell if you're basically decent or bad."

"I'm bad."

"Don't be so sure. You're just twenty-two, and you haven't learned too many wily ways. Can't you seduce somebody like a rich man's young daughter? . . ."

"Hmm, I don't much like young girls."

"That's because you've never had one."

"Mom, you're wicked. . . ."

"I suppose so." Tamae felt that it didn't matter what sin she committed. In ten years she'd lose the taste for it. Everyone is led astray by hypocritical morality. Underneath the hypocrisy, people fight like ferocious lions for the prizes—con-

trol, power, and wealth. Peace and contentment escape like steam from the fric-
tion of human dynamics. For some, there may be laughter. But for Tamae and her
son there was not even a single glimmer of hope. Not even in the bond between
mother and child.[62]

This story chronicles the rift between Saku and Tamae, her growing detachment from her son, and her reaction to the eventual sundering of relations.
From the outset, despite her transparently hollow denials, the mother broaches
her desire for separation. Her shiftless twenty-two-year-old son finally is
offered a job in a coal mine in Hokkaido, and they prepare for what will be a
final separation. She declares that she will not write and will not hear of his
returning even if she becomes ill or dies. Unlike Hayashi's early work, this story
lacks even a hint of sentimentality: at the final parting, the mother thinks her
son looks pathetic, and he, in turn, quickly lets go of her hand. For her, the final
parting is a liberation.

> Aware that now she was all alone, Tamae squared her shoulders and took a deep
> breath. At the end of the year, even the back streets were filled with people.
> Under the blue lights, a succession of store fronts—racks of silver salmon and
> mannequins draped with black velvet—streamed unperceived past her eyes.
> Downtown at this time of year seemed not to have changed a bit from years ago.
> For no particular reason, Tamae imagined she might breathe her last somewhere
> in this tempestuous city. That would surely be the only way to recapture the spirit
> of her youth. She nursed the notion that her life had been snuffed like a candle in
> the wind. In the dark December streets, a girl with her hair up in the traditional
> style and several children were boisterously slapping a shuttlecock with deco-
> rated wooden paddles. The white feathers disappeared into the night, only to
> come streaking across the light of the lamp under the eaves. Ambling out to the
> avenue, Tamae heard a salesman barking hoarsely in front of Morinaga's, mobbed
> with people. "Yes, here are the Morinaga Velvets you all remember. How about
> it?" Mixing with the crowd, Tamae swiped a shining cellophane bag and dropped
> it into her pocket. She felt extremely pleased with herself. At a china store, Tamae
> melted into the crowd and stole a pretty Kutani soy sauce container. More than
> the fact that no one caught her, the weight in her pocket was gratifying. She felt
> she were walking along wearing a mask. All of a sudden, she was happy to be
> alive. Her parting from her son made Tamae feel instantly much younger, and as
> she came to dim Sukiyabashi Street, she took a Velvet from the cellophane bag and
> popped it into her mouth. The sweet melody of a popular song drifted in the air
> from an advertisement. The *Asahi newspaper* electric news raced busily to the
> right, flashing the dissolution of the Diet onto the sky.[63]

Edward Seidensticker heralded this closing image from "Suisen" as among the most memorable of the immediate postwar literature.[64] Mishima Yukio considered "Suisen" his favorite of Hayashi's later works; with it, she had reached "the level of mature art" (*gikō to shitemo enjuku no iki*).[65] In sharp contrast to the rigid conformity of governmentally orchestrated "good wife, wise mother" (*ryōsai kenbo*) perspectives or the didactic moralizing of household or domestic fiction (*katei shōsetsu*), "Suisen" depicts a world bereft of righteousness. By centering on the most common and revered of personal relations, Hayashi reveals the dark underside of ordinary life, perhaps more commonly experienced than the ideals, and she suggests that however resilient the human spirit may be, the real exercise of free will is choosing between distasteful choices.

In "Suisen," as in her other postwar fiction, Hayashi departs from the lyrical sentimentality that characterized *Hōrōki*. In general, her language reflects her tendency, evident in revisions of *Hōrōki*, toward more standard, composed, and complex grammatical constructions. However, perhaps the most striking change in her style is the shift from a fragmented, discontinuous narrative that leaves many incidents either partially or wholly unresolved, toward a more clearly delineated structure, with a standard beginning, middle, and end that unfold to reveal a tightly rendered story line. Even in those later works that were supposed to be autobiographical, such as *Pari nikki*, incidents are presented as a continuous narrative, in chronological order, within a discrete time frame.

The continuities in Hayashi's work, taken as a whole, also are striking. Her characters, predominantly women, possess determination, perseverance, and resilience, despite their unrelenting misfortunes. Most of Hayashi's work illuminated the lives of an underclass, of a *rumpen*, catch-as-catch-can world, that was often drab if not desperate. If her "salary-man" family in her last, unfinished novel, *Meshi*, occupied more of a lower-middle-class station, their circumstances still resonated with the sense of powerlessness that marked her earlier characters. But Hayashi infused a sense of humanity in all these situations and depicted the unextinguished aspirations and inescapable anxieties of those who reside among the debris of broken dreams. Hayashi's fictional world was "of the people" (*minshūteki*),[66] but not from a sense of ideological commitment or political correctness. Instead, Hayashi drew her portraits within a small compass: descriptive depictions of everyday life (*shomin no seikatsu*).[67] Her point of view was always very particularistic, not easily generalizable to a stratum, class, or gender.

The inadequacies of the "woman writer" designation for Hayashi are twofold: such a label fails to capture what was specific to her distinct, somewhat idiosyncratic voice, and it fails to reflect what evolved in her work as she matured. Hayashi may have lacked a larger vision—she avoided directly addressing societal contradictions and profound philosophical or existential questions—but her work merits continued scrutiny on several grounds. Hayashi was a chronicler of a largely unilluminated world, and for many, including Muramatsu Sadataka, it was her portraits of the everyday life of this stratum for which she will be remembered. But for others, such as Edward Seidensticker, her fictional imagination, notably in her postwar stories, succeeded not only in capturing a spirit of the times—a nihilistic disaffection against the backdrop of austerity and injustice—but also in transcending circumstances to present the personal exercise of choice and self-determination.

NOTES

1. Itagaki Naoko, "Atogaki," *Hayashi Fumiko shū*, vol. 19 of *Shōwa bungaku zenshū* (Tokyo: Kadokawa shoten, 1953), p. 407.

2. A chronology of Hayashi's publications appears as an appendix in Joan Ericson, "Hayashi Fumiko and Japanese Women's Literature" (Ph.D. diss., Columbia University, 1993).

3. The prize was first awarded in 1947, to Hirabayashi Taiko. Other early recipients were Amino Kiku (1948), Hayashi Fumiko (1949), none for 1950 or 1951, Yoshiya Nobuko (1952), Ōtani Fujiko (1953), Enchi Fumiko (1954), Tsuboi Sakae (1955), and so on. See *Bungaku shō jiten* (Tokyo: Nichigai Associates, 1985), p. 110.

4. Tamiya Torahiko, "Kaisetsu," *Meshi* (Tokyo: Shinchōsha, 1982 [1954]), p. 221.

5. The roots of this gender-based categorization, as well as the changing terminology and usage by Japanese feminist scholars in the past decade, is examined in Joan Ericson, "Origins of the Concept of Women's Literature," in Paul Schalow and Janet A. Walker, eds., *The Women's Hand: Gender and Theory in Japanese Women's Writing* (Stanford, CA: Stanford University Press, 1996).

6. Fukuda Hirotoshi, "Hayashi Fumiko," *Kokubungaku: Kaishaku to kanshō,* Special Issue "Gendai joryū sakka no himitsu" 27 (September 1962), pp. 43–48.

7. Usui Yoshimi, *Kindai bungaku ronsō (jō)* (Tokyo: Chikuma shobō, 1985), p. 195.

8. Donald Keene, *Dawn to the West: Japanese Literature in the Modern Era*, vol. 1 (New York: Holt, Rinehart and Winston, 1984), pp. 506–17.

9. Cited in Usui, *Kindai bungaku ronsō*, p. 197.

10. Hayashi Fumiko, "Chosha no kotoba," in *Hayashi Fumiko zenshū* (hereafter abbreviated *HFZ*), vol. 6 (Tokyo: Shinchōsha, 1952), p. 249.

11. Hayashi, "Kaki," *HFZ*, vol. 3 (Tokyo: Shinchōsha, 1952), pp. 189–213.

12. The short-story volume was published by Kaizōsha. Fukuda Kiyoto and Endō Mitsuhiko, *Hayashi Fumiko: Hito to sakuhin*, vol. 15 (Tokyo: Shimizu shōin, 1966), p. 77. See also Sakurada Mitsuru, ed., *Hayashi Fumiko: Gendai nihon bungaku arubamu (hito to bungaku shiriizu)* (Tokyo: Gakushū kenkyūsha, 1980), p. 234; and Isome Hideo and Nakazawa Kei, *Hayashi Fumiko, Shinchō Nihon bungaku arubamu* (Tokyo: Shinchōsha, 1986), pp. 67–69.

13. Isome and Nakazawa, *Hayashi Fumiko*, pp. 69, 67.

14. *No mugi no uta* should be considered fictional. The story is rather melodramatic and sentimental: When her husband falls in love with another woman, he divorces Kazuko, telling her that she is as dangerous as a firecracker, and remarries. Kazuko is forced to earn a living as a waitress. She agrees to go to a hot spring with an older customer who turns out to be a famous Japanese-style artist. She decides to become a nude model for a young artist who coincidentally is the son of the older man. The story ends with the young man declaring his love for her despite learning about her brief relationship with his father. *HFZ*, vol. 5 (Tokyo: Shinchōsha, 1952), pp. 107–76.

15. Hayashi discussed her return to this style in her "Atogaki," *HFZ*, vol. 8 (Tokyo: Shinchōsha, 1952), pp. 245–46. Originally published as the afterword to *Hōrōki, Part 2*, in *Hayashi Fumiko bunko*, 10 vols. (Tokyo: Shinchōsha, 1949).

16. Other works that supposedly are autobiographical are *Onna no nikki* (Diary of a Woman, 1936), *Aijōden* (Biography of Love, 1936), *Joyūki* (Record of an Actress, 1940), *Maihime no ki* (Record of a Dancing Girl, 1947), *Onna no seishun* (A Woman's Youth, 1947), and *Yakushima kikō* (Travelogue to Yaku Island, 1950).

17. Miyamoto Yuriko, *Fujin to bungaku; Kindai Nihon no fujin sakka* (Tokyo: Jitsugyō no Nihon sha, 1947), p. 176.

18. See Marleigh Grayer Ryan, trans. and critical commentary, *Japan's First Modern Novel: Ukigumo of Futabatei Shimei* (New York: Columbia University Press, 1965).

19. Hayashi, *Ukigumo*, *HFZ*, vol. 16 (Tokyo: Shinchōsha, 1951). It was partially translated into English by Yoshiyuki Koitabashi and Martin C. Collcott as *The Floating Cloud* (Tokyo: Hara shobō, 1965). For a discussion of *Ukigumo*, see also Donald Keene, *Japanese Literature: An Introduction for Western Readers* (New York: Grove Press, 1955).

20. Nakamura Mitsuo, "Hayashi Fumiko ron," in Nakashima Kenzō et al., eds., *Gendai sakkaron sōsho, Shōwa no sakkatachi II* (Tokyo: Eiōsha, 1955), pp. 93–112. This quotation is from p. 95. Originally published in *Fujin kōron* (June 1953). This has been reprinted numerous times, also under the title "Hayashi Fumiko bungaku nyūmon" in the special issue "Hayashi Fumiko doku hon" *Bungei* 14 (June 1957): 20–27.

21. Nakamura, "Hayashi Fumiko ron," p. 96.

22. In 1950, Hayashi enrolled her adopted son in the first grade of the Peers School (Gakushūin), once reserved for children of the imperial family and nobility. It was made into a private school only after World War II and generally has retained a reputation for exclusiveness, appealing to those with money or a good family name. Kawazoe Kunitomo points out in his chronology of Hayashi's life that we have a better sense of her personality through this detail of where she chose to enroll her son. See Kawazoe Kunimoto, "Nempyō," *Hayashi Fumiko: gendai Nihon bungaku arubamu (Hito to bungaku shiriizu)* (Tokyo: Gakushū kenkyūsha, 1980), p. 236.

23. Miyamoto, *Fujin to bungaku*, pp. 177–78.

24. For a discussion of *tenkō* (political apostasy), see Tsurumi Shunsuke, "Tenkō no kyōdō kenkyū ni tsuite," in Nakajima Makoto, ed., *Tenkō ron josetsu* (Tokyo: Mineruba shobō, 1980); and Honda Shūgo, *Tenkō bungaku ron* (Tokyo: Miraisha, 1964).

Keene notes that "writers of every political affiliation joined [the Nihon bungaku hōkokukai (Japanese literature patriotic association)], including those of the left (like the poet Nakano Shigeharu and the woman novelist Miyamoto Yuriko) in the hopes that membership in this patriotic organization would shield them from charges that they had not truly renounced their former Communist beliefs." See Donald Keene, "Japanese Writers and the Greater East Asian War," *Landscapes and Portraits: Appreciations of Japanese Culture* (Tokyo: Kodansha International, 1971), pp. 300–1.

25. Kawazoe, *Hayashi Fumiko*, p. 233.

26. Her work had been considered too *rumpen* for members of *Nyonin geijutsu* in 1929. Miyamoto Yuriko quoted Hayashi's recollections of 1935: "Proletarian literature was on the rise. I was isolated, without support." Miyamoto, *Fujin to bungaku*, p. 176.

27. Hayashi Fumiko, "Atogaki," in *Fūkin to uo no machi* (Kamakura: Kamakura bunko, 1946), pp. 329–32.

28. "Hayashi Fumiko dokuhon," *Bungei*, Special Issue (June 1957): 263–68.

29. Edward G. Seidensticker, "Hayashi Fumiko," translated from English into Japanese by Saeki Shōichi, *Jiyū*, no. 5 (1963): 122–31. I have translated these passages back into English.

30. Ibid., p. 124.

31. Ibid., p. 125.

32. Ibid., p. 127.

33. Ibid., p. 129.

34. Itagaki points to the experience of Shinchōsha, the publishing house that put out Hayashi's collected works after her death. This set enjoyed unexpectedly strong sales, and when the demand did not let up, the company hurriedly added another three volumes. Itagaki attributes this failure to anticipate the strong market to the disparagement that a woman writer like Hayashi experienced at the hands of the male literati. See Itagaki, "Atogaki," p. 407.

35. Wada Yoshie, "Hayashi Fumiko," *Shūkan dokusho jin*, June 22, 1964, p. 3.

36. Muramatsu Sadataka, "Hayashi Fumiko no dansei henreki," in *Sakka no kakei to kankyō* (Tokyo: Shibundō, 1964), pp. 202–17.

37. Fukuda and Endō, *Hayashi Fumiko*; Itagaki Naoko, *Meiji, Taishō, Shōwa no joryū bungaku* (Tokyo: Ōfūsha, 1967); Hirabayashi Taiko, *Hayashi Fumiko* (Tokyo: Shinchōsha, 1969).

38. Edward Fowler, *The Rhetoric of Confession* (Berkeley and Los Angeles: University of California Press, 1988), p. xviii.

39. My interview with Tsushima Yūko, June 6, 1991, Tokyo.

40. "Gendai joryū sakka no himitsu," *Kokubungaku: kaishaku to kanshō* 27 (September 1962): 10; "Joryū no zensen: Higuchi Ichiyō kara hachijūnen dai no sakka made," *Kokubungaku: kaishaku to kyōzai no kenkyū* 25 (December 1980): 15.

41. In one, Hayashi's name only appears in a list of writers who went to Southeast Asia on the Pen Squad. See Hirano Ken, *Shōwa bungaku shi* (Tokyo: Chikuma shobō, 1963), p. 223.

42. Takemoto Chimakichi, *Ningen—Hayashi Fumiko* (Tokyo: Chikuma shobō, 1985), and *Hayashi Fumiko, Shinchō Nihon bungaku arubamu*, among others.

43. Kawabata Yasunari, "Atogaki," *Sazanami* (Tokyo: Chūō kōron, 1951), p. 267.

44. Kawazoe Kunimoto, "Hayashi Fumiko no 'Bangiku' ni tsuite," *Kokubungaku: kaishaku to kanshō*, September 1951, p. 9. Also see the photograph of the large crowd gathered outside the Hayashi residence on the day of the funeral, in *Hayashi Fumiko, Shinchō Nihon bungaku arubamu*, p. 95.

45. Wada, "Hayashi Fumiko," p. 3.

46. Onomichi dokusho kai, ed,, *Onomichi to Hayashi Fumiko* (Onomichi: Onomichi Public Library, 1974), p. 242.

47. The 1977 Bunsendō collection of Hayashi Fumiko's works is basically a reprint of the Shinchōsha collection. The Nihon kindai bungakkan bought only vol. 16 (essays and chronology) of the more recent collection to add to its shelves.

48. "Hayashi Fumiko ryaku nenpu," in "Hayashi Fumiko dokuhon," *Bungei*, p. 261.

49. Tamiya Torahiko, "Kaisetsu," *Meshi* (Tokyo: Shinchōsha, 1982 [1954]), p. 217.

50. Itagaki, "Atogaki," p. 407.

51. Muramatsu Sadataka, " 'Onna de aru koto' ron," in *Kawabata Yasunari kenkyū sōsho*, vol. 3. Kawabata bungaku kenkyūkai, ed. (Tokyo: Kyōiku shuppan senta, 1979), p. 175.

52. A photograph of the group that included Amino Kiku, Yoshiya Nobuko, Uno Chiyo and Hayashi, during an excursion to Kisarazu in Chiba Prefecture appears in *Hayashi Fumiko, Shinchō Nihon bungaku arubamu*, p. 93. See also Shibaki Yoshiko, "Ukigumo no hito: Shi—Hayashi Fumiko," *Shinchō*, October 1953, pp. 66–71.

53. In 1931, Yasunari Jirō described five views of female readers by newspaper editors, curiously employing the term *gender* written in phonetic Japanese, to explain the rationale for, and means by which, newspapers directed special columns or pages toward either working women or housewives. See Yasunari Jirō, "Shinbun to Fujin," *Sōgō janarizumu kōza*, vol. 9 (Tokyo: Naigaisha, 1931), pp. 1–15.

54. Shibaki, "Ukigumo no hito," p. 71.

55. Yoshida Seiichi, "Kindai joryū no bungaku," *Kokubungaku: kaishaku to kanshō*, March 1972, p. 16.

56. "Hayashi Fumiko dokuhon," *Bungei*, p. 266.

57. Shibaki Yoshiko, " 'Seihin no sho' 'Chairo no me'," "Hayashi Fumiko dokuhon," *Bungei*, Special Issue, 14 (June 1957): 39.

58. Hayashi Fumiko, *Hōrōki* (Tokyo: Kaizōsha, 1930), p. 4.

59. Hayashi Fumiko, *Hōrōki* (Tokyo: Shinchōsha, 1947), p. 5.

60. Hayashi, *Hōrōki* (1930), p. 11.

61. Hayashi, *Hōrōki* (1947), p, 10.

62. Hayashi Fumiko, "Suisen," in *HFZ*, vol. 13 (Tokyo: Shinchōsha, 1951), pp. 53–66. This quotation is from pp. 63–64.

63. Ibid., pp. 65–66.

64. Seidensticker, "Hayashi Fumiko," p. 126.

65. Mishima Yukio, " 'Bangiku' kaisetsu," in "Hayashi Fumiko dokuhon," *Bungei*, Special Issue, 14 (June 1957): 46. Originally published as commentary to the Kawade bunko edition including "Bangiku."

66. Kawamori Yoshizō, "Hayashi Fumiko no koto," *Tenbō*, August 1951, p. 45.

67. Muramatsu Sadataka, "Hayashi Fumiko no dansei henreki," in *Sakka no kakei to kankyō* (Tokyo: Shibundō, 1964), pp. 202–17.

25

When Seeing Is Not Believing: Tsushima Yūko's
"Hikarikagayaku itten o"

◎

VAN C. GESSEL

It is difficult—for me, at least—to survey the landscape of postwar Japanese fiction without being alternately fascinated and frustrated by the extraordinary staying power of the *shi-shōsetsu*, call it "I-novel" or "personal fiction" as you will. While I am in full agreement with perceptive critics like Edward Fowler who argue that this mode of expression has tenacious roots linking it to age-old forms of Japanese literary expression,[1] it remains remarkable that so many Japanese writers of the past five decades—after all their study of other modes of fiction—gravitate so regularly and so comfortably back to the shi-shōsetsu form.

In my own frustration with the likes of Tayama Katai and Shimazaki Tōson for their insistence on reproducing the "truth" about their lives, and thoroughly repulsed by the emotional *seppuku* that Kasai Zenzō commits in his writing, I have warned my students about the pitfalls and shortcomings of this form of writing. I have given entire, hour-long lectures on Katai's failures as a writer, drawing on Fukuda Tsuneari's assertions that Katai was a literary pygmy and moral juvenile who could find meaning in his life only by pretending to be one of the heroes in the works of Western fiction that he was reading.[2]

The occasional antipathy I have felt toward the shi-shōsetsu—and there surely was and is something Orientalist about those feelings—kept me for some time from being able to say anything of interest about the writers I had chosen for my dissertation research —Yasuoka Shōtarō, Kojima Nobuo, and Endō Shūsaku. Ironically enough, I had to go through a fairly long process of distancing myself—the process that one might argue is missing from many "I-novels"—from my three subjects before I could begin a critical evaluation of how and why they reappropriated the shi-shōsetsu in a period of modern history when it seemed possible that the diatribe heaped on the form by the *sengoha* (postwar-generation) writers would finally send it off into retirement.

It is tangential to the concerns of this chapter to explain what I ultimately concluded about the durability and flexibility of the shi-shōsetsu form or about the ways in which I think writers of the 1950s and 1960s transformed it into a mode with significant potential for irony, duplicity, and the creation of an artistic world that could stand quite apart from the realm of an author's narrow personal experience. Simply put, an essential dismantling of the notion of selfhood that had sustained prewar I-novelists was a prerequisite to the transmutation of the form. It was, in fact, my consideration of the ways in which Yasuoka, Kojima, Endō, and also Shimao Toshio sought to present their private experiences and then placed an ironic overlay on them that led me to the thesis that forms the core of the book that slowly grew from my dissertation.[3]

Having said my farewells to that thesis by putting it into published form, my attention in recent years has turned to several female authors who, it seems to me, were extending the process of ego destruction that began in the 1950s among the men. My readings of such novelists as Enchi Fumiko, Kōno Taeko, and Takahashi Takako have convinced me that the disassembly of ego continues in their writings, and sometimes the message that comes across through their works may not be comforting or welcome. In extreme cases, what they may be saying is that the very act of communication is an exercise in futility, that we have lost (if we ever possessed) the power to convey the intensity and import of our personal experiences to another human being.

A distrust of the modes of human communication and a sense of a broken bond are equally strong in the recent work of Tsushima Yūko. She is a logical choice for a study of the ways in which Japanese writers of the postwar period invest their personal experience with literary significance, if for no other reason than that she is Dazai Osamu's daughter. That accident of genealogy holds particular interest for me because it is my sense that the splitting apart of the literary ego in postwar Japanese fiction really gets its start with Dazai, and it is worthwhile to see what happens to that undertaking in the second generation.

My initial readings of Tsushima's work left me somewhat dissatisfied. In some of the early stories, the seams in her writing appear all too obvious, and at times she struggles far too openly to come up with a suitable literary scaffolding on which to hang her sometimes uninteresting personal experiences. Occasionally, she seems almost frantic in her quest to fill a story with as many symbolic images as she can conjure up to decorate the fringes of her autobiography. Even a truly good story like "Danmari ichi" (The Silent Traders, 1982) can strike the casual reader as an all-too-obvious and somewhat labored attempt to draw comparisons between a single-parent mother who tries to establish some kind of link to her former lover, the cats who are tipped over the walls of the Rikugien, and the mountain traders who from time to time come down to the valleys to conduct their mute business. Stories cast in this mode can seem like a second-rate author's desperate stabs at creating some larger literary circle of significance for their personal experience, but failing to convince the reader that a compelling connection exists—in much the same way that Katai's hero, Tokio, fails to persuade me that he is worthy of the same empathy I would grant to any of the Western fictional characters with which he compares himself.

That is not to suggest, of course, that Tsushima's own life lacks the kind of drama that could make good literature. It is perhaps enough to be Dazai's daughter—there is certainly something that could be mined there, though Tsushima wisely avoids it. Her strained relationship with her mother, the death of her retarded brother, her leaving home to live with a boyfriend—all are good fodder for the dedicated I-novelist. Her separation from the father of her two children puts her in that enviable position of speaking for the growing population of single mothers in Japan. She has dabbled a bit in that. And then, of course, there is the fact that in 1985, Tsushima's eight-year-old son drowned in the bathtub while she was in the next room. An incurable cynic could rejoice that she was finally able to find material suitably tragic for autobiographical fiction. A kinder reader might take note in passing of the irony surrounding a writer who has lost both her father and her son to watery graves.

But my interest in Tsushima and her work is not as concerned with the kinds of experiences she is shaping into fiction as with the techniques she employs as a writer to invest her stories with a literary consequence that transcends the borders of the unique and personal. It is simultaneously *makoto* (sincere) and *aware* (moving) to write about losing a child—Ōe Kenzaburō has given us ample insight into that[4]—but simple fidelity to the facts of the matter is not enough. Rather, literature requires probing to the heart of the matter.

One of the most extraordinary literary achievements to emerge from Tsushima's personal tragedy is the short story "Hikarikagayaku itten o" (A Single Glittering Point of Light), which she published in 1988.[5] The title itself seems to suggest something about the potential for connections, grammatical, social, or literary. There certainly are other titles in modern Japanese fiction that end with an inconclusive particle, but I have a hard time thinking of any that so clearly beg for a verb that will grant them some comforting finality. Indeed, the whole issue of frustrating indeterminacy is very much the thesis of this story.

The first section of the story is about a murder. (It may not be unreasonable to assume, even this early, that we have already removed ourselves from the realm of autobiography.) We join the events just as the killing takes place, so we have no clues to its motivation, the identities of the assailant and the victim, or even who our narrator is. We learn that we are seeing events through the eyes of a woman who has come to a park for a high school class reunion and that the two parties to the crime belong to that same group. But our narrator knows no more about what she is witnessing than we do as helplessly unenlightened readers/outsiders. The rest of the women in the group watch silently as the killer stares at the body and then as she does something rather extraordinary: she tries to pick up the body and move it, oblivious to the fact that many people are watching her. When she is physically unable to lift the body, she grabs a leg and begins dragging it away. The watchers continue to watch. As readers we are dumbfounded. Then the killer uses her hands to dig a pointless hole, places the body in the shallow recess, and just barely covers it over with dirt. She then stands up, dusts off her hands, and walks away. The other women, sensing that the party is over, begin to scatter and leave the park. The narrator initially seems to think this is the proper course of action (or nonaction), but when she thinks about having to walk through this park in the days and months ahead, with the possibility that she might step on the corpse and hear a disgusting crunching sound under her feet, she wonders aloud whether they should not contact the police. One woman in the group assures her that this is not necessary—that their work is complete merely because they have witnessed the event. Someone else will find the body and notify the authorities. And time, after all, means nothing to a dead person. Fully persuaded by this logic, the narrator ends her story feeling that she "understands" (*nattoku shita kimochi ni natte ita*),[6] and we must assume that she leaves much as we readers leave her story, feeling absolved of all responsibility for what went on between the pages—mostly because it is so incomprehensible to us, based on the explanation we have been given.

Tsushima then jumps without any warning to the second, seemingly unrelated, section of her story. It is not even clear if the narrator has changed. This section takes place when the narrator's son is eight years old, and we are informed at the outset that this was the summer four years before his death. We get the standard Tsushima catalog of insects and reptiles that delight her boy, and she details the solicitous manner in which she seeks out opportunities to acquire various toads and newts and water scorpions for him.

But the immediate concern of this second story is a recollection of the time the narrator took her children to a forest at night to see flying squirrels (*musasabi*). She goes into great detail about the excursion, even telling us about the infrared flashlights that the guides bring along so that everyone in the group of spectators will be able to see the eyes of the squirrels without scaring them away.

As the mother gropes through the forest with her son, she digresses for a few moments when she begins worrying that she might lose sight of him in the darkness. And she remembers how, around the time her son was born, she had "lost sight of" (*miushinatte iru*) her husband. What if the same thing should happen with her children? Then, from her perspective several years after the events, she notes that her son did in fact die of unknown causes four years after the squirrel hunt and that as a result, he too has become "lost from sight."

But she lingers on that painful memory only for a moment and then takes us right back to the squirrels. In the trees, the eyes of the squirrels redly reflect the flashlights of the guides. Everyone in the group seems to be able to see those eyes. It is a surprisingly intense light given how small the squirrels' eyes are.

Then, as if on cue, the squirrels begin their characteristic leap from tree to tree, appearing to fly. Muffled cries of delighted recognition come from various parts of the group. It seems as though nearly everyone, including the narrator's son, can see the squirrels as they leap; everyone, that is, except the narrator. Struggle though she might to peer through the darkness and catch sight of the airborne figures, she can never locate one. She feels left out, alone, and wonders for a moment whether she should pretend to see so that she can feel a part of the group.

Then we pass suddenly to a peculiar series of events; it seems as though the mother is in confusion after the death of her son and is continuing to search for him in various places where she lived with him in the past, but she can never seem to find him. She goes looking for him at a place where he stayed with a babysitter when he was still an infant. The building is no longer there, and she cannot help wondering why her son is not, either. Her dreams seem to go on and on, and as the fruitless search continues, this segment ends.

The third section is much shorter, and as with the immediately preceding incidents, it can easily be imagined to be based on, or at least suggested by, Tsushima's own experience with the loss of her son. It takes the form of indirect communication—perhaps a letter from the mother of the dead boy to a close friend of hers.[7] Though nothing is stated overtly, it seems reasonable to conclude that we have the same narrator here as for the second part. Nonetheless, we continue to remain in the dark regarding the identity of—or any connection with—the narrator of the first part.

In some respects, the mode of narration in this final section is reminiscent of the approach that Tsushima adopted in her first major work after the death of her son, the novel *Yoru no hikari ni owarete* (Pursued by the Light of Night, 1986), in which a woman who has suffered the same misfortune as herself begins a spiritual communication with the long-deceased woman who wrote *Yoru no nezame* (Wakefulness at Night) in the eleventh century. It is now two years after the death of her son, and the narrator can no longer keep within herself a question that has been haunting her since shortly after the tragic event. Put simply, she wants to know the truth. She insists that this is not a problem that bothers her or that she feels any twinges of guilt; it is merely that she cannot endure the uncertainty. The woman with whom she is trying to communicate came and stayed with the narrator on the night of her son's death. Now, two years later, the narrator begins to wonder what kinds of questions the police must have asked her friend when they were with her alone. Did they not want to know what kind of relationship the narrator had with her son, whether she had ever struck him in anger, whether she might have flown into a rage and killed him?

The narrator is sure that the police would have asked such questions. In fact, every time she passes a police box, she wonders why she is allowed to walk around freely, to make choices about what she will eat and where she will go. Her friend evidently must have given satisfactory answers to the policemen's questions and cleared up all their suspicions. The boy's mother knows full well from her own experience that she had nothing to do with his death. But, she asks, what about people who did not actually witness the event? The whole thing was so unexpected, so bizarre, that she is almost angry that others would believe her version of what happened. No one was with the boy when he died, making it all the more reasonable that doubts should arise about the circumstances of his death.

She proceeds to describe how she discovered the eight-year-old boy floating lifeless in the bathtub. This passage is extraordinarily painful for readers who can imagine how vividly it must replicate Tsushima's own agonizing experience. The narrator goes into great detail about her struggle to pull the boy's heavy body from the tub and of laying him out on the wooden floorboards. At that point, she repeats her diatribe against the police—how can they claim to be in the business of solving crimes if they offer her sympathy instead of challenging her version of the accident? It defies all reason to think they would believe her. So it must be the case that someone intervened to clear away their doubts. And that could be no one other than this friend. Or in fact, were the police still watching her every movement even today, two years later?

She concludes with a muffled but almost desperate plea to her friend to tell her the full truth, to conceal nothing from her. And there she abandons the attempt, tearing up several versions of the letter she was drafting to her friend. She knows that no matter how she phrases the question, she will never be able to elicit a response that she can accept. Perhaps, she concludes, it is better not to know.

One of the most remarkable features of this story is Tsushima's unrelenting repetition of two verbs over and over again in each of the three parts of the story. We are provided with perhaps every possible compound usage of *miru* (to see) that exists in the Japanese language. Tsushima uses more than thirty different verbal compounds suggesting some kind of experience of "seeing": *mimamoru, mienakunaru, mitsumeru, miokuru, mite inai, mirarenakatta, miyaru, mitsukeru, mi ni iku, mitodoketai, hontō ni mita, misete yaritai, miushinatte ita, mishiranu, misadameyō to shita, mitsukedasu, mitorezu niwa irarenakatta, mihakaratte, minasarete iru, miwakeru, mitsukekanete iru, miwasurete shimatte iru, miwakerareru, misenakute wa, mitsukedasō to, mihanasarete imashita, mihararete iru*, and several other combinations that frequently involve, first, the act of seeing and then judging on the basis of that observation. The other commonly recurring phrase in the story is *nattoku suru*, which is used to connote perceiving, understanding, making sense of, and so forth. It appears in the story generally as the action expected of a person after he has seen with his eyes and passed judgment on what he has seen. This process—made to seem like the most normal of all human endeavors because it occurs with such frequency in the story— is straightforward: a person sees something, determines what it is, and then comprehends it. A basic pattern for human behavior.

The litanization of these two key verb phrases throughout the entire fabric of the work is the only link between the first part of the story—the murder in the park—and the second two parts—the squirrel viewing and the letter to the friend after the narrator's son has died. At first reading, these parts seem utterly disjointed, so unrelated to one another that we begin to fear that Tsushima may still be playing her early game of lining up metaphors and just leaving them there, in the hope that her readers will be smart enough to see how they fit together.

But the tensions and incongruities that threaten to tear this story apart at the seams are also what I think give it its remarkable power. In each segment of the story, the relationships among the narrator, listener, and event are quite different. In the first part, the murder scenario, we as readers are presented with what to us as outsiders can only seem to be an irrational description of an incomprehensible incident by the first-person narrator who witnesses it all. In the squirrel segment, we are told about a thoroughly commonplace incident by a narrator who seems unimpeachable. The final portion is a rather transparent claim by a desperate and confused woman that she must be told the truth, all the while insisting that she is not at all desperate or confused by the lack of that knowledge.

Because they are linked by the death of a son, the second and third parts of the story can be easily positioned beside each other, and various kinds of correspondences can be proposed. But the function of the first part lingers as a mystery—there are no self-evident connections between it and any other element in the story. The woman who provides us with commentary on the crime scene appears to be making a valiant effort to describe precisely what she has observed. She is, after all, an official "witness" of the incident and does a good job of creating a sense of immediacy, standing as she does within a few feet of the crime scene. At least insofar as the almost "televised" aspects of the event are concerned, we seem to be well within the realm of believability.

But this credibility begins to break down as we observe how the narrator mentally processes and comes to an understanding of what she has seen. If we inquire into these processes, we will find that she is not as useful a narrator as she might have seemed initially. It turns out, for instance, that at first she does not actually know that a murder has taken place. She hears angry voices as the story opens, but before she even realizes what is going on, the whole thing is over. She sees one body fall to the ground, and she makes a visual note (*mitodokeru*) of the fact that a "reddish pool of liquid" (*akai iro no mizutamari*) is flowing from the body. But at that point, she is unable to conclude that something serious has happened; to her, the woman's crumpled body just looks "slovenly" (*darashinai*). Even when other members of the group start whispering that a woman has been stabbed to death, the narrator cannot bring herself to believe it (*shinjikiru koto ga dekinai mama*), even though solid evidence is directly before her eyes. Only when she shifts her eyes to the woman holding a knife in her hand does the word *murder* finally come into her mind.

From this point forward, we as readers begin to detach ourselves from the narrator and suspend belief in her reliability, even her sanity. The group of women looks on, saying nothing and doing nothing, while the killer drags the body off and starts sprinkling dirt over it. All our expectations regarding normal human reactions are disconnected by this kind of narration; we can no longer believe what we are vicariously "seeing" through the eyes of our informant. If the narrator as privileged observer can come up with nothing more plausible than this, then what reason do we have for accepting what she tells us?

That view is reinforced as we approach the end of this section. Having trickled a little soil over the body, the murderer just walks off, and some of the women who have been watching comment:

"She must think that nobody is watching her."

"Once you've made up your mind that no one saw you, then no one did."[8]

Having neatly settled that into their minds, the women then start to disperse, and that is when we overhear the preposterous discussion about there being no need to contact the police. When she is told why that would be superfluous, the narrator feels that she "understands" (*nattoku shita*).

It is hard as a reader to be persuaded by the logic of this passage, no matter how internally consistent it might be or how much the narrator herself seems to think she has made sense out of it. What makes it all the more peculiar is that this is essentially an eyewitness account, and we normally demand a bit more credibility from sources so close to the events. There is a discomfiting role reversal taking place here—the narrator claims to have seen it all herself and seems to be reporting just what she saw. But her version is incredible, and we, as nonwitnesses, begin to feel uneasy, as though there is some inexplicable subterfuge going on. But what it is, we cannot put a finger on. There is just the nagging feeling that something is being kept from us, leaving us unable to see, to judge, to understand.

I propose some tentative links between this section and the next two. In this opening passage, Tsushima is casting us in the role of skeptical onlookers, a role that will remain in our minds as we observe the mother searching frantically for the squirrels and then for her dead son. Ultimately, we join the ranks of those who were not present to see her son die and who therefore, by definition in this narrative, become doubters of her account of that event. The *mawari no hitotachi*, as Tsushima describes the women in the park, come to refer to her readers as well, because none of us on the outskirts of her characters' experience can participate in, comprehend, or even evaluate what has been described to us. We "see" but do not "comprehend" what is going on. We are as powerless as the woman who blithely worked in the next room as her son was breathing his last.

The mother who narrates the second (and third?) part gives us a detailed, matter-of-fact description of her family's outing to view the flying squirrels. As with the first section, the emphasis is on a visual encounter with a phenomenon. This time, in contrast, the subject of observation is thoroughly benign, mundane, even cute. And unlike the narrator of the murder sequence, the mother here grows increasingly frustrated in her attempts to describe what she is seeing. When the squirrels are still perched motionless and the guide shines a red beam of light toward them, she is able to make out the tiny glittering points of redness that reflect off their eyes. But once the real event begins and the squirrels start to leap from tree to tree, the mother is left as if blinded. It is incredible to her that she seems to be the only one unable to catch even a glimpse of what others can see so effortlessly. Clearly this is a relationship between observer and observed very different from what occurred in the murder sequence. The mother here begins to doubt her own perceptions, to think that perhaps she has seen something flit past the corner of her eye, but she cannot discern what it is.

Then we make that extraordinary shift to her thoughts about "losing sight of" (*miushinatte iru*) her husband and the transference of that anxiety to her dead son. The remainder of the section consists of the narrator's dreams, possibly even hallucinations, involving her search for her son even after he is dead. She seems convinced that he is not gone irretrievably, but is merely lost from view, and that if she turns quickly enough, she will again find him. Perhaps the most moving paragraph in the entire story reads:

> Four years have passed [since we went to see the squirrels], and I'm still having difficulty seeing my son as well. When I think he must be at my side, he isn't. If I think, surely that's him, something is still missing. Even though the natural thing is for him to be standing beside me, I only have the feeling that he is there, and I can't summon him into my arms.[9]

In the third section, we come to realize that a central problem for this mother is that she was not an actual, physical "witness" to her son's death. Whatever it was that happened to him resulting in his death, she was not there "watching" when it occurred. His life has flitted past her eyes like the musasabi. As a result, her mind is unable to fully "accept" (*nattoku suru*) or comprehend the situation. In the first segment, the inexplicable death was "handled," perhaps even settled, by common consent of the witnesses. Even though what they conclude seems, from a logical standpoint, to be preposterous, they are in agreement about the reasonableness of their position, and so the story concludes with collective "understanding." But in the case of the death of this woman's son, the absence of witnesses will not allow even the creation of a plausible explanation. If the mother herself, the one most profoundly scarred by the incident, cannot satisfy her own mind about the death, how can she expect others to understand—especially when they do not even ask her about it? There can be no resolution; she will never be able to come to an "understanding" or even acceptance of her son's death.

As fractured as the elements of this story might seem, this is not, as I mentioned earlier, a completely atypical way for Tsushima to organize a work of fiction. In several other works, she also assembles incongruities into what may initially seem like a haphazard fashion. For instance, in the early "Hana o maku" (To Scatter Flower Petals, 1977)—which I do not think succeeds nearly as well as this story—the elements of the narrative are presented in a disjointed manner. The burden is on the reader to make connections between characters and determine what, if anything, their relationships might be. The time sequence also is disjointed, as if the incidents have appeared in a dream. But Tsushima gives the dream passages the same degree of plausibility as the waking segments, and the narration makes no distinction between the two. Perhaps the disjuncture in narrative fabric is suggestive of the disjointed nature of the families and relationships that Tsushima describes.

In a later story, "Yokushitsu" (The Bath, 1983), the narrator either sees or imagines that she sees her dead brother through the frosted glass of the bath at her mother's home. She recalls visiting the hospital many years earlier on the day her retarded brother died:

> I peeped into the second-floor room that my mother had given me directions to. But no one was there, only a metal bed with the sheets made up neatly. Instantly I sensed in the depths of my heart what had become of my brother; nevertheless, I promptly decided that I must have mistaken the room number. How strange. I leaned my head to one side and looked at the number again. Then I glanced up and down the hall. Which room might it have been? I wondered if my brother had been released from the hospital, since there had been nothing to worry about. Absent-mindedly, I stood in the hallway.[10]

The stubborn refusal to accept death, the continuing quest to find someone who has already died—or, as Tsushima would say, has "been lost to view"—and the delusion that the dead have come back to the land of the living—are elements in common with "Hikarikagayaku itten o."

There are further similarities with "The Silent Traders." In that story, Tsushima focuses on relationships that exist without communication: mother and daughter live together for years without speaking to each other; the daughter and her former lover, who is the father of her children, meet and discuss nothing of any significance, leading Tsushima to compare their mindless bartering with the silent traders who come down from the mountains to sell their wares. The narrator of "Silent Traders" also questions her own memories of past experience: many years after the event, she is not really sure that she and her elementary school classmates actually buried a time capsule in Rikugien park.

In "Hikarikagayaku itten o," a similar breakdown in communication is a major concern. The narrator in the first section is surrounded by women who are not communicating normally, who refuse to report a murder to the police, and who do not believe that being witnesses to a crime necessarily gives them any responsibility for either the victim or the criminal or for a more abstract concept of justice. For the narrator of the second and perhaps third parts, the inability to get reliable feedback on incidents that have transpired in her life propels her into a cycle of doubt surrounding her own experience. If she cannot be certain about those things she has experienced directly, how can she cope with the utterly inexplicable death of her son?

It is almost as though experiences outside the visual range are pushed, by definition, outside the realm of understanding. The flight of the squirrels is, of course, a kind of metaphor for this notion. It is all well and good that others can see the squirrels leaping from tree to tree. The preponderance of evidence provided by those in the narrator's immediate vicinity—the group of onlookers, like those who witnessed the murder—ought to be powerful enough to convince the narrator that the squirrels are, in fact, flying through the dark forest. But the woman who has almost—but not quite—seen the murder in the park, simply by virtue of missing the chance to see that single fleeting, critical moment, has forever consigned herself to the role of tangential observer rather than full participant. As a result, she cannot speak with any authority or credibility about the act itself, about the group's level of complicity in the deed, or persuasively convince others of the need to report the killing to the police. In the same way, the mother has missed the crucial moment when she could have witnessed the squirrels' flight with her own eyes, and so the unique actions of the creatures are forever lost to her. It should, then, come as no surprise that the prospect of "losing sight" of her children, as she did the boy's father, is such a frighteningly real possibility in her mind.

That fleeting moment is certainly the *hikarikagayaku itten*, or single shining point of light, of the story's title. It is at once the moment of violence in part 1; the sparkling eyes of the squirrels in the second segment, as well as the moment when the animals leap; and, most significantly, the instant when the son dies alone, and for no evident—or visible—reason, in the bathtub. The total irrationality of an eight-year-old boy abruptly drowning in a cramped Japanese *ofuro* makes that lost moment of both visual and cognitive contact particularly painful and poignant for his mother. And because of the way Tsushima has prepared us for that moment, by guiding us through several other instances of flickering lights that are either seen and not comprehended or not seen at all, she has made the boy's death equally powerful for us.

By now, the parts of the story that had seemed so incongruent begin to reread one another, and the echoes that are exchanged between them reverberate in a way that both deepens the impact of these experiences and opens them up to a variety of interpolations. The attempt by the murderer to lift the body of her victim is seen again in the desperate attempts by the mother in the third section to pull her son's body from the bathtub. The uncomplicated acceptance of the act and the perfunctory attempt to cover it up in the first part contrasts sharply with the mother's inability to accept either the death itself or anyone's reaction to it. The red light of an "other" that causes the eyes of the squirrels to be "seen" reminds us of the mother's earnest desire to find someone who can illuminate the dark portions of her own soul. The mother's vain curiosity to know what the police might have asked her friend is foreshadowed in the initial narrator's speculation on the need to report the murder to the police.

The painful implications of beginning this story with a murder and ending it with an act that clearly must not be thought of as a murder—like trying to force someone *not* to think about a purple elephant—are self-evident. If the only reality that can be trusted and clung to is the experience that is not only seen with the eyes but also apprehended by the mind, then the possibilities for communication—for, in fact, the simple act of sharing experiences—are slim indeed. Those who actually see the glimmering eyes of the flying squirrels have an experience they can store away in memory—and who knows what will become of it there? But they have nothing they can pass on directly or persuasively to those who have missed the opportunity to see for themselves. Those who "see the light" may in some respect profit from it personally, learn or feel something from it. But the inability to share that insight in any meaningful way surely dilutes the sense of gain. An explanation or definition or retelling of an experience—a literary rendering, as it were—is fine, but the depths to which the listener or the reader can probe the experience, can see into it and comprehend it, are, it would seem, severely limited. There is an insurmountable gap between experience and narration here.

In *The Company We Keep*, Wayne Booth argues that the experience of reading consists of thinking the thoughts of the author:

> Although we usually manage, when we are not totally carried away to a pathological identification, to return to thinking a thought something like what was "ours" before we began listening—full conversions are always rare—a large part of our thought-stream is *taken over*, for at least the duration of the telling, by the story we are taking in.[11]

Tsushima perhaps would acknowledge this notion of the transitory sharing of thoughts by author and readers through the medium of fiction, but her ability to believe that the reader can accept and embrace with any kind of trust the experiences she has described seems limited. The experiences of others, no matter how adroitly they are narrated to us, remain forever foreign. They are rife with potential for doubt, whether doubt about the truthfulness of the experience itself or reservations about the language that was used to define and qualify the emotional scope of the experience.

Here, I would suggest, is where Tsushima has achieved singular success in shaping her personal experience into a remarkable piece of literature. It is not simply a matter of being dissatisfied with the straightforward transmission of her private life to her readers. Instead, in the act of telling us about some of the most intimate moments of her life, the most excruciating experiences one could ever expect to have, she has simultaneously demonstrated to us that the relating of such tales is an act of futility. Her pain is not just the simple pain of a mother who has lost a child to a tragic accident; it is also the pain of someone who knows that her own experiences can never be adequately communicated to another person. And it is the pain of an author who knows that the attempt itself will result in the creation of a fiction and that this fiction, even if it is portrayed as the truth, will never be fully endorsed by another as either reality or fabrication. The beauty and power of this work thus reside not only in the pathetic core of the story itself but also in the way that the whole validity of being a spectator is called into question. Tsushima challenges the belief that reading can be a key to another's experience, and in that sense it is a challenge to the entire history of modern Japanese fiction.

NOTES

1. See Edward Fowler, *The Rhetoric of Confession: Shishōsetsu in Early Twentieth-Century Japanese Fiction* (Berkeley and Los Angeles: University of California Press, 1988).

2. See Fukuda's *kaisetsu* in Tayama Katai, *Futon, Jūemon no saigo* (Tokyo: Shinchōsha, Shinchō bunko, 1952).

3. Van C. Gessel, *The Sting of Life: Four Contemporary Japanese Novelists* (New York: Columbia University Press, 1989).

4. Particularly in a story like "Sora no kaibutsu Aguii" (Aghwee the Sky Monster), 1964, in Howard Hibbett, ed., *Contemporary Japanese Literature*, trans. John Nathan (New York: Knopf, 1977).

5. The story originally appeared in the May 1988 issue of *Shinchō* and was included in the collection *Yume no kiroku* (Tokyo: Bungei shunjū, 1988).

6. Tsushima Yūko, "Hikarikagayaku itten o," in *Yume no kiroku*, p. 262.

7. The vagueness of the language in this section of the story (the narrator addresses her friend

only as *anata*) suggests that the woman might even be writing to her former husband, the one she "lost sight of."

8. Tsushima, "Hikarikagayaku," p. 269.

9. Ibid., p. 273.

10. Translated by J. Martin Holman and published in *Zyzzyva* 4 (1988): 104.

11. Wayne Booth, *The Company We Keep: An Ethics of Fiction* (Berkeley and Los Angeles: University of California Press, 1988), pp. 140–41 (emphasis in original).

26

Translators Are Actors / yakusha wa yakusha

◉

R E B E C C A   L .   C O P E L A N D

> Whenever I get set to teach someone a thing or two about
> carving, I tell him right from the start that I'm not going
> to sit there and explain every little thing. . . . But even if I
> can't come right out and explain to my students all they
> should do, I show them with my hands. I guess it amounts
> to the same thing.
>
> *The puppet maker Tenguya Kyūkichi*[1]

When translators and theorists talk about translation, they generally do so
through a metaphor or an anecdote, which is something of a metaphor as well.
Translation, as ambiguous an act as it is personal, does not easily lend itself to
discussion in abstract terms. For most translators (as for most artists in general), the metaphor of "showing" comes more easily than "telling." The
metaphors for translation have changed over time. In the nineteenth century,
translation was described as a window or a lamp. More recent translators have
presented their art as an "echo" (Benjamin), a "counterfeit" (Seidensticker), a
"reflection of a very dim shadow" (Macadam), or a "cannibalism" (Gavronsky).
And then, of course, there is the oft-cited Italian epigram *traduttore/traditore*
(translator/traitor). Donald Keene, in a challenge to this Italian tyranny,
offered his own metaphor, also in the form of a pun: *yakusha wa yakusha* (translators are actors).[2]

I find this pun to be a very pithy statement of translation theory. Translation
is arguably a performative act.[3] In this chapter, I discuss translation through the
metaphor of performance, using as my primary illustration Arthur Waley's and
Edward Seidensticker's English translations of *The Tale of Genji*.

The Audience

Translations, like dramatic performances, do not occur in a vacuum but "are context bound readings accessible to their time and culture."[4] When Tanizaki Jun'ichirō undertook his first translation into modern Japanese of *The Tale of Genji*, he was obliged to delete scenes that the military censors felt were inappropriate. This example of a readership's influence on a text is somewhat extreme, as few of us translate now for censors. But we do translate for critics (many with censorial propensities) and for editors—those voicepieces for the ever elusive "general reader." More important, we translate for our own perceived audience, and the way we construct this readership contributes to the shape of our translation.

When Arthur Waley first began his translation of *The Tale of Genji*, he was confronted by an audience that knew very little about contemporary Japan and even less about Japan in the eleventh century. "The literatures of China and Japan were the preserve of specialists and of dabblers in quaint exotica," Ivan Morris tells us in *Madly Singing in the Mountains*.[5] Curious and quaint stories had been translated by Lafcadio Hearn and others, but these hardly held their place among the greats of Western letters.

Waley meant to change this attitude. He truly believed that *Genji monogatari* was great literature, "one of the two or three greatest novels ever written,"[6] and he intended his translation to prove his point. But of course, to win any respect for this "Eastern novel," it had to stand up to a comparison with our own Western masterpieces. To wit: Murasaki Shikibu was likened to Fielding, Proust, Austin, Boccaccio, Shakespeare, and Sir John Malory (*sic*).[7] This was particularly important in light of W. G. Aston's earlier declaration that *The Tale of Genji* could never measure up to the masterpieces of the West, especially the works of Fielding, Thackeray, Hugo, and Cervantes. Waley wanted *The Tale of Genji* to appeal to his readers as a Western classic would. Therefore he went to the text "in search of something—certain moral and aesthetic values, a certain kind of hero, certain kinds of anguish. Much of what he sought was incontestably there, but . . . he had no difficulty finding it even where it did not exist."[8] Waley's approach to *The Tale of Genji*—that is, his reasons for undertaking the translation, his perception of his audience's receptivity of things Japanese, and indeed his perception of literary greatness—colored his interpretation and his presentation of the text.

When Edward Seidensticker began his translation of *The Tale of Genji* nearly half a century later, his audience was slightly more sophisticated in its appreciation of Japanese literature.[9] The number of translations of both classical and

modern works had increased since the end of the war, and given the globaliza-
tion of the media, Japan was no longer the "imaginary kingdom" that it had been
for Waley and his readers.[10] Seidensticker could thus make more demands on
his audience. He no longer had to justify *The Tale of Genji*'s status in world literature, because Waley had already done so. He was therefore less constrained by
an impulse to familiarize the unfamiliar and more inclined to concentrate on the
text itself. Yet ironically, since his was a text buttressed by more extensive annotations, it encompassed to an extent the extraliterary commentary that Waley
had lacked and thus had felt compelled to append. But one could argue that this
extraliterary commentary is present in Seidensticker's translation as well,
because it was implicit in his text of *Genji*.

Finally, Seidensticker's reasons for undertaking a new translation were somewhat unlike Waley's for embarking on the earlier translation. First, Seidensticker had Waley's version to translate against. Had Seidensticker felt less dissatisfied with Waley's translation—especially with Waley's omissions and additions—perhaps he would have been less tempted to offer his own.

Seidensticker's reasons were somewhat unlike Waley's, I have said. But only
somewhat. Waley meant to introduce the Western world to a wonderful
Japanese masterpiece, and so did Seidensticker. Seidensticker's version has been
called by some a "retranslation." But in fact it is not, just as Laurence Olivier's
performance of *Hamlet* is not a reperformance of the Elizabethan version. Both
are new. Seidensticker gives us a new *Genji*, and his *Genji* is as dissimilar from its
predecessor as he is from Waley.

The Playwright

Critics of the two translations often write of Waley's *Genji* or Seidensticker's
Genji when they mean to make distinctions. These appellations identify the texts
as belonging to the translator, rather than to the woman designated as the
"author." The distinction is appropriate, for when we read *The Tale of Genji* translated by Arthur Waley, we are in fact reading his reading of a work written centuries ago. It is not that Murasaki Shikibu is not also there. The magic of translation (when translation is good enough to be magical) is that both the author
and the translator coexist in the same text, which is now a new text and not just
an imitation or a copy of the "original."

Translators learn to commune with an author (or, shall we say, with the
"authorial voice") while they translate, even if that author has been dead for centuries and even if that author was never more than the vaguest of existences.

According to Eileen Mikals-Adachi, Enchi Fumiko received visitations from "Murasaki Shikibu" while she was translating *The Tale of Genji* and, as a result, had problems with her eyes. This is not to say that translators slip into some kind of trance or resort to midnight seances while translating (though some may). Rather, they learn to hear the author's voice in the story. Waley did not write a great deal about his theories of translation, but what he did write emphasized again and again that a good translator "simply has to develop the habit of hearing voices talk."[11] In his description of the translation process, he offers a near possession experience: "[A] translator should have been excited by the work he translates, should be haunted day and night by the feeling that he *must* put it into his own language, and should be in a state of restlessness and fret till he has done so."[12] The German translator Christopher Middleton, in a much later essay, describes a similar process:

> When you translate a writer's work, where is the writer? Obviously he is not there, in the place where you walk around or lie or sit, wringing your hands, translating what he wrote, murmuring the words. . . . Yet, afterwards, *he has been there*. Afterwards, I say, he has been there. He has been where you translated him. The work, and the passion of translating, place him there afterwards. Not physically, not altogether fantastically either, but in a sense that we invoke, in all honesty, when we say that rays of feeling surround, penetrate, and situate a particular object. This work of translation, as a kind of sensitive passion, unfolds through two successive moments of *Einfühlung* [empathy]. First, obviously, you enter into a relationship with the writer as a presence which pervades the original text—a presence, that is, rather than a personality. Second, from that relationship, as your translation comes into the open, the writer as a presence is released into the place in which you worked—he steps out into it, that presence.[13]

In order to achieve this kind of connection with the text and the authorial voice or "presence," a translator must have a passion for the text, as Waley indicated. Linguistic skill carries a translator only so far. If translators wish to plum the "vertical" depths of a text, "to enter into the deeper layers of emotional existence so that the atmosphere of these emotions can then be recreated with the possibilities of a new language,"[14] they must have a great love for the text and for their own work. Donald Keene warns those who would believe otherwise: "If he does not feel any love and makes the translation mainly in order to earn some money, the result is likely to be a disaster . . . a highly frustrating experience."[15]

This love for a text does not ask that a translator try to be the author. But he or she should hear the author's voice and, in so hearing, tell the author's tale. The

translator then becomes "the medium—the voice—of the new text."[16] Each
translator hears, of course, a different story and, in turn, tells a different tale.

> Possible versions are not only multiple but infinite, and each "new" story is at
> once quite different and essentially the same, for in each retelling it is digested
> again and provided with a different body. What's more, in the case of poetry and
> much prose, the "story" itself is ambiguous, even ephemeral.[17]

The Script

"An old joke about translating *Finnegans Wake* ends with the punchline, 'But what
are they going to translate it FROM?' Translation, perhaps as much as any critical activity, highlights the difficulty of establishing a 'stable' original."[18] In the
case of *The Tale of Genji*, this notion of the original's "instability" takes on a physical significance as well, with early readers adding to the text, deleting and mis-
copying to such an extent that we cannot even be certain what form the "original" text took. *The Tale of Genji* is certainly more than printed words on a page.
Certainly, that is, if it is actually read. For as modern scholarship has argued, a
text exists only when read, and "it is only and always the version created by the
reader's act of translation."[19] A text, then, is in constant flux. It grows with each
subsequent reading and evolves with time. A twentieth-century reader of *The
Tale of Genji* reads through a filter of time. And a competent translator not only
reads but engages in detailed "research that places the text in the cultural, historical, and aesthetic context of its time."[20]

Understanding the "meaning" of a text—deducing the etymologies of
words, consulting dictionaries, and making sense of vague elocutions—is but a
fraction of what takes place in translation. Waley tells us:

> Hundreds of times I have sat for hours in front of texts the meaning of which I
> understood perfectly, and yet been unable to see how they ought to be put into
> English in such a way as to re-embody not merely a series of correct dictionary
> meanings, but also the emphasis, the tone, the eloquence of the original.[21]

Waley intuited what Walter Benjamin later elucidated as the fleeting manner in
which a translation and an "original" touch each other at the point of meaning.
"Meaning," or "communication," according to Benjamin, is only a small feature
of the translation process, and a nonessential feature at that. "But what is there
besides communication in a literary work—and even the bad translator admits

that this is the essential: is it not the illimitable, the inapprehensible, the 'poetic'?"[22]

Marleigh Ryan refers to just this "illimitable," "inapprehensible" aspect of Japanese literature in her 1980 article on translation:

> It lies on the page, a collection of English words which may or may not "mean" what the Japanese words "mean," but devoid of the feeling permeating the original text. I would argue that without the emotion—in Japanese, inextricably bound to unexpressed language—the translation is profoundly inadequate, for emotion is the substance of Japanese literature. It is where the Japanese genius lies, and failure to convey it in the translation deprives the literature of its greatest value.[23]

The Actors

The perception of emotion is, again, very subjective, and how that emotion is then expressed is equally subjective. Thus a translation is a product, a creation of its translator. It is "a new poem," to quote Ezra Pound. It is not merely an imitation, a reflection of an "original," a copy, a simulacrum, a betrayal, but a text in its own right. Octavio Paz, in arguing for the legitimacy of translations, stated: "All texts are originals because each translation has its own distinctive character. Up to a point, each translation is a creation and thus constitutes a unique text."[24]

It is the translator who gives the translation its "distinctive character," its "voice." Yet, translators' names are frequently not given on translated texts, as if the translator were "the mere delivery person, relegated to the role of a skilled laborer."[25] This notion is so pervasive and so valorized that many translators themselves subscribe to it. The translator is, after all, a humble and "shy character"; otherwise, why would he or she have aspired to such an "insignificant occupation?"[26] But if a translator is to approach the "illimitable, the inapprehensible, the 'poetic,'" the "emotion" of a text, as Benjamin and Ryan tell us he must, how can he remain invisible? Well, he cannot. For "no matter how strong a desire may exist to preserve and transmit the character of the original author's writing . . . the translator's Self is also present in any translation."[27]

Arthur Waley—by all accounts "a shy character"—still seemed to recognize the role his presence played in the translation. To an unnamed French scholar, who admonished the translator to remain invisible behind the text because the texts would speak for themselves, Waley responded: "I have always found that it was I, not the texts, that had to do the talking."[28] Professors Keene and Seidensticker, though not excessively shy characters, seem to prefer invisibility in their translations. But those of us who have known Professors Keene and Seidensticker cannot fail to hear them in their translations. Donald Keene is there in *Oku no hosomichi*, and Edward Seidensticker is present in *Kagerō nikki*. Their presence does not diminish their translations but makes them all the richer. I cannot point to any one sentence in a translation and say, "See, here he is . . . this is vintage Keene!" Nevertheless, I sense his presence between the lines, behind the lines, or, as Christopher Middleton would have it, "afterwards." And I am not suggesting that the visible translator robs the author of his or her due or somehow "steals the show." Rather, as I noted earlier, the author and the translator coexist in the same text.

In this way, translation resurrects an author, or at least the author's presence. Even when the author is still alive, a translation creates the author anew. In a sense, perhaps the "author" of a translated text is a new presence altogether: part original author and part translator—that is, the author as reconstructed in the voice of the translator. As a result, with our two *Genji* translations we now have two Murasaki Shikibu(s). The Murasaki that Waley created for us and the one that Seidensticker gave us are different presences, and I imagine neither is identical to the "real" Murasaki Shikibu. I also imagine that neither is completely dissimilar.

Translations are said to "complete" a text (as I shall explain shortly), but if this is so, then is it possible that a second translation completes the first? Seidensticker's translation has fixed Waley's. It has shown us Waley's errors, and it has shown us the beauty of his poetry and remarkable intuitive powers. But mostly it has shown us Waley. With Seidensticker's translation in accompaniment, we can hear Waley's voice all the better.

For all its faults, Waley's translation served its time, and for many it will remain timeless. Waley brought a small fraction of another world to the lives of those who would otherwise have had no access to it. Furthermore, he proved beyond question that "texts supposed to have been untouchable for cultural reasons"[29] could be translated. For some, perhaps, Waley's translation changed lives. Seidensticker credited it with bringing him to the door of Japanese literature. Once across the threshold, Seidensticker discovered Murasaki Shikibu for himself and, in so doing, found Waley's translation wanting. Seidensticker's translation, in turn, answered a great need, and for many readers it too will remain timeless. This is not to say that it will not be superseded. As Seidensticker himself suggested, there are almost as many readings of *The Tale of Genji* as there are readers.[30] One of these readers, Royall Tyler, is currently at work on his own *Genji*. When he has finished, when he has "completed" Seidensticker's *Genji*—just as Seidensticker earlier completed Waley's—some well-meaning critic inevitably will line up Tyler's translation against the earlier ones and expose its many "flaws" or else use the text to vilify its predecessors.[31]

The Critic

Criticizing a translation is a tricky business. Generally, reviews ignore the translator's efforts altogether, discussing the work as if it had been in English all along. Occasionally a translation will be acknowledged with "reads well" or "rough in places." At worst, critics engage in the smug, nitpicking kind of criticism that Gregory Rabassa described as "poring over both texts in search of warts and hairs."[32] Certainly there will be mistakes. "A few mistakes . . . may be thought inevitable and do not make a bad translation, though mistakes that pass bounds do."[33] Rarely do critics consider the problems that a text poses or the alternatives that the translator faced and chose in resolving those problems.

When critics do tackle the question of translation, they generally balance their arguments among "free and faithful," "poetic and literal," "spirit and letter." Translators have been torn for centuries by these diametric positions. Modest creatures that they are, translators have been placed in an unfair and impossible situation. They can be true to the "original" and betray their own language, or they can be true to their own language and betray the original.[34] Under these terms, translation is always doomed. "The best translation is merely better than the worst to some extent, more or less."[35] And translators so are left with a task that cannot be performed.

In his essay "Translation: What Good Does It Do?" Seidensticker suggests that the very definition for dilemma might describe the process of translation: "a situation requiring a choice between equally undesirable alternatives."[36] But what is this "perfect translation" that is dangled before the translator's nose? Is it to be found in complete fidelity to an original, presented in a poetic language to please readers? No, even this would constitute a "freedom," for as Philip Lewis contends, "the only fidelity is exact repetition—of the original, in the original; and even that, it can be argued, is finally a superficial fidelity."[37] Lewis's argument brings us back to the fluidity of the original, a fluidity a translation makes all the more apparent: "A partial and precious document of a text's vicissitudes may be seen in its translations. What are the many translations of the *Iliad*, from Chapman to Magnien, but different perspectives on an object in motion, a long experimental game of omissions and emphases?"[38]

Waley's translation gives us Waley's reading nurtured by Waley's time, just as Seidensticker's translation gives us Seidensticker's reading in Seidensticker's time. To assign values to each along the poles of free and faithful diminishes the achievements of the translations. That is, to state that Waley's is "free" and "poetic" and that Seidensticker's is "literal," though certainly true on the one hand, limits our reading of the translations. Seidensticker's *Genji* achieves heights of unsurpassed beauty and yes, charm, whereas Waley's, if only by the sheer genius of his intuition, can be very literal to the emotion of the text. Furthermore, to use the original as our only measure of a translation's success dooms the translation to failure. "We do not read the same text twice: why should we be allowed to create it twice?"[39] We cannot. If an exact replica of the original were our only criterion, then we would have no translations. (No readings, either, as we would not wish our readings to be unfaithful to those performed yesterday or centuries ago.) We all would become translators like Borges's fictional Pierre Menard, who translated *Don Quixote* word for word, line for line, without changing a single word. Of course, it took Menard years, and he only managed to complete a few chapters. All in all, his "translation" still was not perfect, even though it was "infinitely richer" than the original.[40] *Traduttore / tradittore*.

If the impossibility of a perfect translation forces us to confer second-class status on translation, then perhaps we have misunderstood its potential and purpose. Perhaps "we have been playing by (or claiming to play by) impossible and inappropriate rules."[41] Rather than dwelling on the loss in translation, perhaps we could consider the gains—the possible. A translation, it has been said, "completes" an original. This statement implies that an original is somehow incomplete, wanting. I found this idea disturbing until I recalled how the puppet maker Tenguya Kyūkichi described his art of carving as always being "somehow incomplete."

> If I was [sic] to tell you what I thought about the gods and the buddhas, then I'd have to explain it like this: Before I start to carve a puppet I have it all clear in my mind how that puppet ought to look. But there's always one part I just can't get no matter how I try—yes, there's always something missing, and it's in that part, that missing part, where the gods reside.[42]

It is in that "one missing piece" that art can be said to flourish. It is the joy of the audience, the viewer, to complete this missing piece, to fill the emptiness with vision. This must have been what Kenkō meant when he insisted on imperfection. "Leaving something incomplete makes it interesting, and gives one the feeling that there is room to grow."[43] A translation, therefore, is "a moment in the growth of the original, which will complete itself *in* enlarging itself."[44] Even a "bad" translation serves the original without unduly damaging it, as Hugh Kenner pointed out in regard to Ezra Pound's translations from the Chinese.

> In laying itself open to being misunderstood and surviving the experience as it does, it demonstrates the persistent virtue of poetry, which can always reassert its true forms as no other means of discourse can. The Chinese poem underwent no real violence, and to its long and honorable history it can now add this distinction, that its supposed qualities reinforced its real ones in helping the post-Symbolist generation to rescue the poetics of Europe from triviality.[45]

In translation, a text lives beyond the means of its time and place and even beyond the imagination of its author. Jacques Derrida suggests that it even "lives more and better."[46]

Cast Party

Derrida's remark reminds me of the classical Japanese course I had with Professor Keene. We were considering Bashō's *Oku no hosomichi* and had come to the "Tsubo no ishibumi" section, where Bashō reaches the monument at Taga Castle. The monument itself is rather nondescript, the inscription of little significance. But Bashō is moved to tears of joy at seeing the words on the monument that have survived, encrusted with moss, for one thousand years. Professor Keene explained it this way:

> Nothing is more important to a poet than words. Here Bashō notes how mountains crumble away and rivers change their course [which is itself a "reading" of Tu Fu], new roads replace the old, stones are buried and vanish in the earth, . . . but WORDS REMAIN. What greater joy can there be for a poet?[47]

Now when I teach this work in my literature class, and I do so in English, I can take Professor Keene's explanation one step further. Words (poems/texts) not only surpass the boundaries of time; they surpass cultural and linguistic boundaries as well. When Bashō wept over the Taga Monument, he could not have imagined that his words, his poems, would be studied centuries later by people on the other side of the world and in a language he did not write. What greater homage can there be to a poet, therefore, than to translate his poems?

The English does not diminish the work. Rather, it contributes to its Derridaian "sur-vival" and its enlargement. Bashō's text, as powerful as it is in Japanese, has been enriched by the addition of Donald Keene's "voice." The two share the stage in a rich performance made complete by its audience of readers.

NOTES

1. Uno Chiyo, "The Puppet Maker," in Rebecca Copeland, *The Sound of the Wind: The Life and Works of Uno Chiyo* (Honolulu: University of Hawaii Press, 1992), p. 128.

2. Donald Keene, "On Translation," *Landscapes and Portraits: Appreciations of Japanese Culture* (Tokyo: Kodansha International, 1971), p. 329.

3. See Carol Maier, "Translation as Performance: Three Notes," *Translation Review* 15 (1984): 5–8.

4. Diane J. Rayor, "Translator/Reader," *Translation Review* 23 (1987): 31.

5. Ivan Morris, "The Genius of Arthur Waley," in Ivan Morris, ed., *Madly Singing in the Mountains: An Appreciation and Anthology of Arthur Waley* (New York: Walker, 1970), p. 67.

6. Ibid., p. 75.

7. According to a review of L. H. Titterton, "The Bridge of Dreams," *New York Times*, June 4, 1933, p. 7.

8. Marian Ury, "The Complete *Genji*," *Harvard Journal of Asiatic Studies* 37 (June 1977) 1: 183–84.

9. I was dismayed to discover that in a class of bright, well-informed comparative literature students, not one had ever heard of *The Tale of Genji*, despite the illustrious comparisons!

10. See Marian Ury, "The Imaginary Kingdom and the Translator's Art: Notes on Re-reading Waley's *Genji*," *Journal of Japanese Studies* 2 (Summer 1976): 267–94.

11. Arthur Waley, "Notes on Translation," in Morris, *Madly Singing in the Mountains*, p. 156.

12. Ibid., p. 163 (emphasis in original).

13. Christopher Middleton, "Translation as a Species of Mime," in Rosanna Warren, ed., *The Art of Translation: Voices from the Field* (Boston: Northeastern University Press, 1989), pp. 23–24 (emphasis in original).

14. Rainer Schulte, "Translation and the Academic World," *Translation Review* 38–39 (1992): 1.

15. Donald Keene, "Translation and Comparative Literature," in Cornelia N. Moore and Lucy Lower, eds., *Translation East and West: A Cross-Cultural Approach: Selected Conference Papers*, vol. 5 of *Literary Studies East and West* (Honolulu: University of Hawaii at Manoa and the East-West Center; University of Hawaii Press, 1992), p. xix.

16. Rayor, "Translator/Reader," p. 31.

17. Maier, "Translation as Performance," pp. 5–6.

18. Richard Francis, "A Rereading of 'Pierre Menard' in Light of Contemporary Translation Theory" (Committee on Comparative Literature, Washington University in St. Louis, 1993), p. 3.

19. Alfred J. Macadam, "Translation as Metaphor: Three Versions of Borges," *MLN* 90 (December 1975): 749.

20. Schulte, "Translation and the Academic World," p. 1.

21. Waley, "Notes on Translation," p. 158.

22. Walter Benjamin, "The Task of the Translator," trans. James Hynd and E. M. Valk, *Delos* 2 (1968): 76.

23. Marleigh Grayer Ryan, "Translating Modern Japanese," *Journal of Japanese Studies* 6 (Winter 1980): 49.

24. Octavio Paz, "Translation: Literature and Letters," trans. Irene del Corral, in Rainer Schulte and John Biguenet, eds., *Theories of Translation: An Anthology of Essays from Dryden to Derrida* (Chicago: University of Chicago Press, 1992), p. 154.

25. Karin Graf, "The Irreplaceable Translator," trans. Sharon Sloan, *Translation Review* 38–39 (1992): 35.

26. José Ortega y Gasset, "The Misery and the Splendor of Translation," trans. Elizabeth Gamble Miller, in Schulte and Biguenet, *Theories of Translation*, p. 94.

27. James A. Hayes, "The Translator and the Form–Content Dilemma in Literary Translation," *MLN* 90 (December 1975): 838.

28. Waley, "Notes on Translation," p. 158.

29. Serge Gavronsky, "The Translator: From Piety to Cannibalism," *Sub-Stance* 16 (1977): 58.

30. See Edward Seidensticker, "A Decade or So for *Genji*," *Delos* 2 (1968): 126–31.

31. See, for example, "A Study on the English Translation of *Genji monogatari*," *Traditions*, nos. 15 and 16 (1981): 7–26 and 7–30. In this piece, which is a translation of excerpts from a book that won the 1980 Mainichi Publication Prize, four Japanese literature scholars compare short passages from Murasaki Shikibu's *Genji* with the translations by Waley and Seidensticker and then comment on the success or failure of the translations. Clearly proponents of the "word-for-word" approach to translation, the point of their exercise is lost in excruciatingly tedious detail.

32. Gregory Rabassa, "Translation: The Recreative Art," *Humanities* 3 (December 1982): 2.

33. Edward Seidensticker, "Translation: What Good Does It Do?" in Jean Toyama and Nobuko Ochner, eds., *Literary Relations East and West*, vol. 4 of *Literary Studies East and West* (Honolulu: University of Hawaii at Manoa and the East-West Center; University of Hawaii Press, 1990), p. 180.

34. See Antoine Berman, *The Experience of the Foreign: Culture and Translation in Romantic Germany* (Albany: State University of New York Press, 1992), pp. 3–5.

35. Joseph F. Graham, "Translator's Note" to Jacques Derrida, "Des Tours de Babel," in Joseph F. Graham, ed., *Difference in Translation* (Ithaca, NY: Cornell University Press, 1985), p. 205.

36. Seidensticker, "Translation: What Good Does It Do?" p. 181.

37. Philip E. Lewis, "The Measure of Translation Effects," in Graham, *Difference in Translation*, p. 39.

38. Jorge Luis Borges, "Las Versiones homéricas," in *Discusión* (Buenos Aires: Emecé, 1966). As quoted (and translated) by Macadam, "Translation as Metaphor," p. 749.

39. Macadam, "Translation as Metaphor," p. 754.

40. See Jorge Luis Borges, "Pierre Menard, Author of Don Quixote," trans. Anthony Bonner, in Anthony Kerrigan, ed., *Ficciones* (New York: Grove Weidenfeld, 1962), pp. 45–55.

41. Francis, "Rereading of 'Pierre Menard,'" p. 9.

42. Uno Chiyo, "The Puppet Maker," p. 124.

43. Kenkō, *Essays in Idleness*, trans. Donald Keene (New York: Columbia University Press, 1967), p. 70.

44. Jacques Derrida, "Des Tours de Babel," p. 188 (emphasis in original).

45. Hugh Kenner, "The Poetics of Error," *MLN* 90 (December 1975): 745–46.

46. Derrida, "Des Tours de Babel," p. 179.

47. This is my paraphrase (or "translation") of a statement made during a class conducted more than ten years ago at Columbia University.

27

Translating Takuboku

◉

C A R L   S E S A R

This is an account of how I went about translating the *tanka* of Ishikawa Takuboku (1885–1912).[1] Along the way I touch on translation as a kind of performance and as a literary genre, go into a few matters of audience and critical response, and cite my personal aspirations for Takuboku's poems in English.

The first task, demanded by the tanka itself, was to establish a sense of form with brevity as a basic ingredient. I attempted a visual, or spatial, solution, using a fixed line count as a matrix, and a restrictive set of orthographic rules, to fashion a sort of word painting, its shapes different from poem to poem, but each in a state of balanced tension, like a Chinese character or a Chinese poem. In this frame, words are juggled to produce voice, phrasings, intonation, and other effects appropriate to Takuboku's texts and his stated aims of colloquial simplicity and directness.

A visual approach may seem a radical departure from the tanka, but Takuboku set a precedent for it when he adopted his contemporary Toki Aika's daring innovation in form, the three-line tanka. Traditionally, the poem's syllable units of 5, 7, 5, 7, 7 were set down in five lines or strung together as one. The new format kept the tanka's metrical structure but, by rearranging its five units into varying three-line combinations, cut across the grain of the traditional orthography. Here, modernizing the tanka didn't mean going to free verse; one simply changed the look of the poem, confronting its readers with a visual field of totally new tensions, rhythms, and voicings. But the American reader, unlike the Japanese, hadn't been looking at traditional tanka orthography for fifteen hundred years, so there was nothing special about a three-line format to make it particularly effective in English. Had the format worked, I'd have used it, but it didn't. In three lines the poem fell flat as a pancake.

I had to come up with a format under different conditions. The American reader in general, or reader of poetry in particular (except for the few interested in Japanese poetry), is not used to, much less amenable to, short poetry. It's a readership that looks on short poems as cute, or precious, or limited at best, a kind of epigram or quip. So I needed a tight format that could command respect as a full and complete poem in English, solid, but with the tensile strength to sustain many variations in structure and pattern and a wide range of feeling. Five lines seemed just right to do that! Maybe a five-unit structure, whatever its arrangement, lends itself perfectly to poetry and accounts for the tanka's amazing longevity. At any rate, it was directly associated with the tanka and a lot newer in English. The syllable count, for Takuboku's poems at least, could not be kept.[2] The one word, one beat of basic English is the polar opposite of polysyllabic Japanese.

For a word picture, the first thing I wanted was a clean, transparent look, a visual and verbal economy that would meld design and semantic content. Simple and apparent, the text would engage the reader as any work of literature does but, like open clockwork or the brush strokes in a bamboo painting, also draw the reader in as a participant in its composition. In this respect, the poem text might be called concrete. But since concrete poetry gets its meanings by manipulating orthography in striking visual departures from standard usage or format, it's easy to forget that the conventional formats of a poem, a newspaper article, or typewritten note—plain words and letters, in fact—just as they are, are no less concrete. A poem text needs no emphatic distortion to attain similar effects (which do not mean images here) but can oscillate between sense and sight in subtle ways that don't insistently reveal themselves to a reader. As I understand it, this in essence is the Chinese idea of the poem as painting, and the painting as poem, and is what I've tried to get in my translations.

Although there is a visual quality to his three-line texts, Takuboku's content, unlike that of haiku, for example, is not largely imagistic. In making a word picture of a Takuboku poem, telegraphic language or one-word image shots can occasionally be used to good effect, but they are not nearly enough to capture Takuboku's poetry. This became magically clear when Takuboku's poems were used, along with some haiku, as exercises in signed poetry for the professional troupe of the National Theatre of the Deaf. Bashō's frog in the pond and Buson's butterfly on a bell were beautifully done using the essentially (but by no means entirely) mimetic qualities of sign language. But it quickly became evident to the troupe that such dramatic sign-mime images were the wrong approach to a Takuboku poem, which required instead signs in their discursive mode—but heightened because of the poem's brief duration—and to arrive at intensity with the plain vocabulary was a challenging problem.

In the same way on paper, Takuboku's poems—heightened yes, and compact—still have to sound like talk. The syntactical thread must run unbroken throughout the interplay of visual and semantic content. The poem cannot cross the border to where graphic design becomes the predominant element; it must look like a sentence, and read like one.

Here I owe the reader an example illustrating some of what I've been saying so far. (For this and other examples of visual effects, the romanized originals have been placed in the notes.)[3]

> feels like
> there's a cliff
> in my head
> crumbling
> day by day

This looks pretty clean. Its shape is compact and self-contained, the five lines balance as a group, and the poem's dozen words (thirteen syllables in all) fit well together. Their meaning is clear, but let's see where sense and sight, and sound also, merge. Reading the poem again, note that it gradually slows down and that by the last two lines the poem is plodding. This happens along with a slow change in verbal textures, from thin, tense, and confined—heightened in the opening lines by tall ascenders narrowing the words—to a thickening, heavy feeling through the next two lines—the words, letters, and sounds widening with *n, m, d, umb,* and *ng*—to the final line, where the poem falls apart into clumps and pieces. The one-word line "crumbling" rumbles onomatopoetically, and the repeating pattern of letters in the last line breaks the word clumps into still smaller fragments. Finally, one literal touch the reader may have noticed is the second line, slightly longer than the others, suggesting the overhanging ledge of a cliff.

Yet when we step back again, we find a locution that is completely natural, its flavor no more than that of an everyday remark in a normal speaking voice. There is no exaggerated minimalism, syntax is there, and the phrasing is ordinary, even predictable.

The effects in this and in many other poems were by no means planned or intended beforehand. In working out the poems, hunting for words and turns of phrase, balancing and breaking lines, and so on, visual and concrete qualities of words and letters become apparent and a factor in the writing. Once drawn into this dimension, it becomes irresistible and a part of one's palette, so to speak. Not every poem is as chock-full of effects as the preceding one, and many of them might not even exist in a larger, more wordy frame. Fragile enough here, they easily pale and vanish. The economy of a text, that clean look, brings them to life.

It's a maxim for both prose and poetry alike that anything, the least little jot or the tiniest comma, can carry great weight and impact. In a small poem of few words, this truth is magnified many times over, in terms not only of meaning but of visual impact also. So to get that clean, transparent look in my small texts, and to have it sustain a visible sense of form, just being concise wasn't enough. I trimmed the orthography to suit as well and, applying a few simple rules to the five-line matrix, set up a format having certain consistent features that readers would come to expect. As it turned out, some of these features enhanced the poems in other ways, too.

The first thing I did was get rid of nearly all capital letters. Let's look at a few versions of a poem side by side and see what happens.[4]

Driftwood	driftwood	driftwood
at the foot	at the foot	at the foot
of a sand dune	of a sand dune	of a sand dune
nobody around	nobody around	nobody around
I talk to it	i talk to it	I talk to it

With a capital, the first poem opens up with a proclamation, like an orator holding forth. The cap is also top-heavy and looks like a bump on the head. In lowercase, the first line sits comfortably with the others and voices the poem in conversational pitch and volume. But that lowercase *i* after the style of e e cummings in the middle version is all wrong, period. The third version is the way I have it. In essence, I kept capital letters to signify proper nouns, and in that function, surrounded by lowercase letters, they acquire a defined presence, as in the following two poems:[5]

sorry place	hard to forget
the streets of Otaru—	Koyakko
unsinging people	her soft

| and their | earlobes |
| gravelly voices | and all. . . |

"Gravelly" for the original's *arasa* (roughness) is an *engo*, or poetic word association, with "streets." The strong first line in the next poem (*wasuregatakari* in the original) came to me only just now, after many years of vacillation between "can't forget" and "never forget," which shows how elusive the obvious can be. The next four lines make up a nice, cuddly word cluster that reads like a *senryū*, a lighter form of haiku. The ellipsis lends a dreamy quality to the poem's fade into silent remembering, and each of the dots quietly stringing out is one of those many things about her.

Here are two special uses of capital letters:[6]

wrote GREAT	'Sad case,
in the sand	that Ishikawa'
a hundred times	say it myself
forgot about dying	sometimes—
and went on home	try to feel sorry

The first poem shows the word as written in the sand. In the second poem, standard orthography for the doctor's remark makes it look and sound natural and helps it to be overheard by Takuboku. Even so, I trimmed it to single quotation marks and left out the period.

The poem texts assume an air of modernity in lowercase, but with proper nouns popping up, one well within bounds and not very daring. Words formally consistent in lowercase, however, take on a generic quality, and this is uncannily powerful. Uniform in style but unique in appearance, meaning, and sound, each word becomes a strong graphic unit. If set in the right combination, the words crystallize into designs vibrating with content. Finally, to get back to details, a capital letter at the beginning of a sentence asks for a period at the end. Either one without the other looks ridiculous, so the choice is all or nothing. Having both—in my texts at least—would lock the poems up. Open-ended, they breathe freely on the page and have a chance to expand in meaning with the tanka's innate capacity for resonance and suggestiveness.

In my zeal for that "look," I decided I didn't want commas all over the place, hanging like caterpillars from the ends of my lines. But without them, the reader would have to stop or read on without any formal signal. In some poetry the lack of commas is meant to let the reader savor, ponder, or decipher lines without their usual punctuation. In my translations, however, to stop or go requires the decision of an instant, and the reader must guess right all the time. If someone hesitates because of doubt, even a blink too long, the poem stumbles. The trick is to avoid ambiguity. When the poem is spoken with hardly a pause, as in

> anybody
> dying of love
> these days
> should go down
> in history

it's no problem at all: just find the right words and balance them.[7] I picked this example because its last three lines also run together with a different meaning, but the ambiguity goes unnoticed in the rush of the simple sentence. But Takuboku's poems usually have two parts, and sometimes more. Here there are only invisible markers of sense to go by, as in the following:[8]

> damn moustache   like a rock
> droops   sliding
> now I   down the hill
> look like   I reached
> the bad guys   today

Note also the arrangement in these poems. The first has a comical shape that helps the wry humor, and the motion of the second does what the poem says. But the flow of sense is sometimes not enough, and to avoid stumbling, when the lines aren't clear-cut, a dash or ellipsis goes in. For these two examples,[9]

> want a place   that item
> I can knock around   in the paper
> all night long—   on the first snow
> think of home   that year. . .
> it leaves me cold   I wrote it

cover them up to see what I mean. There is a workable lightness about the dash and ellipsis because they do force a stop, but not with the finality of a period, and imply something else coming after.

Sometimes a line ending is perfectly clear-cut but needs a dash anyway because it just looks or feels a little off without one.[10]

staring at
pictures in a book—
bored, I try
blowing smoke
at them

Try covering up the dash in this one, too. The *b*'s are good here, I think, suggesting the blubbing of lips, and the blowing of smoke, in the idiocy of boredom.

To wind this up, in translating what may be Takuboku's most famous poem, having made up my mind that both a dash and an ellipsis were needed somewhere in the last three lines, I settled at last in a state of numbness and frustration for a horrible solution that even used a period! For this occasion, however, I found the will to type out the poem once again, cleanly this time, and look at it.[11]

kidding around
carried my mother
piggy-back
I stopped dead and cried
she's so light

I think it works.

Even though a comma almost never appears at the end of a line, every so often I put one inside a line. It's an escape hatch, a last resort when nothing else seems to keep the poem in line. But I have to use this comma sparingly anyway, because its effects turn out to be so pleasing—and even so striking at times— that it can get to be a habit and become too obvious. So it shows up here and there in time to prevent other more usual formats from getting tiresome or predictable. In routine cases, it has a mild slingshot effect that gives the poem a little push in the middle.[12]

fling my
arms and legs
all over the room
then, calmly
get up again

two friends
just like me:
one dead
one, out of jail
now sick

The comma in the first poem sets the stage for a quick change of mood and action; in the second, it springs the man loose from jail. Also, the colon ending the second line puts it behind bars.

Here are two other poems in this format:[13]

always come	late at night
to this gloomy bar	no hat, a man
the late sunset	enters the station
reddening, shines	stands, sits down
right in my drink	finally leaves

For the original's *aka aka to*, the long word suspended before the comma in the first poem catches the slowly setting sun and its darkening red. The comma holds it there a bit before letting it go, and the word after, in one syllable, sharply focuses the light.

The second example, a favorite of mine, breaks all records with its two commas. The text is almost perfectly balanced in structure, and this symmetry, at odds with the punctuated restlessness of its content, produces the tension that animates the scene. The phrase "no hat," coming out of nowhere, sets it in motion.

One typographical symbol I avoided was a clever little ampersand used for *and*, but I kept common signs—the exclamation point and question mark—whenever expected. The absence of a question mark, for example—a good device in some contexts—seemed a trifle affected for Takuboku. So I was surprised to find, when working on a new batch of his poems, one place where it was better left out, and why I think so may sum up this visual approach of mine. Here is the poem:[14]

damn picture
on the wall
how much longer
is it going
to hang there

Its slow burn seems to answer the question it asks. But let's add the question mark and see what happens.

damn picture
on the wall
how much longer
is it going
to hang there?

This is not bad, and seeing them together, might seem even better, since it strikes a clear note of exasperation, but some of its slow burn has been lost. In its own terms, however, with a question mark added, the pause after the second line now seems off somehow, not as natural as before. It needs a dash.

> damn picture
> on the wall—
> how much longer
> is it going
> to hang there?

Now I like it. It rings, everything is set off just right, and I'm tempted to keep it. Hard enough to get one good version, here there are two! Or three, for that matter. What are the critical differences among them? To begin with, both variations with question marks are louder than the first poem. Not the least bit too loud, by any standard, but in the first Takuboku sounds as if he's muttering under his breath, and it's that sullen tone I prefer. Now compare the two variations with the first as graphic units. With question marks, they are well-balanced syntactical word groups, but nothing more. The dash in the third version does pin its first two lines to the page, suggesting a horizontal frame, but that effect doesn't hold up, since it's not a good shape. And even if we take away the question mark here (cover it up to see what I mean), it wants to come back. The first version, completely clean, just hangs there, flat on the page, like the picture it's talking about.

I can't say for sure how much or little readers notice the things shown so far, but most seem to have no trouble reading the poems as I've done them. One reviewer, Roy E. Teele, commenting on the texts, wrote in *Literature East & West*, "The lack of capital letters and punctuation may at first seem artificial, but a few moments' reading proves the form exactly right."[15] This was exactly the response I had hoped for. There was one reader, however, for whom no amount of reading was enough, who turned up in the worst place possible, at the publisher, an American editor who promptly splattered every one of the texts with capitals, periods, commas, colons, and whatnot, and refused to budge. The lengths I had to go to before I forced him to relent, you cannot imagine. But to the idea that the book match the content and look of the texts with a simple design, all were adamantly obtuse; the result was a cute little book-in-a-box to be sold as a novelty in the "orientalia" gift market.[16] The point is that in my working visually with texts, book design was integral to the translation as a whole, and I should have seen to it myself.

To write in a visual dimension is easier than to describe it, but pointing out things may prompt the reader to take a closer look at the poems. Still, just as one takes in a painting, I hope the reader remembers to take a step back. To those who may find what I've said so far dubious, I'll admit that I'm blind to some artists' descriptions of their work. But something is there. And if pains taken, even as figments of the imagination, contribute to the integrity of a finished poem or painting, they become real. Hidden, they are like underpainting, an undeniable part of a finished work, invisible yet visible. For the effects I've tried to create and the means I used, no fixed grammar exists (or if there is one, I'm not the one to explain it). Each poem has a best version somewhere, to be found by trial and error. But in the effort to make certain elements of the poems work within stringent, definitively set rules, no less demanding, and in ways perhaps more so than metrical formulae, I hope some semblance of the powerful and undying tanka form has been achieved.

Up to now I've made little mention of Takuboku's original texts other than with respect to their form. The translations cited have been discussed as poetry in English, which is how they are meant to be read, and maybe there is no other good reason for them to exist. But as interpretive works, they are bound to the originals and would not exist without them. So let's look at some of the interplay between the two.

One way to get a good translation is to preserve the order of the words, phrasings, or images in the original. Somehow, it is felt, the succession of elements has greater cognitive impact than the syntax underlying it, something like the force of a cinematic sequence. In translating the tanka of Saitō Mokichi, Amy Heinrich declares that keeping to this order as much as possible is a priority.[17] Since the word orders of Japanese and English are almost the exact opposite of each other, this self-imposed requirement adds to the strong sense of form in her versions. I didn't strive as intently to do the same for Takuboku, though I did stay alert to the possibility, but if no solution came to mind, I quickly abandoned the attempt. Still, I did get pretty close to the order of the originals every so often. Two examples are

me tozuredo,	shut my eyes
	mind still a blank—
kokoro ni ukabu nani mo nashi.	gloomily
	I open them
sabishiku mo, mata, me o akeru kana.	up again

(ITZ, p. 469)

kanashiki wa,	the trouble is
	(I was the same)
(ware mo shikariki)	scold her
	spank her
shikaredomo, utedomo nakanu ko	the kid won't cry
no kokoro naru.	

(ITZ, p. 488)

The first is a dramatic sequence of events whose order must be kept, and Takuboku mirrors it in his syntax. The second is a rhetorical pattern that just happens to work out naturally in English as well. The translations are typical. In the first poem, I keep the action in the first line clean and make the inflection *-edo* part of an idiom in the second line for Takuboku's "not a thing comes to mind." The three lines left, opening with "gloomily" for *sabishiku mo*, try for a slow, flat, tired, matter-of-fact helplessness. Takuboku's *kana* in his last line seems ironic. Next, as often as Shakespeare uses "sweet," Takuboku uses "sad." Here I take Chikamatsu's advice that saying "it is sad" doesn't make it so,[18] and for *kanashiki wa* I find an idiomatic shade of meaning instead. I could have used "sad thing is" just as well, but trouble and a kid seemed to fit better. A few of Takuboku's many *k* sounds get into the English.

Note the punctuation in the originals that Takuboku had come to experiment with in his later tanka. In his adding punctuation and my subtracting it, we both were going in the same direction. He also began to arrange his three lines in different relative positions, which can't be shown well in romanization.

Sometimes the original text will show you how it wants to be translated. Of course it says what it means, but it also sends out signals about the way it wants to be treated, like this poem:

kishikishi to samusa ni fumeba	tiptoeing
ita kishimu	
	through the cold
kaeri no roka no	suddenly
	in the squeaky hallway
fui no kuchizuke	her mouth on mine

(ITZ, p. 445)

This is a montage-like love scene that you see only in the movies, a chilly morning after, played without dialogue in a silent, stealthy atmosphere, two lovers, a set of takes down a long corridor, a sudden climax, close-up, hold it . . . cut, fin, print. It opens with the sound effect of floorboards creaking underfoot. I mix *kishikishi to* with the footsteps of *fumeba* in the light onomatopoeia of "tiptoeing," so as not to wake the neighbors, and it feels a little shivery in the cold, too. For suspense, I take the unexpected *fui no* away from *kuchizuke* so as to set the kiss up for last, pick up the squeaky floor that was skipped over, and close with the kiss. Instead of an ordinary kiss, the word is broken down into its parts, *kuchi* and *tsuke*, "mouths pressed together" in a good, long kiss that, with its *m*'s, you can feel and taste. *Kaeri no*, meaning that Takuboku is going back to his place, winds up on the cutting-room floor.

Here's another poem that told me what to do, but had a different set of instructions:

oya to ko to	father and son
	minds apart
hanarebanare no kokoro mote	face to face
shizuka ni mukau	
	in awkward silence
kimazuki ya na zo	why—?

(ITZ, p. 404)

Here, by using the common *to* and *to* pattern, plus the reduplicative word *hanarebanare* for "separating in two," and instead of the usual written form of *mukau* 向う , meaning "to face," the Chinese character 對 that basically means "a matched pair," Takuboku establishes a set of three matched pairs to concretize his standoff with his father. This determined the paired wordings in the first three lines of my version, especially in the second and third lines.

Every poem so far has been selected to show what I think are its advantages. Indeed, when busy translating, I had the same luxury, picking and choosing out of a great many only those that seemed to suit me and that I felt I could handle. Those that didn't work out, I threw away. Lest anyone think the rest are perfect gems, however, there are lapses I'm all too aware of and still others I'm not, no doubt. Anyway, for the record, here's something of a blooper, and a well-known poem of Takuboku's at that:

hatarakedo	I work, work
	and still
hatarakedo nao waga kurashi	no joy in my life
raku ni narazaru	

| | I stare |
| *jitto te o miru* | at my hands |

(ITZ, p. 407)

Of course, *raku* doesn't translate as "joy" in this context, but means "to be making a comfortable living." Maybe a better way to do it is

> I work, work
> and still
> can't make it
> I stare
> at my hands

but then again, maybe it isn't. I'm so used to the old version, this one seems like a gruff intruder.

Just as in a poem tale, each of my translations, like the examples I've chosen, has a unique story to tell about itself, but all share certain general features of style. The most conspicuous is their colloquial tone. Vernacular is rich in poetic qualities. I don't mean faddish expressions that quickly date themselves, or argot spoken in closed circles, but the enduring demotic idiom that is common property, the voice of everyday life and experience in any language. Takuboku sought to get the flavor of that into his tanka. But barriers exist between actual talk and written language. Speech often loses voice and color on paper and may need reworking to get it back. In this respect, historically, Takuboku's attempt was transitional. His poems still contain literary language, and their everyday quality comes as much from the subject matter as from the style. Nevertheless, true to his aims, I tried to give the translations a colloquial ring. It's the language I love best, and with no traditional literary diction of a long-established form to overcome, my page was somewhat more open to its usages.

There was a natural joining point in the formal demand for brevity and the laconic quality of American colloquial idiom, and the two came together very well. I didn't have to force colors or accents on a poem, either. All it took was the right turn of phrase here and there to voice it. For example, here in

hetsurai o kikeba	flattery
	riles me—
hara tatsu waga kokoro	pretty sad

| | to know yourself |
| *amari ni ware o shiru ga kanashiki* | too well |

(ITZ, p. 401)

where the second line does the trick for *hara tatsu*. The poem has another instance of Takuboku's frequent use of *kanashiki*, to which I give an idiomatically rueful touch with "pretty sad." Note how in his line breaks here, Takuboku cuts still more deeply across the thirty-one-syllable structure but still preserves it.

A colorful, everyday expression I was happy at the chance to use appears in the first two lines of

yogoretaru tabi haku toki no	give me
	the creeps
kimi waruki omoi ni nitaru	some memories
	like putting on
omoide mo ari	dirty socks

(ITZ, p. 447)

for the original's *kimi waruki*, and in the next poem, serendipity turns a reasonably close rendering of the Japanese into slang in English in my last two lines of

doko yori ka	walking at night
nagare yosenishi	along the sea
yashi no ne no	I feel like a coconut
hitotsu to omoi	washed up
iso yuki yube	from nowhere

(ITZ, p. 185)

for the first two lines of the original, adding some apt overtones. Takuboku composed this poem before he turned to the three-line format, and wrote it down in one line.

A colloquial solution that I think works perfectly for a difficult phrase to translate is the fourth line in

| *nan to naku asu wa yoki koto* | somehow |
| *aru gotoku* | |

colloquial poems, whose tone cues readers to hear something similar. But ordinary language, when sculpted, also has a latent voice that finds its personal ring in the voice of the reader. This is one of the keys to Takuboku's popularity, since it allows readers to hear themselves in his poems.

Takuboku is the subject of every poem he writes. Even in the most detached scene, one senses him there. He found lasting qualities in the minutiae of daily experience, and such fleeting thoughts and incidents in his personal life, brought into sharp focus with telling detail, make up the content of his poems. His aim, as he described it, was to get his real feelings into a poem, "a long and complicated process" of self-discovery.[19] Characteristically, however, Takuboku went much further than that. He denied any difference in quality or kind between his feelings and experiences as a poet and those of anybody else and came to the remarkable insight that to identify oneself as "poet" was a form of self-mystification that could spoil one's writing and sever the crucial link with one's true inner self.[20] Shedding a literary identity, to become "human" first, if you will, Takuboku grips his audience as few poets can. His hold on readers is a personal one. His plainspokenness, writing about daily life out of hard-won self-knowledge and sincerity, gives the poems a living presence that not only wins immediate empathy from his readers (a considerable achievement in itself) but also carries with it a strong sense of mutuality on Takuboku's part that is felt by the reader and results in a close understanding, even a merging of identities, between them.

Shouldn't a translator strive to achieve that same presence? For a poet as personal as Takuboku, there is no other choice except to (pretend to) be the subject of the poems. Since this is so, translating Takuboku becomes not so much a poetic exercise—rendering an image here, a nuance of feeling there—as the creation of a living character, a complete personality running through all of the poetry's swings of mood and temper, in other words, a performance, akin to acting. To be frank, it was not difficult to find that character or persona. All I had to do, it seemed, was keep a dictionary handy. The script was letter perfect and rang bells in me. I am sure many of Takuboku's readers will tell you that. The hard part, the most challenging and exhilarating, was to translate those feelings onto paper. That process I've already described as best I could. In a way, the visual approach to form that I took, composing the poem texts as word paintings, gives them a certain presence of their own. A few notices point to a "fusion" between Takuboku and myself, and in the *Japan Times*, Donald Richie went so far as to say that I had "*become* Takuboku" (emphasis his) in the translations.[21] Those are the things actors like to hear! But such expressions of reader engagement with these versions went far beyond what I had dared hope for.

I've heard the chemistry between poets and translators spoken of as a form of possession in which the spirit of a poet holds someone in thrall, bent to the texts. Some see it the other way around today, the translator fixing like a parasite on a poet's work for exploitation and self-aggrandizement.[22] I won't answer for either. It does start with one person reading what another has written, and these close encounters often are a matter of chance. But sometimes, as in real life, the two may get off to a better start if properly introduced. That's what happened to me in a seminar on Meiji literature, when Professor Keene suggested I read Takuboku's tanka. In Keene's seminars, you produced a paper or translation to be published, and he was quite willing to propose something, not out of a hat, but in light of what he knew about your interests. A year before, immersed in Chinese literature, I took his seminar in nō drama; he promptly suggested I read Komparu Zenchiku's play *Yōkihi*, derived from a poem by the T'ang poet Po Chü-i. That project led to my dissertation, "Nō Drama and Chinese Literature." One might say that that was only to be expected of one's teacher; in fact, the suggestion was so obviously apt, I took it for granted. But what instinct for a student's interest can compare with Professor Keene's introducing me to a poet whose absolute rightness (and practically his very existence) I had no inkling of whatsoever? For that, and obviously more than that, this student is deeply grateful.

My hopes for Takuboku's poems in English are those Takuboku had for his own, to reach a wide audience, one ordinarily shy of most poetry. Takuboku didn't live to see it, but his short poems are some of the most popular texts, traditional or modern, ever composed in Japan. A large audience for a body of modern poetry is especially significant, as the genre is ignored by general readers everywhere, and so despite a view gaining currency that translation as a bridge between cultures is a "weary cliche . . . utterly bereft of any meaning whatsoever,"[23] in the interests of cultural understanding, Takuboku is a rare literary discovery. But Takuboku's tanka do go beyond being solely of cultural interest, since their hold on readers is personal, and being directly and acutely that, giving incidental moments of life poignancy and value, they illuminate the daily world of parents and children, love, marriage, work, friends, troubles, stray thoughts, random impulses—the private, personal world in which each of us lives. Prompting the recognition of oneself so moving for so many Japanese readers, for an American reading them, the poems have an added dimension: they bridge personal worlds across cultures. Neither the incomprehensible "other" nor a utopian vision of universal humanity, they talk to an American reader about what is humanly familiar in a down-to-earth meeting between individuals, as close and true to a real-life encounter as a work of literature can produce.

A vast amount of poetry is being written in America today, the result of thousands of workshops and a boom in poetry-writing programs in colleges and universities, testifying to widespread interest in the art. But all the books and big and little journals printed year after year fail to satisfy the natural hunger that an ordinary reader has for a good poem. Many even of the "best" award-winning works are inbred products that need hype, and often self-induced brainwashing by their small coteries of readers, to establish value or interest in them. All, including the few good poets, are shunned by the general reader. In style and intention, Takuboku's poetry is altogether different from these works, and its popularity, in Japan at least, makes it a proven exception to the rule. The translations try in English to do what he did, and I think that in the attempt—in their language and content, compactness, and visual sense of form—they break new ground in American poetry as well. With luck, in a new edition, they might just win Takuboku a following among American readers, and maybe even influence other poets in their direction also.

NOTES

1. Original texts of Takuboku's tanka are referenced by page number as they appear in Ishikawa Masao, ed., *Ishikawa Takuboku zenkashū* (hereafter abbreviated as *ITZ*) (Tokyo: Kawade shobō, 1964).

2. Not that it can't be done on commission for a small group of tanka in a totally different vein than Takuboku's. See Jonathan Norton Leonard, *Early Japan* (New York: Time-Life Books, 1968), pp. 125–35, for my thirty-one-syllable versions of ten tanka from the sixteenth-century illustrated scroll *Sanjūniban shokunin uta-awase emaki*.

3. *nani ga nashi ni / atama no naka ni / gake arite / higoto ni tsuchi no kuzururu gotoshi* (*ITZ*, p. 408).

4. *sunayama no suso ni yokotawaru ryūboku ni / atari mimawashi / mono iite miru* (*ITZ*, p. 395).

5. *kanashiki wa Otaru no machi yo / utau koto naki hitobito / koe no arasa yo* (*ITZ*, p. 438). *Koyakko to iishi onna no / yawarakaki / mimitabo nado mo wasuregatakari* (*ITZ*, p. 444).

6. *dai to iu ji o hyaku amari / suna ni kaki / shinu koto o yamete kaeri* (*ITZ*, p. 396). *[Ishikawa wa fubin na yatsu da.] / toki ni kō jibun de iite, / kanashimite miru.* (*ITZ*, p. 479).

7. *ima mo nao / koi ni shinu hito / arikakaru / daiji wa shisho ni / shiru subekarikeru* (*ITZ*, p. 93).

8. *waga hige no / shitamuku ga ikidōroshi / konogoro nikuki otoko ni nitareba* (*ITZ*, p. 398). *ishi hitotsu / saka o kudaru ga gotoku ni mo / ware kyō no hi ni itaritsukitaru* (*ITZ*, p. 417).

9. *yo ake made asobite kurasu basho ga hoshi / ie o omoeba / kokoro tsumetashi* (*ITZ*, p. 411). *kano toshi no kano shimbun no / hatsuyuki nokiji o kakishi wa / ware narishi kana* (*ITZ*, p. 439).

10. *uttori to / hon no sashie ni nagameiri, / tabako no kemuri fukikakete miru.* (*ITZ*, p. 470).

11. *tawamure ni haha o seoite / sono amari karuki ni nakite / sampo ayumazu* (*ITZ*, p. 396).

12. *te mo ashi mo / heya ippai ni nagedashite / yagate shizuka ni okikaeru kana* (*ITZ*, p. 400). *ware ni nishi tomo no futari yo / hitori wa shi ni / hitori wa rō o idete ima yamu* (*ITZ*, p. 406).

13. *itsu mo kuru/kono sakamise no kanashisa yo/yūhi aka aka to sake ni sashiiru* (*ITZ*, p. 458). *yoru osoku teisha-ba ni iri/tachisuwari/yagate ideyukinu bō naki otoko* (*ITZ*, p. 461).

14. *itsu made ka,/kono miakitaru kakegaku o/kono mama kakete oku koto yaran.* (*ITZ*, p. 474).

15. Roy E. Teele, *Literature East & West* (March 1967):90–91.

16. Carl Sesar, trans., *Poems to Eat* (Tokyo and Palo Alto, Calif.: Kodansha International, 1966).

17. Amy Vladeck Heinrich, *Fragments of Rainbows: The Life and Poetry of Saitō Mokichi, 1882–1953* (New York: Columbia University Press, 1983), p. xiv.

18. Donald Keene, ed., *Anthology of Japanese Literature* (New York: Grove Press, 1955), p. 388.

19. Kindaichi Kyosuke et al., eds., *Takuboku zenshū*, 8 vols. (Tokyo: Chikuma shobō, 1967–1968), vol. 4, pp. 207–8.

20. Ibid., pp. 213–14.

21. *Japan Times*, February 22, 1967, p. 10.

22. Paul Mann, "Translating Zukofsky's Catullus," *Translation Review* 21, 22 (1986): 7–8.

23. Ellen Elias-Bursac, "Savior, Spy: Thinking About What We Do," *Metamorphoses* 1 (April 1993): 26.

28

The Selected Poems of the Thirty-six Immortal Poets of Fujiwara Kintō

◉

MILDRED TAHARA

The compiler of the *Man'yōshū*, Ōtomo Yakamochi (718–785), wrote about two sages of poetry, one most certainly Kakinomoto Hitomaro and the other either Yamanoue Okura or Yamabe Akahito. By the time the *Kokinshū* was compiled in 905, the two sages of poetry were Hitomaro and Akahito. Ki no Tsurayuki, the compiler of the *Kokinshū*, lists the *rokkasen*, or Six Poetic Geniuses, as Ariwara Narihira, Ono no Komachi, Sōjō Henjō, Bun'ya Yasuhide, Ōtomo Kuronushi, and Kisen Hōshi. In subsequent centuries, other groups of Six Poetic Geniuses were organized. For example, among the "New Six Poetic Geniuses" were Yoshitsune, Jichin, Shunzei, Teika, Ietaka, and Saigyō.[1]

Fujiwara Kintō (966–1041), a court noble whose accomplishments in poetry, music, and art influenced the most talented men and women of the Heian court at its height, compiled such anthologies of *waka* poetry as *Shūishō* (Selections from the Gleanings, ca. 996–97), *Kingyokushū* (Gold and Jade Collection, ca. 1007), and *Shinsō hishō* (Private Selections from the Secluded Chamber, ca. 1008). Kintō's *Wakan rōeishū*, a collection of Japanese and Chinese verse compiled around 1013, was immensely influential for centuries. The poems in this collection were endlessly quoted and alluded to in literary and dramatic works and excerpts copied by famous calligraphers. As a critic, Kintō wrote the treatises *Shinsen zuinō* (Newly Compiled Essentials of Poetry, ca. 1002) and *Waka kuhon* (The Nine Styles of Waka, ca. 1009).

Of lasting influence also was Kintō's selection of the Thirty-six Immortal Poets. Leading artists of the day painted their portraits, and leading calligraphers copied their poems on colorful decorated paper, sometimes with flecks of gold or silver foil, which themselves are treasured works of art. The close tie between image and text can be seen in art collections throughout the United States. For example, the Los Angeles County Museum's Shin'enkan Collection has a handsome pair of six-fold screens of the four seasons by Sakai Hōitsu (1761–1828), featuring Kintō's Thirty-six Poets. Each portrait is accompanied by a poem in elegant calligraphy on a poem card (*shikishi*), sixteen of which are artistically arranged on each screen.[2] The portrait of Saigū no Nyōgo, along with a brief biography and a poem, that belongs to the Agedatami series, is one of the many treasures of the Freer Gallery, in Washington, DC.[3]

Kintō was a poet in his own right and took part in poetry contests, for which he often served as judge. It is believed that Kintō's first list of Thirty Immortal Poets (*sanjūnin*) was based on the Saki no jūgoban utaawase (Former Fifteen-Round Poetry Match). These poets were active when the *Man'yōshū*, the *Kokinshū*, and the *Gosenshū* (ca. 951) were compiled; none of them was from the period of the *Shūishū* (ca. 1006). The Thirty Poets were divided into two teams, the Left and the Right, each represented by an outstanding poem. But this was not an actual poetry contest, as the poems were not judged. Rather, it was an artistic way of presenting what were already recognized to be fine poems. Nonetheless, many examples of image and text pair different poets as though they belonged to opposing teams in a poetry contest. Kintō probably selected the poets of the Nochi no jūgoban utaawase (Later Fifteen-Round Poetry Match), which included him, Egyō, and others of the *Shūishū* period. Kintō selected the two groups of poets between the first month of 1007 and the third month of 1009.[4]

In 1007 or 1008, a ten-round poetry match was held by Kintō, who supported Tsurayuki, and Prince Tomohira, who favored Hitomaro, for the purpose of deciding who had been the superior poet. Although the final judgment was not recorded, each poem—ten by Hitomaro and ten by Tsurayuki—was studied for its strengths and weaknesses. According to different sources, Hitomaro's poem was judged the winner in seven matches, and Tsurayuki's poem came out on top in the remaining three contests. But another source states that eight of Hitomaro's poems were judged superior, one a tie, and one inferior to Tsurayuki's.[5]

Kintō's *Sanjūrokuninsen* (Selected Poems of the Thirty-six Immortal Poets) was compiled after 1007–8. (The *Gunsho ruijū* text used in the *Shinpen kokka taikan* contains 150 poems.) The Thirty-six Poets were divided into two teams, each poet represented by ten or three poems which, we may assume, were Kintō's favorites. No attempt was made to single out the one best poem. On the

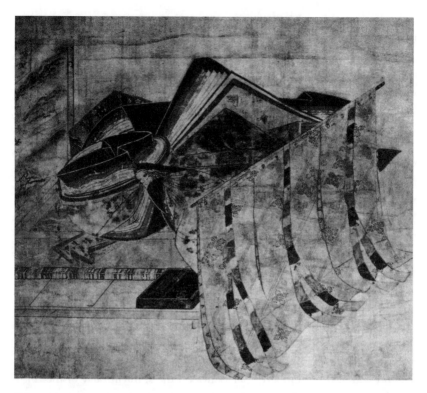

Illustration 28.1.   Portrait of Saigū no Nyōgo from the *Agedatamibon Sanjūrokkasen-e*, thirteenth century. (COURTESY OF THE FREER GALLERY OF ART, WASHINGTON, DC.)

Left team were Hitomaro, Mitsune, Yakamochi, Narihira, Sosei, Sarumaru, Kanesuke, Atsutada, Kintada, Saigū no Nyōgo, Toshiyuki, Muneyuki, Kiyotada, Okikaze, Korenori, Koōigimi, Yoshinobu, and Kanemori. On the Right team were Tsurayuki, Ise, Akahito, Henjō, Tomonori, Komachi, Asatada, Takamitsu, Tadamine, Yorimoto, Shigeyuki, Saneakira, Shitagō, Motosuke, Motozane, Nakabumi, Tadami, and Nakatsukasa.

Of the thirty poets in Kintō's earlier collection, the *Sanjūninsen*, only Fukayabu is missing from the Thirty-six Immortal Poets. Among the 150 poems in the *Sanjūrokuninsen* are 113 poems of the 130 contained in the *Sanjūninsen*. Thirty-seven of the 150 poems are not included in the *Sanjūninsen*, seventeen of which are not found in the *Sanjūrokuninsen*, which was compiled after Prince Tomohira died.

In his research, Kyūsojin Hitaku discovered an expanded version of the *Sanjūrokuninsen*: the "original" 150 plus sixty-nine waka. Kyūsojin does not believe, however, that Kintō oversaw this longer version. A few of these additional poems can also be found in Teika's *Hyakunin isshu*.

There also is a shorter version of the *Sanjūrokuninsen*, with one poem by each of the Thirty-six Poets in the form of an eighteen-round poetry match. Likewise, there are various *kasen-e* (portraits of the immortal poets) dating back to the Kamakura period, such as those referred to as Satakebon, Agedatamibon, Gotoba-inbon, and Narikanebon.

The various texts of the *Sanjūrokuninsen* are thought to have been copied by such luminaries as Koōigimi, Kōzei, Kintō, Shunrai, Saigyō, and Shunzei. By far the most impressive are the Nishi Honganji (a temple in Kyoto) texts which were discovered in 1896, thanks to the efforts of Ernest Fenollosa and Okakura Tenshin.[6] These texts were shown to the public in August 1944, and an exhibition was organized at the Kyoto National Museum in 1952. The poems—more than 6,400—had been copied by some twenty calligraphers, on various kinds of paper.

It is believed that these texts were produced in 1112 to celebrate the sixtieth birthday of Emperor Shirakawa (1053–1129, r. 1072–1086), a patron of arts and letters. Official documents record that celebrations were observed at three different places, the one at the imperial palace in Kyoto being the most elaborate. The beautiful texts, later designated a National Treasure, were probably presented to ex-Emperor Shirakawa on the sixteenth day of the third month of Ten'ei 3 (1112), more than a hundred years after Kintō selected the Thirty-six Immortal Poets.[7]

The Selected Poems of the Thirty-six Immortal Poets

HITOMARO

1	*kinō koso*	Yesterday the old year
	toshi wa kureshika	drew to its close; already
	harugasumi	spring mists have begun
	kasuga no yama ni	to rise and swirl heavenward
	haya tachinikeri	covering Mount Kasuga.

SIS I: 3, *SH* 1, *MYS* X: 1843, *Sanjūninsen* 1, *WRS* 77, Yakamochi 2,[8] Akahito 141

6	*honobono to*	Faintly in the morning
	akashi no ura no	mists of Akashi Bay

Illustration 28.2. From the Nishi Honganji collection, *Sanjūrokunin kashū*, poems by Lady Ise. (Courtesy of the Itsuo Museum, Osaka, Japan.)

asagiri ni	his boat vanishing
shimagakureyuku	among the myriad islands—
fune o shi zo omou	so go my thoughts in its wake.

KKS IX: 409, KGS 47, SH 75, WRS 647, Sanjūninsen 7, SJG 29, Satake 1, Fujifusa, Hitomaro 210

7	*tanometsutsu*	Though I trusted you,
	konu yo amata ni	many are the nights you failed
	narinureba	to come to visit me;
	mataji to omou zo	I spent more nights determined
	matsu ni masareru	not to wait than nights waiting.

SIS XIII: 848, Shō 284, SH 71, WRS 788, Hitomaro 203

Kakinomoto Hitomaro (fl. ca. 680–700). Active in court of Empress Jitō (r. 690–697) and Emperor Mommu (697–707); regarded as saint of poetry; *Sanjūrokuninsen*, poems 1–10.

TSURAYUKI

13	*hana mo mina*	So forlorn the dwelling
	chirinuru yado wa	where all the cherry petals
	yuku haru no	have fallen to the ground,
	furusato to koso	transformed into the old home
	narinuberanare	of the departing spring.

SIS I: 77, Shō 53, WRS 57, KGS 22, SW 115, Sanjūninsen 13, Tsurayuki 8

15	*miru hito mo*	No one there to see
	nakute chirinuru	yet scattered from the trees
	okuyama no	deep in the mountains—
	momiji wa yoru no	the bright leaves of autumn
	nishiki narikeri	are rich brocade seen at night.

KKS V: 297, SW 82, WRS 316, KGS 30, Sanjūninsen 16

16	*sakura chiru*	Balmy is the wind
	ko no shita kaze wa	blowing about the petals
	samukarade	under the cherry trees,
	sora ni shirarenu	and snow unknown to the world
	yuki zo furikeru	falls and carpets the ground.

SIS I: 64, Shō 42, KGS 14, SH 25, Sanjūninsen 17, SW 81, SJG 1, Satake 19, Agedatami, Fujifusa,
Tsurayuki 716

Ki no Tsurayuki (ca. 872–945). Compiler of *Kokinshū*; though of middle rank, a leading professional
poet; patronized by Kanesuke and Sadakata; wrote preface to *Kokinshū* and *Tosa nikki*; compiler of
Shinsen waka; reached junior fifth rank, upper grade, in 943; *Sanjūrokuninsen*, poems 11–20.

MITSUNE

22	*ka o tomete*	Who would not break off
	tare orazaramu	a branch of plum when enticed
	ume no hana	by the blossoms' scent?
	ayanashi kasumi	O cruel mist of spring,
	tachi na kakushi so	do not conceal the blossoms!

SIS I: 16, Shō 15, SH 7, WRS 95, Mitsune 303

24	*waga yado no*	After the blossoms
	hana migatera ni	have fallen from the trees,
	kuru hito wa	I will long for all
	chirinamu nochi zo	who visit me at my home
	koishikarubeki	to view them at their best.

KKS I: 67, KGS 16, SH 20, WRS 124, Sanjūninsen 24, KRJ 4042, SJG 2, Agedatami, Gotoba-in, Fujifusa

28	*kokoro ate ni*	So hard to distinguish
	orabaya oramu	from the first frost that forms—
	hatsushimo no	as I grope blindly about
	okimadowaseru	I may pick a few
	shiragiku no hana	white chrysanthemums—

KKS V: 277, SW 100, KGS 32, SH 55, WRS 273, EGTG 48, HIS 29, KRJ 3744

Ōshikōchi Mitsune (d. ca. 925). Minor bureaucrat; a compiler of *Kokinshū*; highly regarded as professional poet; *Sanjūrokuninsen*, poems 21–30.

ISE

31	*aoyagi no*	The drops of spring rain
	eda ni kakareru	glistening on the branches
	harusame wa	of the green willow

ito mote nukeru	appear like precious jewels
tama ka to zo miru	pierced and strung one by one.

SCSS I: 23, *WRS* 86, *Sanjūninsen* 31, Ise 101

34	*chiri chirazu*	Have all the blossoms
	kikamohoshiki o	fallen from the boughs?
	furusato no	This I'd like to ask of
	hana mite kaeru	one who happens by
	hito mo awanamu	on his return from my old home.

SIS I: 49, *Shō* 30, *KGS* 19, *SH* 24, *Sanjūninsen* 34, *SJG* 4, Ise 95

37	*miwa no yama*	How can I wait
	ika ni machimimu	endlessly on Mount Miwa?
	toshi fu tomo	I know all too well
	tazunuru hito mo	no one will come to visit me
	araji to omoeba	as year after year slips by.

KKS XV: 780, *SW* 357, *KGS* 63, *KS* 69, *Sanjūninsen* 40, Satake 20, Tameie, Fujifusa, Ise 3

Lady Ise (ca. 872–after 938). Daughter of Fujiwara Tsugukage, who served as governor of Yamato and Ise; consort of Emperor Uda (r. 887–897) and mother of daughter, Nakatsukasa, whose father was Prince Atsuyoshi, son of Emperor Uda; *Sanjūrokuninsen*, poems 31–40.

YAKAMOCHI

42	*saoshika no*	In the early morn
	asa tatsu ono no	the stag stands in the meadow;
	akihagi ni	on the bush clover
	tama to miru made	lie the transparent dewdrops,
	okeru shiratsuyu	so resembling glittering gems.

MYS IX: 1598, *SW* 60, *Sanjūninsen* 48, Satake 3, Agedatami, Fujifusa

Ōtomo Yakamochi (717–785). Compiler of *Man'yōshū*; numerous poems in *Man'yōshū*; *Sanjūrokuninsen*, poems 41–43.

AKAHITO

46	*waka no ura ni*	When the tide rises
	shio michi kureba	here at Waka Bay, the waves

kataonami	come rushing in;
ashibe o sashite	crying, the cranes fly across,
tazu nakiwataru	heading for the reedy shore.

MYS VI: 924, *ShokuKKS* XVIII: 1634, *KGS* 48, *WRS* 451, *KRJ* 4353, *SJG* 30, Satake 21, Narikane, Fujifusa, Akahito 115, 352

Yamabe Akahito (fl. early eighth century). Dates unknown; probably served in the court of Emperor Shōmu (r. 724–749); outstanding poems included in *Man'yōshū*; rated highly by Tsurayuki in his kana preface to *Kokinshū*; Akahito compared favorably with Hitomaro; *Sanjūrokuninsen*, poems 44–46.

NARIHIRA

47	*yo no naka ni*	If the delicate
	taete sakura no	blossoms ceased to exist
	nakariseba	in this transient world,
	haru no kokoro wa	so tranquil and unruffled
	nodoke karamashi	would my heart be in spring.

KKS I: 53, *KGS* 15, *SH* 19, *WRS* 123, *SJG* 5, *Sanjūninsen* 44, Satake 4, Gotoba-in, Fujifusa, Narihira 4

Ariwara Narihira (825–880). One of the Six Poetic Geniuses; grandson of Emperors Kammu and Heizei; brother of Yukihira; head chamberlain of junior fourth upper rank; hero of *Ise monogatari*; *Sanjūrokuninsen*, poems 47–49.

HENJŌ

50	*sue no tsuyu*	A drop at the tip and
	moto no shizuku ya	one at the stem of
	yo no naka no	a dew-drenched leaf—
	okuresakidatsu	those who precede us in death
	tameshi naruramu	and those who linger on.

SKKS VIII: 757, *SH* 85, *Sanjūninsen* 41, *EGTG* 66, *SJG* 6, Satake 22, Narikane, Fujifusa, Henjō 15

Priest Henjō (Yoshimine Munesada, 816–890). Served Emperor Nimmyō (r. 833–850), following whose death he became a monk in 850; father of the priest Sosei; one of Six Poetic Geniuses; *Sanjūrokuninsen*, poems 50–52.

SOSEI

53	*ima komu to*	She said she would come
	iishi bakari ni	presently, but the dawn moon

nagatsuki no	in the long ninth month
ariake no tsuki o	is my only visitor
machiidetsuru kana	while I waited for her to come.

KKS XIV: 691, *KGS* 44, *SH* 65, *WRS* 789, *Sanjūninsen* 50, *SJG* 3, *KRJ* 2827, Satake 5, Sosei 24

Priest Sosei (Yoshimine Harutoshi, fl. ca. 890). Son of Henjō; forced by father to become Buddhist monk; major *Kokinshū* poet; active in poetry contests and *byōbuuta*; *Sanjūrokuninsen*, poems 53–55.

TOMONORI

56	*yū sareba*	When evening shadows fall,
	saho no kawara no	the plover that has lost his mate
	kawagiri ni	in the mist that rises
	tomo madowaseru	along the banks of the Saho
	chidori nakunari	River plaintively cries.

SIS IV: 238, *Shō* 143, *KGS* 34, *SH* 48, *SW* 140, *Sanjūninsen* 68, *SJG* 13, Satake 23, Agedatami, Gotoba-in, Tameie, Fujifusa, Tomonori 21

Ki no Tomonori (ca. 845–905). Older cousin of Tsurayuki; prominent poet during Emperor Uda's reign; compiler of *Kokinshū*; *Sanjūrokuninsen*, poems 56–58.

SARUMARU

59	*ochikochi no*	Deep in the mountain,
	tazuki mo shiranu	so dark one cannot tell
	yamanaka ni	where one is heading,
	obotsuka naku mo	I feel a vague uneasiness
	yobukodori kana	when I hear the cuckoo's song.

KKS I: 29, Satake 6, Agedatami, Tameie, Fujifusa, Sarumaru 46

Sarumaru (Sarumaro). Nothing is known about this poet. Some early sources speculated that he was Yuge no Ōkimi, grandson of Prince Shōtoku or Shiki no Miko, son of Emperor Kōnin; mentioned in the Chinese preface to *Kokinshū*; if Sarumaru actually existed, he lived at the end of the Nara or the early Heian period; *Sanjūrokuninsen*, poems 59–61.

KOMACHI

64	*iro miede*	In this wretched world,
	utsurou mono wa	that which grows pale and fades away,
	yo no naka no	never revealing

hito no kokoro no	its true color, is the flower
hana ni zarikeru	in the heart of a man.

KKS XV: 797, *Sanjūninsen* 92, Satake 24, *SJG* 15, Komachi 35

Ono no Komachi (b. before 830). Court lady; one of Six Poetic Geniuses; active around 850 at end of Emperor Nimmyō's reign (r. 833–850); legendary beauty; *Sanjūrokuninsen*, poems 62–64.

KANESUKE

67	*hito no oya no*	Though not in darkness,
	kokoro wa yami ni	truly the heart of a parent
	aranedomo	will become so confused
	ko o omou michi ni	for love of his child,
	madoinuru kana	it knows not where it goes.

GSS XV: 1102, *SH* 86, *Sanjūninsen* 53, *YM* 61, *SJG* 11, Satake 7, Narikane, Tameie, Fujifusa, Kanesuke 127

Fujiwara Kanesuke (877–933). Known as Tsutsumi Chōnagon, since he had a residence on the Kamo River embankment (*tsutsumi*); father of sons Masatada, Kiyotada, and Morotada, of a daughter Sōshi, who became a concubine of Emperor Daigo (r. 897–930); great-grandson of Fuyutsugu; sixth son of Toshimoto; cousin, son-in-law, and close associate of Sadakata; great-grandfather of Murasaki Shikibu; patron of Tsurayuki and Mitsune; gifted poet; rose to the rank of middle counselor, junior third rank; *Sanjūrokuninsen*, poems 65–67.

ASATADA

70	*au koto no*	If we were fated
	taete shinaku wa	never again to meet,
	nakanaka ni	I'll not resent
	hito o mo mi o mo	the one I dearly love
	uramizaramashi	nor regret my wretchedness.

SIS XI: 678, *Shō* 235, *KGS* 45, *SH* 69, *HIS* 44, *Sanjūninsen* 56, *SJG* 12, Satake 45, Fujifusa, Asatada 6

Fujiwara Asatada (910–966). Father, Sanjō Udaijin Sadakata; mother, daughter of Yamakage Chūnagon; served Emperors Daigo (r. 897—930), Suzaku (r. 930–946), and Murakami (r. 946–967); *Sanjūrokuninsen*, poems 71–73.

ATSUTADA

72	*aimite no*	Comparing the way
	nochi no kokoro ni	I once felt about you

kurabureba	to my feelings now
mukashi wa mono mo	following a night of love,
omowazarikeri	I hadn't loved at all before.

SIS XII: 710, *Shō* 257, *SH* 70, *Sanjūninsen* 61, *HIS* 43, Satake 8, Agedatami, Fujifusa, Atsutada 143

Fujiwara Atsutada (906–943). Third son of Tokihira, younger brother of Akitada; rumored to have been killed by vengeful ghost of Sugawara Michizane, whom Tokihira ordered into exile; rose to rank of provisional middle counselor; *Sanjūrokuninsen*, poems 71–73.

TAKAMITSU

75	*kaku bakari*	In this world so full
	hegataku miyuru	of endless sorrow and pain,
	yo no naka ni	how envious am I
	urayamashiku mo	of the unsullied moon
	sumeru tsuki kana	serenely shedding light.

SIS VIII: 435, *WRS* 765, Eiga 3, Satake 26, Narikane, Takamitsu 35

Fujiwara Takamitsu (939–994). Grandson of Emperor Daigo; son of Morosuke, minister of the right (d. 960); became priest and built monastery at Tōnomine; protagonist in *Tōnomine Shōshō monogatari*; *Sanjūrokuninsen*, poems 74–76.

KINTADA

77	*yukiyarade*	I hesitated
	yamaji kurashitsu	all day long to amble on
	hototogisu	along the mountain path;
	ima hitokoe no	I longed to hear once more
	kikamahoshisa ni	the cuckoo's song.

SIS II: 106, *Shō* 69, *KGS* 23, *WRS* 184, *Sanjūninsen* 62, *SJG* 9, Satake 9, Agedatami, Tameie, Kintada 8

Minamoto Kintada (889–948). Grandson of Emperor Kōkō (r. 884–887); excelled in hawking and incense blending; served Emperor Daigo (r. 897–930); son Saneakira married Nakatsukasa; *Sanjūrokuninsen*, poems 77–79.

TADAMINE

80	*haru tatsu to*	They tell me today
	iu bakari ni ya	is the first day of spring;

miyoshi no no	are the misty mountains
yama mo kasumite	of beautiful Yoshino
kesa wa miyuramu	visible this morning?

SIS I: 1, *Shō* 1, *KGS* 2, *SH* 2, *WRS* 8, *Sanjūninsen* 71, *EGTG* 1, *SJG* 7, Satake 27, Gotoba-in, Tameie, Fujifusa, Tadamine 1

Mibu Tadamine (868–920). Of middle rank but active as poet; participated in Kambyō Era Poetry Contest, the poetry contest at the palace of Prince Koresada; a compiler of *Kokinshū*; *Sanjūrokuninsen*, poems 80–82.

SAIGŪ NO NYŌGO

83	*koto no ne ni*	The pine wind sweeping down
	mine no matsukaze	from the mountain peak will blend
	kayou nari	harmoniously with
	izure no o yori	the music of the koto.
	shirabe somekemu	Which strings should I play first?

SIS VIII: 451, *Shō* 514, *KGS* 57, *SH* 87, *WRS* 469, *SJG* 21, Satake 10, Agedatami, Narikane, Gotoba-in, Fujifusa, Saigū 57

Saigū no Nyōgo (Princess Kishi, 929–985). Also known as Shōkōden no Nyōgo; daughter of Prince Shigeakira, fourth son of Emperor Daigo; mother was Kanshi, daughter of Fujiwara Tadahira (Teishinkō); high priestess at Ise shrine from 938 to 946; entered court of Emperor Murakami in 948; mother of daughter Kishi, named priestess of Ise in 975; mother and daughter returned to capital in 984 when En'yū became emperor; *Sanjūrokuninsen*, poems 83–85.

YORIMOTO

88	*tsukubayama*	Harder than ever fall
	itodo shigeki ni	the maple leaves of red and gold
	momijiba wa	on Tsukuba's peak;
	michi mienu made	buried under the fallen leaves
	chiri ya shinuramu	the path is no longer seen.

Satake 28, Agedatami

Ōnakatomi Yorimoto (d. 958). Son of Sukemichi, provincial governor of Higo; father of Yoshinobu; excelled in waka; active in court of retired Emperor Uda; composed silk screen poems and congratulatory poems; served as head priest of Ise shrine; *Sanjūrokuninsen*, poems 86–88.

TOSHIYUKI

89   *aki kinu to*   That autumn has come
      me ni wa sayaka ni   isn't immediately clear
      mienedomo   when I gaze about me,
      kaze no oto ni zo   but I can't help being startled
      odorokarenuru   by the sound of the blowing wind.

KKS IV: 169, *WRS* 206, *Sanjūninsen* 65, Satake 12, Agedatami, Toshiyuki 14

Fujiwara Toshiyuki (d. 901). Father, Fujimaro; mother, daughter of Ki no Natora; son-in-law of Ki no Aritsune; brother-in-law of Narihira; head chamberlain, junior fourth upper rank; favorite of Emperor Uda; *Sanjūrokuninsen*, poems 89–91.

SHIGEYUKI

92   *yoshinoyama*   When did the mantle
      mine no shirayuki   of snow on Yoshino's peak
      muragiete   melt away and in
      kesa wa kasumi no   the chill of early morning
      tachiwataru kana   the swirling mists enshroud the land?

SIS I: 4, *KGS* 3, *Sanjūninsen* 74, Satake 29, Agedatami, Shigeyuki 221

Minamoto Shigeyuki. Dates unknown; grandson of Prince Sadamoto; son of Kanenobu; later became adopted son of his uncle Kanetada; served as provisional governor of Sagami; close associate of Taira Kanemori and Fujiwara Sanekata; *Sanjūrokuninsen*, poems 92–94.

MUNEYUKI

95   *tokiwa naru*   With the coming of spring,
      matsu no midori mo   even the vibrant green
      haru kureba   of the young pine
      ima hitoshio no   turns into a darker lovely
      iro masarikeri   emerald hue.

KKS I: 24, *SW* 11, Satake 11, Agedatami, Narikane, Muneyuki 9

Minamoto Muneyuki (d. 939). Grandson of Emperor Kōkō (r. 884–887); son of Prince Koretada; nephew and friend of Emperor Uda (r. 887–897); senior fourth rank, lower grade; *Sanjūrokuninsen*, poems 95–97.

SANEAKIRA

99   *koishisa wa*   Your love for me
    onaji kokoro ni   may not be as great as mine,
    arazu to mo   but won't you tonight
    koyoi no tsuki o   gaze up as I do at the moon
    kimi mizarame ya   with a yearning as intense?

SIS XIII: 787, *Sanjūninsen* 82, Satake 30, Gotoba-in, Tameie, Fujifusa, Saneakira 33

Minamoto Saneakira (910–970). Son of Kintada; provincial governor of Bingo, 947–953; husband of Nakatsukasa; governor of Wakasa, Shinano, Echigo, and Mutsu; *Sanjūrokuninsen*, poems 98–100.

KIYOTADA

101   *nenohi shi ni*   The seedling in the field
    shimetsuru nobe no   marked off for the Day of the Rat—
    hime komatsu   do not uproot it yet—
    hikade ya chiyo no   wait till it casts a shadow
    kage o matamashi   a thousand years from today.

WRS 33, *Sanjūninsen* 83, Satake 13, Narikane, Kiyotada 6

Fujiwara Kiyotada (d. 958). Second son of Kanesuke; excelled in composing silk screen poems; junior fifth rank, lower grade; provincial governor of Kii; *Sanjūrokuninsen*, poems 101–103.

SHITAGŌ

104   *mizu no omo ni*   When I count the months
    teru tsukinami o   while gazing at the lovely moon
    kazoureba   reflected in the pond,
    koyoi zo aki no   I realize this evening
    monaka narikeru   marks the midpoint of autumn.

SIS III: 171, *Shō* 115, *WRS* 251, *Sanjūninsen* 86, *SJG* 26, Satake 31, Agedatami, Narikane, Fujifusa

Minamoto Shitagō (911–983). Son of Kozoru; one of Five Poets of Pear Pavilion; joined Poetry Bureau in 951; a compiler of *Gosenshū*; died when provincial governor of Noto; excelled in both *kanshi* and waka; *Sanjūrokuninsen*, poems 104–106.

OKIKAZE

108   *tare o kamo*   Since the dark green pines
      shiru hito ni semu   of Takasago are not
      takasago no   my friends of bygone years,
      matsu mo mukashi no I wonder who I can turn to
      tomo naranaku ni   as my soul's companion.

KKS XVII: 909, *SW* 204, *WRS* 740, *HIS* 34, Satake 14, Okikaze 28

Fujiwara Okikaze. Poet-bureaucrat active during Emperor Uda's reign, together with Toshiyuki, Tomonori, and Tadamine; participated in Kambyō Era Poetry Contest and Teiji no In Poetry Contest; *Sanjūrokuninsen*, poems 107–109.

MOTOSUKE

110   *aki no no no*   If only I might have
      hagi no nishiki o   in my garden the brocade leaves
      waga yado ni   of the bush clover
      shika no nenagara   in the autumn meadow
      utsushite shi gana   and the stag that sadly cries.

WRS 285, *Sanjūninsen* 96, *SJG* 16, Hōbutsushū 441, Satake 32, Narikane, Gotoba-in, Fujifusa, Motosuke 23

Kiyowara Motosuke (908–990). Grandson of Fukayabu; son of Harumitsu; son of daughter of Takashina Toshinari; father of Sei Shōnagon; provincial governor of Suō and Higo; *Sanjūrokuninsen*, poems 110–112.

KORENORI

113   *miyoshino no*   A lovely mantle
      yama no shirayuki   of pure white snow lies deeply
      tsumorurashi   on Yoshino's peak;
      furusato samuku   here in my old village
      narimasarunari   the cold intensifies.

KKS VI: 325, *KGS* 38, *SH* 60, *WRS* 382, *SJG* 17, *Sanjūninsen* 93, *KRJ* 229, Satake 15, Korenori 23

Sakanoue Korenori. Dates unknown; father of Mochiki; participated in Kambyō Era Poetry Contest of 893, imperial excursion to Ōi River in 907, and Teiji no In Poetry Contest of 913; *Sanjūrokuninsen*, poems 113–115.

MOTOZANE

116 *toshigoto no*
     haru no wakare o
     aware to mo
     hito ni okururu
     hito zo shirikeru

How painful it is
to part with the spring each year;
I who am always
bidding friends farewell
know all too well this sadness.

KGS 67, *SH* 89, *WRS* 639, *SJG* 18, Satake 33, Gotoba-in, Tameie, Motozane 191

Fujiwara Motozane (fl. ca. 950). Dates unknown; third son of Kiyokuni; junior fifth rank, lower grade; active during Tenryaku era (947–957) of Emperor Murakami (r. 946–967); *Sanjūrokuninsen*, poems 116–118.

KOŌIGIMI

119 *iwabashi no*
     yoru no chigiri mo
     taenubeshi
     akuru wabishiki
     kazuraki no kami

The vows we exchanged
on the stone bridge that night
are bound to be broken;
O god of Kazuraki,
how sad it is at dawn!

SIS XVIII: 1201, *Shō* 469, *KGS* 64, *SH* 91, *Sanjūninsen* 99, *SJG* 22, Satake 16, Agedatami, Gotoba-in, Fujifusa, Koōigimi 12

Koōigimi. Also read Koōgimi or Kodai no kimi; called Sakon when serving in crown prince's palace; dates unknown; one source states that Koōigimi was a daughter of Prince Shigeakira and of Teishinkō's daughter, thus a sister of Saigū no Nyōgo; *Sanjūrokuninsen*, poems 119–121.

NAKABUMI

122 *ariake no*
     tsuki no hikari o
     matsu hodo ni
     waga yo no itaku
     fuke mo yuku kana

I waited patiently
for the lovely moon to shed
its radiant light
at dawn; as I did so
the night of my life advanced.

SIS VIII: 436, *Shō* 501, *KGS* 68, *SH* 90, *Sanjūninsen* 102, *SJG* 19, Satake 34, Agedatami, Narikane, Gotoba-in, Fujifusa

Fujiwara Nakabumi (923–992). Grandson of Okinori; son of Kinkazu; acquainted with Fujiwara Yoritada, Kaneie, and Michikane; friend of Kiyowara Motosuke, Ōnakatomi Yoshinobu, Fujiwara Kintō, and Sugawara Sukeaki; *Sanjūrokuninsen*, poems 122–124.

YOSHINOBU

126   *momiji senu*   By its own cries,
       tokiwa no yama ni   the lonely stag dwelling
       tatsu shika wa   on Mount Tokiwa,
       onore nakite ya   where the leaves have yet to turn
       aki o shiruramu   crimson, knows that autumn's here.

SIS III: 190, *Shō* 102, *WRS* 336, *KGS* 29, *Sanjūninsen* 106, Tameie, Fujifusa, Shigeyuki 26

Ōnakatomi Yoshinobu (921–991). Son of Yorimoto and father of Sukechika; grandfather of Ise Tayu; one of Five Poets of Pear Pavilion; compiler of *Gosenshū*; head priest of Ise shrine; *Sanjūrokuninsen*, poems 125–127.

TADAMI

128   *nenobi suru*   No seedling pine have I
       nobe ni komatsu no   to celebrate the New Year's
       nakariseba   out in the meadow.
       chiyo no tameshi ni   What, then, am I to present
       nani o hikamashi   to wish my lord life eternal?

SIS I: 23, *Shō* 20, *KGS* 8, *SH* 13, *Sanjūninsen* 108, Narikane, Tadami 85

Mibu Tadami. Dates unknown; son of Tadamine; middle rank but active as court poet; participated in Tentoku Era Poetry Contest; active during Tenryaku and Tentoku eras (947–960); *Sanjūrokuninsen*, poems 128–130.

KANEMORI

131   *kazoureba*   When I pause to count,
       waga mi ni tsumoru   many are the months and years
       toshitsuki o   I have muddled through.
       okurimukau to   Why are people so eager
       nani isoguramu   to see in another year?

SIS IV: 261, *Shō* 162, *KGS* 39, *SH* 62, *WRS* 396, *Sanjūninsen* 111, *SJG* 27, Satake 18, Agedatami, Gotoba-in, Fujifusa

132   *miyama idete*   Did the cuckoo emerge
       yowa ni ya kitsuru   from within the mountain's depths

hototogisu	in the hush of night?
akatsuki kakete	I hear its melodious song
koe no kikoyuru	in the first faint flush of dawn.

SIS II: 101, *Shō* 65, *Sanjūninsen* 112, Kanemori 97

135   *kurete yuku* The autumn drawing
   aki no katami ni to a close leaves behind it,
   oku mono wa as a memento,
   waga motoyui no a thin layer of white frost
   shimo ni zarikeru on the cord that binds my hair.

SIS III: 214, *Shō* 133, *KGS* 31, *SH* 52, *WRS* 278, *Sanjūninsen* 115

Taira Kanemori (d. 990). Grandson of Prince Koretada; son of Atsuyuki, governor of Chikuzen; identified in *Fukurozōshi* as father of Akazome Emon; composed many *byōbuuta*; *Sanjūrokuninsen*, poems
131–140.

NAKATSUKASA

142   *uguisu no* Were it not for
   koe nakariseba the sweet song of the warbler,
   yuki kienu how would the village
   yamazato ikade in the mountains high above
   haru o shiramashi ever know spring is here?

SIS I: 10, *Shō* 6, *KGS* 4, *SH* 6, *WRS* 74, *Sanjūninsen* 122, *SJG* 28, Satake 36, Gotoba-in, Fujifusa

143   *isonokami* When I make my way
   furuki miyako o to the ancient capital
   kite mireba of Isonokami,
   mukashi kazashishi I see at their height the blossoms
   hana sakinikeri the courtiers once wore in their caps.

SKKS I: 88, *SH* 15, *WRS* 529, Narikane, Kiyotada 7, Nakatsukasa 24

145   *sayaka ni mo* How often tears spring
   mirubeki tsuki o to my eyes as I gaze
   ware wa tada up at the moon above!
   namida ni kumoru Such breath-taking loveliness

ori zo ōkaru   should always be bright and clear

SIS XIII: 788, *Sanjūninsen* 125, Saneakira 34, Nakatsukasa 191

Nakatsukasa. Dates unknown; daughter of Ise and Prince Atsuyoshi, minister of central affairs (Nakatsukasa no kyō); friend of Fujiwara Saneyori, Taira Kaneki, Prince Motoyoshi, and Prince Tsuneaki; wife of Saneakira; participated in poetry contests; composed many *byōbuuta*; *Sanjūrokuninsen*, poems 141–150.

Abbreviations of Poetry Collections

EGTG	*Eiga taigai*
GSS	*Gosenshū*
HIS	*Hyakunin isshu*
KGS	*Kingyokushū*
KKS	*Kokinshū*
KRS	*Kokinrokujō*
KS	*Kindai shūka*
MYS	*Man'yōshū*
SCSS	*Shinchokusenshū*
SH	*Shinsō hishō*
ShokuGSS	*Shoku Gosenshū*
ShokuKSS	*Shoku Kokinshū*
Shō	*Shūishō*
SIS	*Shūishū*
SJG	*Saki no jūgoban utaawase*
SKKS	*Shinkokinshū*
SKS	*Shikashū*
SSZS	*Shinsenzaishū*
SW	*Shinsen waka*
WRS	*Wakan rōeishū*
YM	*Yamato monogatari*

Index of First Lines (from the *Sanjūrokuninsen*)

au koto no (70)

chiri chirazu (34)

hana mo mina (13)

haru tatsu to/iu bakari ni ya (80)

hito no oya no (67)

honobono to (6)

ima komu to (53)

iro miede (64)

isonokami (143)

iwabashi no (119)

ka o tomete (22)

kaku bakari (75)

kazoureba (131)

kinō koso (1)

koishisa wa (99)

kokoro ate ni (28)

koto no ne ni (83)

kurete yuku (135)

miru hito mo (15)

miwa no yama (37)

miyama idete (132)

miyoshino no (113)

mizu no omo ni (104)

momiji senu (126)

nenobi shi ni (101)

nenobi suru (128)

ochikochi no (59)

sakura chiru (16)

saoshika no (42)

sayaka ni mo (145)

sue no tsuyu (50)

tanometsutsu/konu yo amata ni (7)

tare o kamo (108)

tokiwa naru (95)

toshigoto no (116)

tsukubayama (88)

uguisu no (142)

waga yado no/hanamigatera ni (24)

waka no ura ni (46)

yo no naka ni (47)
yoshinoyama (92)
yukiyarade (77)
yū sareba (56)

NOTES

1. Kyūsojin Hitaku, *Sanjūrokuninsen* (Tokyo: Hawawa shobō, 1960), p. 29. The *Shinrokkasen* were compiled by both unknown and historical figures. Some of the collections include five poems by each of the Six Poets; others only four or even one poem each. Retired Emperor Gomizuno'o selected only poems on the cherry blossoms, for example, and Karasumaru Mitsuhiro chose only autumn poems by each of the six.

2. The poems selected are included in Kintō's *Sanjūrokuninsen*, with the exception of the *Gosenshū* poem (GSS, vol. 1, poem 19) accompanying the stylized portrait of Mitsune. This choice of a lesser-known spring poem by Mitsune probably reflects the personal tastes of either the calligrapher or the patron. A handsome reproduction of this pair of six-panel screens may be found in Miyeko Murase's *Masterpieces of Japanese Screen Painting* (NewYork: Braziller, 1990), pp. 161–66.

3. She is the only one seated on a raised tatami in the Satake series and is often represented only by a curtain of state in group depictions of Kintō's Thirty-six Poets, such as those of Ogata Kōrin and Sakai Hōitsu.

4. Kyūsojin, *Sanjūrokuninsen*, pp. 33–36.

5. Ibid., pp. 37–40. The competition, I imagine, was as intense and serious as the image and text competition described in the "E-wase" chapter and the perfume-blending and calligraphy contests described in the "Umegae" chapter of *The Tale of Genji*. The emphasis here was on the aesthetic refinement of the two arbiters and their familiarity with the waka tradition.

6. Examples from the *Mitsune shū* (one of the most exquisite), *Ise shū* (known for its superb collage), and *Tsurayuki shū* are striking. *Ise shū* and *Tsurayuki shū*, vol. 2, were fragmented and sold; mounted fragments can be seen in art museums (including some in the United States) and private collections.

7. Sources for this chapter are Akiyama Ken, ed., *Nihon bungaku zenshi—Chūko* (Tokyo: Gakutōsha, 1978); Kinoshita Masao, *Sanjūrokunin kashū (Nihon no bijutsu)*, no. 168 (Tokyo: Shibundō, May 1980); *Kokuhō Sanjūrokuninshū* (Tokyo: Kabushikigaisha bijitsu shoin, 1947); Komachiya Teruhiko, *Ōchō no kajin*, vol. 7 of *Fujiwara Kintō* (Tokyo: Shūeisha, 1985); Kyūsojin Hitaku, *Nishi Honganjibon Sanjūrokuninshū seisei* (Tokyo: Kazama shobō, 1966); *Sanjūrokuninshū* (Tokyo: Hanawa shobō, 1960); Taniyama Shigeru et al., eds. *(Shimpen) kokka taikan*, 5 vols. (Tokyo: Kadokawa shoten, 1986).

8. When a poet's name is mentioned following a translation, it refers to the Nishi Honganji text. In this example, it is poem number 2 in the Nishi Honganji text of the *Yakamochi shū*.

29

Translating Modern Japanese Plays: A Case for Cultural Transformation

TED T. TAKAYA

There is a long tradition in America of the professional performance of plays translated into English. When great works—from Ibsen's *A Doll's House* and *Hedda Gabbler* and Chekhov's *Three Sisters* and *The Cherry Orchard* to more recent modern plays—are presented, the public assumes they will be given in English, unless otherwise indicated. Although scholars may argue over the relative merits of the translations, the professional theater offers a wide range of plays, especially those written in European languages. By contrast, such performances of modern Japanese plays in English have had a rather brief and sporadic history. I saw my first performance by professional actors while I was attending Columbia University as a graduate student. Two of Mishima Yukio's modern nō plays, *Hanjo* and *The Lady Aoi*, were given as experimental theater on November 15, 1960, at the Theater de Lys by ANTA (American National Theater and Academy). Previous performances from Mishima's series of modern nō plays had been given in New York, Honolulu, San Francisco, and Newport, Rhode Island. The other notable performance, which I attended, was the American premiere of Abe Kōbō's *Friends*, presented by the Milwaukee Theater Company for a six-week run beginning January 27, 1978, at the Todd Wher Theater in Milwaukee, Wisconsin. All these plays were translated by Donald Keene.[1]

The outstanding success of *Friends* clearly demonstrated that a modern Japanese play addressing important themes affecting all humanity would appeal to an American audience. Although certain aspects from the Japanese cultural tradition may still seem exotic and even puzzling to some Americans, this fact should no longer discourage modern Japanese plays from being considered for the professional stage. Nonetheless, despite Donald Keene's pioneering efforts, there has been little progress in preparing Japanese plays for performance in American theaters.

In the meantime, the growing number of modern Japanese drama groups performing abroad have received international recognition and prestigious awards, especially in Europe. These theatrical productions are undoubtedly of the highest caliber, and the members cited for their accomplishments are deserving of the honors accorded by their professional peers in other countries. But it still seems important to question how well an average audience appreciates such a performance presented entirely in Japanese. A theatergoer may grasp some aspects of the play through the intonation and gestures of the actors, the makeup, wardrobe, music, set design, and other nonverbal features, and the program notes may further illuminate the plot, acts, and scenes. In addition, with the aid of surtitles, subtitles, and wireless earphones providing simultaneous translations and running commentaries, even an uninitiated audience may go away feeling that their theatrical experience was on a par with that of an audience that understands Japanese. But viewed more critically, even the up-to-date electronic devices are just stop-gap measures that cannot provide the vital missing link, the opportunity of totally involving the hearts and minds of the entire audience, which is the goal of every performing art.

Because English versions of plays in European languages have had a long history on the American stage, perhaps this same approach—translating the plays—could be the solution. At the present time, essentially one type of published modern Japanese play is available. They often are accompanied by a brief introduction providing background for the general reader; others may offer a more detailed analysis of the characters, themes, and ideas, which may be of greater interest to students, scholars, and professions with a special interest in the field. The dialogue of most of these translated plays, however, reveals an uneven mixture of literary and theatrical styles. How could this occur when the original Japanese plays were written for the stage?

I believe that most of these translated plays use the same familiar conversational style found in the novels and short stories of modern literature, whose authors intended to be read in the context of the ongoing narrative. On the other hand, the dramatist designs the dialogue of a play to be spoken by the actors, who in turn, through both words and action, convey to the theater audience the playwright's intended meaning. Whereas the author addresses the reader, the dramatist addresses the actors and the audience, always aware that they are crucial participants in the complex process of transforming a stage dialogue into a live theatrical performance.

But why even bother raising this issue of "stage worthiness" when few contemporary Japanese plays ever find their way to the professional stage in America, and even amateur productions on college campuses are rare? Perhaps Japanese playwrights should look for professional recognition elsewhere than on the stage. After all, only a handful of contemporary Japanese plays are translated into English each year, but even being read in translation is preferable to total obscurity. Besides, an English translation offers far greater exposure nationwide than would a theatrical performance that may run for even several weeks but may be limited to one location. Finally, why should a Japanese dramatist demand more of a translation than that it meet the stringent editorial standards of an established publisher and is read as literature by an appreciative readership whose opportunity to see a stage production is probably nonexistent?

The recurring question is whether the translator owes the Japanese dramatist any obligation beyond the formal agreement covering the permission to translate the play and comply with the publisher's guidelines. Must contemporary Japanese playwrights abandon any hope of having their plays performed in English, or even of protecting their reputation as dramatists, by demanding the same standard of excellence already employed by translators who create English versions of modern European plays? Is there a place for translations of modern Japanese plays that takes into account the artistic aspirations of the original playwright, whose goal is to communicate directly with the theater audience?

I believe that in striving to bring out the stage worthiness of the original work, the translator must be able to move the play into a different cultural context. In other words, a conscientious translator must find words, phrases, and lines in English as close as possible in meaning to those of the original play, even though it will be performed for an entirely different audience.

I know of no simple way to describe the cultural transformation required to translate a play so that it may be presented on the stage, but the following incident, related to the opening of *Friends*, may be useful. In a discussion held in Tokyo during January 1978, John Dillon (artistic director of the Milwaukee Repertory Theater), Abe Kōbō, and Donald Keene were exchanging views on how eel, a favorite Japanese dish mentioned in the play, should be treated in the English version. The American director suggested hamburger as a better choice, but finally they settled on veal cutlet. As Keene explained,[2] eel is not an ordinary food that Japanese eat everyday. On the other hand, it would not be on the menu of a first-class restaurant; it was something in between. Those familiar with both Japanese and American food would know that veal cutlet had a better chance of being accepted without hesitation or resistance by the Milwaukee audience. Indeed, at the very mention of eel, if the audience started to laugh, scream, or react inappropriately, it might destroy the mood that the play was trying to create. The troublesome eel is part of a dialogue in which the family members are thinking of possible places where their next victim might be found. The lines are recited to a guitar accompaniment, and the specific reference occurs when Grandmother says, "They're eating eels and rice." (*Friends*, scene 6, p. 56). This popular dish is prepared by grilling fillets of eel over hot charcoal and placing them on top of hot, freshly cooked rice served in large individual bowls. Interestingly, the reference to eel was a rare instance of "exoticism" found by the American director in a translation otherwise tailor-made for the Milwaukee audience. Later on, Young Son whispers, "*Kobone bakari no niboshi mitai ni*" (Like a dried sardine, with only little bones) (scene 6, p. 56). In the Japanese text, the fish is *niboshi*, any small dried fish—including sardines—used for making stock. Sardines, however used, should not trouble an English-speaking audience.

If a successful play translation is one that can communicate the dramatist's intent to the English-speaking audience, the translator must first decide whether the play was intended to be read or to be performed. Although stage plays from William Shakespeare to Tennessee Williams do make good reading, they were written to be performed. Similarly, a play translation that is meant to be presented on the stage also may be enjoyable to read, reconfirming its ability to communicate effectively with the audience.

In fall of 1979, I wrote the following preface to my collection of modern Japanese plays: "All the translations . . . are intended primarily to be read as dramatic literature and not to be used in their present form for immediate stage presentation."[3] This matter of stylistic discrepancy is relevant only when the English versions of contemporary Japanese plays are measured by the professional standards of a stage play. Insofar as stage worthiness is not a criterion in the assessment of these play translations, my statement still seems relevant.

In a book of translations of plays by Abe Kōbō, Donald Keene describes the inseparable link between the dialogue and the actors, referring to the translator's difficulty in formulating lines for the stage that can be spoken easily: "Such problems, faced by every translator, are particularly troublesome when translating dialogue that must flow naturally from the mouths of actors and actresses. I hope that if these plays are performed in English the actors will modify the words to accord most easily with their own speech."[4] This statement shows Keene's concern for the frustration of those actors who must deal with badly written lines and reveals his approach to translating modern Japanese plays to be performed on stage.

Rather than dwelling on the negative aspects of current play translations, however, a more constructive approach might be to provide several examples from *Friends* illustrating how one translator (Donald Keene) of modern Japanese plays created a script that can be both read and staged. It is important to remember that Keene states nowhere in his translation of *Friends* that it was designed for the stage. Nevertheless, he demonstrates that his main goal went beyond the reading public to a theater audience reached only through a stage performance.

Some of the scenes in *Friends* deal with commonplace, daily conversation heard in a family setting, but the ease with which the audience can follow the action on the stage does not mean that the original text was written in rather elementary Japanese. The translator, fully aware of how differences in generation, gender, age, and other aspects of the Japanese cultural tradition are conveyed in spoken Japanese, has meticulously transformed them into a more familiar context for the English-speaking audience. Another point to keep in mind is that the reader of a play translation may judge the translator's skill by the more striking, climactic scenes. In a play script, however, the translator may be better judged by the intervals in which dramatic action is relatively absent, and the translator must use greater ingenuity and effort to sustain the audience's attention. To do this, the translator must find expressions in colloquial English that convey the meaning of the original text and must avoid any lapses that might diminish the sense of credibility while the play is being performed.

The following extended excerpt from *Friends* illustrates how a rather ordinary scene can still be theatrically absorbing. In this scene, a minor family conflict develops when Man, being held captive by the family of the title—who barged into his apartment one day and took total control of his life—accuses Grandmother, searching for a package of cigarettes, of being a sneak thief:

MAN	(*suddenly becoming aware of Grandmother's suspicious activities*):
	It's all very well for you to talk, but what are you doing there, anyway?
GRAND-MOTHER:	I was just looking for a cigarette.
MAN:	Cut it out! Stop acting like a sneak thief!
GRAND-MOTHER	(*with exaggerated dismay*): Oh—I'm a sneak thief, am I?

FATHER: Of course you're not a sneak thief. I ask you all to refrain from mak-
                 ing remarks that might cast aspersions on anyone else's character.

ELDER SON: How about setting a fine of 100 yen on any remark decided by the
                 majority vote to be offensive?

FATHER: An excellent suggestion. Yes, that appeals to me. There's no such
                 thing as being too discreet when it concerns a person's character,
                 is there?

GRAND-
MOTHER   (*more engrossed than ever in her search for cigarettes*): Imagine calling
                 me a sneak thief! A cigarette only turns to smoke, no matter who
                 smokes it.

MAN: Stop rummaging that way through my desk!

                 (*Man, thinking he will stop Grandmother, steps forward automatically, only
                 for Elder Son to stick out his foot adroitly and trip him. Man flops down
                 magnificently.*)

ELDER SON: Oops—Excuse me!

                 (*The family at once rushes over to Man in a body and surrounds him, lifting him
                 to his feet, massaging his back, brushing the dust from his suit, and otherwise
                 showering him with extreme attentions.*)

ELDEST
DAUGHTER: Are you sure you're all right?

MOTHER: You haven't hurt yourself?

YOUNGER
SON: Can you stand okay?

GRAND-
MOTHER: No pain anywhere?

FATHER: No broken bones?

MAN   (*freeing himself*): Lay off for God's sake!

ELDER SON   (*apologetically*): I'm sorry. I was just worried you might get so carried
                 away by your feelings you would resort to violence.

MAN: Wouldn't you describe what you did as violence?

YOUNGER
SON   (*cheerfully*): We won't let you get away with that! Allowing yourself to
                 get involved in a quarrel is just the same as starting one. You'll have to
                 pay a fine. Or would you rather make amends in kind?

ELDER SON   (*dejectedly*): I don't have to tell you how hard up I am for money.

ELDEST
DAUGHTER: But even if he prefers to make amends in kind, it won't be easy. How can anybody trip himself?

YOUNGER
SON: Can't you think of anything better to do than butt into other people's business? Do you plan to go on removing nail polish forever? It's just a matter of time before you dissolve your finger tips. (*to Man*) I wonder if you'd mind tripping my brother back?

MAN   (*angrily*): Don't be an idiot!

YOUNGER
SON: It can't be helped, then. I'll take over as your substitute.

(*As soon as Younger Son finishes speaking, he gets up and deftly trips Elder Son, who falls over with a loud groan. Younger Son at once drags Elder Son to his feet, only to trip him again, without allowing him an instant's respite. He repeats this a third time and is about to trip him a fourth time when Man, unable to endure any more, cries out.*)

MAN: That's enough, for God's sake!

MOTHER   (*relieved*): At last, he's forgiven you.

ELDER SON   (*grimacing with pain and rubbing the small of his back*): Thanks.

YOUNGER
SON: Well, what do you know? Perspiring seems to have relieved my hangover a little.

(*scene 6, pp. 32–34*)

A few examples of the changes by the translator to facilitate the transformation from one cultural context to another show how it is done:

MAN: The insurance agent in the apartment below is a nut for *poker*. (emphasis added)

(*scene 1, p. 14*)

In the Japanese text, the game of chance is mah-jongg, a game imported from China but now a popular pastime in Japan. The translator could have left it as a Chinese game, but "nut for poker" perfectly conveys the sense of what Man really meant to say.

GRAND-

MOTHER: The proof of the pudding is in the eating.

(scene 6, p. 31)

Ron yori shōko is a proverb corresponding to the lexically adequate translation, "Action speaks louder than words," but because Grandmother is constantly identified with cooking and the kitchen, she is more likely to say "Proof of the pudding."

GRAND-

MOTHER: Let me see, how did it go again? It's all written down in *Mother Goose*.

(scene 6, p. 57)

Iroha karuta, a popular recognition game, uses the Japanese phonetic syllabary, usually forty-seven in case of this parlor game, and requires the players to know all the proverbs made up from each kana in the syllabary comprising the reading set. Each card in the companion set spread before the players contains a single syllable and a picture describing the proverb. The object of the game is to pick up the most matching cards while the proverbs are read aloud. A number of verses in *Mother Goose* were probably familiar to Grandmother when she was a child, and both the Japanese game of cards and the English rhymes involve popular sayings, the point she is trying to make.

YOUNGER

SON: But there's no use crying over spilled milk.

(scene 13, p. 93)

The irony of this English line becomes apparent if compared with the Japanese text, whose meaning is roughly "what's done is done." In fact, the translator "improves" on the Japanese line by underscoring the shocking action of Middle Daughter, who makes a habit of putting a fatal dose of poison in the milk, always the prelude to the departure of the mysterious family to adopt another "friend" who will become their next victim.

Donald Keene translates all of his plays as though they are intended for the American professional stage. For him, stage worthiness is the responsibility of the translator of a drama; that is, the translator must preserve the artistic integrity of the original play while translating it into a viable stage script in English. But up to the opening of *Friends*, such an opportunity for a professional theatrical presentation with an extended run had not been available—nearly ten years after its publication.

It should be evident by now that the first qualification for translating plays is a high level of proficiency in Japanese. Only an experienced translator can bring to the English version the assurance of authority and credibility after the translation has been transformed into another cultural context. But even for someone fluent in Japanese, creating a successful play script is a slow and painstaking task.

A bit of literary style in the dialogue of a translated play that otherwise observes a conversational style may not be disturbing to most readers. But if such lines are spoken on the stage, they may sound stilted and unnatural. A beautifully conceived dialogue overflowing with brilliant literary expressions, though a joy to read, can cause problems for actors trying to articulate them on stage.

Perhaps ideally, the most comprehensive test for a play translation in English is an actual stage production given by professional actors under the management of an established director and presented before a live audience. To make a proper assessment, both the Japanese playwright and the translator should be present to evaluate the audience's response and to determine how closely the translation meets their expectations. Interestingly, the American professional premiere of *Friends* held in Milwaukee included all these components for conducting such a test. This performance, however, did not come about by chance. Donald Keene's reputation as a scholar and translator of Japanese literature and drama had already been well established for more than two decades before *Friends*. He also was a long-time personal friend of Abe Kōbō and thoroughly familiar with the author's many works; he had attended many of the Abe plays and had often visited his acting studio. Furthermore, he had already translated the original version of *Friends* some years before (1969). In addition to translating Abe's plays, Keene had translated a number of plays by Mishima Yukio, another literary giant, and these plays had already been staged in America.

Unless more plays approaching the level of performability attained in Donald Keene's translations become available, there is little hope for modern Japanese plays to become serious contenders for the professional stage. The present practice of settling for readability alone and overlooking the dramatic capabilities of modern Japanese plays does a disservice to both the publishers and the Japanese playwrights.

From my own experience, a translation that tries to serve as a play script requires more time and effort than one meant primarily to satisfy the reading public. But who would be willing to assume such a seemingly unrewarding task?

In creating a viable play script, the translator must always keep in mind that a play must be performed within a prescribed time with no needless interruptions or delays that may distract the audience. On the printed page, a poor choice of words may be shrugged by the reader off as a minor annoyance and may not interfere with the reading itself. On the other hand, for the stage, the translator must sustain a smooth flow of dialogue so that the audience can easily follow without interruption each word or line spoken by the actors: a single discordant moment can shatter the mood of a critical scene.

Today, when there is no pressing demand for professional productions of modern Japanese plays, English translations meant for the stage may remain largely unnoticed and recognized only as literature to be read. But perhaps it is too early to despair, for after all, the future director of the Milwaukee Repertory Theater read Donald Keene's original version of *Friends* when he was still in college, and it was his dream to one day put it on stage. Years later, in 1978, under his direction, the first professional performance of a full-length modern Japanese play in America opened to a capacity crowd that attentively sat through the entire performance, easily grasping Abe's sardonic commentary on the destruction of the individual in an urbanized society. As a member of the Milwaukee audience, I, too, shared in appreciating the Japanese dramatist's sardonic humor and felt that the playwright's artistic intention had been communicated accurately.

The performance of *Friends* provided a spectacular view of Donald Keene's painstaking care in translating the original Japanese work. In short, that evening was an unforgettable exercise in demonstrating why the translator must maintain a constant dynamic balance between promoting the theatrical element of the English dialogue while preserving the accuracy of the original Japanese text. Keene readily drew the audience into the dark and macabre mood of the Abe play and prompted their spontaneous response to certain scenes and lines rendered in English that might usually be expected of an audience that actually understood the dialogue in Japanese.

My first venture into the area of theatrical performance happened under the most unlikely circumstances. Only a year had passed since *Friends* played in Milwaukee as the first modern Japanese drama on the American professional stage, and so the possibility of a similar production elsewhere in America seemed out of the question. Moreover, my *Modern Japanese Drama* was to be published in a few weeks, requiring last-minute work to meet the deadline. In the midst of this activity, in late March 1979, my neighbor, a free-lance writer, invited me to a small gathering for David Wassermann, who had written the stage script for *Man of La Mancha*, the celebrated Broadway musical (1965–1971). On the morning after our proposed meeting, I was scheduled to fly to Los Angeles for a discussion with my editor on the upcoming book.

When *Man of La Mancha* opened in Tokyo in 1969, its translated version with an all-Japanese cast had a very successful run, and Dave Wasserman was a familiar name among theatergoers in Japan. When we met, we shared views on presenting a theatrical production in another language. In the course of our discussion, I gave him a short summary of the play *Hokusai Sketchbooks*, which traces the flamboyant career of the celebrated nineteenth-century artist, and, at Wasserman's request, gave him a copy of my English translation. He was struck by the remarkable similarities between Hokusai and Don Quixote, both of whom displayed an indomitable, dauntless spirit in the pursuit of their own ideals, although in different historical and cultural contexts. The talk soon turned to the possibility of putting *Hokusai Sketchbooks* on the American stage. Wasserman encouraged me to contact the East West Players, a well-established repertory theater in Los Angeles, noted for its outstanding productions focusing on Asian Pacific themes. When I arrived in Los Angeles, I telephoned them and was asked to send the manuscript for review. After several weeks, my translation was accepted and later became part of the 1980–81 season. I was not asked to do any rewriting. At the premiere of *Hokusai Sketchbooks* in February 1981, which I attended with its Japanese playwright, Yashiro Seiichi, I found to my relief that the dialogue had undergone no major revisions. The *Los Angeles Times* (February 18, 1981) called the production "one of East West's classiest," and the play ran for two months.

Flattering as it was to have an English version selected for a stage production, if the translator attends the opening performance, he or she must be prepared to confront the reactions of the critics and the theatergoers. The translator also faces the more personal concern of how the audience's response will affect the dramatist if he has made a special trip from Japan to attend the American premiere. There is no guarantee that a production will be successful, a risk inherent in any artistic endeavor. Yet here lies the unique thrill of an opening night, at which the translator can savor the satisfaction of having shared in a worthwhile creative goal with a Japanese playwright—the realization of a theatrical performance given in English.[5]

There is an ephemeral aspect to all performing arts. Like the proverbial soufflé, a successful play script requires a master chef, who must serve it quickly to an eagerly awaiting customer, who in turn must eat it quickly before it collapses, leaving not a trace behind. Granted, consuming an evening's performance at the theater may take a little longer, but once it is over, the only substantial evidence that such an event ever occurred may be the play translation itself, whose dormant stage magic will not be released until the next opening curtain.

In the current state of modern Japanese plays in America, where the goal of the translator has not yet been defined, Donald Keene has upheld the best interest of the Japanese playwright, striving to make each of his translations into a viable play script.[6]

NOTES

1. Translations appear in Abe Kōbō, *Friends*, trans. Donald Keene (New York: Grove Press, 1969). Citations in the text refer to this edition. Mishima Yukio, *Five Modern Nō Plays*, trans. Donald Keene (New York: Knopf, 1957).

2. This episode is from the interview with John Dillon in "John Dillon: The Director's Perspective," in *Prologue* (Milwaukee Repertory Theater Company), January 27, 1978.

3. Ted Takaya, ed. and trans., *Modern Japanese Drama: An Anthology* (New York: Columbia University Press, 1979), p. x. The following plays are included: Abe Kōbō's *You, Too, Are Guilty*; Mishima Yukio's *Yoroboshi: The Blind Young Man*; Yashiro Seiichi's *Hokusai Sketchbooks: A Play in Three Acts*; Yamazaki Masakazu's *The Boat Is a Sailboat: A Play in Three Acts and an Epilogue*; Betsuyaku Minoru's *The Move: A Play in Six Scenes with a Solemn Epilogue*.

4. Donald Keene, *Three Plays by Kōbō Abe* (New York: Columbia University Press, 1993), pp. xii-xiii.

5. By that time, my translation of *Yoroboshi: The Blind Young Man*, one of Mishima Yukio's *Modern Nō Plays*, had premiered at the Open Space Theater in Soho, New York City, in May 1980—more than a year earlier than *Hokusai Sketchbooks*—and it ran concurrently with another play in the Mishima cycle, *Sotoba Komachi*, translated by Donald Keene. In March 1988, Betsuyaku Minoru's *The Move* had its world premiere during the Japan Today Festival held at the Riverside Theatre on the campus of the University of Ulster, Coleraine, Northern Ireland.

6. I also believe that his play translations reveal the best of all the most admirable qualities of Donald Keene as both a scholar and the teacher I encountered as a graduate student many years ago.

Once, the regular instructor for a Japanese class had fallen ill, and Donald Keene turned out to be the temporary replacement; I had never had him as a teacher before. Rather than using the regularly assigned text on contemporary Japanese reading, he chose Kawabata Yasunari's *Yukiguni* (Snow Country). Laying aside the usual line-by-line method of literal translation, stressing grammar and syntax, he allowed us to work out our own English version, focusing on what the author was really trying to say. It was my first encounter with this approach to translation, that the real challenge was the opportunity to exercise one's creative imagination.

One day when I was taking Keene's advanced course on classical Japanese theater at Low Memorial Library, he came into class with a copy of his own translation. We currently were reading *Meido no hiyaku* (Courier for Hell) by Chikamatsu Monzaemon, the foremost Edo playwright for the puppet theater. He told us rather casually that his translation (*Major Works of Chikamatsu*, 1961) would need more revisions before it would be ready to be submitted for publication. Since he already had an international reputation as both a scholar and a translator, it made us deeply aware of how far we still had to go before we could ever hope to reach his standard of excellence. I also recall how he generously put on library reserve copies of several play translations he intended to include in his Chikamatsu volume, since there were no up-to-date English versions of the plays for his introductory course on Japanese literature in translation.

I have many more recollections of Donald Keene as a teacher and scholar. These memories have often served as helpful road signs suddenly flashing in front of my headlights to guide me in the proper direction while driving along an unfamiliar, precarious route on a foggy night—such a night often encountered in the pursuit of credible play translations that I hope may approach his well-established standard.

Contributors

◉

Janine Beichman, born and educated in the United States, received her doctorate in East Asian languages and cultures from Columbia University and has lived in Japan since 1969, where she is professor of Japanese literature at Daitō Bunka University. She is the author of *Masaoka Shiki* (Twayne, 1982), a biography of the haiku poet Masaoka Shiki; "Drifting Fires," *Asian Theatre Journal 3* (1986):233–60, an original English-language nō play that has been performed in Japan and the United States; and translator of two books by Ōoka Makoto, *A Poet's Anthology* (Katydid Books, 1994) and *Beneath the Sleepless Tossing of the Planets* (Katydid Books, 1995). In 1991–92, Beichman held a National Endowment for the Humanities fellowship in support of her research on the modern poet Yosano Akiko. Her major fields of research are nō and Japanese poetry.

Joanne Bernardi is assistant professor of Japanese and film at the University of Rochester. Her undergraduate work in photography and film studies included one year in Japan, and after completing her degree she became a student at Columbia University. Under Professor Keene's guidance, she completed her Ph.D. in Japanese studies in 1992 with a dissertation on the pure film movement and scenario writing in Japan during the 1910s. From 1987 to 1992, Bernardi taught courses in Japanese cinema at Ibaraki University, Japan. She has published articles on early Japanese film, and her current research includes a reassessment of the scenarios of Tanizaki Jun'ichirō.

Karen Brazell is professor of Japanese literature and theater at Cornell University. Her major publications include a National Book Award–winning translation, *The Confessions of Lady Nijō*, originally published by Doubleday/ Anchor Press in 1973 and often reprinted; *Nō as Performance: An Analysis of the Kuse Scene of Yamaba* and *Dance in the Nō Theatre* (3 volumes), both coauthored with Monica Bethe and published in Cornell's East Asian Papers series; and *Traditional Japanese Theater: An Anthology of Plays* (forthcoming).

Michael C. Brownstein is associate professor of Japanese at the University of Notre Dame. He received his Ph.D from Columbia University in 1981 for a dissertation on Kitamura Tōkoku (1868–1894). In addition to translations of several modern Japanese short stories, Brownstein has published articles on Tōkoku and on Meiji-period literary history. He is currently working on a study of Chikamatsu Monzaemon's *sewamono* (domestic dramas).

Rebecca Copeland, who studied with Donald Keene from 1978 to 1983, is assistant professor of Japanese at Washington University in St. Louis. Her publications include *The Sound of the Wind: The Life and Works of Uno Chiyo* (University of Hawaii Press, 1992); entries on Hiratsuka Raichō, Okamoto Kanoko, and Uno Chiyo in *Japanese Women Writers: A Biocritical Sourcebook*, edited by Chieko Mulhern (Greenwood Press, 1994); *The Story of a Single Woman* (Peter Owen, 1992); and other translations of works by Uno Chiyo.

Mary-Jean Cowell is associate professor and coordinator of the dance program in the performing arts department at Washington University, St. Louis. She has performed with companies such as the St. Louis Repertory Dancers and the Katherine Litz Company, choreographed more than fifty works, and worked with the Abe Kōbō Studio in Tokyo in 1975 as the modern dance instructor and choreographer for two productions. She received her Ph.D. from Columbia in 1983. Cowell's publications include "Mishima Yukio's Modern Noh: An Effort to Revive a Classic Genre," *Theatre Studies*, Summer 1989, and "East and West in the Work of Michio Ito," *Dance Research Journal*, Fall 1994.

Stephen Dodd received his B.A. in oriental studies from Oxford University in 1980 and his Ph.D. from Columbia University in 1993. He taught modern Japanese literature at Duke University before returning to England in 1994 where he is now lecturer in Japanese at the School of Oriental and African Studies, University of London. His article "Fantasies, Fairies and Electric Dreams: Satō Haruo's Critique of Taishō" appeared in *Monumenta Nipponica* 49 (1994).

Joan Ericson was raised in Hiroshima Prefecture, near Hayashi Fumiko's "home town" of Onomichi. She is the author of "The Origins of the Concept of Women's Literature" in *The Woman's Hand,* edited by P. Schalow and J. Walker (Stanford University Press, 1996), and of a book on Hayashi Fumiko that includes a translation of *Diary of a Vagabond,* forthcoming from the University of Hawaii Press. Ericson is currently assistant professor of Japanese at Colorado College and lives in Colorado Springs with her husband and two daughters.

Felice Fischer is curator of Japanese art and acting curator of East Asian art at the Philadelphia Museum of Art. She has published frequently in the *Philadelphia Museum of Art Bulletin*, including the articles "Meiji Painting from the Fenollosa Collection" and "Japanese Buddhist Art." Fischer's other publications include "Murasaki Shikibu: The Court Lady," in *Heroic with Grace*, edited by C. Mulhern (Sharpe, 1991), and is a coauthor of *Japanese Design: A Survey Since 1950* (Philadelphia Museum of Art and Abrams, 1994 and 1995).

Van C. Gessel is professor of Japanese and chair of the Department of Asian and Near Eastern Languages at Brigham Young University. His publications include *The Sting of Life: Three Contemporary Japanese Novelists* (Columbia University Press, 1989) and *Three Modern Novelists: Sōseki, Tanizaki, Kawabata* (Kodansha International, 1993). He has translated six works by Endō Shūsaku, including *The Samurai, Scandal*, and *Deep River*, and coedited *The Shōwa Anthology* (Kodansha International, 1985). He served as literary adviser for a joint production by the Milwaukee Repertory Theater and the Subaru Company of a 1995 stage adaptation of Endō's *Silence* by American playwright Steven Dietz.

Carol Gluck is the George Sansom Professor of History at Columbia University and the president of the Association for Asian Studies for 1996–97. Her major publications include *Japan's Modern Myths* (Princeton University Press, 1985), *Showa: The Japan of Hirohito*, coedited with Stephen R. Graubard (Norton, 1992), *Asia in Western and World History*, co-edited with Ainslie Embree (Sharpe, 1996), and the forthcoming *Versions of the Past: The Japanese and Their Modern History*.

Amy Vladeck Heinrich is the director of the C. V. Starr East Asian Library at Columbia University, where she received her Ph.D. in 1980. She is the author of *Fragments of Rainbows: The Life and Poetry of Saitō Mokichi, 1882–1953* (Columbia University Press, 1983), as well as many articles on Japanese literature and East Asian library resources. From 1991 through 1995, she served as the founding chair of the National Coordinating Committee on Japanese Library Resources. For many years, she has had her own Japanese *tanka* published in the journal *Uchūfū*.

Eileen Kato was born in County Mayo, Ireland, in 1932 and studied at the National University of Ireland's Galway College, majoring in French, in which she received the NUI master's degree. She did postgraduate studies at the University of Poitiers and the Sorbonne in France. After marriage to a Japanese and moving to Tokyo, she became a Japanese citizen and took up Japanese studies, receiving a master's degree from Columbia University. After New York, Kato spent prolonged periods in Paris, Beijing, Cairo, and Brussels. Now widowed, she lives in Tokyo and is a free-lance translator.

Laurence Kominz received his Ph.D. from Columbia University in 1985 and is professor of Japanese language and literature at Portland State University. He is a devoted student, teacher, and fan of Japanese drama, has done *kyōgen* and *Nihon buyō keiko* for many years, and has produced, directed, and performed in professional and university shows ranging from nō dance to avant-garde drama. Recent publications include *Avatars of Vengeance: Japanese Drama and the Soga Literary Tradition* (Michigan University Press, 1995) and "Ichikawa Danjūrō V and Kabuki's Golden Age," in *The Floating World Revisited*, edited by Donald Jenkins, with the assistance of Lynn Jacobsen Katsumoto (University of Hawaii Press/Portland Art Museum, 1993).

Susan Matisoff received her Ph.D. from Columbia University in 1973, having started teaching at Stanford in 1972. Still at Stanford, teaching both undergraduate and graduate courses, Matisoff is a member of the faculty of the Asian Languages department and has also served as director of the Center for East Asian Studies. Her recent research has been on the relationship between performing arts and popular religion of the medieval and early Edo periods. Previous publications include *The Legend of Semimaru, Blind Musician of Japan* (Columbia University Press, 1978); articles on Zeami's last work, *Kintōsho*, and "Lord Tamekane's Notes on Poetry: Tamekanekyō Wakashō," coauthored with Robert N. Huey, in *Monumenta Nipponica*; and "Holy Horrors: The Sermon-Ballads of Medieval and Early Modern Japan," in *Flowing Traces: Buddhism in the Literary and Visual Arts of Japan*, eds. James H.

Sanford, William R. LaFleur, and Masatoshi Nagatomi (Princeton University Press, 1992).

Carolyn Morley is associate professor and chair of the Japanese department at Wellesley College. Her publications include *Transformation, Miracles, and Mischief:The Mountain Priest Plays of Kyōgen* (Cornell University East Asian Papers, 1993), and "The Tender-Hearted Shrews: The Woman Character in Kyōgen," *Journal of the Association of Teachers of Japanese* 22 (1988) 1.

Herbert Plutschow was born in Zurich, Switzerland, and was educated in Switzerland, England, Spain, and France before receiving his Ph.D. in Japanese studies from Columbia University in 1973. He taught at the University of Illinois and is currently a professor of Japanese literature at the University of California, Los Angeles. Plutschow also taught as a visiting professor at the University of Zurich, Switzerland, and the International Christian University, Tokyo. He is the author of thirteen books and sixty articles. His most important publications are *Nihon kiko bungaku binran* (Musashino shoin, 1975); *Four Japanese Travel Diaries of the Middle Ages* (Cornell East Asia Papers, 1978); *Chaos and Cosmos: Ritual in Early and Medieval Japanese Literature* (Brill, 1990); *Tabi suru Nihonjin* (Musashino shoin, 1983); and *Japan's Name Culture* (Japan Library, 1995).

Peipei Qiu received her Ph.D. from Columbia University in May 1994. Her dissertation, which was completed under the guidance of Professor Donald Keene, deals with Taoist traits found in both Bashō's *haikai* and Chinese poetry. While writing her dissertation, Qiu taught at Fordham University as instructor and assistant professor of Japanese language and literature. Since 1994 she has been assistant professor of Japanese language and literature at Vassar College, coordinating Vassar's Japanese program.

J. Thomas Rimer is chair of the University of Pittsburgh's Department of East Asian Languages and Literatures. He has written widely on various aspects of Japanese literature, theater, and culture. His most recent publications include *Mori Ōgai: Youth and Other Stories* (University of Hawaii Press, 1994) and *Kyoto Encounters* (Weatherhill, 1995). He is currently completing an English-language adaptation of a book by the critic Senda Akihiko on contemporary Japanese theater.

Barbara Ruch is professor of Japanese literature and culture at Columbia University and director of the Institute for Medieval Japanese Studies. Until

1990 she served as founding director of the Donald Keene Center of Japanese Culture at Columbia. In addition to her numerous studies of medieval Japan, she has edited three books in Japanese on *Nara ehon* in European, American, and Japanese collections. Her most recent publications in English are "The Other Side of Culture in Medieval Japan" in *The Cambridge History of Japan*, vol. 3 (Cambridge University Press, 1990), and "Coping with Death: Paradigm of Heaven, and Hell and the Six Realms in Early Literature and Painting," in *Flowing Traces: Buddhism in the Literary and Visual Arts in Japan*, eds. James H. Sanford, William R. LaFleur, and Masatoshi Nagatomi (Princeton University Press, 1992). Her book (in Japanese) *Mō hitotsu no chūsei zō* (Another Perspective on Medieval Japan) (Shibunkaku, 1991) led to her selection as the first Minakata Kumagusu Prize winner in the humanities in 1991, and in 1992 this book was awarded the Aoyama Nao Prize for Women's History, the first awarded to a non-Japanese author. Since 1993 Ruch has directed the Imperial Buddhist Convent Research Project, cosponsored by the National Institute of Japanese Literature (University of Tokyo) and the Institute for Medieval Japanese Studies (Columbia University).

Marleigh Grayer Ryan was the first Columbia student to receive her Ph.D. under Donald Keene. Her dissertation was published by Columbia University Press in 1967 under the title *Japan's First Modern Novel: "Ukigumo" of Futabatei Shimei* and won the Van Am Distinguished Book Award the following year. It was also accepted into the UNESCO collection of representative works, Japanese series, and was recently reissued as the first item in the Michigan Classics in Japanese Studies. In 1975, she published *The Development of Realism in the Fiction of Tsubouchi Shōyō* (University of Washington Press). She taught at Columbia from 1960 to 1972, was chair of the department of Asian languages and literature at the University of Iowa, and from 1981 to 1990 served as dean of the faculty of Liberal Arts and Sciences, State University of New York at New Paltz, where she continues as professor of Japanese. The research for this chapter was conducted while she was a fellow of the Woodrow Wilson International Center for Scholars of the Smithsonian Institution.

Carl Sesar holds a degree in Latin and Greek from the City College of New York and a doctorate in Chinese and Japanese from Columbia University. He founded the Department of Asian Languages and Literature at Wesleyan University, Middletown, Connecticut, where he taught and served as its chair from 1967 to 1975. In addition to work on the modern *tanka* poet Ishikawa Takuboku, Sesar's publications include a translation of the ancient Roman lyric poet Gaius Valerius Catullus and *Hey*, a book of short poems printed by hand under the imprimatur of the One Shot Press, which, with two stamp pads, red and black, and 102 rubber stamps, is the smallest press in the world. He is now busy doing more translations for another volume of Takuboku's *tanka*.

Haruo Shirane graduated from Columbia College, received his master's degree from the University of Michigan, and his Ph.D. from Columbia University. He taught at the University of Southern California before coming to Columbia University, where he is now Shinchō Professor of Japanese literature. He has written extensively on Japanese fiction, poetry, and poetics and is the author of *The Bridge of Dreams: A Poetics of the Tale of Genji* (Stanford University Press, 1987), which also appeared in Japanese and won the Kadokawa Prize for the best study of Japanese literature, and *Traces of Dreams: Landscape, Culture Memory, and the Poetry of Bashō* (Stanford University Press, 1997). He is currently working on a project on canonization and Japanese literature.

Amanda Mayer Stinchecum is a historian specializing in a broad approach to the cloth and clothing of Ryukyu and Japan. Her published works include "Who Tells the Tale? 'Ukifune': A Study in Narrative Voice," *Monumenta Nipponica* 35 (Winter 1980) 4; *Kosode: 16th to 19th Century Textiles from the Nomura Collection* (Japan Society/Kodansha International, 1984); and *Mingei: Japanese Folk Art*, coauthored with Robert Moes (Art Services International/Thames and Hudson, 1995). A special research fellow at the Institute for Okinawan Studies, Hosei University, Tokyo, Stinchecum also writes about Asian culture, food, and travel for *Natural History*, *The New York Times*, and other publications.

Mildred Tahara, a doctoral candidate at Columbia University from fall 1965 to spring 1969, is associate professor of Japanese literature in the East Asian languages and literatures department of the University of Hawaii at Manoa. She is the translator of *Kōkotsu no hito* (The Twilight Years) and *Kinokawa* (The River Ki) by the Japanese woman writer Ariyoshi Sawako (1931–1984). In recent years Tahara has been focusing on the classical court poetry of the tenth thorough thirteenth centuries, with a special interest in imperial anthologies and image and text.

Ted T. Takaya is professor of Japanese at the University of the Pacific. He is the author of *Modern Japanese Drama: An Anthology* (Columbia University Press, 1979) and eighteen articles, including the lead article on Kabuki theater for the *Encyclopedia of Japan* (Kodansha International, 1983). Takaya previously taught at the University of Wisconsin, Madison, and the University of Washington, Seattle.

Etsuko Terasaki holds a master's degree from Yale University and Ph.D. from Columbia University. She was a faculty member at Cornell University for a number of years and subsequently held the position of visiting scholar or visiting fellow in the East Asian Program, again at Cornell. Currently she is an associate in research in the same program and recently received a National Endowment for the Humanities grant. Terasaki's published works include reviews, translations, and articles on Japanese literature. Her recent critical textual studies on Japanese medieval nō plays are "Images and Symbols in *Sotoba Komachi*: A Critical Analysis of a Nō Play," and " 'Wild Words and Specious Phrases': *Kyōgen kigo* in *Jinen Koji*, a Nō Play," both published in the *Harvard Journal of Asiatic Studies*; and an essay entitled "Is the Courtesan of Eguchi a Buddhist Metaphorical Woman? A Feminist Reading of a Nō Play in the Japanese Medieval Theater," in *Women's Studies: An Interdisciplinary Journal*, 1992. She is now preparing a book dealing with rhetorical reading of several early nō texts.

Royall Tyler is reader in the Japan Centre at the Australian National University in Canberra. His books include *Japanese Tales* (Pantheon, 1987), *The Miracles of the Kasuga Deity* (Columbia University Press, 1990), and *Japanese No Dramas* (Penguin, 1992). He is currently translating *The Tale of Genji*.

Paul Varley is the Sen Sōshitsu XV Professor of Japanese Cultural History in the department of history of the University of Hawaii at Manoa and professor emeritus of Japanese history in the department of East Asian languages and cultures at Columbia University. He is the author of a number of books on Japanese history, including *Japanese Culture* (3rd ed., University of Hawaii Press, 1984) and *Warriors of Japan, as Portrayed in the War Tales* (University of Hawaii Press, 1994); and is coeditor with Kumakura Isao of *Tea in Japan: Essays on the History of Chanoyu* (University of Hawaii Press, 1989). Varley is currently writing a book on Japan in the sixteenth century.

Index